AMERICA INSECURE

AMERICA INSECURE

Arms Transfers, Global Interventionism,
and the Erosion of National Security

by

Miles D. Wolpin

McFarland & Company, Inc., Publishers
Jefferson, North Carolina, and London

British Library Cataloguing-in-Publication data are available

Library of Congress Cataloguing-in-Publication Data

Wolpin, Miles D.
    America insecure : arms transfers, global interventionism, and the
erosion of national security / by Miles D. Wolpin.
        p. cm.
    Includes bibliographical references and index.
    ISBN 0-89950-529-5 (50# alkaline paper : lib. bdg.) ∞
    1. United States—National security.   2. Military assistance,
American.   3. Munitions—United States.   4. United States—Military
relations.   5. Developing countries—National security.
6. Munitions—Developing countries.   I. Title.
UA23.W63   1991
355'.033073—dc20   90-52570
                                                                   CIP

Manufactured in the United States of America

McFarland & Company, Inc., Publishers
  Box 611, Jefferson, North Carolina 28640

For
my father,
Charlotte, Mary and Ralph

Table of Contents

Acknowledgments

Initial inspiration and support for this work were provided by Sherle Schweninger and the World Policy Institute. While they bear no responsibility for the final form of what was intended to be an article on United States arms transfers, their generosity was essential for the project's gestation. I am also grateful to the International Peace Research Institute, Oslo, for the use of its facilities.

Preface

While American society as a whole benefited during the 1950–1970 era from the United States' global military role, since then the sharply rising costs of that posture have undermined the economic infrastructure, social well-being and political cohesion of the citizenry.

De-industrialization has resulted from the foreign policy goal of promoting overseas investment, particularly when arms transfers and a broad range of security activities contribute to that goal. These activities tend to reduce investment costs abroad by systematically targeting reformist parties and movements. Thus taxes, wages, and occupational and environmental safeguards are minimized. Consequently, it becomes more difficult to address those needs domestically without adding incentives for "runaway plants" and "outsourcing."

Budgetary militarization has pre-empted fiscal resources for vital domestic infrastructural investment, civilian research and development, health, educational and housing needs. The transformation of America into the leading world debtor nation (the national debt was close to $600 billion in mid-1989) symbolizes the country's global erosion of stature. So does the new domestic austerity, which has subverted the lower-middle and working classes' historic "American Dream" that each generation will enjoy a higher living standard and quality of life.

Even worse, the growth of a "security" substructural state within a state has led to virtually unpunished official lawlessness and an eclipse of democratic accountability, eroding the very values that were to be "secured." Just as Watergate flowed from earlier illegal repressive tactics against the left, so the Iran-Contra Affair was a natural sequel to law enforcement failures vis-à-vis the Nixon clique and the CIA in the 1970s. A major consequence of recent scandals has been the decline of congressional stature, which in turn has been accelerated by Congress's growing dependence upon campaign funding from corporate special interests—including the military-industrial complex. Systematic use of such wealth for high-tech "political consultant" propaganda has increased the alienation of citizens and, in conjunction with growing "national security" secrecy as well as duplicity, further contributed to erosion of popular sovereignty.

American security—understood as the people's safety and well-being—

can be restored only if major foreign policy goals involving Third World inter-vention and its related nuclear "escalatory dominance" posture are changed. These changes in turn require the re-emergence of a reformist popular move-ment dedicated to giving the ordinary American a higher degree of economic security and quality of life in the social realm. Self-consciously "patriotic" in the best (non-aggressive) sense, such a coalition should take advantage of historic symbols that resonate with the body politic, e.g. the flag and the con-cept of a "Second New Deal." This strategy, rather than internationalism or a narrow focus upon eliminating weaponry, should be adopted by the peace movement if that movement is to become relevant to the lives and perceptions of average Americans.

Drawing upon historical and empirical data published for the most part between 1980 and 1989, this book provides a critique of American national security policy in the 1970s and 1980s. It is distinctive from other works on the subject in four respects: First, it addresses the linkage between the East/West and North/South security issues, with an emphasis upon the primacy of the latter. Second, it focuses upon America's domestic corporate-dominated power structure as a primary source of Washington's foreign and interventionist security policies. Third, it contains an integral critique and explanation of the ineffectiveness of both liberal arms control advocates in the 1970s and peace movement activists during the Reagan-Bush era. Finally, as implied in the preceding paragraph, it offers an alternative populist strategy to enhance the prospects not only for peace, but also for real security and prosperity for or-dinary Americans in the 1990s. This strategy encompasses an "alternative security" policy which is neither interventionist nor isolationist. Rejecting pacificism as well, it stresses a strong yet non-offensive United States–based military posture — including new criteria for arms exports — along the lines ad-vocated by Admiral La Rocque's Center for Defense Information and Randy Forsberg's Institute for Defense and Disarmament Analysis in Cambridge.

Many contemporary works approach national security narrowly, in terms of particular issue areas (e.g. arms transfers) or decisions. With such an ap-proach the domestic context is either assumed or left unquestioned. Others portray the international system or irrationally aggressive behavior of others as primary determinants. This work attempts to address national security ques-tions through a synthesis of a systemic and an historical perspective. It is hoped that this framework will enable readers to comprehend the structural sources of the Bush Administration's propensity for interventionism as well as its asym-metrical and snail's-paced response to Soviet arms control initiatives.

To the extent that the "Communist Conspiracy" bogey recedes, "narco-terrorism" and "Democracy" will be projected as rationales for Washington's global imperium. This process generates domestic anomie and foreign enmity more than it inspires admiration from either quarter.

A nation that continues year after year to spend more money on military defense than on programs of social uplift is approaching spiritual death.

Martin Luther King, Jr.

The problem in defense is how far you can go without destroying from within what you are trying to defend from without.

Dwight D. Eisenhower

1. "National Security": Symbolism and Perversion

One of the ironies of late twentieth-century America is that despite the enjoyment of impressive material wealth and military capabilities, in the psychological realm — particularly with respect to nuclear proliferation, terrorism and, until recently, Soviet capabilities — the nation is experiencing unparalleled levels of insecurity. While scholars like Lifton and Falk (1982) analyze the social implications of this dilemma, Scheer (1982), McMahan (1985), Landau (1988), Leslie Cockburn (1988) and other analysts focus upon the Reagan Administration's abortive effort to restore the post–World War II epoch of unchallenged American military hegemony. The current era is a strange time for Reagan to have launched this drive to recapture an earlier global primacy. Other powers have long since recovered from World War II's devastation and their consequent dependence upon United States aid or diplomatic leadership. The European Economic Community is emerging as an autonomous and in some respects challenging rival to the American economy, while its members assert greater military and especially diplomatic independence. At the same time Tokyo has become virtually the leading financial center of the world as Japan itself appears well on its way (Hartcher, 1988:20–22; Okitu, 1989) to becoming one of the major military powers again. Already her military budget ranks third globally.

In contrast, the superior economic performance, unsurpassed living standards and societal cohesion which underpinned American hegemony after World War II have been seriously attenuated if not lost. The dollar has been totally divorced from the gold standard; trade imbalances have become chronic; unemployment levels have continued their secular rise, assuming structural significance; and transit deterioration, urban decay and high crime rates have taken on an endemic character. The rapid post-war rise in the American standard of living — which supported the historical expectation undergirding traditional American optimism — fell off and then ceased in the late twentieth century. Thus (Hempel and Tiffany, 1989:1) "according to a recent University of Michigan Survey Research Center study, in a 10-year period, fully one-third of Americans [expect] to see their standard of living temporarily drop by 50% or more and 25% [expect to] live in poverty for at least one year."

1

Parallel to these expectations, there has been growing political alienation reflected in part by declining mass support for both major political parties and three decades of diminishing participation in the system, reaching an all-time low in 1988. Tax changes, the "chastening" of the labor movement and major curtailment of social expenditures imply that the real costs of Reagan's two trillion dollar militarization program have been imposed upon ordinary Americans. This imposition will increase disenchantment and intensify citizen alienation among the non-affluent 80 percent of the populace.

Several lines of argument will be developed in this work: first, that the quest for global military dominance has decreased rather than strengthened American security—psychological as well as physical. Second, that the East-West nuclear arms race was intimately related to the Third World militarization that both blocs fomented through arms transfers. Put succinctly, there is a deadly connection between competitive intervention in the developing areas and Washington's drive for global strategic superiority. Third, I shall argue that arms exports to and intervention within the Third World not only impede development but indirectly diminish American safety and well-being. Finally, I shall propose an alternative "defensive" and non-hegemonic American national security approach premised upon a renunciation of interventionism. By reducing tensions, this approach will facilitate East-West efforts to negotiate an end to the qualitative nuclear arms race—one whose "modernized" weapons systems in many cases imply greater instability in future crises.

The initial focus of this discussion, then, will be weapons—the key instrument of security policy. Particular attention will be directed at the motives for arms transfers to the South.[1] My underlying thesis is that a major change in American foreign policy toward the Third World is a necessary condition for significant East-West progress toward a nuclear test ban, a "freeze" upon production and optimally elimination of all destabilizing (i.e., vulnerable or counterforce) weapons systems. Thus effectiveness in fundamentally altering military policy toward the East presumes simultaneous change of American foreign policy (i.e., hostility) toward nationalist and other movements for egalitarian social change in the developing areas. For as then Republican Foreign Relations Committee Chairman Percy (U.S., Sen., CFR, *Conventional Arms Sales,* 1981:2) and many others have acknowledged, "arms sales are, first and foremost, an instrument of U.S. foreign policy." And as such, they (Gansler, 1980:212) "have been a major issue since the 1976 presidential campaign."

This has not always been the case. Before the League of Nations Covenant and the United Nations Charter delegitimized armed force as a means of resolving conflicts, for example, the mere sale of weapons for economic gain was seldom a source of opprobrium or a reason for defensiveness. Today, however, American officials rarely and often only as an afterthought refer to profits or economic advantages as a primary justification for selling destructive weaponry to others. A more hallowed, indeed quasi-sacred, "security" rationale to legitimize such transactions has been formulated. It functions to insulate proponents from critics who charge them with being imperialists or in league with what the Nye Committee in the aftermath of World War I aptly called the "merchants of death." Particular firms have employed this rationale as a hedge against competition from lower-cost foreign producers. Thus according to a recent report (Fitchett, 1988:1) on the global protectionist trend:

> In the United States, where ball-bearing makers recently tried to get protection from foreign competition, calls to safeguard a national "defense-industrial base" often are simply code for non-tariff barriers, and the national security umbrella increasingly shelters protectionism and services.

In particular, the report states, "new categories of industry—from machine tools to semiconductors and even clothing manufacturers engaged in making military uniforms—are seeking relief from imports on national-security grounds, saying that over-reliance on foreign sources poses a threat to defense."

Profit-sensitive proponents of the "national security" theory seldom specify exactly how the importing of particular items or components would adversely affect security in event of nuclear war or even a crisis involving conventional forces. Indeed (as Chapter 6 will make clear), primary weapons contractors have, with Pentagon approval, subcontracted production abroad for decades. Other firms have traditionally imported—even from the Soviets—"strategic" minerals, alloys, etc.

"National security" is a vague abstraction which at bottom connotes a feeling that the physical existence and well-being of the nation are safe from threats by others. The former head of the USAF's "Star Wars" program under Presidents Ford and Carter (Bowman, 1989:1) emphasizes that:

> Security, after all, means more than military strength. It means an informed electorate, a healthy environment, a strong economy, and a just society. We are endangered not just by nuclear weapons, but also by pollution of our air, rivers, lakes, and oceans, by leaking nuclear waste dumps, by the hole in the ozone layer, and by the greenhouse effect. We are endangered not just by foreign economic competition, but also by drugs, illiteracy, and disease, by unregulated corporate greed, and by the wasting of our technical talent in the weapons' industry.

Such a broad conceptualization is favored by Jordan and Jordan (1984) as well as many other contemporary analysts. Fischer (1984:528), on the other hand, largely restricts it to the politico-military domain while acknowledging imprecision:

> It may be difficult to measure "national security" in precise quantitative terms. It will be related to a country's ability to avoid a war, and to its citizens' probability of survival in case of war. It will also depend on people's ability to

maintain their own way of life, free from foreign domination (otherwise living in a concentration camp would be compatible with national security). Even if the concept is somewhat vague, it is essential to deal with it, because it is so central to thinking about defense. The choice of concepts should be made on the basis of their relevance, not their elegance. Too often, intellectuals give in to the temptation of dealing with concepts for which statistical data are readily available or which permit sophisticated manipulations, but which have little to do with the fundamental problem to be addressed.

Historically, the term was seldom used prior to World War II. Nor does it seem to have conditioned, before that time, Washington's decisions to wage war. In a careful study of America's entry into six major foreign wars between 1812 and 1941, Small (1980:295–309) concluded that none involved either a "threatened . . . military attack" or commercial interruptions likely to adversely affect the country's "standard of living." Pride of power—often euphemized as "honor"—and domestic political opportunism or electoral advantage in a context of traditional chauvinistic *machismo* were considerably more important in leading politicians to forsake diplomatic compromise.

In the aftermath of World War II, United States primacy was unchallenged except locally in Eastern Europe and perhaps within an extremely impoverished Chinese mainland. One would be hard put to demonstrate an actual threat in either of these remote areas to the physical safety and well-being—material or spiritual—of the atom bomb–brandishing American nation. Yet a new posture involving a permanent global base structure and presence was initiated with "national security" as the legitimating metaphor. Senator Vandenberg warned President Truman he would "have to scare the hell out of the country"—this to induce multibillion dollar congressional appropriations essential for strengthening the old socio-economic order in Western Europe and incorporating those countries *and their colonies* into an American-led (i.e., -dominated) Atlantic Alliance. While the Soviets were by no means innocent bystanders in the division of Europe, it seems clear that the initial animus and drive in this American-Soviet polarization process emanated, as McKinlay and Mughan (1984:253) argue, from Washington.

> The United States in fact opted for an intermediate strategy that was designed to exclude the USSR from this new, US-dominated order by way of containment. The immediate effect of choosing this option was to institutionalise the USSR as an enduring problem for the United States since it deliberately juxtaposed the two states against each other in a system of international apartheid in which the "dark" part of the world was to be led by the USSR and the "light" part by the United States. In the longer term, this juxtaposition also laid the basis for a zero-sum conflict that characterises the relations between the two states to this day. To state the matter simply, a loss for one of them means a commensurate gain for the other.
>
> If it comes to apportioning blame, the United States must bear primary responsibility for this situation. Its action of dividing the world into "light" and

"dark" parts, apart from being hardly flattering to the USSR, was not achieved by negotiated settlement, but was imposed by US fiat. It was a division, furthermore, that did not entail a partnership of equals, being characterised instead by a gross asymmetry in favour of the United States. The United States then set about protecting its dominance by organising Western Europe through NATO and the Marshall Plan and surrounding the remainder of the USSR with countries that were tied to the United States through various bilateral and multilateral defence treaties. In minor image terms, the functional equivalent of the US policy of containment through exclusion would be for the USSR to arm and politically organise neighbouring countries to the United States. Given the current US concern, even paranoia, over what it sees as communist penetration of Cuba and a number of Central American states, its failure to appreciate that the USSR could only interpret containment as an aggressive and threatening action can only be explained by severe myopia or gross hypocrisy on its part.

Another explanation suggested by recent archival scholarship (Nasser, 1989) is a deliberate intent to coercively intimidate Moscow as early as the 1945 Potsdam conference. This was reflected by Truman's belligerently changed attitude after the successful explosion of an atomic bomb as well as his decision to demonstrate a willingness to use them upon two Japanese urban centers.

The onset of the first Cold War was associated with massive threat inflation, whose object, as Vandenberg counseled, was to alarm American and West European public opinion with the specter of advancing Red hordes. Until recently, with the exception of a short-lived detente era between the late 1960s and mid-1970s, policy-making elites and mass media in the United States constantly employed this quasi-paranoid theme of multifarious threats to national security.[2] Even during the temporary attenuation of Cold War rhetoric referred to above, demonized monolithic "Communist totalitarianism" continued to be portrayed as a cancerous threat in Latin America, Asia and parts of Africa. As Ege (1983:15–20) demonstrates with respect to allegedly Soviet-backed "international terrorism," domestic fears may be manipulated by falsely attributing the origins of terrorist threats to the Kremlin while simultaneously exaggerating the incidence as well as gravity of such threats. Although such threat inflation and symbolic manipulation were used to decrease opposition to the CIA's new covert domestic operations function, these techniques have also been commonly employed by elites (Landau, 1988) with a bias favoring reliance upon military force (i.e., "force projection"), paramilitary interventions and weapons transfers abroad. I shall refer to such proponents of a narrow, force-oriented national security approach as "militarists" after Vagts (1967).[3]

An important caveat is that such militarists are not necessarily guided or constrained in day-to-day decision-making by the legitimating national security frame of reference they effortlessly invoke. On the contrary, several hundred interviews with high-level Reagan Administration officials by Lars

Schoultz (1988), whose concern was "understanding the intellectual process by which U.S. policy-makers link Latin American 'instability' to U.S. 'national security,'" found:

> Top officials of all persuasion welcome the simplification their subordinates provide through "enhanced" data, contrived options and the flagging phrase "national security." [M]ost policy-makers do not ask whether [Latin American] instability has any significant consequences for U.S. security. They assume it does.

The author concluded that "national security rhetoric has been used to sell a less palatable agenda of imperialism." Given Bush's unqualified defense of the Reagan Administration's foreign affairs role, his active participation in Reagan's Central American policy and the general move from moderate to rightist Republicanism during the 1980s and of course his invasion of Panama, there is a clear line of continuity with the preceding administration.

Historically these militarists have been found predominantly if not exclusively to the right of center. They have included civilians as well as many in the armed forces, for "militarism" is not the exclusive province of the military; indeed, a few military leaders like Eisenhower have been sensitive to the limits and uncertainties as well as the moral implications of employing armed forces in the nuclear era. Along with many civilians, a small minority of officers (such as the previously quoted former Star Wars head Col. Robert Bowman) have recognized the danger that excessive militarization may be counterproductive and even undermine the socio-economic foundations of national security.[4] A broad civilianist "national security" critique of this genre has even found favor with a few Republicans. Thus during the height of the Reagan Administration's militarization drive, Senator Charles Mathias (Coffin, 1983a:3) counseled the New York City Bar Association:

> It is important to remember that national security does not rest on military strength alone, or even primarily on military strength. Our national security rests on the minds, talents, energies and spirit of our people.
>
> We cannot afford to misuse these precious assets or to neglect them. If economic stagnation and unemployment destroy the hope for the future of the working men and women of America, no army in the world can save a society destabilized by despair. The real foundations for real security rest in a healthy society, in a productive economy and in an educated citizenry.

Widely shared material well-being, high cultural levels, and spiritual cohesion are also essential for maximum combat effectiveness of military personnel.[5] These societal attributes in conjunction with industrial strength are both the bedrock and the object of national defense capabilities. Even more important, they constitute resources to undergird diplomatic agreements that can enhance security without resort to war.

A broad national security framework is civilianist, then, in that it manifests a bias favoring diplomatic compromise. Although recognizing the legitimate need for armed forces in the current interstate system, "civilianists" are more prone to question what I shall term the "threat inflation syndrome" that characterizes militarists. They take a balanced view which is sensitive to socioeconomic costs and dangers generated by an uncontrolled and unprecedented global militarization process. Those dangers include the likelihood that excessive or even primary reliance upon military means may jeopardize the very quality of societal institutions which are to be protected. And when militarization diverts resources needed to prevent socio-economic decay, that decay adversely affects the most vital human factor in defense capabilities.

Washington's determination to achieve "strategic superiority" in the 1990s is also increasing the likelihood of nuclear war because of both the intense animus necessary to sustain the process and the "first strike" character of many weapons systems. Even if the Soviets stick to their apparent intention to accept "sufficiency" with much lower force levels, the United States will continue the "modernization" drive and sharply limit voluntary weapons cutbacks. The latter will be minimal with respect to bases, surface naval vessels and other force components intended for intervening ("Does America," 1989:28–29) in Third World countries. The "security" shibboleth will be employed to obtain, through manipulation, public acquiescence to covert and overt military operations against a plethora of self-generated and fabricated threats. At some point in the nineties, the "threats" may include Japan and even, less probably, China or the Soviet Union again.

Ultimately, this book will show how contemporary American militarism is serving a corporate-oriented hegemonic global design that is undermining rather than enhancing our security.

2. Weapons Exports and Third World Militarization

What I have termed a "balanced" civilianist perspective in the first chapter may also be distinguished from the militarist orientation by a willingness to perceive security threats, not only as generated by our own elites and foreign political protagonists, but also as indirect consequences of the *militarization process itself*. Thus, one Stockholm International Peace Research Institute (SIPRI) analyst (Ohlson, 1982:212) comments:

> There is now, within the disarmament community and elsewhere, a growing appreciation that the arms trade is extremely dangerous, perhaps even the most dangerous aspect of world armaments at the present time. By and large this concern appears to stem from the fact that the political, military, and economic rationales for the arms trade, upon scrutiny, seem inadequate in relation to the scale, pace and consequences of the flow of weaponry. To casual and professional observers alike, the impression gained is one of more or less uncontrolled escalation which is exacerbating regional tensions and fueling local rivalries and instabilities, thereby increasing the risk of open conflict.[1]

This concern arises from (Pearson, 1981:43) "an evident arms sales race especially in the sale of major weapons which increased fourfold in the 1970's compared to the 60's, and eightfold compared to the 50's. The yearly increase is put at 25 percent from 1975–80 compared to 15 percent from 70–75 and 10 percent from 65–70." Before turning to the forces catalyzing this process and its consequences, it may be useful to give some picture of the magnitudes involved.

NORTH/SOUTH PATTERNS

A Congressional Research Service study (Klare, 1982: 64) for example reported that "arms transfer *agreements* from North to South rose from $10.5 billion in 1973 to $41.2 billion in 1980 (in current, non-inflated dollars). Total orders during this period amounted to a staggering $199.2 billion, an amount that easily exceeds the total value of economic assistance given to Third World countries by the industralized nations."[2] These arms transfers represent more than a quarter and possibly a third of Third World military expenditures.[3] LaRocque and Goose (1982:19), of the Center for Defense Information, add that "during the 1970's, Third World Nations—some 130 of the world's 161 nations—spent more than $800 billion on military forces and munitions."[4] Analyst Landgren-Backstrom (1982:206, 208) of SIPRI stresses that by 1981, fully 67 percent of total major weapon exports were being shipped to the developing nations. She proceeds to note for that year alone

> The arms trade registers list 1100 individual arms deals. Of these, 40 per cent consist of new major weapon systems, 20 per cent are for second-hand weapons and 40 per cent are for refurbished weapons. This means, in practice, that the large customers in the Third World in principle opt for the same weapons systems as their counterparts in the industrialized world ... for example, the Mirage fighter, the Sheffield destroyer, the Exocet missiles, and the Leopard tank.

This widely noted trend toward importing or producing more complex as well as more destructive (i.e., "sophisticated") and costly weapons along with substantial replacement of grant aid by sales credits may account in some measure for the impressive rate of growth in military spending. According to SIPRI analysts (Ohlson and Tullberg, 1983:130), between 1974 and 1978 the average annual real increase in world military expenditures was 2.2 percent, while it was 3.8 percent for 1978–1982.

By 1983, the arms trade (Power, 1983:4) was in excess of $35 billion annually with an estimated three-quarters of the North's exports going to the South.[5] Institute for Policy Studies analyst Michael Klare's (1982d:45) figure, which may include the burgeoning clandestine trade as well as small arms weapons, is considerably higher. He emphasizes that "record-breaking arms sales by France, West Germany, the Soviet Union and other producers—including such novice suppliers as Brazil and Israel—have pushed total world figures to over $50 billion per year and are expected to go higher in the years ahead." Apparently the growing economic crisis for many heavily indebted developing nations forced a cutback in imports during the mid-80s. Sivard (1987:42) reports that between 1983 and 1985, major arms imports (in constant dollars) by Third World countries dropped sharply from $30.3 to $20.2, while those by developed nations declined only slightly from $9.2 to $8.2. The Third World's proportion, however, remained close to 75 percent. Pentagon (USAC-DA, 1989:69) data also indicate a sharp 1987 upswing following the 1984–86 import decline. Thus in the most recent year for which figures have been published, almost $39 out of $47.4 billion in arms were imported by "developing" countries. This foreign exchange drain represented close to 30 percent of total Third World military outlays.

The foregoing numbers suggest the magnitudes involved, but vary because of data availability, reliability, exclusionary criteria and interpretive biases. For example, since the Carter Administration the Pentagon has massively inflated the dollar values of Soviet military spending and arms transfers.

The great disparity in dollar values also reflects the fact that SIPRI-based financial data is restricted to major weapons transfers. Smith (1985:6) reports, "It has been estimated that small arms and minor weapons systems may constitute up to 50% of the arms trade, but to date there have been few efforts to monitor or define this section of the arms trade." Michael Klare, now the Director of Peace and Security Studies Program at Hampshire College, is one of very few Americans to scrutinize American small arms exports because of their unique potential for repressive uses by Third World regimes. Indeed, the significance of such items is analyzed at length in his *American Arms Supermarket* (1984:183–203) and underscored by Brogan and Zarca's (1983) description of Interarms, the world's largest private arms trading corporation, whose inventory is sufficient to equip at least 40 divisions or close to a half million troops! To this may be added clandestine exports. Those involving outright theft by American military personnel in the mid-1980s ("Black Market," 1985:30) reached a magnitude of half a billion or more dollars. Thus exports of such major weapons as helicopters, tanks and field guns represent only one—albeit an important—segment of this booming lethal trade.

RECENT DEVELOPMENTS

In the early 1980s two new trends in major weapons exports were discernible. Most salient was a change in the patterns of Soviet and United States dominance over the Third World arms trade. During the decades of the '60s and '70s, America had been the foremost supplier of arms to the world. And between 1979 and 1983, both the relative position and absolute value of Soviet exports declined. Dollar totals for exports by the USSR, according to SIPRI (1984:25, 28), dropped from $6.9 to $4.1 billion in constant 1975 dollars. As the Soviet share plummeted from 46.1 percent to 30.3 percent, that of the United States increased from 26.0 percent to 39.1 percent, while the constant dollar value rose from $3.9 to $5.3 billion. These trends are vividly portrayed in Figure 1 and Table 1. Between then and the mid-1980s this imbalance was attenuated by a sharp rise in Soviet vs. American shipments. Yet the Center for Defense Information ("U.S.–Soviet *Military* Facts," 1988:6) predicts, "If the U.S. continues to export the amounts that are planned for this year (over $20 billion) . . . it should soon regain the lead." And indeed, in 1988 (Pear, 1989), "total American sales rose 66 percent from 1987, and Soviet sales fell 47 percent." Despite the apparent equality of the two superpowers, the imbalance remains high and is growing. For America's allies still play a vastly larger role than did Soviet ones in exporting weapons to developing areas. Even in 1979 total Western shipments were far in excess of the East. For the 1979–1983 period as a whole, North Atlantic Treaty members accounted for about $40 billion compared to roughly $29 billion for Warsaw Pact states. In 1983 alone, the former figure was *almost double* the latter!

While this disparity was sharply reduced by the mid-80s due to acute

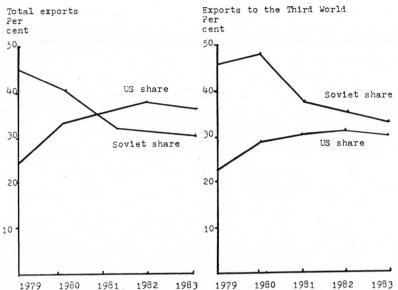

Figure 1. Soviet and U.S. shares of world exports of major weapons: Total exports and exports to the Third World, 1979–83. Source: *SIPRI (1984:28).*

Country	1979	1980	1981	1982	1983	1979–83	Per Cent of total exports to Third World, 1979–83
USSR	6921	6486	4962	4736	4070	27174	
	46.1	42.4	33.8	32.7	30.3	37.2	69.1
USA	3901	5512	5519	5704	5264	25900	
	26.0	36.0	37.6	39.3	39.1	35.5	50.3
France	1633	1194	1292	1227	1192	6539	
	10.9	7.8	8.8	8.5	8.9	9.0	79.3
UK	446	515	601	743	527	2831	
	3.0	3.4	4.1	5.1	3.9	3.9	77.3
Italy	483	377	526	579	458	2424	
	3.2	2.5	3.6	4.0	3.4	3.3	93.3
FR Germany	468	295	403	284	750	2201	
	3.1	1.9	2.7	2.0	5.6	3.0	55.4
Third World	349	271	396	438	332	1785	
	2.3	1.8	2.7	3.0	2.5	2.4	97.3
Others	810	660	989	792	856	4106	
	5.4	4.3	6.7	5.5	6.4	5.6	65.4
Total	15011	15310	14688	14503	13449	72960	

Table 1. Largest major weapon-exporting countries: Values and respective shares for 1979–83. Source: *SIPRI (1984:25).* Note: *Figures are SIPRI trend indicator values, as expressed in U.S. $ million, at constant (1975) prices; shares in percentages. Figures may not add up to totals due to rounding.*

foreign exchange shortfalls and Western success in undermining OPEC earnings, NATO members and their allies continued to dominate most Third World markets. And while the relative exporting position of Moscow diminished somewhat within the WTO, the United States and France together ("Western," 1988:14) in 1985 accounted for 80 percent of all NATO weapons exports, up from about 75 percent in 1977. The Western nations and allies increasing their share were the United States (15 percent), France (80 percent), and Japan (90 percent), whose share nevertheless remains quite modest.

The previously mentioned upsurge in Reagan era sales during the latter half of the 1980s may well diminish the relative importance of Washington's major allies, the latter having resisted a complete turnover of their domestic markets (Fitchett, 1988:1, 14) to United States military producers. By late 1988, "the NATO allies [were] already cutting out U.S. defense contractors for reasons of domestic politics and 'Europe-building,' the U.S. Ambassador to West Germany, Richard R. Burt, warned recently." Fitchett adds that in 1986 France opted to create her own new fighter while Japan insisted upon domestic production of all parts for the FSX—a new version of the F16 which Tokyo agreed to co-produce as a consequence of intense "U.S. pressure."

But, as far as Japan is concerned, a new relationship is in the offing with respect to domestic production as well as export rivalry. For earlier Fitchett warns that:

> An emergent arms industry is seeking protection to develop into a full-fledged supplier capable of replacing many of the combat aircraft and warships that once were major imports that helped redress the Japanese trade surplus with the United States.

Hartcher (1988:20–22) adds that:

> The Japanese government has always been anxious to keep a functioning domestic arms industry. Since the U.S. started urging Japan to rearm, the Japanese government has effectively subsidized it. The Defense Agency procures its equipment and arms from Japanese manufacturers and suppliers wherever possible. In most cases, this means paying more than it would if it bought from abroad—in some cases, double. As a result, Japan is highly self-sufficient in arms: 99 percent of its ships are from Japanese makers, as well as 89 percent of its aircraft, 87 percent of its ammunition, and 83 percent of its firearms....
>
> A confidential Japanese private-sector study stated that if allowed to export, Japan could control 60 percent of world warship construction, 40 percent of military electronics, 25 percent to 30 percent of the aerospace market, and 46 percent of the demand for tanks and motorized artillery.

Indeed, not only is Tokyo's military budget the third largest after the two superpowers, but it has unparalleled capacity for further increases since a far smaller percentage (1.6) of her GNP is so allocated than other major powers whose range is 4–12 percent.

But Japan is not the only emergent and perhaps rival giant. Even traditionally subordinate allies like the United Kingdom have become far more
independent—rejecting the new M-1 Abrams tank recently in order to develop
a new British one, safeguarding a traditional manufacturing and export potential. It is evident that in the 1990s, the "new Europe" will join Japan in ex-
hibiting greater pluralism in military and diplomatic roles as well as in the
crucial area of competitive arms exports. Indeed, even U.S. "leadership" and
NATO as an instrument of dominance appear to be rapidly eroding—though
the pace is more gradual than the deflation of Soviet influence in Eastern
Europe.

Notwithstanding the upsurge in the role of Western weapons exports—
with $3.1 billion (Pear, 1989) in arms exported during 1988, accounted for
largely by Washington's and in lesser measure France's impressive increase in
weapons transfers since the early 70s (Wulf, 1988:326)—there has been a second change worth noting. Klare (1985:16) records a moderate decline in the
relative importance of both the Soviets and Americans paralleled by an even
greater downturn for Washington's major West European allies—Britain,
Federal Republic of Germany and Italy—between the late 1970s and early
1980s. Table 2 reveals the emergence of a new tertiary supplier group comprised by such countries as Belgium, Czechoslovakia, Poland, Spain, Switzerland, Israel, Brazil, both Koreas and Singapore. More recently, China has
joined this group, and Japan may in the next few years. While several belong
to the Third World, most of these emergent arms exporters are tied as de facto
or treaty allies to the United States (8) or the USSR (2). Thus the decline in the
relative "superpower" role in arms exports, while real, has been somewhat less
significant (especially for the United States) than the mere proliferation of tertiary exporters implies. Israel, for example, has developed both training and
equipment supply links with many repressive right wing regimes that were also
backed by the Reagan Administration. Indeed there have been some instances
(e.g. Guatemala, South Africa) where that country has acted as a surrogate
(Perera, 1985) because diplomatic or domestic political constraints temporarily
inhibit Washington from providing weaponry.

Most of this new tertiary exporting group are tied to the so-called superpowers or their major allies in other ways as well. The unbalanced and limited
industrial-technological development of many of these new producers means
(Wulf, 1979:340) that "there is virtually no major weapon system produced in
developing countries that does not rely on the import of licenses, production
technology, knowledge, or components from industrialized countries.[6] In
numerous cases such dependence often exists even for relatively unsophisticated military equipment as trucks, tanks and rifles." On the other
hand, the growing diversity of technology suppliers as well as expanded local
production have modestly enhanced the range of options (Anthony, 1989) and
situational autonomy during a crisis for most developing nations. It can also

<u>Percentage of Weapons Exports</u>

Source	1976-1979	1980-1983	1983
Superpowers	65	53.0	55.5
Major U.S. Allies	24	23.5	14.5
Other	11	23.5	30.0

Table 2. Tertiary arms exporters to the Third World. Source: *Klare (1985:16).*

be said that arms manufacture by developing countries also contributes modestly to their independence by tending to decrease (Looney, 1989) imports.

Similar consequences flow from another major though perhaps temporary alteration in Third World equipment import patterns. This change in consumer demand has contributed to the emergence of new exporters among the semi-industrialized developing countries that appear in Table 2. Thus, concerning preferences by importing states in the early 1980s, Klare (1985:16) reports, "a conspicuous de-emphasis upon . . . high-technology hardware. . . . Now, however, they tend to concentrate on purchases of medium- and low-technology munitions: trainer aircraft and counterinsurgency planes, helicopters, jeeps and trucks, small arms and so forth." He adds that this shift towards less sophisticated weaponry is due to three factors. First, lower tech light weaponry is less expensive when growing numbers of Third World nations are unable to amortize or even meet interest payments on their external indebtedness, now totaling over a trillion dollars. Second, in both the Falklands War and recent Syrian/Israeli aerial combat, "success was largely attributed to superior tactics, training and leadership rather than to superior weaponry."[7] Klare (1985:16-17) pinpoints the third reason for this trend toward "rugged low-technology hardware particularly suited for use in underdeveloped areas" by noting that "some analysts also suggest that large-scale acquisitions of high-tech weaponry can actually undermine the combat readiness of Third World armies, by tying up extensive repair and maintenance capabilities (always in short supply in the Third World) and by saddling these forces with sensitive equipment that often breaks down under rugged battlefield conditions."

Despite this recent movement in the direction of light weaponry, one primarily catalyzed by increasingly insupportable debt burdens, developing countries have accumulated a vast reservoir of complex weapon systems. This is

	Tanks[a]	Light Armor[b]	Field Arty[c]	SAMs[d]	MSL Boats[e]	Jet Cmbt Acft[f]	Helicopters[g]
1966	2	13	7	0	0	6	9
1971	7	14	10	1	0	10	11
1976	12	29	19	2	2	15	22
1981	18	36	36	8	6	21	31

Table 3. Numbers of sub–Saharan African countries possessing selected items oj military equipment. Source: The Military Balance, *IISS London 1971–72, 1976–77, 1981–82; and Adelphi Paper #27, IISS London, 1966. As reproduced in Thom (1984:37).*

Notes:

a. *Tanks = All; from MBTs (main battle tanks) to light tanks.*
b. *Light Armor = Armored cars, Armored Personnel Carriers, Infantry Fighting Vehicles, etc. Excludes "homemade" lightly armored trucks.*
c. *Field Artillery = All sizes; self-propelled and towed.*
d. *SAMs = All permanent and mobile launchers, excluding hand-held/shoulder fired weapons.*
e. *Missile Boats = All vessels smaller than major combatant size that mount surface-to-surface missiles.*
f. *Jet Combat Aircraft = All, including combat capable trainers, listed in source material as combat aircraft.*
g. *Helicopters = All regardless of service assignment.*

illustrated by Table 3. Furthermore, the 1- to 5-year lag between sales agreements and actual deliveries of many weapons in the pipeline suggests that the early and mid-1980s have been a period of maximum influx of armaments. Thus despite a sharp drop in 1983 to $24.7 billion, sales agreements in 1980 and 1982 respectively totaled $46.2 and $46.8 billion according to Klare (1985:15). This backlog will literally flood the developing areas with arms and munitions of all sorts. Not only that, but we have already referred to the late '80s upsurge in United States sales which increasingly emphasize "user friendly" semi-high technology weapons (Miller, 1988:18–20) and intelligence devices for "low-intensity" conflicts.

Insofar as particular geographical regions vary, it is clear that at the close of the 1960s most imports — roughly 70 percent — were by Europe and the Far East with less than 15 percent by the Middle East. Yet a mere decade later, an unprecedented change had occurred: Europe and the Far East now accounted for 26 percent "while the Middle East's share had risen to thirty-seven percent." Klare (1982:65) adds:

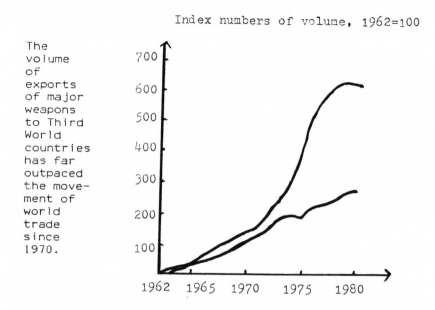

Figure 2. Major weapons exports to the Third World and the growth of world trade: 1962–1980. Source: *SIPRI Yearbook, 1982. Reprinted from Landgren-Backstrom (1982: 202).*

This shift reflects the dramatic increase in arms imports by the Third World over the past decade. According to the U.S. Arms Control and Disarmament Agency (ACDA), imports by Middle Eastern countries rose by 82.5 percent between 1969 and 1978 (from $820 million to $7.6 billion, in current dollars), while imports by Africa rose by 3,500 percent (from $145 million to $5.2 billion), and those by Latin America by 536.6 percent (from $205 million to $1.1 billion).

With the decline of East-West detente (1978–1982), however (Ohlson and Loose-Weintraub, 1983:271), a slightly different pattern emerges. The Middle Eastern share dropped from 54.3 to 44.7 percent over the preceding four years, whereas all other regions increased their shares: Africa, 19.3 to 22.3; Far East, 9.9 to 13.1; Latin America, 10.5 to 10.7; and South Asia, 6.0 to 8.8. While the Latin American increase obscures a dramatically larger one for Central America, the overall global rate of growth in major weapon imports between the periods 1973–1977 and 1978–1982 was on the order of 50 percent, in contrast to a 100 percent increase for earlier five-year periods since 1963.

Ohlson and Loose-Weintraub (1983) maintain that the lessened rate was occasioned by temporary market saturation and the diminished global economic performance of recent years. Despite this lower rate of increment, it is clear from Figure 2 that since 1965 and more starkly from 1972 the rise in weapons imports has exceeded by far the growth of world trade. Thus to a very substantial yet indeterminate degree, the mushrooming arms trade has contributed to the specter of Third World bankruptcy or inability to maintain payments under prior indebtedness.

In terms of present day reality, World Bank President Barber Conable ("Third World," 1989:741) has himself finally been willing to address the issue, acknowledging that approximately one-third of the $1.3 trillion foreign debt of developing nations "is the result of military spending." It is unclear whether this includes the "grey" area of illegal arms trading.

Less indeterminate is the American contribution, if not total responsibility, for this financial albatross. For we have also seen that since the mid–1980s the United States has reasserted its role *vis-à-vis* the Soviets as the paramount direct and indirect provisioner for Third World militarization. With the further erosion of Soviet interest in developing areas at the close of the 1980s, this disparity of militarization (almost by default) between the United States and the USSR has become even more stark. Is it simply the high returns to weapons producers and middlemen merchants of death that explain the Yankee preoccupation with diffusing them to all corners of the global "free market?" To better understand the salience of arms transfers in Washington's relationships with developing countries, we shall briefly analyze the historical linkage between specific foreign policy goals and the flow of massive amounts of weaponry of all types to armies or "security forces" in the South.

3. American Arms Exports in Historical Perspective

For more than a century and a half, arms exports have at times been employed to promote foreign policy goals. At least since the early 1820s, American diplomats and weapons were intervening (Campos, 1963:107, 153, 192) in support of some South American struggles against Spanish mercantilism or rule. In the 1830s, arms exports were used to promote an insurgency against Mexico in Texas as they were subsequently by colonists in Hawaii. Prior to the close of the nineteenth century, furtherance of commercial exports was clearly the predominant if not exclusive policy goal. Since then, interventionism to influence the specific character, policies, or very existence of foreign governments has increasingly complemented and constrained the earlier general primacy accorded to commercial gain for weapons exporters. By 1980 only 10 percent of United States arms transfers (Pearson, 1981:39) were officially designated as "commercial" sales, most of which went to American allies. Of 30,000 commercial license applications, 20 percent were classified as "controversial." Reflecting the salience of political constraints, however, was the fact that *all* had to be approved by the State Department's Munitions Control Office.[1] Licenses are denied when the importing government (e.g. the Sandinistas of Nicaragua) is an object of administration hostility. Exceptions are made when "friendly" officer factions in the armed forces of such countries (e.g. Indonesia, 1963–1965; Chile, 1971–1973; Ethiopia, 1974–1977; Sudan, 1985–1989) need reinforcement and cover for covert intelligence liaison in preparation for an eventual coup d'état.

AN INTERVENTIONIST HERITAGE

While Latin America and in much lesser measure the Far East—both primary areas of American colonialism and intervention—were important American markets prior to World War II, the largest volume of weapons by far went to European buyers during the World Wars and in the two decades following the Second World War. As the weakened European colonial empires disintegrated and nationalist movements emerged in developing areas—occasionally with very limited Eastern arms supplies—the United States gradually intensified military and covert activities in such areas. Thus two veteran CIA officers, Agee (1975) and McGehee (1983), maintain that their agency's primary function is not to gather intelligence, but to weaken progressive and even reform-oriented nationalist movements through paramilitary and covert political intervention.

What must be borne in mind from an historical standpoint is that at least since the Aguinaldo insurgency in the Philippines at the turn of the century if not before (e.g. Boxers, Cuban independenistas, etc.), the United States has opposed nationalist movements and especially those of an egalitarian reformist or socially radical character in the developing areas — denying economic aid to them, withholding recognition, imposing trade embargoes, promoting organizational splits, attempting to coopt leaders or more often providing arms for use against these national liberation struggles.[2] The most frequent interventionism of this neo-colonial character — often overtly on behalf of investor interests — occurred in Central America, the Caribbean and the Pacific from 1896 until World War II became imminent.[3]

Hence well before and even in the total absence of Soviet encouragement, American policy elites defined Third World nationalism (or "instability") as a "problem," and more recently as a threat to national security. Chomsky (1985:6) pinpoints an underlying rationale for such reactive negativism:

> One thing you'll notice, if you look over the years, is that the United States quite consistently tries to create enemies (I'm not being sarcastic) if a country *does* escape from the American grip. What we want to do is drive the country into being a base for the Russians because that justifies us in carrying out the violent attacks which we *must* carry out, given the geopolitical conception under which we organize and control much of the world. So that's what we do, and then we "defend" ourselves. We engage in self-defense against the Great Satan or the Evil Empire or the "monolithic and ruthless conspiracy."

More recently, a relatively conservative analyst (Pfaff, 1989:4) has offered a similar diagnosis:

> A curious feature of American political life during the past 30 years has been willingness to turn inherently unimportant challenges into major and self-destructive problems that cannot be solved at acceptable cost.
>
> Washington made the existence first of Fidel Castro, then of Moammar Gadhafi and now of Manuel Antonio Noriega into dramatic domestic political issues and crises of foreign policy. In practice unable to do anything about these people, the president of the day has consequently been damaged. Why was an intrinsically minor nuisance in foreign relations allowed to become a test of the nation and of a president's own position?

The author, in contrast to Chomsky, is less preoccupied with the sources of such behavior than the counterproductive policy effects. He warns: "The result of this attention to the Noriegas, Castros and Gadhafis has naturally been to augment their influence, not diminish it." The Noriega ouster, of course, sharply intensified "anti–Americanism" throughout the hemisphere, resulting in South American opposition to Bush's "drug war" proposals.

Not only is the "drug war" being lost ("Losing," 1990:20–22), but in being redefined as the latest threat to national security, it has served to rationalize further militarization, says Pfaff.

> The State Department and the Drug Enforcement Administration had the lead in the drug war, but now that drugs have become a national-security issue, the Pentagon has become the lead agency responsible for stopping the flow of narcotics into America.
> Though it expects little from the Andean summit, the administration is committed to spending $2.2 billion in the region over the next five years. Much of that will go to military forces.

This spending will enable United States special forces to intervene against Sendero Luminoso, a growing leftist nationalist insurgent movement that has protected peasants' interests in the face of both drug traffickers and the military-dominated regime in Peru.

Occasionally, officials unwittingly reveal their neo-colonial goals even today despite their general preference for altruistic and anticommunist rhetoric. Thus in defending the largest arms sale in recent history (U.S., Sen., CFR, *Arms Sales Package,* Part 1, 1981:61), then Chairman of the Joint Chiefs of Staff General David Jones announced, "As the President said in his press conference, we are not going to let happen in Saudi Arabia what happened in Iran" (referring to the deposition of the Shah of Iran and the assumption of power by the Ayatollah Khomeini). Analogously, while speaking in favor of the same $8.5 billion weapons "package" in a subsequent hearing, then Senate Foreign Relations Committee Chairman Charles Percy (U.S., Sen., CFR, *Arms Sales Package,* Part 2, 1981:61) stated: ". . . we do have $35 billion of contracts with Saudi Arabia. The Saudis have always tried to favor American corporations."

Kelly (1983:8–10) cites a number of public declarations by then CIA Director Casey attributing responsibility for "international terrorism" to the USSR. Yet in a less publicized address (early 1980s) to the United States Chamber of Commerce, Casey pinpointed economic "nationalism" in the developing areas—particularly its unreceptivity to transnational corporate profiteering—as being at the root of "instability" and by defintion *his* foreign policy problem:

> Today we live in a world of increasing nationalism, increasing terrorism, and vanishing resources. These three realities illustrate the new kinds of problems of concern to intelligence.
> First, the tide of nationalism is running strong in the less-developed countries of the world. There is hostility and negativism toward free enterprise.

> There are potential dangers there for American, European, and even Japanese multinational corporations. Local politicians cannot always manage this distrust of foreigners. Free enterprise from abroad suddenly appears as foreign domination or neo-colonialism. It is difficult to predict when and where this hostility will break out.
>
> Nationalism is not new. Its manifestations range from restrictive policies to outright expropriation. What is new today is that it is accompanied by global distress. This is caused by the explosive growth of energy costs—in both industrialized countries and the less-developed ones.
>
> The enormous cost of fueling economic activity is forcing the less-developed countries into austerity and no-growth policies. They are running out of credit. They cannot meet the very high interest rates required. All this intensifies instability.

It is worth noting that Casey was recruited from the investment banking community. As one of the closest officials to Reagan, he personally supervised provisioning of the Contras against the socialist-oriented "Marxist" Sandinista Revolution.

A noted peace researcher, William Eckhardt (1977:9), summarizes a number of historical studies to conclude that investor protection has been the dominant motif in American foreign policy. And like Agee (1975) and McGehee (1983), he regards this also to be one of the covert functions of the CIA:

> Since the late 19th century U.S. foreign policy was designed to promote and protect foreign investment, finance, and trade (Klare, 1972:23). However, the 160 U.S. foreign interventions from 1798–1945 recorded in the Congressional Record (Klare, 1972:24) would suggest that U.S. imperialism on a global level was already well under way by the late 19th century, at which time the U.S. began to take the lead over England in ruling the world. Since the end of the second world war, the U.S. has engaged in more major military interventions than any other country (Eckhardt & Azar, 1977).
>
> Following the second world war U.S. foreign policy moved from massive retaliation and nuclear deterrence under Truman and Eisenhower in the 1950s to counter-insurgency under Kennedy, Johnson, and Nixon in the 1960s (Klare, 1972:33–38), when it was realized that any direct military threat from the Soviet Union was a myth, but that the threat to U.S. business by Third World revolutionaries (in or out of government) was a reality (Aronson, 1971:336).
>
> This shift of emphasis in U.S. foreign policy from nuclear deterrence to counter-insurgency brought the CIA into a more prominent role in the promotion and protection of MNC interests abroad, because there was a greater need for secrecy in fighting starving people in poor countries. . . .

Indeed, at the outset of the first Cold War, State Department architect George Kennan (1948)—who elaborated both the "containment" rationale and the so-called Marshall Plan—warned his colleagues:

> We have 50 percent of the world's wealth, but only 6.3 percent of its popula-
> tion. This disparity is particularly great between ourselves and the peoples of
> Asia. . . . Our real task is to devise a pattern of relationships which will permit
> us to maintain this position of disparity without positive detriment to our na-
> tional security. To do so we will have to dispense with all sentimentality. . . .
> We should cease to talk about vague, and for the Far East, unreal objectives,
> such as human rights, the raising of living standards, and democratization.

Historically, of course, such "vague and unreal" aspirations were initially articulated by nationalists and socialist movement elites opposing Western
domination of Third World peoples. They were given moral support by the
Bolshevik-sponsored Comintern Baku Congress as early as 1922.

The national security metaphor, as noted earlier, was not customarily
employed during the half-century (1896–1946) of intervention against both
nationalist movements and rival powers seeking to establish spheres of influence in the developing areas. Existing military technology in conjunction
with geophysical insularity would have denied "security" claims even a faintly
credible basis. Instead, the era of continental conquest (Van Alstyne, 1965;
Brown, 1972) in the name of Manifest Destiny or Providence was followed by
intervention primarily in the Caribbean area and Asia. The rationales were
often commercial in character (e.g. the goal of an "open door" for trade on the
same terms as others) and political in the sense of opposing sphere-of-influence
extension by major European powers or Japan.

This opposition was frequently portrayed (e.g. in the Monroe Doctrine)
as a desire to preserve the independence of other peoples. Such a principle was
no more uniformly applied in practice (Moon, 1926) than are contemporary
security related rationales (Parenti, 1984, 1988) such as freedom, self-determination and democracy. In cases of enforced economic privileges for American
investors, the forced imposition of protectorates (e.g. Cuba, Haiti) or even the
overt creation of colonies (e.g. Hawaii, Philippines, Puerto Rico), the inconsistent ideology became obvious to the inhabitants of these countries and even
to more perceptive United States citizens.

Anti-imperial nationalist- and socialist-oriented movements proliferated
in the underdeveloped areas during the 1920s and early 1930s. They were encouraged not only by the previously mentioned Soviet moral and quite
marginal material support, but increasingly by Japanese, Italian and German
denunciations of Western hypocrisy. The relatively enlightened and reformist
Roosevelt New Deal Administration reacted in part to these developments in
1933 by enunciating a Good Neighbor policy renouncing military interventionism in Central America and the Caribbean. Although not wholly honored
in practice, it appeared to mark a major departure. By 1936, the Philippines
were being promised independence within a decade, and no more than a shipping and limited trade embargo was imposed upon Mexico in 1938. (At that
time, United States oil corporations, which refused to respect that country's

new labor code, were nationalized.) Promises of economic aid and a continued New Deal after the Second World War inspired admiration from many Latin Americans, Filipinos and others as the United States joined the Soviet Union and Western colonial powers in a common effort to defeat the nakedly exploitative and militantly aggressive fascist regimes of Germany, Italy and Japan. War propaganda depicting the struggle in Manichean terms escalated post-war expectations in developing countries, as did the example of the American-Soviet alliance and mutual respect during the conflict and in elaboration of the United Nations system. Indeed, despite the Soviet feat in turning the tide against almost 90 percent of Hitler's military machine, America's quantitative superiority in war output — if not her strategic or tactical brilliance — played a truly impressive role in defeating both the Nazis and, particularly, Japan. It has been estimated (Kennedy, 1985:32) that during the Second World War, the United States was "spending three or four times as much on arms as any other combatant. . . ."

A NEW "MANIFEST DESTINY"?

Thus one can readily understand why there was an era immediately after World War II when the United States was widely regarded as "the arsenal of democracy." Throughout much of the world Americans were both envied and admired — yet only rarely feared. Continued military presence in Europe supplemented by massive economic grants and emerging alliance military ties not only safeguarded capitalism from popular leftist movements, but structured a newly hegemonic position in the West for Washington. As late as 1988, a relatively liberal national security expert for the ill-fated Michael Dukakis presidential campaign (Nye, 1988:117) opposed a reduction in United States military presence in analogous terms:

> Providing for the defense of other countries is a source of American influence and regional stability. It affects the way Western Europe and Japan respond to U.S. interests in the economic as well as the military and political areas.

While the contemporary desire for such leverage or political inequality is but a pale reflection of United States dominance between 1945 and 1965, it continues to function as a sacrosanct imperative for "realist" policy elites of both major parties. Yet as the decades have passed, an entirely new situation has evolved. Western Europeans and the Japanese no longer envy America's wealth. Standards of mass welfare in the United States, as well as the general quality of urban life, are in varying degree often surpassed (Nagle, 1985) by their own. In the developing areas, envy is becoming ever more intertwined with resentment, fear and hostility — what America arrogantly tends to label as anti–Americanism, xenophobia or "extremism."

Such pervasive antipathy in its multifarious forms is founded upon neither irrationality nor a facile conjuration of Soviet-inspired disinformation and conspiracy. It is in considerable degree the legacy of our own "national security" policy, i.e., nearly four decades (Kolko, 1969; Chomsky and Herman, 1979; Parenti, 1988) of aid and comfort for corrupt, repressive, comprador-type regimes.[4] Thus one expert (Pierre, 1982:31) on arms exports has cautioned, "Quite apart from moral considerations which democratic governments cannot or ought not overlook, the transfer of arms can be a source of deep embarrassment to the supplier country if they are then used for internal repression and to crush dissidents." But even when weaponry is not directly employed for suppression, it adds to the resources of repressive regimes and has an intimidating effect.

Not only was there relative indifference to violent repressiveness in the 1960s, but somewhat surprisingly Schoultz (1981:155, 161–163) found a strong positive correlation between United States aid and repressive regime behavior by Latin American countries in the mid-1970s—Washington's human rights rhetoric notwithstanding:

> The correlations between the absolute level of U.S. assistance to Latin America and human rights violations by recipient governments . . . are uniformly positive, indicating that aid has tended to flow disproportionately to Latin American governments which torture their citizens.
> . . . . By far, the largest portion of U.S. military aid to Latin America—89 percent in FY1975 through FY1977—is in the form of FMS credits.
> Each of the military aid/human rights correlations . . . is positive; most are stronger than those generated by U.S. economic assistance programs. As in the case of economic aid, however, major fluctuations occur over short periods of time. . . . The positive correlation between military aid and human rights violations existed not only because the United States favored three repressive regimes but also because the non-repressive governments of Latin America received almost no military aid. . . .

Similar patterns appeared when Schoultz used per capita aid.[5] Further, since repressiveness was only weakly (– .13) related to low per capita GNP, the author (1981:166–167) concludes that "the positive relationship between U.S. aid and [low per capita GNP] is not a justification for the equally strong positive correlation between aid and human rights violations. . . . At any given level of human need during FY1975–FY1977, U.S. aid remained positively correlated with the level of human rights violations in Latin America."

While analogous studies are lacking for other regions, it is probable that similar patterns would be revealed. Wolpin (1983a: Table 25) found that out of 33 major American arms transfer recipients in various parts of the world between 1961 and 1979, 32 of them were highly repressive in 1980. Two-thirds were characterized by the use of extremely violent suppressive practices such as torture, execution, "disappearances," etc. It is not so much that United States policy-makers preferred brutally repressive recipients, though there is considerable evidence of such culpability (McClintock, 1985; Huggins, 1987), at least in Central America. More generally, as McKinlay and Mughan (1984: 261) argue, this is an inherent by-product of the primacy accorded to an anti-leftist animus.

> In opposing socialism, whatever form it took, these [arms] transfers have often been seen to support repressive, anti-socialist regimes rather than to promote liberal ones. Indeed, they have often upheld clique regimes that are themselves among the biggest obstacles to structural change in the direction of liberalism. In other words, the United States has shown a propensity to associate with the forces of reaction rather than those of progress.

The Reagan Administration's general disregard for brutal human rights violations in pro-capitalist countries, and major arms shipments to corporate-oriented Saudi Arabia, Morocco, Pakistan, Israel, El Salvador, and Honduras, indicate that the relationship was, if anything, strengthened during his tenure as President. So does what Hitchens (1983:230) referred to as "rising" United States aid for a highly repressive Turkish military dominant regime — already close to "the $1 billion mark." The absence of this issue as it affected right-wing regimes in the 1988 presidential campaign, and Bush's record so far of "aid and comfort" to such regimes provided that they are subservient, indicate that little change can be expected.

DEVELOPMENT AND HUMAN RIGHTS PATTERNS

The consequences of such a global policy bias are more far-reaching than those epitomized by Pierre's "morality" or "embarrassment." Most of these "moderate" governments are not employing economic resources to promote rapid growth, and even the few that do generate relatively little spillover (Wolpin, 1983) into mass welfare. On the contrary, austerity is being ubiquitously imposed upon lower middle and working class sectors. As Lens (1983) argues, United States aid to such anti-popular repressive regimes is actually counterproductive in that it generates internal support for anti–American nationalist — often socialist — oriented opposition or resistance movements, which further increase the costs of maintaining an "informal empire." And these material burdens are ever more taxing on resources that might otherwise enhance mass welfare and the quality of life of average Americans. Not only are billions of dollars diverted from needed investments in American highways, housing, schools, adult literacy programs and health needs, but the aid to these regimes and its associated global military infrastructure are major factors (roughly 85 percent of official military expenditures) in rising federal tax burdens and national debt expansion. The latter increases long-run mass tax burdens.

Even worse, corrupt "comprador" regimes repress labor unions so that artificially low market wages attract runaway American industrial plants and jobs. The mere threat of such a move often induces workers in the United States to reject unions and accept forced wage reductions and fringe benefit erosion — thus contributing to the present decline in working and lower middle class living standards as well as the spectacular growth of personal indebtedness and insecurity. Secular and particularly recent rises in penal incarceration rates, youth suicide and hostility towards the rights of women and minorities attest to the damaging effects of this process upon American cohesion, spiritual health and general quality of life. These manifest threats to the American dream are more fully documented in Chapter 8.

Indirectly, then, as well as in more immediate fashion, America's national — as opposed to transnational corporate — well-being is diminished rather than enhanced by close association with such repressive "open door" regimes. And this is even more the case (Wolpin, 1981, 1983a) than it would be if socially radical nationalist counter-elites won control of those societies. The latter tend to improve living standards and mass purchasing power — for American exports among others. For example, in 1983 Lippard (p. 22) reported that Nicaragua's Sandinistas

> . . . in four short years, under the most economically and military embattled cir-
> cumstances, have achieved a 16-point gain in the Overseas Development Coun-
> cil's (a private Washington-based organization) "physical quality of life" index,
> which includes literacy (from 12 percent *to* 50 percent), infant mortality and
> life expectancy — the greatest improvements in this hemisphere. A people who
> have wiped out polio, begun to provide housing for the poor other than card-
> board and thatch huts, who despite shortages and subversion from within are
> resisting demoralization.[6]

Thus only when one accepts some variant of the anti-socialist paranoid style in American politics — a style that masks a neo-imperial ideological orientation (Thompson, 1983; Lens, 1983) — does the kind of conflict which Betts (1980:109) and other mainstream liberals perceive arise between so-called "Realpolitik" and "moral" norms:

> *Moral* norms should be primary in inhibiting [arms] sales where they overlap
> completely with *Realpolitik* (e.g., South Africa), secondary where the
> odiousness of the regime and the extent of the threat to it are both moderate
> (as in the cases of much of black Africa and Latin America), and tertiary where
> the objectionableness of the government pales beside the threatening alter-
> native (for instance, South Korea).

The question excluded from this framework is why a leftist or even Marxist government in South Korea should be regarded as so "threatening" an alter-native? North Korea is no less independent than Yugoslavia or China. Both of the latter have been given or sold military material by the Reagan and/or Bush administrations — this notwithstanding Beijing's support for Pol Pot's deposed Kampuchean regime, one notorious for sanguinary repression.

In Table 4, I have classified approximately one hundred developing countries on the basis of both repressiveness and the use of overt violence against opponents.[7] If we look at the twenty largest Third World major weapon-importing countries for the period 1977–1981 as listed in Table 5, sixty percent are in the violently repressive category and three-quarters of these are military-dominant. Close to two-thirds of the total are military-dominant, while among all 102 countries in Table 4, the military-dominant proportion is but slightly over two-fifths. The military-dominant were far more likely than civilian governments to be violently repressive, to treat minorities poorly and to be confronted by ethnically based insurgencies. Violent repressiveness was also strongly correlated with the presence of United States military personnel.

Sixty percent of the largest major weapon importers are "open door" oriented, while only 10 percent are state socialist. The last category (Wolpin: 1981, 1983) exhibits the best economic development and social welfare improvement, while the open door approach — especially for military-dominant regimes — generally exhibits the poorest. Thus in terms of both repressive and "structural" violence, the largest arms importers are quite salient.[8]

If we turn to the seven countries slated to receive 84 percent of United States FY1984 Foreign Military Sales Generated Credits in Table 7, we see that six out of the seven were military-dominant and the seventh, Israel, is a militaristic power that (as emphasized earlier) has provided arms to Zaire, Argentina, Guatemala and other violently repressive military-dominant regimes as well as to South Africa. Furthermore, when we exclude the two civilian-governed — but not yet wholly civilian-ruled — European recipients, 80 percent of the remaining five are military-dominant, and three-quarters of these fall into the violently repressive category. All of the recipients are characterized by an open door policy to foreign capital.[9]

REAGAN: INITIATIVES AND CONTINUITY

As I have already suggested, the Reagan Administration's nearly total indifference to human rights in developing countries of a rightist hue set it apart from a certain ambivalence which characterized the Carter era. This departure was clearly manifested in Reagan's arms exports policy. Aside from "a tendency to consider arms transfers almost exclusively in an East-West context," Landgren-Backstrom concluded in 1982 (p. 203) that "the Reagan guidelines are basically a restatement of the so-called Nixon doctrine of the early 1970's — Third World countries shall be armed as a substitute for U.S. military presence there." Or in the more colorful expression (Pierre, 1982:65) of a State Department official, "This is the currency in which foreign policy now deals.... We can't sign treaties anymore, we can't deploy forces abroad — so how the hell else do you do it?"

While offensive military actions against Grenada, Libya, Lebanon, Egypt and Iran were on a much smaller scale than those of the Nixon era in Southeast

	Violent		Institutional		Minimal	
	Civilian	Military	Civilian	Military	Civilian	Military
	Angola (SC)	Argentina (OD)	Albania (SS)	Algeria (SC)	Botswana (OD)	Nigeria (OD)
	Afghanistan (SC)	Bangladesh (OD)	Cameroun (OD)	Benin (SC)	Centr. Afr. Rep. (OD)	Panama (OD)
	Bahrain (OD)	Bolivia (OD)	China (SS)	Burma (SC)	Costa Rica (OD)	Portugal (OD)
	Chad (OD)	Brazil (OD)	Cuba (SS)	Burundi (SC)	Cyprus (OD)	
	Guinea (SC)	Chile (OD)	Equador (OD)	Congo (SC)	Dominican Rep. (OD)	
	Haiti (OD)	Colombia (OD)	Gabon (OD)	Egypt (OD)	Fiji (OD)	
	India (OD)	El Salvador (OD)	Gambia (OD)	Ghana (OD)	Jamaica (OD)	
	Iran (SC)	Ethiopia (SC)	Guyana (SC)	Madagascar (SC)	Malta (OD)	
	Mexico (OD)	Guatemala (OD)	Israel (OD)	Niger (OD)	Mauritius (OD)	
	Philippines (OD)	Honduras (OD)	Ivory Coast (OD)	North Yemen (SC)	Senegal (OD)	
	Saudi Arabia (OD)	Indonesia (OD)	Jordan (OD)	Peru (OD)	Trin.-Tobago (OD)	
	South Africa (OD)	Iraq (SC)	Kampuchea (SS)	Rwanda (OD)		
		Liberia (OD)	Kenya (OD)	Taiwan (OD)		
		Libya (SC)	Laos (SS)	Togo (OD)		
		Mali (SC)	Lebanon (OD)	Upper Volta (OD)		
		Mauritania (SC)	Lesotho (OD)			
		Pakistan (OD)	Malaysia (OD)			
		Paraguay (OD)	Malawi (OD)			
		Somalia (SC)	Mongolia (SS)			
		South Korea (OD)	Morocco (OD)			
		Sudan (OD)	Mozambique (SC)			
		Syria (SC)	Nepal (OD)			
		Thailand (OD)	Nicaragua (SC)			
		Turkey (OD)	North Korea (SS)			
		Uganda (OD)	Oman (OD)			
		Uruguay (OD)	Sierra Leone (OD)			
		Zaire (OD)	Singapore (OD)			
			South Yemen (SS)			
			Sri Lanka (OD)			
			Swaziland (OD)			
			Tanzania (SC)			
			Tunisia (OD)			
			Venezuela (OD)			
			Vietnam (SS)			
			Yugoslavia (SC)			
			Zambia (SC)			
			Zimbabwe (OD)			

Importing country	Total value*	Percentage of Third World total	Repressiveness**
Saudi Arabia	3797	8.0	M
Iran	3514	7.3	H
Iraq	3033	6.3	H
Syria	2913	6.1	H
Libya	2833	6.0	H
Israel	2676	5.6	–
Jordan	2626	5.5	M
South Korea	2042	4.3	H
Morocco	1350	3.0	H
Vietnam	1220	2.6	M
Peru	1126	2.4	H
Egypt	1126	2.4	M
Ethiopia	1096	2.3	H
South Yemen	1026	2.1	M
Algeria	986	2.1	M
South Africa	970	2.0	H
Argentina	859	2.0	H
Taiwan	848	2.0	H
Indonesia	685	1.4	H
Chile	671	1.4	H
Others	9885	21.0	
Third World Total	47829	94.0	

Table 5. Rank order and repressiveness of the twenty largest Third World weapon-importing countries: 1977–1981. Source: SIPRI Data Base. Reproduced from Landgren-Backstrom (1982:207); and Sivard (1982:17). Notes: *Figures are SIPRI trend indicator values as expressed in U.S. $ million at constant (1975) prices. The values include license-production. **Repressiveness in 1980: H = high. M = medium.

Asia, they marked a clear departure from the relative restraint which characterized both the Ford and Carter administrations. In other respects too the Reagan-Bush Administration exhibited continuity with the Nixon entourage. The Iran-Contra scandal mirrored Watergate (LaRue, 1987) in its disregard for Constitutional and common law norms. Similarities were also revealed by 1) an emphasis upon sophisticated weapons; 2) a shift to Third World recipients; 3) the effort to use proxies and mercenaries for regional intervention; and 4) support of military and other repressive regimes against domestic radicals.[10]

In general, arms transfers had also played a major role (Sorley, 1983) in the Nixon Adminstration's foreign policy. Domestic reaction to its failure in Vietnam and the Administration's insensitivity to human rights abroad—

Opposite: Table 4. Composite index of global state repression: 1980. Sources: Amnesty International (1981, 1982); U.S. Dept. of State (1981); Gastil (1981); Sivard (1982); Wolpin (1983a: Tables 3 and 6). Note: Development Orientations are OD = Open Door; SC = State Capitalist; SS = State Socialist.

epitomized by a catalytic role in overthrowing Allende's democratically elected government in Chile as well as flagrant disregard for America's own democratic process (i.e., Watergate)—engendered a sharp intra-elite division and mass disillusion. The latter was reflected by a sharp rise in political alienation among ordinary citizens (Gilmour and Lamb, 1975), a broad disaffection with the military-industrial complex and military interventionism, and a willingness by more committed liberal elites to challenge (Raskin, 1979; Barnet, 1981) the paramilitary, repressive and imperial policy manifestations of the so-called "National Security State" during the 1973 to 1976 period. While many of the Vietnam generation earnestly hoped that liberals in the subsequent Carter Administration would complement detente with a new global noninterventionist role, they were soon to be disillusioned. How this came about is discussed in the next chapter.

4. Carter's Interregnum:
The Eclipse of Liberal Human Rights and Arms Restraint Policies

Worth pondering is the gestation of detente under two Democratic administrations — those of John Kennedy and Lyndon Johnson — to be followed by its virtual funeral in the era of Carter, also a Democrat. This created a milieu in which Reagan's rampant militarism could triumph. By scrutinizing what occurred under the Carter Administration, we can better understand why liberals within the Democratic Party were incapable of *effectively* confronting the challenge of militarism and interventionism even when public opinion, along with a substantial elite sector (Kriesberg, 1982), favored Carter's initial "arms restraint" and "human rights" policy rhetoric. I use quotation marks because in a very real sense such policies were imposed (Schoultz, 1981:155): "Over the open and intense opposition of the Nixon, Ford and Carter Administrations, since 1973 Congress has added human rights clauses to virtually all U.S. foreign assistance legislation."

CONGRESSIONAL HUMAN RIGHTS INITIATIVES

Even before Carter's election, then, this new public mood of revulsion against military interventionism, subversion of foreign governments and support for authoritarian regimes was being reflected by congressional investigations of the CIA and proscriptions upon military aid to Chile, Argentina and Guatemala. In 1974 the Nelson Amendment (Pierre, 1982:50) "obligated the executive branch to give twenty-days advance notice of foreign military sales of over $25 million, during which time a sale could be blocked by the passage of a concurrent resolution of disapproval by both houses of Congress." The same source goes on to note that after President Ford vetoed an even stronger version of this restriction, new legislation was enacted in June 1976 which provided the statutory basis for the policy subsequently espoused by Carter. Its provisions were striking in both their specificity and their departure from past practice:

The International Security Assistance and Arms Export Control Act was the most significant piece of legislation dealing with arms transfers since the enactment of the Mutual Security Act more than a quarter of a century earlier. It sought to shift the focus of of U.S. arms sales policy from that of selling arms to controlling arms sales and exports. The act emphasized public disclosure and review procedures. All sales of over $25 million in weapons or ancillary services to non–Nato countries were to be handled through government-to-government rather than commercial channels, thereby eliminating most of the direct or exclusive dealings between U.S. companies and foreign governments; the time during which a concurrent resolution could block a sale was lengthened to thirty days; the president was called upon to submit information to the Congress on arms transfers on a quarterly basis; U.S. military assistance advisory groups (MAAGS) in foreign countries were to be severely reduced in both number and size, and their remaining personnel were subsequently instructed to avoid any activity that could stimulate host country requests for military equipment; prohibitions were placed on arms transfers to countries that violated human rights; "agents' fees" (often, although not always, a euphemism for bribes) and political contributions related to arms sales had to be reported to the Department of State. Through this act Congress secured its role in dealing with the process of arms transfers and gave voice to its continuing interest in restraints. The act expressed the "sense of the Congress" that annual aggregate sales should not exceed then current levels.

The same legislation also mandated "that the president make an annual country-by-country evaluation for the Congress on human rights conditions to aid it in making judgments on security assistance." In the first such report, compiled by the Carter administration in March 1977, it was found that in most of the eighty-two countries that receive some form of security assistance—the exceptions being the Western European nations and a few others—human rights were being violated in some degree.

Other restrictions on foreign assistance in the mid-1970s were the Clark and Symington amendments, which respectively prohibited military aid to CIA- and South African–backed Angolan counterrevolutionaries, and to countries developing nuclear weapons (i.e. Pakistan).

This moralistic (or what some critics later depicted as "soft-headed") liberal orientation was not wholly unrelated to assumed Realpolitik benefits. In subsequent congressional testimony (U.S., House, CFA, 1981: 42), leverage against repressive regimes as well as enhancement of American interests by disassociation from brutal "security" forces were stressed.[1] Not only would American prestige be enhanced globally as well as among opposition elements who often eventually come to power, but such human rights pretensions were also viewed as useful in promoting some liberalization in Eastern Europe, where the door might be opened further to American ideology and corporate investments. The second dimension of "Carter's" arms restraint policy was even more Realpolitik. Klare (1982:45) recalls:

> In a 1976 study of which Cyrus Vance was a principal author, the U.N. Association of the United States warned that "the massive introduction of new weapons systems" into potentially explosive regions of the Third World would influence local rivalries and thus increase the likelihood of violence. This

concern was shared by top aides to President Carter, who on May 19, 1977 adopted a "policy of arms restraint" designed to reduce U.S. military exports. Arguing that "the virtually unrestrained spread of conventional weaponry threatens stability in every region of the world," Carter also pledged to seek multilateral curbs on the arms trade.

Like the newly articulated concern for human rights criteria, this pledge marked a new policy, for previously, as Pearson (1981:27) notes, "there was no formal general U.S. policy on the sale of arms."[2]

What was really new, however, was the *symbolic* commitment to restraint and ostensible sensitivity to the human rights record of recipients. Hereafter arms transfers were to be treated as "exceptional," and a global ceiling was set. Moreover, Presidential Directive 13 proscribed development of weapons specifically designed for export, excluded flagrant and persistent violators of human rights, promised a progressive reduction of the global ceiling, and eschewed transfers of offensive sophisticated weaponry. In addition, military and diplomatic officials were instructed by a so-called "leprosy letter" *not* to assist the sales efforts of weapons marketers.

OUTMANEUVERING THE LIBERALS

Given the post–Vietnam milieu of strong public opposition to military interventionism during the mid-1970s, the best that right-wing military-industrial and allied bureaucratic sectors could obtain was a series of exemptions or loopholes as well as presidential waiver authority for "friendly countries" when "extraordinary circumstances" necessitated maintenance of "a regional balance." Also exempted were countries with major defense treaties such as Taiwan and Israel. Nor did the ban extend to infrastructural or support programs — training, technical assistance, construction of runways, etc.

So long as Paul Warnke, Cyrus Vance, and other "arms controllers" exercised influence or remained within an increasingly polarized administration, the "arms restraint" policy was at least partially implemented. But with a well-intentioned though indecisive president in the White House, the heavily financed unrelenting rightist propaganda campaign (Sanders, 1983a) gradually affected both elite and mass attitudes by equating the erosion of Western influence with gains by Moscow in the developing areas. At the same time, Soviet efforts to narrow the strategic gap as well as their modest yet growing role in the Third World were grossly exaggerated.

Those few Carter Administration top officials who would have treated the Soviet Union with the sense of equality and respect due any great power were eclipsed and forced out, as were others (like Andrew Young) who wished to accord similar respect to Third World nationalist movements such as the PLO. The Soviet intervention in Afghanistan simply accelerated a pattern that had begun to characterize the Administration within a year of its inauguration and was powerfully catalyzed by an event with which the Soviets had little to do: the Iranian Revolution and hostage crisis. A year earlier (1977) the Soviets had been deliberately excluded from Middle East Peace Accord negotiations with Israel and Egypt. And the CIA's "Team B" — a legacy of George Bush — had grossly inflated Soviet military spending by gearing it to dollar equivalents and changes in United States budgets.

As in the case of previous presidential efforts to make significant arms control progress, the military-industrial complex (Wiesner, 1985) assumed the character of a veritable state-within-the-state. Yet in the context of Carter's weak leadership, militarist sectors managed not only to block ratification of the Strategic Arms Limitation Treaty but also to subvert detente as well. These actions were possible because most moderate liberals themselves tacitly shared neo-imperial premises which, as McKinlay and Mughan (1984) as well as Wallensteen (1985) cogently maintain, implied a free hand for the United States in developing areas, as well as strategic superiority to back it up, while simultaneously denying parity to the USSR.[3] When the Soviets declined to accept permanent second class status premised upon such a double standard, much of the liberal American center in politics and the media joined rightists in denouncing Russian perfidy.

Thus the successes of the arms restraint policy were quite temporary and limited. They resulted from a few decisions made by committed though increasingly harassed officials in the first year or so of the Carter Administration. LaRocque and Goose (1982:20) of the Center for Defense Information — an anti-militaristic lobbying organization in Washington headed by retired military officers — note that military aid was denied or "significantly reduced . . . to over a dozen regimes recognized as consistent and gross violators of human rights." Further, although a substantial number of sales licenses have been denied by all administrations, the significance of Carter's first year is underlined by the fact that (Pierre, 1981/1982:276) an impressive "614 requests from 92 countries totaling more than one billion dollars were turned down in the first 15 months of the Administration."

Yet LaRocque and Goose also record that total weapons exports rose from less than $5 billion at the beginning of Carter's tenure to "the near-record level of $17.4 billion in 1980. About $40 billion in arms were sold to Third World nations . . . including controversial sales to Iran and Saudi Arabia." Undersecretary of State for Security Assistance Buckley (U.S., Sen., CFR, *Conventional Arms Sales,* 1981:10) acknowledged that "the total dollar value of agreements under the foreign military sales (FMS) program did drop from fiscal year 1976 to fiscal year 1977, but it began rising steadily thereafter. . . ." Although such offensive equipment as long range fuel tanks for Saudi Arabia's purchase of 62 F-15s was denied, many exceptions were made (Pierre, 1982:59) with respect to licensed joint production in "friendly" authoritarian Third World regimes. Pierre states:

The largest number of exceptions was made for the prohibition against co-production agreements with other countries for significant weapons, equipment, and major components. Most of these exceptions were made for co-production arrangements with countries friendly to the United States and involved low technology items such as grenade launchers, artillery pieces, and unsophisticated missiles. Nevertheless, South Korea is to co-assemble F-5Es; and Japan, which is exempt from the controls because it is a treaty ally, is to co-produce the F-15.

Iran was also exempted illegally as a de facto ally under the Shah's brutally repressive rule.

Clearly there were so many loopholes in Carter's arms restraint policy as to doom it from the outset. Indeed, one unsympathetic analyst (Pearson, 1981:41–42) demolishes or at least casts doubt upon several alleged accomplishments. First were "delayed approvals," which could be circumvented if the customer was "willing to pay." Second was a much touted decline in sales to the Third World in 1979. But Israel and certain Arab states were excluded from this statistic, and sales to NATO rose sharply. Further, the Iranian Revolution rather than the pro–American Shah's torture of opponents ended transfers to Teheran. Third, some weapons such as A-7s and F-18s were vetoed for the Shah's Iran, and another sale of F-16s to South Korea was also blocked. But these decisions were due only to firm resistance and the "personal influence" of Warnke, who was soon forced out of the Administration.[4] Fourth, while 1977–78 saw the greatest decrease in transfers, this was partly due to Pentagon preferences not to release "sophisticated technology" to certain African, Latin American, and Asian countries. Hence "when commercial sales are added to FMS, the sales decline during the Carter years is much less pronounced and really confined to the year 1977." Thus as Carter's policy-makers gradually succumbed to militaristic pressures to heighten tensions with both Third World nationalist movements and the Soviets, arms restraint became a dead letter. According to one careful student (Betts, 1980:105) of the matter, "during the second half of the Administration, the policy was put on ice in effect if not in theory."[5]

While (as noted previously) there were a few early denials on human rights grounds for several Central and South American countries, attack planes were nevertheless sold to Chile. Some formal refusals were inspired by fears of an arms race in Central America. Yet in several of these cases, Israel was encouraged to furnish substitute weaponry to sanguinary regimes in Africa and especially to the terrorist Guatemalan military and others in the Latin American region. Thus, Perera (1985:43) reports that "since the mid-70s, about 50 to 60 percent of all Israeli arms exports have gone to 18 Latin American nations." The dominant Israeli attitude — one reflecting Tel Aviv's disposition to serve as a willing neo-imperial proxy — was reflected in a 1981 public declaration by that country's Economic Planning Minister, Ya'acov Meridor: "We will say to the

Americans: Don't compete with us in Taiwan; don't compete with us in the Caribbean or in other places where you cannot sell arms directly. Let us do it. . . . Israel will be your intermediary." The United States has taken Israel's offer at face value, most recently in persuading Israel to sell to the Nicaraguan contras an array of Soviet-made PLO armaments that it captured in Lebanon. Why this was necessary is unclear as the CIA itself controlled the contra operation and presumably shipped weaponry from its own stocks.

Indeed, at least since early 1983, according to Greve and Warren (1984:1), the 160th Task Force of the 101st Airborne Division has been carrying out combat missions within Nicaragua in support of contra attacks. And of course funds from the Medellin Cartel as well as overpriced arms sales to Iran by the Casey-Gregg-North conspiracy to subvert congressional authority (Parry, 1988) ensured a flow between 1983 and 1987. The contra military command is headed by brutal ex–Somoza officers, while manpower shortages have been filled by an increasing reliance upon mercenaries (Lawrence, 1984) who also harbor few scruples when it comes to committing atrocities against civilians.

Interestingly, one anomaly in Carter's so-called arms restraint policy involved exhibition of greater caution by Pentagon officials than their State Department counterparts. (Ultimate responsibility was vested in State for implementing P.D. 13.) Neither human rights nor regional stability considerations explain the Pentagon's greater restraint. The explanation lies in the fact (Pearson, 1981:42) that the equipment in question was not yet available to U.S. forces: 155mm rounds, Maverick and Stinger missile motors, and coproduction of advanced helicopter designs. Thus restrictions upon such sophisticated weapons may reconcile this irony apparent in the Defense Department's ACDA being more of a restraining force than the State Department.[6] Yet ACDA actually raised objections to but 15 percent (199) of the 1360 proposed sales in FY1979.

The interplay of bureaucratic politics as well as ACDA's very limited influence—especially after Warnke's departure—is delineated (Pearson, 1981:37–38) in the following summary of the conflict over developing a specially designed export fighter bomber, the F-X (now the F-20):

> Functional bureaus concerned with P.D. 13 questions often line up across departments in opposition to the regional bureaus which somewhat more frequently favor sales. In fact certain DOD agencies were more critical of F-X development than certain State Department agencies. DOD estimated that the technological gap between the F-5 and the F-16 and 18 was narrower than State maintained, and would be closed even further by the time an F-X was marketed and obsolescence set in on the 16 and 18. However, such DOD views are tempered by the Joint Chiefs' priorities for support of cooperative military establishments around the world; the Joint Chiefs' staff tends to assume that target countries can be controlled through the military, and that the military are the logical leaders for many Third World states.

The last sentence in the quotation underscores a primary ongoing political objective (Wolpin, 1973) of military aid—one which helps us understand why Washington's neo-imperial political elites have recoiled against the arms restraint initiative.

Most experts concluded that Carter's arms control policy was a total failure. Only Pearson (1981:47) in a very limited sense and Klare (1982f:142) found the effort at all worthwhile. The former viewed it as a mechanism for enhancing "skepticism" about sales as foreign policy "levers."[7] Klare in highlighting that Reagan's early measures included authorization of three sales (F-16s to Korea and Venezuela plus the AWAC package for Saudi Arabia) held up by the Carter Administration, suggests that the policy had not been rendered completely nugatory.

More typical of overall assessments was the view (Betts, 1980:82, 84, 86) that "even before they were promulgated, the actual limitations were whittled to small proportions by the Administration's excessive commitments." After emphasizing some fast-footed bureaucratic maneuvering which enabled the Shah of Iran to get most of what he wanted,[8] the author aptly concludes that "the program of arms trade restraint had been crumbling from the moment of its inception. Philosophically flawed, practically unfeasible, and never seriously implemented, the policy needed only the *coup de grace* administered by the Soviets in December 1979."

THE NEO-COLONIAL DIMENSION

What other post-mortems offer useful insights for us? We have already seen that where it was a matter of maintaining a proxy or "sub-imperial" military (e.g. Iran), the restraint criteria were basically ignored as were human rights scruples. This also applied (Pierre, 1982:33) to South Korea and the Philippines, where United States bases assumed paramount importance. As for early denials to a few regimes due to brutal repressiveness, the consequences were to weaken Washington's neo-colonial leverage:

> Argentina and Uruguay announced that they wanted no American assistance at all, while Ethiopia closed some U.S. facilities and ordered American personnel to leave the country. Brazil, which had been cited in the human rights evaluation report for torture of political prisoners as well as arbitrary arrest and detention, canceled a twenty-five year-old military assistance treaty, rejected U.S. military credits, and loudly expressed resentment against American moral imperialism and the intolerable interference in its internal affairs. This occurred, it should be added, precisely when Washington was attempting to gain Brazil's support on a nuclear non-proliferation policy that was implicitly at odds with an important new Brazil-West German nuclear accord. Not surprisingly, the criticism of human rights and the end of the arms transfer relationship (subsequently Brazil was denied even spare parts for U.S. weapons already in its inventory) had a damaging effect on U.S. non-proliferation efforts.

Put more succinctly (Gliksman, 1981:81), the "inconsistent application" of human rights criteria "against Argentina but not against Korea, for instance — created bitterness and loss of influence."

Further, the existence of alternative suppliers such as the German Federal Republic, Great Britain and France in addition to Israel, has led some analysts (U.S., House, CFA, 1981:42) to conclude that only a joint supplier's agreement might have offered a real chance of effectively curtailing Third World militarization and repression.[9] Although we shall return to this point, another of equal significance is highlighted by testimony before congress (U.S., House, CFA, 1981:33) concerning the ineffectiveness of denials to Batista, Trujillo, Somoza and the Ecuadorian junta:

> This is not to argue that the United States should have provided arms in any of these four cases. It is rather to point out that arms transfers as an instrument of United States policy in Latin America are only effective if they are carefully coordinated with all other aspects of our policy, presenting a single, clear message to the individual nations of this hemisphere.

Yet the real issue, aside from coordinating disparate bureaucracies, remains: in these instances, human rights were not accorded the priority that is a *sine qua non* for such policy coherence. So long as suppressing social revolution and economic nationalism along with promoting corporate investment are the most salient policy goals, human rights are destined to receive rhetorical rather than orchestrated instrumental support.

Human rights promotion actually impedes attaining such goals. The maintenance of neo-colonial hegemony can be secured only by military training and its concomitant ideological indoctrination (Wolpin, 1973), arms, covert activities and the reinforcement that comes from a global military infrastructure of United States bases and alliances. Thus the human rights scheme at the outset was utopian in character. Even more shameful was the apparent willingness of some liberal arms control proponents — Warnke excepted — to go along with not only the use of "loopholes," but also the "juggling" of figures (Betts, 1980:84).[10] Indeed, another critic (Pearson, 1981:25), referring to the "loopholes," and "new accounting methods," went so far as to maintain that "arms transfer restraints are often designed to be circumvented."[11]

Pierre (1982:57) concludes that the result of such manipulation of accounting procedures "was that, while the ceilings were respected, giving appearances of reductions, in reality total U.S. arms sales actually increased." To this Pearson (1981:46) adds that at the close of the Administration, moves were afoot to broaden exemptions: "Even in Jimmy Carter's last days as President efforts were underway to modify the Arms Export Control Act to allow presidential authority to permit sales in emergencies, to eliminate advance Congressional notification of FMS sales to allies, and to 'clarify' restrictions on the types of defense 'services' U.S. advisors could lend to countries engaged in 'self-defense' or other military operations."[12]

The upshot of Administration backtracking was also epitomized by its January 1980 reversal on whether to develop *export-designed* supersonic fighters more sophisticated than the F-5. This decision was actually portrayed (Pearson, 1981:37) as an "arms control" measure:

> In 1979–80, six months of inter-agency review went into consensus building on the controversial development of an F-X intermediate jet fighter solely for export, an explicit contradiction of a P.D. 13 provision. Remarkably, spokesmen came to justify the decision to proceed as an arms control maneuver. Since there was no suitable aircraft for export to replace aging F-5's around the world except the sophisticated F-15, F-16 and F-18, production of an upgraded F-5, the F-X (technically Northrop's F-5G was the leading F-X candidate) would provide an alternative to the "necessity" of exporting America's most advanced systems. When arms control is taken to mean the development of alternative jet fighters and when decision-makers admit they would have "no choice" but to sell high technology aircraft upon request, the momentum for arms sales in all parts of the Federal bureaucracy, as well as the symbolic uses of one P.D. 13 provision to negate another, become evident.

The "momentum" also reflected an overall intensification of the militarization process during the 1978–1980 period. Congressman Dellums (1983:3) underscores this point: "In 1977, when the Carter Administration assumed office with a pledge to reduce military spending by $5–$7 billion in its first year, the total military budget was slightly less than $100 billion. Four years later it was $173 billion, but Carter left office asking for a further increase to $194 billion."

Earlier in this chapter we noted that a handful of Latin American regimes were antagonized by denials of arms on human rights grounds — really a consequence of pre–Carter congressional prohibitions. No other region, however, seems to have been so affected. With respect to Africa, for example, the chief of the State Department's Arms Licensing Division, Joseph Smalldone, testified (1983:215) that Reagan's arms transfers exhibited an essential *continuity* with Carter's — who also opposed Soviet influence and radical forces.[13] Between 1976 and 1980, he observes that aside from $15 million to South Africa, the seven major United States arms recipients were Egypt, Morocco, Ethiopia, Kenya, Nigeria, Sudan and Zaire. Table 4 shows that five of the seven were military-dominant while six were highly repressive — half violently so.

Only revolutionary Ethiopia was not deferential to foreign investor interests, and its arms flow was terminated in 1977 despite pleas via Israeli intermediaries for continuance. This is not to imply that the Derg was necessarily hostile to all investing corporations or Washington — only that it was dominated by nationalistic junior officers who aspired for independence, non-alignment and a socialist-oriented developmental mobilization. Washington's arms embargo may have sought to provoke a coup by United States–trained rightist officers since the American-equipped armed forces were dependent upon imported spare parts, etc. To exacerbate instability in the Derg or ruling Revolutionary Council, Saudi Arabia was encouraged to finance a Somali invasion of Ethiopia, which then moved further left and sought Cuban as well as Soviet assistance. The United States in turn encouraged both Egypt and China to provide arms to the Somalis. Both of these countries were de facto allies to whom shipments of military related material or weapons were being stepped up (especially to Egypt).

It is no wonder, then, that as early as December 1977 the Senate Foreign Relations Committee (U.S., Sen., CFR, *Conventional Arms Sales,* 1981:1) released a Congressional Research Service Study which concluded that "arms sales [had] continued with 'business as usual,' and that the policy was 'a victim of its own rhetoric.'" Former Congressman Armistad Selden, who served as State Department Counselor during the first three years of the Carter Administration and as Undersecretary for Security Assistance in the last year, subsequently (U.S., Sen., CRF, *Conventional Arms Sales,* 1981:95–96) recalled:

> I think someday, if a historian goes through and looks at the reality of actual sales, I believe one would find that there were very few sales that were actually turned down that another administration might have made. There probably were some, but not very many.
> But as I recall, last year the total sales of the United States in terms of contracts signed were about $15 billion. That has steadily moved up over the past years. I do not think there were many significant sales that were turned down.
> Second, regarding the rhetoric of the Carter administration, it was really unrealistic. There is one sentence in PD-13 which I have never been able to explain. It says that arms sales shall be "exceptional." They obviously are not exceptional, since we do $15 billion worth of sales. We have thousands of sales, and everyday they crossed my desk.

This perspective is also consistent with Pearson's overall (1981:36, 39–40) assessment that the restraint policy did little more than ease bureaucratic life by providing "clear ... checklists" and "excuses if they wished to turn down a sale without embarrassment."

> While ACDA spokesmen have noted in Congressional testimony that the qualitative controls dampen the proliferation of arms production capabilities in third world countries," they claim it is not possible to put a dollar value on sales turned down or turned off (quick discouragement), or to compare them to years before P.D. 13. Several hundred cases have been turned down, but few agency officials interviewed stressed the reduction of sales volume as one of the key benefits of P.D. 13 or Congressional review....
> On the whole then, P.D. 13 and accompanying legislation have been seen throughout the bureaucracy as a useful management tool though not necessarily very relevant to arms control. These provisions allow for more systematic sales priorities, quicker turndowns and turnoffs with less embarrassment when

administrators do not want to dispatch arms, quicker and better notice of companies' foreign sales promotions, easier protection for U.S. inventories and procurement needs, clearer evaluative criteria and checklists, and overall, more
order in a complicated and sometimes chaotic policy arena. . . . Such benefits
may make life easier for bureaucrats. . . .

He adds that "priorities for operational deployment of systems with U.S. forces
seem to have been successfully enforced, but assuring that U.S. personnel do
not promote sales abroad, especially in light of military consultation, the use
of agents and intermediaries, and close government-company relations, has
been extremely difficult."

Even more stark is the retrospective appraisal by Matthew Nimitz, Carter's
Undersecretary for Security Assistance, who in the course of a Senate arms
transfer hearing (U.S., Sen., CFR, *Conventional Arms Sales,* 1981:45) maintained: "Though greatest attention has been placed on the differences between
the Reagan Administration's approach to this issue from [sic] that of the Carter
Administration's approach, I believe it is important to note that the differences
are greatest in the rhetoric used. When one looks under the rhetoric, there are
important elements of continuity." The unmistakable conclusion, then, is that
in contrast to their bureaucratic-industrial opponents, the Carter Administration's arms controllers were "too weak" (Klare, 1982f:141–142) to have much
impact. Klare continues by noting that "the Administration became more and
more concerned about Soviet military activities in the Third World and thus
found itself less inclined to resist the powerful corporate and bureaucratic
forces which coalesced behind each major arms transaction."

In the final analysis, the most that can be said for Carter's arms restraint
policy is that it gave the issue of weapons exports to the Third World more
prominence, and rendered the arms transfer process somewhat more systematic
in administrative terms. The former achievement was largely negated by the
progressive militaristic shift in American policy during Carter's reign. Thus the
only durable legacy (Pearson, 1981:39) pertained to its having "improved
bureaucratic management, albeit while promoting bureaucratic redundancy,
and for this reason elements of it may be retained in the 1980's but it did not
fundamentally alter bureaucratic priorities. . . ." Pearson's prediction is borne
out by the testimony of a Reagan Administration official (U.S., House, CFA,
1981:24) who conceded that "the overall management and organization of our
arms transfer and security assistance program is not substantially different from
Carter's."

One of the factors contributing to the defeat of liberal arms control enthusiasts was the claim by militarists—conservative and liberal alike—that
unilateral arms restraint was utopian if not self-defeating. Not only would
American exporters suffer economically, but weapons producers in other nations were waiting to take over their markets. At the same time, the United
States would sacrifice political "leverage" and possibly generate resentment by

Third World political elites while rivals might move into the so-called "vacuum." The persuasiveness of such arguments—for those in the center and even liberals accepting the underlying neo-colonial foreign policy premises— was underscored by the growing ineffectiveness of Washington's non-military instrumentalities for controlling events beyond America's borders. Thus a recent study (Hammond *et al.*, 1983:76) concluded that "persistent trends in U.S. foreign policy since the fifties have loaded on arms sales more and more of the functions previously performed by other instruments of U.S. policy." Noting that the overriding goal of such transfers has been to promote deferential pro–American regimes in the developing areas, the same authors maintain that since the late 1960s, arms sales have become the primary mechanism for achieving such a goal, due to reductions in economic aid as well as unwillingness and inability to use United States forces or create new alliances.[14] Similarly, a heightened emphasis upon sales to Europe in the sixties— extended to Third World recipients during the following decade—was required by the rising costs of United States overseas bases, declining export competitiveness reflected by the deteriorating balance of trade, growing European, Japanese and Arab economic strength as well as other factors. As Hammond *et al.* (1983:76–77) stress, arms transfers—increasingly sales—had become ever more important "as a foreign policy instrument" since the late 1940s. By the late 1970s, they "were simply too useful for too many purposes to be extensively curtailed" or treated as an "exceptional instrument"—the purported goal of Carter's P.D. 13.

ILL-FATED ARMS EXPORT RESTRAINT NEGOTIATIONS

Proponents of restraint endeavored to meet this multifaceted challenge by arguing that benefits to the United States would outweigh costs if other major suppliers joined the United States in a mutual agreement to limit exports. Precedents did exist in related areas such as the "London Suppliers Club" of "major nuclear technology producing countries" which (Wulf, 1985:3–4) sought "to prohibit the proliferation of military relevant technology." Yet it was no more successful than the United States–United Kingdom embargo on arms shipments to India and Pakistan during their 1965 war. At that time, Turkey evaded the requirement of United States authorization for re-exportation by first sending fighter bombers to Iran, whence they were immediately flown to Pakistan. To these experiences one might add the United Nations embargo on weapons shipments to South Africa which had been notoriously flouted by the United States and a number of its allies including Italy, France and Israel.

Hence it is no wonder that Rand Corporation specialists (Ronfeldt and Sereseres, 1977:36) voiced pessimism on the eve of a Carter Administration effort to negotiate mutual arms transfer restraints for Latin America—an area of then relatively low militarization.[15] Despite such skepticism, the Vance-

Warnke arms control faction argued vigorously for efforts to reach multilateral agreement restricting transfer through what came to be called the Conventional Arms Transfer (CAT) negotiations. Thus in early 1977 (Pierre, 1981/1982:283) when Administration officials "broached the subject of cooperative restraints on arms sales with the European allies, responses ranged from expressions of interest and support to skepticism. A consistent theme in European responses was the need to involve the Soviet Union at the first stage." Or in the words of Richard Burt, a Reagan State Department official (U.S., House, CFA, 1981:22), the allies "argued that the United States and the Soviet Union had to work out an agreement first."

Between December 1977 and the collapse of the talks one year later, four sessions were held in Mexico City. Klare (1982g:44) recalls that "among the measures reportedly considered before the suspension were a ban of introduction of new high-technology weapons into Third World areas, limits on sales of nuclear-capable systems, and an embargo on especially odious weapons like napalm, 'cluster' bombs and incendiary devices." Pinpointing intra-administration dissension between what Sanders (1983a) aptly describes as "militarists" and "managerialists" rather than Soviet intrasigence, Wulf (1985:5–6) summarizes the progress of these ill-fated talks:

> After differences of opinion with the U.S. administration on a regional versus a technical approach had been decided in favour of regional regulations, the Carter administration suggested the establishment of working groups on regions and proposed Latin America and Sub-Saharan-Africa, given the relatively low levels of arms transfers by either side to these areas. The Soviet delegation was however more interested in legal principles regulating global arms transfers, particularly in defining criteria for potential recipients. The suggested guidelines were intended to permit arms transfers to those countries that needed arms for self-defense but not to those countries that used arms in wars of aggression. A compromise including legal, technical and regional criteria as well as guidelines was ultimately negotiated. After Latin America and Sub-Saharan-Africa had been discussed the Soviets proposed consideration of China and the Persian-Arabian Gulf. At that time U.S.-Chinese relations were somewhat normalized while the U.S. Gulf region policy was being delicately influenced by the instability of the regime of the Shah of Iran. The U.S. National Security Council suggested stopping the negotiations in order not to endanger U.S. foreign policy in these regions. Despite the fact that the Soviet government had accepted the U.S. proposal to expressly discuss geographic regions the U.S. delegation was not entitled to take up the Soviet suggestion.

Thus the final collapse was triggered when (Pierre, 1981/1982:283), "the American delegation was instructed at the last minute to refuse to even listen to any discussion of the Soviet proposed regions of West Asia and East Asia...."[16] Pearson (1981:26) also underscores that the breakdown occurred because of Washington's refusal even to discuss restraints in the Middle East and Asia (China) though "just fifteen years ago U.S. officials lamented the

U.S.S.R.'s refusal to 'listen to reason' and discuss mutual arms limitations to the Middle East. . . ." Now that Moscow had accepted the Carter Administration's geographical criteria, Washington was placed in an acutely embarrassing position. The impasse was resolved after the "managerialist" arms control faction was forced out of the Administration. In December 1979 (Kende, 1983:39) Washington broke off the discussions.

Pearson (1981:37) ultimately pins responsibility upon uncontrolled bureaucratic infighting and hard-liner Brzinski's influence with the President, which seems gradually to have eclipsed that of Cyrus Vance, who resigned when Carter approved the ill-fated special forces attack upon Iran.

> Indeed the Conventional Arms Transfer talks themselves seemed to fail largely because of the conflicting priorities of those at the State Department's Bureau of Politico-Military Affairs in Carter's early days, and the National Security Advisor. . . . Others with high level experience at ACDA lay the blame for the eroding emphasis on arms control under P.D. 13 to the influence of the National Security Advisor.

This assessment squares with Pierre's (1981/1982:283) post-mortem that "a deep split had developed between the American negotiators, headed by Leslie Gelb of the Department of State, and the White House." The militarists opposed detente, seeking instead to use military aid offers to entice pro–American elements in the Iranian armed forces to overthrow the revolutionary Islamic Government and similarly to "play the China card" against the Soviet Union. Pierre concluded that "the Conventional Arms Transfer talks with the Soviet Union collapsed more because of internal feuding within the Administration and a lack of clarity as to aims than because of substantive disagreements with the Soviet Union at the negotiating table. . . . But the split also reflected conflicting conceptions within the Carter Administration regarding policy toward the Soviet Union, especially with respect to the East-West competition in the Third World." It is no wonder that by April 1979—fully eight months before Soviet troops intervened in Afghanistan to support the Karmal faction—a Senate Foreign Relations Committee Report (U.S., Sen., CRF, *Conventional Arms Sales,* 1981:1) warned that the arms export restraint negotiations were "on the brink of failure."

Two and a half years later, during the height of Reagan's anti–Soviet rhetoric, the State Department responded (U.S., House, CFA, 1981:56) to an inquiry from House Foreign Affairs Committee Chairman Clement Zablocki as follows: "We have no plans to initiate supplier restraint discussions, given the apparent lack of interest of the Soviets and our allies when the issue was raised during the previous Administration."

RESURGENT MILITARISM: FROM CARTER TO BUSH

Before turning to the Reagan Administration's approach to arms transfers and their "deadly connection" to its drive for strategic superiority, it is crucial to stress that the militaristic faction's veto of strategic arms reduction proposals between 1986 and 1988 wasn't really a consequence of weak leadership from the President. Not only was his lack of foreign affairs expertise paralleled by a one-sided personal commitment to both human rights and arms restraint, but concerned elite sectors within the Reagan-Bush coalition couldn't appeal to a broad organized base backed by considerable resources either within or beyond the Democratic Party—itself little more than an undisciplined symbolic coalition of opportunistic personalities.

Militarist elements had long been dominant within the Republican Party. The Democrats, with the nomination of Carter, their most conservative major candidate, began a decade-long drift in the same direction, albeit with less zeal than the Republicans. This corporate-funded bellicose movement which overwhelmed both major parties did far more than make a mockery of human rights, Third World arms restraint initiatives and the ill-fated Conventional Arms Transfer negotiations. The ouster of the Vance-Warnke-Young arms control faction symbolized the unilateral American repudiation of detente. Even in 1977, prior to total demise of this detente faction, West Germans were being pressured to solicit the so-called Euromissiles—first-strike weapons such as the Pershing II and Cruise missiles. Although the West Europeans insisted upon negotiations by the two superpowers (i.e., the so-called "dual track" decision) prior to Euromissile deployment, disillusionment was quick to set in (Birnbaum, 1985a:10):

> Even before Ronald Reagan came to power, the ruling Social Democrats had begun to criticize American policy, [and] Chancellor Helmut Schmidt . . . wanted the United States to negotiate seriously with the Soviet Union before deploying the weapons, whereas U.S. officials regarded the Geneva talks on limiting intermediate-range missiles as a public relations device.

This because such emplacements were integral to the new war fighting preemptive as opposed to retaliatory strategy (Leitenberg, 1981), codified in Presidential Directive 59.

Years earlier General Eisenhower had become convinced (Houweling and Siccama, 1988:50–52) toward the end of his second presidential term that a disarming first strike was impossible. He then opted for nuclear armed yet relatively inaccurate Poseidon SLBMs to provide an invulnerable retaliatory capability. After winning the presidency with a militaristic campaign alleging a non-existent "missile-gap" in 1960, Kennedy backed higher military spending in order to restore a "first strike option" while retaining submarine and other (e.g. SAC) retaliatory or second-strike weapons systems. What had been "lost" with Soviet development in the late 1960s of a relatively invulnerable retaliatory capability (a modest yet "sufficient" number of ICBMs and SLBMs) is pointed up by Houweling and Siccama (1988:51):

America's absolute escalation dominance corresponds with a situation of
military preponderance; giving rise to inequality in bargaining power and leaving no doubt upon the question which side will give in during a crisis. . . . From
the moment the U.S. was no longer capable of taking out the Soviet strategic
nuclear weapons capability in its entirety, a switch was made to a doctrine of
deliberate gradual escalation.

Although the priority drive to develop high-speed, extremely accurate pre-
emptive weapons had begun in the early 1960s, it ironically was Carter's fate
to officially codify the United States commitment to their first or pre-emptive
use. The militaristic faction demanded deployment when such systems became
available in the late 1970s. And at the same time that the Soviets were reducing
their rate of increase in military spending and seeking a second SALT, the Carter
Administration was soliciting Congressional authorization for substantial
military expenditure increases for fiscal 1979 and 1980. These increases were
modest only in comparison with those of the Reagan-Bush Administration,
which took advantage of this new Cold War trend.

Other manifestations of the incremental militaristic takeover of Carter's
Administration can be discerned in his failure to control — let alone reduce —
the military budget, his reversal of a pledge to remove one of the United States
divisions from Korea, the arms race control rather than arms reduction content
(Johansen, 1979) that infused the SALT in its final version, Carter's disinclination to present even that watered-down treaty to the Senate, his willingness to
discredit an accurate assessment of his own CIA by allowing team "B" to inflate
Soviet military expenditures, dismissal of Andy Young because of his efforts
to negotiate with PLO representatives at the United Nations, and Cyrus
Vance's resignation over the militaristic hostage rescue mission in Iran. To
these might well be added Carter's ineffective and self-defeating 1980 grain
embargo against the Soviet Union. Sanders (1983a) describes in utmost detail
the origins and rise of a resurgent corporate-financed militaristic coalition, as
well as its veritable capture or at least intimidation of the Carter Administration. The Reagan/Bush 1980 victory signaled the culmination of such tendencies and, as we shall see, the unchallenged hegemony of the military-industrial
complex over and within an emerging American "garrison state."

5. The Salience of Arms Transfers and Threat Inflation in Reagan's "Containment" Policy

If the Reagan Administration's rationale for intensifying the nuclear arms race was premised upon an image of the USSR as an "evil empire" and the fact that the Soviets had attained a credible deterrent force (i.e., relative strategic parity), it was also fueled by Vietnam as America's first "lost war" and a perception of eroding Western and particularly American hegemony in the Third World.[1] Commenting upon the multifaceted identity crisis gripping many middle Americans, one astute observer (Kimball, 1988:435) recalls:

> In Vietnam, American national policy and military strategy met with defeat, or at least with failure; thus, America lost the war or at least was unable to emerge victorious. Battles were lost at the small-unit, tactical level. The army was humiliated and under criticism, its morale in shambles. Two presidencies fell victim to the war; one major political party underwent an upheaval in leadership, and another seemed doomed to an even smaller minority status than it then held. To some at the time, American society seemed to be undergoing a social, intellectual, and political "revolution." In addition, the U.S. economy was under increasing strain, and American foreign and military policy doctrines were in tatters. There followed a postwar period of economic crisis and perceived political confusion. Then, in the presidential election of 1980, a rightist "counterrevolution" achieved power through allusions to betrayal in Vietnam and calls for the revival of patriotic pride, stronger foreign and military policies, and more law and order at home.

Thus Reagan—exuding personal magnetism in emphasizing strength and confidence—rode to power on a program committed to reactionary socioeconomic policies at home and expansionist militarism abroad.

RESTORING AMERICAN PRIMACY

Externally, Reagan's unrestrained militarization of the early 1980s seems little more than a response to the dual failure of Washington's prior containment and detente policies. Although the latter policy could be differentiated in certain respects—civility of style, cultural exchange, arms control, expanded trade—both hinged upon the same (McKinlay and Mughan, 1984; Wallensteen, 1985) premises.[2] The first was that the Soviets could be prevented from playing a normal great power role beyond their borders in Europe, and particularly in the Third World. Ironically, the Soviets' "failure" to isolate themselves from the developing areas was in part a function of Washington's own interventionist behavior (Wofsy, 1985:12):

> The Third World governments and liberation movements that are most beleaguered by American military pressure and interventionism generally seek support from the USSR. The Soviets will not accede to exclusively American rights in the Third World. But they lack the economic motivation that underlies U.S. policy. Nor do they have the military and political range, the tremendous emphasis on rapid deployment forces and far-flung bases, that characterize Reagan's world-wide police mission.

In Europe, too, American hegemony was attenuated by West European economic strength, desires for autonomy, expanded trade and normalcy of relations. Equally, CIA-inspired uprisings (McGehee, 1983) in Berlin (1953) and Budapest (1956) failed to weaken the Soviet sphere of influence and security buffer, as was also the case with respect to more sophisticated destabilization efforts in the GDR (1961), Czechoslovakia (1968) and Poland (1979–1981). The virtual collapse of Russian dominance there was, ironically, a consequence of Soviet (Gorbachev's) reform inspired foreign policy departures.

The second faulty premise of the containment and detente policies— directly linked to the first—was that no change would occur that seriously altered the Soviet Union's strategic inferiority of the 1950s. Concretely, this meant that in any imaginable confrontation, the Soviets could not hope to credibly threaten unacceptable damage—even in the form of a retaliatory strike—upon the United States.[3] Or in the somewhat revealing terminology (Morrison, 1985:34) of Richard Wagner, Reagan's Assistant Secretary of Defense:

> "The final reason for accelerating advanced technology in the DOE program," he told a congressional subcommittee in the spring of 1983, "relates to what I call . . . keeping the Soviets in a deterred frame of mind. . . . What it comes down to in the end is for us to keep their image of themself [sic] inferior to their image of us, so that if a crisis comes along, they will have a gut feeling that they won't be able to measure up against us. It is a lot more than just numbers of weapons, the sizes and yields."

What he is alluding to is not only an expanded global base infrastructure but a qualitative lead symbolized by third-generation space- (i.e., "Star Wars") and land-based "tailored effect" weaponry, which would restore credibility (Bowman, 1985; Bowman, 1988) to future American threats to employ nuclear weapons.[4]

Long before Wagner made these allusions, a Joint Chiefs of Staff post–Hiroshima planning document (Makhijani, 1985:10) had anticipated the intimidating potential of being able to threaten nuclear attack with impunity:

> In the face of . . . the bomb's demonstrated power to deliver death to tens of thousands, of primary military concern will be the bomb's potentiality to break the will of nations and of peoples by the stimulation of man's primordial fears, those of the unknown, the invisible, the mysterious. We may deduce from a wide variety of established facts that the effective exploitation of the bomb's psychological implications will take precedence over the application of the destructive and lethal effects in deciding the issue of war.

That this was no idle musing is underscored by the boasts or claims of all American presidents and national security managers that such threats (Kaplan and Blechman, 1978) were directed at the Soviet Union during the 1946–1973 period. The specific occasions as extracted by IPS (1988:78) from the previously mentioned and other reputable United States sources were:

When the U.S. Threatened: Incident	Date
U.S. aircraft shot down by Yugoslavia	November 1946
Inauguration of president in Uruguay	February 1947
Security in Berlin	January 1948
Security in Berlin	April 1948
Security in Berlin	June 1948
Korean War: Security of Europe	July 1950
Security of Japan/South Korea	August 1954
Guatemala accepts Soviet bloc support	May 1954
China-Taiwan conflict: Tachen islands	July 1958
Suez Crisis	October 1956
Political crisis in Lebanon	July 1958
Political crisis in Jordan	July 1958
China-Taiwan conflict: Quemoy and Matsu	July 1958
Security of Berlin	May 1959
Security of Berlin	June 1961
Soviet emplacement of missiles in Cuba	October 1962
Withdrawal of U.S. missiles from Turkey	April 1963
Pueblo seized by North Korea	January 1968
Arab-Israeli War	October 1973

The only Soviet threat occurred in October 1962 during the Cuban missile crisis. Another may have been prompted by the Anglo-French-Israeli invasion of Suez, six years earlier.

While such Soviet threats may have contributed modestly to Kennedy's willingness to compromise, they were dwarfed by American "brinksmanship." Yet nuclear weapons, which account for approximately 15 to 20 percent of the

United States military budget, have also been tacitly threatened in a context of overt conventional intimidation. Afheldt (1988:27) draws upon the work of a British researcher (Sabin, 1987:59) to underscore the inherent dangers of such posturing.

> A detailed study of American demonstrative military actions in the three decades up to 1975 found that the U.S. got its way in nearly every case when strategic nuclear or major conventional forces were brandished.... Such actions retained their force despite the advent of nuclear parity, because the threat is not so much to go deliberately to nuclear war as it is to participate and persevere in an escalatory process, even though it might *result* in nuclear war. The risk of displaying resolve through such action is, of course, that events *will* get out of hand and that the superpowers will slide into an unintended conflict.

Fear by the late seventies — in the aftermath of "losing" Vietnam — that the USSR had developed an effective retaliatory capability accounts in part for the Reagan/Bush campaign's "window of vulnerability" rhetoric.

Thus, the essence of Reagan officialdom's militarization policy was reactionary; it sought to restore "relative escalation dominance" that flowed from the immense strategic superiority (Houweling and Siccama, 1988:52–53) of "containment" as it had functioned two or more decades earlier when the Soviets lacked significant retaliatory strategic capabilities. Yet, as Sanders (1983:27) observes, even this description is actually a misrepresentation of "an *offensive* strategy [which] has been characterized as containment." Referring to Weinberger's "Fiscal Year 1984–1988 Defense Guidance Plan," Sanders concludes that it "represents in effect . . . an expansion of the counterforce strategy set forth in skeletal form in PD-59."[5] He goes on:

> In addition to nuclear war-fighting, the Pentagon plan envisioned an improvement in covert operations over the next five years as well as an even greater emphasis on military aid to "friendly nations." Demonstrating once again the misnomer by which an offensive strategy had been characterized as containment, Fiscal Year 1984–1988 Defense Guidance also revealed that "particular attention would be given to eroding support within the Soviet sphere of Eastern Europe." Finally, according to the *Times*' account, the planning document asserted that "the United States and its allies should, in effect, declare economic and technical war on the Soviet Union," a tactic that would shortly be put to the test in the Administration's attempts to block construction of the trans–Siberian pipeline.

The foregoing seems to suggest an aggressive if utopian drive to enforce a hostile "Pax Americana" against the USSR as well as nationalist forces in the Third World — a posture incompatible with significant negotiated strategic arms reductions. This posture, it may be added, can be traced to Truman's related mid-1945 decisions (Nasser, 1989) to gratuitously employ nuclear weapons against a virtually defeated Japan then suing for peace, and his disregard of understandings integral to the Yalta accords.

The passage of three and a half decades witnessed the globalization of Washington's neo-imperial *Weltanschauung*. Thus, Richard Burt, the State Department's Bureau of Politico-Military Affairs director, defended (U.S., House, CFA, 1981:10) his administration's arms transfer policies by alleging that "vital American interests are challenged in almost every region of the world." Such a sweeping hegemonic perspective was proclaimed in simplistic paranoid terms of vaguely defined "real potential threats" by other high officials. State Department Undersecretary for Security Assistance James Buckley (U.S., Sen., CFR, *Conventional Arms Sales,* 1981:8) averred when referring to Afro-Asian nations:

> They will include a larger number of developing countries which desperately need more effective means of defending themselves against very real potential threats, countries with which we want to develop cooperative relationships so that in times of crisis we may be able to more effectively project our own power....

Upon occasion Administration officials and their congressional supporters (U.S., Sen., CAS, 1981:6–9) candidly distinguished "extremist" or "radical" regimes (U.S., Sen., CFR, *Arms Sales Package,* Pt. 1, 1981:27, 186, 190) as a "security threat" or even acknowledged (Cepeda and Glennon, 1983:1) that "some threats arise independently of the Soviet Union." At times both these and Soviet "pressures" were treated as *dual* threats justifying an actively "offensive" (Klare, 1982a) posture. Thus in attempting to defend $8.5 billion in sales to Saudi Arabia, Buckley threw down the following (U.S., Sen., CFR, *Arms Sales Package,* Pt. 1, 1981:33) challenge to skeptical members of the Committee on Foreign Relations:

> Will the United States be seen as supportive of a strong anti–Soviet posture by the free nations of Southwest Asia, or will they be forced to trim their foreign policies to accommodate new political and military pressures from the Soviet Union and the more radical states in the Arab world.

Although twice (32, 36–37) "the threat" was depicted as arising independently from "radical" Arab states, Buckley stressed (30, 33) the alleged Soviet menace.

Such threat inflation was equally manifest in the Administration's quick decision to give several billion dollars in military aid, including F-16s, to General Zia's highly repressive and corrupt Islamic dictatorship in Pakistan. This aid was granted despite Pakistan's export of heroin along with a nuclear weapons development program and the likelihood of destabilizing the regional balance of power with India. Harrison (1981/1982:96–97) reports:

> Administration officials often explain their new tilt toward Pakistan by arguing
> that India, with its extensive military reliance on Moscow, has become a virtual
> Soviet ally. But this explanation is a dangerous oversimplification. India turned
> to the Soviets for arms in the 1960s only after it had made an unsuccessful bid
> for large-scale U.S. military aid. Moreover, India has consistently attempted to
> minimize its dependence on Moscow. As one example, key components of the
> Indian-style Mig-21 aircraft made in India under a Soviet license are imported
> from the West. In recent years, New Delhi gradually has been increasing
> military procurement in Western Europe.

Yet the overwhelming mass of Administration justifications were reduc-
tionistic anti–Soviet and anti-radical imperatives at best, and some type of
conspiracy theory at worst.[6] Typically, in his FY1984 Annual Report to Congress (U.S., DOD, 1983:19) Weinberger alleged "the Soviet empire" was
the primary source or aggravator of most threats, including threats by
others.

Dogmatic rigidity was a consequence of the thinly veiled hatred
characteristic of Reaganism. Ideological animus easily distorts perception and
results in *a priori* rejection or discounting of evidence indicating that local (i.e.,
non East-West) grievances often fuel conflicts in particular countries or regions.
Hence, the rationales of state managers (Schoultz, 1988) and their congressional supporters were immune to their own Rand or CIA intelligence reports
suggesting such complexity. Similarly ignored were works by such scholars as
Raskin (1979), Barnet (1981), Halliday (1983), McKinlay and Mughan (1984)
and Cohen (1985, 1986) along with a host of others. Only direct personal exposure (in October 1986) to Gorbachev as a human being dedicated to improved relations enabled Reagan to transcend earlier rigidities. This new
dynamic, along with the encouragement by the president's influential wife,
Nancy, led to the ouster of some of the most fanatical die-hard opponents of
moderation within his Administration. The balance was gradually tipped
against belligerence and rigid obstructionism.

The dovish recalcitrance of many officials and moderates in Congress may
be attributed to their lower levels of antipathy toward the Soviets as well as
greater intellectual sophistication. Yet while neither fanatics nor militarists,
they still — with few exceptions — share a neo-imperial interventionist outlook.
Noteworthy examples of this modest but important distinction include former
Republican Senator Mathias' perspective on national security quoted briefly in
the first chapter. More outspoken has been a small band of prominent liberals
such as Congressman Dellums (1983:3), who publicly deplored a "national
security psychosis" that has been carried to a dogmatic extreme. This was put
more euphemistically by Matthew Nimitz, former State Department Under-
Secretary for Coordinating Security Assistance Programs, in a July 1981 Senate
Foreign Relations Committee (U.S., Sen., CFR, *Conventional Arms Sales,*
1981:50) Hearing on Conventional Arms Transfers:

The Argentine-Chilean dispute over the Beagle Channel, the long-standing territorial disputes among Peru, Ecuador, Bolivia and Chile that resulted in armed incidents just months ago, long-standing disputes among Central American states, and the historic rivalry, now quiescent, between Brazil and Argentina, have almost nothing to do with the United States–Soviet relationship. And there are other areas of the world, such as Sub-Saharan Africa, the Indian sub-continent and the China-Taiwan issue, where regional problems and the persistence of historic disputes or divisions are central to the arms transfer issues that we will face. In dealing with them, we must be mindful of Soviet ambitions and activities in the region, but these are often not the dominant considerations. I believe the administration will soon become aware of this reality of arms transfers. But I fear the East-West rhetorical framework for its policy may mislead some into thinking that these issues are easy ones....

Others, like Carter's second, and more interventionist, Secretary of State, Edmund B. Muskie, have warned (TRB, 1983:6) of the Administration's "anti–Communist paranoia," while former United States Ambassador to El Salvador Murat Williams offered a parallel diagnosis (Coffin, 1983a:1):

We are blind to believe that supplying helicopters and weapons and Green Beret training is the way to solve the problems in El Salvador. You just don't solve social problems by military means. You can't keep the lid on the boiling cauldron of popular aspiration by using machetes and guns. Our government has been unwilling to recognize this fact. A lot has to do with the basic philosophy of the Reagan Administration, which is that we are in a confrontation with the Soviet Union.

It's all wrong to let our policies be determined by fear. We are too big and too strong a country to be governed by anti–Soviet or anti–Castro paranoia. The problems in El Salvador existed long before Castro was born or even before the Soviet Union came into being.

Coffin (1983a:3) continues by reporting that "the ranking minority member of Senate Foreign Relations, Claiborne Pell (D-RI), has stated, 'At the very highest foreign policy levels, the Cubans have strongly signaled their willingness to cooperate in far-ranging negotiations with the U.S.' which would include discussions of mutual concerns in Central America. Cuba has also signaled its desire to lessen its dependence on the Soviet Union." Other countries about which the same might be said include Nicaragua, Angola, Vietnam and Afghanistan. Even Ethiopia had made such overtures.

Reaganite responses in these and other cases, including that of the PLO (until 1988), were to turn a deaf ear or even to continue hostile destabilization operations! The underlying animus was so extreme that it precluded the minimum respect necessary for negotiated agreements that markedly improve the underlying relationships. Thus when Paul Nitzi, a prominent Administration negotiator, actually sought (perhaps for his own prestige) an agreement

at the Euromissile INF "talks" in Geneva on matters unobjectionable to the
JCS, he was immediately disavowed.[7] Cohen (1988:307) explains that "the
modest progress in arms control [i.e., the 1987 INF accord] achieved since 1985
has been due largely to a long series of concessions by Gorbachev." Tragically,
this Soviet unilateralism, which was necessary to neutralize the most extreme
militarist sector (Weinberger, Adelman, Buchanan, Pearle, *et al.*) in Reagan's
entourage, has if anything made future progress more doubtful. For both 1988
presidential campaigns not only stressed "toughness" but also that future concessions would again have to be "asymmetrical." And the Bush campaign emphasized its unyielding commitment to carrying the arms race into space,
although the SDI label may be dropped as a symbolic concession. Predictably,
Bush's 1990 budget called for higher SDI funding.

It may be reasonable to infer that at bottom we are dealing with a
"paranoid projection syndrome" that masks, not what some refer to as a containment policy, but rather what Klare (1982a), Draper (1983) and Sanders
(1983) demonstrate to be an *offensive* militarist drive to eradicate Third World
nationalism, social radicalism and quite possibly the Soviet Union.[8] Catalyzed
by fundamental hatred, this strategic posture systematically employs threat inflation to rationalize militarization, interventionism, unqualified support for
stable pro-capitalist authoritarian regimes, etc. It is clear that hostility towards
"Communists" diminishes almost proportionately to their willingness to open
their systems to corporate takeover of existing investments. Even more important is the destabilization of the socialist regime itself, both politically and in
terms of its military base.

Referring again to the previously mentioned Geneva INF "talks" on
Euromissiles (Cruise and Pershing II missiles), another analyst (Paine, 1984:18)
provides a clue to why the Reagan Administration, in this area as well as others
where agreement was relatively easy (e.g. banning underground detonations
or anti-satellite interceptor testing), opted for public relations rhetoric rather
than serious negotiations:

> The "need" for the Pershing II stems not from any inability to retaliate after
> a Soviet attack on Europe. Its purpose, rather, is to make more credible NATO's
> ability to launch pinpoint strikes against the Soviets with an "incentive" not to
> further escalate any conflict, and to end it on NATO's terms. As Richard Perle
> told the Senate Armed Services Committee in March 1983, "We will continue
> to make clear that we have the capability to escalate a conflict, and that we will
> take whatever steps are necessary to halt aggression against us or our allies."

While the 1987 INF accord contributes to stability by modestly lengthen-
ing Soviet "launch on warning" reaction times and establishes the useful precedent of on-site verification, it fails to diminish the United States drive for
escalatory leverage. Not only did Gorbachev dismantle three warheads for
every one removed by the United States, but the disarmed warheads can be

modified for re-use. The significance of this and other "loopholes" is pointed up by Paul Rogers (1988, "Nuclear Connection," pp. 20–21), who appraises the INF within the broader "modernization" context:

> The strategic nuclear programs of the 1980s have enhanced the offensive "counterforce" strategies aimed at destroying the enemy's missiles and command structures.
> The most significant developments, some of which are still in early stages, have been the following:
> • major improvements in the accuracy of MIRVed (multiple-warhead) missiles;
> • earth-penetrating warheads;
> • offensive strategies to destroy missile-carrying submarines;
> • improvements in command, control, communications, and intelligence, especially to facilitate rapid retargeting;
> • stealth aircraft and "smart" standoff missiles designed to locate and destroy even mobile targets from a safe distance.
> Even a strategic arms reduction (START) agreement involving deep cuts, which may look attractive, could simply dismantle obsolete systems and even encourage the shift toward counterforce weapons. The INF Treaty will dismantle some counterforce weapons, but the treaty could be bypassed by increasing and modernizing sea-based forces and the short-range systems not covered by it. As with strategic weapons, the trend is toward increasing accuracy. Ultimately, third-generation warheads may be tailored to focus the energy of a detonation to destroy a military target with almost no collateral damage. This would further weaken the political and psychological threshold separating conventional from nuclear war.

Longtime Soviet expert Stephen Cohen (1988:306) cautions:

> Nor is the cold war over, contrary to euphoric reports in the media inspired by four Reagan-Gorbachev summit meetings since 1985. The nuclear and conventional arms race goes on, its fast-paced technology speeding far ahead of the political half-measures taken to constrain it. The ratified intermediate-range nuclear forces (I.N.F.) treaty, which promises to remove and destroy American and Soviet medium-range missiles in Europe, is important as a first symbolic act of nuclear abolitionism. But the two sides have given themselves three full years to abolish missiles capable of carrying, at most, only 4 percent of their stockpiled nuclear warheads. Discussions now focus on a so-called START agreement that would eliminate 30 to 50 percent of the strategic arsenals. By the time it is negotiated, ratified, verified and fully implemented, technological geniuses on both sides are likely to have invented new nuclear weapons that formally comply with the treaty but are even more deadly than those to be abolished. Meanwhile, both sides contemplate a "modernization" of conventional weapons, and a full range of underlying cold war conflicts—ideological, political and regional—continue to rage around the world.

Cohen's cautionary note is especially apt in light of Bush's initial deferral of nuclear test ban negotiations (Smith, 1990) in early 1990, "a move that could anger both Moscow and Congress, and his FY1991 budget featuring only cosmetic changes in force structures ("Experts," 1990) and weapons development ("Bases," 1990). Even the *Washington Post*—hardly a bellwether of the peace movement—deplores ("More Budget," 1990:6) the insignificance of Bush's proposed budgetary reductions:

> On the spending side, a modest $3.2 billion is cut from defense. Even that is achieved only by another "management savings" of $2.3 billion; almost none of the pruning of the weapons list that sensible military and fiscal policy both require is done.

Aside from modest cutbacks—primarily involving extending acquisition of new weapons (raising unit costs) and bringing a few more military contingents back to the United States—Congress is unlikely to sharply reduce military allocations in the proposed budget.

As Forsberg (1984: 295–98) argues, it is toward the unceasing struggle for politico-economic "hegemonialism" in the Third World that both the configuration of United States conventional forces and the drive for nuclear superiority are geared. Thus the Soviets' major unilateral conventional force reductions and deployment changes, as well as specific proposals for a non-intervention regime, a convention to eliminate chemical weapons, further conventional reductions in Europe, a 50 percent diminution of strategic weapons—all highlighted (Farris, 1988:1, 6) in Gorbachev's United Nations address—failed to elicit reciprocal proposals offering equal or, indeed, *any* concessions by either Reagan or Bush. After all, such initiatives would, if reciprocated, undermine not only the arms race dynamic but also the quarter-century drive to restore American escalatory dominance in any East-West confrontation. For at bottom the nuclear arms build-up in the North is designed to ensure the credibility of escalatory threats in the event that American clients, proxies or forces are on the verge of defeat in the developing areas or elsewhere. In fact, Forsberg (1988: 49–50) goes so far as to argue that "making superpower forces defense oriented in a limited geographic region—especially Europe—while they remain non-defense oriented everywhere else in the world is impracticable."[9] Thus in a dual sense United States interventionism helps explain Washington's virtual paralysis insofar as major arms control reductions are concerned.

To forestall the need for "escalatory dominance" (Forsberg, 1984), the Reagan-Bush Administration—as shown in Chapter 3 and discussed subsequently in this chapter—sharply stepped up military training and arms transfers to developing countries. Similarly, it assigned unparalleled priority to developing (Klare, 1989) both doctrine (at the Army–Air Force Center on Low-Intensity Conflict in Langley, Virginia) and administrative structure for expanded low intensity interventionist capabilities. With respect to the latter, Miller (1988:18) underscores:

Congressional enthusiasm for the concept rivals that of the Administration. With little fanfare, in 1986, lawmakers created a new job at the Pentagon for Special Operations and Low Intensity Conflict.

At a doctrinal level, "low" refers to modest rather than massive commitments of special forces or other troops in the newly created "light" infantry divisions assigned to the expanded Central Command. Nevertheless, it seems clear that, as Miles (1989:155) shows, the doctrine encompasses a wide range of possibilities.

> As less attention is paid to reform, LIC may simply degenerate into repression and special operations, carried out by a combination of elite US forces, foreign mercenary soldiers, and private businesses. It may mean broader coalition warfare by the US in alliance with third countries such as Egypt, Jordan, Pakistan, Turkey, Korea, Taiwan, and others. Other, non-military LIC activities will be carried out that, in the words of Sam Sarkesian "fight without appearing to fight, and wage war through peaceful enterprise." And a greater degree of secretiveness in all of these activities is much more likely: the fact that responsibility for LIC is spread out through the bureaucracy may actually help future operations to maintain a lower profile.

The Bush Administration's 1989 invasion and occupation of Panama may reflect an escalatory "high-intensity" alternative when "low profile" subversive operations fail. Certainly the unilateral dispatch of the S.S. *Kennedy* to nearby Colombia deviates markedly from maintaining a "low profile." Hence, the doctrine per se should not be taken too seriously as an operational constraint.

Of perhaps greater significance, then, is a concomitant policy emphasis upon the development of ("appropriate") semi-high tech weaponry such as sensors, remotely piloted vehicles, robots, microwave weapons, aperture radar, and other exotically labeled yet user-friendly arms. Of these Miller (1988:21) recounts:

> SAMs, SARs, LIDs, RPVs, and their kin are the weapons of the future, the arms that, barring nuclear war, will actually do the killing. In the words of "Discriminate Deterrence," a top-level Defense Department study of long-term strategy, the Pentagon is looking at the armaments that will be in service well into the next century. Issued this year, that document reveals that the Pentagon is quietly moving its frontlines of attention to suppression of Third World insurgencies, while also maintaining its financial and public allegiance to anti–Soviet nuclear strategies.

While largely symbolic arms control agreements with the Soviets along with their retrenchment from Eastern Europe and Moscow's sharply reduced support for Third World nationalism will lessen the use of anti–Soviet "threat inflation," it is unlikely that anti–Sovietism will disappear as a dominant American cultural bias. Unless, of course, the Soviets open the door to uncontrolled corporate investment.

Whether or not all those who focus upon drug or other "terrorism" or "the Soviet menace" unwittingly believe their own exaggerations is problematic. Sanders (1983:7, 13–14), who elsewhere traces the rise of this reductionist perspective — one akin to that of the McCarthy era — to a heavily financed domestic campaign since the early 1970s by the Committee on the Present Danger, is skeptical.

> As I have tried to show elsewhere, this worst-case perception of Soviet capabilities and intentions, which has now become official dogma, represents a deliberate distortion of reality for purposes of partisan gain. Even though the Soviets have made significant military improvements over the last decade to reach a point of strategic parity with the U.S., the alleged "window of vulnerability" (the current version of the "Soviet threat") has no basis in fact and appears to be as calculated as previous apocryphal threats, gaps, and exaggerations of Soviet capabilities and intentions that have been well documented over the course of the Cold War.

Similarly, Johnstone (1983:22) in the course of reviewing Fred Kaplan's doctrinal analysis *(The Wizards of Armageddon)*, contends that "the U.S. security establishment, by projection, has created a fictitious monster called the USSR, which is largely the mirror image of strategic threats dreamed up by the American wizards ('national security' intellectuals) for their own side."

A more recent interview-based study (Schoultz, 1988) focused upon how three hundred top Reagan Administration officials employed "national security" goals when dealing with "instability" in Central America. The importance of this study is underscored by the probability that many of the officials were carried over to the Bush Administration. Predictably, rather than guiding or constraining policy, "national security" was rhetorically used to legitimize decisions to maintain an imperial sphere of influence. Enhanced data and contrived options were routinely provided by subordinates to decision-makers who welcomed such simplifications because of their own frequent inability to comprehend the data. Worse, when policy alternatives existed that might have enhanced American security with greater efficiency though at the cost of promoting regional dominance, they were systematically excluded as appropriate or viable options. Hence, in their own (rhetorical) terms, policy-makers often weakened the very security they claimed to be furthering.

It is probable that deliberate distortion characterized the work of officials, politicians, and intellectuals who were sophisticated or well-educated and highly competent. Others whose antipathy was especially intense and whose previous experience had not qualified them for their positions were likely victims as well as manipulators of such rhetoric. While the late CIA Director Casey, Bush, Haig, McFarlane, Burt, Enders, Buckley and perhaps Schultz seem to fall into the first group, Reagan, Buchanan, Clark, Pearle, Adelman and possibly Weinberger were characterized by expressive fanaticism, mild paranoia and/or the Peter Principle. Kelly (1983: 8–11) provides us with a poignant example of the cynical manipulation perpetrated by the more sophisticated sector of officialdom, showing how Casey found it necessary to purge CIA officials such as David MacMichael, whose integrity prevented them from fabricating or inflating data on "terrorism" and imputing Soviet responsibility.

Subsequently, after generating and publicizing such "facts" by, among other things, innuendo, and classifying "potential" terrorist threats as terrorism, Casey in an address to the United States Chamber of Commerce (quoted in the third chapter of this study) attributed most actual "terrorism" to the "instability" generated by "nationalism" and "economic austerity" in the developing areas. At least some intelligence officials (Alexander Cockburn, 1985:102–103) sought to inform top decision-makers that little evidence supported repeated allegations concerning Soviet sponsorship of a global terrorism network. That these officials were routinely ignored reflects intense animus and the perception that the allegations against the Soviets—reinforced by an anti-left network of *agents provocateur* (Lawrence, 1985) and other redundant disinformation—were valuable psychological warfare resources.

SOVIET INTENTIONS AND CAPABILITIES: DUAL THREAT INFLATION

At the core of this publicized threat inflation is an attribution of demonic character to the Soviets. Beyond the pale of humankind, or at least the American moral code, their nefarious "evil empire," as painted by the Reagan-Bush Administration, was so unscrupulous that only force would effectively counter compulsive aggressiveness. Such a Manichean perspective is naturally devoid of the respect and equality of status necessary for serious arms reduction negotiations let alone durable agreements that promote the genuine cooperation necessary to resolve the Israel-Arab or other war-threatening crises. Neither Christian humility nor self-criticism has characterized American officialdom when declaiming or testifying about "the Soviet threat." The blatant hypocrisy as well as the potential for mass violence which inheres in this crude reification has even astonished the Roman Catholic hierarchy—not noted for "softness" toward communism. Questioning such a tacit justification for waging World War III, the United States Bishops' Conference (National Conference, 1983: B16) admonished:

> To pretend that all evils in the world have been or are now being perpetrated by dictatorial regimes would be both dishonest and absurd. But having said this, it is imperative that we confront reality. The facts simply do not support the invidious comparisons made at times, even in our own society, between our way of life, in which most basic human rights are at least recognized even if they are not always adequately supported, and those totalitarian and tyrannical regimes in which such rights are either denied or systematically suppressed....
>
> We see with increasing clarity the potential folly of a system which threatens mutual suicide, the psychological damage this does to ordinary people,

especially the young, the economic distortion of priorities—billions readily spent for destructive elements while pitched battles are waged daily in our legislatures over much smaller amounts for the homeless, the hungry and the helpless here and abroad. Negotiations on arms control agreements in isolation, without persistent and parallel efforts to reduce the political tensions which motivate the build-up of armaments will not suffice....

Our government has sometimes supported repressive governments in the name of preserving freedom, has carried out repugnant covert operations of its own, and remains imperfect in its domestic record of insuring equal rights for all....

Sensible and successful diplomacy, however, will demand that we avoid the trap of a form of anti–Sovietism which fails to grasp the central danger of a superpower rivalry in which both the U.S. and the U.S.S.R. are the players....

But the Soviet people and their leaders are human beings created in the image and likeness of God. To believe we are condemned in the future only to what has been the past of U.S.-Soviet relations is to underestimate both our human potential for creative diplomacy and God's action in our midst which can open the way to changes we could barely imagine.

The quasi-hysterical reaction of the Reagan Administration to the unsoftened first draft of this statement was conditioned ideologically by strategic hatred underlying what I have previously referred to as a paranoid projection syndrome. Almost a decade later, policy elites have yet to fully assimilate the document's prescient counsel.

Despite scholarly research by Ravenal (1980), Forsberg (1984) and many others showing Soviet behavior as well as influence to be sharply at odds with such caricatures, no reappraisal as yet promises to affect the basic United States posture. Indeed, three years of initiatives by Gorbachev evoked little more than stylistic moderation by the Reagan Administration. Similarly, the 1988 presidential campaign indicated that neither Bush nor Dukakis was open to experts who would meet Gorbachev's new thinking with some of their own. Thus Stephen F. Cohen (1988:106), writing during the height of the campaign—before Bush pulled ahead—deplored the fact that

> ...a great many influential Americans in both major political parties are sternly warning the next Commander in Chief against any such policy. Some of them are theological cold warriors for whom there can never be an alternative U.S.-Soviet relationship, no matter how great the necessity or possibility. But the majority of these influential advisers belongs to the self-described "bi-partisan center"—a large company that includes many of yesterday's officials and policy intellectuals whose worn concepts obscure today's historic changes and opportunities. They speak of policy toward Gorbachev's Soviet Union in abstract jargon and empty cliches about "toughness" and "negotiating from strength," as though everyone else advocates dealing from weakness. In effect, by insisting that U.S. policy never deviate from "bi-partisanship" and the center, they reflexively oppose the new anti–cold war thinking and measures that America so urgently needs.

While there are significant differences between our wild-eyed cold warriors and statesmanlike centrists, they are united by their opposition to a fundamentally new course in U.S.-Soviet relations. Their recommendations vary, from a policy of escalated cold war and arms race to one of indifference or business as usual toward Gorbachev's leadership.

Bush's commitment to restoring the escalatory leverage ("strategic superiority") lost in the mid-1960s when the Soviets acquired an invulnerable retaliatory (second-strike) capability suggests that unless an improbably continuous succession of unilateral concessions emanates from the Gorbachev leadership, the now "potential" Soviet threat (should conservatives oust Gorbachev) will continue as the unifying sacrosanct assumption of American policy elites.

Ullman (1988), like Stephen Cohen (1988), warns that interim failure to go halfway will strengthen Gorbachev's hard-line opponents—thus restoring the "threat" as traditionally portrayed. Others warn that the charismatic Soviet President's possible success in politico-military and economic reform goals will so strengthen Soviet appeal and systemic capabilities that the USSR will become an even more threatening superpower. It seems, then, that American elites may share a functional need for an external threat of such dimensions that it can be employed to weaken forces seeking even reformist socio-economic *perestroika* both domestically and in the developing areas. For it is far more difficult to discredit such counter-elites without being able to link them to a real or imaginary Soviet menace that foments "instability" and "terrorism" in the Third World. Recently, although association with the "Soviet menace" still serves handily in Central America, Africa and Asia, indigenous communists, Marxist-radicals and "narco-terrorists" are (at least for the present) being projected as functional equivalents to justify perpetuation of massive interventionist forces. Thus if one form of "threat" recedes, surrogates will be accorded greater prominence in the struggle against economic nationalism and de facto political independence.

The corollary to the "Soviet threat"—one shared unfortunately by a majority in both houses of the United States Congress—implies that one should embrace and depict as "moderate" the most despotic rightist regimes if they appear useful (Herman, 1982) in holding back the tides of egalitarian (McGehee, 1983) social change and nationalism—regardless of the degree to which the Soviets support such tides. This perspective has been dominant since the eclipse of detente in the latter 1970s. Hence in the course of defending (U.S., Sen., CFR, *Arms Sales Package,* Pt. 2, 1981:84) the previously mentioned sale of AWACs and other offensive weaponry to the flagrantly corrupt authoritarian regime in Saudi Arabia, Weinberger stressed: "we would be equally concerned with any problem that might arise internally...." Not to be outdone in demonstrating they had learned little from past close identification with such despots as Haile Selassie, Somoza and the Shah of Iran among others, the pro–Administration majority in the Senate Committee on Armed Services (U.S., Sen., CAS, 1981:9–10) approvingly reported:

> Saudi leadership is sensitive to prevailing and potential internal problems, particularly since religious fanatics seized the Grand Mosque at Mecca in November 1979. Saudi society remains strongly traditional, religious, and oriented toward tribal institutions. This orientation and the presence of the House of Saud throughout the Kingdom's bureaucratic structure act to create a stable internal situation.
>
> At present, opposition to the Saudi government is reported to be weak and disorganized.

Similarly, Senate Foreign Relations Committee Chairman Percy had the following exchange (U.S., Sen., CFR, *Arms Sales Package,* Pt. 2, 1981:75) with then State Department Counselor and subsequent National Security Advisor Robert McFarlane:

> [MR. PERCY.] Is there not more of a democratic process in their own way than really is fully understood in the West?
>
> MR. MCFARLANE. That is right, Mr. Chairman. In all of our dealings with the Saudis, we have been impressed by the deliberation and care with which decisions are made. They clearly reflect collegial exchanges within the hierarchy of the royal family.

Portrayals by the Reagan Administration and these two key committees were dogmatically maintained notwithstanding considerable contradictory testimony from the likes of General George Keegan (Ret.), former Assistant Chief of Staff of Air Force Intelligence, who warned (U.S., Sen., CFR, *Arms Sales Package,* Pt. 1, 1981:270–271) that many young American-trained Saudi officers were highly nationalistic and that it was therefore unwise to be so intimately linked to the existing oligarchy:

> The Saudi regime, whatever its friendship for the United States or not, is in fact one of the last great despotic feudal regimes on Earth. You have to go and you have to see for yourself what passes for civil rights in the country. . . . These people are going to make a revolution, if not tomorrow, then next year, sometime.

It is conceivable that General Keegan, like the minority of professional officers referred to in the initial section of this study, reflects a broad or civilianist national security perspective—one that neither defines the Saudi regime as democratic nor views a suppressed domestic opposition as necessarily threatening American safety and welfare, i.e. national security.

Perhaps the most ubiquitous manifestation of threat inflation has been the systematic exaggeration of Soviet military capabilities and successes. It is true that the former have increased relative to America's since Kennedy "humiliated" Khrushchev in the 1962 missile crisis, and particularly after Nixon played nuclear blackmail during the 1973 Yom Kippur war. However, as Kaplan (1982), Ege (1983) and others have emphasized, in such crucial areas

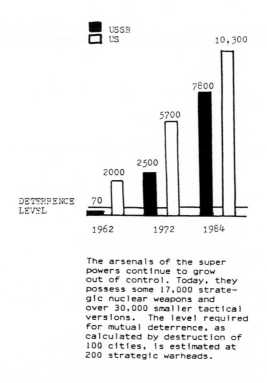

The arsenals of the super powers continue to grow out of control. Today, they possess some 17,000 strategic nuclear weapons and over 30,000 smaller tactical versions. The level required for mutual deterrence, as calculated by destruction of 100 cities, is estimated at 200 strategic warheads.

Figure 3. Strategic nuclear weapons of the superpowers. Source: *Sivard (1982), adapted.*

as warheads, electronics, accuracy and overall quality, the United States remains far ahead. Even Weinberger (U.S., DOD, 1983:303) boasts of "the qualitative superiority of U.S. security assistance," i.e., weaponry and training.

Figure 3, Table 6, and Figure 4 are instructive in this regard. Table 6 and Figure 4 were produced by the Defense Department, whose budgetary insatiability would incline it if anything to minimize American and NATO superiority. By 1988, according to the Center for Defense Information ("U.S.-Soviet," 1988:1), the United States had "more than 16,000 nuclear weapons" it could explode "on the Soviet Union," compared to 11,000 such weapons the USSR could explode on the United States. And in the area of "deployed military technologies," the CDI ("NATO and Warsaw Pact," 1988:4) emphasizes the great NATO "advantage" in "weapons quality" in tanks and combat aircraft — "two of the most important weapons categories" — as well as elsewhere.

This advantage is reflected in, for example, the greater accuracy of NATO anti-aircraft and anti-tank missiles. In a 1988 estimate the Pentagon rated the U.S. superior to the Soviet Union in 15 categories of deployed weapons technologies —

BASIC TECHNOLOGIES	U.S. SUPERIOR	U.S./U.S.S.R. EQUAL	U.S.S.R. SUPERIOR
1. Aerodynamics/Fluid Dynamics		X	
2. Automated Control	X		
3. Conventional Warhead (including Chemical Explosives)			X
4. Computer	X		
5. Direct Energy		X	
6. Electro-Optical Sensor (including IR)	X		
7. Guidance & Navigation	X		
8. Microelectronic Materials & Integrated Circuit Manufacture	X		
9. Nuclear Warhead		X	
10. Optics	X		
11. Power Sources (Mobile)		X	
12. Production/Manufacturing	X		
13. Propulsion (Aerospace)	X		
14. Radar Sensor	X		
15. Signal Processing	X		
16. Software	X		
17. Stealth (Signature Reduction Technology)	X		
18. Structural Materials (lightweight, high strength)	X X		
19. Submarine Detection (including Silencing)	X		
20. Telecommunications	X		

Table 6. *Relative U.S./U.S.S.R. standing in the 20 most important basic technology areas.* Source: *FY1984 DOD* Report on Research, Development and Acquisition. *Reprinted from Ege (1983:16).*

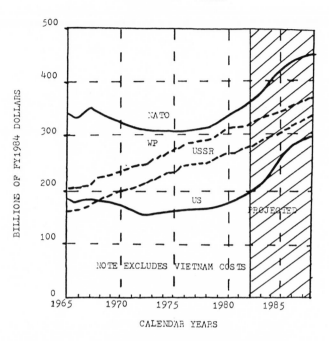

MILITARY EXPENDITURES OUTLAYS

Figure 4. A comparison of NATO military expenditures with estimated dollar cost of Warsaw Pact defense activities. Source: *FY1984 DOD* Report on Research, Development and Acquisition. *Reprinted from Ege (1983:17).*

including, for example, attack helicopters, combat aircraft, and surface warships — equal in ten categories, and inferior in only six. Similar disparity exists with respect to military expenditure increases for the major "superpowers." Between (IPS; 1988:74) 1979–85, the U.S. average was four percent while that of the Soviets was two percent.

Equally at odds with Reaganite threat inflation is Table 7, indicating relative stability for Soviet production of major weapons. In fact, between 1977 and 1981 there were declines for no less than fourteen items and increases for but six — only one of which was of substantial magnitude. This trend, documented by the prestigious Stockholm International Peace Research Institute (SIPRI), is also consistent with CIA (1985) data:

> Based on satellite surveillance, the CIA estimated that since 1976 the annual growth rate of Soviet military spending has sunk to two percent or even lower, according to Leonard Silk in *The New York Times,* January 23, 1985.

Military Item	1977	1978	1979	1980	1981
GROUND FORCES MATERIAL					
Tanks	2500	2500	3000	3000	2000
Other armoured fighting vehicles	4500	5500	5500	5500	4500
Towed field artillery	1300	1500	1500	1300	1500
Self-propelled field artillery	950	850	250	150	200
Multiple rocket launchers	550	550	450	300	400
Self-propelled AA artillery	300	300	300	200	200
Towed AA artillery	250	100	-	-	-
AIRCRAFT					
Bombers	30	30	30	30	30
Fighters/fighter-bombers	.1200	1300	1300	1300	1350
Transports	400	400	400	450	350
Trainers	50	50	25	25	10
ASW	10	10	10	10	...
Helicopters	900	650	700	750	750
MISSILES					
ICBMs	300	200			
IRBMs	100	100			
SRBMs	200	250			
SLCMs	600				
SLBMs	175				
ASMs	1500				
SAMs	50000				
ATGMs	35000				
NAVAL SHIPS					
Submarines	13	12	12	13	9
Major combatants	12	12	11	11	9
Minor combatants	55	50	50	60	45
Auxiliaries	6	4	7	5	5

Table 7. U.S. Defense Intelligence Agency estimates of Soviet output of certain military items: 1977–1981. Source: "Allocation of Resources in the Soviet Union and China — 1982," Statement of Lt. General James A. Williams before the Joint Economic Committee (Defense Intelligence Agency, Washington, D.C., 29 June 1982, as reproduced by Ohlson and Tulberg [1983:155]).

According to a study by Richard Kaufman, assistant director of the Joint Economic Committee of Congress, data from official intelligence sources shows a decline in production of certain strategic offensive systems which "were the most costly." Deployment shows a similar trend: the Soviet land-based ICBM force declined by 70 missiles in 1973–77 and by 79 missiles in 1978–82. Nuclear-powered ballistic missile submarines rose by 34 in 1973–77 but only by one in 1978–82.

Appraising the Kaufman study, John Steinbruner of the Brookings Institution criticized the Pentagon for a "systematic overestimate that ignores Soviet

restraint." He stated that Defense Secretary Weinberger is responsible for the
non-disclosure of the information concerning Soviet restraint in the production
and deployment of offensive weapons. Steinbruner correctly emphasizes that
"fears about the Soviet military that are rendered immune from any disproof
or qualification will ultimately become self-fulfilled."

These studies belie the familiar contention of the Reagan administration that
the USSR "has conducted the greatest military buildup in the history of man."
This false contention has been the pretext for the massive increase in the
military budget during Reagan's first term. Now, too, it is being used as the
excuse to raise military spending by six per cent above inflation. Of course, such
a raise is also sharply inconsistent with Reagan's promise to seek arms reduction
in his second term.

Similar reports of a slowdown in the growth of Soviet military expenditures
during the Carter era even come from the Western alliance ("NATO," 1985:230)
in Brussels. It is no wonder that Ege (1983:15) recounts:

> "Today, in virtually every measure of military power, the Soviet Union enjoys
> a decided advantage." (Ronald Reagan, November 22, 1982)
> When Reagan was asked several weeks after he made that statement whether
> he would trade U.S. forces for Soviet forces, he replied, "No." The Chairman
> of the Joint Chiefs of Staff, General John Vessey, gave the same answer in a
> 1982 Senate hearing.
> There are certainly some areas in which the Soviet Union has at least a quan-
> titative advantage. Reagan officials acknowledge, though, that the U.S. has an
> overall technological lead over the Soviet Union [Table 6]. In other areas, e.g.
> the number of "strategic" warheads—which appears to be a rather crucial
> one—the U.S. even has a numerical lead [Fig. 3].

A SIPRI (1984:9–10, 22) report emphasizes that in addition to having a lead in
warheads, the United States boasts a superior "mix" of strategic weapons
systems from the standpoint of surviving a first strike. Indeed, recent
assessments by the Center for Defense Information ("U.S.-Soviet," 1988) and
the Institute for Space and Security Studies (Bowman, 1988a) document a pattern of NATO superiority in both conventional and nuclear force areas. This
pertains not merely to spending and quality but also to numbers in most areas.
Thus while Table 8 seems to suggest Warsaw Pact tank superiority—a pet
theme of those prone to threat inflation—the Center for Defense Information
("NATO and Warsaw Pact," 1988:4) underscores the need to qualify such apparent disparities:

> According to a 1983 report by Rudolf Hilmes, currently the Assistant Chief of
> the tank technology section of the West German Ministry of Defense's procure-
> ment office, NATO tanks are superior to Warsaw Pact tanks in 29 key criteria
> of effectiveness, equal in three and inferior in only eight. These advantages in-
> clude, for example, more accurate guns and better armor.
> Another way to measure NATO's advantage in tank quality is to break down

	NATO*	Warsaw Pact	China
Population	646 million	396 million	1.1 Billion
GNP	$9.0 Trillion	$3.3 Trillion	$0.5 Trillion
Military Spending	$440 Billion	$344 Billion	$25 Billion
Military Manpower	5.5 million	5.0 million	3.2 million
Strategic Nuclear Weapons	12,683	10,470	c.200
Total Nuclear Weapons	c.31,000	c.25,000	c.400
Tanks	31,200	68,700	12,050
Anti-Tank Weapons	400,000	Not Available	
Other Armored Vehicles	65,300	77,400	2,800
Combat Aircraft	12,900	11,400	6,200
Helicopters	14,200	6,000	500
Major Surface Warships	537	306	53
Attack Submarines	239	272	117

Table 8. Where they stand: Military resources of NATO, Warsaw Pact and People's Republic of China. Source: Center for Defense Information. "U.S.-Soviet Military Facts," The Defense Monitor, XVII:5(1988):4. Based upon data from: NATO, ACDA, DOD, CIA, IISS, CDI. Notes: * NATO totals include France and Spain. ** Excludes border guards, internal security, railroad and construction troops.

the tank inventories of the two sides into first and second-line tanks. Only some 30 percent of the 53,100 tanks that the Warsaw Pact could use in a fully rein-forced attack are relatively modern T-64s, T-72s, and T-80s. In contrast, about 70 percent of the 28,200 NATO tanks opposing such an attack would be first-line tanks, such as the U.S. Army's M-1 and M-60.

An even greater relative edge for NATO's tanks is seen by Col. Robert Bowman (1988a:6) who maintains that what is most meaningful "is the number of tanks which could be deployed at the front during the critical first weeks of an engagement. For the WP, this is somewhat less than 25,000 to about 19,000 for NATO. Even this slim WP numerical advantage is deceptive, because most of their tanks are inferior or altogether obsolete. They could bring into battle only about 5,000 modern tanks, whereas NATO would be defending with nearly 18,000. What's more, even comparing the 'modern' tanks of each side, NATO's are clearly superior in speed, turret maneuverability, gun rate of fire, muzzle velocity, range, and ammunition load." The same holds for the few other weapons systems in which the Warsaw Pact appears to hold a numerical lead such as submarines in Table 8. Thus Bowman goes on to note that NATO's subs "have big advantages in speed, depth and quiet," while "the Soviet Navy is largely bottled up in Vladivostok and the Baltic and Black Seas." And the Center for Defense Information ("U.S.-Soviet," 1988:3) adds:

- 88 percent of the 942 Soviet strategic submarine-launched ballistic missiles (SLBMs) are liquid-fueled. All 624 U.S. SLBMs are solid-fueled. Solid-fueled missiles are more reliable and safer.
- The most modern Soviet SLBM is the SS-N-23 which is carried on four Delta IV submarines. The U.S. Director of Naval Intelligence told Congress this year that none of the four Delta IVs has gone on patrol and that the SS-N-23 "apparently has suffered reliability problems."
- U.S. Trident and Poseidon submarines are at sea 66 and 55 percent of the time respectively. According to the Joint Chiefs of Staff, "only about 15 percent of the Soviets first line nuclear fleet . . . operates away from port at any given time."
- Currently, the U.S. has 19–20 submarines at sea at all times. These submarines, which are virtually invulnerable to Soviet attack, carry approximately 3,000 nuclear warheads.

Most Soviet strategic subs, on the other hand, are vulnerable due to new tracking sensors deployed by NATO. Furthermore, the latter ("NATO and Warsaw Pact," 1988:6) boasts 35 aircraft and helicopter/STOL carriers to four for the Warsaw Pact.

Two other areas that deserve passing mention involve artillery and antitank weapons. Despite the WTO's "2–1 advantage in the number of artillery pieces," Bowman (1988a:6) emphasizes "the range of NATO's pieces exceeds that of the WP's by about two to one. How many Soviet piees are going to get close enough to fire before being wiped out?" He adds that NATO has "nearly 500,000 antitank weapons to about 70,000 for the Warsaw Pact." Not only does the Soviet Union have a vast territory to defend, but its neighbor China a decade ago established military links with the Pentagon and is currently modernizing her forces.

What should be borne in mind is that the Reagan and Bush administrations' exaggerations of Soviet capabilities were distinguished not only by their grossness, but also by the unwillingness of West European allies or Japan to pay them more than polite lip service. A zenith (or nadir) was reached by President Bush when he suppressed and ignored a May 1989 intelligence analysis indicating Moscow was in the process of implementing major force structure changes and reductions. Between then and October—when the report was leaked—the Bush-Quayle team continued to publicly insist that a Soviet buildup was in progress. No wonder that by early 1990, West European NATO members were beginning to pressure the United States to make significant force structure reductions in their theatre.

No other NATO country except Norway has sharply increased the military share of its national budget since 1980 (SIPRI, 1948:8, 23), while the United States proportion rose 24 percent. It is in these and other respects, such as the abortive economic warfare pressures or sanctions against New Zealand for not wanting American nuclear weapons in its harbors, that the Reaganites including Bush have isolated (Radway, 1985) the United States from its allies. This collapse of American leadership may be attributed to pathological militarism — also reflected in highly provocative maneuvers ("War Games," 1984) and other hostile deployments of U.S. military forces against Grenada, Libya, Nicaragua, and Panama — rather than Washington's mere espousal of an anti-Soviet perspective.[10] The latter, of course, has characterized all post–World War II administrations.

Indeed, anti–Soviet threat inflation in less extreme form has been routinely employed by our policy elites since the late '40s. In their *Soviet Strategic Forces: Requirements and Responses* (Washington DC: Brookings Inst., 1982), Robert P. Berman and John C. Baker

> document that the development of the Soviet Union's missile and bomber arsenal is primarily a response to threats posed by U.S. nuclear weapons systems. This process began immediately after World War II, the authors write, when the Soviets hoped to "offset" the "American monopoly on nuclear weapons" by maintaining a large army. The U.S. government, however, used an inflated . . . assessment of Soviet strength to rapidly increase its nuclear weapons arsenal.

The reviewer ("Inflating," 1983:57–58) goes on to underscore that the authors

> provide evidence that the Soviet arms buildup was usually geared toward catching up with a U.S. lead in weapons development, and state that gaining parity with the United States has been one of the most important objectives of the Soviet government.

Illustrated in Table 9, this reactive process is understandable in light of the historic American post–World War II disinclination to accord the Soviet Union the respect and equality of status essential for peaceful reconciliation of conflicts between great powers.

George Kennan (1982), the previously cited author of the "containment doctrine," now concedes that his primarily political view of the Soviet challenge was consciously distorted by American cold warriors. In restrospect he concludes that United States preference for dominating and militarizing Western Europe since the late 1940s negated his and other proposals for negotiations. Such negotiations, by recognizing legitimate Soviet security concerns, could have avoided the long-run danger of a Europe divided into antagonistic nuclear-armed military blocs. Instead, the options for disengagement, neutralization and Soviet acceptance of enhanced East European

US 1945	atomic bomb	1949 ˙USSR
US 1948	intercontinental bomber	1955 USSR
US 1952	thermonuclear bomb	1953 USSR
USSR 1957	intercontinental ballistic missile (ICBM)	1958 US
USSR 1957	man-made satellite	1958 US
US 1959	photo reconnaissance satellite	1962 USSR
US 1960	submarine-launched ballistic missile (SLBM)	1968 USSR
US 1966	multiple warhead (MRV)	1968 USSR
USSR 1968	anti-ballistic missile (ABM)	1972 US
US 1970	multiple independently-targeted warhead (MIRV)	1975 USSR
US 1982	long-range cruise missile	1984 USSR
US 1983	neutron bomb	198? USSR
US 1985	new strategic bomber	1987 USSR
US 1986?	anti-satellite rocket (direct ascent)	199? USSR
US 199?	stealth bomber	199? USSR

Table 9. Action-reaction in the nuclear competition. Source: *Sivard (1985:16).*

autonomy were foreclosed by Truman's unwillingness (Nasser, 1989) to abide by the Yalta accords once the nuclear fission process was perfected.

As for the Reagan era inflation of Soviet military expenditures, Ege (1983:15–17) pinpoints several sources — including official ones — that underlie his conclusion of gross exaggeration. In the same vein, Coffin (1983b:4) color-fully recalls:

> Congressman Les Aspin (D–Wis.), the former Pentagon whiz kid, a key member of House Armed Services, sends me a copy of his study "Are the Russians really coming?" Les writes that the report "shows how some of the facile comparisons used by the Administration give a distorted view of the East-West balance."
>
> The Congressman shows, for example, that attempts to explain Soviet military expenses are largely bunkum, since the Defense Department calculates what it would cost for Soviet arms and manpower in the U.S. This "dollar comparison" has a built-in bias that exaggerates Soviet defense spending. The Soviets draft men and pay them less than a ruble a week. Manpower is cheap, so they use lots of it. . . . In dollars, the Russians spend a little more than the U.S. In rubles, the Russians spend considerably less.
>
> Another point: Production within the Soviet Union, whether consumer or military goods, is inefficient, so that "we now know it costs them 2½ times as many rubles to build one ship than we had previously calculated. . . . It will be much more difficult for them to expand (militarily) without pushing their people to the wall."

Furthermore, as we noted earlier, the capabilities of North Atlantic Pact allies are substantially greater than those of Warsaw Treaty allies, who in any case

Exporting Country	Total Value*	Percentage of World Total Major Arms Exports
1. USA	29,978	42.5
2. USSR	19,923	28.2
3. France	7,687	11.0
4. Italy	2,679	3.8
5. UK	2,512	3.6
6. FR Germany	2,132	3.0
7. Third World	1,666	2.4
8. Norway	1,184	1.7
9. Netherlands	707	1.0
10. Brazil	624	(0.8)
11. China	480	0.7
12. Israel	414	(0.6)
13. Australia	377	0.5
14. Sweden	304	0.4
15. Switzerland	292	0.4
Others	616	0.9
World Total	70,537	100.1

*Table 10. Rank order of the twenty largest major weapon exporting countries in the world: 1977–1981. Source: SIPRI Data Base. Reproduced from Landgren-Backstrom (1982:207). Note: * Figures are SIPRI trend indicator values, as expressed in U.S. $ million, at constant (1975) prices. The values include license-production.*

Country*	1962-66	1967-71	1972-76	1977-81**
USA	29	34	38	37
USSR	42	42	33	33
France	9	7	10	12
Italy	1	1	2	5
UK	12	10	9	4
Others	7	6	8	9
Total	100	100	100	100
Total Value	7,870	14,583	25,755	47,829

*Table 11. Shares of exports of major weapons to the third world regions by supplier: 1962–1981. Source: SIPRI Yearbook 1982. Reprinted from Landgren-Backstrom (1982:204). Notes: * Countries are listed in rank order according to their shares for 1977–1981. ** Percentages are based on SIPRI trend indicator values, as expressed in U.S. $ million, at constant (1975) prices.*

would be unreliable for offensive operations against Western Europe, and perhaps in the case of some units, even for defensive ones. Similarly, there are also good reasons (Andrew Cockburn, 1983; Mellenthin, Stolfi and Sobik, 1984) for doubting the general offensive capabilities of the Soviet military not only in terms of weaponry but equally from the standpoint of tactics, organization and morale. Even the efficiency and capabilities of Soviet air and naval defenses in their most sensitive regions (Walden and Bello, 1983; David Pearson, 1984) are problematic! And beyond all of this distortion is the tactical norm of 3–5 to 1 as the necessary ratio for a successful land offensive. Warsaw Pact Army ratios in Central Europe have never aproached this level—a ratio that should be tripled in view of tactical nuclear artillery, mines and missiles. (In World War II, the victorious Soviet ratio on the Eastern front was 1 German to 7 Soviet divisions.)

When one turns to the strategically related area of arms transfers, a similar picture emerges. In the previously cited hearings, administration officials and sympathetic congressmen inflated the threatening significance of the actual rise in Soviet major weapons exports to the Third World. They *ignored* several crucial facets of this process. First, as Table 10 reveals, when licensed co-production — largely by American allies — is included, the United States export lead remains impressive. The growing importance of such integrated or cooperative activity as well as the domestic dominance of the military-industrial complex is underscored by National Security Industrial Association lobbyist Walter R. Edgington in testimony (U.S., Sen., CFR, *Conventional Arms Sales,* 1981:87–88) before the Senate Foreign Relations Committee:

> We in industry are regularly involved with multiple European and Canadian corporations in various business opportunities, joint ventures, licenses, and marketing activity....
> We are pleased to see that the current arms transfer policy has, in essence, responded to our recommendations or acknowledged the basic issues of concern to us, such as co-production agreements and third-country transfers....

If one proceeds to add allied exports for each superpower, the gap is truly immense. Even when we exclude co-production as in Table 11, the United States share has actually increased since the early sixties. For a more recent period, Table 12 reveals only a 1 percent reduction in the American lead. Closer scrutiny indicates that as stressed in Chapter 2, since 1979 United States global exports have been rising in proportional as well as absolute terms while the converse holds for the Soviets. That these trends apply to both the North and the South is apparent from Figure 5. If one adds weapons exports from North Atlantic Pact allies for the 1978–1982 period, and especially the last year, Western dominance is overwhelming.

Relative stability of this imbalance is suggested by Pierre's (1982:14) observation that "as much as 67 percent of arms transfers to the Third World were undertaken in 1978 by members of NATO, while the Warsaw Pact accounted for another 29 percent." Even the Pentagon's own biased calculations (USACDA, 1988: 134) attest to a continued if diminishing NATO preponderance in sales between the periods 1977–81 and 1982–86, when the Western alliance went from $97.3 to $120.8 billion in global terms while the WTO increase was from $75.1 to $102.5. During this time the USSR's relative dominance over Eastern sales declined (her allies' export share doubled) while the United States sharply increased her share from about 42 percent to more than 55 percent of NATO sales. Put differently, sales agreements by Moscow between the two periods increased by about 30 percent while the United States figure was nearly 70 percent. And as we saw in Chapter 2, if the last years of the Reagan era had been included, the disparities undoubtedly would have been higher. Similarly, when one restricts one's focus to the developing areas, while the overall

Country	1978	1979	1980	1981	1982	1978–82
USA	8136	4011	4966	4958	4962	27033
	47.8	26.6	34.7	33.8	37.7	36.4
USSR	4274	6460	5750	4990	4005	25479
	25.1	42.9	40.2	34.0	30.4	34.3
France	1734	1677	1175	1298	1312	7196
	10.2	11.1	8.2	8.9	10.0	9.7
UK	651	533	454	558	683	2899
	3.8	3.7	3.2	3.8	5.2	3.9
Italy	417	531	413	560	669	2590
	2.4	3.5	2.9	3.8	5.1	3.5
FR Germany	559	488	317	389	195	1948
	3.3	3.2	2.2	2.7	1.4	2.6
Others	1258	1350	1243	1903	1346	7078
	7.4	9.0	8.6	13.0	10.2	9.6
Total	17029	15070	14318	14656	13172	74232
	100.0	100.0	100.0	100.0	100.0	100.0

*Table 12. Largest major-weapon exporting countries: values and respective shares for 1978–1982. Source: Reprinted from Ohlson and Loose-Weintraub (1983:269). Note: * Figures are SIPRI trend indicator values, as expressed in U.S. $ million at constant (1975) prices; shares in percentages.*

commitments of the two blocs have become almost equal ($86.7 for WTO vs. $88.0 for NATO), the United States increase has been on the order of 90 percent compared to 25 percent for Moscow.

Furthermore, West European, Israeli, and other exports resulting from licensed co-production must be approved by Washington. Since the early 1960s and particularly during the 1980s, major weapons exports by such American allies as Italy, West Germany, Israel, Brazil and especially France, as we saw in Chapter 2, sharply increased.[11] Some of these allies such as Italy and particularly Israel (Ohlson, 1982:216–217) replaced Britain and France as major suppliers to South Africa.

> The U.K., South Africa's primary supplier before 1963, substantially reduced its deliveries in the late 1960s, but France and Italy offered assistance in the form of licensing arrangements that circumvented the ban on direct arms sales. In the late 1970s, when France reduced its support due to pressure from Black African states, Israel instead emerged as a major supplier of arms and technological knowhow.

Ohlson goes on to note that "U.S. military assistance and credits cover about half of the Israeli defense budget. The Israeli arms industry has now grown so large that it is in many areas competing with the U.S. industry that helped it

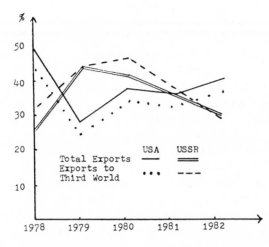

Figure 5. U.S. and Soviet shares of world exports of major weapons: total exports and exports to the Third World, 1978–1982. Source: *Reprinted from Ohlson and Loose-Weintraub (1983:269).*

to be set up." Indeed, Israel's Begin, according to Evans and Novak (1983:31), gave "high priority" to "acting as arms merchant for right wing pariah governments around the world." Thus, as we saw in Chapter 4, Israeli weapons were consigned to Guatemala during Carter's "arms restraint" policy, while another recipient, South Africa, in turn exported armored cars to Morocco and SAMs to Chile.[12]

Moreover there is some evidence (Cavanagh, 1983:50–53, 59) of covert United States indirect shipments to South Africa. These and others to Nicaraguan counter-revolutionaries are said to have been arranged by the CIA. Hence Cepeda and Glennon (1983:3) reported:

> Last November, *Newsweek* magazine and the *New York Times* printed articles detailing CIA operations against Nicaragua. According to the stories, an estimated 50 to 150 CIA personnel are working in Honduras. Their major role is providing money and military equipment to train ex–Guardsmen for sabotage and paramilitary operations. Attacks on Nicaragua by these forces have been steadily increasing, causing more and more casualties.

Neither this weaponry, which was targeted primarily against civilian noncombatants, nor war materials shipped since early 1979 to Afghan contras (Harrison, 1981/1982:97) are included in United States arms transfer data cited in this study. The same could be said for CIA-supported paramilitary forces (McGehee, 1983; Peterzell, 1984) attacking the governments of Angola, Kampuchea and Ethiopia.

A salient focus of the Reagan-Bush Administration's threat inflation rhetoric infusing a plethora of speeches, testimony, and articles pertained to Soviet "gains" in the Third World since the early seventies. These utterances implied that friendly relations with Moscow and limited influence in, say, Syria, Cuba or Angola were tantamount to total subordination or permanent "loss" of one's proprietal domain. Hence it was blithely alleged that such governments lacked any autonomy or flexibility — a perception of their own interests. Such imperial arrogance ignored the fact that many of these governments, including Nicaragua, had initially sought friendly relations with Washington only to be rebuffed. In the instance of Iran, relations with the Revolutionary Government were initially soured by Carter's refusal to dissociate the United States from the highly corrupt deposed Shah, whose unpopular rule was brutally repressive.

Similarly, as already noted, feelers from the new Ethiopian revolutionary leader, Mengistu, were spurned. Shipler (1983:11) reports:

> According to well-placed Israeli and foreign officials, Colonel Mengistu, has maintained close, secret ties with Israel for many years. In 1977, the Ethiopian leader is reported to have asked for Israeli help in restoring good relations with the United States, which turned away from Ethiopia when it switched into the Soviet camp after the 1974 overthrow of Emperor Haile Selassie.
>
> Consequently, Prime Minister Menachem Begin, as the first item in his first meeting with President Carter, urged a reversal of United States policy toward Ethiopia, the officials said, much to the astonishment of the Americans.

Shipler, writing for the prestigious *New York Times,* portrays Carter's policymakers as innocent if not ignorant. In doing this along with purveying falsifications (e.g. Ethiopia being in "the Soviet camp" by 1974) he exemplifies the mass and prestige media's obsequiousness to state managers on foreign policy issues — one that has been carefully documented by Chomsky and Herman (1979), Said (1981), again more recently by Herman (1984), Dorman (1985:18, 21), Seldes (1987), Chamorro (1987), and Said and Hitchens (1988).[13]

Given the virtual creation of Ethiopia's modern armed forces by the Pentagon during the two preceding decades when it was (along with Iran) one of the two major aid recipients (Wolpin, 1973), the Ethiopian officer corps was permeated with sources for United States intelligence. Thus even after the abrupt United States termination of military aid in 1977 (not 1974) induced that country's government to become dependent upon Soviet assistance, it was known — as it is today — to be as autonomous and nationalistic as other radical "Marxist" or "Socialist" Third World regimes. A Pentagon analysis (Rand Corporation, 1985:11), presumably intended to inform top decision-makers, concluded

> despite the growing communist orientation of the Derg, U.S. economic aid programs continued without interruption, and military support actually increased. The Derg itself is closed to Soviet and Cuban advisers, and Mengistu

has been very successful in excluding outside advisers from his military and security forces.

Second, the Soviet Union dragged its feet in supporting Mengistu and the Derg with military arms or economic aid. The first Soviet-Ethiopian military aid agreement was signed in 1976, two years after the revolution.

But after the Somali-Ethiopian war, it was Mengistu who kept a political distance from the Soviets. He delayed in establishing a political party, fearful of Soviet and Cuban dallying with potential rivals. . . .

Mengistu attempts to present a nationalist orientation to Ethiopians, but there is no evidence that he is trying to imitate the Soviets' territorial pattern by restructuring the country along national lines.

Hence when a United States client regime was overthrown by a revolutionary one, there was neither a "vacuum" nor a one-to-one replacement by Soviet influence. While there is an accretion of the latter—if only because of the need by the regime to defend itself from American destabilization—the essential replacement for Washington's tutelage is indigenous nationalism.

And because dependent capitalism has failed to meet the developmental challenge in most Third World countries (White, *et al.,* 1984; Nagle, 1985), the content of this nationalism is frequently "socialist" in aspiration if not practice. This means that "revolutionary governments" seek to control their own economics—an objective that Syrians, Libyans, Angolans and Nicaraguans have shown includes a continuing role for foreign corporate investment provided profits are modest rather than exorbitant. Even the pariah of them all, Libya, was not adverse to amity provided that Washington was respectful toward Palestinian and other nationalist aspirations. Indeed, Washington asked American oil companies to pull out of Libya. Yet Khadafy was depicted as a Soviet proxy by administration officials who off the record acknowledged (*Chicago Tribune,* 1983:4) that he was an object of Soviet "distrust." Thus the process here resembles a self-fulfilling prophecy! Initial American arrogance or hostility by Washington catalyzes a cycle (Chomsky, 1985) generating intense antipathy toward nationalist elites who then have little alternative but closer ties with Moscow.

Even then, as we have seen in the Ethiopian case, revolutionary Third World governments—not excluding those describing themselves as Marxist or Marxist-Leninist—remain autonomous and national (White, *et al.,* 1984) to a considerable degree in most cases. This is especially true where there is a broad popular support internally, complemented by offers of friendly or at least normal ties from other Western and Third World nations. Not only has Moscow intervened militarily far less (Wallensteen, 1982) than has the United States in developing areas since 1945, but a recent analysis (Schmid, 1985) clearly establishes that the Soviet pattern has not been consonant with a design for global hegemony. Even George Kennan, the State Department architect of the 1947 "containment" rationale (1988:33–34) now firmly rejects such fear as unreal and symptomatic of "mass neurosis":

> But suppose there had never been any reality to this assumption in the first place. Suppose the Soviet leaders never had either the desire or the intention or the incentive to do any of these things. I ask you to consider this because I, as one who has been involved in the observation of Soviet-American relations longer, I believe, than anyone now in public life on either side. I have never seen any evidence of any desire, intention or incentive on the Soviet side to do any of those things. And if this is true, has it not then been a tremendous abuse of popular understanding to reiterate on thousands and thousands of occasions a word that carries the opposite implication?...
>
> So wildly overdrawn is this view — so great is here the gap between image and reality — that I can only assume it to be rooted in the effort to repress some sort of inner insecurity by the unreal image of an "external danger."

On the other hand, the USSR's behavior until recently was not as "conservative" as ultra-leftists and others claimed — maintaining that the Soviets have betrayed Marxism. There was, as Halliday (1983) and Schmid (1985) concluded, support for radical and friendly nationalist regimes. And intervention, when it rarely occurred, often was a consequence of "pull factors" after the initiation of military assistance, when the regime was threatened by externally (i.e., Western) backed rebels.

While I do not wish to defend their acts in Afghanistan, critics uniformly ignore the CIA's role in assisting a counterrevolutionary uprising (Peterzell, 1984:13) months *prior* to the entry of Soviet troops. Clearly the Soviet armed intervention there has involved great bloodshed, yet similar American military involvements (Wolpin, 1986a) have been far more sanguinary in terms of civilian casualties. Further, Washington's unwillingness to respect provisions barring new weapons shipments in the United Nations–mediated Afghan-Pakistan 1987 accord reveals that peace is less a United States objective than expanding its influence along Soviet borders.[14]

Initial Reagan Administration belligerence and denunciations of the Russians had, despite Soviet reluctance, destroyed the last threads of detente and embittered relations during the 1980–85 period. Hoffmann and Laird (1982), Stephen F. Cohen (1985), and Hough (1985), like Spechler (1978) before them, focused upon genuine factional conflicts between Soviet "modernizers" or "reformers" and "conservatives." Influential but not even marginally dominant prior to the Andropov investiture, the former emphasized the interdependence of socialist and capitalist economies as a consequence of the "scientific technological revolution." Consequently they were salient policy proponents of detente, caution in the Third World, increased trade and arms control with the West. The Soviets' attitude toward arms control ("Unilateralism," 1985), and particularly their flexibility in the CAT talks described in the preceding chapter, also imply that this faction or "current" within the Party had developed significant influence by the late 1970s.

Unfortunately, both American administration testimony and exchanges in congressional hearings are almost wholly devoid of humility or self-doubt concerning the evolution of East-West relationships—blame invariably rests elsewhere. Nor were American political motives ever assumed to be less than the honorable once the 3-mile limit was traversed. As illustrated by official and media reactions to Gorbachev's March 1985 six-month freeze upon SS-20 deployments, his July unilateral test-ban initiative and more recent proposals for conventional force reductions, any Soviet gesture involving balanced reciprocity or a real halt to the arms race tends to be dismissed as a ploy. Such negativism masks not only animus and militarism, but equally what then Senator J.W. Fulbright aptly termed the "arrogance of power." Even worse, there was blatant evidence of mendacity by top Reagan Administration officials as well as media complicity.[15]

For those paralyzed by such a mindset, it was wholly understandable that little account would be taken of the many instances in addition to the previously mentioned case of Ethiopia, when the Soviets have *failed* to maintain, let alone enhance, their influence notwithstanding prior or promised military assistance. Thus one strongly anti–Soviet analyst (Pierre, 1981/1982), reminds us:

> The record, in fact, is strewn more with failures than successes. Arms to Indonesia did not inhibit Sukarno from adopting a pro–Chinese foreign policy and after the abortive 1965 coup from ousting the Soviets from the country. Weapons for Peru have done nothing to enhance Moscow's position on the South American continent as a whole. The Congo, Ghana, Guinea and other parts of sub–Saharan Africa have witnessed a long string of Soviet failures to establish a permanent presence. The Russian navy was summarily forced out of Berbera, the Soviet Union's largest overseas naval base. Arms supplied to Syria and Iraq have not made them fully pliable to Moscow's political wishes. Damascus has refused to give the Soviets as many military facilities as it seeks, and Bagdad condemned the invasion of Afghanistan.
>
> The most striking failure has been in Egypt, where the Soviets penetrated the Egyptian military as they did in no other country. Egypt's armed forces were reorganized in Soviet style, and at the peak there were 17,000 Russian military personnel in place, some actually manning air defense sites and flying on patrols. Yet this did not prevent Sadat—after, it should be noted, consistent disputes with the Soviets regarding the adequacy of their arms deliveries—from breaking ties with Moscow and sending the Soviets home. In sum, the Soviet experience confirms that the provision of arms often does not readily translate into lasting influences.

Pearson (1981:43) agrees that "arms transfers frequently do not bring the type of influence abroad major powers have sought." Acknowledging that there have been other countries where Soviet influence may have increased in the late 1970s, Pearson continues by stressing that "spokesmen in both the Carter and Reagan Administrations have seen Soviet 'successes' in the Third World as due to U.S. passivity and weakness rather than to unique and isolated local or regional conditions."

Finally the "threat inflation" by Reagan's entourage, focusing upon Soviet-inspired Communist expansionism, along with Bush's campaign claims that Reagan's policies turned the tide is belied by the actual stagnation of the even then very limited Soviet influence during the two decades prior to the Reagan era. According to the Center for Defense Information ("U.S.-Soviet," 1988:7–8), after starting "with influence in 9 percent of the world's nations," the USSR today has "significant influence in 18" of the "164 countries in the world today," or not quite 11 percent. The CDI goes on:

- The Soviets have been successful in gaining influence primarily among the world's poorest and most desperate countries.
- Soviet foreign involvement has to a large extent been shaped by indigenous conditions and the Soviets have been unable to command loyalty or obedience.
- Soviet setbacks in China, Indonesia, Egypt, India, Iraq and Afghanistan dwarf marginal Soviet advances in other countries.

Most of the setbacks antedated the "stand-tall" Reagan Administration, which discredits the notion that its militarism was a significant factor in the exclusion of Soviet influence. Indeed, the deployment of massive United States forces in Southeast Asia during 1964–74 had the opposite effect. Indochina is now more dependent upon the Soviets than it would have been had Washington not sought and militarily failed (Stanton, 1985) to replace the French as the dominant regional power. (And the Nicaraguan Sandinistas, like Cuba's Castro, initially sought weapons to defend their revolution in the West.)

This assessment is shared by other serious analysts. Rather than viewing Soviet arms transfers as integral to a plan or design for world empire, Pierre (1981/1982:273) anticipates Schmid (1985) by maintaining that "Soviet military assistance has long been applied opportunistically, taking advantage of instabilities created by regional conflict or international crisis." Even more categorically rejecting the Manichean perspective associated with the paranoid projection syndrome, West Berlin's Free University's foremost military expert, Ulrich Albrecht (1983:365–366), presciently contends:

Against this rather simplistic view, there is a good deal of evidence to suggest that Soviet arms trade policy has been much less uniform and much less coherent than this. It is not difficult to show that the Soviet Union does not simply pour in arms wherever there is an opportunity. The regional distribution is marked by unevenness and massive local concentrations with little evidence of any strategic plan....

...[T]he regional distribution of Soviet weapons does not fit the hypothesis that this trade is mainly meant to serve the objective of world revolution; it is only necessary to consider some of the substantial arms deliveries which have been made to governments which suppress the Communist Party—for instance Egypt, Libya, Guinea and Algeria.

...[I]t is no longer possible to neglect the commercial motives of Soviet arms sales. It is true that when the Soviet Union began to transfer arms to Third World countries, credit terms were very generous and payment could be made in cotton or some other national produce. Those days seem to have passed. Countries which buy modern Soviet arms now have to pay in cash, apparently hard currency, even if they are 'friends' in an emergency (during the 1973 October War, Egypt had to pay in cash for equipment brought in by Soviet airlift). The Soviet Union recalls only too well the enormous losses which it suffered from generous arms transfers. The cancellation of repayment by Egypt is estimated to have cost the Soviet Union $5 billion; the collapse of relations with Indonesia led to a loss estimated at $3 billion. Now transfers on generous terms appear to be the exception rather than the rule. It is estimated that military equipment accounts for more than 10 percent of all Soviet exports; together with sales of energy and gold, arms sales are one of the main sources of hard currency.

Indeed, the Soviets here have followed the American and one might say general trend of shifting from grants to cash or credit sales. And some Warsaw Pact allies, such as the Germans, Bulgarians and particularly the Czechs, appear (Brogan and Zarca, 1983) oblivious to any political criteria when seeking hard currency through the export of arms to a limited number of rightist pro–Western regimes.

Given these realities and Soviet efforts to restore detente in the mid-1980s, it is difficult to conclude that the untempered ideological dominance of aggressively militaristic anti-communism of the first five to six years of the Reagan era constituted a reasonable, let alone balanced, response to the gradual erosion of American global hegemony. The zealous primacy accorded to military and paramilitary instruments in a context of unrestrained psychological warfare indicated that current policies, including those governing arms transfers, were no mere continuation (Smalldone, 1983:216) but rather represented "a complete break" (Klare, 1982f:144) with the Carter Administration.[16] This hiatus was reflected not only by the rhetoric of Reagan's officialdom but by the sharp escalation in arms budgets, exports and paramilitary operations, as well as the Administration's open endorsement of brutal rightist governments, its unilateralism in militarily attacking such Third World countries as Nicaragua, Grenada, Iran and Libya, and its consequent gradual alienation of traditional advanced capitalist allies in Europe and elsewhere.

These trends have moderated since 1984 with the emergence of the "nuclear freeze" movement in the context (Nye, 1988:112) of "growing congressional resistance" to the wild military spending binge. Particularly important were Reagan's three summit encounters with Gorbachev between October 1986 and May 1988. Yet the most significant change was an elimination of the Administration's vitriolic rhetoric. While this and the one-sided INF agreement have enhanced the East-West political climate, the Bush campaign's strident attacks upon Dukakis' foreign and military policies and unqualified identification with maintaining Reagan's doubled level of arms spending indicate that at most only minor accommodations (e.g. a different policy-mix toward Nicaragua) can be the anticipated. Thus despite the emergence of a Soviet leader firmly committed to both domestic reform and external demilitarization (Gorbachev, 1987), it appears that Bush has been coopted by the intelligence and military-industrial complexes, which will impede him from taking advantage of an "historic opportunity" (Stephen F. Cohen, 1988; Ullman, 1988) to substantially reorder long-term American interventionist and first-strike military (Forsberg, 1988; Houweling and Siccama, 1988) priorities. Indeed, Reagan himself after the first term moved in the direction of restrained or "moderate" toughness toward the USSR coupled with praise for one-sided Soviet concessions. A less benign posture characterizes American policy toward nationalist leaders (e.g. Ortega, Arafat, Ghadafy, Noriega) in the Third World. In Eastern Europe only anti–Soviet manifestations of nationalism are supported. After briefly examining the economic and bureaucratic forces which undergird such policies, we shall delineate precisely how this militarization process is attenuating America's security both internationally and with greater effect, domestically—Bush's alleged moderation and bipartisan disposition notwithstanding.

6. Military-Industrial and Transnational Corporate Interests

The momentum behind American militarization is explained on one level by "pride of power" or a drive for world hegemony in an era when nonmilitary instrumentalities of domination appear increasingly inefficacious. But the forces that fuel this drive for a militarized "Pax Americana" are both ideological and of a more socio-economic character. Corporate interest has been a reinforcing catalyst of demonic antinationalism, the "war" on drugs, and the previously examined "communist" threat inflation. It is the economic counterpart to what Congressman Dellums calls the American "national security psychosis." These structural sources of militarism include the aptly denoted "military-industrial complex" of which General Eisenhower prophetically warned upon leaving the White House. Yet aside from this relatively recent accretion, an even more significant yet indirect long-run interest generating foreign policy interventionism has been the profit-maximizing imperative of the transnational corporate sector.

INTEGRATION AND CORPORATE DOMINANCE

Although an increasing proportion of American automotive and electronics transnational corporations have moved (Shaw, *et al.,* 1985) into the "defense" area while many of the major military contractors have, as Table 13 also indicates, joined the ranks of the largest corporations, an appreciable number of the latter continue as essentially civilian-oriented producers. Their interest in maximizing returns from overseas markets and investments has been increasingly threatened both by nationalist aspirations of developing countries and by growing inroads of frequently more efficient competition by the transnational corporations of other advanced capitalist states.

The expanding overseas role of America's corporate sector helps us understand why the historical policy patterns discussed in Chapter 3 were hostile to nationalist movements from the Boxer Rebellion of the 1860s to that of the Sandinistas in the 1920s as well as more recently. Yet from the standpoint of America's own heritage of a republican (i.e. radical) independence revolution (i.e. a national liberation movement) against mercantile privilege, the United States should express sympathy for such national movements even when they

Top Companies *	Fortune 500 Ranking	Ranking Top 100 Defense Contractors
Aerospace		
United Technologies	20	3
Boeing	34	6
Rockwell	42	8
McDonnell-Douglas	43	2
General Dynamics	46	1
Lockheed	56	5
Signal	69	55
Martin-Marietta	108	10
Northrop	158	12
Grumman	177	11
Fairchild	281	82
Electronics and Appliances		
General Electric	11	4
ITT	16	40
Western Electric	22	72
Westinghouse Electric	31	13
Raytheon	58	9
Litton	68	15
Texas Instruments	79	24
Warner	92	-
Motorola	98	58
Emerson Electric	110	80
N.A. Phillips	122	44
Allegheny	142	-
Singer	155	36
Motor Vehicles		
General Motors	2	26
Ford	5	20
Chrysler	29	-
TRW	66	21
Intl. Harvester	73	-
Bendix	86	32
American Motors	139	39
Eaton	147	49

Table 13. Military contractors ranked among top 500 corporations. Source: Los Angeles Times. *Reproduced from* Syracuse Post-Standard, *August 4, 1983, p. A-11.* Note: * *"There are 63 companies on the Fortune Magazine list of the top 500 manufacturing companies that are also listed among the top 100 defense contractors by the Department of Defense. For some of these companies, defense contracts account for only a small percentage of their business. However, all 63 companies are to some degree dependent on the Pentagon for their livelihood."*

espouse egalitarian socio-economic policies akin to the American Declaration of Independence dictum that "all men are created equal." Can it be that the interests of corporate capital have—like those of the military-industrial complex—subverted this dimension of America's patriotic heritage? Worth pondering in this regard is Table 14's indication that foreign market penetration and production have become crucial sources of profit-taking for top American-based corporations. As a percent of all United States profits, those reported (grossly understated) from United States–owned overseas facilities had increased (IPS, 1988:9) by almost 300 percent, from 5.9 percent in 1965 to 15.6 percent in 1980.

	Foreign Revenue ($ millions)	As % of Total	Foreign Profit ($ millions)	As % of Total
Exxon	$61,815	69.7%	$2,913	54.0%
Mobil	32,629	58.7	1,010	67.2
Texaco	25,157	62.8	900	73.0
Phibro-Salomon	20,100	67.5	235	50.0
IBM	17,058	42.5	2,142	39.1
Ford	16,080	36.2	351	18.8
General Motors	14,913	20.0	258	6.9
Gulf	11,535	43.4	604	61.8
SOCAL	10,952	40.1	755	47.5
DuPont	10,816	30.8	436	26.6

Table 14. *Top ten transnational corporations, 1983.* Source: Forbes, *July 2, 1984.*

Corporate loyalties are to their own profit-maximizing potential even if that dictates the impoverishment of American industrial towns or massive tax avoidance. Hence, the term "transnational" — the nation state being merely a *base* of operations rather than an object of commitment. Historically, most of the major corporations have not only paid their workers as little as they could get away with given existing constraints, but they have routinely disregarded criminal and other legal norms to enhance the bottom line. Thus in reviewing one of the latest (Mokhiber, 1988) "muckraking" investigations — a genre with more than a century-long lineage — Sherrill (1988) encapsulates the "reality":

> Mokhiber offers us thirty-six cases of corporate misconduct that killed people or destroyed the environment. Many of the episodes are several years old: Most of them were widely reported and commented on when they occurred, or shortly thereafter. No doubt the establishment press, being loath to force ethical conduct on its corporate peers in the fashion proposed by Mokhiber, will dismiss the book as "old stuff." But criticizing the age of the material misses the point entirely. Mokhiber is not dealing in "exposés." He is reviewing history for the purpose of suggesting reform. . . .
>
> Corporate crimes were not impersonal ones. When General Motors or McDonnell Douglas or J.P. Stevens did violence to their workers or to the public, it did not happen in the manner of a landslide or flood. It was not an accident, or an act of God. There was plenty of *mens rea* involved, which Mokhiber, a lawyer, will remind you is a "legal term used to identify the mental element in crime." The decision to risk lives, or to ignore warnings that people were dying or might die from company actions, or to fight attempts to help the victims — these decisions can't be nullified or neutered by the word "corporate." *Men,* thinking men, in those corporations, consciously made the decisions. In many instances, it seems to me the deliberateness — the premeditation — that went into those decisions, given the results, would have made first-degree murder charges perfectly justified.
>
> There are many, many murders done in these pages: sly, calculated, cold-

blooded and often (though, thank goodness, not always) highly profitable murders.

When I say calculated, I mean among other things that a common theme running through these cases is a conscious contempt for life. Mokhiber will introduce you to corporations that persisted in marketing a dangerous product and took no thought for the consequences, even though they could have made the product safe very easily and cheaply.

The same applies with even greater force to the cost-plus military sector contracts. Here firms have often delivered dangerous or malfunctioning weapons, and even ignored safety in their production facilities. Illustrative is Wald's (1989:3) report:

> At least four workers who complained about safety and environmental problems at four military nuclear plants run for the government by private contractors say they were ordered by their superiors to see psychiatrists or psychologists.
>
> The workers and their lawyer all say they believe that the orders came as retaliation for the allegations they made. In two highly publicized cases the allegations against the contractors have been confirmed; in the others they have been denied.
>
> Each of the workers says that the implication that he was suffering from mental problems was part of a long campaign of harassment that included such tactics as demotions, ridicule in front of co-workers and threats to revoke the security clearances that are required for such jobs....
>
> Thomas Carpenter, a lawyer representing the four workers, complained about the referrals in a letter July 13 to James D. Watkins, the secretary of energy.
>
> "The use of psychiatric fitness-for-duty examinations in whatever context essentially has been retaliatory, punishing dissidents by labeling them mentally incapable of service to their country," wrote Mr. Carpenter, who is with a watchdog group, the Government Accountability Project.
>
> Representative Ron Wyden, Democrat of Oregon, said of the psychological sessions: "This is an old strategy that goes on in totalitarian countries. It's incredibly grotesque that it's being pursued here."

"Whistleblowers" have been victimized by even more severe sanctions. Another example will be discussed shortly—a man who paid an extremely high price for his revelations.

Even foreign criminality benefits from relative indifference or connivance (Coffin, 1988:1, 3–4) by United States executive officialdom in the State and Defense departments as well as the CIA. Tolerance and even "protection" exist so long as the Hondurans, Panamanians, Turks, Pakistanis, Mexicans, Afghans, etc., cooperate in opposing leftist or nationalist forces which promise to limit corporate exploitation and maldevelopment (Trainer, 1989:482–90) of Third World resources. Financial or employment dependency of high government officials upon corporations or closely linked (Domhoff, 1967) institutions explains the endemic historical pattern of psychological complicity at or near the policy-making levels. Many in this stratum are, of course, directly recruited from the corporate owning upper class. Very few look benignly upon Third World economic nationalism.

From an explanatory standpoint, it is only by factoring in this array of underlying bureaucratic and corporate interests that one can reconcile the patterned inconsistencies and sheer vacuousness of the military-related official rationales and rhetoric (to be dissected in the next chapter). Thus as we saw, even ardent advocates of weapons transfers like Betts (1980:87) acknowledge that "revival of containment does not justify all sales, because some customers are not proxies of either superpower, and want arms for purposes unrelated to U.S.-Soviet competition. . . . [P]roponents of arms sales often make dubious arguments about how these sales benefit more than just our pocketbooks." The multibillion dollar contribution of commercial arms exports and especially DOD-sponsored foreign military sales to the "pocketbooks" of top American TNCs and specialized weapons producers is depicted in Tables 15 and 16.

Interests of this character as well as bureaucratic careerism and aggrandizement are easily masked and reinforced by invoking the paranoid projection syndrome or more generally by anti-radical national security rhetoric. Thus in his prepared statement (U.S., House, CFA, 1981:45–46) for two subcommittees of the House Foreign Affairs Committee, Caesar Sereseres—a research analyst for the Pentagon's own Rand Corporation—willingly concedes:

> Seeking "influence," posturing that the Soviets seek world domination, or defining instability, violence, and anti–Americanism in terms of Communist ideology and subversion tactics is not a security assistance/arms transfer doctrine. What often fuels the pace and direction of security assistance is the self-perpetuation of the bureaucracy itself. The case of El Salvador in the early months of 1981 is an example of this. As one U.S. military officer stated after his fifth visit to El Salvador, the only military crisis that exists is the one in Washington. It is overreaction. Everybody wants in on the act. Nobody wants to be left behind on this. It is "show-and-tell" time for all the services. God save the Salvadorian military from Wsahington! There is no security assistance in doctrine.

Gansler (1980:217), in turn, reminds us that economic and other interests were supposed to be "secondary" to the "sole legal justification" for transfers—which is their contribution "to the overall U.S. defense posture."

> Yet in almost all foreign military sales effort there are major interdepartmental conflicts—for example, the efforts of the Department of Commerce to encourage exports and the political needs of the State Department (including requests for arms from our friends and allies overseas) versus the security need of the Department of Defense to control equipment and technology. Even within the DOD there is a conflict between the "marketing department" (the Defense Security Assistance Agency) and the various "control" groups. In this conflicting interdepartmental arena there is no "higher court" to resolve the

Company	FY 1977 Sales	Rank	FY 1978 Sales	Rank	FY 1979 Sales	Rank	FY 1980 Sales	Rank	FY 1981 Sales	Rank
Lockheed Corp.	$102,394	1	$190,503	1	$ 49,369	6	$133,525	1	$198,662	1
Hughes Aircraft	29,925	8	78,577	4	23,489	11	52,261	6	121,372	2
Nisso-Iwai American	19,960	15	32,406	11	44,177	8	64,300	4	79,857	3
Raytheon Corp.	19,204	17	81,360	3	187,049	1	47,702	7	75,551	4
Boeing Corp.	47,489	3	41,536	8	80,496	2	25,406	12	67,658	5
Teledyne Inc.	-	-	-	-	17,882	17	60,931	5	61,639	6
Texas Instruments	-	-	-	-	16,970	19	26,504	11	47,007	7
Olin Mathieson	23,869	11	38,026	10	47,589	7	25,109	13	45,482	8
Singer	10,615	23	30,868	12	21,426	12	39,689	8	39,768	9
Bendix Corp.	-	-	-	-	-	-	-	-	36,401	10
Nittler Forwarder	-	-	-	-	-	-	27,856	10	35,894	11
AVCO	23,049	13	38,338	9	27,290	10	-	-	29,897	12
Electric Memories	-	-	13,223	21	15,592	21	-	-	26,717	13
Luigi Serra Inc.	-	-	16,954	17	16,854	13	15,143	21	25,888	14
Colt's Inc.	21,617	14	-	-	20,891	-	14,845	22	24,090	15
Emery Air Freight	-	-	-	-	-	-	19,299	17	21,929	16
NAPCO Industry	-	-	-	-	-	-	-	-	21,510	17
FMC Corp.	-	-	-	-	-	-	17,112	20	20,897	18
Smith & Wesson	10,336	24	-	-	-	-	-	-	20,455	19
Sperry Rand Corp.	-	-	-	-	-	-	13,487	25	19,916	20
Sumitomo Shoji	-	-	-	-	13,783	23	14,161	23	19,892	21
Thiokol Chemical	-	-	-	-	-	-	-	-	19,353	22
Northrop Corp.	41,005	5	53,341	6	30,643	9	-	-	19,171	23
Litton Industries	-	-	-	-	-	-	-	-	17,181	24
United Technologies	40,015	-	65,772	5	52,688	4	86,059	2	17,110	25
Other (Top 25 Companies)	322,088	-	333,262	-	233,862	-	226,862	-	-0-	-
	$711,566		$1,014,146		$900,050		$910,251		$1,113,298	

issues, only the president. Consequently, arbitrary decisions get made at the lower levels for valid short-term objectives.

Nevertheless, this chaotic bureaucratic maze of infighting or politics remains generally consonant with, and functions within, the overall pro-corporate interventionist politico-military infrastructure.[1] Such constraints explain arms embargoes including pressure upon allies not to sell to Nicaragua and other nationalist regimes whose armed forces lack sufficient autonomy to depose the government. But when we come to friendly armed forces or "open door" (i.e., corporate-investor oriented) governments, "national security" criteria may obscure, as we have seen, other operative yet vital relationships among weapons producers, procurement officials and others whose careers are enriched by promoting overseas sales.

Tables 15 and 16 listed the major corporations and respective sales volume for the fiscal years 1977–1981. Two patterns are worth noting: first, the immense disparity between much higher publicly subsidized and concessional foreign military — as compared with commercial — sales; and second, the relative stability of the latter in contrast to a sharply rising trend for the former. Thus, Carter's "leprosy letter" which instructed officers not to assist arms merchants, appears to have been "layered" by the military bureaucracy. The influence of such prime military contractors is implied by the fact that many were ranked in Table 13 among Fortune's Top 500 United States corporations. These companies are a continuing (Etzioni, 1984:102–130) source of massive political "contributions" to elected officials as well as post–Pentagon employment for thousands of retired officers. Table 17 depicts the complex's infamous "revolving door."

Predictably, fraud, defective products, and overpricing are endemic to the procurement process, where sanctions have seldom been enforced (such enforcement as exists tends to be symbolic in nature). Given this reality and the fact that whistleblowers are seldom rewarded, it is unsurprising to discover (Coffin, 1990:3) that "profits for military contractors average some 56 percent higher than profits for businesses serving the civilian sector."

Underlying the growth of the enormously powerful military-industrial coalition is the previously described interventionist foreign policy which purports to legitimize both mounting arms transfers to the Third World and the overarching drive for strategic hegemony. Weapons producers routinely employ former executive as well as legislative officials as lobbyists and finance advisory "councils," "committees" and "think tanks" (Sanders, 1983; Blumenthal, 1987/88) that inundate the body politic with inflammatory anti-radical and even anti-liberal propaganda. A dynamic mutually reinforcing process of

Opposite: *Table 15. Commercial export sales of top 25 corporations: FY1977–FY1981.*
Source: *Reprinted from U.S.G.A.O. (1982:96).*

Company	FY 1977 Sales	Rank	FY 1978 Sales	Rank	FY 1979 Sales	Rank	FY 1980 Sales	Rank	FY 1981 Sales	Rank
McDonnell Douglas	$446,134	2	$273,857	5	$638,853	1	$471,238	4	$1,211,480	1
United Technologies	87,102	12	115,302	11	249,058	5	749,047	3	632,465	2
Vinnell Corp.	-	-	103,726	12	110,842	9	-	-	409,591	3
General Dynamics	303,322	4	1,475,524	1	517,928	2	992,958	1	377,124	4
Al Huseini	-	-	-	-	205,622	6	-	-	323,890	5
Hughes Aircraft	156,092	7	156,188	10	86,423	14	95,533	20	259,678	6
Westinghouse	70,986	16	56,403	17	85,266	15	140,101	15	187,907	7
Raytheon Corp.	149,028	8	271,046	6	132,113	8	435,468	5	184,829	8
General Electric	220,956	6	175,657	8	101,422	13	175,597	11	174,542	9
Northrop Corp.	853,022	1	266,978	7	472,282	3	859,401	2	164,341	10
Lockheed Corp.	305,226	3	297,292	4	141,812	7	148,536	13	135,442	11
Ex Cell O Corp.	-	-	-	-	-	-	-	-	122,042	12
Grumman Corp.	252,814	5	69,992	14	-	-	-	-	116,112	13
FMC Corp.	-	-	70,683	13	65,267	20	232,933	7	106,049	14
Chrysler Corp.	-	-	-	-	-	-	197,089	10	102,170	15
Science Applications, Inc.	-	-	-	-	-	-	-	-	93,410	16
Teledyne Inc.	21,241	24	26,871	25	53,237	23	108,541	19	86,242	17
Sperry Rand Corp.	-	-	-	-	75,138	16	72,705	23	83,526	18
Ford Motor Co.	42,260	17	65,642	15	-	-	-	-	78,664	19
AT & T	26,773	20	28,176	24	61,832	21	78,773	22	72,150	20
Saudi Tarmac, Ltd.	77,247	14	-	-	-	-	-	-	64,475	21
General Motors Corp.	-	-	31,969	22	50,692	25	109,071	18	64,334	22
Saudi Maintenance Corp.	-	-	-	-	-	-	128,834	17	60,585	23
Hyun Dai Const.	-	-	-	-	-	-	58,338	25	55,744	24
E. Systems, Inc.	-	-	-	-	-	-	-	-	54,099	25
Other (Top 25 Companies)*	683,074	-	1,382,226	-	936,988	-	1,277,732	-	-	-
Total**	$3,695,277		$4,867,532		$3,984,775		$6,331,895		$5,220,891	
Total foreign military sales	$4,449,536		$5,805,480		$5,329,876		$8,157,571		$7,590,486	

Company	Total Flow	Flow to Company DOD Military	Flow to Company DOD Civilian	Flow TO DOD
Boeing	398	316	35	37
General Dynamics	239	189	17	32
Grumman	96	67	5	16
Lockheed	321	240	30	34
McDonnell-Douglas	211	159	12	29
Northrop	360	284	50	16
Rockwell	234	150	26	47
United Technologies	83	50	11	12
Total	1942	1455	186	233

Table 17. Personnel transfers between Department of Defense (DOD) and major military contractors, 1970–1979. Source: Adapted from Gordon Adams, The Iron Triangle: The Politics of Defense Contracting *(New York: Council on Economic Priorities, 1981), p. 84. As reproduced in Russett (1984:78).*

ideological threat inflation is fomented by the military-industrial complex and in lesser measure by the transnational corporate sector. The consequences are heightened priorities for diverting public resources to the militarization process.

The payoffs to legislators in the form of jobs and millions in campaign contributions (Etzioni, 1984:102–30) are supplemented by the allocation of contracts to their districts. These and the corporate impetus for the Reagan-Bush "Star Wars" trillion dollar boondoggle are documented by a Center for Economic Priorities (Mashinot, 1985:4) report on what Paul Warnke called the "great pork barrel in the sky."

> According to the CEP, 77 percent of the prime space weapons contracts awarded in fiscal years '83 and '84 were given to states or districts represented by Congress members who sit on the Armed Services Committee and the Appropriations Defense subcommittees—four committees with key roles in Star Wars decision-making. Members from these four committees had received an average of $34 million in strategic defense contracts—six times the amount awarded to districts of non-members.
>
> The report also said that the seeds for entrenched political support for Star Wars are being sown in other ways on Capitol Hill. The nation's top 10 defense contractors have been awarded 87 percent of the strategic defense awards. Since Star Wars is projected to be the fastest growing Department of Defense Research and Development program—jumping from 3.7 percent in 1984 to 13.1 percent in 1990—the top firms will become increasingly dependent on Star Wars to keep their profit margins high.

Opposite: *Table 16. Foreign military sales top 25 U.S. Corporations: FY1977–FY1981. Source: Reprinted from A.S.G.A.D. (1982:95). Notes: *All top 25 companies not listed. **As of September 30, 1981. Totals may not add due to rounding.*

> . . . [T]he one brake on the institutionalization of Star Wars — the "independent panel" appointed by President Reagan to assess the technical feasibility of the program — is filled with industrialists from major defense contractors, including the chairperson, who's the president of a major weapons firm, R & D Associates.

Omitted from this portrait are the scientists, engineers and bureaucrats in the Department of Energy whose own careers (Morrison, 1985) require research and development on a "third generation" of "tailored effect" nuclear weaponry. Bowman (1987:19) emphasizes the two-way flow of influence by stressing that "one of the major objectives" of "SDI spending" "has been to create a constituency or 'buy' political support. Thus official SDI spending has been spread around to about 500 companies plus something like 100 different universities and 100 nonprofit organizations." He then proceeds to identify the multibillion dollar top twenty contracting corporations.

Not only has this constellation of interests enormously increased the obstacles to avoiding an arms race in space (Stares, 1985), but former presidential science adviser Wiesner (1985:102–103) recounts how major presidential initiatives toward arms control have been sabotaged for almost three decades.[2] He captures the lawless dynamic and ultimate irrationality of this process using as an example Carter's pyrrhic effort to halt the now-operational B-1:

> . . . After the project was shut off by the Carter Admnistration, funds from the space shuttle and other government projects were fraudulently diverted to keep the B-1 alive. A story in the April 7, 1984 *San Francisco Examiner* details how the manufacturer then scattered contracts so widely that almost every state and hamlet in the country had a stake in the B-1's future. Even though it is generally agreed that the B-1 is unnecessary, the campaign succeeded.
>
> The contracts were worth an average of $700 million per state. The states of the 20 senators who lobbied hardest for the aircraft were scheduled to get sums ranging from $1 to $9 billion. Even more disturbing is the fact that labor unions and chambers of commerce lobbied vigorously for this marginally useful aircraft at a time when budget deficits were destroying the U.S. economy and the infrastructure of the American society. This irrational behavior is only possible because we, the citizens of the nation, permit it. It is no longer a question of controlling a military-industrial complex, but rather, of keeping the United States from becoming a totally military culture.

Wiesner's pessimism and perception of irrationality are echoed by both Evans (1984) and Etzioni (1984:102–130). The former, a Marine Corps colonel on staff assignment to the Office of the Secretary of Defense, pinpoints both the dubious efficacy of gold-plated (high tech) weaponry and the utter waste due to the hegemony of military service parochialism and primacy rather than national defense criteria governing procurement by what he aptly denotes as a voracious "Runaway Pentagon."[3] Etzioni, once a Carter Administration adviser, like Fallows (1981), amplifies the critique, arguing that no operative strategic assessment or doctrine governs the procurement process.

That process, as we also see in the Star Wars context, is a non-rational out-come of petty service rivalries, corporate or interest group leverage and congres-sional constituency dependence. These pressures, in turn, have not only precluded reasoned debate over strategic alternatives, but have resulted in billions of squandered resources through redundant and inappropriate weapons systems, inadequate funding of personnel and maintenance com-ponents and even the needless loss of lives through deployment of inappro-priate or insufficiently tested (e.g. the M-16 in Vietnam and the B-1 crackups in 1988) defective weaponry. Even worse, the entrenched influence and effec-tive veto power of the military-industrial complex also explain continuing White House refusals to join the Soviets in a mutual nuclear and missile test ban or even a no-first-strike pledge (the former despite a unilateral initiative by Moscow which ended nuclear tests from mid-1985 until the end of 1986). Indeed, in 1986, presidential options were further constrained (Previdi, 1988) by creation of a general staff under tighter centralized control of the Chairmen of the Joint Chiefs of Staff.

THE "IRON TRIANGLE" IN ACTION: COSTS TO AMERICANS

Reality is today symbolized by a veritable "iron triangle" comprised of three major military-industrial complex sectors: industry, congress, and bureaucrats (civilian as well as military). Minor components include publicists from academia and journalism along with a few labor leaders and veterans' groups. The importance of the iron triangle is underscored by a leading inter-national relations scholar, Bruce Russett (1984:71–78), who concluded after an empirical analysis of external and domestic arms race catalysts that the military-industrial complex along with "sphere of influence" goals were the most salient underlying forces for militarization. Thus with respect to the upsurge of arms transfers during the post–Vietnam public opposition to high Pentagon budgets, Russett comments:

> Especially during the post–Vietnam War years, arms exports became a major prop to the military-industrial complex. United States arms exports of $10 billion in 1974 and 1975 amounted to over half as much as the total of U.S. government arms purchases for the American armed forces.

The inferential thesis is that when procurement for United States forces declines due to a shift in public mood (i.e., disillusionment over Vietnam), the military-industrial complex's influence will ensure profitability via an escalation of exports. Similarly, when Third World countries in the late 1970s found escalating indebtedness in the context of global economic stagnation to be inhibiting new purchases, especially of exorbitantly costly complex weaponry, new domestic procurement—fueled by threat inflation—took up the gap. Thus we see the functional significance of Reagan's Star Wars in the context of his overall escalation of procurement.

Hartung and Nimroody (1985:200) recall that "a declassified 1982 Pentagon study made public . . . by Republican Senator Larry Pressler puts the cost of deploying the most effective possible space-based laser defenses at $500 billion, and former Secretary of Defense James Schlesinger estimates that deployment could cost as much as $1 trillion." The authors set this within a context of the SDI's doctrinal and corporate implications:

> . . . Experts in the Pentagon now admit that the most likely role for the strategic defense initiative (S.D.I.) will be to "enhance deterrence." The apparent shift in the program's military goal merely underlines what has been its purpose from the beginning: to preserve the nuclear weapons program of the 1980s while planting the seeds of the major weapons programs of the 1990s and beyond.
> Not surprisingly, the companies that are receiving millions of dollars to find a way to "protect" us from nuclear weapons are the same firms that manufacture them. . . .
> As . . . nuclear weapons programs pass their peak production levels . . . Star Wars research awards will tide the companies over until the next major upsurge in military spending. . . . One Pentagon expert on S.D.I. contracting explained it succinctly: "This isn't just a new area of opportunity for the major contractors; they've adopted the attitude that this is their future. That's it's life or death. That either they're in or they're out."

What stands out here, as in the area of "national security" (Schoultz, 1988) policy decision-making, is the fluidity or malleability of strategic doctrine when confronted by concrete corporate profiteering interests.[4]

A ranking of the major initial beneficiaries and proponents of SDI appears in Table 18. Financial statements (Gerth, 1985:D1) of "10 of the largest weapons makers showed that, on the average, they realized a 25 percent return on equity in 1984. By contrast, the average return for manufacturing corporations of all sorts was only 12.8 percent, according to figures the Census Bureau released last week." Table 19 highlights such profit-taking disparity in this most political of businesses. Recent figures are lower, though this may reflect increased manipulation of official data in the Reagan-Bush era.

Thus Coffin (1990:3) contends that "the military budget has become a colossal welfare scheme for much of Corporate America and overseas contractors. Profits for military contractors average some 56% higher than profits for businesses serving the civilian sector." Based upon a critical editorial by Richard D. Hartel in *Challenge* magazine, the percentage disparity may represent pretax profits rather than return on equity. The latter tends to be considerably greater in the military production sector. Another possible explanation is that the returns to smaller—usually more efficient—contractors are lower.

It is not only external threat inflation, then, which enhances returns but the increasingly complex (hence costly) weapons systems opted for by political appointees who operate largely within a cost-plus rather than competitive bidding framework. Similarly, the political influence of the military-industrial complex is increased along with that of the corporate sector generally by the

Company	Value of Pentagon Awards for S.D.I., 1983–84 (in millions of dollars)	Total Pentagon Awards to Firm, 1984 (in millions of dollars), and Rank	
Boeing	$364.3	$4,563.8	(5)
Lockheed	240.1	4,967.5	(4)
McDonnell Douglas	236.8	7,684.2	(1)
L.T.V.	211.0	1,655.3	(14)
Teledyne	115.4	425.8	(44)
Rockwell International	88.7	6,219.3	(2)
T.R.W.	76.4	982.5	(24)
Hughes Aircraft	34.8	3,230.5	(7)
AVCO	30.6	872.8	(27)
Litton	25.3	2,440.7	(10)

Table 18. Top ten recipients of Star Wars R & D contracts fiscal years 1983 and 1984. Sources: *Council on Economic Priorities,* The Strategic Defense Initiative: Costs, Contractors, and Consequences; *and* Aerospace Daily, *April 26, 1985. As reproduced in Hartung and Nimroody (1985:202).*

sharply rising costs of electoral propaganda (campaigning). Coffin (1988b:3) recalls that:

> From 1980 to 1982, spending on Congressional races rose 43% to $332 million. From 1984 to 1986, the increase was 20% . . . .
> Organized groups, using the political action committee device spent $13.7 million on the 1980 presidential race and nearly $17.5 million in 1984.

So extreme is the situation of dependence that Senator Ernest F. Hollings (D–S.C.) estimates "twenty-five percent of the time of a U.S. Senator is expended in the collection of money." Analysts who have probed various facets as well as the growth of the military industrial complex or what appears on the way to becoming a de facto state-within-a-state include Lens (1970); Cooling (1977); Koistinen (1980); Gansler (1980); Fallows (1981); Tobias (1982); Melman (1983); and Sanders (1983a).

Naked careerism and conflicts of interest in the Pentagon may partly explain the immense waste that is periodically exposed. Some of the more gross examples of this corrupt profligacy appear in Table 20. These were revealed more than a year after a "report by a Presidential commission on Government spending . . . said that $92 billion could be saved by reducing waste and mismanagement in the Pentagon." When questioned (Halloran, 1983:A-13) about this, Deputy Defense Secretary W. Paul Thayer admitted

Contractor	Profits As Percent of Equity	1984 Profits (In millions)	Percent of Sales to U.S. Government
Lockheed	42%	$572	85%
General Dynamics	30	382	86
Northrop	29	167	84
Martin Marietta	28	176	76
Boeing	26	787	42
Grumman	24	108	62
Rockwell International	21	496	63
Raytheon	18	340	49
Litton	16	277	41
McDonnell Douglas	16	325	69

Table 19. Profits at 10 large military contractors. Source: *U.S. Census Bureau, 1984 Annual Reports. Reprinted from Gerth (1985:D1).* Notes: *Average return on equity for this group: 25%. Average return for manufacturing, mining and trade corporations: 12.8%. Profits are after provisions for tax and are for company as a whole. Equity, defined as paid-in capital plus retained earnings, is as of January 1984. Profits and equity are based on continuing operations.*

that Government and industry officials appeared to have been negligent in paying excessive prices for spare parts for aircraft engines. . . .

Mr. Thayer's comments were in marked contrast to testimony before Congress by other senior Administration officials who have repeatedly asserted that the Administration had not asked for more than was necessary for military spending.

Mr. Thayer has taken a different line. He said earlier that military contractors increased prices 10 to 30 percent to cover products that had to be remade because they were made improperly the first time.

It is instructive that Thayer, like other whistleblowers (such as Francis Fitzgerald, who disclosed massive cost overruns on the C-5), was subsequently ousted from the Defense Department. He was also subjected to an SEC investigation which resulted in prosecution for insider trading—a notoriously commonplace violation of the Securities and Exchange Act.

Thayer's revelations, notwithstanding the price he paid for his perceived disloyalty, help us understand one of numerous sources of excess profits in cost-plus military contracting. Another is inflated wage costs.[5] These problems are integral to the general problem of institutionalized fraud. Senator William Proxmire, one of the few remaining outspoken critics of the military-industrial complex, has linked such notorious practices (Coffin, 1985b) to the absence of meaningful sanctions:

ITEM	MANUFACTURERS PRICE	WHAT THE GOVERNMENT PAYS WITH YOUR TAX DOLLARS
Door Gasket	$ 5.67	$ 94.50
Bolt	$13.45	$ 328.00
Screw	$ .03	$ 91.00
Wrench	$ .12	$9,609.00
Diode	$ .04	$ 110.00
Cutting Tool	$ .07	$ 980.00
Plastic Cap	$ 1.00	$1,000.00
Claw Hammer	$15.00	$ 435.00

Table 20. Official military parts price list form #A0654. Source: *Committee Against Government Waste — 499 S. Capitol Street, SW — Suite 102 — Washington, DC 20069 (1985).*

General Electric, the nation's sixth largest defense contractor, pleaded guilty to defrauding the Air Force of some $800,000 by doctoring its books on the Minuteman missile project. What individual person was prosecuted? No one. Who went to jail? No one, as GE continued its trip around the defense monopoly board. Instead, the Government settled for $2 million every eight hours.

In July, an internal Pentagon memorandum revealed that of 400 cases of suspected defense contractor fraud uncovered over the last five years, only 11 had resulted in prosecutions. In other words, defense contractor fraud does pay. It is one of the safest games in town. Even if the Pentagon catches you, there is less than a 3% chance you will be brought to justice. And even if you are prosecuted, as previous examples demonstrate, you will walk away free, with an undiminished profit forecast.

One likely explanation for the pattern of symbolic and hence ineffective sanctions are the close personal linkages (detailed by such scholars as Mills, Domhoff and others referred to later in this chapter) between top corporate and Federal Executive officials. About a year before G.E.'s slap on the wrist, George Bush (then Vice President) was negotiating a 3.2 billion dollar aid package with Pakistan's (now deceased) dictator General Mohammed Zia al-Haq. In the words of a highly reputed and personally connected South Asian expert (Lifschultz, 1988:492):

According to numerous Pakistani sources close to the talks, Bush also intervened to secure a $40 million contract for the General Electric Company to supply Pakistan with gas turbine units for a power plant — even though G.E. had been fairly outbid by tenders from the Japanese firm Mitsubishi and a German-based multinational, the Brown-Boveri Corporation.

Zia, whose country "according to European police sources . . . was furnishing 70 percent of the world supply of high-grade heroin," also agreed to funnel $2 billion additional to "the largest U.S. 'covert' operation since the Vietnam War." Unsurprisingly, the American Ambassador was with Zia when both died in a mysterious plane crash. Since then, the Pakistani military—still dominant in that country—has been exempted from Bush's so-called war on drugs because top officers willingly serve CIA proxy roles *vis-à-vis* Afghanistan and possibly in the Middle East.

Even as an elected President, Bush has continued (Auerbach, 1990:15) to lobby foreign governments on behalf of transnational corporations seeking lucrative contracts:

> Top officials of the U.S. government, led by President George Bush, took the unprecedented step of intervening this month with their counterparts in Tokyo and Jakarta to help AT&T in its effort to win an Indonesian telecommunications contract that could be worth as much as $2 billion, according to administration and company officials. . . .
>
> In the AT&T case, top administration officials said they acted following reports from Jakarta that Japan might be using its $2.1 billion in annual aid to Indonesia as leverage to swing the contract to NEC.

Despite Indonesia's 1975 invasion of East Timor and genocidal killing of an estimated 300,000 during the succeeding decade, economic sanctions were never considered. On the contrary, U.S. based as well as Tokyo's TNCs have used their government access in a fierce rivalry for the lucrative petroleum-based market.

Personal linkages may explain the pattern of successful "tax avoidance" by major military contractors. Citizens for Tax Justice reported ("Economic Clips," 1984:11) that:

> five of the nation's top dozen military contractors earned profits in each year between 1981 and 1983 but paid no federal taxes. The five companies, with profits of $10.5 billion in the three year period, were among 17 major American corporations that paid no taxes or received refunds and other tax benefits worth $1.2 billion. Of the five contractors, Grumman Corporation and Lockheed paid no federal taxes in three years, and General Dynamics, General Electric, and Boeing received cash refunds.
>
> The five companies accounted for more than $15 billion in Pentagon contracts in 1983 alone. Excluding the privately held Hughes Aircraft, the report notes that the top twelve American military contractors paid a total of $296 million in federal income taxes, while reporting more than $19 billion in profits in the three year period. This amounts to an average tax rate of 1.4% on reported profits—44.5% less than the statutory rate of 46%.

Equally successful were the military-industrial complex's efforts in blocking NATO weapons standardization that would save an estimated (Hartley, 1983) $10 billion annually.

Another major source of waste and corruption occasioned by politically in-sulated military management involves incredibly poor inventory control and outright theft of sophisticated equipment ("Black Market," 1985:1, 30) by slothfully officered army and naval personnel. In 1983, the General Account-ing Office tactfully admonished that "(t)he magnitude of the inventory ac-curacy problem is much greater than has previously been recognized by the Department of Defense." Two years hence, it became public knowledge that perhaps billions of dollars' worth of ammunition, lethal small arms, including machine guns, grenades and components for high tech weaponry, had been stolen. Such items were sold in the burgeoning American underground economy — estimated to range between $300–$400 billion. In California alone, Federal officials disclosed that "Navy employees and others stole several hun-dred million dollars worth of weapons and related equipment, including parts for Phoenix missiles and F-14 fighter planes, from Navy warehouses in San Diego and from the aircraft carrier *Kitty Hawk* over the last five years." Other major thefts at Fort Bragg, N.C., and from the army's ammunition plant at Lake City, Missouri, are referred to in Chapter 11. Indicative of the quality of military management is the fact that "Pentagon security officials, who by law are supposed to be told of thefts so they can correct security problems, say that in many cases, when thieves are caught they do not learn of the incidents until they hear about them through the press." Or in the words of the Pentagon's deputy inspector general: "The problem is pretty widespread. It leads us to believe there are a lot of holes in the supply system. . . ." Whether this includes overseas depots is unclear.

Even more directly related to the Third World and intercorporate officer linkages are repeated General Accounting Office (U.S., G.A.O., 1980:7, 10) complaints of over- and underbilling of Foreign Military Sales recipients due to endemic corruption and chaotic record keeping.[6] Pearson (1981:49) adds that "DOD was unable in some cases to specify the weapons purchased from manufacturers. . . . Furthermore, the GAO has found discrepancies in export values in 50% of all expired or returned 1976 or 77 commercial licenses reported by the State Department." A year later the same Congressional watch-dog (U.S., G.A.O., 1982:36) complained that "the purchasing government is responsible for paying all costs associated with the sale. We have issued numerous reports showing that DOD does not recover full cost." This may be explained *in part* by the salient political objective of maximizing influence with recipient elites, most of which are at least as prone to gross speculation as American corporate executives who engage frequently in various forms of illegal behavior (Green and Berry, 1985; Rothschild, 1985). Gansler (1980: 209–210) highlights this reality from a somewhat broader perspective:

> Bribery appears to be a major factor in the international competition for arms sales. In the United States, many of the major arms suppliers are or have been

under investigation in connection with foreign bribery charges. Lockheed has
been accused of paying bribes in at least fifteen countries, and in at least six
of them it has caused serious governmental crises. It has been claimed that
Lockheed and Northrop have paid off officials from Japan, Southeast Asia, the
Middle East, West Germany, the Netherlands, and South America. Over a
three-year period Northrop is alleged to have put out $30 million, which is
about equal to Northrop's total net income during the same period. The stakes
in this competition are very high. Bribes are used for two purposes: most obviously, to get customers to buy from the company making the bribe, but also
to encourage the country to buy weapons it might not otherwise even buy.

Whether best explained by corruption, a desire to maximize influence or
bureaucratic sloth, failure to recover amounts lost functions as a taxpayer subsidy as do other practices to be mentioned elsewhere in this chapter. All must
be subtracted from short-run national economic benefits imputed to such
sales.

While some analysts (Pierre, 1982:71) minimize the importance of foreign
military sales to weapons producers, arguing that few depend heavily upon
them, when one selects other years or takes a longer view (see Table 16) as do
some corporate executives, a somewhat different picture emerges. Gansler
(1980:201–212) for example, amplifying Russett's point cited earlier in this
chapter, notes:

> • In 1975 the United States procured for itself only $17 billion worth of
> military equipment, compared with the $12 billion worth it bought from the
> U.S. defense industry for foreign governments. Thus, in many areas, foreign
> military sales were the predominant demand factor; for example, the U.S.
> Army Missile Command bought 70 percent of its equipment for foreign sales.
> • From 1970 to 1976 the top 25 defense contractors had a 45.5 percent in-
> crease in foreign military sales, but their U.S. defense business in this same
> period fell 23 percent (both figures in constant dollars). More military aircraft
> and more Army missiles were built in the United States in 1975 for foreign sales
> than for the American military. . . .
> • In 1976, eight of the top 25 defense contractors had over 25 percent of
> their total defense business in foreign military sales: Northrop, Grumman, Lit-
> ton, Raytheon, FMC, Textron, LTV, and Todd Shipyards. Another five of the
> top 25 had over 15 percent of their total defense business in foreign sales. In
> total, the percentage of foreign relative to domestic military business for these
> top 25 defense firms rose from 4 percent in 1970 to 20 percent in 1976. . . .
> • The heavy debt of many large U.S. defense contractors has been partially
> alleviated by large foreign military sales, which have frequently provided better
> cash payment arrangements than domestic sales.

Clearly, absent increased domestic procurement, even a 5 to 10 percent decline
in sales — especially for more highly remunerative export items — can make the
difference between an outstanding net earnings performance and a mediocre
or dismal one. The latter directly affects executive careers and earnings, as it

does credit terms, dividends and capital gains for those including high government officials who speculate in such stocks.

Reflecting the Reagan Administration's extraordinary level of interpenetration and government-industry rapport (an attribute of the Bush team as well), Walter R. Edgington testified on behalf of the National Security Industrial Association (U.S., Sen., CFR, *Conventional Arms Sales,* 1981:89) before the Senate Foreign Relations Committee to the effect that "U.S. industry believes that the current policy and its approach are well thought out, pragmatic, and flexible, a policy within which U.S. industry can meet its goals." Even under the Carter Administration's "arms restraint" policy, it appears that weapons manufacturers exercised leverage sufficient to avoid arms transfer denials that would have allowed competitors to pre-empt their potential market. Then-Congressman Mike Barnes — revealing acute sensitivity for this commercial interest despite his strong liberalism — pointed out (U.S., House, CFA, 1981:48):

> There are a number of specific cases in which we made the judgment not to enter into the sale and they did not turn to somebody else and did not try to obtain or did not obtain, in fact comparable equipment. We turned down sales of the F-5A for Guatemala, the A-7 for Pakistan, the F-4 for Taiwan, the F-4G for Iran. There are specific instances all over the world in which the United States said we are not going to sell it and our competitors did not necessarily benefit as a result of that decision.

It seems, then, that the market position by United States arms corporations was virtually unaffected by Carter's policies. In fact, the State Department could identify only three sales that were lost to other Western competitors.[7] And this in turn helps one appreciate why Edgington, in his previously cited congressional testimony, argued that "there is no apparent advantage in retaining the commercial ceiling. Our experience in the last Administration proved that very few, if any requests were denied. We applaud the Committee's recommendation to do away with the ceiling."

The growing intimacy between what the Nye Committee once colorfully depicted as the "merchants of death" and an ever more subservient Pentagon is also manifested by the veritable transformation of the latter into a sales agency for the corporate arms sector. Gansler (1980:205–206) thus delineates this new function as it came to be performed even prior to the overt subservience of the Reagan team:

> The U.S. government now plays a more significant and direct role in assisting U.S. firms in the sale of their military goods and services to foreign countries. This began with the executive branch (particularly the Department of Defense) playing a major role in the foreign marketing activities of American companies, and reached a peak with such programs as the sale of the F-16 aircraft to a consortium of NATO countries. Here the DOD became the major sales organization

in combating the joint efforts of the foreign competitors and their governments.

His reference to the F-16 sale to Denmark, Norway and the Netherlands is especially noteworthy. Dörfer's (1983) case study of this sale indicates that allied economic security was actually diminished by State and Pentagon pressure. This resulted in these allies incurring greater costs than necessary. An unusual number of crashes spurred greater disenchantment.

Insofar as Americans are concerned, the costs of such DOD sales efforts constitute a taxpayer subsidy which along with other unpublicized corporate welfare subsidies must be offset against short-run direct economic benefits attributed to arms exports. Gansler (1980:207) adds that even prior to Reagan's heightened militarization, the "present trend is toward corporate dependency by many prime defense contractors in the United States on their foreign sales of military commodities." And while this was diminished by an unprecedented rise in domestic orders between 1982 and 1986, by the late eighties (as documented in Chapter 2) exports would again assume much greater importance.

The salience of what is now approximately $30 to $40 billion in arms production annually (including about $12 billion for export) is also underscored by a *Los Angeles Times* (1983:A11) report that "today, the importance of defense in the total economy is no less pronounced. It accounts for 10 percent of the nation's manufacturing output and 38 percent of its export sales." This export sector is given added importance because of the growing trade deficits over the 1970s and 1980s. Thus Klare (1982c:41) recalls:

> When the United States suffered a foreign trade deficit in October 1971 (its first in 78 years), President Nixon ordered the Pentagon to step up its marketing of U.S. arms abroad. The results were dramatic. Foreign military sales rose from an average of $1.3 billion per year in fiscal 1970–71 to $4 billion annually in 1972–73. This upward drive gained even more momentum in December 1973, when the Organization of Petroleum-Exporting Countries announced a fourfold increase in the posted price of crude petroleum, adding an estimated $16 billion to America's 1974 oil import bill. Foreign military sales orders from the Persian Gulf states rose from $861 million in 1972 to $6.5 billion in 1974. Although Government spokesmen have not openly linked arms sales to oil imports, most analysts agree that this dramatic increase in military exports to the oil-producing countries was at least partially motivated by a desire to compensate for the increase in overseas oil payments.

From fiscal year 1974 through 1982, the United States Department of Defense (1982:1–2) reported that foreign military sales agreements with countries of the Middle East and South Asia totaled in excess of $51 billion. This figure excludes commercial exports and other transfers (e.g. "excess defense" articles, MAP, CIA, etc.). Furthermore, as noted earlier, there is a conservative bias in such DOD data.

The Middle East according to the same report "received 60 percent of all Third World (arms) imports" between 1961 and 1980, making it another prime example of vacuous security rationales and the tendency of arms manufacturers to absorb newly acquired Third World foreign exchange earnings. Indeed, the editor of *South,* Altaf Gauhar, has fielded the proposition (1982:11) that the more wealth a developing country acquires, the greater the propensity for weapons exporters to siphon it off.[8] Even if Gauhar's thesis is slightly overdrawn and undue significance attached to the influence of arms merchants, his argument is in some measure persuasive and warrants careful attention — particularly in view of subsequent empirical findings (Looney, 1989) that arms imports are highly correlated with resource availability — especially in financially burdened countries.

This is especially true in light of the problematic attainment of official military and political objectives for such sales — discussed in the next chapter and in varying degree elsewhere in this study. Even the progressively widening trade imbalance since 1976 was only modestly offset. Thus between 1983 and 1987, SIPRI (1988:177) records conventional arms sales by the United States exceeded $52 billion (in 1985 constant dollars). The total current dollar balance trade deficit (IPS, 1988:8) for those years surpassed $620 billion. Thus even if inflation were excluded in calculating exports, their loss would add but 10 percent to the trade imbalance.

FOREIGN POLICY IMPLICATIONS: THE "FREE MARKET" CONTEXT

Although the foregoing corporate profit maximizing goals appear to be of paramount immediate importance, others of a more long run or systemic nature reinforce the impetus to expand weapons exports. Klare (1982:41–42) touches upon one:

> Rising oil prices affect not only the balance of payments but also the very survival of the world capitalist system. This is so because the Middle East oil countries are accumulating oil payments (or "Petrodollars") faster than they can spend them on internal economic development. According to one Senate report, the OPEC countries collected $89.1 billion in oil revenues in 1974, of which only half (or $46.7 billion) was spent internally; the rest of this money ($42.2 billion) was deposited in short-term accounts in major banks around the world.
>
> Such huge concentrations of capital represent a major potential threat to international monetary stability. Even $10 billion, if unloaded on the money market all at once, could precipitate a major financial crisis. Thus a major goal of U.S. policy-makers is to "repossess" these petrodollars by persuading the OPEC countries to increase their spending on U.S. goods and services. The biggest long-range problem facing the United States in the Middle East, a top Pentagon official told me in 1973, is to find a way to get the Arabs to spend their dollars without getting control of our economy.

This assumes added significance when it is recognized (Kende, 1983:38) that OPEC's share of world arms imports between 1973 and 1981 increased from 37 percent to 57 percent. The additional billions which Saudis and other "moderate" Arabs have invested in the North have given them a major interest in world capitalist stability.

It is no coincidence that Kuwait and Saudi Arabia have endeavored through share acquisitions in British Petroleum (22 percent) and Aramco (60 percent) respectively, to acquire interests in refining, transportation and distribution networks of advanced capitalist countries. Reinvestments in other corporate sectors from the highly profitable "downstream" operations will enhance the already impressive Arab investments in the more developed economies.[9] To assure long-term Western markets (Rolfe and Vidal-Hall, 1988:52) the latter have effectively opposed "OPEC and non-OPEC pleas for production cuts to increase prices." These and other monarchic regimes were in turn strengthened by United States military measures since 1983 to lessen the appeal of Iran's Islamic Revolution by altering the balance in that country's war with Iraq. By 1988 the Iranians were forced to sue for peace on terms acceptable to the Iraqi aggressor, and a sense of fatalism temporarily enervated nationalist movements. They were confronted by the reassertion of regional military dominance symbolized by the American naval flotilla in the Persian Gulf and its aggressive posture.

In a broader sense, the shared antagonism of Americans, Saudis, and other "moderate" arms recipients toward economically nationalistic and socially radical regimes — regardless of the degree of Soviet support — may preserve privileged access to raw materials and markets. Here there is a certain functionality to the paranoid projection syndrome's threat inflation and anti-radical administration rhetoric — a style that in more muted form also colored predecessor administrations. This antecedent "structural" dimension of United States foreign and military policy is underscored by Eckhardt's (1977:11–12) summary of several pertinent empirical analyses:

> Rosen (1974) has shown for five developing countries in Asia, Europe, and Latin America since 1960, that leftward shifts in their governments (usually resulting from elections) have led to reduction of U.S. aid, investment, and trade, while rightward shifts (usually resulting from military coups) have led to increased U.S. aid, investment and trade.... "If we project continued expansion of multinational investment in the future, counter-revolutionary tendencies in U.S. foreign policy may also be expected to increase" (Rosen, 1974:135–137). In other words, U.S. foreign policy and CIA activities would seem to be not so much concerned with "national security" as with multinational profits.
>
> While Rosen combined U.S. economic and military aid since 1960 in his five case studies, Odell (1974) concentrated on U.S. military aid from 1950 to 1965 in his statistical study of 119 nations, finding that more military aid was given to those nations (1) whose raw materials were more essential to U.S. industry, (2) where there was more U.S. private investment, and (3) which traded more

with U.S. business. These results provided further evidence that U.S. foreign policy was concerned with multinational profits, and that the U.S. military-industrial complex was a complex of "fully armed business concerns," that is multinational empires.

Moran (1974) found that Chilean liberal and conservative governments and conservative business interests "acted with complicity in the exploitation of their own country ... to serve their particular domestic interests rather than the broader national interest" (p. 174) in their policy toward the U.S. copper companies of Anaconda and Kennecott. This was only one instance among many documented collaborations between Third World elites and multinational corporations or the CIA....

Underlying this growing linkage between the transnational corporate class, their indigenous comprador or military dependents and the need for "security" against radical nationalists is the sharp rise (Magdoff, 1969) in foreign investments by United States corporations since World War II and particularly in the 1960s and 1970s. Total overseas corporate investment increased (IPS, 1988:6) from a mere $31 billion in 1960 to $213 billion in 1980; by 1986 the figure had reached $260 billion. Although in the past many of the investments were in such areas as extraction, finance and other services, the de-industrialization of the United States has been reflected by a sharp rise in foreign manufacturing investments. Hence, between 1977 and 1988 (IPS, 1988:7), the assets of United States affiliates abroad as a percent of all United States manufacturing assets rose from 6.3 percent to 12.1 percent.

In the developing countries, which, as Table 4 reveals, accounted for in excess of $51 billion in direct 1983 American investment, "there has been a massive proliferation of branch plants whose high profits have been largely financed by locally and internationally borrowed capital rather than newly invested funds from the United States" (World Bank, 1988: viii, xii). As Trainer (1989:494) underscores, "foreign investors in general bring into the Third World around 15% or less of the capital they invest there...." This along with transfer pricing and capital flight explains why such investments have resulted over time in more money being taken out of these countries than being brought in by the "investing" corporations.[10] Between 1981 and 1987 the total disbursed and outstanding long-term debt—public and private—zoomed from $498 billion to $930.5 billion. The projected amount for 1988 was $980 billion. When short-term debt and IMF credits are included, the 1988 projected total exceeds a trillion dollars—up from 672 billion in 1981 to 1,135 billion. These and other factors—some associated with such economic dependency—have contributed to the virtual bankruptcy (MacEwan, 1989) of most developing countries.[11]

The perception by administration and congressional elites during the "liberal" 1960s that arms transfers and especially foreign officer training do, and should, promote receptivity to American corporate investment is

	All Industries	($ billions) Mining	Petroleum	Manufacturing	Trade, banking, finance, and other industries
All countries	$226.1	$6.7	$59.8	$90.1	$69.5
Developed countries	169.6	3.9	38.9	71.7	55.0
Canada	47.5	2.1	10.9	19.8	14.7
Europe	102.5	---	23.6	44.0	34.8
U.K.	30.9	---	9.3	13.1	7.5
W. Germany	16.0	---	3.3	9.9	2.8
Japan	8.6	---	2.0	4.7	1.6
Australia	8.6	1.7	1.5	2.6	2.2
S. Africa	2.3	.2	---	1.1	.5
Developing countries	51.0	2.8	16.6	18.4	19.9
Latin America	29.5	2.2	6.8	14.7	5.7
Brazil	9.0	.1	.3	6.1	2.4
Mexico	5.0	---	---	3.7	.8
Other African	5.2	.4	3.5	.5	.7
Middle East	3.0	---	.9	.2	.8
OPEC	8.6	.1	4.7	1.3	2.4
Other Asia & Pacific	13.3	---	5.3	2.9	3.9

Table 21. United States direct investments abroad: 1983. Source: *U.S. Dept. of Commerce,* Survey of Current Business, *8/84. Reprinted in Hansen (1985:9).*

documented by Wolpin (1973:22–24). Relying upon congressional testimony and exchanges during hearings in the late 1970s, Zwick (1982:27) also concludes that Washington officialdom "believes that military presence reinforces trade patterns, willingness to accept direct foreign investment and retards protectionist pressures which would affect U.S. markets." Sklar (1984) and Miles (1989) echo this conclusion with respect to the Reagan-Bush Administration's aggressive posture of expanding United States force levels abroad.

Wolpin's (1983a) comparison of 105 developing nations in turn reveals a strong correlation between violent state repressiveness and United States military presence. And since an immense majority (Kriesberg, 1982:40) of Americans disdain interventionism "to promote capitalism," Washington's political elites naturally resort to "national security" threat inflation to secure acquiescence. Their ties and frequent identity with corporate elites are detailed by Kolko (1969), Horowitz (1969a), Sklar (1980), and Dye (1983). Indeed, by 1983, as Tables 14, 15, and 16 reveal, many of the largest and most influential United States corporations relied upon foreign activities for a very sizable proportion of their profits.

Today, the only countries that are not objects of corporate expansionism are those few like Nicaragua, Cambodia and perhaps Angola or Afghanistan, which actively support economic nationalism and egalitarian domestic restructuring. These are targeted for destabilization. The remainder, including some nominally Marxist-led systems such as Yugoslavia and China which cooperate with the United States "security" apparatus in opposing revolutionary movements, are actively—if quietly—being pressured by American officials and executives (Pacific Forum, 1984:1–12) to further open the door to greater opportunities for profit-taking by United States–based transnational corporations.

CONTRIBUTING TO AMERICAN PROSPERITY: TRENDS AND PATTERNS

Until the Vietnam War era, a modest net benefit to American mass welfare—and hence to national security—was engendered by such interventionism. Low raw material prices and global economic dominance of markets by American based transnationals at relatively modest cost, ensured a "trickle-down" manifested by rising living standards. The New Deal legacy of progressive reforms—largely undermined today—also contributed to this outcome by increasing mass purchasing power and status. Even so it is problematic whether the public would acquiesce in military interventionism on the premise that a particular regime (e.g., Cuba or Vietnam) posed an immediate or long-run (i.e., the demonstration effect) threat to our "national security" by independently driving a harder (i.e., more costly) bargain with transnationals.[12] Higher foreign taxes, wages and improved working conditions would have inhibited U.S. de-industrialization (i.e., runaway plants).

If from a "trickle down" perspective such threat inflation actually may have promoted on balance national welfare in the past (though even then the contribution was modest), since the Vietnam era it has become dysfunctional if not suicidal. Transnationals including weapons producers (Tuomi, 1983: 148–160) have, as we have seen, increasingly relocated their production and reinvestment abroad while integrating an enlarged number of operations with European and Japanese firms. Growing de facto autonomy, profitability and tax exemptions for transnational corporations (Barnet and Muller, 1974; Sklar, 1980) have paralleled a rise in domestic tax, industrial unemployment and, with the exception of the 1983–87 period, inflationary burdens for mass sectors. This in conjunction with public sector austerity since the late 1960s has at least temporarily frustrated the common American's historic optimism for an ever rising standard of living and quality of life. As the Third World economic nationalism referred to earlier in the Casey excerpt has diffused and intensified with modest though diminishing Soviet support, the escalating economic costs of a global infrastructure (i.e., state services) to protect and promote transnational corporate interests have surpassed the declining benefits to mass sectors.

As its inception, not only did America's world military system provide markets for surplus and new arms, but it was touted as low cost because of reliance upon the so-called doctrine misnamed "massive retaliation."[13] Even then, however, this was actually a coercive first-strike action as opposed to public policy.[14] By the end of the fifties, Kennedy's missile gap threat inflation generated the flexible response doctrine. After the Vietnam disaster, the national security establishment ostensibly renounced use of Americans in favor of proxy troops under the aegis of the Nixon Doctrine. Its failure to stem social radicalism and economic nationalism—often vacuously portrayed as Soviet gains—resulted in a new Carter and particularly Reagan buildup carrying, as Tables 8 and 9 reveal, unparalleled economic costs for the American public and unprecedented profits for the now dominant military-industrial complex. Begun in the late 1970s and catalyzed by the virtual exclusion of civilianist national security approaches from the Reagan Administration—particularly epitomized by the removal of fringe moderates such as White, Hinton, and Enders—the new orientation stresses clear nuclear strategic superiority backing massively expanded rapid deployment forces under the central command. These and, if possible, allied units will generate flexibility of response in the event that counterrevolutionary client forces falter. Allies, however, have historically proved to be as unreliable as the latter.

Hence it is ironic that arms transfers and concomitant military aid have been officially rationalized as economically cost-effective mechanisms for reducing the growing American financial burden. A salient neo-colonial rationale reiterated over the decades is the lower cost of foreign as compared to American personnel. The 1982 *SIPRI Yearbook* (Kende, 1983:40) quotes from a speech that Kennedy himself planned to make in Dallas:

> Our assistance makes possible the stationing of 3.5 million allied troops along the Communist frontier at one-tenth the cost of maintaining a comparable number of American soldiers....
> It is far cheaper, and less politically troublesome, to send arms abroad than to send U.S. troops.... Furthermore, arms transfers improve the foreign trade balance, provide some 800,000 jobs in the U.S.A., and make U.S. domestic arms procurement cheaper.

Similar short-run economic benefits were touted by Undersecretary of State Buckley in his presentation of the Reagan Administration's arms transfer policy to the Senate Foreign Relations Committee (U.S., Sen., CFR, *Conventional Arms Sales,* 1981:13):

The marginal U.S. dollar loaned under the FMS to the Turkish Army or the Thai or Pakistan Air Force is a dollar that we would otherwise have to spend outright on our own forces to do a job that Turks and Thais and Pakistanis can do better and at less cost. Not only are security assistance dollars spent in the United States for U.S. equipment, not only are they ultimately paid back even if the interest charged may sometimes be at less than market rates, but we get the security benefit of the force improvements these dollars buy for friendly foreign governments.

This may be properly termed the mercenary rationale. The three recipient dictatorships boasted not only de facto military regimes but also were characterized by torture, thousands of political prisoners, executions or disappearances. The citizens of those countries, of course, will incur greater austerity as the military sales debts are amortized.

An equally hard-headed emphasis upon economic benefits was articulated by former Bechtel Corporation executive Caspar Weinberger (U.S., DOD, 1983:301) early in his tenure as Reagan's hard-line Secretary of Defense:

> ...the security assistance program is not a giveaway. Almost all the financing for foreign military sales, the Economic Support Fund, and the funds for International Military Education and training are spent in the U.S. Thus, the program has economic benefits associated with economies of scale, production line smoothing, expansion of the defense industrial mobilization base, and expanded pipeline availability.

Such commercial profit-maximizing considerations may contribute to Washington's propensity in the late 1970s and more recently to export the most sophisticated weapons systems—sometimes even before American forces were fully equipped. Indeed, in some cases advance foreign orders may engender Pentagon orders. Gansler (1980:209) attributes this to the fact that "the large firms with extensive R & D and marketing organizations are in a better position to capture this market, and thus to use the foreign sales volume to enhance their position in the U.S. market." Klare (1982c:41) adds that "many leading U.S. defense contractors—recognizing that the award of lucrative procurement contracts often depends on the acquisition of sufficient foreign military sales orders—launched aggressive export campaigns of their own (in some cases involving bribes or other illicit payoffs)."

If such economic rewards accrue primarily to the corporations and their owners, other benefits like foreign exchange earnings, multiplier effects, and employment generated *do* have a broader short-run societal impact. Yet these presumed spillovers are themselves incidental to corporate profit maximization. Thus the previously noted (Tuomi: 1983) trends toward increased coproduction under license, overseas investment in subsidiaries, and the export of components to foreign corporations adversely affect potential United States–based production, employment and even exports to third countries. Evans and Novak (1983:31) refer to but one example:

Shultz's markedly more pro–Israeli predecessor Alexander Haig, in 1982 backed Israeli purchase of jet engines with $180 million in U.S. aid under Foreign Military Sales (FMS) — a program supposedly limited to off-the-shelf American military items.

Pratt & Whitney (a subsidiary of United Technologies, where Haig has worked before and after his tenure at State) then sold the engines to Israel.

That was not the end of U.S. taxpayers' subsidy, direct and indirect, for a foreign plane competing with U.S. rivals. Licenses for technology transfer were needed. Besides, nobody would be able to control Israeli diversion of FMS money into the Lavi. . . .

The upshot of the deal is familiar indeed. The U.S. is subsidizing, directly and indirectly, a new Israeli weapons system clearly destined for the world market. The U.S. and Israel have reached another agreement rejected by Arab states.

The only ostensible beneficiary here was Pratt & Whitney, since the Lavi project was shelved a few years later.

There are also other frequently ignored important taxpayer subsidies which offset short-run export returns and adversely affect employment within the United States. Gansler (1980:211) reports:

> Since 1965 the U.S. government has been involved in extending credit for foreign military sales. Since 1969, loans from U.S. commercial banks and the Export-Import Bank have become increasingly important to the foreign military buyers. A good deal of the military equipment sold abroad has been built in U.S.-government-owned plants and with U.S.-government-owned manufacturing equipment, frequently contained within company plants. Until recently, these sales were made on a rent-free basis. Numerous other "hidden costs" have been absorbed by the U.S. government. Many of the countries buying U.S. equipment are now requiring "off-set agreements," in which the United States agrees to buy from those countries a certain amount of equipment in exchange for their having bought U.S. equipment — with full waiver of the "Buy American" act. These offsets help the U.S. prime contractors to consummate sales at the expense of the U.S. subcontractors and parts suppliers. In many cases, a "foreign" company involved in multinational coproduction or licensing is simply a U.S. multinational firm's overseas division selling the product and technology it received under license or direct transfer from its U.S. sister division.

The same analyst concludes that "such actions clearly profit the firm; the question is their effect on the overall U.S. defense position and whether the U.S. government gets its money's worth."

Collateral, indirect, long-term costs to the American public and economy — as opposed to transnational corporations which are the major beneficiaries — are commonly ignored by such liberal analysts as Betts, Gansler, Pearson, Pierre and even Klare. Obviously "force projection" facilities are secured in part via arms transfers and otherwise through multibillion dollar escalating "rental" payments as in Spain, Greece and the Philippines. Hundreds of such bases (thousands if one includes smaller sites) require the existence of American units in the United States, Europe or elsewhere that can utilize such facilities. Logistical equipment, nuclear weapons, naval units—in short, the overall complement for deployment as in the Grenadan or Lebanese invasions of 1983, and that of Panama six years later, is integral to this hegemonic posture. The same may be said for reinforcements and so-called strategic "deterrent" forces.[15]

Given this and the fact that arms transfers are officially defined as integral to the global "security" posture and foreign policy context, only by including the overall strategic arms race and militarization of space can their ostensible "benefits" be placed in perspective. It is more than coincidental that Betts (1980:96) discovered "many opponents of arms sales also opposed high U.S. defense spending." While arms transfers themselves yield some often exaggerated short-run direct economic benefits (primarily to the corporate owning class), multi-trillion dollar socio-economic costs consequential to the United States military buildup over the years—essential for credibility in threatening Third World conflict escalation—are often ignored by those with a narrow sectoral or temporal frame of reference.

The net adverse impact of related heavy military burdens upon civilian industrial exports, employment, infrastructural investments (transport, education, health), price stability, innovation, productivity, economic growth, crime, etc., has been analyzed or described in a plethora of articles, monographs, books and reports. (Many are cited in the next chapter.) By early 1983, the "guns vs. butter" tradeoff had become both obvious to and opposed by a majority of Americans. Cepeda and Glennon (1983:4) reported that "public opinion polls reflect growing opposition to the Reagan budget from the grass roots. A *Washington Post*/ABC poll found 59% of Americans opposing cuts in social programs." The 300,000 citizens who demonstrated in Washington during late August 1983 also shared this perspective as do a growing number of national legislators who oppose further increases in military spending.

Coffin (1983c:1) reports that "Senator Robert Byrd (D–W.Va.) said, 'Speaking for the people of my state, which has an unemployment rate of 21%, I wish the Administration would be more concerned about our own people than keeping a wealthy few people in power in Central America.'" Indeed, public opinion polls revealed that a majority of citizens voting for Reagan opposed his militaristic and inegalitarian economic policy biases. But while Byrd's quoted remarks were applicable nationally, he and others were unable to effectively counter a highly manipulative ultrasophisticated (Perry, 1984) corporate-funded campaign effort which Reagan's backers organized. Similar high-tech tactical prowess, albeit with a less appealing personality, gave Bush a narrower triumph four years later. Dukakis' failure to adopt a Jesse Jackson–type populist campaign (Meyerson, 1989) until too late in his campaign ensured the Republican victory.

Of particular long-run importance is the fact that future productivity of the civilian economy, its export and employment potential are being further undermined by a key datum (Cepeda and Glennon, 1983:2): "The military will claim almost two-thirds of all federal research and development spending in the FY 1984 budget, placing yet another obstacle in the way of domestic economic recovery and growth." Or as William Winpisinger, former head of the International Association of Machinists, more recently (Coffin, 1990:2) observed: "among the 14 Western industrialized nations and Japan, the U.S. ranks first in military research and development, first in military spending, but fifth in civilian R & D, tenth in civilian spending, eleventh in economic growth, thirteenth in annual real wage increases, and tenth in wage levels." Worse, the hidden subsidies to weapons exporters discussed in earlier parts of this chapter offset and lessen direct short-run economic benefits to the nation. Yet even when these hidden subsidies are ignored, administration claims outrun the conclusions of several official studies.

Pearson (1981:48) notes that in "a peak sales year, 1975, officially reported military sales accounted for only 2% of U.S. exports."[16] Furthermore, two important analyses (Pierre, 1982:69–70) by the U.S. Congressional Budget Office (1976) and the U.S. Treasury Department (1977) suggest that arms sales contribute relatively little to either employment or the balance of payments at the national level.[17] Pierre (1982:25) states that these "economic benefits are less than is generally assumed." As questionable as that general assumption was Defense Secretary Weinberger's allegation that unrestrained arms exports are essential "to preserve a military-industrial base." Landgren-Backstrom (1982: 205) points to a striking alternative:

> Japan remains as a unique example among the leading industrial nations, with a large and expanding domestic defense industry, but operating under such heavy arms exports regulations that there is almost a total prohibition on arms sales. During 1980 and 1981, for example, Japan does not appear in the SIPRI arms export statistics at all. The Japanese example, if it lasts, may serve to refute the claims made worldwide by defense industry representatives that they have to export to survive.

If in the American setting "survival" of particular corporate entities such as Lockheed became doubtful, recourse could be made to General B.B. Somervell's proposal (Coffin, 1983b:4) at the outset of World War II to nationalize the arms industry. As procurement head, he "argued this was the way to get guns cheaply and efficiently." The War Production Board, however, was unresponsive.

Nationalization would also sharply reduce that industry's autonomous role in the national political arena, where it has actively lobbied domestically at taxpayer's expense while routinely corrupting foreign decision-makers. Furthermore, nationalization would probably reduce cost inflation due to corruption arising from conflicts of interest among procurement and other officers who aspire for industry jobs after retirement. With even greater certitude it would eliminate some publicly subsidized threat inflation propaganda while weakening militaristic policy support and concomitant diversion of societal resources. Worth pondering again is the coincidence between a temporary decline in domestic procurement during the final years of the Vietnamese disaster and the sharp escalation of arms transfers. Did the latter offset the former for this highly influential weapons producing industry? And is it a mere coincidence that the tapering off of arms sales agreements in the early 1980s was paralleled by skyrocketing domestic military appropriations? Or, to press the point, when procurement leveled off—albeit at higher levels—in the late 1980s, that another upsurge in programmed military sales occurred? Recalcitrance due to defense industry protectionism in Europe and Japan (Fitchett, 1988), more intense European and even Third World competition, and, most crucially, virtual financial bankruptcy (MacEwan, 1989) in much of the Third World indicate that the success of this latest export drive will be problematic for the Bush Administration.

Ultimately, then, it would seem that the primary civilian beneficiaries of the militarization of American foreign policy are the military-industrial complex and the ever more integrated transnational corporate sectors. This of course pertains to past decades but not necessarily the future. As we shall see in the next chapter, historic "power-projection," which once may have been a "rational" approach to securing spheres of influence, has increasingly become a source of instability in developing areas and inferentially at the world level as well. In the context of unparalleled planetary militarization and an East-West arms race in space, it is even more difficult to disjoin regional from global security.

7. Official "Security" Rationales and Liberal Critiques: The Underlying Imperial Dimension

Given their salience and the ubiquitous concern over the "bottom line" within the corporate sector, it is ironic though understandable that economic considerations are generally added as an afterthought or reinforcing argument to official security justifications. The public or declaratory policy rationales are wholly devoid of references to profit enhancement for weapons producers or structuring a favorable overseas investment environment for transnationals by supporting "moderate" elites or insurgents (e.g. the Nicaraguan contras) against nationalistic domestic opponents. In the early sixties when economic nationalism was less salient and United States hegemony more secure, there was greater willingness by high level officers, administration representatives and congressmen to be explicit (Wolpin, 1973:15-24). Thus Percy's remarks, other congressional excerpts, and CIA Director Casey's Chamber of Commerce address quoted in earlier chapters constitute exceptions to contemporary reticence. Greater candor can be found—as Chomsky (1985:2-3) demonstrates—in classified State Department and other official planning documents.[1]

A PANOPLY OF GOALS

This points to one of the major problems for "security assistance" analysts. Arms transfers and military aid often serve multiple objectives. Some goals are more publicly defensible than others. It is easier to defend CIA weapons transfers to Nicaraguan counterrevolutionaries in Honduras if the end is portrayed (falsely) as interdiction of material bound for guerrillas in military-ruled El Salvador. Serious legal, diplomatic and even domestic political problems would arise if it were conceded on one hand that most guerrilla supplies were captured or purchased from the military within El Salvador, that effective interdiction of small shipments was very difficult, and in any case the real objective was to destroy the Nicaraguan Revolution, i.e., overthrow the Sandinista government. Only in September 1983, after the Soviet downing of the Korean passenger "spy" (Pearson, 1984) plane was used to heighten tensions, was the

114

interdiction pretense abandoned. Tom Wicker (1983) feigned surprise at belated disclosures by Undersecretary of Defense Fred C. Ikle before the Baltimore Council on Foreign Affairs: "Now we know. By its own declaration, the Reagan Administration seeks 'military victory' rather than a negotiated settlement in El Salvador. And it aims to 'prevent consolidation of a Sandinista regime in Nicaragua' rather than merely to interdict whatever arms that country supplies to the Salvadoran guerrillas."[2]

This candor underscores the continuing relevance of the Report of the Draper Commission—appointed by President Eisenhower to review American security assistance policies toward developing areas—which emphasized (U.S., President's Committee, 1959) the need for a distinction between "public policies" and "action policies" toward Third World countries. The Reagan (and Bush) Administration's systematic use of such duplicity is analyzed generally in terms of its campaign by Perry (1984), particularly in the foreign affairs area by McMahan (1985), and specifically with respect to Nicaragua by Kornbluh (1987), as well as Panama, where the invasion was obviously given a green light at least a month ("U.S. General," 1989:3) before the planned provocative incident.

Such institutionalized trickery is necessitated by public opinion in the United States, which has opposed unprovoked military intervention—more strongly since Vietnam—in developing areas even though it is precisely in such regions that Washington must rely upon coercion, as Chomsky (1985) brilliantly demonstrates, to assure privileged raw material access and market dominance against forces seeking to use indigenous resources to promote economic development and end mass impoverishment. High post-intervention approval ratings of 85 to 90 percent reflect low mass self-esteem and information levels as well as the value accorded to success. To this one may add the cultural fascination with violence and its intense chauvinistic particularism.

Hence arms transfers are most defensible when they are portrayed as strengthening our balance of trade or overall military and strategic posture. Seldom, however, is the vast military buildup in the North and particularly the goal of superiority for "war fighting" publicly linked to the deployment of force in developing areas. Sanders (1983:24–25) illustrates the delicate nexus of these strategic interdependencies:

> Once adopting such a pantheon of East-West struggle it then became, in the words of senior White House aide Ed Meese, "entirely possible" that the U.S. would take direct action against Cuba. Quite candidly he explained, this was all part of Reagan's larger policy "to have America's foes go to bed each night uncertain what Washington's next move might be." Such a strategy, in turn, would require a vast military buildup to make the threat credible. As NSC-68 had emphasized over a quarter century before: "Without superior aggregate military strength, in being and readily mobilizable, a policy of 'containment'—which is in effect a policy of calculated and gradual coercion—is nothing more than a policy of bluff."

For Containment Militarism, "arms control" was as pernicious to its aims as "human rights." If human rights undermined the legitimacy of support for repressive regimes, arms control acted as a similar foil to the nuclear threat that helped keep them in power. As the CPD stressed repeatedly in its analyses, "The strategic deterrent is the fulcrum upon which all other use of military force pivots." The logic of the position was explained as follows: "If the Soviet dominance of the strategic nuclear level is allowed to persist, Soviet policymakers may — and almost certainly will — feel freer to use force at lower levels, confident that the United States will shy away from a threat of escalation." In its familiar elliptical style the barely concealed message was that "U.S. policymakers" as much as their Soviet counterparts would also be "freer to use force at lower levels" with superior nuclear capabilities at their disposal.

Rather than specifying such linkages in the overall strategic balance, official rationales tend to be limited to regional power projection or war coalitions without referring to plans to threaten escalation (i.e., escalatory leverage) to global East-West nuclear war. Thus under the rubric "strategic," Weinberger's *FY 1984 Annual Report* (U.S., DOD, 1983:301) to Congress specified a cluster of "force projection" objectives in pinpointing that "the specified security assistance program supports our efforts to obtain the access, overflight, and base rights the Defense Department needs abroad. Furthermore, this program helps us move toward greater equipment standardization and interoperability, which enables friends and allies to move, shoot, and communicate with U.S. forces in coalition warfighting situations."

What this means in terms of Klare's (1982a) reference to a new "offensive" posture is implied (U.S., Sen., CFR, *Arms Sales Package,* Pt. 1, 1981:57) by Joint Chiefs of Staff Chairman General David Jones' justification of the widely criticized sale of 5 AWACs, several hundred Sidewinder missiles and long range fuel tanks for F-15s to Saudi Arabia: "We have increased U.S. presence in the region with combatant forces, naval forces, increased power projection capability; but very important to our defense capability in Southwest Asia is friendly relations with nations of the region, improving facilities, and developing some infrastructure." In even greater specificity, State Department Undersecretary for Security Assistance Buckley revealingly defended this largest arms sale ever to a Third World regime (U.S., Sen., CFR, *Arms Sales Package,* Pt. 2, 1981:65) in essentially if not exclusively neo-imperial terms:

> The bedrock that we are establishing is one based on the mutuality of interests. We have almost as large a stake in the protection of the Saudi oilfields as they have. If we establish the kind of relationship that we want and propose, in which we have a natural American presence in support of systems and equipment that are totally compatible with ours, we will see flowing out of that facilities that are compatible with our equipment, spare parts, repair shops, communication systems that fit right into ours, runways of the appropriate length — all of these things that mean that in case of an emergency we will be able to have an American presence there which can be effective on the date of arrival.

This is actually a much more efficient way in these strident times for the United States to be able to project a credible deterrent presence in different parts of the world.

We also have the matter of access. You have automatic access if you are working with people. We don't have bases in Oman; we have access. We don't have bases in Somalia; we have access. We are discussing access with Egypt. So we respectfully submit that from the point of view of American security we are really getting something better.

The despotic character of the Saudi regime was not mentioned even though Buckley's State Department was denouncing the Soviets ad nauseum for human rights violations.

At another hearing earlier that year (U.S., Sen., CFR, *Conventional Arms Sales*, 1981:6) Buckley in presenting Reagan's "new policy" pursuant to a July 8, 1981, presidential directive, specified four "factors" to be considered in future arms transfer decisions.

A. . . .the military justification . . . including the nature of the threat. . .
B. . . .the ability of the recipient to absorb the transfer. . .
C. . . .the effect of the transfer on regional stability. . .
D. . . .whether the needs of U.S. forces would be adversely affected.

Although a residual "other factors" criterion ostensibly encompassing "human rights considerations" was added, the four listed above are criteria that lean heavily in a military direction. The significance of the military dimension at the *de jure* level is highlighted by Gansler (1980:217):

It is important to note that the sole legal justification for all military assistance — whether sales or grants, and whether through the federal government or directly from U.S. companies — is its value to the overall U.S. defense posture. This is the criterion under which the export license reviews are made. Other rationales, such as improving the balance of trade and providing jobs, are clearly intended to be only secondary considerations.

Yet at the operational level, this appears to be what the Draper Commission (U.S., President's Committee, 1959) depicted as the "public" or declaratory policy. As we saw in preceding chapters and will again below, the "action" policy implies additional goals which are often accorded greater *de facto* priority.

The same need to engineer consent through threat inflation helps us understand the existence of a public *vs.* policy dichotomy — one of considerable historic lineage. Thus a conservative military aid specialist, Edgar Furniss (1957:1–2, 37), acknowledged years ago that a "chasm" existed between the publicly stated and real purposes of such "assistance." The latter, according to a recent interview-based scholarly study (Schoultz, 1988), pertain far more to imperial dominance than to security. Other pertinent decision-making attributes were ideological fanaticism, empirical apathy and analytical vacuity. Thus while publicly diffused military aid or arms transfer rationales may be relevant, no particular weight should be attached to them—official source notwithstanding.

Frequently specified immediate objectives are compensation (i.e., payoffs) for bases (e.g. Philippines or Morocco), intelligence facilities (e.g. Turkey, China, or Ethiopia prior to 1977), and alliance support (South Korea, Greece, Pakistan, Taiwan). Even the stationing of troops (e.g. in Honduras) to train third-country (e.g. Salvadoran) soldiers and perhaps support CIA operations against fourth (e.g. Nicaragua) countries may require costly payoffs in terms of both dollars and arms. Thus a report by Taubman (1983) noted that Honduran strongman General Gustavo Alvarez had announced at a Washington press conference that the Pentagon "had agreed" to ask Congress for a major increase in military aid from $37.3 and $41 million for FY 1983 and 1984 to $400 million over the next several years. In turn, the "Honduran Government agreed last month to permit the United States to send more than 100 additional military advisers to Honduras, tripling the current number, and to open a training base there for Salvadoran and Honduran soldiers."

Again, as Gliksman (1981:39) indicates in another example, the impetus for such expansion of a massive global force projection antedated the Reagan Administration:

> Current interest in sales to Morocco began in the last year of the Carter presidency, when the Afghanistan invasion highlighted Morocco's strategic importance as a transit point for the movement of forces to the Gulf region. A Carter sale of $135 million in aircraft was the first down-payment to a new relationship with King Hassan. In March 1981, Reagan offered 108 M-60 tanks, an offer that Hassan has had to defer for lack of finance. Gaining rights to the air bases might require giving the tanks away, perhaps together with additional equipment that the King needs in his war against Algerian-supported Polisario guerrillas in the Sahara.

Since then, United States officers (Wenger, 1983:54–55, 59) have played active intelligence and combat advisory roles on the Saharan battlefield, while American diplomats have energetically endeavored to exclude the Saharan Democratic Republic from the OAU. Yet, this is not to imply that the military objectives of arms transfers are unimportant or invariably a mask for other less defensible neo-colonial goals. In any case the belligerent anti-nationalist posture of the Reagan and now Bush Administration leaves less to inference. Furthermore, many weapons export objectives are mutually reinforcing.

On the other hand, the Draper Commission distinction is useful in understanding why arms transfers are steadfastly defended regardless of criticism, such as Klare's, that weakens or vitiates the purely defensive security-based rationales. The Saudi case, as mentioned previously, involved three controversial components: fuel tanks to extend the range of the F-15s sold in 1978; Sidewinder missiles; and five AWACs aircraft. Some of the major objections and gross deficiencies of a military character were summarized (U.S., Sen., CFR, *Arms Sales Package*, Pt. 2, 1981:88) by the ranking Democrat on the Foreign Relations Committee.[3] During the hearings it was acknowledged that the Saudis lack even minimal capability to operate the AWACs and that the F-15 enhancement package gives that aircraft a distinct offensive capacity. Although "power projection" via future base access for the Rapid Deployment Force still provided a residual military rationale, Weinberger himself when pressed admitted (U.S., Sen., CFR, *Arms Sales Package*, Pt. 1, 1981:92) that while the AWACs package might not be militarily optimal, the key consideration was that *the Saudis wanted it.* This in turn can be reconciled with former CIA Director Stansfield Turner, who, while viewing (U.S., Sen., CFR, *Arms Sales Package*, Pt. 1, 1981:206–207) the sale as lacking military justification, favored it nevertheless to immunize the Saudi regime from Arab nationalism:

> The position the Saudis are in, and the reason I favor the sale, sir is this. If they don't show some return for their limited association publicly with the United States, they will be under increasing pressure from the PLO and other radicals in the Arab world and to agree to some sovereignty infringing arrangement would be tantamount to subjecting them to intense criticism from the rest of the Arab world.... The radical Arab world so closely associates the United States with Israel, so if the United States rebuffs the Saudis, the Saudis will have to step up and in some way express considerable displeasure.

In a subsequent hearing (U.S., Sen., *Arms Sales Package*, Pt. 2, 1981:87), Foreign Relations Committee Chairman Percy recalled Turner's endorsement and argued that such evenhandedness with Egypt's assassinated military ruler, Sadat, had been instrumental to the latter's willingness to break with the Arab League:

> In 1978, if Congress had opposed the sale of F-5s to Egypt there would not have been a peace process. Few dispute now that Camp David would not have occurred without the reassurance of American support that Egypt received in the 1978 sale. This has been reconfirmed to us by President Sadat and by now–President Mubarak. A defeat would have destroyed U.S. credibility as an unbiased participant in the Camp David process.

In both instances, a neo-colonial militaristic bias or perceptual framework inhibits Turner as well as Percy from imagining an alternative evenhanded approach: reducing weapons exports to Israel as a basis for denying Egyptian and Saudi requests! Even better, pressure Tel Aviv to make concessions on the West Bank, Gaza and the Golan Heights in return of recognition and normal relations with her neighbors including a small Palestinian state. By inviting the

Soviets to participate in a joint effort followed by a general Middle East peace conference, some real gain in regional security might well have been attained. Only when such "unthinkable" alternatives are considered do we begin to see that immediate advantages — support for a client state's expansionism, hostility to Arab as well as Palestinian nationalism, and perhaps enhanced profits for the military-industrial complex — were the major "action policy" determinants.[4] Lebanese instability following the Israeli invasion and United States arms transfers to a government dominated by the aggressive Likud minority faction underscore the irrelevance of such "military diplomacy" to a peaceful settlement.

Percy's reward for backing the AWACs deal was his ouster from the Senate by the *crème de la crème* of the Zionist lobbying complex — the American-Israeli Public Affairs Committee. It is not, however, such funds and propaganda that account for the symbiotic United States–Israeli Nexus. The Nexus adopted a fierce anti-nationalist and anti–Soviet foreign policy line after the 1973 war and PLO movement toward a bi-state solution in 1973–74. Thus, as Zunes (1988:16) cogently argues:

> The actual reason for the direction of U.S. policy ... may have more to do with the role Israel plays for the United States. Israel has successfully crushed radical nationalist movements in Lebanon and Jordan, as well as the Occupied Territories. It has kept Syria, an ally of the Soviet Union, in check. Its air force controls the skies from Morocco to Iran and from Turkey to Ethiopia. It has been a conduit for U.S. arms to regimes too unpopular to get direct miliary assistance — such as South Africa, Iran and Guatemala. Israeli military advisers have assisted the Nicaraguan contras, the Salvadoran junta and foreign occupation forces in Namibia and Western Sahara. Its secret service has assisted the U.S. in intelligence-gathering and covert operations. Israel has missiles capable of reaching the Soviet Union and has cooperated with the U.S. military-industrial complex with research and development for advanced weapons technology.
>
> As a result, the U.S. has been encouraging the most chauvinistic and militaristic elements in the Israeli government, undermining the last vestiges of Labor Zionism's commitment to socialism, non-alignment and cooperation with the Third World.

Zunes concludes that "continued U.S. 'support' will likely increase Israel's militarization and isolation in the world community, encourage greater intransigence by its enemies and may ultimately lead to Israel's destruction."

Despite the PLO's willingness to accept normal relations (Chomsky, 1988) between a future Palestinian mini-state and Israel, the 1988 elections of Shamir and Bush — both hard-liners against return of the West Bank and Gaza — underscore the relevance of Zunes' prescient analysis. For if anything, a nuclear-armed Israel is an overall liability to genuine U.S. security — threatening to suck America (Chomsky, 1988) into a nuclear conflagration as Arab states acquire long-range missiles and eventually primitive atomic ordnance. The Egyptians, Syrians and Saudis already possess ballistic missiles (Karp, 1989) capable of striking Israeli territory.

Similar non-defense (i.e., "security") considerations explain an early Reagan Administration decision to provide the oil-producing but fiscally bankrupt Venezuelans several squadrons of ultra-sophisticated F-16s. The fact that they cannot maintain or conduct effective combat with such equipment was dismissed, as was their active dissatisfaction with the Guyana boundary (Venezuela claims about a third of Guyana). Instead, Administration arguments (U.S., House, CFA, 1981:14–25) centered on what I earlier described as the paranoid projection syndrome. Criticisms of its premises — no matter how gently articulated, even by Rand expert Sereseres (U.S., House, CFA, 1981:37, 39, 44) as an invited witness at hearings — were blithely disregarded. In the course of his testimony Sereseres questioned Venezuela's technical absorptive capacity (45), placing the payoff (40, 45) for this F-16 transfer in the diplomatic and political realm. They serve "a useful institutional and symbolic function. . . . Within the region prestigious weapons are as significant for diplomatic symbolism as for operational military capabilities in affecting relations between neighbors. Among other things, arms acquisitions must also be seen as a form of diplomacy."

In truth the Administration rationale did point to Caracas' "cooperative" role vis-à-vis Central America. Pierre (1981/1982:279–280) also stresses that "the government . . . has supported U.S. policy in Central America and the Caribbean, including the Reagan Administration's approach to El Salvador. In addition, the United States imports about four percent of its crude oil from Venezuela. . . . Nonetheless, Venezuela has no serious security problem which justifies the F-16."

The sphere-of-influence operational goal was best phrased by Richard B. Burt, the State Department's Director of Politico-Military Affairs (U.S., House, CFA, 1981:8), in his blanket justification of transfers to the region: ". . . the price of inattention to the security requirements of friendly states has been a weakening in our bilateral relationships. This can decrease our ability to influence them in areas that are important to us."

A neo-colonial "military" benefit briefly mentioned in the preceding chapter was low cost proxy troops — a legacy of the now uncelebrated Nixon Doctrine which we saw had antecedents in the Kennedy era. Historically, of course, both the British and French empires relied upon such units to control natives. According to Brookings analyst Betts (1980:95):

> The least ambiguous intersection of arms trade with defense policy is the effect on U.S. military capabilities. Transfers to allies who supplant our own deployments can function as an extension of American forces. Sales can also increase net cost-effectiveness by using cheaper indigenous manpower. By one estimate, South Korea can maintain twenty troops for the cost of one U.S. soldier; for Turkey the ratio is twelve to one.

Superficially persuasive, this rationale which infuses arms transfer/military aid justifications consistently ignores offsetting costs such as the arms sales subsidies by American taxpayers discussed in the preceding chapter, as well as manpower diversion and other security liabilities. Gansler (1980:216), for example, notes:

> American military commanders raise an even more immediate concern about these military sales by pointing out the large amount of DoD manpower devoted to training and logistics activities for these foreign governments. (These resources must come directly out of the manpower ceilings established by Congress for the DoD.) This potentially weakens the U.S. defense position in order to support foreign sales. The counter argument states that foreign military sales are only allowed (by law) if they are "in the U.S. defense interest;" thus, the manpower being used in support of foreign military sales strengthens our allies' position and should, in the end, result in a reduced requirement for U.S. military manpower. In the case of many military sales today, the support for the latter argument is very hard to trace.

Gansler's reservations concerning this defense rationale are given salience by the fact that, with few exceptions, proxy troops are poorly motivated, ineptly led, directed by unreliable governments and often incapable of effectively employing even non-sophisticated weaponry. They may also be difficult to control (e.g. Israel). Wulf (1979) stresses that "due to poor logistics, lack of specific military infrastructures (like airfields and fortified bridges), and inferior training of soldiers the modern equipment could be used only marginally or not (at) all." Similarly, Ronfeldt and Sereseres (1977:23) refer to the "more costly and sophisticated items obtained through U.S. military programs" in Latin America, and conclude that "it is even doubtful, as noted above, that MAP programs of the 1960's contributed much to the defeat or containment of rural guerrillas." More recently, Gliksman (1981:36) adds:

> For Third World nations, training soldiers to fight and operate military equipment can add substantially to the price tag. Of the $55 million given to El Salvador in early February, 25 million is aimed at the replacement of helicopters and aircraft, much of the rest will go for training. One official conceded that El Salvadoran soldiers "just don't know how to fight." The biggest problem is teaching troops to use the equipment they have rather than the provision of more weapons.

Again the performance of such heavily aided, and generally corrupt, armies as those of China (1946–1949), Korea (1950), Cuba (1957–1958), Vietnam (1958–1975), Nicaragua (1968–1979), Chile (1973), Zaire (1978), El Salvador (1979–1988), the Nicaraguan "Contras" (1982–1989) and the Philippines (1985–1989) are invariably ignored. What is clear here is that these weapons were used often indiscriminately to terrorize (Herman, 1982) the civil population. Excepting an uncombative Thai unit and a South Korean mercenary division, none of these countries provided "cheap" and militarily useful proxy units in Vietnam during the United States intervention.

One other exception is Israel, which since 1967 and particularly after the United States impeded total conquest and occupation of Egypt in the 1973 war, transformed intself into a staunchly anti–Soviet and anti-radical ally of exceptional military proficiency—a model proxy. Yet in Lebanon their invasion—despite a blank check from the Reagan Administration—proved to be ineffective destroying the PLO or imposing a client government in Beirut.

Peiris (1982:35) records that "after every 'unauthorized' use of U.S. arms by Israel, the U.S. administration forgives its prodigal son and replenishes the arsenal he has squandered." Indeed, under the Carter Administration, Israel was exempted from arms restraint criteria and treated as a de facto ally. The AWACs package for Saudi Arabia was justified by the Administration as being targeted against revolutionary Iran and possibly the USSR. Furthermore, considerable emphasis was placed by Reagan's Undersecretary of State for Security Assistance, James L. Buckley (U.S., Sen., CFR, *Arms Sales Package*, Pt. 2, 1981:39), upon a statement attributed to Israel's Chief of Intelligence that the package would *not* be a threat to Tel Aviv. The real "threat" in the early 1980s was the Saudi-supported moderation of both Arab League and PLO positions on the Palestinian issue. But again, the United States refused to impede (and may have provided intelligence for) the Israeli 1985 bombing raid upon the PLO offices in Tunis. Similarly, it failed to join the U.N. Security Council in condemning it!

This, like the ill-fated 1985 attack upon an Egyptian airliner and the botched 1986 bombing (assassination) raid upon Libya, may be explained by a reported (Snyder, 1988:6) "secret strategic co-operation agreement signed in 1982" between Washington and Tel-Aviv. Although not covered by the media, in mid-1988 approximately 4,000 U.S. marines arrived at the northern Israeli Port of Haifa:

> They stormed ashore from five landing crafts. According to military sources in touch with Reuters, the marine exercise is the latest step in increasingly close military ties between the United States and Israel. . . .

Thus it is clear that while Washington consistently endeavors to divide Arab "moderates" from radicals, in all major showdowns, it ultimately lines up with its most useful if unruly proxy in the area. Even brutal repression of the 1987–88 *intifada* has evoked only the most tepid pro forma criticism by the Reagan and Bush administrations.

And as the PLO moved toward de facto recognition of Israel, Washington's reply was to illegally deny its most moderate leader and chief spokesman a visa to address the United Nations. Amidst world condemnation, the session was moved to Geneva. Even after Arafat virtually humiliated himself by unilaterally conceding to all State Department conditions for talks, those talks had to be virtually forced upon Washington when the entire Arab world unanimously called for negotiations. Congress remains adamantly opposed to an independent Palestinian state — the core aspiration of that people's nationalism. Yet if a subservient pro–American leadership emerged, the Bush team would probably move to a dual state solution.

The fear of Islamic social revolution in Iran is candidly admitted, and parallels apprehensions of other socially radically and economically nationalist forces or ideas. Hence the United States maintains its open-ended commitment to the Saudi and similar "comprador" regimes which are ubiquitously threatened by indigenous popular movements for social change. Occasionally, when the social-change movements are supported by nearby "radical" regimes, sophisticated weapons are transferred — largely for symbolic (i.e., psychological) reasons. But what is often ignored is the systematic provision of light arms and counter-revolutionary weaponry. Klare (1982c:39) underlines this flow in a neo-colonial interventionist context:

> With the decline in military assistance appropriations, foreign military sales and related training programs are playing an increasingly significant role in the Pentagon's efforts to reinforce threatened pro–U.S. regimes in the Third World. Thus, helicopters and counter-insurgency planes (such as the Rockwell OV-10 Bronco and the Cessna A-37B Dragonfly) form the bulk of U.S. aerospace exports to Latin America and Southeast Asia. U.S. counter-insurgency hardware is also being delivered in quantity to Iran and Saudi Arabia — nations which embody potentially explosive social, ethnic and religious divisions. (The much publicized contract between Saudi Arabia and the Vinell Corporation for training of the Saudi National Guard is intended primarily to stiffen Riyadh's internal security capabilities, rather than, as reported in the press, to defend Saudi oil fields against enemy attack — a job which is assigned to the regular Saudi Army.)

Thus repressive paramilitary intimidation and suppression of domestic nationalists are catalysts for light arms transfers — ones that may be rhetorically eclipsed by more dramatic controversies over Sidewinder missiles, AWACs, F-16s and other sophisticated yet largely symbolic prestige-enhancing weaponry integral to what Ronfeldt and Sereseres (1977) depict as "military diplomacy." That diplomacy, of course, is ultimately oriented — as we have seen in the Venezuelan case — toward isolating and extinguishing socially progressive movements or governments that threaten investor interests in all regions of the Third World.

Finally, it should be mentioned that any net military advantage from arms transfers — like other initiatives such as space militarization ("Star Wars") — must assume non-response by perceived adversaries. Pierre (1981/1982:279) notes that the sale of F-16s to the brutal Zia dictatorship in Pakistan was likely to trigger India's acquisition of Mirage 2000s or MIG25s. Harrison (1981/1982:

102) essays the range of possible Soviet reactions to these and other forms of military "force projection"

> if the United States should manage to get Rapid Deployment Force bases or electronic intelligence facilities in Pakistan or if the United States should give a more sophisticated level of equipment to the Afghan resistance. Moscow might very well retaliate by supporting Baluch insurgents. Such Soviet retaliation could in turn lead to conflicts not only between Islamabad and Kabul but also between Punjabis and ethnic minority groups in Pakistan.
>
> A Soviet-American confrontation and the concomitant growth of tensions between Islamabad and New Delhi clearly would strengthen the forces working for the Balkanization of Pakistan. For this reason, U.S. strategists should tread very warily in South Asia. American policies should be damage limiting rather than risk inviting. They should not be governed by immediate U.S. objectives in the Persian Gulf, Afghanistan, or Pakistan, but should rest on a broader recognition that the entire region from India to Iran is wired up together in an incendiary network of interacting rivalries.

While the Soviets may have eschewed fomenting Baluchi ethnic separatism, they responded to Washington's belligerence by introducing Scud missiles, slowing army withdrawals and providing logistical backing for Afghan bombing runs against rebel staging areas in Pakistani territory. And to Washington's surprise, the Afghan Government did not collapse following the withdrawal of Soviet troops in 1988.

A related dimension of the problem is that arms exports are generally portrayed for "public" policy purposes as reactive to ungenerated indigenous requests or external threats. In the Saudi case, pro–Israeli Senator Biden homes in on this threat mania by facetiously recounting (U.S., Sen., CFR, *Arms Sales Package*, Pt. 2, 1981:91) the alleged menaces:

> We have heard the rationale and there have been several offered, and I think I can catalog them all very briefly: one, the Russian threat; two, the threat from across the gulf—that is, from Iran and/or to the north from Iraq or even possibly Syria; the threat from Aden or the threat from Yemen; the threat from radical Arabs and Communists within the Arab world; the threat to peace process, the implication being if we don't sell, the peace process will not be supported by the Saudis.

Seldom, however, do official arms transfer proponents acknowledge that stimulating local arms races reduces the prospects for diminished tensions and the spirit of compromise essential for peaceful settlements or security. Nor do they readily concede that new weapons inputs may invite similar reactions by others, neutralizing whatever real security gains originally envisaged. As Gauhar argued in the preceding chapter, this appears to be the non–zero-sum net effect of high reciprocal military expenditures in the Middle East.

THE CRITICS' DILEMMA

Despite the foregoing limitations, those fanatically committed to a global struggle against radical (i.e., non-moderate) economically nationalist regimes—even those with marginal or no Soviet support—will define almost any short-run military increment as cost effective. The critic may point to denials, after extensive "aid," of intelligence facilities in Ethiopia and Pakistan, or to similar losses of base facilities in Morocco, Libya and Panama. Defenders simply reply that new access rights have been obtained elsewhere, cite the overthrow of left-nationalists Goulart and Allende (Ronfeldt and Sereseres, 1977:51), similar ousters of rightists who were no longer responsive like Marcos, Duvalier and Noriega, or stress that the Honduran Army is actively cooperating with American troops to deter an effective Nicaraguan defense against an escalation of counterrevolutionary assaults. Similarly, Klare (1982c:37) recalls that "in Latin America, the Nixon Administration thus expedited weapons sales to Brazil's military rulers, who pledged to combat revolutionary movements in the hemisphere, while holding up such deliveries to Peru's leaders, who opposed Washington's preponderant role in Latin America affairs." Defenders of this use of arms transfers ignored the Brazilian dictatorship's death squads, its growing unpopularity, the collapse of its "economic miracle" and the continued "margination" of half or more of its citizens. They stressed its suppression of social radicals, and the eventual ouster of Peru's radical nationalist military leadership in 1975. Today the willingness of both armies to tolerate civilian government would also be touted as a benefit.

Other gains include bases in Bahrein, Oman and Somalia along with shore facilities in Kenya. These can be used for interventions against nationalist regimes or to deter the currently indifferent Soviets from backing them. Hence as with other policy instruments, so long as such liberal critics themselves share a consensus on anti-nationalist and anti-radical goals, the most one can do is focus upon selected imperfections and high costs. Defenders counter by pinpointing "successes" and argue that these costs are not excessive, and are in any case necessary. This helps us understand why critiques by such liberals as Pearson, Betts, Pierre and Klare have for the most part failed to affect policy.

A similar dilemma faces the liberal critic with respect to the political influence that is viewed to flow from arms transfers and the concomitant training which engenders personal ties and indoctrinates (Wolpin, 1973) officers against economic nationalism and nonalignment. Or as Pierre (1982:14–15) puts it:

> A major political rationale for arms transfers has been the influence the supplier gains in dealing with the recipient nations....
>
> Arms may provide access to political and military elites. This has been the traditional justification for many of the U.S. military assistance programs to Latin American nations, where often there was no serious military threat or need for arms.

The salience of this preoccupation is underscored by Pearson (1981:38) whose study of Carter's arms restraint policy was based upon interviews with Pentagon and State Department officials. After observing that ACDA and the Pentagon opposed some sales or projected export weapons such as the F-X that were favored by the State Department, he adds the previously cited caveat that "such DoD views are tempered by Joint Chiefs' priorities for support of cooperative military establishments around the world; the Joint Chiefs' staff tends to assume that target countries can be controlled through the military, and that the military are the logical leaders for many Third World states."

While stressing both the importance and difficulties in attaining such control, Ronfeldt and Sereseres (1977:52) emphasize that "where effective, the presumed leverage requires constant renewal in the form of further arms transfers, whose utility is of short-duration and non-cumulative as a form of political investment currency." Klare (1982c:38–40) details various dimensions of this compulsive drive for leverage within what political scientists call "penetrated," "porous," or "soft" states of the Third World:

> Arms sales . . . provide continuing access to foreign military leaders, who in most Third World countries play a decisive role in national politics. Such contact usually begins with the sales negotiations themselves, which are often conducted by a country's top military officers, and also occurs during the training programs that follow as well as during negotiations over service and maintenance contracts, technical assistance, etc. If handled skillfully, these contacts can lead to a close working relationship with a recipient's military personnel and result in significant political advantages as well as further military sales. And when these officers move into (or seize) high government offices, Washington can utilize these links to propagate its strategic vision. . . .
>
> Such leverage (also) stems from the fact that most modern armaments require spare parts, training aids and maintenance that can only be obtained from the original supplier. The more sophisticated the item moreover, the greater the dependence. . . .
>
> There is an additional negative factor which might be called preemptive action, that is, Washington will often conclude a sale with the primary motivation of locking out an alternative supplier. . . .

Ronfeldt and Sereseres (1977:50–51) also pinpoint both re-supply dependence and pre-emptive market control as immediate objectives.

Resentment against such neo-colonial domination and concomitant resource exploitation has spread from Latin America to the remainder of the Third World. Often misrepresented as irrational or xenophobic "anti–Americanism" in subservient United States media (Chomsky and Herman, 1979), it signals a new global phenomenon that in recent years has even affected in lesser measure the West European (Radway, 1985; Birnbaum, 1985; Wolpin, 1986) alliance core.[5]

Thus the objective of maximizing neo-colonial leverage through such dependency is becoming ever more difficult to attain. In the 1960s Pakistan

(1965) and Israel (1967) employed American weapons to attack neighbors despite Washington's nominal opposition. Rather than attempt to exert restraining leverage in 1982 when Israel invaded Lebanon, Washington actually seems to have encouraged the attack whose primary objectives were to install a pro–United States regime and obliterate the PLO as a viable organizational entity.

Gansler (1980:214) argues that such "blackmail" possibilities as may have existed in the past have been eclipsed in large part by the emergence of competitive alternative suppliers for sophisticated weaponry.[6] Iraq's 1980 attack against Iran, like Somalia's invasion of Ethiopia several years earlier, certainly demonstrated this with respect to the Soviet Union. In the Saudi AWACs case, one senator (U.S., Sen., CFR, *Arms Sales Package,* Pt. 2, 1981:109) was unmoved:

> People tell me that they are going to go to Britain and France and buy the equipment there. Well, I say let them. Maybe it would be a good thing if Britain and France shared the defense needs of that area. Perhaps, if Britain, France, and the United States were all involved in protecting the security of the Arabian Peninsula and the Persian Gulf that protection would be enhanced.

While the goals of maximizing American corporate earnings and hegemony were ignored, the alternative here did not involve threats of either radicalism or potential friendly ties with the Soviets. Moreover, the congressman in this case probably benefited from generous support by the influential Zionist lobby in the United States. Even so, American companies might have lost some future Saudi contracts to their European rivals.

A HEGEMONIC DRIVE?

What becomes manifest from administration prophecies, reactions and fears is that at bottom there is an imperialist drive, or at least aspiration, for exclusive influence within what is a de facto protectorate. Thus then Undersecretary of State Buckley warned (U.S., Sen., CFR, *Arms Sales Package,* Pt. 2, 1981:34-35) that unless the AWACs sale was approved:

> ...we will see ... a revival of questions as to the reliability of America as a security partner. We will see an inevitable distancing by these states from the United States as they seek alternative means of assuring their own safety and security....
>
> The Saudis are not going to sit on their hands if we deny them weapons which every military expert will testify are of a kind required to safeguard their most precious assets....
>
> If we are not a supplier, they will turn to other suppliers, to the British, for example, for the Nimrod. They will also be broadening their base of procurement and go perhaps to the French.

The same inference may be drawn from then Defense Secretary Weinberger's (U.S., Sen., CFR, *Arms Sales Package,* Pt. 2, 1981:80) apprehensions:

> I think they would turn to the other plan, which we believe is very good but not quite as good, as a second choice. I think it is important that since they do want to have close and continuing working relationship with us, and since we do not have a surplus of countries feeling that way in the world, it would be a very unfortunate thing to lose that kind of relationship or that kind of atmosphere.

Concretely this "kind of atmosphere" is one of influence or responsiveness that may be used internally to favor American corporations with contracts yielding high profits as well as externally in pursuit of anti-radical military (Somalia, Afghanistan) and diplomatic (e.g. OPEC pricing, pressure on the PLO or Sandinistas') goals. It is what Betts (1980:98) calls an American "hegemonial policy" — an active pursuit of power that is impeded by allied Western powers and more resolutely by economic nationalists and Marxists including the pre–Gorbachev Soviets.[7]

The value of formal alliances such as NATO is that of facilitating leverage against allies seeking commercial gain or a small "place in the sun" for themselves. Thus Gansler may exaggerate the de facto ability of nationalist Third World states to shop around "when the U.S. denies arms." Cuba attempted this in 1959–1960 before opting for Soviet support. The diminished autonomy of Britain and France resulted in those countries' succumbing to United States pressure against the sale of even light arms to Havana.[8] Despite the weakening of NATO cohesion over recent years, a similar fate befell the Sandinistas. As early as September 1979, the Carter Administration stonewalled the Sandinistas' requests for small arms even after they were attacked (Black and Matthews, 1985:129, 148–49) by Somoza's National Guard remnants ensconced in Honduras. Prior to Reagan's inauguration, Nicaraguan officers seeking to commercially export helicopters from Texas were arrested. When Managua sought similar defensive equipment from France, alliance loyalty was used to pressure the Socialist Mitterand government to veto a prior sale of merely two helicopters.[9] Like Cuba, Nicaragua was forced into virtually total dependence upon Soviet (and Cuban) arms aid.

The imperial dynamic operating in these and other—particularly though not exclusively Latin American—cases is cogently encapsulated by Chomsky (1985:5–6):

> The people who are committed to these dangerous heresies such as using their resources for their own purposes or believing that the government is committed to the welfare of its own people and so on, may not be Soviet clients to begin with and, in fact, quite regularly they're not. In Latin America, they are often members, to begin with, of Bible study groups that become self-help groups, church organizations, peasant organizations, and so on and so forth. But by the

time we get through with them, they will be Soviet clients. The reason . . . is
that they will have nowhere else to turn for any minimal form of protection
against the terror and the violence that we regularly unleash against them if
they undertake programs of the kind described.

And this *is a net gain* for American policy. One thing you'll notice, if you
look over the years, is that the United States quite consistently tries to create
enemies . . . if a country *does* escape from the American group. What we want
to do is drive the country into being a base for the Russians because that justifies
us in carrying out the violent attacks which we *must* carry out, given the
geopolitical conception under which we organize and control much of the
world. So that's what we do, and then we "defend" ourselves.

While Latin America has traditionally been regarded as a proprietary region
by Washington policy-makers, since World War II, other areas have become
increasing objects of what Fulbright called the "arrogance of power." And this
has extended even to former colonies of allies that had lost the ability or desire
to coercively maintain an exclusive neo-colonial sphere of influence.

A prime example of such intra-alliance rivalry and presidential arrogance
was epitomized by the disinclination of Britain and particularly Greece to
pressure the non–Marxist though neutralist and democratic government of
Cyprus to provide territory for U.S. base facilities. In his review of Christopher
Hitchen's *Cyprus*— a rendition of how that island state became partitioned—
Chomsky (1985a:19) recalls:

> In 1964, Lyndon Johnson delivered an important lesson in political science to
> the Greek ambassador, succinct, accurate and more enlightening than many
> weighty tomes. Johnson hoped to convince the Greek government to accept the
> "Acheson plan" designed to partition the independent Republic of Cyprus be-
> tween Greece and Turkey. The purpose was to remove the threat of Cypriot
> neutralism (a potential "Cuba of the Mediterranean"), to secure an important
> U.S.-British intelligence and military base, and to prevent war between two
> NATO powers. . . .
>
> When the Greek ambassador said that "no Greek parliament could accept
> such a plan," Johnson responded as follows: "Fuck your parliament and your
> constitution. America is an elephant, Cyprus is a flea. Greece is a flea. If these
> two fellows continue itching the elephant, they may just get whacked by the
> elephant's trunk, whacked good. . . . If your prime minister gives me talk about
> democracy, parliament and constitution, he, his parliament and his constitu-
> tion may not last very long." For good measure, he added: "Maybe Greece
> should rethink the value of a parliament which could not make the right deci-
> sion," where "right" is understood. . . .
>
> Shortly after, the people of Greece were properly whacked. In 1967, a
> military coup installed the first new fascist government in Europe since Hitler,
> also the first government headed by a CIA agent (Colonel Papadopoulos was
> the liaison between the CIA and its Greek counterpart, virtually a subsidiary).

This episode underscores the bipartisan continuity of such hegemonic imperialism, which embraced not only liberals such as Johnson and Kennedy,[10]

but in a somewhat less arrogant style also distinguished socio-economic conservatives like Carter and Ford.

Even under Reagan, few congressional Democrats publicly opposed the 1983 invasion of Grenada or the provocative maneuver followed by military attacks upon Libya in the mid- and late 1980s. Some form of aid to the Nicaraguan contras was invariably appropriated (Frank Donner, 1985a) by bipartisan congressional majorities. And such aid continued through the decade to sustain the contra army despite its clear violation of the Central American peace accords. As late as 1986, a majority (Marc S. Miller, 1988) of Democrats supported the still actively interventionist Reagan Administration's desire to assign much higher priority and resources to massively expanded special forces units—a veritable elite quasi-autonomous foreign legion of what once were called shock troops:

> Congressional enthusiasm for the concept rivals that of the Administration. With little fanfare, in 1986, lawmakers created a new job at the Pentagon. Assistant Secretary of Defense for Special Operations and Low-Intensity Conflict.

The mere availability of such mobilized expeditionary units under the Central Command increases the likelihood of intervention should United States–supplied indigenous forces falter or prove recalcitrant—as we saw in Panama, another invasion boasting bipartisan support.

Nor have there been objections to militarizing the drug problem, let alone its facile definition as a national security threat. At the very same time that some, including prominent conservatives, are tending to favor legalization and medical treatment, Bush has ignored policy and economic needs while pressuring Colombia (Bagley, 1989–90) to accept United States military personnel and largely military aid. This bias is, of course, the essence of a militaristic ethos. One should not be surprised if military autonomy in Colombia today is transformed into overt seizure of power in the near future.

One of the ironies found in discussions of leverage flowing from arms aid to Third World countries is the frequent minimization of consequential influence by establishment experts. The provision of weaponry is generally viewed in isolation from the total web of relationships which they structure and, in turn, reflect. Further, particular instances of "failure" are selected, or misrepresented, while others of a more successful character are ignored.[11] In some cases, for example, it is argued that attempts to sell weapons viewed by the Pentagon as most "appropriate" or "economical" have been stymied by what might be called "reverse leverage."[12] Yet, despite such reiterated potency problems—perhaps because domestic profit maximizing by military contractors is the paramount immediate catalyst—arms control and human rights groups have never had sufficient congressional support to veto a sale.[13]

In one abortive veto attempt, Senator Cranston (U.S., Sen., CFR, *Arms Sales Package,* Pt. 2, 1981:103–104) echoed what we might call this "impotence thesis" by highlighting a Saudi $400 million subsidy to the PLO and the fact that

> if the Saudis were to pay us for the AWACs it would be with our own dollars, dollars they have garnered from American consumers by raising the price of oil from $2 to $32 a barrel for the past two decades. Specifically, they raised the price from $12 to $32 since the Senate last submitted to a litmus test amidst hopes for Saudi moderation by approving the 1978 sale of advanced fighter planes to the Saudis.

Yet administration defenders of the $8.5 billion sale facilely retorted that Saudis had favored American corporations, helped pressure the PLO into moderation and a Lebanese ceasefire, created an oil glut and financed weaponry to intensify the counterrevolutionary civil war in Afghanistan. Ege (1988a:51–55) after describing Kabul's efforts to negotiate with both domestic rebels and Karachi with which it had experienced less success, assigned responsibility for diplomatic failure to Washington:

> Bringing an end to the foreign intervention carried out by the United States, Pakistan, China, Egypt and Saudi Arabia is key to peace and further progress in Afghanistan. . . .
> A political settlement is possible in Afghanistan—in fact, dramatic steps have been taken in that direction through the government's negotiations with rebel military commanders and with tribal leaders. An overall political settlement which would facilitate the withdrawal of Soviet troops from Afghanistan is being held up by the intransigent posture of the Reagan administration.
> The U.S. government, through the CIA and allied regimes in the Middle East and Asia, is waging a "secret war" against Afghanistan, just as it is waging a "secret war" against Nicaragua.

Indeed, another major arms transfer recipient, Egypt, is also furnishing what appear to be Saudi-financed weapons to Pakistan-based Afghan tribal counterrevolutionaries.

These are probably the most sanguinary of several "secret wars" promoted (Peterzell, 1984) by Reagan's militaristic team. Its militarism as applied to the Nicaraguan and Afghan wars was epitomized by the use of arms transfers and aid to Central America and Pakistani clients to subvert diplomatic initiatives. Nor, as was emphasized earlier, did the arms flow cease after the United Nations–brokered 1987 peace accord between Kabul and Islamabad which stipulated its termination as well as the withdrawal of Soviet forces.[14] Continued arms exports and massive financial handouts to Israel have similarly been instrumental in reinforcing Jerusalem's opposition to a diplomatic settlement which recognized Palestinian rights to their own homeland on the West Bank and in Gaza. These cases, among others, condition Pierre's (1982:15) conclusion that "the most important political benefits of arms transfers may be leverage over other countries' sensitive foreign policy decisions," assuming high donor nation interest in exerting such leverage.

If we turn to other alleged potency problems, a similar balance must be struck. F-16s and other arms may not be sufficient to induce Pakistan to suspend nuclear weapons development, but they bring enough responsiveness to obtain intelligence and naval facilities. Similarly, in Africa, a sharp increase in arms transfers (Smalldone, 1983:191) occurred during periods of acute instability in Ethiopia (1975–1977) and Liberia (1980). Success might only be claimed in the latter case where pro–American Sgt. Doe emerged as a brutal dictator.

The foregoing episodes as well as Schoultz's (1988) findings compel us to dismiss defense or security rationales as spurious. Their primary audience is the ill-informed ordinary American who must bear the staggering fiscal costs of such hegemonial pro-corporate interventionism. Beyond that, of course, are the related yet no less significant bureaucratic and financial interests of the military-industrial complex. The inability of liberal critics to come to grips with the underlying transnational corporate imperative and its concomitant anti-nationalist dogma has invariably rendered their critiques vulnerable, thus easing the militarists' task of putting such liberals on the defensive through accusations of "softness" on communism, terrorism or most recently drugs; "wimpiness" toward the "real" challenges; naivete; etc.

Was this not the sobering lesson of Michael Dukakis's ill-fated presidential campaign? Even militant black leaders like Jesse Jackson have folded under such withering attacks. In this context Alexander Cockburn's (1985a:231) pugnacious critique of Jackson's reaction is illuminating:

> The defeat sustained by Jesse Jackson at the hands of Jerry Falwell in the September 4 *Nightline* debate on South Africa provides a number of lessons. First, our side has simply got to stop apologizing. Every time Falwell invoked the Communist menace and asked the audience if it would care to see the red flag flying over Cape Town, Jackson ran for cover. Lesson number two: Defy their premises.
>
> FALWELL: If there is a Soviet-Cuban takeover in South Africa—
> JACKSON: Stop right there. Standards of health, education and nutrition are higher in Cuba than anywhere on the Latin American continent, Reverend Falwell. If the average South American black were to wake up in Cuba, he would think he had gone to heaven.
> FALWELL: What about Ethiopia, Reverend Jackson?
> JACKSON: Well, what about Ethiopia, Reverend Falwell? Let's talk about conditions in Ethiopia when the U.S. supported Haile Selassie there. Let's talk about Uganda after your friends in Israel had installed Idi Amin. Let's talk about Zaire, shall we, Reverend Falwell?
> FALWELL: Who does Bishop Tutu represent?
> JACKSON: Who do you represent?

The trouble with progressives is that they always panic at the sight of the red-baiter's paintbrush. This is what finished off the nuclear freeze movement.

Yet what precisely the "political and security interests" are invariably remains vague. Dominance or more euphemistically "leadership" or "responsibility" for promoting "stability" is the ubiquitous liberal rationale for interventionism. Now "terrorism," "drugs" and even "Democracy" have been added to the security pantry. Beyond occasionally doubting the effectiveness of particular acts, few liberals ever endeavor to explain or identify the linkage between such imperatives to corporate domestic dominance and its expansionism or growth imperative.

Hence, unless like Ravenal (1980), Richman (1984), Parenti (1984) and Forsberg (1984), one rejects arms transfers by first renouncing neo-colonial objectives and by denouncing their association or "deadly connection" with the immense costs of the strategic buildup, it is difficult to effectively refute all of the defender's articulated advantages. That there is such a linkage with "global" United States "interests" as well as aggressive pursuit of internal policy leverage is even implicitly conceded in the following passage by a Reagan-Bush Administration State Department official (Smalldone, 1983:213–214), a liberal director of the Munitions Control Office (i.e., commercial exports):

> The following conclusion emerges clearly from these studies and the data presented in this chapter. Although U.S. arms transfers to Africa are designed to serve a multiplicity of policy objectives, historically the magnitude and distribution of U.S. security-assistance programs in Africa have been determined principally by the political and military-strategic *importance of the recipient to U.S. global and regional interest....* Whereas global arms transfers to Africa are best explained by internal pull variables, U.S. arms supplies to Africa correlate highly with U.S. policy objectives. Rather than responding to African demand in a classical demand-supply-response model, U.S. arms transfers are an instrumentality to further American political and security interests in the region. [Emphasis added.]

Ultimately, then, one must confront the actual interests that guide the policy. Put differently, how do revolutionary Angola or Ethiopia really threaten American safety and welfare? Both countries have actively sought friendly relations with the United States.

Does endeavoring to control through arms transfers and other often related means the domestic, foreign and military policies within "developing" nations measurably enhance American safety and living standards or the vitality of the democratic process, i.e., national security? I have argued that the material costs to average Americans now far exceed such benefits, and added the obvious fact that this global strategic posture is associated with an unrestrained qualitative nuclear arms race that is becoming increasingly dangerous. Former Defense Department analyst Earl Ravenal (1983:22–24) also emphasized the linkage between the drive for an increasingly unstable "first strike" counterforce strategy and the commitment to "extended deterrence" or an interventionist "iron hand" in the developing areas. Deliberate provocations of Cuba (and possibly the Soviets) by aggression against Grenada, Libya, Iran, Afghanistan, Nicaragua and Panama are but the most recent illustrations of such militaristic danger. Despite greater competence by Bush, the underlying commitment to open-door anti-nationalist interventionism in conjunction with the industrial-military complex's political dominance will ensure not only continuance of the arms race drive for escalatory dominance but also the consequential crisis instability due to enhanced first-strike vulnerability of unilaterally scaled-down Soviet forces. This notwithstanding a temporary improvement of the political climate since the mid-eighties and even more "arms control" accords, which nevertheless exclude testing, production and exports. Hence, America's safety (i.e., national security) is also becoming less rather than more secure while mass sector prosperity becomes ever more elusive. In the chapters which follow we shall scrutinize more closely specific domestic costs imposed upon ordinary citizens and particular dangers shared by all, before charting a way out.

8. The Domestic Costs of Pentagonism: Whither the American Dream?

I have argued that the inability of what has been called "cold war liberalism" to seriously impede either the expansion of weapons exports or domestic militarization flows from its shared consensus upon the underlying "open door" or pro-corporate interventionist foreign policy goals. In a world pervaded by mass impoverishment, economic underdevelopment and the radical nationalist movements which respond to such challenges, liberals who counsel restraint, moderation and humaneness are usually outmaneuvered by unscrupulous or rigidly ideological perpetuators of threat inflation. This was the sorry tale of our preceding chapter. An unceasing barrage of anti-leftist conservative propaganda — heavily funded by sectors of the corporate-owning upper class — has shifted the political spectrum or range of legitimate policy options. Provocative rhetoric concerning Soviet weapons capabilities (greatly exaggerated), terrorist conspiracies, espionage rings, Libyan "hit squads," "yellow rain" and assorted "evidence" of "communist" barbarities or revolutionary export has resulted in the effective removal or intimidation of most firmly anti-militaristic liberals from the American political scene following their short-lived heyday during the post–Vietnam disillusionment of the period 1970–1977.

THE DECLINE OF LIBERALISM

The majority of those surviving the post-1973 corporate and far right propaganda onslaught (Sanders, 1983: Perry, 1984) heavily funded by an upsurge of corporate PACs (Etzioni, 1984, Sherrill, 1988) have defected to neoliberalism or outright conservatism. The national Democratic Party today not only lacks effective leadership, but has all but forsaken (Meyerson, 1989) its New Deal heritage. Indeed, an unprecedented minority of Democrats at state and national levels did in the early 1980s actually desert (Donner, 1985a) their party to become Republicans. Meanwhile, Republicanism was almost totally purged of its residual liberal minority faction.

But the foregoing denouement of liberalism, shared in lesser measure by the Democratic Party, obscures a process of erosion that actually began with the onset of bipartisan Cold Warriorism in the late 1940s. Its genesis was symbolized by the willingness of Congress to override President Truman's 1948 veto of the Taft-Hartley Act legislation designed to weaken both the left and the trade union movement as a whole. The gradual emergence of a warfare state has paralleled an erosion of the welfare state—given a certain time lag. Throughout the McCarthyite Cold War era of the 1950s and since, with the partial exception of the four-year "Great Society" interregnum of Lyndon Johnson, socio-economic measures have been whittled down in scope and increasingly denied adequate funding.

By the close of the sixties, employer influence was sufficient to block (Thurow, 1985:48–49) expansion of federal jobs programs to counter cyclical and rising structural unemployment.[1] The consequence was an immense growth of a welfare "underclass" in the Nixon-Ford era which dwarfed those of predecessor administrations.[2] Working class Americans then became increasingly resentful toward not only "affirmative action" (Edsall, 1989:405), but also the steadily rising tax burdens imposed upon their earnings to offset welfare transfers. Ultimately, as we shall see, a rising portion of the unemployed during the Carter and especially the Reagan Administration have been denied even these welfare payments.

Liberalism's other great feat—civil rights enforcement—has suffered an equally pronounced erosion since the late 1960s and particularly during the 1980s. What contributed to the weakening of liberalism's socio-economic promise was its growing inability to deliver for ordinary working and lower middle class citizens when confronted by a combination of rising resource needs of the militarization process and spectacular tax breaks for the upper classes. While the illusion of having "guns *and* butter" was sustained for a period by simply postponing payment via expansion of the national debt, by the mid-1970s and especially in following years the chickens came home to roost.

FISCAL AND SOCIO-ECONOMIC PATTERNS IN AN ERA OF CORPORATE DEREGULATION

As the largely (60 to 80 percent) military-related national indebtedness has risen—indicated by Table 22 and Figures 6 and 7—so has the tax burden upon ordinary Americans both to service the debt and to cover other current government outlays.[3] At the same time the overall tax system has become increasingly regressive. The proportion represented by corporate taxes has diminished as that represented by wage taxes has moved steadily upwards.[4] These trends, highlighted in Table 23, Figure 8, and Table 24, actually began early in the Cold War era. According to Navarro (1985:38):

> Between 1953 and 1974, direct taxes paid by the average income family doubled from 11.8 percent of income to 23.4 percent of income, while the tax burden of a family with four times the average income went from 20.2 percent to 29.5

Year		Amount (billions)	Per Capita
1865	End of Civil War	$ 2.27	$ 75
1900	Pre-World War I	1.26	17
1920	After World War I	24.30	228
1930	Start of Depression	16.19	138
1945	Height of World War II	258.00	1,849
1975	End of Vietnam War	553.00	2,496
1980	Start of Reagan Administration	900.00	3,969
1984	End of Reagans 1st Term	1,800.00	7,000
1989	C.B.O. Projection	3,100.00	10,000

Table 22. United States federal debt. Source: *Kahn (1985:11).*

percent, an increase of less than half. Between 1969 and 1980, social security taxes increased by 92 percent. And since social security taxes apply to only the first $37,700 of wages, the major portion of this increase was on the non-wealthy. During the same period, corporate income tax collections fell 14 percent, and capital gains rates were cut by 20 percent.[5]

Similarly, between 1955 and 1985, the corporate income tax as a share of the federal budget fell (IPS, 1988:46) from 27 percent to 9 percent! In 1986 alone, tax loopholes (Coffin, 1985a:1) "for corporations ... cost the Treasury $120 billion." As for individual income tax payers during the Reagan era, an estimated ("The Reagan Legacy," 1988:1) $1 trillion was lost from those in the upper brackets due to a sharp reduction in tax rates—much greater than for those in middle and low income strata.[6]

Contributing even more to this regressive trend has been the growing importance of items "explicitly exempted from taxation" infelicitously termed "tax expenditures." In the words of one analyst ("The Economy," 1988:23):

> Since the federal government began publishing its tax expenditure report in 1967, federal tax expenditures have almost doubled as a percentage of direct total expenditures. . . .
> . . . all states are riddled with tax breaks that reward corporate behavior and protect those most able to pay. . . .
> In 1975, tax expenditures equaled 28.7% of direct government outlays: by 1987: that amount had risen to 37.5% . . . . Furthermore, from 1979 through 1986 the increase in tax expenditures outpaced the overall growth in the budget.

During the same period, the number of tax exemptions rose from 75 in 1975 to 88 in 1980 and further to 108 in 1987. Although the imminent bankruptcy of the government forced a halt to this loophole expansion in 1987, subsequent reductions in IRS resources imply continued massive upscale tax evasion.

Between 1980 and 1984 alone, the income tax as a percent of family income (IPS, 1988:34) changed as follows: for an income of $10,000, .04 to .05; $20,000, no change; $35,000, .19 to .18; $50,000, .24 to .22; $100,000, .36 to .31. Etzioni (1988:306) cautions that this is but part of the story:

> Social Security taxes have always been very regressive because there are no exceptions: A poor family that earns only $6,000 a year must pay the tax from the first dollar on up. Further, while the tax base has been widened somewhat, those with an income above $45,000 do not pay Social Security tax on any earnings above that mark. If a person's income is $50,000, $100,000, $1 million or $20 million, that person will pay the same amount to Social Security as a person with an income of $45,000. Thus, the *rate* is much lower for the rich.
>
> Reagan, by cutting all other taxes but increasing the Social Security tax, has shifted us away from the relatively progressive income tax. The numbers tell the story: While Social Security provided only 5 percent of the total Federal revenues in 1950, it now accounts for 27 percent.

In terms of social structure, the Congressional Budget Office says ("Economic Clips," February 1988:16) that such "reforms" will result in the following:

> The poorest one-tenth of the population will pay 20% more of their earnings in federal taxes for 1988 than they did in 1977, and the richest one-tenth will pay 20% less. Between 1977 and the end of this year, 80% of all families will have seen their real income decline, while the richest 10% will see their income rise by 16%, and the richest 1% will see a 50% increase.

Although this process antedated the 1980 Reagan-Bush victory, it has accelerated since then.

As mentioned previously, the initial weakening of populism and economic egalitarian political tendencies began in the late 1940s with the onset of Cold War militarism. During the first two decades (1948–1968) liberalism, though divided and in some measure repressed by the bipartisan Cold War consensus, fought back and suffered only minor economic defeats while making some social gains. But in the 1970s and 1980s, the last social reformist elements were all but forced out of the Republican Party on the national scene, or became, like Bush, "a Reaganite over the past eight years" ("Tomorrow: George Bush," 1988:33). And since the late sixties, the Democrats have moved steadily to the right on socio-economic issues (Kotz, 1988; Sherrill, 1988; Etzioni, 1988) as the party has become increasingly dominated by corporate fat cats. Illustrative of this tendency is Abelda and Mann's (1988:9) report:

> The progressivity of the U.S. federal income tax system has been significantly eroded in recent years. The top rate has fallen from a high of 70% in 1978 to

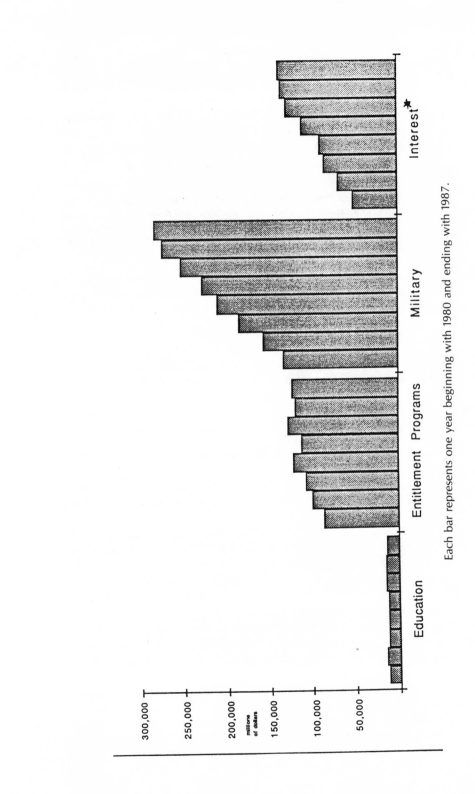

Each bar represents one year beginning with 1980 and ending with 1987.

just 28%, the rate scheduled to take effect next year. A measure of just how taboo taxes have become was the resounding defeat at the Democratic Party Convention of Jesse Jackson's proposal to restore the top rate to its pre–Reagan level.

Significantly, Michael Dukakis, the party's ill-fated nominee, was a technocrat with a reputation of deference to the corporate sector in Massachusetts.

By the mid-1980s, approximately 42 percent of the national budget and 75 percent of its discretionary portion (i.e., "federal funds") was being devoured ("Economics of Military Spending," 1984:8–9) by military-related uses. Between 1981 and 1984, while military spending moved sharply upward by more than $144 billion, spending at the national level for social programs was cut in excess of $110 billion. The implications of what Navarro (1985:39) aptly calls "the fiscal version of class struggle" are vividly illustrated by Melman (1985). Among the many items in his list of "butter" (domestic spending for social programs) traded off for "guns" (military spending) are

460 meals for the homeless in Grand Central Terminal	= $439	= One 155-mm. (conventional) high-explosive shell
Proposed 1986–87 cuts in federal funding for subsidized lunches for New York City schoolchildren	= $8.7 million	= 800 Army multiple-launch rockets
Proposed federal cuts in housing for the elderly and handicapped, and the cut in energy assistance for poor people	= $1.5 billion	= One projected (LHD-1) Marine amphibious assault ship
Estimated cost of cleaning up 10,000 toxic-waste dumps that contaminate the nation's soil and water	= $100 billion	= The Navy's Trident II submarine and F-18 jet fighter programs

By the late 1980s, military-related expenditures (Friends Committee, 1988:3) were still consuming almost 70 percent of the discretionary budget while a mere 13 percent was devoted to domestic poverty. The growth of the national deficit and especially the gross federal debt ("The Reagan Legacy," 1988:1) from less than one trillion to 2.8 trillion dollars during the Reagan era—roughly equal to the cumulated rise in military spending—will seriously

Opposite: *Figure 6. Sources of United States government deficit: 1980–1987.* Source: *IPS (1988:42). Based upon* Economic Report of the President, *1988, p. 338.* Note: **Interest payments are directly proportional to budget categories.*

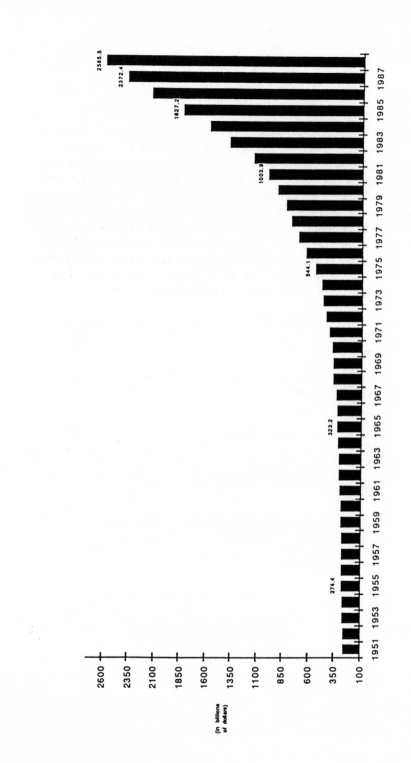

Fiscal year	Individual income tax	Social insurance tax	Corporate income tax	Excise and state taxes and all other revenue sources
1960	44.0	15.9	23.2	16.8
1965	41.8	19.1	21.8	17.4
1970	46.9	23.0	17.0	13.0
1975	43.9	30.3	14.6	11.3
1980	47.2	30.5	12.5	9.8
1984 (est.)	44.8	36.8	7.8	10.5

Table 23. Sources of United States federal revenues (as percent of total). Source: *T.B. Edsall,* The New Politics of Inequality *(New York: W.W. Norton, 1984), p. 212, Table 6.4.*

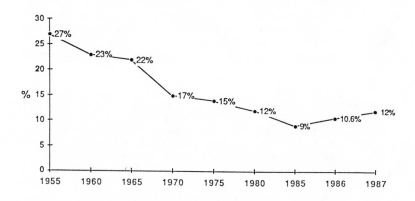

Figure 8. Corporate income tax as a share of United States federal budget: 1955–1987. Source: *IPS (1988:46). Based upon United States Student Association.*

constrain future mass living standards as well as social programs by Washington.

These are but the tip of the iceberg. A plethora of studies (Wolpin, 1983:23–41) reveal that not only do high levels of military expenditures over time adversely affect health and especially educational outlays, but they also are often associated with declines in civilian investment growth rates, innovation, productivity growth rates and export competitiveness. Even within the financial community there is concern. The socially progressive Calvert Investment Fund (Coffin, 1988b:2) warns:

Opposite: *Figure 7. United States gross federal debt: 1951–1987.* Source: *IPS (1988:23). Based upon* Economic Report of the President, *1988, p. 331.*

Year	1974 dollars	Current dollars
1975	$11,145	$12,159
1976	11,049	12,750
1977	11,025	13,550
1978	11,000	14,553
1979	10,869	15,999
1980	10,282	17,181
1981	9,636	17,768
1982	9,786	19,151
1983(e)	10,013	20,227

Table 24. Real after-tax income: All United States families. Source: *Monthly Tax Features, 7-8/84, Tax Foundation. Reprinted in "Taxes" (1985:5).* Note: *This is the median real after-tax family income for all families with one earner employed full-time, year-round. It does not factor in unemployed or part-time workers. As a result, it is an underestimation of the situation for the working population as a whole.* e = *estimated.*

When we look at the workings of our economy, by far the biggest bottleneck seems to be the amounts of resources being spent on military commitments. We must begin to redefine our national security needs and missions. Military spending is essentially non-productive, and almost half of our current military budget goes for defending our allies who are now our economic competitors.

While we spend about 6.6% of the GNP on defense, our NATO allies spend about 3.3% and Japan spends 1% or in per capita terms, $453 by each West German, $163 by each Japanese, and a whopping $1155 by each American.

The comparative military burden and productivity growth patterns in Figure 10 are poignant reminders of this tradeoff. Gordon reported in 1985 (p. 80) that:

The productivity slowdown persists. Overall improvement in the economy's efficiency can be measured by comparing growth in hourly output from the peak of one business cycle to that in the next. That index of productivity growth has dropped by two-thirds over the last twenty years. The improvement between 1978 and 1984, by the most recent available data, was approximately 0.9 percent, the same as it was between 1973 and 1978—hardly evidence of rejuvenation.

Since the recovery has essentially passed, there is little reason to think that any of the most regressive trends of the past four years will be reversed during Reagan's second term. More and more Americans will live in poverty. Teenagers, members of minority groups and many women will increasingly

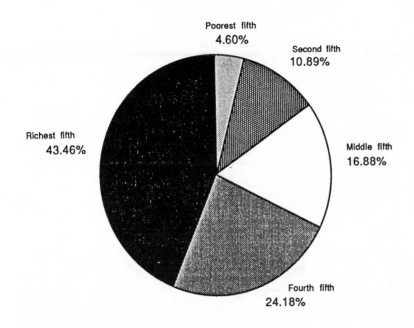

Figure 9. Distribution of income in the United States in 1985. Source: *IPS (1988:35).* *Based upon U.S. Bureau of the Census,* Money, Income and Poverty Status of Families and Persons in the U.S., *August 1986.* Notes: *Totals may not add up to 100 percent because of rounding off of decimals. The percent of income received by three lowest fifths was the smallest since this information has been collected (1947). The share of income received by the top 5 percent was 16.7 percent.*

suffer job and wage discrimination. Foreclosures of family farms are likely to reach epidemic proportions. Union membership as a percentage of the labor force will probably continue to decline. Production and nonsupervisory workers' share of the total national income, which fell from 52 percent in 1978 to about 48 percent in 1984, is likely to erode, particularly because growing numbers of them are moving into relatively low-wage jobs.[7]

What is remarkable is that despite the 1985–1987 "recovery," virtually all of Gordon's prognosticated trends were unaffected. Even the rate of productivity growth (IPS, 1988:22) was less than 1 percent for the period 1979–1986. This was half the rate for 1966–1973 although somewhat better than the .5 percent rate for 1973–1979.

The .5 percent Reagan era "improvement" may actually mask the opposite as far as civilian industry is concerned. According to Mandel (1988), "Much of it is a one time phenomenon" and can be attributed to the assault upon labor—a phenomenon that cannot be repeated indefinitely and which will be discussed later in this chapter. Second, when many corporations closed

Income group by decimals	1977 avg. income	1988 avg. income	Percentage change	Dollar change
First	$ 3,528	$ 3,157	-10.5%	-$371
Second	$ 7,084	$ 6,990	-1.3%	-$94
Third	$ 10,740	$ 10,614	-1.2%	-$126
Fourth	$ 14,323	$ 14,266	-0.4%	-$57
Fifth	$ 18,043	$ 18,076	+0.2%	+$33
Sixth	$ 22,009	$ 22,259	+1.1%	+$250
Seventh	$ 26,240	$ 27,038	+3.0%	+$798
Eighth	$ 31,568	$ 33,282	+5.4%	+$1,714
Ninth	$ 39,236	$ 42,323	+7.9%	+$3,087
Tenth	$ 70,459	$ 89,783	+27.4%	+$19,324
Top 5%	$ 90,756	$124,651	+37.3%	+$33,895
Top 1%	$174,498	$303,900	+74.2%	+$129,402
All groups	$ 24,184	$ 26,494	+9.6%	+$2,310

Table 25. United States average after-tax family income: 1977–1988. Source: *IPS (1988:39). Reproduced from* U.S. News & World Report, *July 25, 1988, p. 68. Basic data from the Congressional Budget Office.*

plants or moved them abroad, the least productive ones were shut. To continue this would deprive the country of its remaining industrial base at a time when Miller and Castellblanch (1988:6) note already "manufacturing's share of output has declined significantly: from 22% in 1977 to 18% in 1987."

Although some automation has been introduced, much of the Reagan era new capital investment has been for military production when, because of non-competitive pricing, the value-added is very high. Thus the boost is largely spurious because of the one-time factors and the weapons procurement process which actually competes with rather than strengthens the civilian industrial base. Perhaps more significant is the report (Coffin, 1990:2) that "in the U.S., for every $100 available for domestic capital formation, $46 is spent on the military, compared to $14 in West Germany and $3.70 in Japan." Admittedly, this pertains to not only industrial investment but socio-economic infra-structure—a major source of "external economies" to the former. But the trends add significance to the foregoing. For (Garten, 1990:6) "in the past decade, Japanese investment (excluding housing) rose to 19 percent of GNP from 15 percent, while that in the United States dropped to 10 percent from 12 percent." Of related significance is the fact ("Determine," 1988:1) that

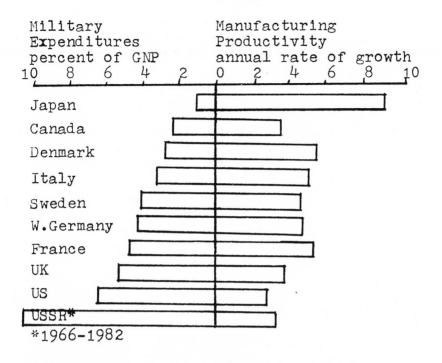

Figure 10. *United States military burden and productivity, 1960–1963.* Source: *Sivard (1985:23).*

> Two-thirds of all federal research and development funds go to the military: one third relates to civilian research (Source: National Science Board). This compares with Europe's 70% for civilian research. We are spending $600 million on military applications of super computers while Japan spends $100 million on the commercial applications of such computers.

Even worse, while the Pentagon "currently controls 71% of all Federal funds for academic computer science research, up from 45 percent ten years ago," there are likely to be even fewer spillovers than in the past. This, according to Selvin (1988:563–64), is because of a new emphasis upon applied weapons systems. Selvin reports that "basic research now accounts for less than half of federally funded research: five years ago it represented more than three quarters."

In terms of manpower, America's economy has been undermined by the diversion of between one-fourth and one-third of the nation's best scientific and engineering talent to the long-term military buildup. This has adversely affected civilian technological innovation. Jonquires (1985:27) notes that "the EEC share of U.S. patents rose from 14 percent in 1962 to 21 percent in 1981."[8] During roughly the same period, the competitiveness of United States manufacturers declined as a growing trade deficit assumed chronic proportions. While it was but 29.2 billion dollars in 1977, the negative imbalance progressively deteriorated (IPS, 1988:8) to 107.9 in 1984 and 171.2 for 1987. Of this total, Miller and Castellblanch (1988:6) underscore that fully "138 billion was in manufacturing." This along with a speculative binge on the stock market set the stage for "Black Monday" and the subsequent loss of confidence in the dollar.

By mid-1988, it was reported ("Economic Clips," July/August 1988:15) that "the ten largest banks in the world are now all Japanese-owned. The falling dollar pushed U.S. banks out of the top 25 for the first time in three decades. Citibank now ranks 28th...." Thus Tokyo replaced New York as the world's financial capital. By late 1989, after strengthening, the dollar again declined as the United States' net external debt moved beyond $600 billion. Predictably, as its largest single donor, Japan began urging — against staunch Bush Administration opposition — that the seat of the International Monetary Fund be moved from Washington to Tokyo.

The financial eclipse or at least growing external dependence is closely linked to an erosion of the international competitiveness (i.e., market dominance) of United States exports. Like the employer assault upon both unions and the welfare state, the deteriorating trade imbalance has reflected the absolute and comparative decline (Mandel, 1988:17) in the rate of productivity growth. A substantial though imprecise causal factor has been the diversion of top engineering talent and capital to the militarization process as well as militarization's corrosive effects (Melman, 1988) upon managerial quality. Yet the productivity growth rate decline also reflects other secular phenomena including the very welfare state and other "public infrastructure" cutbacks championed by the business-backed Reagan-Bush team. Thus, according to Chicago Federal Reserve Bank economist David A. Aschauer (Lynde, 1988:20–21), "two statistics have declined in tandem."

> The study finds a connection between the decline in U.S. profits during the 1970s and early 1980s and a similar decline in public spending on the economy's infrastructure — roads, sewers, bridges, and other public works.

One might add education given the known importance of this variable for a highly productive work force. Mandel (1988:19) observes that among industrialized countries, "the [United States] ranks low in the proportion of the population participating in adult education."

The supply-side tax cuts combined with an unprecedented peace time escalation of the resource-depleting military budget also effectively pre-empted the revenues necessary for social and public infrastructure, but not, ironically ("Did You Know That," 1989:7), for an "added 310,000 white-collar civilian federal employees" during eight years of the supposedly belt-tightening Reagan

Administration. While the tax giveaway to the rich was rationalized as essential to provide capital for productivity-enhancing manufacturing investment, this ignored the fact (Mandel, 1988:16–17) that in industrialized nations with even higher tax rates, productivity growth was superior and remained so! Released savings were instead channeled into exorbitant executive compensation, leveraged stock repurchases, mergers, foreign acquisitions and other speculative areas — such as the stock and bond markets — where short-run returns were higher (Mandel, 1988:18) than they would have been in re-industrializing the American economy. Industry opted instead to enhance profits not only by rolling back prior improvements in wages and working conditions, but also (Lynde, 1988:21) by "cut[ting] costs in another way — through 'deferred maintenance' on their own plant and equipment. As a result, the private capital stock is depreciating at a faster rate now than it was in the 1960s."

Finally, it is likely that our dismal productivity growth rates also reflect the monopolistic tendencies promoted by de-regulation, an absence of effective anti-trust law enforcement and rising salience of the un-competitive industrial-military complex in the increasingly concentrated and interlocked (Dye, 1983) corporate sector. Nye (1988:123), for example, recalls that "the economist Mancur Olson, in his study *The Rise and Decline of Nations,* found that falling productivity and growth are linked to declining domestic competition." Of course, the indirectly monopolistic "conglomerate" phenomenon (virtually unrelated economic activities under one financial roof) was unknown to most of the societies Olson studied. This last trend has also contributed to the erosion of high mass purchasing power by (Moberg, 1989) weakening organized labor's bargaining position.

In any case, as American capital has "exported jobs" — increasingly industrial in character — by taking over heretofore nationally owned companies or establishing new plants in such low wage repressive Third World countries as Taiwan, South Korea, Singapore and Mexico, the United States has endeavored to offset its growing trade deficit by inducing foreign business sectors to acquire American debt obligations and equity. High interest rates made such bonds and notes extremely attractive so that gradually by 1985 the United States became a net debtor nation for the first time in a half-century. As mentioned earlier, by the close of the eighties, net external indebtedness had surpassed $600 billion — assuring America's status as the Number One global debtor nation. Rising public interest payments also redistributed income from ordinary to "upscale" citizens as well as foreigners.

Simultaneously, American real and corporate property was being sold to foreigners on an unprecedented scale. A 1985 *Wall Street Journal* report ("Economic Clips," 1985a:14), for example, noted that "between 1980 and 1983, the latest year for which figures are available, Japanese investment in U.S. manufacturing facilities rose 63%. And the 1983 total could easily double in the next few years, judging from the dozens of additional projects announced since then." Many of these investors of course raise a substantial portion of their capital by borrowing the savings of Americans. Within a short time their international profit remissions will further exacerbate the U.S. balance of payments since these tend to exceed the inflow of new investment capital. The alternative, of course, is to take over more American land and businesses.

One might add that the early 1980s had also been characterized by an unprecedented wave of corporate and (personal) bankruptcies as well as an enormous number (Bruck, 1988) of mergers and acquisitions. Those acquisitions as well as stock repurchases by many corporations have been financed with high-interest "junk bonds," which also contributed to a national debt binge. In addition to the previously mentioned $2.8 trillion federal debt as of 1987 (IPS, 1988:25), there were $2.7 trillion in consumer debt, .2 trillion in farm debt, $2.5 trillion of corporate debt. The pace of such debt expansion in leveraged buyout "financial plays" is indicated (Kelley, 1988/89:3) by the fact that as of "1989 non-financial companies will have doubled their debt to $1.8 trillion in just six years."

If most of the debt capital had been used for industrial research and productive industrial investment rather than for speculation and consumption, this potential source of a disastrous economic decline might have been warranted. But we have seen that much of the growth of the federal share mirrored the cumulative increase in military expenditures during the Reagan era, when roughly three trillion dollars was allocated to such ends. A parallel tax break for the rich cost $1.5 trillion. The consumer debt expansion partly constituted a short-term offset for lower middle and working class Americans whose real wages had declined. This along with the fact that the upper middle class shared in the credit binge helps explain why Americans' rate of savings is the lowest — having declined (Coffin, 1988b:1) "from 7% in the 1970s to 3% in the 1980s" — in the industrialized world. Even so, Rothstein (1988:24) notes that "in the 1980's, U.S. bank deposits were as likely to be lent for speculative as productive activity." Between 1980 and 1983, $212 billion was spent on corporate mergers. For the next three years, the figure (IPS, 1988:14) was $454 billion. Comparatively, between 1980 and 1986, $307 billion was spent on research and development by all industries.

Thus mergers, stock buy-backs and parasitical speculation accounted for much of the corporate debt expansion. Not even "home equity loans" and mortgage debt are being increasingly used for consumption or speculation. By mid-1988, the head of the Federal Deposit Insurance Corporation (Hershey, 1988:D1) estimated that "the savings and loan industry continues to pile up heavy losses and that some $50 billion would ultimately be required to rescue it." This turned out to be a gross, and probably a deliberate, understatement. One investment advisory service ("Special," 1988) cautions:

Over 200 banks failed in 1987 — more than in any year since the Great Depression. And another 800 more banks operating today are technically bankrupt. Almost one third of all Savings and Loans are now insolvent and their insurer, the FSLIC is officially bankrupt, according to a recent report by the General Accounting Office. To make matters worse, the FDIC has only $8 billion in liquid assets to cover $175 trillion in insured deposits!

By early 1989 ("News," 1988:11; NPR, "Evening," Jan. 10, 1989) the FSLIC had allocated $16 billion with $4 billion in tax breaks "to rescue insolvent thrifts, primarily in Texas and Oklahoma. Incredibly, less than $300 million in additional capital has been put up by the investors purchasing these institutions. This corporate welfare subsidy or handout to the wealthy was but the beginning. Private and congressional estimates were in the range of $100 billion for the entire savings and loan bailout operation. If anything, the public bailout subsidy will be considerably higher than this conservative figure. By late 1990, the figure exceeded $500 billion — assuming no recession.

To obtain such funds, the national government will either have to further expand its indebtedness or escalate tax burdens upon (and prices to) ordinary Americans. With customary deception, the indebtedness has been defined as "off-budget" thus avoiding clear violation of the Gramm-Rudman proscription. To further soften mass reactions, ordinary Americans are being told they have to end their consumption "binge." Yet, as one economist (Henwood, 1989:44) admonishes:

> In fact, all this talk of "binges" is a covert attempt to solidify the heritage of Reaganism: the military buildup, the war on the welfare state and the upward distribution of income. Those in the austerity crowd typically suggest only cosmetic reductions in the military; they don't seem to care that all but the richest fifth of Americans have seen real income fall over the past decade, or that the Federal tax system, even after the 1986 reform, is still less progressive than before.

Yet this reality is ignored even by liberals like Harvard's Joseph Nye (1988:114), a top advisor to 1988 Democratic presidential candidate Dukakis, who warned that "in the future Americans will have to cut consumption and increase savings to defray the Reagan debt. The adjustment may be painful. . . ." This recalls the recession engineered by the Federal Reserve to curb inflation (Greider, 1988) during the first term of the Reagan Administration — one which savaged both economic security and higher living standard aspirations for the lower 80 percent of American Society.

The next "recession" — whether government-induced through high interest rates and spending cuts or triggered (Metz, 1988) by some event — will not only scale down mass consumption and wipe out debt, but further reduce the opportunity to get ahead for ordinary citizens. As it is, "some nine out of every 10 new (Day, 1988:3) businesses go broke within five years." The rate of failure zooms up with an economic downturn—for old as well as new businesses.

THE ECLIPSE OF ORGANIZED LABOR AND ECONOMIC SECURITY

During the 1980s, the previously mentioned official tolerance for the use of potentially productive capital to finance buy-outs, mergers and conglomerates has not only strengthened monopolistic tendencies in the economy but seriously weakened the position and well-being of American workers. In the course of reviewing Bruck's (1988) analysis of federal permissiveness toward insider trading and other forms of Wall Street white-collar crime, Winslow (1988:20) details some of the ways such concentration has

> affected American labor and many local communities. For example, once a merger was completed, new management often had to shut down factories, postpone new investments, cut jobs and negotiate cheaper union contracts in order to pay off its junk bonds. Not surprisingly, this bitter medicine was often forced on the most troubled sectors of the economy. Over half of all mergers in the '80s were in manufacturing or mining; nearly half of America's 1,000 largest companies—companies that have the most high-paying union jobs—have undergone a merger or significant financial restructuring.
>
> The result transferred billions of dollars from employees, especially organized labor, and local communities into the pockets of corporate raiders and Wall Street firms like Drexel, but failed to solve the problems that created the economic crisis: management's failure to make long-term investments to increase productivity and international competitiveness. Worse, a decade of takeover speculation has dramatically increased corporate debt. And with more than just $185 billion worth of junk bonds outstanding, up from only $15 billion in 1976, it is even more unlikely that corporate America will invest in its long-term future.

Equally improbable is the preservation of most remaining jobs when many of these highly leveraged (over-indebted) corporations go under. Thus AFL-CIO economist Markley Roberts, referring ("Worth Noting," 1989:4) to the approximately five million white-collar workers laid off between 1983 and 1988 alone, notes that "a significant share of the displaced white-collar workers" were the victims of ... 'corporate cannibalism'—their jobs devoured by corporate mergers, acquisitions, takeovers and leveraged buyouts." By definition then, the new entities were "leaner," and in some cases, stronger.

Efforts to attract domestic investment and to slow the tax and foreign policy encouraged a "runaway plant" trend—one which has cost American workers several million industrial jobs in the past decade—have involved extraordinary state-backed pressures against a much weakened (Moberg, 1989) trade union movement, whose decline is traced in Figure 11. Similarly, the dramatic reduction in militance or strike activity is graphically though perhaps spuriously contrasted by Alexander Cockburn (1988c:226):

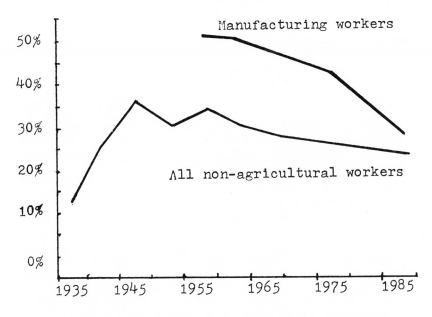

Figure 11. Union membership, 1935–1985: Percentage of workers belonging to unions. Sources: *Bureau of Labor Statistics; Statistical Abstract.* Economic Notes, *Oct. 1985.*

When the strike rate goes down, the murder rate goes up. According to *Midnight Notes #9* (available from Box 204, Jamaica Plain, MA 02130), if we distinguish two major American postwar eras—1947–73, when the average weekly wage rose 2.3 percent a year on average, and 1974–87, when the average weekly wage fell 1 percent a year on average—and then calculate the average percentage of estimated work-time in "days idle" because of work stoppages involving 1,000 or more workers per year in each period, we get .17 percent for the earlier period and .08 percent in the later one. Roughly speaking this constitutes a 53 percent drop in workers' militancy. There's a correlated rise in drug abuse and murder, which is now the fourth-ranked cause of death in the United States, after heart attack, cancer and accidents. Capitalism obviously prefers murders to strikes. Most murders are committed by the poor against the poor anyway. It's like a Phillips curve, written in blood.

While the correlation may reflect the growth of poverty and the erosion of an effective welfare state rather than the decline of strikes—particularly successful ones—the falloff undoubtedly has reflected an increasingly hostile political environment. Consequently, there has been a failure of even unionized workers to keep up with the cost of living or to halt the sharp drop in the proportion of the workforce represented by trade unions. Ferguson and Rogers (1985:164) emphasize:

> Average first-year wage increases in major private collective bargaining agreements set a record low at 2.4 percent last year, lagging, for the third year in a row, significantly behind inflation. This dismal bargaining performance in part reflects the spectacular decline in union membership over the Reagan years, a decline recently confirmed by the Bureau of Labor Statistics, which reports a 22.4 percent drop in unionization rates for the private sector from 1980 to 1984. Unions now claim only 15.6 percent of the private sector work force and an even smaller proportion in growth sectors like finance, insurance and real estate (2.7 percent), services (7.2 percent) and wholesale and retail trade (8.2 percent). This membership level cannot even be preserved, let alone strengthened, at the current rate of organizing. In 1984, for the third year in a row, unions organized fewer than 100,000 workers through representational elections before the National Labor Relations Board.

The overall percentage of the public and private workforce in unions had plummeted (Amott, 1988:7–8) to 17 percent in 1988 from nearly 25 percent fourteen years earlier.

> This decline in labor's position is no accident. An employer offensive against unions, macroeconomic policies aimed at preserving profitability by maintaining high unemployment, capital flight to low-wage countries, unfriendly labor law administrators, and slack government enforcement of labor standards have all contributed to an erosion in labor's bargaining power. With labor weakened, the unemployment rate fell steadily for six straight years without the improvements in pay and working conditions that workers had historically been able to achieve in tightening labor markets.

Thus by "1986, the average major collective bargaining contract called for a minuscule 1.6% increase over the life of the contract, compared to 8.3% in 1981." While the rate increased to 2.6 percent in 1987/1988, all of these figures were well below the actual rate of inflation. These reductions in employee purchasing power reflected, as previously emphasized, the declining ability of workers to wage successful strikes due to personal indebtedness, the increased use of strike breakers—professional as well as traditional—from the growing reserve of unemployed, and governmental hostility. Moberg (1989) analyzes the contribution of these and other factors—some endogenous to the labor "movement" itself.

    Ironically, organized labor's precipitous decline had been accelerated by the global pro-corporate interventionist policies to which the AFL-CIO leadership has long been committed. Repression of the reformist and radical left divides and weakens labor in developing countries. Efforts by congressional liberals to restrict trade preferences or subsidies for repressive anti-labor regimes have for the most part been ignored by the Reagan and Bush administrations. Witt (1989:9), for example, recalls:

The Reagan administration twisted the intent of amendments passed by Congress, denying GSP trade preferences to Nicaragua, Romania and Paraguay while ignoring the major worker-rights violators among U.S. trading partners. Benefits for Chile were suspended only after a congressional outcry. The administration refused even to hold hearings on petitions for review of GSP privileges for El Salvador, Guatemala, Indonesia, the Philippines, Thailand and Turkey. Only Romania, Nicaragua, Ethiopia and Paraguay have been removed from OPEC programs on worker-rights grounds.

The Bush admimistration has shown a similar lack of enthusiasm for enforcing worker-rights provisions of trade laws. In April, the U.S. trade representative, Carla Hills, rejected petitions from labor or human-rights groups on worker-rights violations in Malaysia and Israel, postponed action on Haiti, Syria and Liberia, and removed GSP privileges only from the Central African Republic and Burma.

Lower wages and fringe benefits resulting from anti-leftist regimes backed or imposed by the United States in turn attract "runaway" American industrial plants.

Mexico under the "technocrat" Salinas is (Reding, 1989) a prime example. Thus just south of the Rio Grande are more than 1300 "maquiladoras" or "twin plants"—most being subsidiaries or affiliates of U.S. corporations. According to a recent (Juffer, 1988:24) investigative report, such assembly operations

are booming with their numbers expanding at an annual rate of 25 per cent. The boom began with the 1980 devaluation of the peso, which made Mexican laborers among the cheapest in the world. Those in Hong Kong and Singapore make more than three times the Mexican wage, and even those in Costa Rica and the Dominican Republic make half again as much.

U.S. companies hire a largely young, organized female work force, at wages of $25 for a forty-eight hour week. The near finished goods they assemble are then transported without import tax to the United States where they are packaged and sold for huge profits.

The returns are also swelled by lax Mexican enforcement of safety and environmental laws.

From 1973 to 1980 alone, such "outsourcing" resulted in the loss (IPS, 1988:13) of more than 387,000 industrial jobs. Since then the job loss has continued to rise albeit at a slower pace. Other jobs are lost and the trade imbalance is adversely affected by new investments being located abroad rather than in the United States. Between 1975 and 1985, imports from such investments or acquisitions (IPS, 1988:10) rose steadily from approximately $5 billion to more than $30 billion per annum. Over that decade United States imports produced by United States corporations abroad totaled almost $170 billion. One economist (Henwood, 1989:44) adds that while "the government doesn't collect such statistics, private economists estimate that one-third to one-half of our trade deficit is the result of U.S.-based multinationals importing goods from foreign subsidiaries or sub-contractors." An example of corporate patriotism?

Another major consequence has been the downgrading of America's blue collar employment opportunity structure. As Table 26 and Figures 12 and 13 reveal, the greatest proportionate shift in the work force has been from traditionally highly paid and unionized industrial and craft sectors to poorly remunerated and difficult to organize clerical and service sectors. Harrington and Levinson (1985:421–22) underscore the dual consequences of automation and plant closures by citing a Bureau of Labor Statistics study of "5.1 million workers whose jobs were abolished or plants shut down between January 1979 and January 1984." In the latter month, almost 60 percent were worse off as they either found jobs at lower wage rates or joined the ranks of the unemployed, including more than 14 percent who dropped out of the labor force altogether. Of the 10 million ("Worth Noting," 1989:4) white and blue collar workers who "lost their jobs as a result of plant closings and layoffs from 1983 to 1988 . . . seven out of 10 of these workers [had] found new jobs as of January 1988." Fully "44% had to settle for pay cuts—some in excess of 20%—when they went back to work" according to a Bureau of Labor Statistics study.

Similarly, a recent report by Congressman Willian H. Gray III ("Following," 1988:5) refutes

> the Bush claim that the Reagan Administration created 17 million jobs [and] 'the majority of them paid an average of more than $22,000 a year.' Gray says not even the administration's Bureau of Labor Statistics will defend that claim. In the eight years of the Reagan Administration about 15.8 million new jobs were created, a pace slower than the job creation rate under the Carter Administration, Gray says.

Ledbetter (1988:427) records that "nearly half the jobs created between 1979 and 1987 pay less than $7,400 a year." Even worse, according to recent Census data (Wicker, 1988:A27), "85% of newly created jobs have been in the lowest-paying industries, while the number of jobs in the highest-wage industries—service as well as goods producing—has declined." Indeed, William Julius Wilson's (1987) study of the emergence of an allegedly permanent underclass in America's cities assigns great significance (Hill, 1988:17) to the "loss of millions of low and semiskilled jobs in America's large urban manufacturing centers."

Between 1981 and 1987 alone, Coffin (1988:1) points to approximately "two million well paying factory jobs that have been lost." Miller and Castellblanch (1988:6), referring perhaps to a broader range of industrial jobs, recall that

Occupation:	1950	Shares in Total Labor Force: 1985	1995	1982*
Professional, technical workers	8.6%	16.3%	17.1%	$410
Managers	8.7	9.4	9.6	430
Sales Workers	7.0	6.9	6.9	317
Clerical Workers	12.3	18.8	18.9	248
Craft Workers	14.2	11.4	11.6	375
Machine Operaters	20.4	12.8	12.1	252
Service Workers	10.5	16.0	16.3	207
Laborers	6.6	5.8	5.5	243
Farm Workers	11.8	2.7	1.9	186
Total:	100	100	100	$309

Table 26. United States labor force trends. Source: *Bureau of Labor Statistics, in Robert Samuelson, "Middle-Class Media Myth,"* National Journal, *December 31, 1983. As reproduced in Harrington and Levinson (1985:424).* Note: *Average weekly earnings.*

Employment in manufacturing declined from 27.3% of the non-agricultural work force in 1973, at the peak of the post-war boom, to 19.5% in 1985. Even in absolute terms, there were fewer manufacturing workers in 1985 than in 1973.

Earlier they noted that "more than five million manufacturing workers lost their jobs permanently between 1981 and 1985 thanks to plant closings and layoffs." Apparently this phenomenon continued into the late 1980s for ("Worth Noting," 1989:4) according to the Bureau of Labor Statistics, "nearly 10 million American workers lost their jobs as a result of plant closings and layoffs from 1983 to 1988, with the impact falling across the board on blue-collar and white-collar workers alike...." This de-industrialization is also given salience by the fact (Thurow, 1985:52) that "not so long ago (1981), adult men had unemployment rates significantly below those of adult women. Today the reverse is true."

Deterioration of mass welfare is further underscored by rising structural or endemic unemployment as well as official understatements of cyclical joblessness in Table 27 and Figure 14. By mid-1988 in the midst of a much heralded sustained "recovery," the real jobless rate ("Economic Clips," July-August 1988:14) was 11.6 percent—one which encompassed discouraged workers, those with special employment needs, and involuntary part-time workers, calculated for hours lost. And if the military were not included with

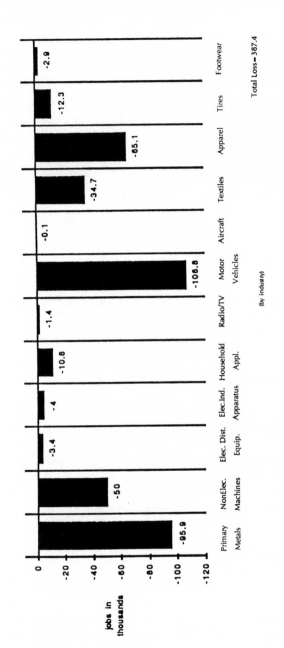

jobs in thousands

Primary Metals **-95.9**

NonElec. Machines **-50**

Elec. Dist. Equip. **-3.4**

Elec.Ind. Apparatus **-4**

Household Appl. **-10.8**

Radio/TV **-1.4**

Motor Vehicles **-106.8**

Aircraft **-0.1**

Textiles **-34.7**

Apparel **-65.1**

Tires **-12.3**

Footwear **-2.9**

(by industry)

Total Loss= 387.4

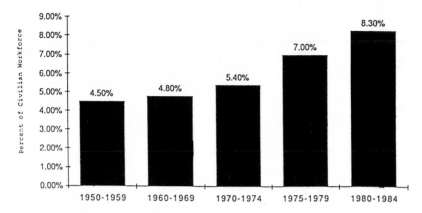

Figure 13. United States secular unemployment trends: 1950–1984. Source: *IPS (1988:17, 19). Based upon* Economic Report of the President, 1985. Note: **Between 1979–1984, approximately 11 1/2 million workers were displaced.*

the productive labor force (a Reagan Administration innovation), the actual full-employment unemployment rate would be around 13 percent!

In addition to such methodological revisions, necessary because of an unprecedented increase in official data distortions (which also understate trade and budgetary deficits), others indicating the real extent of hardship would focus upon roughly 25 percent of the workforce who at some time during a year experience joblessness. This encompasses not only victims of layoffs but also millions who are dismissed or quit—often consequential to autocratic and exploitative managerial styles. Such management is critiqued in Robert Reich's recent study *Tales of a New America.* Damage to potential productivity improvement is implied, according to the author, by the response of workers (Peters, 1987:53) "when asked the much more practical question: 'Who would benefit most from an increase in [worker] productivity.' Some 93 percent of Japanese workers thought that they would benefit while only 9 percent of American workers felt that way." While an exploitative ethos may be one factor, the example of management self-enrichment patterns during an era of union busting and other austerity measures to reduce real wages may also be relevant. The average top executive "earnings" package ("International Recruitment," 1988:6) in the United States exceeds a half million dollars. This can be compared with Japan ($315,000), West Germany ($260,000) and France ($250,000).

Although primarily concerned with the need for a more effective management style to enhance productivity, Thurow (1985:54) highlights the enormous

Opposite: *Figure 12. Job loss in the United States due to outsourcing: 1973–1980.* Source: *IPS (1988:13). Based upon Barry Bluestone* et al., Shadows on the Horizon.

	1977	1978	1979	1980	1981	1982	1983	1984	1985	1986	1987
BLS Civilian Labor Force	99,009.	102,251.	104,962.	106,940.	108,670.	110,204.	111,550.	113,544.	115,461.	117,834.	119,865.
BLS Civilian Employment	92,017.	96,048.	98,824.	99,303.	100,397.	99,526.	100,834.	105,005.	107,150.	109,597.	112,440.
BLS Unemployed	6,991.	6,202.	6,137.	7,637.	8,273.	10,717.	10,717.	8,539.	8,312.	8,237.	7,425.
BLS Unemployment Rate	7.1%	6.1%	5.8%	7.1%	7.6%	9.7%	9.6%	7.5%	7.2%	7.0%	6.2%
Part-Time Employment	21,204.	21,441.	22,918.	22,930.	26,012.	25,439.	24,895.	24,427.	24,682.	25,226.	28,007.
Discouraged Workers	1,026.	863.	771.	993.	1,103.	1,568.	1,641.	1,283.	1,204.	1,121.	1,026.
Civilians Not in the Labor Force Who Want Jobs	5,775.	5,446.	5,427.	5,675.	5,835.	6,559.	6,503.	6,070.	5,933.	5,825.	5,714.
Jobless Persons	14,048.	12,981.	12,907.	14,877.	15,878.	19,546.	19,725.	16,791.	16,320.	16,154.	18,542.
Jobless Rate	14.4%	12.9%	12.5%	14.4%	14.9%	17.9%	17.8%	15.0%	14.3%	13.9%	15.8%

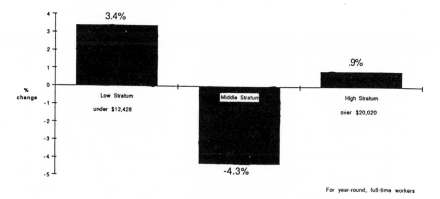

Figure 14. United States employment change by wage level: 1979–1986. Source: *IPS (1988:30). Based upon Economic Policy Institute,* The State of the Working Class, *1988.*

insecurity implied by the fact that "within any one year the average American company loses about half its total labor force—about half of those quit and half are fired."[9] Quotations of this nature, of course, obscure the trauma to individuals and families. Some social consequences will be addressed shortly.

Even worse, figures on joblessness don't reveal that unemployment compensation no longer functions as a significant safety net. When first introduced in the New Deal Era, benefits averaged about 50 percent of earnings; by the early 1980s the proportion had plummeted to half of that. (This is less than one-third the average in highly developed Scandinavia.) Compounding the harm, Congress responded to the militarization-induced fiscal crisis of the state by failing to review the Federal Supplemental Compensation (FSC) program in March 1985. The "FSC provided 8 to 14 weeks of benefits to jobless workers who have exhausted state-funded unemployment benefits (which usually run 26 weeks)."[10] Levinson (1985:395) adds that "this occurs at a time when only 34 percent of the unemployed were receiving unemployment benefits in an average month in 1984—the lowest level ever recorded. With the end of FSC this level is likely to fall below 30 percent in 1985. This compares with 50–70 percent of the unemployed receiving benefits in the late 1970s." The same author notes that these percentages exclude approximately one million workers who have given up looking for jobs and therefore are ineligible for unemployment compensation. Thus, in 1984 about 75 percent of the jobless were not covered.

Opposite: *Table 27. Comparison of BLS civilian unemployment rate with jobless rate: 1977–1987.* Source: *IPS (1988:29). Based upon United States Department of Labor, Bureau of Labor Statistics,* Employment and Earnings, *various issues, 1978–1988.* Note: **Figures in 000's.*

The direct impact of the recent militarization-induced reallocation of priorities is similarly underscored by a Congressional Budget Office study ("Economic Clips," 1985:14) revealing that the proportion of unemployed receiving benefits had plummeted from 45 percent in 1979 to 25 percent in 1984. While the rate of unemployment has declined somewhat since then, it remains in real terms close to 12 percent. Continued government belt-tightening has further restricted the availability of unemployment benefits and particularly cost of living increases.

INCOME, WEALTH AND POVERTY TRENDS

It is no wonder, then, that the 33.7 million who were poor in 1984 was higher than the number of poor in 1964, when President Johnson declared his "war on poverty." Although in percentage terms Census Bureau data show a slight decline from 15.3 percent in 1983 to 14.4 percent in 1984, Muwakkil (1985) adds that the percentage "is still the highest since 1966, except for the recession years of 1982 and 1983." When those on the margins of poverty or the near poor are taken into account, an astounding (Ferguson and Rogers, 1985:164) "100 million live below the Bureau of Labor Statistics' 'low standard city budget for a family of four.'" A large number of those who were ineligible for or exhausted their unemployment benefits are even ineligible for "welfare" (i.e., social assistance) if they attempt to maintain intact families.[11] Unsurprisingly (Coffin, 1988a:4), "a study by the Physicians Task Force on Hunger in America finds that 20 million Americans, particularly workers dropped from manufacturing jobs and now in service areas, as well as infants and the elderly, do not get enough to eat." Coffin (1988b:2) informs us that "a U.S. Conference of Mayors report finds that the demand for emergency food assistance increased an average of 18% in 23 of 28 major cities in 1987. Two-thirds of the requests were from families with children."

According to a recent ("Updates," 1988:5) study by the Washington-based Center on Budget and Policy Priorities, a smaller proportion (26 percent) of families with children were lifted out of poverty in 1987 than in 1979 (38 percent) by federal and state programs. Similarly, "another recent study found that government benefit programs in Australia, Canada, Norway, Sweden, the United Kingdom and West Germany surpassed the United States. Of the countries studied only Switzerland provided less support for poor families and their child poverty rate was still only one-third the U.S. rate." Finally, analogous patterns were identified ("Child Poverty," 1988/89:4) by a recent Urban Institute study, *The Vulnerable,* which concluded that a

> greater percentage of children grew up poor in the United States than in Australia, the United Kingdom, West Germany, Switzerland, Sweden, Norway and Canada. This occurs even though family incomes were higher in the United States than in most of the other seven nations studied....
>
> The book's co-editor, Timothy Smeeding ... believes the problem has

gotten worse in recent years for children in the United States. He cites a Census Bureau report that estimates 20 percent of U.S. children lived in poverty in 1987.

While not highly accurate, the Census reports are suggestive. In any case their official sponsorship by an administration that has massaged data elsewhere (foreign trade—excluding shipping and other import costs—and employment—including the military while excluding discouraged workers) implies, if anything, an understatement of the problem as does the under-counting bias for urban slums in data collection.

Also according to the Census Bureau ("No Kidding," 1988:5), "32.5 million Americans lived under the government's official poverty line in 1987, 8 million more than in 1978." In the former year 32.5 million Americans— one-seventh of the population—lived beneath (Wicker, 1988:A27) the ar-tificially low federal poverty line. This represents ("Trends," 1988:12) "a 25% increase since 1975." The same Census data revealed (Wicker, 1988:A27) that 20 percent of all children and more than 34 percent of households headed by women fell into this category.

Despite the much heralded 1987 business recovery, there was no signif-icant change in the poverty rate. Indeed, a report of the 1988 Commission on the Cities (Squires, 1988:16), convened by former Oklahoma Senator Fred Har-ris, concluded that "poverty is worse now that it was 20 years ago. . . . Overall unemployment in the U.S. is twice what it was 20 years ago. And unemploy-ment for blacks is now twice what it is for whites." With respect to race and the quality of urban life, the portent (Harris, 1988) was particularly ominous:

> To a considerable extent the residents of city ghettos are now living in separate and deteriorating societies, with separate economies, diverging family struc-tures and basic institutions, and even growing linguistic separation within the core ghettos. The scale of their isolation by race, class and economic situation is much greater than it was in the 1960s, impoverishment, joblessness, educa-tional inequality and housing insufficiency even more severe.

Broad patterns of deterioration in mass education and housing are essayed toward the close of this chapter.

Urie Bronfenbrenner, an expert on children (Rosenfeld, 1988:4), cites three major societal changes which have adversely affected child welfare in the United States: working mothers, single parents, and increased levels of poverty.

> He cites statistics from the U.S. Census Bureau and the Children's Defense Fund to argue that the percentage of families with children under 6 who live in poverty was the same (25 percent) in 1986 . . . as in 1959. In 1969, following the War on Poverty, the percentages had declined to 14 percent.

Such poverty is not simply a matter of stunted aspirations or opportunities. It is literally a desecration of the right to life. Ledbetter (1988:428) informs us that "from 1980 to 1985, the number of U.S. children who died because of poverty, hunger and malnutrition was greater than the total number of U.S. battle deaths in the Vietnam War."

Equally injurious consequences are pointed up by Green (1989:126), who also deplores the fact that "the infant mortality rate among minorities in the United States exceeds those of many Third World nations."

> The simultaneous increase in single-parent families and decline in real value of the minimum wage, for example, have produced a poverty rate among children (at least 20 percent) that is the highest of any industrial democracy. The 1970s and 1980s also saw an unprecedented influx into the work force of women and children—without safe, affordable, quality child care. There has been a large increase this decade in reported cases of child abuse, teen-age pregnancy and school dropouts.

The plight of such youth will be discussed later in this chapter.

Virtually all recoveries from economic recessions over the past several decades have been associated with higher post-recession levels of unemployment. While some rightists in recent years have blamed this upon the growing labor force participation of women, what tends to be ignored is that such job seeking increasingly reflects not merely women's liberation but also a desire by many wives or divorced mothers to prevent a deterioration of prior living standards in the face of declining family purchasing power. Thus one liberal ("The Reagan Legacy," 1988:2) public interest group cautions that:

> the decrease in unemployment rates has not translated into increased well-being for American families, for two reasons: 1) It now takes two workers per family to provide what one worker used to provide. 2) Of the new jobs being created, only about half pay wages that clear the poverty line.

Even official data (Kilborn, 1990:3) confirm these sources of growing stress:

> The Bureau of Labor Statistics found in a sampling of the work force last May that the number of women with two or more jobs had quintupled, from 636,000 in 1970 to 3.1 million last May, while the number of men who moonlight rose at a slower pace, from 3.4 million to 4.1 million. . . .
> The bureau survey found in its sampling that the number of women with two or more jobs had jumped from 2.2 percent of 28.9 million working women in 1970, to 5.9 percent of 52.8 million who were working last May.
> The percentage of moonlighting among men declined from 7 percent in 1970 to 6.4 percent last May.
> The survey also showed that most men who held two jobs were married, while most women who moonlighted were divorced, separated, widowed or had never married.

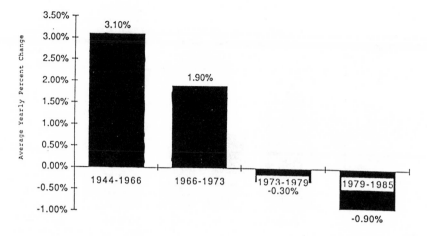

*Figure 15. Decline in United States production workers' wages—average annual change: 1944–1985. Source: IPS (1988:18). Based upon Business Conditions Digest. Note: *Adjusted for Inflation.*

Noting that full time female employees received 30 percent less pay on the average than male counterparts, the director of the Women's Policy Research Institute emphasized:

> Government statistics show that for men and women, the incentive to moonlight has risen as it has become harder for employees to manage on one paycheck.
> When increases in the cost of living are taken into account, hourly wages have slipped by about 5 percent in 20 years.

Predictably, real average gross weekly earnings ("Economic Clips," March-April 1988:14) fell 11.3 percent between 1979 and 1987.

An unparalleled expansion of consumer indebtedness and often unpleasant low-wage jobs for wives have been necessary to prevent the median family living standard from falling between 1973 and 1987. And as the tables and figures on pages 157–166 indicate, this trend will intensify in the absence of foreign policy changes to prevent the exportation of industrial jobs to administration-backed repressive low-wage sweatshops in Mexico, Singapore, Taiwan, South Korea, etc. Between 1977 and 1984 ("Corporations," 1984:12), foreign employment by 3,540 United States–based transnational corporations rose from 7.2 million "to about 10 million" jobs. As noted earlier in this chapter, many were exported or not created in the United States because the highest rates of return are in developing countries, where in 1977 United States

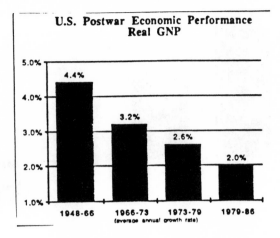

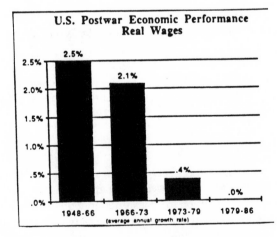

Figure 16. United States postwar economic performance—real GNP and real wages: 1948–1986. Source: IPS (1988:22). Based upon Economic Report of the President (1987).

investors paid $1.74 in average hourly compensation. And the wage disparity has not altered over the past decade.

Thus the assault upon ordinary Americans' living standards by what Fred Cook once called "the warfare state" has had a dual character. First the tax

	Percent of the Population*	
Reference Point	1978	1983
Below The Poverty Line	15–	15
Between The Poverty Line And Low Budget Line	15+	25
Between The Low And Medium Budget Lines	25+	20
Between The Medium and High Budget Lines	30	20+
Above The High Budget Line	15	20–
Total:	100	100

Table 28. Squeeze on the working class. Source: *Steven Rose,* Social Stratification in the United States *(Baltimore: Social Graphics Co., 1983), p. 11. As reproduced by Harrington and Levinson (1985:425).* Notes: **Because the budgets are for an urban family of four, our estimates are imprecise. Therefore, the figures are rounded to the nearest 5 percent with a plus or minus.*

The changes from 1978 to 1983 are dramatic considering that this is such a short period. In 1978, 55 percent of the population lay between the low and high budget lines. By 1983, this figure had shrunk to just above 40 percent with most falling below the budget line and a few rising above the high class budget marker. Thus, the number of people in the "middle middle class" has fallen while the percentage of those below the low budget line has jumped from 30 to 40 percent.

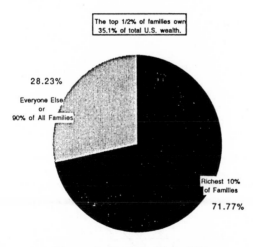

The top 1/2% of families own 35.1% of total U.S. wealth.

28.23%
Everyone Else or 90% of All Families

Richest 10% of Families
71.77%

Data represents net assets after deduction of debt.

Figure 17. Distribution of U.S. Wealth Including Home Ownership: 1983. Source: *IPS (1988:36). Based upon Joint Economic Committee,* The Concentration of Wealth in the United States, *p. 24.* Notes: *The 1986 JEC study [chart source] is the most comprehensive study of wealth in the U.S. ever undertaken, including a special effort to measure the top of wealth distribution. Yearly income can be deceiving in that "tax loopholes," the occasional bad year, and other financial resources do not get reflected; therefore a better indicator of economic equality in America is the overall wealth distribution.*

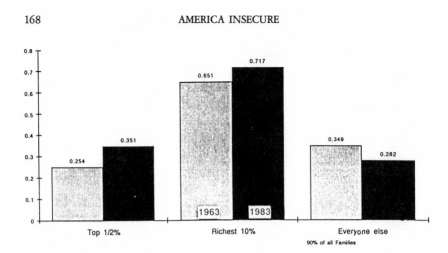

Figure 18. Change in the Distribution of United States Wealth: 1963–1983. Source: *IPS (1988:38). Based upon Joint Economic Committee,* The Concentration of Wealth in the United States, *p. 24.*

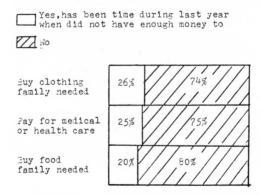

Figure 19. Dimensions of United States Poverty: 1984. Source: *Survey by the Gallup Organization, January 27–30, 1984.*

burden became greater as well as more regressive while real social spending was being diminished. Thus ("Economic Clips," January/February 1988:16):

> Between 1980 and 1987, government spending jumped 70% to just over one trillion dollars. Military spending doubled and interest payments on the national debt rose 150%. The share of the federal budget marked for social programs fell from 41% in 1980 to 28% in 1987.

Secondly, as noted previously, to further reduce costs for the corporate-owning class, the trade union movement became a target of sustained attack by both the corporate and state sectors. Illustrative of this—though only the "tip of the iceberg"—is the transformation of the National Labor Relations Board. Ferguson and Rogers (1985:165) deplore the fact that its "anti-union decisions continue. Since Reagan appointee Donald Dotson became chair, unions have lost an average of 57 percent of contested cases decided by the board (compared with 16 percent from 1974 to 1976, under the last Republican-dominated board) and have lost fully 86 percent of the cases brought against them." It is unsurprising, then, that average wages—adjusted for inflation—have not risen for almost two decades.

Even more seriously, they have fallen since 1977, and according to some estimates, from as early as 1973. Thus Lester Thurow, a noted liberal economist, informs us (Harrington and Levinson, 1985:418) that "relative to the price of capital, American wages were 37 percent lower in 1983 than in 1972. After correcting for inflation, wages have fallen 6 percent in absolute terms. This has not happened in Europe." More recently, Thurow (1990:4) indicated an accelerated rate of decline for the 1983–1989 period: "Inflation-corrected wages of nonsupervisory workers have fallen 16 percent since 1972 and are now falling by 1 percent a year." Others (Ferguson and Rogers, 1985:164) note that "despite the record-shattering political business cycle engineered by the Reagan Administration, real average gross weekly earnings in 1984 stagnated at levels 12.5 percent below their 1972 peak." According to yet another observer (Muwakkil, 1985):

> Most analysts blame the drop in real wages on the decline of manufacturing jobs and the growth of jobs in the service sector. Says David Dembo of the Council of International and Public Affairs, "The hourly wage in retail trade is only 62.9 percent of the hourly wage in manufacturing. Similarly hourly wages in the finance, insurance and real-estate sector, and in other service sector employment averages 83.3 percent and 83.1 percent respectively of those in the manufacturing sector." Those jobs are not just lower paying, he notes, but are often part-time as well.
> "Unfortunately," Dembo adds, "most of the new employment in the last couple of years has been in the lowest-paying sectors."

The changes in employment patterns, which Dembo refers to as "pauperization," are fundamentally due to the decline of organized labor. This decline is manifested by labor's inability to prevent plant closures or to win adequate wage increases, setting a pattern for unorganized sectors. "Economy in Review" (1988:8) notes that:

> Up until 1974, union wage increases outpaced consumer prices, resulting in a rising standard of living for workers. Since 1974, contracts have failed to keep up with inflation, and the standard of living has stagnated. Only by increasing the number of earners per household was the average union family able to keep up its standard of living.

And in the most recent period, what the previously noted minimal contract gains imply, is ("Economic Clips," March-April 1988:14) that:

> Real wages for union workers have fallen in three of the last four years. Part of the decline is due to the fact that COLA clauses have been surrendered. Only 37% of all workers covered under major agreements negotiated in 1987 had COLAs, down from 60% in 1977. The portion of union contracts with lump-sum payments increased from 6.5% in 1984 to 52% in 1987.

It is unremarkable, then, that there has been an actual decline in family earnings.

Even official 1988 Census data report (Wicker, 1988:A27) *at best* stagnation of the median family income over the 1973–1987 period. And these data ignore the adverse effects of job insecurity, consumer indebtedness and tax burdens—all having sharply risen—upon actual living standards. Indeed ("Worth Noting," 1989:4), according to "a recent study by the Economic Policy Institute," at least "40% of American families" reported "a decrease in their buying power in the 1980s." This notwithstanding an increase in the number of working wives "from 55.4% to 66.1%" between 1979 and 1986.

The squeeze upon America's much heralded "middle-middle" or working class—forcing many more downward than it allows to climb upward—is shown in further detail by Table 28. Although actual deterioration may have been less stark since 1978 represented a business cycle peak while the year 1983 was one of partial recovery, there can be no doubt of the deepening hardship confronting almost two-thirds of the population. Correspondingly, there has been an extraordinary rise in personal and consumer indebtedness so that by the mid-1980s, a majority of Americans were either net debtors or owned less than $500 in assets after mortgage and consumer debt were subtracted. Their diminishing economic status was also reflected by skyrocketing personal bankruptcies. As one report has it ("Economic Clips," 1985:14), between late 1979 and the last quarter of 1984 those bankruptcies rose nearly 60 percent. Continued high personal bankruptcy rates have been paralleled during the 1980s by similar disaster for many family farms which have been foreclosed, abandoned or sold to pay off creditors. It is clear that the foregoing trends have been accentuated by the stridently pro-corporate and military policy bias of the Reagan Administration and its support by a "moderate bipartisan" congressional coalition.

It appears that inequality has actually been increased among social classes in recent years. As Thurow (1985:47) points out, the growing disparities are even more pronounced for the distribution of wealth than income.

> Between 1969 and 1982 the income share going to the bottom 50 percent of all American families has fallen from 23 to 20 percent of the total; the income share going to the next 40 percent has fallen from 48 to 47 percent, while the income share of the top 10 percent of the population has risen from 29 to 33 percent of the total. . . .
>
> If one looks at the distribution of wealth (net worth), inequalities are larger and growing more rapidly than those of income. While the top 10 percent of the population receives 33 percent of total income, they own 57 percent of total net worth. Almost 20 percent of all American families have zero or negative net worth.

Without explicitly specifying militarization process tradeoffs, Thurow nevertheless identifies declining productivity and export competitiveness as well as social spending cutbacks as contributory factors.[12]

In fact, Congressional Budget Office and other Census Bureau studies demonstrate that this deterioration actually commenced before the Reagan era.[13] As argued earlier, the onset can be dated to the Vietnam War if not the fifties, with further decline during Carter's Administration. Reagan, of course, with Democratic congressional support, sharply intensified the assault against the working and lower middle classes. The 1988 Census Report (Wicker, 1988:A27) crystalizes this trend. Between 1967 and 1987, the poorest one-fifth of American families saw their share of total income reduced from 5.5 percent to 4.6 percent—an 18 percent decline. The erosion for the next 60 percent was from 54.1 percent to 51.7 percent. The top one-fifth experienced a gain from 40.4 percent to 43.7 percent. Much of the last group's gain is accounted for by its upper and upper middle class sectors. Hence "Economic Clips" (Jan./Feb. 1988:16) predicted: "Between 1977 and the end of this year, 80% of all families will have seen their real income decline, while the richest 10% will see their income rise by 18%, and the richest 1% will see a 50% increase."

More dramatic changes (IPS, 1988:36, 38), as suggested earlier by Thurow, have characterized the distribution of wealth (including homes). According to the Joint Economic Committee of the United States Congress, between 1963 and 1983, the share of the top ½ percent (1.4 million persons) increased from 25 percent to 35 percent. For the richest 10 percent of families it rose from 65 percent to 72 percent while declining from 35 percent to 28 percent for the remaining 90 percent. When homes were excluded, the top ½ percent held 45 percent, the highest 10 percent had 83 percent, while the bottom 90 percent possessed 17 percent of the nation's wealth in 1983. And it seems clear that while these trends began before the era of Republican administration dominance in the 1980s, recent policies (Green, 1989:124) accentuated their impact:

> The results? Savings and investment *fell* after enactment of Reagan's tax and budget programs in 1981, and the distribution-of-wealth gap predictably widened. The planned, massive redistribution from labor to capital produced the greatest disparity between the wealthiest fifth and poorest fifth of American families in forty years, as $9.50 in income was added at the top for every $1 lost at the bottom. While the average American worker earned $281 a week in 1983, he or she earned only $276 a week (in constant dollars) by 1988.

The anti-egalitarian offensive has affected minorities and women with a particular vengeance.[14] And it continues under Bush despite "kinder and gentler" rhetoric.

THE UNDERCLASS AND BASIC NEEDS: A HUMAN RIGHTS DEFICIT?

The symptoms of general social decay are quite visible in a broad range of areas. Featured prominently among them is the emergence of a degraded and permanently unemployed underclass. A parallel development is the appearance of the so-called "homeless"—millions of rootless people of all ages living in doorways, subways, bus stations, and abandoned buildings. Hartman (1985:A34) calls our attention to the tragic plight of "outright homelessness, [which] is growing by 10 percent a year, according to conservative estimates by the Department of Housing and Urban Development—the total number of homeless may be anywhere from 250,000 to 2 million." By late 1988, even some conservatives were urging the victorious Bush ("Conservative," 1988:3) to diverge from the outgoing administration's indifference toward the by now "250,000 to 3 million" estimated homeless.

Lerachman (1989:118) attributes the homeless phenomenon primarily to a lack of affordable housing:

> During the Reagan years, Federal support for low- and middle income housing practically ceased, and the homeless population in suburbs as well as cities, in dangerously radical Massachusetts as well as staunchly conservative Orange County, California, exploded. At least 3 million are homeless, including many whole families, few of them out of yearning for fresh air, the hypothesis of good old Ed Meese.

The homeless account for a substantial minority of the approximately thirty-two million Americans who are actually suffering from hunger or undernourishment. These two categories of what economists call "structurally unemployed" join the 20 to 25 percent of the labor force victimized annually by some form of official unemployment as well as those employed at low or recently "rolled back" wages who constitute a rising proportion of the citizenry state agencies (conservatively) classify as impoverished.

Often ignored by those who focus upon the structurally unemployed and the need for job training or "workfare" rather than "welfare" is a change ("Economy in Review," 1988:8) that now distinguishes the United States from most other industrialized democracies. In great measure "the safety net that supported workers was shredded. Cuts in unemployment compensation, food stamps, Aid to Families with Dependent Children, along with the eroding buying power of the minimum wage significantly reduced the cushion workers could fall back on during hard times." The safety net's collapse, or at least its lowering, reflected not only the bipartisan political leadership's desire to divert greater resources to the militarization process, but also a conscious determination to drive "welfare bums" into the workforce and to deter other lower class persons from "going on the dole."

But this determination—and lowering the minimum wage—has made mass impoverishment "structural" or epidemic, for it is clear ("Trends," 1988:12) that:

> Much of the poverty exists among the "working poor." In 1985, more than 9 million working Americans failed to earn enough income to raise their families out of poverty—a 40% increase since 1979. Nearly a third of these workers were employed full-time and year round. Seventy percent of poor minimum wage earners are their family's principal bread winner. A principal cause of rising poverty is the fall in real earnings of low-wage workers....
>
> Eighty-four percent of all current minimum wage earners are over the age of 18. Sixty percent are women and many of these women are the sole support for their chlidren.

Although in 1988 the minimum wage was raised slightly, in real terms it remains below the level of a decade ago. The same applies to future adjustments, as do loopholes for employment.

One of the most salient parameters of low income is malnourishment which is particularly damaging to both intellectual and emotional development for children. Writing a few years ago, Nina George (1985:8) deplored the fact that

> Children often seem to be the hardest hit by Reagan's slashing of poverty programs. Over 14 million of the hungry poor are children, 47% of whom are Black, 38% Latino and 15% white. "If you are under 6 years old in the U.S., you are six times more likely to be poor than if you are over 65," declared Sen. Daniel Patrick Moynihan (D–N.Y.). "We are the first industrial nation in the world in which children are the poorest age group."

Returning to what this poverty means in terms of the "right to life" for these future citizens, a few trends—slowed perhaps but not reversed since then— might be worth further study.

Steffens (1984:18–19) deplores the growth of outright "hunger" since 1980, warning that:

> More children are malnourished. More babies die at birth or during their first year. The Congressional Black Caucus reports that between 1981 and 1982, infant death rates of white and Black infants increased in 13 states and that Black infants are more than twice as likely to die before their first birthday as white infants. The report by Congressman Julian Dixon attributes most of the increase in infant mortality to the increase in poverty and points out that this Administration has made cuts in maternal and child health programs, migrant health programs and Medicaid which have intensified the effects of increased poverty.
>
> A House Committee reports that the number of poor children increased by 2 million between 1980 and 1982 alone: "Today, one of five children and one out of two Black children live in poverty. . . ."
>
> The Census Bureau tells us that 15 percent of the total population or more than 34 million Americans now live below the monthly poverty line of $682 for a family of four. As with all "official" figures, this one grossly understates poverty despite the fact that it represents a 25 percent jump in the ranks of the officially poor since 1980.

We see clearly that the real poverty stricken group is a large minority and may even be a majority today since the 1986–1987 "recovery" hardly touched them. At its extreme, even polls reported by the rightwing American Enterprise Institute's *Public Opinion* magazine—summarized in Figure 19—reveal that in 1984 between one-fifth and one-fourth of the population complained they lacked enough money for food or clothing. Given subsequent trends in real wages and social policy, this situation—despite administration exercises in statistical manipulations—has stagnated at best and will deteriorate with the oncoming (Batra, 1988) recession to levels that surpass the current 20 to 25 percent range.

ILLITERACY AND EDUCATIONAL DYSFUNCTIONS

An even higher proportion are totally or functionally illiterate. By 1989, American Federation of Teachers head Albert Shanker (1988/89:7) was defensively warning that "the national estimated 20 million to 60 million 'functional illiterates' are in the spotlight." Drawing upon a number of inexact yet suggestive studies a few years earlier, Kozol (1985) and Dammerell (1985) estimate that roughly 25 million adults are totally illiterate while close to 35 million are unable to use their language conceptually or even to fill out simple forms. This is also true (NPR, November 2, 1988) for 15 to 20 percent of those leaving high school. All forms of illiteracy, according to the same report, are on the rise. Focusing on the same problem, a recent Pentagon study (Shanker, 1988/89:7) revealed that among "young adults," 47 percent read at the fifth to ninth grade levels while 5 percent were below that.

There is a certain irony in a militarization process that culturally impoverishes those who are supposed to be protected by diverting funds needed for schools and adult literacy programs. Such funcational illiteracy rebounds adversely upon the national security capabilities of the armed forces through damage to equipment by personnel who cannot read or understand manuals. One analyst (Duffy, 1985:438–39) points out that:

> The median reading grade level (RGL) of entering recruits is 9.5 as compared to a national average of 9.6. Approximately 40 percent read below the ninth-grade level and 6 percent below the seventh grade. . . .
> The higher the literacy skill of the personnel the more likely they were to use the [manuals]. At all literacy levels, the performance of personnel who used the [manuals] was better. . . . At a less empirical level, there are reports of multi-million dollar losses in equipment due to failures to either read or comprehend the technical instructions.

As a consequence, the armed forces have found it necessary to demand even more funds for repairing weapons and internal literacy instruction which itself has yet to avoid "multi-million dollar losses" of equipment. Indirectly, mass functional illiteracy also undermines the industrial basis of national security. It likewise helps in understanding the relative and absolute declines in the rate of productivity growth. The preference of Canadian employers for American workers *after* European and Asian may also be suggestive.

Contributing to the growth of de facto illiteracy have been a number of factors, including widely acknowledged deterioration of standards in, and available financing for, public educational systems. For example, funding has been cut for one of the most effective early childhood enrichment motivational programs for underprivileged children—Project Head Start. It has been reported ("What's Next," 1988/89:4) that "currently, Head Start reaches only 16 percent of the 2.5 million children eligible for service. Militarization also has literally devoured resources which could have upgraded the quality of education by paying enough to attract and hold more capable persons as teachers for disadvantaged children most in need. Similarly, funds for both adult education and inner city schools have been virtually frozen or cut back due to reductions in federal aid. Thus for more than two decades since the early 1960s, public schools have been awarding an increasing proportion of diplomas to functional illiterates.

This educational failure is partially—though as the following (Beck, 1988) makes clear, not wholly—a function of national spending priorities that favor even a diminished number of billion-dollar first-strike "stealth" ("The Brave New World," 1988) B-2 bombers, which according to one (Coffin, 1990:3) senator "lacks any essential mission." Beck states:

> The fact that American children and teenagers are consistently outscored in math, science and other subjects by their peers in Japan, Taiwan, China and several European nations should be well known by now. That may seem to be

a matter of only academic interest, worth a few seconds on TV on a slow news night, except that other countries are also beginning to outproduce and out-market us too. Dumbing down hurts in lots of ways.

In many school systems, geography has been mixed with history and melted down into social studies. Social studies has been dumbed down by readability scales for textbooks, processed into "teacher resource packages" and robbed of good writing, excitement, color and any ideas that aren't certifiably "safe." What's left is too simplistic, too gray and too deadening to hold students' attention.

Thus, as in industry, one of the sources of decline is poor managerial (leadership) quality. And with a touch of irony we may note that just as warfare state procurement policies have weakened the discipline of industrial management, so its concomitant "threat inflation" has made public school social studies intolerant of the type of teacher who would dare put "unsafe" questions to students. The ironic upshot is that perhaps even more than college-bound Soviet students, Americans fail to develop critical faculties or even a capability of independent thought. The analytical deficiencies of those "promoted through" secondary schools are so extreme that they cannot hold officials accountable—the essence of any democratic process. During early 1990 ("Lessons," 1990:50): "In what has become a depressing quadrennial exercise, a government-sponsored National Assessment of Educational Progress report indicated that most 17-year-olds cannot read well enough to understand a newspaper editorial."

Indeed, the sharp decline in SAT scores since the early 1960s and their continued (NPR, November 2, 1988) erosion—despite ubiquitous cram courses in how to take the tests—indicate that most secondary students cannot manipulate simple concepts, use their language effectively to convey ideas, or even memorize for achievement tests. Neither available salary levels nor working conditions in repressive school systems are sufficient to attract the more capable university students to teaching.

Within colleges themselves, declining student capabilities were evidenced (Evangelauf, 1985) by a National Center of Educational Statistics survey that found enrollment increases in remedial (i.e., secondary level) courses between 1978 and 1984 at 63 percent of the colleges and universities offering them.[15] Educational decay is symbolized by higher education that is not "higher" and secondary diplomas awarded despite failure to achieve minimum competence for graduation. What this means for youth who do not realize that they are the primary victims of grade inflation and an erosion of standards is pointed up ("Geography," 1985) by a survey at the University of North Carolina (one of America's better state universities):

> [The survey administered a] basic geography test . . . to 1,875 students at the Chapel Hill campus. In their answers, students indicated that the Soviet Union

is between Nicaragua and Panama, that Africa is the largest nation in the Americas, and the world population for 1980 lies somewhere between 100,000 and 238 billion. Nearly 95 percent of the students failed the test.

The Educational Testing Service's (ETS) test of the geographic knowledge of more than 3,000 undergraduates at 185 higher education institutions corroborated the North Carolina findings: the ETS-tested students received a mean score of 42.93 out of a possible 101.

Concerned about the patterns revealed by this and similar tests, the National Geographic Society sponsored a massive cross-national Gallup poll ("Lost," 1988:31) of more than 10,820 persons 18 years and older in the United States, Mexico, Canada, Sweden, West Germany, Italy, France and the United Kingdom.

> Sweden was the second best while the United States was sixth, ahead of the U.K., Italy and Mexico. (Among the Americans, 14 percent could not pick out the United States on a world map. Perhaps Gallup should have included a helpful "You are here" pointer.) And among 18–24 year-olds, Americans finished dead last.
>
> Besides map identifications, Americans were asked questions that relate geography to current events, politics and history. In many instances, the results were poor. Only half knew that the Sandinistas and contras have been fighting in Nicaragua, and that Arabs and Jews were quarreling in Israel. One in three cannot name any of the members of NATO; 16 percent think the Soviet Union is a member of the group.

Fully 20 percent of the American 18–24 group could not locate their own country on a map and (Shanker, 1988:E7) "more than half of U.S. adults couldn't find Japan on a map." Roughly the same proportions couldn't place the United Kingdom or South Africa on a map; nor did the same group know that South Africa "is where apartheid is official policy." Similarly almost a third could not identify a single member of NATO while only a similar proportion knew Poland was a WTO member. "On an outline map [of the United States] the average American could identify fewer than six of ten states."

More ominous, even, than the documentation of pervasive mass ignorance is the secular trend — known for more than two decades — and the inability to reverse it. For the National Geographic Society's Gallup Poll "also reported that young people now had much less overall knowledge of geography than did students in 1947." Similarly, the ranking of Americans as a whole as sixth while the 18- to 24-year-old group placed at the bottom confirms extreme deterioration that is absolute as well as relative.

When and how much deterioration has occurred are open to question. Even in the early 1980s, approximately three-quarters of adult Americans were ignorant of basic security policies, Jay Rosen (1988:4) recalls:

> A May 1982 CBS/New York Times poll showed that, while most of the popula-
> tion said it favored the freeze, only 30 percent knew that Ronald Reagan op-
> posed it, and 59 percent thought that the issues involved in the freeze were too
> complicated for the public to decide. . . .
> A 1984 Public Agenda Foundation study found that 81 percent of Americans
> are unaware that the U.S. has declined to adopt a "no first use" policy.
> Seventy eight percent do not know that it is U.S. policy to use nuclear weapons
> to repel a massive Soviet invasion of Western Europe with conventional
> weapons.

If the educational institutions have been failing to engender even a modest
level of awareness or interest, the deterioration probably began as early as the
Vietnam War era and has only been accelerated during the Reagan era.

Reflecting both the decline of student capabilities and pervasive institutional corruption is the rising number of "colleges" which simply sell degrees.
Thus, the American Council on Education ("List," 1985) has identified "'145
organizations operating now or in the recent past that are clearly fraudulent,'
another 114 organizations 'for which records exist that appear to be legal but
are grossly marginal'; and at least 200 more are ephemeral diploma mills." By
1984–1985, a number of major institutional studies deplored the "crisis" (i.e.,
deterioration) of American education, emphasizing in part the need to end
austerity funding.

At the significant though perhaps less important physical level ("Repairs,"
1988/89:3), the decline in federal aid is manifested by overt decay.

> Leaky roofs, drafty classrooms, outdated laboratories, poorly ventilated
> stairwells, faulty electrical wiring, collapsing ceilings, crumbling courtyards:
> From the granite foundations to the wooden spires, higher education's physical
> infrastructure is decaying.
> Many campuses' comfortably shabby exteriors hide more than absent-
> minded neglect of temporal matters, say experts. Rundown facilities are a sign
> of a ticking time bomb called deferred maintenance, and the price tag for deal-
> ing with the problem in the here and now could come close to $70 billion.

Since public institutions account for three-fourths of those in higher education, this suggests that the bulk of college students from lower middle and
working class homes will be deprived of suitably equipped facilities. Worse
still, they are being exposed to greater risks of bodily injury—and not only
because of "deferred maintenance." "According to the center for the Study and
Prevention of Campus Violence at Towson State University, campus violence
is increasing 10 percent annually." ("Waging War," 1988/89:8.)

Meanwhile a sharply rising proportion of upper middle class children—
and even the children of the better paid public school teachers—are being sent
to private schools and colleges. Although private sector education has been
favored over public institutions by Reagan-era fiscal and social policy bias, it

too has experienced belt-tightening. One approach has been to emphasize programs that "sell" — usually 60 percent narrowly and prematurely vocational. As a recent National Endowment for the Humanities' report ("Students' Interest," 1988:2) demonstrates, the trend has clearly favored such training over education.

> A third fewer students are majoring in the humanities today as compared to 20 years ago — even though the number of B.A. degrees has almost doubled since 1966.
> And the NEH says colleges themselves aren't helping to reverse the trend. It notes that more than 37% of American colleges and universities don't require their students to take history courses, while 62% don't require philosophy and 77% don't require studies in a foreign language.

The rarity of foreign language requirements is particularly revealing for a nation that has imagined itself to be a world leader, let alone a superpower, for almost a half-century. (At a more practical level, the inability of executives to use foreign languages is another important reason why United States corporations fail to compete effectively with linguistically versatile European and Asiatic rivals.)

While premature vocationalism has affected public sector institutions even more than higher status private counterparts, both have resorted to hiking fees for college attendance — this at a time of cutbacks in government financial aid for higher education, which are another consequence of the militarization process — induced fiscal crisis. Thus according to one ("What's Next," 1988/89:4) report:

> Although college costs have risen 49 percent in the last five years — three times the Consumer Price Index — the past eight years have seen repeated attempts by the administration to reduce or eliminate loans for middle-income families. This has also occurred at a time when enrollment of minority students in higher education has declined.

Higher costs have saddled youth with heavy indebtedness and frozen more from the lower middle and working class majority out of the opportunity to complete even a vocational program at a state or junior college. Thus a recent study ("Poor Students," 1988:2) "found that four years after graduation, 88% of the most affluent students had enrolled in post secondary education, compared to 73% of those with medium-high incomes, 57% with medium-low incomes and 42% with the lowest incomes."

Appraisal of these figures requires recognition that lower income youth drop out at all levels of the system at far higher rates than upscale students. Further, they attend inferior colleges whose level often is much lower than a European academic secondary school or gymnasium. A disproportionate number enroll in semi-vocational or teachers' programs whose cost-effectiveness and quality are so marginal that ("What's Next," 1988/89:4) "almost half of new teachers are predicted to leave the classroom within five years." This "waste," of course, may reflect the unprofessional and highly authoritarian administrative practices in many public schools, as well as inappropriate admission criteria and curricula in the teachers' colleges. Both probably are reflected ("Science Faculty," 1988/89:3) by the willingness of secondary schools to employ and expose students to "as many as 60,000 math and science teachers who are not qualified." As with mental institutions, the impoverished public educational sector increasingly resembles a custodial dumping ground for the working and lower middle class majority.

SOCIALLY DESTRUCTIVE YOUTH BEHAVIORAL TENDENCIES

Related social pathologies include a sharp rise in youth suicides which by 1985 had reached (NPR:1985) 6,000 per annum with attempts ranging between 30,000 and 50,000. In a violent society with an estimated 100,000 guns in private possession, it is unsurprising that guns are employed ("Teen Suicide," 1985:7) in nearly two-thirds of suicides by those in the 15- to 24-year age cohort. One psychologist who had studied the youth suicide phenomenon—a 300 percent increase since 1950—attributes it to a rising incidence of divorce or family desertion, increased child abuse, and growing fear of nuclear war. An educational peace researcher (LaFarge, 1988) found ("Political Booknotes," 1988:59) that "vast majorities of children claim . . . [a] fear of nuclear war, and increasing numbers—a third of high school seniors, according to one poll—say they'll perish in one." Another researcher whose work we have already cited, Urie Bronfenbrenner (Rosenfeld, 1988:4) "is one of a small band of child-development experts trying to answer the questions of why the rates of drug abuse, child abuse, teen-age pregnancy, infant mortality [the worst of 20 industrialized nations], divorce [highest in the world] and delinquency in the United States keep going up." Bronfenbrenner

> cites a Finnish study that followed a group of children from ages 8 to 30 and showed instability in a family was the strongest predictor of later anti-social behavior. By instability he meant frequent changes in day care arrangements, or in parental employment, location and schedules.

As noted before, Bronfenbrenner maintains that the rise in the number of working mothers, single parents and levels of poverty have adversely affected child welfare including the instability factor. The consequences of "conservative" assaults upon mass earnings, the welfare state and militarization of resources have combined to aggravate this situation.

By the end of the decade (Barden, 1990:3), a study revealed that due to "drug abuse, financial pressures and a growing number of single-parent families, hundreds of thousands of adolescents are running away or being forced out of their homes every year...." The federally funded research "found that there are about 500,000 runaways and 'throwaways' under 18 each year. They are joining a growing number of homeless youths...." Approximately a million young people, then, including those in institutions or foster homes, lack any sort of intact (even one-parent) family nurturing.

The erosion of youths' well-being is, of course, symbolized by drug usage rates, which again place the United States in the number one position among industrialized societies. According to an official (NPR, January 14, 1988) government survey which certainly understates the incidence, 42 percent of high school seniors reported using illegal drugs during the preceding years. High school seniors are, of course, the primary recruiting base for the armed forces as well as industry.

Given the national security implications of these patterns along with the functional illiteracy of at least 20 percent of high school leavers, another dimension warrants some attention. This pertains to a study by military-sponsored researchers (Rimland and Larson, 1981) who found the decline in the emotional stability and intellectual quality of military enlistees in the 1970s was a result of a parallel decline in the quality of the civilian youth pool from which they recruited. Interestingly, they concluded the emotional and intellectual deterioration was occasioned by the growing toxicity of fetal and infant environments—not only from such substances as lead or other pollutants, but also from increased use by women of cigarettes, alcohol, and a broad range of drugs (tranquilizers, stimulants, etc.). The economically forced entry of many young women into low paying work, frequent changes of employment, high evidence of divorce, poverty and insecurity are highly stressful, often leading to drug dependence.

ENVIRONMENTAL AND OCCUPATIONAL SAFETY: WHENCE THE THREAT?

The political elites' weakening of protective regulation, and budgetary priorities favoring the military sector, have both rendered the environment more toxic to children and adults. Coffin ("The Job Ahead," 1988d:1–2) notes that "the EPA admits that 'one quarter of U.S. lakes, rivers and estuaries remain too polluted for swimming and fishing.'" Not only do such activities occur, but drinking water is also drawn from such sources. Unsurprisingly, then:

> The Center for the Study of Responsive Law, a [Ralph] Nader outfit, finds that nearly one in five public water systems are tainted with chemicals, many of them toxic. Treatment with activated carbon filters can remove at least 87% of the organic chemicals at a cost of 21¢ per 1,000 gallons. The Environmental Protection Agency proposed to demand seration or carbon treatment of contaminated water supplies. When the Reagan Administration came to town in 1981, the EPA withdrew the proposal.

Equally or more baneful is "a May 1987 National Research Council study [which] suggests that pesticide residues in domestically grown food may add an estimated 20,000 more cases of cancer every year. Nearly 80% of the risk is from 15 foods, with tomatoes, beef, potatoes, oranges and lettuce at the top." Ironically this very same chemical intensive "agro-export" development model (Karliner, 1989) is being imposed upon Third World countries.

The foregoing is but the tip of the proverbial iceberg of "structural violence"—institutional policies that needlessly engender premature mortality. By acquiescing in the militaristic right's "shredding of the safety net" on the bottom while simultaneously weakening the shield of protective regulation above, the moderate center has increased not only death but also disease and injury rates. A few more examples will serve to illustrate the shameful trend—a clear affront to the "right to life."

One of the greatest hazards is nuclear and other toxic waste. Yet Coffin ("The Job Ahead," 1988:4) informs us that "the Superfund Law was passed in 1980, but as of last June only 13 sites had been cleaned up and scratched off the list of the nation's 961 most dangerous waste sites." Among these are some with long-life radioactive materials from nuclear warhead component factories operated by the Department of Energy, whose budget under Reagan (Ridley, 1988:484–85) became "more than 60 percent" military-related. "The cost of cleaning up similar contamination at seventeen weapons plants has been put at $110 billion by the D.O.E. which projects that the task will take fifty-seven years." The damage, according to a DOE report (Schneider, 1988:3) made public after the 1988 election, is "much worse than previously admitted."

> The report said that in many instances radioactive and toxic chemicals have migrated beyond plant boundaries and contaminated public water supplies with radioactivity and toxic substances....
> The report described pollution from plutonium, cesium, strontium, PCB, chromium, arsenic, mercury, and a variety of solvents used in producing nuclear weapons. These compounds are known to cause cancer and other chronic diseases in humans and animals, but the report does not quantify the risk....

Very serious health problems have arisen from highly toxic waste sites near military bases. Yet of several hundred, only a handful have been decontaminated. Out of a total of 3700 toxic dumps (PBS, 1988, "Frontline"), the Pentagon claims to have cleaned up 207 while a GAO report puts it at less than a hundred!

Even the Pentagon's own hospitals are becoming death traps. Blaylock (1988:11) reports:

> In the Veterans Administration, we are down to a ratio of 1.5 employees for each patient. That includes everyone from housekeepers, nutritionists, lab

technicians to doctors. For any hospital to get certified in any state today the minimum qualification is 5.5 employees per patient. So that tells you what kind of treatment the veterans are receiving — not because the federal workers in those hospitals don't want to give the care but because the resources have been reduced to the point where they can't give the proper care.

How much infection and premature mortality occur is anyone's guess. What is clear is that incidence of both is high and demonstrates disrespect for those who have served in the armed forces. Yet historically this fits the pattern. For with the exception of World War II (a total — largely civilian — mobilization), a lack of gratitude (Severo and Milford, 1989) and shabby treatment have been the norm for veterans of America's wars.

Just as the corporate sector favors weapons acquisition over personnel expenses, it has also specially targeted two regulatory agencies for impotence. One, the Environmental Protection Agency — created in the 1960s — is a mere shadow of its former self. We have seen the inefficiency in several key health hazard areas. Not only does it inform companies prior to inspections, but Ferguson and Rogers (1985:165) report "a massive recent study of the agency by the Office of Technology Assessment (O.T.A.) confirms [that] enforcement levels have slid to a point where they provide virtually no deterrent to violations of the Occupational Safety and Health Act. The O.T.A. estimates for example, that manufacturers who violate the act can expect on average, a penalty of only $6.50." This would be less a cause for concern if the union movement were strong and growing. There would be an effective alternative to inept government monitoring.

Yet the situation, despite some exceptions, vests authority without real accountability with management. Berman (1988:19–20) informs us that

> in most large industries in the U.S., a military model for the delivery of occupational health services prevails: the company sets the rules and the workers obey, at the risk of firing. The director of safety and director of security are usually the same person, and many company physicians are retired military personnel looking for "easy" jobs with relatively high benefits and fewer of the stresses of normal medical practice. Naturally such persons are reluctant to raise disturbing questions about production practices which might harm the workers' health, and fight tooth and nail against sharing their knowledge and power with the workers they are supposedly trying to protect, despite the 1970 passage of the federal Occupational Safety and Health Act which theoretically guaranteed a limited sharing of information and power over working conditions.
>
> In the nuclear industry, even where workers were organized into labor unions, an iron curtain of secrecy descended over information about the health effects of radiation levels, and it was considered "unpatriotic" or "communistic" for workers or in-house physicians to raise questions about the safety of working conditions.

A recent study (Schmidt, 1988:24) by the Chicago-based National Safe Workplace Institute informs us that:

more workers died in workplace accidents in the 1980's than should have, given
statistical trends of the late 1970's. The report calculates that workplace deaths
declined at an annual rate of 2.2 percent from 1975 to 1980 but have gone down
only about two-tenths of 1 percent a year since then. The report attributes the
difference to what it calls "the failure of the Federal job safety program to keep
pace with the progress of the 1970's" and concludes that 9,115 worker fatalities
that have occurred since 1980 should not have happened if earlier trends had
prevailed.

Job-related injuries and illnesses increased (NPR, October 15, 1988) substantially from 5½ million (79/1000) in 1986 to 6 million (83/1000) in 1987.
Similar consequences have occurred in another area targeted for deregulation
by the right and center, as noted by Peters (1988:8): Major U.S. airlines in 1987
had the highest number of accidents in 13 years and the most deaths in
five years, while commuter airlines had their worst safety record of this
decade...."

MENTAL ILLNESS AND CRIMINALITY

Some might agree that a nation with this record which simultaneously
imagined itself as a model for global leadership and committed future generations to a multi-trillion dollar space militarization boondoggle could be lacking a certain degree of psychological balance. In an earlier chapter, we cited
George Kennan's view that America's anti–Soviet phobia smacked of a
pathological "collective neurosis." The eminent historian Richard Hofstadter
(1965) has dissected "the paranoid style in American politics." It may be no
wonder, then, that a study by the National Institute of Mental Health (Albee,
1985:60) "reported that 19 percent of American adults (43 million people) are
mentally ill." Although, as with all studies, criteria for inclusion may be problematic, it is noteworthy that neurotics were excluded. Inclusion of the highly
neurotic would more than double the percentage. The report's conservatism
is also implied by its official sponsorship. Governments, especially those of a
rightist hue, tend if anything to minimize social problems—that is, unless
those problems can be privatized; i.e., attributed to personal deviance from
traditional moral norms.

I add that these findings are consistent with Figure 20's upsurge in suicide
for almost all white male age cohorts (Coleman, 1985:C1) since the onset of
the Reagan era. For those under 35—black as well as white—the rate has been
rising since 1960.[16] Some of this is probably consequential to increased
economic hardship—induced stress, neglect, and anomie in an ever more
violent culture. Even some pro-military spokesmen, oblivious to their own
responsibility, have deplored such manifestations of social decay. Thus
Republican Senator D'Amato (1984) simulated concern to his constituents by
reporting "two-thirds of American youth try drugs before finishing high
school" while "65,000 to 93,000 children are sexually abused" annually.

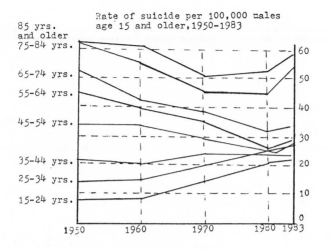

Figure 20. Suicide in white male Americans. Source: *National Center for Health. As reproduced in* The New York Times, *October 8, 1985, p. C1.*

Each year 150,000 children disappear forever.... 20,000 to 50,000 are abducted by strangers and never seen alive again. Some children abducted by strangers are sexually abused, forced into prostitution or child pornography, or murdered.

Many, of course, are assimilated into the closely interlocked worlds of drugs and crime. It is unclear what proportion of these belong to the half-million annual runaways and "throwaways."

Coffin (1988b:3) informs us that "the supply of cocaine, the most commonly abused drug, has grown steadily. The number of drug users in the U.S. remains near its all-time peak." Indeed, a General Accounting Office study reported (Coffin, 1988:1) that in 1987

Americans bought an estimated 178 tons of cocaine, 12 tons of heroin, and more than 600,000 tons of marijuana. Hospitals reported a 167% jump in cocaine-related emergencies from 1983 to 1986. The number of cocaine-related deaths rose 124% during the same period.

Senator Claiborne Pell (D–R.I.) explains the problem: "On the streets of our cities and even in our small towns and rural areas, the price of drugs is down and supply is up. Perhaps 20 million of our fellow citizens have tried cocaine. Five million are regular cocaine users, up to one million of whom are addicts. An additional 500,000 Americans are addicted to heroin."

Even among high school seniors reported illegal usage of heroin and cocaine (Kerr, 1988:5) between 1978 and 1987 remained the same or increased, while that of marijuana, hallucinogens and alcohol decreased. Kerr cautions:

> But statistics indicate and experts say the tale is more complex than it seems from the campaign oratory and news reports. It is a tale of a nation with two drug problems: one that may be getting better for the more affluent and one of accelerating despair and social disintegration among the poor.
> The surveys, however, did not measure drug use among high school dropouts and homeless people and thus may not have accurately measured trends in the underclass.
> Many experts agree that cocaine use in the city's poorest, most troubled neighborhoods appeared to be on the rise, particularly over the past two years with the arrival of crack, the smokable and far more addictive form of the drug.

Even among more middle class seniors in high school, any *reported* drop in cocaine or heroin use is more likely to reflect fear of heightened Bush era repressive intrusion and criminalization policy than behavioral modifications by youth. Indeed, to the extent that Bush's "war" on drugs temporarily diminishes supplies from abroad, it will drive up the street prices and crime rates.

The consequences, of course, are visited upon other citizens who become victims of drug-related crimes. Pell (Coffin, 1988:1) notes that:

> "More than half the criminal cases pending before the courts involve drug-related crimes. It is estimated that the economic costs associated with drug use and abuse in the U.S. could be as high as $100 billion a year in lost productivity, associated health care costs, and the need for increased law enforcement." The National Institute on Drug Abuse claims that one working person in six has a drug problem.

It seems obvious, then, that despite its rhetoric, the corrupt Reagan Administration was less inept in militarizing the budget than in using its resources to confront this problem. Even a conservative like General William E. Odom (1988:22), former head of the National Security Agency, decries the Reagan-Bush team for not being "really serious," and concludes that "against the forces of major narcotics cartels, without a unified approach and the assistance of its intelligence community, the U.S. now looks like a Division III football squad competing in the National Football League."

Without belaboring the point by stressing the high general incidence of crime in America—a phenomenon that also has risen to crisis levels since the early 1960s—we can merely note that for the vast majority of citizens, a sense of personal security and physical safety can no longer be taken for granted. Even more demoralizing than the rampant non-violent criminality (Green and Barry, 1985) of the corporate elite is the acute generalized climate of fear indicated ("Opinion Roundup," 1984a) by the 49 percent of the populace who worry a "good amount" or a "great deal" about their home being burglarized, the 20 percent who have been threatened or shot at with a gun, and the 40 percent who say they have been physically assaulted. Such response patterns antedated the upsurge in homicides during the mid-1980s, which along with a rise in motor vehicle accidents and AIDS fatalities resulted for the first time in a decline in black life expectancy for two successive years. Hilts (1988:3) reports that:

> Recently there has been "a tremendous increase in homicides among both young whites and blacks," he added. But it has hit blacks harder, with a 15-percent increase in homicides among blacks for 1985 and 1986, compared with a 5-percent increase among whites.
>
> Some officials attributed part of the problem to economic policies of the Reagan administration, which they said had increased homelessness, cut aid and health care to the poor and otherwise hurt blacks disproportionately....
>
> It was the first time since 1962 that life expectancy for any race has declined two years in a row, and the only time this century that the life expectancy for blacks has dropped while the figure for whites has risen.

Violent crime has risen despite the impressive 41 percent (NPR, 1984) rise in prison inmates between 1978 and 1983.

By the late 1980s, prison expansion was one of the few dynamic growth areas in the social welfare area. If we look at the period between December 1985 and June 1989, the prison population (Wicker, 1989:4) "increased by more than 6 percent each year, and by 14.6 percent in the first six months of 1989." The number in local jails has risen by more than 6 percent annually over the same period. Thus by 1990, there were an estimated "731,978 in federal and state prisons and 341,851 in local jails—1,055,829 altogether." This represents a 200 percent increase over 1972, when the respective numbers for prison and jail inmates were 200,000 and 150,000. America's incarceration rate has made it number one among industrialized societies.

HOUSING AND HEALTH CARE NEEDS

It is to be expected that the response of militaristic state managers to lower class penal infractions will be coercive. The abysmal conditions of prison existence in conjunction with the generally worsening socio-economic situation for the bulk of the population suggest that further decay may be the most reasonable prognosis. One need only look at the housing situation or health trends for symptoms. Both are integral to any assessment of the quality of life in the modern era.

With respect to the situation for ordinary citizens, the trend has been one of sharp deterioration in the availability of affordable or good quality homes. For working class Americans, reality is vividly conveyed by millions of dilapidated or abandoned apartment buildings that blight urban life. In rural areas, tens of millions have found that only rapidly depreciating mobile homes are affordable as housing. America's housing standards have long since been surpassed in central and northern Europe.[17]

Sharply rising consumer indebtedness in conjunction with the proliferation of low-wage jobs and the postponement of marriage may partly account for the fact ("Did You Know That," 1988:9) that "the average age of first time home owners is now 37, that's up from 32.4 in 1977." Worse, as more youth are forced to rent, Reagan-era tax benefits for condo conversions and total diversion of funds from public housing to militarization have generated a sharp rise in the proportion of income that goes to landlords. Shields (1988:9) underscores this trend:

> Between 1970 and 1983, rents rose twice as fast as incomes. By 1986, the real median income of all renters had fallen 10% from its 1972 level....
>
> Federal housing programs, primary targets of Reagan's henchmen, once offered some reprieve, but no longer. When Reagan took office, the military got seven dollars for every federal dollar spent on housing. As the end of his tenure approaches, that ratio will be 44 to 1. Exacerbating the cuts in public-sector housing programs, the current administration implemented tax and banking policies that discourage the private sector from providing low-rent housing.

In terms of all renters (22 million), more than 37 percent were paying more than 25 percent of their income for rent in 1970. By 1983 ("The Rising Burden," 1988:23), this proportion had surpassed 45 percent. For the end of the 1980s, it was certainly close to 50 percent—given the bias of housing policy and the slump in housing construction. At the same time, the continued fall in real wages forced a growing renting sector to go deeper into debt or subject its consumption to belt-tightening.

The quality-of-life gap for ordinary citizens is equally great and widening in the health area. Navarro (1985:49–50) for example, emphasizes that "by whatever criterion one can think of (infant mortality, low birth weight, life expectancy, etc.), U.S. health indicators do not compare favorably with those of other countries. And the situation is deteriorating in many important areas."[18] We have already discussed the relationship between high infant mortality as well as some other health short-falls and the growth of poverty. Beyond that, the United States is also near the bottom ("Whispering," 1988:4) of 20 industrialized countries in providing health services to another highly vulnerable group—its youth. In the crucial area of family planning, a recent Alan Guttmacher Institute study found that "U.S. teenagers have much lower rates of contraceptive use and much higher rates of pregnancy, childbearing and abortion. The new report shows the same is true among older Americans, notably those in their 20s."

Perhaps the greatest shame is the unparalleled disparity between the quality of health care available to the upper class on the one hand and the 80 percent in America's lower middle, working and underclasses on the other. Despite spending proportionately more — 11.1 percent in 1987 — of the United States GNP on this need, "almost half" of the industrialized nations ("Better Health," 1988:4) boast a superior "general level of health care" according to conservatively biased official data from the United States Health Care Financing Administration. Two decades ago, no more than two or three nations surpassed the United States in general health care, life expectancy, etc. The same pattern appears in related areas. Not only does the United States rank eighteenth ("Determine," 1988:2) in physicians per 1000 population and infant life expectancy, but it stands out as the only modern industrial society without a comprehensive national health insurance system. Commenting on the wastefulness and inefficiency involved, Coffin notes (1988a:1) that:

> Our 1987 bill for health care was $500 billion. . . . Our total health spending is greater than any other nation's both in dollars per capita and as a share of the Gross National Product. Yet all other industrial democracies provide health care coverage to each of their citizens. People in these other nations are healthier, enjoying greater longevity and lower infant mortality.

While it is difficult to determine how much "healthier" the citizens of other industrialized nations are, it is clear that Americans feel (Barsky, 1989:3) they are suffering from more illness than in prior decades:

> polls . . . report *less* satisfaction with our health compared with the 1970s. We are visiting doctors *more* frequently (an average 5.7 times a year for women and 4.4 for men). We complain of *more* symptoms. We report 250% more yearly episodes of acute (non-chronic) illness compared with 60 years ago, despite the intervening introduction of antibiotics — and we are *disabled longer* by these minor complaints.

Whether this reflects the growing toxicity of our environment, rampant hypochondria (40 to 60 percent of complaints cannot be medically diagnosed), or the collective neurosis of an increasingly narcissistic (Lasch, 1979) culture remains to be determined. Certainly it cannot be fully explained by reference to other societies with full national health insurance nor by American coverage increases which still often exclude non-major medical treatment in part or completely.

Fully 15 percent of Americans according to the Census Bureau ("Economic Clips," 1985:14) "lack any kind of health insurance," while most of the remainder have only partial coverage due to deductibles, exemptions and limitations of most policies. Navarro (1985) sees the remedy in a national insurance scheme that would reduce the waste and medical profiteering that characterize the present non-system.

Nowhere is the gap between skyrocketing costs and quality delivery more apparent than in care of the elderly. Quoting from *The Gray Panther Network*, Coffin (1988a:2–3) deplores the fact that:

> Older people now pay [with Medicare] a larger proportion of their income to health care than they did before the program was enacted. Poor and near-poor people devote 25% of their income for health costs.... In many states elderly people must impoverish themselves before getting on Medicaid....
> Other realities: Today, about 1 of ten seniors in nursing homes is receiving skilled nursing care, and Medicare is picking up less than 2% of the tab, according to a government study. The other 99% receive mostly custodial care, providing assistance with dressing, eating, walking, etc.

This of course parallels the situation in most public mental institutions.

Even worse, by the late 1980s, approximately 85 percent of the increasingly corporate dominated United States nursing homes ("Sorry Marks," 1988:92) failed to met minimum standards in all key areas. A study of 15,000 nursing homes, released after the 1988 election, by the Health Care Financing Administration

> found that only 2,300 nursing homes met minimum standards on 32 key measures of the quality of care, from cleanliness and privacy to prompt care of bedsores and proper administration of medication. In addition, the vast majority of homes failed to meet minimum standards on at least one of the 32 requirements. HCFA officials say the standards for most of the 32 evaluation categories were "minimal."

At least 20 percent failed in one or more of the following: rehabilitation (22 percent); contagion (25 percent); medication (29 percent); hygiene (30 percent); food (43 percent). How many die prematurely due to such deficiencies? Even in general hospitals, 27 percent of elderly patients fail to survive due to negligence!

Ironically, the proliferation of such nursing homes has been associated with the closing of generally higher quality hospitals. Brennan and Dooley (1988:15–18) comment that "the *New England Journal of Medicine* reports that between 1980 and 1986, 414 hospitals nationwide closed, resulting in 56,628 less beds and 46.7 million fewer inpatient days." And despite a greater need for nurses, almost a half-million nurses have dropped out of active work partly due to poor working conditions, status and inadequate salary progression (i.e., weak unions). The acute shortage will worsen due to a 25 percent decline in undergraduate enrollments to study nursing associated with the disappearance of government funding for such programs.

Bronfenbrenner (Rosenfeld, 1988:4) concludes: "The industrialized nations that have better numbers for prenatal care, infant mortality, birth weight, maternity leave, day care and so on, all have higher taxes." These of course might be avoided by a reallocation from the Pentagon of major resources that in turn would require a sharp curtailment of missions with perhaps a redefinition of national security so that socialist or radical elements abroad were not defined *a priori* as a threat. The underlying irony is that no real military reduction or tax increase would be needed were such a redefinition to occur. For in that case an allegedly socialist universal national health system that could control the greed of some health professionals and corporations would also be acceptable. The only remaining alternatives would be to further increase tax burdens as well as alienation of ordinary Americans or to increase the already crippling national deficit. Such options, however, would endanger the political and economic foundations of American society.

9. Constraining Third World Socio-Economic Development Prospects

In this chapter I shall briefly look at some of the ways in which American arms and interventionism impair the developmental prospects of many Third World countries. We have already seen in the preceding chapter how the mounting costs of a mammoth global military infrastructure, the quasi-autonomous military-industrial "complex," and the associated economic policies espoused by the transnational corporate sector have weakened the American economy. One serious domestic consequence since the early 1970s was a decline in the historic optimism of ordinary Americans aspiring for higher standards of material and socio-cultural well-being. Militaristic hegemonialism has indirectly contributed to rising mass alienation over the past two decades — a process accelerated under the Reagan Administration.

IMPLICATIONS OF THE "OPEN DOOR" AND THE "FREE MARKET"

Symptomatic of its indirect costs have been the runaway plants that lay off well-paid workers at home to relocate in repressive low-wage and virtually tax-free open door regimes which we saw were the primary beneficiaries of United States aid and comfort. Although historically, control over primary commodities and minerals pricing was the initial object of investment in such areas, increasingly labor intensive assembly operations have been located in Latin American and Asian client states. This also accounts for a substantial portion of United States foreign direct investment, which as we saw in Table 21 includes a very appreciable portion located in developing countries. The sharp rise in foreign investment since the onset of the first Cold War is delineated on Figure 21. The manufacturing proportion has increased markedly as have investments in financial, insurance and commercial activities.

Perhaps because of a desire not to embarrass the gravely weakened AFL-CIO which ironically has actively collaborated with the state and corporate sectors for decades in efforts to impose an open door policy upon developing countries, "vital" or "security" interests in the Third World are seldom defined in terms of the need for cheap labor to exploit in such assembly type manufacturing or processing operations. Similarly, little mention is made of another (Susan George, 1984) trend — investments in agricultural exports including

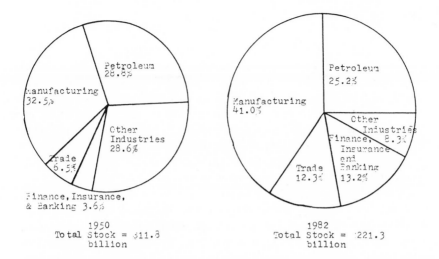

Fig. 21. Distribution of Stock of USDIA by Industry, 1950 and 1982. Source: *U.S. Department of Commerce, BEA. As reproduced in "Investment" (1984: D).*

Commodity	Total Exports ($ million)	Percentage marketed by 15 largest transnationals[a]
Food		
Wheat	$16,556	85-90%
Sugar	14,367	60
Coffee	12,585	85-90
Corn	11,852	85-90
Rice	4,978	70
Cocoa	3,004	85
Tea	1,905	80
Bananas	1,260	70-75
Pineapples	440[b]	90
Agricultural raw materials		
Forest products	54,477	90
Cotton	7,886	85-90
Natural rubber	4,393	70-75
Tobacco	3,859	85-90
Hides and skins	2,743	25
Jute	203	85-90
Ores, minerals, and metals		
Crude petroleum	306,000	75
Copper	10,650	80-85
Iron Ore	6,930	90-95
Tin	3,588	75-80
Phosphates	1,585	50-60
Bauxite	991	80-85

Table 29. Corporate Control of the Global Commodity Trade: 1980. Source: *IPS (1988:49). U.N. Conference on Trade and Development secretariat estimates, based upon extensive research and interviews with traders and marketing specialists. The figures represent orders of magnitude only.* Notes: *(a) In most cases, only 3 to 6 transnational traders account for the bulk of the market. (b) Four-fifths consist of canned pineapples and one-fifth of fresh pineapples.*

vegetables, beef, grain, etc. Produced by impoverished peasants who have been forced from subsistence food plots, these exports have been characterized by unstable prices and declining terms of trade. Thus this emergent "agro-export" model or pattern has contributed not only to the problems of pollution and environmental devastation (Karliner, 1989), but also external indebtedness and malnutrition (George, 1984) in so-called "developing" areas. Indirectly through repressed wage low-priced exports, it has contributed to the growing incidence of bankruptcies and sales by American family farmers to corporations and land speculators—foreign as well as domestic.

Given the domestic political sensitivity of such proliferating investments in Third World branch plants and agricultural commodity production, most American open door rationales tend to focus exclusively upon access to vital minerals (e.g. cobalt, titanium, platinum, etc.) and fuels such as petroleum. In absence of an alternative qualitative rather than growth oriented development model for the U.S., the need for such resources is of course real—as indicated by Table 30. Access (i.e., control) is assumed to constitute a justification for intervention because of national security. For multitudes of uninformed Americans, this in a context of "the Communist threat" becomes a cover rationale for the entire interventionist infrastructure that is targeted against developing countries on a global scale.

Trainer (1989:501) views the interventionism in the context of "a system which invariably functions to deliver most wealth to the rich few," i.e., where one-fifth of the global population consume four-fifths of the planet's "resource output." This inequality "produces much of the violence in the world." In turn, it also requires

> the major beneficiaries of the system, the developed countries and their transnational corporations, to engage in the vast military preparation needed to secure the empire against dissent from within (indigenous revolution) and threat from without (subversion or attack by the USSR, Iran etc.).
>
> *Important for the maintenance of the empire is the reproduction of particular climates of public opinion in the core countries which will guarantee that intervention in the Third World is perceived as legitimate.* As has been noted, the main device employed to this end is the evocation of fear concerning "the Russian threat" whereby any sign of rebellion in the Third World can be attributed to communist subversion and therefore attacked without objection from within the rich Western countries. *This mechanism has been the main factor responsible for the Cold War.*

Whether the eclipse of Moscow's support for Third World nationalism and "socialism" will diminish hostility to the low prices accorded by the "international market" to what is taken out of the South, remains to be seen. If anything, the pressure upon labor and natural resource endowments in the low-income countries is likely to increase unless, as Trainer goes on to argue, they and the industrialized nations forsake market-determined "indiscriminate

	United States		European Community	Japan
	Total Imports Percentage	Imports from Third World Percentage	Total Imports Percentage	Total Imports Percentage
Aluminum	88	63	31	93
Chromium	90	29	100	90
Cobalt	99	50	100	100
Copper	20	10	76	93
Iron	17	9	59	100
Lead	19	11	70	67
Manganese	98	48	99	87
Nickel	72	6	100	100
Phosphates	6	--	100	100
Tin	84	73	87	90
Tungsten	64	35	100	100
Zinc	59	14	73	74
Petroleum (1973)	37	n.a.	98	100

Table 30. Western Imports of Raw Materials (1974). Sources: *Sewell,* United States and World Development *(1977); Hansen,* United States and World Development *(1976: 163), International Economic Report of the President (U.S. Government Printing Office, 1975). As reproduced in Nagle (1985:256).*

growth" approaches to development. Only then will control and the voracious consumption of cheap raw materials or labor not be defined as vital to American "national security" or that of its allies.

The impoverishment of Third World countries is manifested by their escalating indebtedness required in part to offset net capital outflows (Nagle, 1985:248–60) and deteriorating terms of trade. During two and a half decades (1960–1983) of Western and particularly American opposition to commodity production and price agreements, the situation has worsened. According to UNCTAD (IPS, 1988:48) data on 41 primary materials, terms of trade improved for 7, while 16 deteriorated. Even the World Bank, which unlike UNCTAD has been dominated by the United States and other industrialized Western nations, now concedes—"with some very important qualifications"—the "declining terms-of-trade argument." According to its recently published ("Commodities," 1988:1) study:

The new data show ... from 1900 to 1986 a cumulative fall of about 40% in the market prices of nonfuel primary commodities relative to those of manufactured products—and a decline of 36% in the relative prices of all commodities (including fuels). Though substantial, the declines are not as pronounced as those in previous series. Nonfood agricultural product prices fell at the rate of 0.84% a year; metal prices went down 0.82% a year and agricultural food products 0.36% a year....

In the nonfood agricultural category, the trend is clearer.... Non-food product prices fell strongly and steadily in relation to internationally traded manufactured products. Since 1900 the purchasing power of these products in terms of manufactured products has fallen by more than 50%. The slide is particularly apparent between 1953 and 1986.

The report took pains to emphasize that *all* developing countries were not equally or even adversely affected—particularly a small number of fuel and manufacturing exporters (NICs), food importers and those which do not export metals.

That control by the United States over access and pricing of Third World exports is vital to American security is both largely mythological and inherently tautological. First, the very creation of a global military infrastructure and the concomitant arms racing to restore strategic superiority itself requires ever increasing amounts (Hveem and Malnes, 1980) of strategic resources—the ostensible object of this public policy rationale. Second, even though some of these resources are vital to the American economy as now organized, and to a given level of "defense" capabilities, it is equally true that domestic substitutes or alternative resources can be developed to replace imports. America, for example, has a vast coal, natural gas, solar, and shale oil as well as traditional petroleum potential. The cost of some of these may be higher only because the cost of the global military infrastructure to enforce Middle Eastern and other "access" is excluded from calculations. Third, even the USSR during our genocidal (Gibson, 1988) Vietnam intervention was supplying the United States with titanium—a vital component for supersonic bombers. Fourth, with the emergence since the early 1960s of the Soviets and such Eastern European allies as Bulgaria, the German Democratic Republic and Czechoslovakia as major aid givers in the form of factories whose ownership vests in the recipient government, Western transnational corporations have for the first time confronted competition offering developing countries much better terms. Finally, Third World countries have eagerly sought markets in the North for their products. Thus, the real problem is not access but pricing, tax avoidance and suppressed labor costs—all contributing to far higher profit rates on equity investments in the South. These are enhanced even more in the North by (Mokhiber, 1988) the relative immunity of corporations when they knowingly market unsafe products or fail to take adequate measures to safeguard employees, local populations and environments. Further, despite their infusion of technology and capital, the former is often unduly complex or capital intensive (i.e. "inappropriate"), while much of the latter (ca. 85 percent) is borrowed or locally generated rather than constituting a new infusion from developed countries.

Worse, there has been a tendency to acquire or subordinate locally owned "national" firms rather than invest in new facilities. Trainer (1989:490) notes that "approximately 40% of Third World industrial production is now carried out by transnational corporations, which means it is largely unconnected with the needs of most Third World people." Through transfer pricing and other forms of capital flight by the transnationals as well as local supportive elites, the low income countries suffer far more capital drainage than by official profit remissions. Much of the foreign aid has provided the hard currency necessary for capital transfers to the industrialized countries—leaving instead escalating indebtedness and almost half of their populations completely marginated from the development process. That process, when subject to market forces, ignores basic needs while favoring small indigenous elites and especially the rich in the North. Ironically, then, the open door imperative not only denies developing countries a fair return for their labor and resources, but also deprives them of the means to buy more American exports.

But, as I have argued, such damage is seconded by the impoverishment and underdevelopment being imposed upon most Third World countries by dominant military elites committed not only to their own corporate interests, but also to a continuing influx of weapons necessary to suppress movements that might challenge the free market unsustainable growth model. In addition to the exploitation of their natural resources and peoples, the very flow of arms representing the iron fisted underpinning of such asymmetrical interdependence has itself functioned directly to exacerbate the poverty, indebtedness and violence so endemic in these countries. Consider that between 1961 and 1971 alone, official arms imports by the Third World were in excess (Sivard, 1981:9, 16) of $122 billion. In Chapter 2, I noted that between 1973 and 1980, weapons orders adjusted for inflation reached (Klare, 1982:64) almost $200 billion, "an amount that easily exceeds the total value of [all] economic assistance given the Third World countries by the industrialized nations." Pierre (1982:36, 37, 38) echoes Klare's concern by relating this resource loss to absolute levels of underdevelopment and external indebtedness.[1] Figure 22 depicts the latter's portentous acceleration. By 1990, the total—despite some write-offs and debt-equity swaps—surpassed 1.3 trillion dollars. Pertinent findings by more than a dozen researchers (Wolpin, 1983) tend to support Pierre's (1982:38) unduly conservative conclusion that "it is far from clear that channeling funds through defense budgets is a constructive way of pursuing economic development and meeting civilian needs."[2]

Iran and the Philippines represent two poignant "free market" examples of the real human as well as developmental costs of this militarization process. Pearson (1981:26) recalls that the "unrestrained weapons transfers to Iran

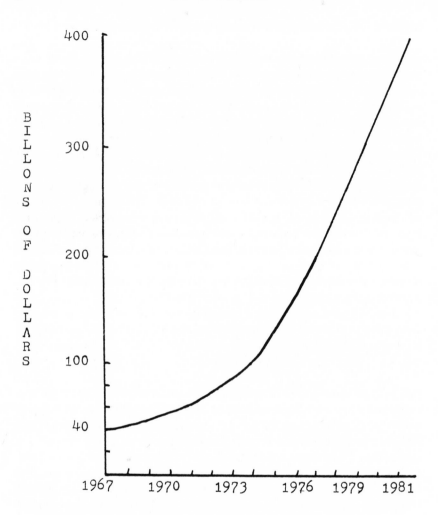

Figure 22. Debt Burden of Non-OPEC Developing Countries. Sources: *Adapted from Sewell,* United States and World Development *and* Spiegel, *Vol. 36, no. 36 (September 6, 1982), West Germany. As reproduced in Nagle (1985:257).*

during the 1970's ... [not only failed] ... to protect the incumbent regime from internal collapse, but they contributed to the revolutionary brew by draining much of the country's revenues from needed internal development programs." The sharp rise in petroleum revenues was recycled back to the North for weapons, luxury consumption and investments by the small comprador bourgeoisie which benefited from the Shah's regime. Between 1973 and 1979, Teheran imported (U.S. ACDA, 1985:108) 10.5 billion dollars in arms.

Zwick (1983:20–23), focusing upon the United States–backed Marcos regime in Manila, emphasizes that the initial purchase price of modern weaponry is often only a fraction of the total life cycle costs, and further that recent coproduction of some arms had transformed but not lessened external "dependence." The need for more foreign exchange to finance not only weapons imports but also imported components and license payments increases government incentives to subsidize exports as opposed to import substitution and domestic food production. Relating this policy bias to prior social conflicts involving unmet popular aspirations in the Philippines, Zwick (1983:25) continues:

> Export promotion further exacerbates this pattern by requiring sufficiently low wages to attract foreign investment, and the vulnerability of the economy to crises in international markets is also heightened. These conditions, in turn, dictate such repressive policies as the outlawing of strikes and demonstrations in the urban areas, increased military presence in the rural areas to quell revolts and protect foreign investments, and increased military control over the civilian population in general. The added costs of these military operations lead to further foreign exchange shortages and the cycle outlined by Luckham is intensified.
>
> It should not be surprising, then, that while the government has established that a family's annual income must be at least 15,000 pesos to lead a "decent life," 83% of all Filipino families earn less than 8,000 pesos per year while an additional 12% earn less than 15,000 pesos annually. Export-oriented industrialization, which is both cause and consequence of militarism, dictates such conditions by requiring low wages both to make Philippine products competitive in world markets and to attract foreign investment.

As Washington stepped up its paramilitary intervention and training of elite counterinsurgency units in the late 1980s, economic analysts (Chase, 1988:4) deplored the corruption and incompetence of Corazon Aquino's "reform" administration. Unsurprisingly, when a military faction attempted to unseat her in 1989, mass sectors were unwilling to demonstrate support for her regime — one now openly subservient to the United States.

In only three decades, a country that was probably the richest in Asia after Japan had become as poor as Indonesia. Neither democracy nor economic progress is served by the mounting costs of poor planning, a landless peasantry and a rich oligarchy. In a country of 56 million, roughly 60 percent of the population lives below the poverty line, which is officially set at $120 a month for a family of six. Corruption — so-called crony capitalism — an underdeveloped agricultural sector, a poor export-oriented industrial base and a crushing debt burden, all contribute to the economic disaster that nurtures the insurgency. Total foreign debt approaches $30 billion. In the budget for 1989, no less than 44 percent of spending was set aside for debt servicing. Thus, as James Chase points out, even massively increased "economic aid is no solution. There is little assurance that it would not find its way into external bank accounts and prove a windfall for the corrupt crony capitalists."

The alternative for the Bush Administration will be to intensify Reagan's resource flow to the expanding coercive apparatus of a "death squad democracy" noted for torture, executions and disappearances. Its agrarian reform loopholes (Wise, 1988) predictably preserve the dominance of large corporate operations thus confirming Albrecht, Lock and Wulf's (1974) view that such "military aid" and weapons are integral to a global structure of North vs. South corporate economic exploitation, a view likewise expressed in a number of studies referred to by Eckhardt (1977:2–16) and Nagle (1985:213–93). Thus we see one of the major functions of the Third World arms imports which according to Sivard (1985:14) accounted for approximately 75 percent ($233 billion) of total weapons imports between 1964 and 1983.

MILITARY AID AND THIRD WORLD MILITARISM: DEVELOPMENT IMPACTS

It is unsurprising, then, that the sharp increase in arms transfers has been associated with or paralleled rising military expenditures, armed forces growth, and higher military-to-population ratios. Thus between 1968 and 1977, Third World military expenditures in constant dollars (USACDA, 1979:27) rose from 54 to 92 billion. By 1983, the figure was in the vicinity (Sivard, 1985:12) of $160 billion, rising to $173 billion in 1985 (USACDA, 1988:43). During the 1970s alone, "Third World nations—some 130 of the world's 161 nations spent more than $800 billion on military forces and munitions" (LaRocque and Goose, 1982:19).

It is demonstrable that the relative burden of arms purchases upon failing economies is growing. Sivard (1985:23) reports that "for the poorest half of the world population . . . the military share of GNP rose from 4.8 perent in 1960 to 5.8 percent in 1982, a burden out of all proportion for countries with yearly [per capita] incomes averaging less than $300." Because of the widespread concealment of military spending we noted in Chapter 2, these percentages may seriously understate the burdens upon their economies for which there are precious few collateral "spillover" (Wolpin, 1983) benefits.

A preponderance of studies summarized by Wolpin (1983:44–55) indicate trade-offs between high military burdens and economic growth or social welfare. Illustrative of this type of "substitution effect" analysis (Power, 1983:4) is the following:

> Laurie Taylor of the Massachusetts Institute of Technology studied the economic performance of 69 developing countries in the 1950s and 1960s. She concluded that for each 1 percent increase in the military's share of a given country's gross national product, the proportion of the GNP spent on industrial investment fell by 23 percent.

Although some studies do fail to identify such tradeoffs, they represent a small minority and generally involve low or moderate rather than high military expenditure levels. The latter adversely impact not only investment and economic growth, but also health, education, and employment. Arms spending for weapons imports exacerbates unemployment by diverting funds from more labor-intensive activities. Except for a few items, even licensed domestic arms production employs imported capital-intensive technology in regions where between a fourth to a half of the population are unemployed partially or totally. Ball (1988) provides an incisive analysis of pertinent research.

MASS AUSTERITY AND THE DEVELOPMENT CRISIS

Sivard (1985:27) points out that "among youth, which represent the largest proportion of the jobless (at least 40–50 percent of the total), increasing alienation has led to a sharp increase in outbreaks of violence in the cities, and rising crime rates." She calls our attention to the fact that while in 1983 only 31 million workers in OECD countries were unemployed (three times the rate a decade earlier), ILO estimates for the Third World countries were 500 million "unemployed and underemployed." More ominously "a sample of 21 developing countries indicated that the number of unemployed has more than doubled in one decade."

For most workers, there is neither (Nagle, 1985:268) unemployment compensation nor welfare as a safety net against destitution, which according to Sivard (1985:26) afflicts one billion people. At the same time, these underdeveloping countries forego immense potential production of goods and services which gainful employment could generate. And while conscription may reduce short term unemployment, for the most part this adds one more unproductive burden upon the remaining population. For very few armies produce even part of the food they consume, let alone the other resources they require.

Other investigations emphasize the relative impoverishment of particular groups or types of developing countries. Trainer (1989:484) points out that

> The few World Bank figures available indicate that half the Third World's income goes to the richest 1/5 and the poorest 2/5 receive about 15%. This suggests that the world's poorest 520 million people average annual incomes of $87, and that over the 20 years of the boom these incomes increased annually by about 73 cents....
>
> African GDP per capita fell 11% between 1980 and 1985, and in the Middle East the fall was 19.2%. UNICEF reports 10–15% falls in living standards between 1983 and 1987, and worsening welfare indicators in the 32 poorest countries.

The same author concedes that some "development" has occurred, but concludes that it has been skewed towards the rich rather than the basic needs of 40 to 60 percent of the citizens in such countries.

Looney and Frederiksen (1983:633, 643) "hypothesize that relatively poor countries tend to cut back high-growth development expenditures in favor of maintaining defense programs, while relatively rich countries are much less likely to abandon development expenditures given a constant level of defense

	Scientists and Engineers			Physicians and Surgeons			Teachers			Total		
	United States 1962-72[1]	Canada 1963-72	United Kingdom 1964-72	United States 1962-72[1]	Canada[2] 1963-72	United Kingdom[3] 1964-72	United States 1962-72[1]	Canada 1963-72	United Kingdom 1964-72	United States 1962-72[1]	Canada 1963-72	United Kingdom 1964-7
Asia	35,708	6,132	3,239	16,239	8,792	11,628	NA	5,055	8,818	51,947	19,979	23,685
Africa	2,334	523	1,035	912	302	3,845	NA	501	5,296	3,246	1,326	10,176
Latin America	6,974	207	1,402	5,704	199	495	NA	159	496	12,678	565	2,393
All Other Developing Countries	3,226	3,784	2,708	2,187	6,622	13,499	NA	5,377	7,967	5,413	15,783	24,174
Total, Developing Countries	48,282	10,646	8,384	25,042	15,915	29,467	NA	11,092	22,577	73,284	37,653	60,428

preparedness. Thus we should expect a negative relationship between defense and growth in the poorer countries but a positive relationship in the richer countries." And their cross-sectional regression analysis of 37 developing countries was consistent with this hypothesis. "Countries suffering from a relative lack of foreign exchange and government revenues, on the other hand, experience the reverse. For these countries defense expenditures apparently siphon funds away from more productive domestic investments with a subsequent detrimental effect on growth."

During the first half of the 1980s even richer Third World countries including some OPEC members experienced acute foreign exchange shortages and sharply diminished growth rates. Stagnation, inflation and a massive brain drain depicted in Table 31 have—along with practices of expatriate investors—impeded the technology transfers necessary to stimulate an economic takeoff in all but a handful of semi-peripheral cities and countries. (Singapore, Hong Kong, South Korea and Taiwan have benefited from unusual circumstances.) Trainer (1989:487–92) argues cogently that natural resource limits and environmental constraints, as well as the 80 percent of global resources consumed by the North, preclude most Third World countries from successfully imitating the North's indiscriminate growth model.

Yet efforts to pursue that model were imposed upon bankrupt Third World governments by the IMF and World Bank (Stevenson, 1989) during the 1980s. Not only has this exacerbated growing social inequality (Nagle, 1985:283–87), but by 1989, external debt servicing was forcing many of the poorest nations to sharply cut back their previously inadequate nutrition, housing, health and education programs. According to a UNICEF (NPR, December 20, 1988) study, monthly child mortality consequently rose by 500,000 for countries that were now "sliding backward."

The gravity of these adverse socio-economic effects was pointed up by the United Nations Group of Governmental Experts on the Relationship between Disarmament and Development (UNSG, 1982:25) who warned of "the large and widening gap in standards of well-being between developed and developing countries." Similarly in terms of per capita income growth, Sivard (1981:20) notes that "in absolute terms, the gain since 1960 has been over ten times more for developed countries, $3,600 in constant dollars, as against $240 for developing." As Table 32 indicates, the per capita income gap between these two regions has been widening for nearly three decades. This despite a slightly higher rate of growth in the South. Other data (Nagle:272) project the same trend into the twenty-first century.

Opposite: *Table 31. The Brain Drain from Developing Countries to the United States, Canada, and the United Kingdom, 1962–1972.* Source: *Adapted from ILO (1976), p. 130. As reproduced in Nagle (1985:282).* Notes: *(1) Excluding 1970. (2) Includes dentists, graduate nurses, medical and dental technicians. (3) Doctors, dentists, and nurses. NA = Not available.*

	Population (1976, Millions)	Annual Population Growth Rate Percentage (1960–75)	GNP/Capita Growth Rate Percentage (1960–75)
Mexico	62.3	3.5	3.2
Brazil	110.2	2.9	4.3
Nigeria	64.7	2.5	3.4
Kenya	13.8	3.2	3.2
Egypt	38.1	2.5	1.5
India	620.7	2.3	1.3
Indonesia	134.7	2.2	2.4
Averages			
Third World		2.7	2.3
Liberal Democracy		0.9	3.7
Communist		1.2	4.0

Table 32. *Third World Population and Economic Growth.* Source: *World Bank Atlas (1977). As reproduced in Nagle (1985:242).*

Austerity and hopelessness are generally experienced by part (albeit 60 to 80 percent) but not all of each population. Only a small oligarchic sector – in large measure linked to transnational capital – manages to benefit from existing structural dependency patterns. This failure of the open door or free market diffusion model in conjunction with superior socialist socio-economic performance at low levels of development, explains the endemic and continuing appeal (Wolpin, 1983; White, Murray and White, 1983; USSR, 1985) of socialist mobilization systems or models in such impoverished underdeveloping areas. While United States–aided "low-intensity" (yet highly disruptive) warfare – backed by major economic sanctions – against Nicaragua, Angola, Cambodia and Afghanistan induced these governments to "moderate" their immediate goals in the late 1980s, this trend is best viewed as short-run pragmatic adjustment. Hence the functionality of American arms and induced militarization along with other instrumentalities (Nagle, 1985:295–304) in deterring breakouts from the existing structure of transnational corporate domination.

The overthrow of Panama's General Noriega resulted from his growing independence vis-à-vis U.S. determination in the 1986–1987 period to create a pretext for invading Nicaragua. Previously his well known drug dealings, like those of other imperial collaborators, were overlooked and even protected for years by Bush and other (Morley and Byrne, 1989; Johnson, 1989; Buckley, 1990) high "national security" officials. Unsurprisingly then, those installed to head the new post-invasion regime were and are heavily involved or linked to (Labaton, 1990:1, 6) narcotic money laundering operations for druglords.

In other cases, U.S.-backed sanctions against nationalistic regimes of an equally mild genre have actually increased government tolerance of drug production and export. Lee (1988:505) notes that:

> In Peru and Bolivia, traffickers who repatriate hard currency are protected by government decree from tax penalties and to some extent from criminal investigation. Such money now replaces the international loans which are no longer forthcoming from commercial bankers. Peru's nationalistic economic policies exclude it from receiving loans from any international sources, and Peruvian banking officials make no secret of their view that cocaine dollars partially substitute for foreign investment and bank loans.[16] In an apparent effort to draw in more cocaine dollars and to keep them in Peru, the government has overvalued the local currency (the INTI) and provided high INTI interest rates for depositors. In sum, drug dollars create pockets of prosperity, stimulate certain industries, stabilize the currency, and help finance exports. Were the industry suddenly shut down, economic chaos would reign in Bolivia and Peru, and possibly in Colombia too.

Thus it can be said that the disastrous economic consequences of dependency and financial bankruptcy in the 1980s have created an irresistible incentive to generate foreign exchange by exporting whatever is in high demand on the "free market." Even here, however, rising Third World exports of cocaine suffer the same fate as do others. For Lee (1988:501) adds that "Cocaine wholesale prices in the United States dropped from $55,000 per kilo to $15,000 in mid-1988."

The global significance of the widening gap between industrialized and dependent capitalism in terms of premature mortality or what Kohler (1978:7) defines as "structural violence" is delineated in Table 33.

> "Structural violence" is a term used in contemporary peace research and is to be distinguished from armed violence. . . . [S]tructural violence is violence exerted by situations, institutions, social, political and economic structures. Thus, when a person dies because he/she has no access to food, the effect is violent as far as that person is concerned, yet there is no individual actor who could be identified as the source of this violence. It is the system of food production and distribution that is to blame. The violence is thus exerted by an anonymous "structure." The measurement of the number of persons killed through structural violence uses statistics of life expectancy. By comparing the life expectancy of affluent regions with that of poor regions, one can estimate how many persons died in a poor region on account of poverty and poverty-related conditions (e.g. lack of doctors, clean water, food, etc.), which can be interpreted as "structural violence."

Little improvement seems to have occurred even during the late 1960s when the North was relatively generous in providing large doses of "aid" to the South. Nagle (1985:293), for example, cites a study by a scholar (Hoivik, 1979) at the International Peace Research Institute, Oslo. Using 1970 data, "Hoivik's

A.   Estimated world totals, 1965 Deaths from:

	international violence	11,500-23,000
	civil violence	92 000
	structural violence	14,000,000-18,000,000

B.   Distribution of violent deaths, 1965   (World = 100% in each
                                            category)

Affluent 'North'	population	30.6%
	international violence	9.1%
	civil violence	.1%
	structural violence	4.2%
Poor 'South'	population	69.4%
	international violence	90.9%
	civil violence	99.9%
	structural violence	95.8%

Table 33. The Inequality of Global Violence. Source: *Gernot Kohler and Norman Alcock. "An Empirical Table of Structural Violence."* Journal of Peace Research, *12:4 (1976): 345-349. As reproduced in Kohler (1978:8).*

figures indicate that over 18 million human lives are lost each year through systematic inequality of access to basic diet, housing and health needs." Regional breakdowns were as follows: Europe, 90,000; North America, 90,000; Japan, 20,000; the USSR, 100,000; Latin America, 800,000; Africa, 3 million; and the Third World areas of Asia, 14 million.[3] The linkage between so massive a denial of human rights or the "right to life" and underdevelopment is obvious.

Of equal importance is the destitution associated with enormous social inequalities which deny access to basic needs. Illustrative is the estimate (Sivard, 1985:27) that contemporary "deaths related to hunger and starvation average 50,000 a day." What we may name the "Canvas of Preventable Citizen Mortality" is painted in broad strokes but with a keen eye for the particular by Geras (1983:105):

> 40,000 children die every day; ... of the 122 million born in 1979, 17 million (nearly 14 percent) will die before they are five; between 350 and 500 million people are disabled, the major cause of this being poverty: about 100 million have been disabled by malnutrition; ... 180 million children are not getting enough food to sustain health and minimal physical activity: protein deficiency, which can lead to mental retardation, affects 100 million under five in developing countries ... over half the people in the third world have no access to safe water and ... water borne diseases kill some 30,000 people every day and account for about 80 percent of all illnesses: every year 400 to 500 million are affected by trachoma and 6 million children die of diarrhea ... in the tin mines of Bolivia a miner's life expectancy is reduced to 35 because of silicosis and tuberculosis; ... 375,000 or more people in the third world will this year be poisoned by pesticides....

Eckhardt (1977:7–14) in turn, drawing upon the work of Alcock and Young, concludes that Western "economic imperialism contributed to the structural violence of poverty."[4]

Although noting that for the 1970s "up-to-date" global estimates of structural violence are not available, Kohler (1978:8–9) suggests that

> (a) The world total of deaths due to structural violence seems to have declined slightly despite the rise in world population. It can be assumed that the distribution of fatalities between the North and the South remains as unequal since 1965 as it was in 1965.
>
> (b) The world total of deaths due to large-scale armed violence, both international and domestic, does not exhibit a steady trend but fluctuates considerably from year to year and period to period. Between 1965 and 1976, a peak was reached in 1971 when the Pakistan-Bangladesh-India war and the war in Vietnam sent the annual world total of deaths in this category to about 1.5 million or more. From 1973 to 1976, the corresponding world figure may have been around 100,000 deaths, with the inequality between the North and the South remaining undistributed.

During the decline of detente for a decade from 1977 to 1987, it is quite probable that war casualties exceeded the levels of Kohler's years. At least that is the inference which may be drawn from LaRocque and Goose (1982), Kende (1983) and other references to Third World warfare that are discussed in the following chapter. Similarly, the debt-induced austerity of the eighties may have reversed the "slight" decline in structural violence estimated by Kohler for the 1966–1976 decade. Figures cited by Hoivik and Sivard in the preceding paragraph appear to be inconsistent with Kohler's optimism. So are the IMF/WB imposed reductions in social spending and food subsidies (Stevenson, 1989) of the early 1990s.

THE COMPLICITY OF INDIGENOUS ELITES

Given the pivotal role of military "aid" (Wolpin, 1973, 1983; Chomsky and Herman, 1979; Parenti, 1984; Nagle, 1985:296–304) and weapons sales in perpetuating repressive, structurally violent regimes, the question arises whether responsibility for this flow is shared by elites in peripheral as well as core states. Although it is clear that destitute mass sectors in the South are harmed by dependency to a far greater extent than their counterparts in the North, we should not equate their victimization with the more subtle psychological humiliation of military and civilian oligarchies who govern Third World politics. It is obvious that regimes which are subservient to transnational corporate interests do need considerable quantities of small arms to suppress movements for revolutionary social change. Further, there are non-rational prestige motivations enhancing the attractiveness of ultra-sophisticated aircraft, etc. At best, then, such gold-plated extravagance may reflect the fact that, as Ungar (1985:32) put it, "poor countries sometimes buy advanced weapons for the same reasons that the poor in the United States buy Cadillacs: They are expensive to maintain and they may soon fall apart for lack of maintenance, but they make the owners feel good in the meantime."

A number of analysts have attempted to discern whether rising arms imports are primarily a result of "push" (external) or such "pull" factors. In Chapters 6 and 7 respectively, Gauhar (1982) and Smalldone (1983:209–211) — the latter citing several quantitative studies — recognized the salience of "pull" factors such as growth in energy and economic output. Yet Gauhar also vehemently denounced the role of "arms merchants," while Smalldone highlighted the primacy of United States politico-military interests (i.e., "push" factors) for American transfers to Africa.[5] This apparent contradiction is easily reconciled. Overall growth or wealth governs ability to finance higher total arms imports. Yet the U.S. was actively endeavoring — especially under Reagan — both to supplant traditional allies (e.g. France, Britain) and to increase the absolute volume of arms exports to Africa. The same may be said of the Middle East — an historic Anglo-French sphere of influence. Aronson (1985) records:

> From 1978–82 the U.S. transferred more than $14 billion in arms to the Mideast — 50 percent more than was sold to NATO countries and more than twice as much as was sent to Asia. Israel topped the list with $4.4 billion, followed by Saudi Arabia with $3.5 billion, Iran with $3.1 billion, Egypt with $1.5 billion and Jordan with $850 million. Arms purchased but not delivered assure that the arms pipeline will run at full capacity for years to come.

During the first two post–World War II decades the United States imposed itself as the dominant supplier first in Latin America and then, excepting two or three countries, in Asia. The Middle East followed in the late 1960s and particularly the 1970s, with Africa's incorporation only in the 1980s. This ill-fated drive for global dominance has meant that certain military establishments under the effective control of "unfriendly" (i.e. independent) governments could not receive American weaponry. Beyond that constraint, there has only been the understandable Pentagon interest in being the first to obtain new top-of-the line systems.

As we saw, neither human rights violations nor a recipient country's mass destitution has limited the drive to export arms. Chapters 3 and 4 also made clear that repressive anti-radical regimes had been favored recipients of arms transfers. Underlying the great impetus and partially explaining fluctuations in arms exports over time are the increasingly hegemonic interests of the military-industrial state-within-a-state discussed in Chapter 6. Indeed, in contradistinction to its major allies whose military-industrial complexes are less autonomous or dominant, the United States, as mentioned in the preceding chapter, is distinguished (Smith, Humm and Fontanel, 1985) by an inverse relationship between arms exports and military expenditure (rates of increase as well as actual levels). Put differently, when there is an upsurge in domestic procurement, pressure is eased for the taxpayer-subsidized expansion of Third World markets. With restraints (since 1987) or cutbacks (the 1970s) in the former, the arms merchants direct their profit-maximizing energy flow to the South. Whether Third World peoples can afford to import more weapons is seldom if ever a criterion since credits or loans can postpone the day of reckoning. Nor is the intensity of repression or eclipse of civilian rule a consideration. Further, such criteria are inoperative as constraints regardless of whether arms exports are rising breathlessly as they did during the 1970s, or tapering off as they did under Reagan when the massive 1981–1986 diversion of domestic financial resources (via civilian program cuts and deficit expansion) took up the procurement slack.

REPRESSION AND MILITARY DOMINANCE

Interestingly, if we look at global data (USGAO:1982) on four United States arms transfer–related activities (Foreign Military Sales Financing Program, Licensed Commercial Exports, Military Assistance Program and the International Military Education Program), a revealing pattern emerges.[6] I compared only countries which Sivard (1982) classified as high or low in repression, contrasting those which manifested only decreases in all such programs with others characterized by increases in at least three of the four programs. The base figure was the FY1979–FY1980 average. It is clear from Table 34 that Third World recipients of increased arms transfers were considerably below those whose programs were being reduced on Sivard's (1982) global ranking of socio-economic standing! Further, a majority of those in the increasing category were military-dominated according to her classification, while a majority in the decreasing category were civilian-governed. Thus those least able to afford increased arms imports and generally more repressive military regimes were slated for higher arms transfers by Reagan.

This points to another trend that has accompanied growing arms transfers—the rising proportion of military-dominant systems in the developing areas. Between 1960 and 1980, their share increased (Wolpin, 1983:2) from about 13 percent to 43 percent. By 1985, Sivard (1985:25) calculates "the count had gone up to 57 military controlled out of 114 independent governments."[7] Nominally civilian government such as those in the Philippines, South Korea and Honduras are frequently subject to policy veto by the armed forces—a veritable state-within-a-state. For example, Ungar (1985:32, 33), prior to bemoaning the fact that "as many African countries become steadily poorer, their military budgets become more bloated," points out a more fundamental dilemma:

> Even in relatively prosperous African countries under reasonably stable civilian rule, such as Cameroon and Kenya, military expenditures represent a

High Repressiveness	Decrease Only		Increase***	
Military Dominant	1979 Rank**		1979 Rank	
	Bolivia	91	El Salvador	82
	Iraq	56	Guatemala	86
	Syria	75	Haiti	122
	Afghanistan	136	Honduras	92
	Libya	39	Turkey	75
			Pakistan	118
			Thailand	86
			Somalia	123
			Zaire	114
				-
Civilian				
	Iran	69	Colombia	68
	India	115	Peru	72
	South Africa	65		
Average Rank		81		94
Low Repressivenesss Civilian*				
	Cyprus	37	Ecuador	64
	Qatar	31	Portugal	41
	Mauritius	62	Oman	73
			Botswana	84
			Zimbabwe	99
Average Rank		43		87

*Table 34. United States Arms Transfer Increase or Decrease for FY 1979–1983 with Repressiveness and Socio-Economic Ranking in 1979. Sources: Sivard (1982: 17,30–32): U.S.G.A.O. (1982:5–13, 23–25, 28–31, 88–93). Notes: *There were no military domi-nant systems in this category. **Average ranking of 140 nations for GNP per capita, education and health. The indicators "chosen for education and health represent both input of national effort (e.g. public expenditures, teachers) and output (e.g. literacy, infant mortality)." ***An actual or projected increase in at least three of the following four programs: Foreign Military Sales Financing Program; International Military Educa-tion and Training Program; Military Assistance Program; Commercial Exports Licensed Under Arms Export Control Act.*

growing percentage of national budgets, and the arms trade composes a sig-nificant part of the nation's commerce with the outside world. Indeed, it is now a given of African politics that whatever the nature of a government, it cannot survive unless it keeps its military happy. It cannot convince its people that it is truly in charge unless it can stage frequent, ostentatious displays of elaborate modern military equipment.

Even in Latin America, where armies have been traditionally subservient to the property owning upper classes, an autonomous tendency has emerged in recent decades — reinforced by United States or Israeli weapons and training em-phasizing unique "national security" missions for the armed forces. Lernoux (1988:556) notes that in Guatemala, where the armed forces have endeavored to obliterate Mayan cultural institutions in a savage campaign, the military no longer views itself as an agent of the upper classes but rather as an equal and potentially more powerful partner. In a more indicative reflection of its new status, the military forced the country's large landowners and industrialists to accept a tax reform in 1987, arguing that the oligarchy owed the 40,000-man army a "security debt," for saving it from the guerrillas. Defense Minister Hector Gramajo put it succinctly during a meeting with Guatemala's industrialists and large landowners: "You people have been using us to kill your Marxists for the past 400 years."

This should not obscure the propensity of high-level officers during the past decade to become large landowners themselves by seizing indigenous lands nor their traditional appetite for wives from oligarchic families. ("Marry up" is an ancient and ubiquitous military maxim.) Underlying their contemporary systemic autonomy, however, has been the vast buildup of their coercive resources since the CIA sponsored overthrow of Guatemala's last freely elected government in 1954. At that time, President Arbenz had dared to propose a serious land reform that would have expropriated uncultivated fields of the United Fruit Company and similar lands owned by the oligarchy.

Two Rand Corporation experts, Ronfeldt and Sereseres (1977:24), are both advocates of arms transfers and "corporativist" style regimes, but they nevertheless concede that "some MAP and FMS programs, especially in regard to schooling and training, may have inadvertently contributed to the [Latin American] trend toward dictatorship." Wolpin (1973) found less "inadvertence" by Washington insofar as its anti-nationalist (i.e. pro–open door) political indoctrination of Third World officers was concerned, and moderately pronounced rightist global effects for countries with a high proportion of officers trained. Pierre (1982:38) in turn observes "that many of the military governments have proved to be grossly inept in handling economic problems." They have been found by numerous analysts (Wolpin, 1983, 1983a) to be more repressive, less responsive to mass welfare needs and in some though varying degree to be associated with lower economic growth rates.

THE DIFFUSION OF WEAPONS MANUFACTURING

Two additional trends which adversely affect Third World development prospects have become more pronounced since the early seventies. First there was a shift (emphasized in Chapter 2) from military grant aid to cash or credit sales. This has contributed significantly to the escalation of external indebtedness. So has the trend toward licensed arms and munitions production in the Third World. As in the previously discussed Philippine case, such local manufacturing has in most instances replaced import dependency with licensed technological dependency while often (Tuomi, 1983:155) making such weapons *more* rather than less costly.[8] Among approximately 24 Third World countries manufacturing or assembling weapons, only a handful export significant quantities—Brazil, Israel, Singapore, and South Africa. Of these "Brazil and Israel account for approximately two-thirds of all Third World arms exports ... Libya and Saudi Arabia are the main 're-exporters.'" LaRocque and Goose (1982:21) go on to note that Israeli sales are at the level of about a billion dollars with Brazil's twice that. Referring to the experiences of India and Israel, Wulf (1979) stresses that:

> Producers in underdeveloped countries are entirely dependent ... on licenses and technology whenever technologically complex arms are to be produced and exported. The two most ambitious arms production programs in the periphery, those of India and Israel, prove that either intensive government subsidies and incentives for foreign investment have to be made (with all the negative side effects on the whole economy) or exports remain negligible.... The burden placed on the societies will, however, hardly be compensated by aggressive export strategies. Rather internal conflicts will be exacerbated.... [E]mpirical results prove that, due to technology transfers from industrial countries, [nationalistic] expectations were not met. Additional aims of both industrialization and indigenous arms production like saving hard currency, enlarging the qualified work force, creating new jobs, and spin-off effects were likewise unattainable. Instead difficulties in utilizing installed production capacities emerged....

For most of these developing nations, then, there is continued dependency and higher costs are imposed upon civilian sectors resulting in a transformed widening mass welfare gap with the North. But domestic production often does lessen (Looney, 1989) imports, and China, which joined Brazil as a major Third World exporter in the late 1980s, may have escaped (Brzoska, 1989:515–17) higher costs. The same can be said for Brazil and South Africa.

Yet these few are but partial exceptions to the pattern. For the quasi-bankrupt financial condition of a significant and rising proportion of heavily indebted developing nations will itself reduce their ability to transcend pre-existing or new military dependency relationships. Looking at Africa and certainly overestimating the relevance of petroleum exports (Nigeria, Egypt, Algeria and Angola are burdened with immense debts) as well as "defense" needs, Arlinghaus (1983:226–227) observes that

> the financial dependency of African states ... will continue to determine the pattern and scale of conventional arms transfers in the region. Since they cannot meet their own perceived defense needs without arms, yet cannot afford to purchase them on a cash basis (comparable to most Middle Eastern nations), they will be forced to acquire arms from those states able and willing to grant them military-sales credits. Although the non-oil producing African nations might prefer to purchase Brazilian or other nonaligned arms, they will most likely be forced in most instances to make their purchases from the more traditional suppliers, East and West.
>   In addition, these simple facts of international financial life will reinforce supplier-nation confidence in the ability of arms transfers to influence African nations. Since the demand for arms is so great, even in the face of enormous

political and economic costs, the supplier nations must respond. Any attempts to limit arms sales to Africa will be interpreted as a lost opportunity to influence a region.

His deterministic frame of reference assumes the neo-colonial hegemonialism which was viewed in Chapter 7 as the crucial underpinning of American arms exports and military aid. The major catalysts and primary beneficiaries of this imperial drive are the transnational corporations whose operations extend to the Third World. They in a growing number of instances have also begun to market weapons and military technologies. In this way, as well as through interlocking directorates (Domhoff, 1967; Dye, 1983), the corporations have become closely linked to traditional military contractors.

CAPITAL OUTFLOWS AND RECYCLING

What should be underscored here is that historically military dependency is associated (Albrecht, Lock, and Wulf, 1979; Kaldor, 1981) with economic dependency. Insofar as ties with Western industrialized or core nations are concerned, this economic dependency, as noted in Chapter 6, has involved net outflows of wealth. Transnational corporate profit remissions in conjunction with adverse terms of trade, less generous (i.e., "concessional") economic aid and Third World economic slowdown since 1979 have contributed to an enormous growth of external indebtedness. That indebtedness, as I have argued, is further exacerbated by escalating arms transfer and licensed co-production costs. Weapons and related imports alone have, according to the highest officials in both the IMF and World Bank ("Third," 1989), accounted for about one-third of the South's 1.3 trillion dollar external indebtedness.

Finally, capital flight may well explain another third of the debt albatross. Though often ignored in discussions of the world financial crisis, there has been a massive export to the North of several hundred billion dollars in capital by indigenous military and civilian elites during the past three decades. Some of these funds are banked in numbered Swiss accounts or recycled to the United States or other advanced capitalist countries for safekeeping or speculative investments. This flow of funds to the North constitutes a capital drain that parallels the brain drain and deepens the South's financial crisis.

The loss is grossly enlarged as a consequence of corruption that is furthered (Nagle, 1985:319–23) by transnational corporations in order to enhance the return on their own investments. Arms exporters are among the most prominent beneficiaries and sources of such speculation. After recounting many "scandals," Sampson (1977:286–287) concludes:

> In the industrial countries, Lockheed and Northrup appear to have wasted a good deal of their slush funds. But in the Third World, the bribes have been much more important, as the means not only of competing with rivals, but of enlarging the market. Whatever the ethics and problems of bribery in ordinary

business, it has always had a special significance in the arms trade to the Third World.... [B]ribery has been part of the unique character of the arms companies in which (in the words of the 1936 Royal Commission) "the success of one firm doesn't mean the failure of another, but rather increases its chances of doing business." Thus in Colombia and the Philippines, Lockheed used their bribes to foist arms on their client; and thus today Lockheed and Northrop can get rich together in the Middle East, even using the same agents, confident that the arms market has plenty of room for them both.

But the real importance of the Lockheed and Northrop revelations lies not so much in the details of payoffs as in the relentless pressures that lay behind them, to sell arms at all costs. The mounting bribes were only the symptoms of the growing frenzy to push weapons into the new markets, in the midst of an arms race without precedent over the past thirty years.

Sampson's account also indicates that there may be considerable merit in Gauhar's (1982) thesis that the "arms merchants" have played an important role in recycling Middle Eastern, and inferentially, other Third World wealth that is vitally needed for developmental investments. Today these, for the most part, are being maximized only in the less corrupt low-income socialist-oriented (White *et al.,* 1983) mobilizational systems—particularly those not under paramilitary assault by Western-supported counterrevolutionary forces.[9]

ESCALATING INDEBTEDNESS AND POSSIBLE DEFAULT

During the decade of the eighties, conditions for new IMF-approved loans required greater mass austerity (DeCormis, 1983:21; Stevenson, 1989) as well as an even more hospitable climate for transnational investors. Those investors often introduce technology that is very costly and even inappropriate (Wulf, 1979; Trainer, 1989) for societies with surplus labor and a scarcity of highly skilled technicians. This mutually reinforcing process exacerbates dependency, intensifies mass distress, heightens popular discontent, necessitates repression along with further arms imports, and creates a favorable setting for even more ubiquitous domestic militarism and instability. Despite modest debt relief initiatives during the late 1980s, several major developing countries or a larger group may default on their external indebtedness, setting off a chain of *de jure* bankruptcies in the South which will both disrupt American exports and bankrupt many irresponsible (Moffitt, 1983) American financial institutions.

According to a March 1983 *New York Times* report (Dixon, 1983:7): "About two-thirds of total LDC debt, roughly $350 billion of it, is owed to transnational banks. Of that amount, more than 22% (upward of $80 billion) is owed to just nine United States transnational banking institutions. This far exceeds the total equity capital of these banks." The deepening crisis (Magdoff and Sweezy, 1988) arises from the *de facto* bankruptcy of growing numbers of developing nations. DeCormis (1983:21) notes that "at least 34 of them, including some of the biggest borrowers, are unable to make the orginally scheduled payments on the debt." She adds:

One suggestion, made by New York investment banker Felix Rohatyn and others, is to stretch out the maturities of loans by converting them into long-term bonds. As Euromoney points out, a stretch-out would "act as a bulwark against the threat of default, and would reduce the need for new bank loans."

However, even some bankers criticize such proposals as ducking "the real issue, which is", as one international banker put it, "how to get new money to these countries."

A British banker gets to the point: The banks will be willing to go on lending to developing countries provided they are guaranteed against losses. "Any new balance of payment debt," he recently told Euromoney, "must be incurred outside the international banking system." Stretched-out debt converted into bonds or other third world bonds "need(s) to be guaranteed, so that if there is a default the whole developed world bears the weight and not just the banks. . . ."

Although a temporary decline of interest rates since 1983, a willingness to prolong repayment periods, and increased loss reserves by major banks, along with other moves such as "debt equity" swaps (which further denationalize Third World economies), have postponed the eventual day of reckoning, the American economy itself has become burdened by unprecedented indebtedness as have those — albeit to a lesser degree in some cases — of other advanced capitalist states. A sharp rise of interest rates, should there be a run on the dollar — in conjunction with a marked fall in American imports in the ensuing economic downturn — is a likely catalyst of the anticipated wave of defaults.

Even if foreign and interlocked American banks were "bailed out" as Lockheed and other major United States corporations have been (Penn Central, Chrysler, etc.), it would be ordinary American taxpayers and consumers (i.e., inflation) who in the final analysis would be forced to "socialize" such losses on the order of hundreds of billions of dollars. This is already occurring with respect to the $300 billion savings and loan bailout, and to a lesser degree via increased contributions to such global financial conduits as the IMF and World Bank. Thus regressive indirect tax burdens are already being quietly increased.

Nor is it likely that the Bush Administration will reverse the growing concentration of wealth that has deepened class divisions for more than a decade. Insofar as the material welfare and societal cohesion of American citizens continue to deteriorate, so will the country's national security. At the same time, barring structural change of the international system, the basic plight of peoples in the dependent countries of the South will also continue to worsen. This plight, as the following chapter demonstrates, is not simply a matter of mass destitution, structural violence or national indignities. The current North/South system is one that also foments organized violence and global insecurity.

10. Fomenting Arms Races and Warfare in the Underdeveloped Areas

We have seen that in addition to greater austerity which governments are required to impose to refinance rising external indebtedness, every debt or cash payment for weapons imports deprives societies of capital that could be used in the short run to generate employment and enhance mass welfare. General Eisenhower, ironically the only American president who effectively confronted (Ambrose, 1984) the military-industrial complex, warned shortly after his inauguration (1953):

> Every gun that is made
> every warship launched
> every rocket fired signifies,
> in the final sense, a theft
> from those who hunger
> and are not fed,
> those who are cold
> and are not clothed.
> This world in arms is not
> spending money alone.
> It is spending the sweat
> of its laborers,
> the genius of its scientists,
> the hopes of its children.

Further, it is equally clear—as Table 33 demonstrated—that welfare issues in developing areas are also life and death ones for millions. Continued "structural violence" directly threatens the safety of mass sectors.

In this chapter we shall elaborate the view that arms transfers or other military aid reinforces oligarchical "moderate" elites whose policies perpetuate the social status quo. These and auxiliary inputs promote not only structural violence, but also domestic repression as well as civil and at times even international wars. Here it will be assumed that the imperial or dependency context and its relationship to global militarization and arms transfers—all dissected in earlier chapters—are understood. Rather than making references to such linkages, or to the socio-economic costs this system imposes upon ordinary citizens in the advanced capitalist and particularly the hypermilitarized United States economy as well as the peripheral developing countries, I shall focus almost exclusively upon the repressive employment of the weapons upon Third World peoples. With even greater detail, we shall scrutinize uses to which they are put along with the destabilizing consequences of arms flows for regional and global security—including America's own.

WEAPONS EXPORTS AND ARMED CONFLICTS INTENSIFICATION

While reasons abound and motivations vary, it seems obvious that without these multi-billion dollar continuous injections of lethal weaponry, the incidence and especially levels or intensity of organized violence would be appreciably diminished. For it is clear that the proximate cause of most violence is the weapons themselves. Gansler (1980:208) helps us visualize these as homicidal engines of mass destruction by recalling that "between 1965 and 1975, the United States transferred to foreign governments 866 F-4 jets, 2,375 helicopters, 185 destroyers and destroyer escorts, 1,500 Hawk antiaircraft missiles, 25,000 Sidewinder air-to-air missiles, 28,000 antitank missiles, 16,000 armored personnel carriers, 25,000 pieces of artillery and 28,000 tanks, plus enormous stocks of weapons, spare parts, and services." Increasingly these sources of indiscriminate firepower along with the small arms transfers reported by Klare and Arnson (1981) are routinely employed to mutilate domestic civilian dissidents who are often struggling against regimes that engage in ethnic discrimination or perpetuate class orders associated with high structural violence. Such relationships were analyzed in Chapters 3, 4 and particularly 9.

Here we only reiterate that the arms flow patterns summed up in Chapter 2 cannot but enhance the repressive resources of the 114 developing countries studied by Sivard (1985:25): "Over two-thirds of the military controlled regimes resorted to torture, brutality, disappearances, and political killings frequently enough to appear to have institutionalized violence as a matter of policy."[1] By 1987 (Sivard, 1988:26) only two of fifty-nine such regimes did not engage in such practices. The situation had improved apparently since in only half of them "terror tactics were so frequent as to appear institutionalized." On the other hand "ten times as many civilian as military governments had no record of human rights abuses," although the former represented a minority (48 percent) of the 113 countries in the comparison. Similarly, less than 20 percent of the civilian governments routinely engaged in the more brutal forms of repression. In the area of voting rights, denials or limitations were also far more ubiquitous among the military regimes. The latter, of course, diverted far more societal resources to themselves.

> Relative to population, they have two and one-half times as many men under arms. Their military expenditures per capita also average twice as high as in other developing countries.

While helicopters, tanks and even artillery are occasionally so used for repression, primary reliance continues to be upon small arms.

Other weapons, perhaps most of those listed by Gansler in the preceding paragraph — are also commonly deployed for potential use against neighboring states. They increase the intensity of violence, casualty levels including civilians, and at times, the probability that war will be opted for. Thus when announcing his policy of arms restraint in 1977, President Carter warned, "The virtually unrestrained spread of conventional weaponry threatens stability in every region of the world." Brookings analyst Betts (1980:86) cautions that "the same assertion prefaces every brief for global limitations on arms trade, and the assertion is wrong. It mistakes a necessary or proximate cause for a sufficient or significant cause." Here we have an example of what might be called "critique inflation" — commonly articulated by intellectual apologists for the status quo. Few if any critics of America's escalating arms exports maintain that weapons imports are themselves a primary source of conflicts over boundaries, treatment of ethnic groups, religious adherents or underclasses.

Instead, fears center upon the prospect that, as Landgren-Backstrom (1982:202) warned, "possession of ever more sophisticated weaponry facilitates the choice of military solutions to political conflicts." Vietnam's invasion of Kampuchea, Argentina's of the Falklands, Somalia's of Ethiopia, Iraq's of Iran, and Israel's of Lebanon illustrate how availability of modern equipment can facilitate military options that eclipse diplomatic alternatives such as negotiation and mediation. Klare (1982c:34, 43–44) notes:

> ...[M]any analysts agree with Edward C. Luck of the United Nations Association that "the massive transfer of armaments . . . can exacerbate local tensions and increase the likelihood of conflict. This danger is particularly acute," Luck argues, in "explosive Third World areas like the Middle East where the introduction of innovative and highly sophisticated weapons . . . may magnify uncertainties in the perceived military situation, leading to overconfidence or insecurity between rivals." In such an environment, any new deliveries of offensive arms and/or equipment used in launching a surprise attack "may increase the incentive to strike first."

This militaristic temptation arises because, as I emphasized in Chapters 2 and 4, imports that enhance military capabilities of one side of a hostile dyad (e.g. Israel) will induce a compensatory reaction by the other side (e.g. Syria).

Or as Johansen (1983:33) puts it: "Today new arms usually stimulate counter armaments that pose new threats to oneself." Landgren-Backstrom (1982:209) in turn cautions, "The largest arms importers per region turn out to be mutually hostile powers, competing for regional influence — for example the Arab world and Israel, Argentina and Brazil, India and Pakistan, etc." Further, counterforce or nuclear weaponry may exacerbate pre-emptive temptations. Thus Israel's development of a nuclear arsenal encompassing several hundred weapons may have stimulated Arab acquisitions of ballistic missiles and in some cases, chemical weapons. At least twenty countries (NPR, "Evening: Chemical," 1989), including the United States which began in 1987, produce chemical weapons despite international legal proscriptions against their use.

How this destabilizing pattern is promoted by United States exports is implied by an American security analyst's (Betts, 1980:91) contention that the United States decision to export A-4B's to Argentina inspired Chile to purchase Hawker Hunters, which in turn led Peru to import advanced weaponry. Similarly, another establishment expert, Richard L. Millett, in testimony before the House Foreign Affairs Committee (U.S., House, CFA, 1981:30), unsuccessfully opposed the F-16 sale to Venezuela by citing territorial conflicts with both Colombia and Guyana. At the same time Millett saw no "threat" emanating from Cuba that could warrant such a sale. Getting to the heart of the matter, yet another security specialist (Pierre, 1981/1982:280) warned of several likely consequences of this transfer:

> . . . Venezuela has no serious security problem which justifies the F-16. Testifying before the Senate Foreign Relations Committee, Under Secretary of State Buckley cited the threat to Venezuela emanating from Cuba. Surely this is a highly questionable justification. Selling the F-16 to Venezuela would break the tacit threshold on sophisticated jet fighters to Latin America and would be a matter of real concern to neighboring Colombia. It would, moreover, make it more difficult to turn down other nations which requested the F-16 without a legitimate security need for it. If Venezuela is to receive it, why not Argentina, Chile, Peru or Mexico?

Millett in the previously cited testimony (U.S., House, CFA, 1981:31–32) underscored that this approach not only ignored the primary source of "turmoil," but was actually likely to engender greater regional strife:

> Most of the region is currently in the midst of a severe economic slump, a problem compounded by massive debts, high interest rates, and spreading internal conflicts. . . . Economic and social problems, not the lack of modern combat aircraft, submarines, and tanks, lie at the root of the increasing turmoil in Latin America, and any major diversion of scarce governmental resources into efforts at a new arms buildup will prove counterproductive to our basic interest in regional stability.

This perspective, however, was predictably ignored by Reagan Administration officials who were unsuccessfully trying to buy enough support for their campaign to isolate and overthrow the Sandinista Revolution.

It is clear that, as Klare (1982d:46) warns, "new regional arms races are emerging in more and more Third World areas." Furthermore, once initiated, such arms races themselves aggravate tensions and fears because of intrinsic difficulty of measuring (Klare, 1982b:44–45) whether a balance of power exists.

> There is no real way for instance, to compute the "balance" between competing arms even when they are designed to perform a similar function: there is no true equivalence between, say, a Soviet MIG-25 jet and its closest American counterpart, the F-14 Tomcat. Furthermore, the long lead-times involved in most major military sales deliveries insure that some imbalances will always occur. All of these problems are compounded by the effects of another military principle, the doctrine of "worst-case analysis." This principle holds that a certain degree of error is unavoidable in any intelligence estimate of enemy capabilities, and hence the prudent military planner must prepare for the worst possible scenario rather than the most plausible one. This normally means that countries will tend to overcompensate for deliveries to their rivals, rather than balance them.

Consequently, "while it is undoubtedly true that a power balance can inhibit conflict under certain conditions, analysis suggests that such a balance is intrinsically unstable in situations where there is no agreement between suppliers to restrict their weapons deliveries to conflict-prone areas."

Analogous reasoning characterized most contributors to a 1978 Harvard conference on Northeast Asian security (Weinstein, 1982), who emphasized the precarious nature of the balance of forces in the region. Bello and Hayes (1983) go so far as to cogently argue that the tensions generated by this Reagan-sponsored regional arms race played a major indirect role in the Soviet downing of a Korean airliner in September 1983. Since then Washington has continued its offensive naval buildup and unrestricted, often provocative, maneuvers not only in the Soviet north Pacific but also near Murmansk — Moscow's only warm water, year-round open access to the Atlantic. At the same time, until 1990 the United States steadfastly declined to include naval armaments in any arms reduction negotiations. Minor changes may be in the offing provided that Moscow continues to make most of the concessions.

At best, as Pierre (1982:20) notes, "one nation's perception of balance may be another nation's imbalance. The risk of a process of competitive acquisition, leading to a local arms race, is often present."[2] At worst such rivalry, as in the cases of Somalia/Ethiopia and Iraq/Iran, may prompt a decision for war due to miscalculation of temporary advantage or the prospect of its imminent loss (Pakistan vs. India in 1965). Ironically, such a decision usually occurs when there is relative equality of capabilities, i.e., a "balance of power." Singer (1981:10–11) refers to the "relatively consistent" findings of researchers on this point. Citing studies by Garnham, Weede, Barringer and Wright, he cautions "that nations that were approximately equal in material capabilities were significantly more likely to carry their disputes to war" than were nations of discernible disparity. Another researcher, Mihalka, found "that once military force was threatened or used, the greater disparity in capabilities of the disputants, the less likely the dispute was to escalate to hostilities." Singer's own Correlates of War project, which quantified the parameters of interstate wars between 1816 and 1965, revealed "that while only 13% of all major power militarized disputes since 1816 escalated to war, that figure rose to 20% when the parties were approximately equal in military terms, and to 75% if such parity was combined with rapid military buildup during the three years prior to the dispute."

Given this corpus of research and findings, one must view as problematic the official American rationale claiming that arms transfers will promote peace by maintaining or restoring a "balance." Other objectives of a less noble sort may of course be served—profits for weapons exporters, political leverage, strengthening of an unpopular but friendly repressive client regime, or as in the case of Nicaragua, Afghanistan or Cambodia, overthrowing a socially leftist regime. Similarly, in Peru and the Philippines, suppressing left-led nationalist "communist" movements has been an objective. In Colombia, ELN guerrillas and an autonomous narcotics cartel are the targets of an enhanced weapons flow.

Another favorite U.S. rationale for arms transfers is to neutralize the "threat" of Islamic radical nationalism to "moderate" comprador regimes in the Middle East. Although the United States furnished (NPR, "Morning," August 18, 1988) 4 percent of Teheran's arms, this amount was dwarfed by as much as $20 billion that Washington, London and Bonn provided to the Gulf states. More than $27 billion—a veritable sales bonanza—in arms from ten or more countries fueled the Gulf War. Many of these countries, including the United States, were selling to both sides. When it appeared in 1985 that Iran had recovered from the Iraqi invasion and was about to go on the offensive, Washington stepped up aid to Iraq and dispatched a flotilla of warships, prolonging the war. Arms shipments continued despite Iraq's use of nerve gas against both Iranians and its own Kurdish nationals. Other important suppliers included the USSR, China, Egypt, Brazil, and France—the last being most important in this respect. Clearly this is but a part of the vast flow of arms into the region—continuously upsetting and restoring the so-called "balance." Thus the Center for Defense Information ("U.S.-Soviet," 1988:7) records that:

> Almost one-half of the arms deliveries to the Third World over the last ten years have gone to the Middle East, the most volatile region in the world. Noncommunist nations have provided $77 Billion of arms during the last decade, communist nations, $68 Billion.

Fortunately by the end of the decade world arms sales ("Early Warnings," 1988:4) were "beginning to slump as peace accords are achieved in troubled regions, the large Third World market sinks into deeper economic crisis, and weapons costs rise. Top arms exporting nations have reported losses up to $800 million in 1987 and expect worse in 1988." Nevertheless, an intensified arms race involving state-of-the-art, high-tech weaponry continues between Israel and its neighbors, where miscalculation can easily trigger a pre-emptive attack. And, as pointed out in Chapter 2, U.S. arms sales have experienced a sharp upsurge since 1987.

QUALITATIVE WEAPONS "MODERNIZATION"—ENHANCING DESTRUCTIVENESS

Another facet of the increasingly sophisticated weaponry being exported is its unprecedented destructiveness. Pearson (1981:26) highlights this with the observation that the "regional disputes reach levels of astounding destruction—as in Arab-Israeli warfare—in part because of the advanced weapons which are pumped in for political reasons." A similar view is offered by LaRocque and Goose (1982:20) with respect to the Iraqi-Iranian war. One of the small number of "international" wars in the contemporary era, it has accounted for (Sollen, 1989:47) approximately 400,000 fatalities. If one adds the simultaneous and partially linked Kurdish civil insurgency, the total exceeds 600,000—not counting the wounded and dispossessed. And as mentioned previously, these conflicts marked the first resort to poison gas since World War I—if United States use of dioxin in Agent Orange against the Vietnamese is excluded.

As for El Salvador, Cepeda and Glennon (1983:3) report that such weaponry inflicts particularly heavy casualties upon civilians: "The use of United States–supplied jets and helicopters by the Salvadorean Air Force in recent weeks has increased the number of civilian casualties, as cities and towns are being rocketed and bombed." In both El Salvador and the Israeli invasion (Sivard, 1982:14) of Lebanon, civilian suffering has been further intensified by the use of American manufactured cluster bomblets. This underscores the meaning of Klare's (1982b:45) conclusion that "while the role of massive arms sales in provoking conflict may be disputed, few can disagree with Frank Barnaby's observation that 'such levels of armaments make conflict much more violent once it begins.'" Some illustrations are provided by Miller (1988a: 17):

> LIC [low-intensity conflict] proponents—inside and outside the executive branch and in both parties—are quietly but consistently engaging in a permanent, offensive war. The battlefield reaches the Philippines, where U.S. dollars fund the Aquino government's war against the New People's Army. It foments civil war in Afghanistan, where Congress appropriated more aid for the rebels than the administration requested. And it finances aggression in Angola, where the U.S. collaborates with South Africa. In every case, the enemy is ostensibly communist subversion, but the targets and the victims are self-determination and the potential for a constructive, democratic U.S. foreign policy.

One can add — taking account of the conduct of United States–directed warfare within both El Salvador and Nicaragua — that when indigenous personnel cannot deploy such destructive weapons systems with efficiency, American officers will assume tactical command. Such a situation, after successive United States–inspired coup attempts were foiled by General Noriega, may explain the apparent November decision ("U.S. General," 1989:3) to invade Panama by Christmas.

In the United States–sponsored insurgency against the Sandinistas — one which deliberately targeted civilian schools, clinics, and farms — the devastation has been unparalleled. Thus, Miller (1988a: 17), while noting that "among LIC's [Low Intensity Conflict's] greatest advantages . . . are its low profile and emphasis on surrogates and covert actions," goes on to emphasize that:

> In Nicaragua, LIC makes sense of seemingly irrational contra attacks on health centers, schools, churches, farms and international workers. Says Miles, "there is a conscious effort to remove successful social programs that generate goodwill for the Sandinistas. Columbia University public health researchers Richard Garfield, Thomas Frieden and Sten Vermund attribute declines in hospitalization and in feeding programs for undernourished children to closed health centers — contras have completely or partially destroyed 65 clinics — and to the need to mobilize more than 5,000 health-care workers into the militia.
> . . . That civilians should suffer from LIC is not surprising, since it is a doctrine of war. But attacks on noncombatants can jeopardize international and domestic acceptance — and congressional funding.

Indeed, loss of acceptance and funding is precisely what has happened due in part to Latin American and world criticism of this intervention and its exceptional level of civilian fatalities. According to one calculation (McAffee, Brickner and Ruether, 1988), "the percentage of Nicaraguans killed in this Low Intensity Conflict is larger in proportion to the population than the total number of U.S. citizens who died in World War I, World War II, the Korean War and Vietnam COMBINED."

Although the Carter Administration's arms transfer policy initially proscribed the development of new weaponry specifically designed for export, we noted in Chapter 4 that a decision was made during 1979 to develop a so-called F-X fighter bomber somewhat less sophisticated than the F-16 but more so than the F-5 (at $6 million without spares, etc.), a popular defensive interceptor. Such an intermediate fighter would, it was claimed, lessen Third World interest in America's first-line weaponry and safeguard against the Falklands' experience where some of the most sophisticated imported weaponry was turned, with Israeli resupply and American transport facilitation, against a former Argentine military supplier and a United States ally — the United Kingdom.

The fateful consequences of Carter's F-X decision, which was fully implemented (i.e., the F-20 Tigershark at $12 million each plus spares, etc.) by an enthusiastic Reagan Administration, are (Pearson, 1981:44–45) expanded markets for weapons producers and enhanced prospects of warfare in the developing areas.[3]

> The overall potential for Third World warfare will escalate sharply, both because of "export only" sales and the "trickle down" of the second or third hand weapons from states purchasing newer models. The escalation might be sharper than would be the case if the choice remained between selling standard U.S. forces' technology vs. no sale. The higher cost of U.S. arsenal systems, and the greater potential American governmental reluctance to release them could do more to dampen Third World arms races than the supposed benefits of selling less refined and advanced systems.

Interestingly, Northrop was given the F-20 contract to replace its F-5 export—at roughly double (SIPRI, 1989) the price of the earlier strike fighter. Meanwhile F-16s flow to petroleum producers at $20 million plus, and others able to afford them.

Even more significant has been the Pentagon fascination with developing new simple-to-use intelligence devices and highly lethal weapons (Klare, 1989) for low intensity conflicts.[4] These would be deployed by United States troops and exported to proxy forces. Referring to a series of papers by the Army–Air Force Center on Low-Intensity Conflict in Langley, Virginia, Marc Miller (1988:18–19) notes that one

> sums up the dominant view on how to use technology against Third World insurrection: "We can take a lesson from the terrorists here. They don't normally use complicated weapons. What really counts is simplicity and reliability.". . .
> In search for simplicity, CLIC proposes that a more basic gadget for detecting mines—one that even a child could use: "Inexpensive remote control vehicles such as toy cars equipped with appropriate micro-sensors could be designed, permitting rapid searches ahead of the operators.

Even as a Third World buyers' market for major weapons narrows further due to financial crisis, United States weapons producers are determined to find opportunities to equip armies in the South with a new generation of user-friendly, relatively low-cost arms. If the development of these "export" weapons is associated with arms races, the tightening of alliances and "system wide increases in military expenditures," the overt conflict prognosis is ominous. For among the findings reported by Singer (1981), all three of the foregoing in tandem with higher military capabilities increase the likelihood of interstate warfare. Toward the end of this chapter we shall see that the high incidence of contemporary warfare in developing areas conforms to Singer's prediction.

NUCLEAR PROLIFERATION
The decline in global security, then, is a direct consequence of intensified great power rivalry and export of increasingly lethal modernized weaponry. Three particularly dangerous aspects of this erosion of security are (1) nuclear

proliferation; (2) a North to South diffusion of military power in a context of growing Third World frustration over most of the North's rigid opposition to a New International Economic Order along with the marginal impact of OPEC; and (3) to some extent the fear of suppliers that new technology may be compromised by the losing side in a regional conflict. Whether the Bush Administration's response to recent Soviet concessions and initiatives will eventually culminate in a non-intervention regime is uncertain at best. Washington has flatly rejected Moscow's offer of such a regime.

While China has possessed nuclear weapons since the early 1960s, there is widespread belief in the arms control community that such countries as Israel, South Africa, India, Pakistan, Brazil, Argentina and even Chile ("Thatcher," 1983) either possess or will be capable of producing nuclear weapons in the very near future. Despite Israel's unprovoked 1982–85 invasion of Lebanon and her arsenal of a dozen to two hundred nuclear warheads, she is one of the most heavily aided U.S. satellites. Similarly, despite Islamabad's drive to develop atomic weapons, a report (Marshall, 1983:5) on Reagan's $3.2 billion military and economic aid—including 40 F-16s—to Pakistan noted that "President Zia has enhanced his image as an international negotiator by managing to obtain U.S. help without compromising his country's controversial nuclear program." The effects upon India were, as we saw in Chapter 5, ignored, and the fact that "about 60 percent of the heroin reaching the United States comes from the frontier area" was depreciated after referring to claims that Zia's officials were assisting in a "joint effort to control" the trade. More weighty was the willingness of Zia's regime to allow its territory to be used as a massive CIA center for paramilitary warfare against Afghanistan's Soviet-supported Revolutionary Government.[5] This reflects the traditional and current Bush bias in so-called "drug wars." Proxy and covert action cooperators are tacitly or overtly supported.

But the proliferation of nuclear capability is, like chemical warfare plants, also a function of commercial (Johnstone, 1985) profiteering—one suspects in approximately the same measure as are weapons exports. There are already approximately 2,500 nuclear facilities and "activities" (Arkin and Fieldhouse, 1985) now integral to a global nuclear infrastructure encompassing four oceans as well as fully 65 countries and territories. One cautious analyst (Leventhal, 1985:12–15) warns that "the underlying proliferation dilemma . . . is the current trend toward accumulation of vast stores of weapons—usable materials by dozens of nations throughout the world, under the cloak of legitimacy provided by the NPT and IAEA safeguards." The shortcomings of International Atomic Energy Agency inspection procedures and policing authority exacerbate these dangers as does the related treaty on non-proliferation of nuclear weapons exemption of fissionable materials for "peaceful" uses.[6] Leventhal adds that the risks are further magnified by "the *laissez-faire* attitude toward unsafeguarded nuclear activities."

Under Reagan, even the minimal caution concerning safeguards and exports to Third World nations was diminished. More seriously, failure of the "superpowers" to negotiate major reductions of their own armaments—an obligation under the NPT—has rendered the agreement one-sided and perhaps nugatory. This absence of mutuality or equity (Castrioto, 1989) enhances incentives to tacitly develop nuclear and chemical weapons potential—perceived as a mechanism for attenuating their military disadvantage *vis-à-vis* the major powers. The same can be said with respect to Washington's blind eye toward Israel. The latter's manufacture, as noted above, of several hundred atomic bombs and warheads was a consequence of French-supplied technology for the Dimona plant and fissionable material illegally smuggled from the United States. Tel Aviv, in turn, may have carried out joint testing and development with South Africa.

Of related concern is the dual nuclear capability of first line fighter-bomber exports like the F-16—soon to be produced by Japan. Referring not only to such aircraft, but equally to the 155mm and 8" howitzers as well as other recently improved weaponry, Landgren-Backstrom (1982:202) warns that "a number of the conventional weapons widely exported today are capable of delivering nuclear weapons. Thus, the acquisition of nuclear weapon carriers may facilitate the spread also of nuclear weapons in the future—a carrier may be purchased and the nuclear warheads may be locally produced." While Reagan Administration officials argued that new sophisticated conventional arms may diminish the desire for nuclear weapons, some security analysts (Pierre, 1982:30–31) are dubious:

> ...If a nation believes that its existence is so threatened that it must base its security upon an independent nuclear weapons capability, it is unlikely to be dissuaded by an uncertain supply of conventional weapons from abroad.... Moreover, the nuclear decision is likely to be made in many countries for reasons quite separate from a rational calculation of security requirements. These include factors of prestige, the desire to achieve regional dominance or to catch up with another state in the area, the interests of indigenous scientific and bureaucratic communities, or the pressures of domestic politics in which nuclear issues—involving, as they do, notions of sovereignty and status—can often become key ingredients of the national debate. In none of these considerations would conventional arms be viewed as real alternatives to nuclear weapons.

The interest in nuclear arms, already demonstrated by those countries mentioned previously along with Iraq and possibly Libya, Turkey, or Japan, may well be the harbinger of a global proliferation process in the coming decades.

MODIFYING THE GLOBAL BALANCE OF POWER

The growing market for nuclear and chemical materials, supplemented by the virtually unrestrained export of highly destructive sophisticated or first-line weapons, has been viewed by Betts (1980:94) and Pierre (1981/1982:269) among others as effectively reducing the military superiority of the North over the South. The former expresses apprehension that

> the long term consequences of diffusion of military power are unpredictable, and by no means will they all benefit American security. In the past decade, suppliers contracted for over $140 billion of arms transfers to LDCs. As Leslie Gelb—then Director of Politico-Military Affairs at the State Department—testified, "most of this equipment has not yet been delivered, much less absorbed. When these arms are delivered and when the recipients learn to use them, they will change the face of world politics . . . in the process, our own technological advantage will recede."

The trend toward greater equalization of military capabilities and the fact that America and other Western powers continue for the most part to firmly oppose nationalist aspirations as well as related demands for a NIEO suggest that the Falklands episode may be but a portent of future disasters.

Even in the late 1960s the Israelis had risked sinking the *Liberty,* an American intelligence vessel, involving many casualties. Several years later, the North Koreans used modern naval and aircraft to capture another *Pueblo.* More recently, Cambodians fired upon the *Mayaguez,* and Libyans may have attacked American reconnaissance fighters for violating their territorial airspace. Even Lebanese irregulars destroyed a major Marine encampment. Klare (1982e) notes that "a $1-million boat or plane can fire a $200,000 missile and sink a $100-million destroyer such as the *Sheffield*—or even a $2-billion aircraft carrier such as the USS *Nimitz.*" Similarly, small "satchel-sized" A-bombs as well as deadly biochemical agents can be smuggled into American harbors—a danger likely to increase in coming years unless United States military interventions and support for brutally repressive regimes are ended. Similarly, we can expect a long-term rise in low level attacks by terrorists upon vulnerable American individuals and corporate targets.

The desire for the latest equipment may be what Sereseres (U.S., House, CFA, 1981:51) diagnoses as "a universal disease." If that be the case, it would appear to be transmitted by suppliers via training (Wolpin, 1973) and demonstration effects. Some of those currently afflicted are surveyed by La-Rocque and Goose (1982:20):

> The major Third World recipients of sophisticated U.S. arms are Israel, Saudi Arabia, Egypt, and South Korea, closely followed by Pakistan, Venezuela, and Morocco. These nations have received such items as F-15 and F-16 fighter aircraft, AWACS reconnaissance/command and control aircraft, a variety of advanced missiles, high-speed vessels, electronic radar and countermeasure devices, M-60A tanks, AH-1S attack helicopters, and self-propelled howitzers and artillery. These are front-line weapons being used by the U.S. armed services.

The major Third World recipients of Soviet arms are Syria, Iraq, and Libya, followed closely by Cuba, Ethiopia, South Yemen, and Vietnam. These nations have received MIG-23 and MIG-25 aircraft, Mi-8 and Mi-24 attack helicopters, several advanced missiles, Osa-II fast patrol craft, T-62 and T-72 tanks, and self-propelled howitzers and artillery.

It could well be that as Klare (1982e) puts it, such "conventional weapons are 'conventional' only in the sense that they are non-nuclear." Clearly, the electronic breakthroughs that have facilitated production of highly accurate "smart bombs" and precision guided missiles mark a new qualitative stage in the arms race as does the mass production of "tactical" nuclear warheads.

In opposing the sale to the Saudis of hundreds of Sidewinders (U.S., Sen., *Arms Sales Package,* Pt. 2, 1981:92) — a frontal attack missile previously denied the "neutral" Swedes — Senator Biden added

> ...I am quoting from the minority report by the Armed Services Committee:
> The AIM-9L must be of high-priority interest to the Soviet Union, which can be expected to devote substantial resources and strenuous efforts to acquiring access to these systems. The technology of the AIM-9L missile is sufficiently advanced and sensitive now and for many years to come that no avoidable risk of its compromise should be taken.
> This takes me back to square one. The burden should be upon those who argue that the sale must go through to show that there is some superseding, overwhelming reason why we should, in fact, take a risk which could be avoided.

Fellow Senator Patrick Moynihan, another member of the powerful Zionist congressional lobby, gave substance to this apprehension by stressing that "one-quarter of the armed forces in Saudi Arabia is Pakistani. That is how fragile a country this is.... [T]he idea of the largest arms sale in the world to a regime so fragile is unwise, sir." But so paramount are the commercial motives of the industrial-military complex and the desire to maximize influence over the Saudi proxy regime that such security concerns are dismissed out of hand. So, for that matter, are others of an even more compelling nature.

RISKS OF ESCALATION

LaRocque and Goose (1982:21) highlight a danger of far greater magnitude. Although especially pronounced in the Saudi, Moroccan, Egyptian, Nicaraguan, Philippine and El Salvador cases, this danger characterizes many "troublespots" and arises from "the fact that advanced weapons delivered by the U.S. are usually accompanied by a large contingent of U.S. military and civilian technicians to train indigenous personnel and to help maintain and operate the weapons systems. These technicians become so active in the day-to-day operation of the foreign military establishment that the danger of their becoming involved in any attack on the host nation, whether the U.S. desires to be involved or not, is great. The number of U.S. technicians overseas implementing arms sales has risen 25 percent in the past two years." Such a danger of direct involvement is enhanced if a client is facing defeat. Both Korea and Vietnam were cases in point. So for that matter were the reverses experienced by the Salvadoran military in the early 1980s and the advances more recently by the revolutionary nationalist movement in the Philippines. In both of the latter cases as well as Nicaragua, there has been direct tactical participation by United States military personnel.[7]

In the immediate future, this danger seems greatest in the Philippines, where United States personnel are actively involved in training and otherwise directing (Bello, 1988:685–86) the intensification of the regime's counter-revolutionary repression. In 1989 they openly intervened to suppress a military uprising against the corrupt and inept Aquino Administration. More than 300,000 American officers and enlistees operate from a vast base complex in that country. Many, of course, are uninvolved. Yet in the view of nationalists, including but not limited to those leading the revolutionary movement, their presence plays a key role in the context of the overall American operational presence. Although put perhaps too harshly, Sison's (1988:8–9) critique conveys well the fierce outrage that drives the insurgent and civilian opposition movement:

> The United States wants to reverse the revolutionary trend by using what it calls the "low-intensity conflict" strategy, a vicious and brutal policy of using Filipinos to kill Filipinos and terrorizing the people with psy-war and dirty tricks. On mere suspicion of being connected with the revolutionary movement, people in both urban and rural areas are targeted for massacre, assassination, torture, strafing and bombing, zoning, and forced evacuation. The entire U.S.–Aquino regime, the military, police, and paramilitary forces are responsible, but there are frequent attempts to make these barbarities appear as having been perpetrated solely by paramilitary forces and even by ordinary civilians.
>
> The low-intensity conflict scheme is supposed to preempt the commitment of U.S. troops. But, in fact, it prepares for a blatant U.S. war of aggression because U.S. advisors, trainers, Pentagon and CIA covert operatives, U.S. ground and navy patrols with the AFP, U.S. air and naval surveillance operations, direct U.S. funding for death squads and vigilante groups through the CIA, as well as indirect funding through international and anticommunist organizations, and Pentagon-directed coup rumors and mock coup attempts have increasingly come into play. The U.S. military bases in the Philippines, which did not originate in a treaty between two independent states, have signified uninterrupted aggression since the beginning of the twentieth century and are launching pads of currently intensifying U.S. intervention, which has already reached the point where the national question has come to the fore and the revolutionary forces have decided to target U.S. military personnel and installations.

This may also help us understand why, according to CIA Director William Webster (1988), approximately half of "terrorist attacks" in the world target Americans, and why such attacks have escalated from 500 in 1981 to 800 by 1985.

The escalatory effect may also arise from what Klare (1982f) calls supplier "credibility" when an important client regime is losing, as well as
acute fear that advanced weaponry will be captured by the other side.[8] He
adds that such superpower intervention almost occurred when "during the
1973 Arab-Israeli war, both the United States and the Soviet Union trans-
ported arms directly to their allies in the war zone, narrowly averting a head-on
collision."[9] A future war between Israel on one hand, and Syria, Iraq and
possibly Iran on the other, poses similar risks. Gorbachev leadership may have
lessened Soviet "credibility" in withdrawing troops from Afghanistan as the
United States did in Vietnam. Yet the Kabul regime has managed to hold its
own with only material aid unlike that in Saigon. Nevertheless it is too
soon to write off "credibility" as a major motivating force for any state
with superpower pretensions. And while it is unclear as yet whether the
Soviets have completely or permanently renounced such pretensions, there
can be little doubt that the Bush Administration remains wedded to an imperial mission.

Whether a collision is initiated with conventional weapons is becoming
less important as the threshold or firebreak between tactical nuclear weapons
(e.g. mines, artillery shells, etc.) and increasingly potent conventional explosives diminishes. Not only will the latter result in "wars . . . fought at higher
and higher levels of violence and destructiveness," but this development in
conjunction with the previously mentioned deployment of dual capability
delivery systems and nuclear warheads gives added weight to Klare's (1982b)
view that "any realistic assessment of likely war scenarios would suggest that
a nuclear war probably would begin as a conventional war, when the superpowers intervene in a local conflict."

Related to this prospect is Sanders' (1983:25) reminder that "U.S. and
allied strategies for deterring or coping with major conventional conflicts are
dependent on a credible threat of nuclear escalation."[10] Reagan's drive for
(Scheer, 1982; Klare, 1982a; Bello and Hayes, 1983) an offensive superiority
sufficient to "win" a nuclear war was, as I argued in Chapters 3 and 5, designed
to enhance the credibility of such threats. This is the operational meaning of
"deterrence" — in the context of a first strike. The militarization of space is the
logical outcome of this drive, even though it is no more likely (Karas, 1983)
than existing counterforce strategy to protect American society from some
retaliation and nuclear winter. That Bush remains fixated upon SDI and this
goal is unsurprising given his assertion of basic administration continuity with
his predecessor.

Thus we better perceive the direct tie or "deadly connection" between the
nuclear arms race and competitive intervention in the Third World. Referring
to the Committee on the Present Danger which in 1976 introduced the doctrinal perspectives subsequently adopted by the Reagan-Bush Administration,
Sanders (1983:25) notes:

Limitations on nuclear arms from the CPD's perspective would therefore constrain and diminish the credibility of intervention through conventional means in regional and internal conflicts. Conversely, closing the publicly-proclaimed "window of vulnerability" through the continual modernization of nuclear forces would widen the privately-coveted vista of opportunity for intervention. In a very direct sense, then, nuclear weapons occupy a central role in dissuading challenges to the present world order—if, that is, one can achieve an edge so that their threatened use will be perceived as credible. Conversely, arms control, which is based on parity, works against the achievement of such a "state of confidence."

For this reason, rationalized earlier by paranoid projection rhetoric, we can understand not only administration opposition to any nuclear freeze that is not a source of one-sided advantage, but equally the dim prospects—even before the Korean airline incident according to Warnke (Judis, 1983)—for substantive reciprocity in negotiations with the Soviet Union. Washington's unprovoked aggression against Grenada, Nicaragua, Libya, Afghanistan, Cambodia, Panama and arguably Iraq, similarly reflect this militaristic animus.

Thus the dangers to America's own security are underscored by the propensity of Reagan, and in equal measure, Bush, for interventionism in the Middle East, Asia, Central America and Africa. Most war today occurs at least initially in developing areas and is seldom wholly endogenous. Like Kohler (1978:8), Sivard (1982) and Kende (1983), Ohlson (1982: 211) fastens our attention upon this parameter of the global system: "Not only does conventional weaponry absorb the bulk of resources devoted to armaments, but all wars since 1945 have been fought with these weapons. Nearly all of these some 130 conflicts have been or are being, fought in the Third World and, furthermore, almost exclusively with weapons supplied by the industrialized countries."

WAR PATTERNS AND CIVILIAN VICTIMIZATION IN AN EAST/WEST CONTEXT

In Table 33 we saw that in 1965 alone, the overwhelming proportion of war casualties—in excess of 90 percent—were in the South. The figure rises to more than 99 percent if we limit our focus to civil violence. And to bring the matter closer to date, Power (1983:4) informs us that "according to one estimate, two-thirds of all nations of the world were caught up in physical violence last year, almost all of them in the Third World." Several years later, Sivard (1987:28) reported that "twenty-two wars were underway in 1987, more wars than in any previous year in recorded history." Not to be outdone, Sollen (1989:46–47) "counted thirty-two wars in progress in 1988." Thus neither the arms transfers from the North nor the buildup of forces supposedly to deter attack in the South has promoted peace or stability. Indeed, the very historic incidence of warfare demonstrates the vacuity of "deterrence" as an effective doctrine.

Even more ominous is the declining proportion of military to civilian casualties—a pattern likely to be accentuated by the previously discussed commitment to expanded low-intensity warfare capabilities. Westing's (1982) data on twentieth century wars suggest that between 60 and 70 percent of fatalities are civilian. These estimates roughly dovetail Sivard's (1985:9) tabulation. She emphasizes that "excluding the two world wars, 83 wars started before 1945, 120 since then; four times as many deaths have occurred since World War II than before it." More recently, Sivard (1987:28) observed the overall trend:

> In the 18th, 19th and most of the 20th century, civilians represented about 50 percent of war-related deaths. Recently the proportion of civilians in the death toll has been going up. In the 1960's civilians accounted for 52 percent of the deaths; in the 1970's, for 73 percent; so far in the 1980's, for 85 percent.

As for the 22 wars in progress as of September 1987, she recounts that "the total death toll in these wars so far is at least 2,200,000—and rising fast. Incredibly, many more civilians than soldiers are victims, civilians account for 84 percent of the recorded deaths."

While a preponderance of these wars have been primarily internal wars of an ethnic, religious or class nature, many of them have an international dimension, and almost all are fueled by arms preponderantly from the West, or in lesser measure from the East. Sivard (1985:9) takes pains to stress that "with the heavy flow of advanced weaponry from the industrialized to the poorer countries, no hamlet, no matter how remote, is far from the battlefield. Death rates in wars are poorly recorded. Where fatalities are available for both civilians and soldiers, civilian deaths are sharply higher. Wars are now more life-threatening for non-combatants than for the men fighting them."

While it would be foolish to assume the non-existence of major damage to civilian life in the absence of superpower involvement, that intrusion obviously contributes to both the incidence and the destructiveness of Third World warfare.[11] Noting that after Reagan's first year in office, fully 37 of 40 existing wars were in the developing areas, LaRocque and Goose (1982:21) add that "weapons provided mainly by the Soviet Union and United States have permitted these wars to continue, perhaps encouraged their escalation, and certainly increased dramatically the power of small nations to kill and destroy." We have already mentioned Washington's role in Afghanistan, Cambodia and the Philippines at the beginning of the 1990s. Similar effects appear destined for Peru, and Iraq—Kuwait—Saudi Arabia, among others. This exogenous dimension symbolizes a trend that has become more rather than less pronounced over the post–World War II period.

Analyzing military conflicts between 1945 and 1970, Kende (1973:73–82) found a positive correlation between military expenditures and arms imports on one hand, and war on the other. Whynes (1979:91) underscores the strength of that association: "When examining the aggregate figures . . . we find a really striking similarity between their trends, especially those in wars and arms imports. . . . Kende's intuitive conclusion is supported by regression analysis—the relationship between war and imports gives a coefficient of correlation of 0.821, and this figure increases slightly if imports are lagged by one year." The "wars were preponderantly domestic rather than international." Most occurred within the Third World, increasingly so as the twenty-year post–World War II period progressed. The average duration of internal wars tended to lengthen, a phenomenon most likely to occur when there was foreign intervention. The United States was the most ubiquitous foreign participant in such conflicts.

Pentagon combat involvement has been associated (Wolpin, 1986a) with the highest incidence of civilian as well as military casualties. Even more than Korea or World War II, where restraints were largely on paper (Schaffer, 1988), in Vietnam per capita casualties reached a zenith with the execution of a "production model" or "technowar" (Gibson, 1988). Indeed, while the human dimension was depreciated, more ordnance than in the entirety of World War II was targeted—with few (Kimball, 1988) de facto restraints—upon the inhabitants of Laos, Cambodia, and particularly Vietnam. My Lai was a metaphor, rather than an aberration.

These patterns were consonant with Sivard's (1981:8) finding that 95 percent of "the 125 or more conflicts which have occurred in the world since World War II" have been in the Third World. "In most cases foreign forces have been involved, western powers accounting for 79 percent of the interventions, communist for 6 percent, other developing nations for the remainder." Eckhardt (1977:14) concludes that "so far as overt military interventions in major world conflicts may be taken as a sign of military imperialism, 78% of 306 such interventions from 1945 to 1975 were conducted by Western nations, 11% by Middle Eastern nations, less than 7% by communist nations, and 4% by Asian nations (Eckhardt and Azar, 1977)." The same author adds that "many civil wars and other civil conflicts were also a function of imperialism as shown by Eckhardt and Young (1974b, 1975, 1977). Kemp (1977) found that MNCs [Multinational Corporations] stimulated arms expenditures and international war from 1923–37 and 1950–64. Consequently, both civil and international wars have been related to imperialism by empirical and statistical studies."

The significance of improved East-West relations is revealed by a follow-up study for the 1976–1980 period. Kende (1983) reports a continuation of the trend of foreign—especially American, and in lesser measure NATO and Communist—military interventions. These involvements and the incidence of war diminished appreciably despite a rise in arms transfers between the late 1960s and mid-1970s—an era of detente. A marked increase in such wars and Western—particularly U.S.—interventions characterized the late 1970s and the 1980s. A spectacular rise in interventions can be linked to Washington's hardening resolve to repudiate detente over the 1980s. Lebanon, Chad and Grenada are the most recent manifestations. Again, however, the improvement in Soviet-American relations in the last two years of the Reagan Administration may have some ameliorating effect. If, as seems probable, the less belligerent—even, in some areas, cooperative—posture is sustained by the Bush Administration, this is likely to be the case.

A more respectful East-West framework might also lessen the incidence of another new phenomenon identified by Kende (1983). This development has been the growing interventionism of Third World nations as "proxies" (e.g. Honduras, Zaire, South Africa, Pakistan, Israel) or for their own purposes (China). Both of these post-detente trends enhance in varying degree the probability of nuclear escalation. While efforts to limit forms of involvement and the operational theatre as in Vietnam may be effective in a substantial number of cases, miscalculation and other manifestations of human error subsumed by Murphy's Law imply the growing risk of eventual nuclear weapons use as the militarization process proceeds in the South, and at a reduced pace, in the United States.

In this chapter we have seen that while the notion of a "global village" may be exaggerated, the idea contains considerably more than a grain of truth. Western militarization, arms transfers and interventions contribute to the depletion of raw materials in the South as well as the perpetuation of both structural and repressive violence. Interstate wars and insurrectionary national liberation movements—in varying degree previously supported by the increasingly cautious (Cassen, 1985) Soviets—have also contributed to a climate of armed conflict which threatens and often involves Americans or their close allies. It is increasingly apparent that the ever-growing ecological damage and material costs of diverting unending resources to the arms race encompassing a global array of military installations are being imposed upon the ordinary citizens of both North and South. While most of the human costs have thus far been exacted in the Third World, interventionist trends, concomitant exacerbation of tensions and escalatory risks suggest that a still possible world war would certainly impose human casualties upon the North that dwarf the 50,000,000 associated with World War II. Even this rests on the highly dubious (Schell, 1982) assumption that there will be no nuclear winter, i.e., life will return to normal under the aegis of strong civil authority. It is far more probable that whatever life does survive will be, to use the Hobbesian phrase, "nasty, brutish, and short."

11. The Nascent American Garrison State

It has been argued by Falk (1984) and others that the prospective use of nuclear weaponry is itself incompatible with the existence of political democracy. While this diagnosis would have been premature during an era of massive retaliation, the adoption of a pre-emptive counterforce posture, in tandem with the escalatory potential of extended deterrence since the late 1950s, means that ordinary citizens have in a real sense lost control over their very lives. Even armed interventionism threatens to escape the democratic process now (Miller, 1988:18) as recent formulation of "low intensity conflict doctrine mandates a combat role for the U.S. military in the absence of declared war and popular support for such declaration." Official scenarios predict that nuclear war—if it occurs—is most likely to escalate from a regional conflict rather than result from a premeditated surprise attack.

Ultimately there can be no *a posteriori* accountability by a commander-in-chief of a nuclear warfare state when war itself is tantamout to suicide for a majority of citizens. Analogous reasoning holds for those living in allied countries which are even indirectly integrated into a superpower's global nuclear infrastructure. And in the event of a nuclear winter following an exchange of strategic warheads, citizens of both peripheral allies as well as neutral countries in the northern and probably even the southern hemisphere would become victims of radioactive contamination, famine or worse—annihilation without representation. Explored in Chapters 3 and 5 as well as tangentially in 10, these ultimate dangers to our very existence are simultaneously threats to all values, including political freedom, since the latter is seldom stable without a certain measure of shared affluence. Even the most optimistic scenario of a nuclear war that terminated with survivors would almost certainly be succeeded by authoritarian regimes in the more politically democratic contemporary systems. Contingency planning for post-war environments assumes that. Furthermore, widespread famine, disease and destitution in a context of societal breakdown hardly constitute a firm basis for democratic give and take, let alone pluralistic tolerance!

Less dramatic perhaps is the contemporary erosion of accountability and liberty within a state whose energies become ever more focused upon preparation for total war. Since the late 1940s, as we saw in early chapters, this has been the course followed—with a possible hiatus under President Eisenhower toward the close of the 1950s. During the first five Cold War years, Marxists, populists and even liberals firmly opposed to global interventionism and dogmatic anti–Sovietism were purged from public life. Since that era, the institutionalized impact of McCarthyism (Donner, 1980; Meranto and Lippman, 1985) has had a "chilling effect" upon opinion leaders and political aspirants who questioned the hegemonial premises of the foreign policy "consensus." The easiest way to be discredited and perhaps to sacrifice one's career was to be denounced as "soft" on communism (Joel and Erickson, 1983) or a "dupe." Internal advocacy of even socialism was treated as tantamount to support for demonic Marxist totalitarianism. Not only did the absence of distinctions (Miliband and Liebman, 1985) markedly narrow the legitimate range of democratic discourse concerning national security goals, but a tacit by-product was to bias assessments of foreign policy instrumentalities in favor of military means.

LASSWELL'S MODEL

Ironically, even before the outset of the first Cold War, Harold Lasswell, a distinguished political scientist, predicted that a long-term high expectation of international violence in an environment of total war would bring in its wake an emerging "garrison state." Drawing upon the main features of what has proved to be an uncannily apt prognostication of contemporary reality, Fitch (1985:31–32) first points to the increasing dominance at the national level of "specialists in violence," who "are typically not traditional military elites, but modern military professionals with extensive expertise in management, technical operations, and public relations." Second, the new civilian-military elite is constrained by a pre-eminent interest "in diverting resources to military expenditures." Third, this budgetary bias requires heavy reliance upon internal propaganda and coercion purportedly legitimized by the now sacrosanct national security metaphor:

> National security therefore requires a conscious effort to maintain domestic morale and legitimates symbolic manipulation and coercion as necessary instruments for internal control. . . . In order to maintain popular willingness to forego immediate consumption, the garrison state will depend on war scares, more than on actual fighting. Because of the preoccupation with danger, tendencies toward repetitiousness and ceremonialization will be prominent.

Reassessing his model at the time of the missile crisis and deepening involvement in Vietnam during the early 1960s — roughly two decades after its initial elaboration — Lasswell "again emphasized the trend toward an increased expectation of violence and the increasing prominence of experts in violence." Their reaction to the narcissistic hedonism and social fragmentation of advanced capitalist societies would be to reaffirm traditional moral values "with the increasing use of coercion to ensure conformity to those norms."[1] (Take, for example, the United States' domestic "war on drugs" and anti-abortion crusades of the 1980s with their reliance upon expanded penal [Wicker, 1989:4] infrastructures, intrusion upon privacy, and criminalization.)

Yet this does not imply overt authoritarianism. In his first elaboration of the garrison state model Lasswell was reacting to the rise of fascism and its racist Nazi variant. Fitch (1985:32) acknowledges that Lasswell's revised paradigm did not have to "be characterized by the overt abolition of democratic institutions. The external *forms* of democracy might continue to exist, but effective power would be concentrated in the hands of a loosely knit elite of civilianized military officers and militarized civilians, with increasing integration of corollary skill elites — the police, party and interest group leaders, scientists, and educators — into a growing military-industrial complex." And it is this same industrial-military complex that we noted in Chapters 5, 6 and 7 habitually engaged in ceremonial demonization and threat inflation with respect to the Soviet Union, "communist subversion" and, reified recently as the fashion (Falk, 1988) goes, "international terrorism."

Clearly, what I have at times called the paranoid projection syndrome is a *sine qua non,* for (Falk, 1988) "without enemies, the expectation of violence could not be maintained nor could high defense budgets or domestic repression be legitimized." The overt collapse of the Soviet threat metaphor has thus generated not only "nostalgia" (Tarnoff, 1989:4) for Cold War II, but a genuine quandary among civilian militarists at the pinnacle of the military-industrial complex. After four full years of asymmetrical Soviet peace initiatives and concessions, Bush ("Bush," 1990:1) "told troops at a desert training exercise ... that 'uncertainties and dangers' in the world justify increased military spending...." Those "dangers" are now, at least temporarily, attributed to the Third World, notwithstanding the disproportionate and inappropriate force structures. Some relatively conservative analysts (Hoagland, 1990:4) have already underscored the spuriousness if not absurdity of the new "national security" rationale:

> Despite the wishful thinking by American strategists hurrying to find a new global military role for the United States beyond Europe and the Cold War, Panama does not represent the wave of the future. This invasion is more likely to be seen in retrospect as a late example of a major power using disproportionate military power in the Third World to resolve a problem that better political and diplomatic management would have avoided in the first place.

For militarists, however, terrorism and drugs will be wedded to radicalism as the new "threats" necessary to maintain the basic institutional interests of the military-industrial complex. Saddam Hussein was but the latest example!

CLASS DIMENSIONS

The class bias of the emergent garrison state is a dimension neglected by both Lasswell and Fitch as well as most of the small number of liberals who articulate principled opposition to contemporary American militarism. As we saw in Chapter 4, their failure to take account of several key socio-economic infrastructural underpinnings fatally weakens their critique of the policy bias favoring interventionism and its strategic reinforcers. Put differently, it renders them vulnerable to charges of utopian idealism, softness or a lack of realism. Even Michael Dukakis, whose relative centrism sharply differentiated his campaign from Jesse Jackson's, fell victim to such charges by Bush.

In the first place, this liberal remnant tends to ignore the fact that major transnational corporations over the past decade have, through acquisitions and subcontracting, joined the traditional arms merchants as primary weapons contractors. At the same time, interlocking occurs through common board membership and equity holding by the corporate-owning upper class. The upper and upper middle investing classes, with insignificant exceptions, do not discriminate against firms on the basis of what is produced as opposed to anticipated earnings and capital gains. Profit yields on invested capital by corporations engaging in military production resemble those of investors in "friendly" developing countries in one important way. On the average, they are close to double or more that of United States–based civilian production. Further, because of sharply rising campaign costs and the growing role of PACs which now account for more than 50 percent (Green, 1989:124) of congressional campaign funds, upscale and corporate dominance of the political system, and especially the Democrats (Etzioni, 1984; Meyerson, 1989), has increased considerably over the past several decades. Conversely, civil rights, women's organizations and above all labor on the left have seen their influence progressively diminished as the systemic symbolic bias tilted in a conservative direction. Indeed, Bush successfully tarnished Dukakis by associating him with the "L-word" — Liberalism.

This brings us to the second point: Garrison state militarism is not directionless. Like other institutions and cultural biases (Heilbroner, 1985), it generally promotes corporate investment and capital accumulation abroad. The autonomy of the weapons producers and the military-industrial complex has been constrained generally by the global or transnational class interests (Targ, 1984) of American-based transnational capital. Thus countries (Guatemala, 1954; Egypt, 1955; Cuba, 1959; Libya, 1970; Angola, 1975; Iran, 1978; Nicaragua, 1979) which nationalized or heavily taxed foreign investments, enhanced the status of labor, vigorously extirpated corruption and championed nonaligned foreign policies were systematically denied weapons even if they sought to pay cash. The only exceptions were those whose armies remained largely intact, had been penetrated and impacted by prior American or at least Western indoctrination, and therefore — as in Arbenz's Guatemala, Allende's Chile, Keita's Mali, Sukarno's Indonesia, Goulart's Brazil, or Nkrumah's Ghana — offered good prospects for overthrowing the economically nationalist and socially reformist regime (or at least for forcing upon it a more "moderate" course as in Portugal, Peru, Guatemala and the Philippines). Thus, the interests of transnational corporate investors have continuously shaped the overall posture of American neo-colonial military policy and its garrison state infrastructure.

While dogmatic anti-communism has been deeply ingrained as a sacrosanct legitimating ideological rationale, a plethora of equally virulent corollaries and euphemistic symbols have been employed when opportune. These ranged from Dulles' "immorality" of neutralism, Kennedy's denunciation of "indirect aggression" and "subversion," to "instability" and Nixon and Carter's stress upon "access" to Middle Eastern oil as "vital interests," to the most recent Reaganite *bête noir*—"terrorism." Terrorism has been variously linked to drugs, Libya and "communism"—the last even after "Evil Empire" rhetoric evaporated in the face of Gorbachev's peace and reform initiatives. Thus Bush has had to rely upon "international terrorism" and "Narco-terrorism" more recently as his major foreign threat inflators. Their manipulative function is carefully dissected by Falk (1988). With the emergence of active anti-interventionist movements in the United States during the late 1960s, many of these distorting ideological slogans have been ritualistically employed ad nauseam to narrow the appeal for domestic opponents of militaristic hegemonialism. Thus the 1990 Iraqi episode evoked silence.

REPRESSIVE TENDENCIES

Lasswell's (1962) perspicacity is nowhere better revealed than in his prediction "that if peace movements began to win significant support, their success would generate increasing pressure for tighter controls on 'subversive activities.'" His revised work was published about a year before Kennedy's assassination, which itself occurred some months after Kennedy compromised to settle the missile crisis and subsequently sought to move toward a policy of detente with the USSR. This policy was associated with a radical shift in policy toward Cuba from previous invasion commitment to "containment." And shortly before his death Kennedy had, according to the late Senator Wayne Morse, taken the latter to the "privacy" of the White House Rose Garden and expressed his decision to withdraw a substantial number of United States military personnel from Vietnam. Kennedy, in short, was so traumatized by the missile crisis that he rejected militarism in favor of civilianism.

It may be coincidental that two prominent American black leaders—both with large and rapidly growing followings—were assassinated a year or so after they adopted strong anti-interventionist stands and openly opposed militaristic hegemonialism. Martin Luther King's death in 1968 followed by three years that of Malcolm X. The assassination of Robert Kennedy—who was moving in the same direction by mid-1968—ensured that the two major party nominees that year would be inoffensive to the vested interests of the military-industrial complex, and the Mafia-linked intelligence substructure.

The virtual collapse of the anti–Vietnam war movement and Nixon's landslide over his "radical" Democratic opponent, McGovern, in the aftermath of the 1970 Kent State massacre of protesting students by National Guardsmen who to this day have gone unpunished, eliminated another potential challenge to the incipient garrison state. But even prior to that event a pattern of official lawlessness toward domestic dissenters (Donner, 1980; Glick, 1988; Churchill and Van der Wall, 1988) had appeared. Disrespect for the Constitutional rights of arrested black rioters in urban ghettos during the 1960s culminated in ubiquitous police brutality and even murder of "Black Power" and other militant civil rights advocates. Like their organizations, those of the anti-war movement were the targets of FBI informers and provocateurs. In fact, an operation labeled COINTELPRO was introduced to disrupt and otherwise weaken groups strongly opposed to militaristic interventionism in the Third World. Other intelligence agencies like the CIA as well as several within the armed forces also actively endeavored to weaken antiwar groups.

Not only was the McGovern peace candidacy targeted for dirty tricks and the "radical" (i.e., unpatriotic) smear, but considerable rivalry emerged between the quasi-autonomous CIA and the FBI. In fact one exhaustive investigation (Hougan, 1985) attributes the Watergate burglary to the CIA's interest in wielding much enhanced domestic leverage over both Democratic and Republican figures in the congress and possibly even the Nixon Administration. Paradoxically, the operation may have been "blown" by an FBI endeavoring to preserve its monopoly over confidential information on potentially embarrassing behavior by apparently respectable mainstream pols.[2] In any event, the episode dramatized the pronounced growth of warfare state lawlessness and intimidation against insiders once such practices had become institutionalized or routine against so-called radicals.

While state efforts to undermine those opposed to interventionism lessened during the 1970s in the wake of the Watergate scandal and withdrawal from Vietnam, this decrease also may have reflected past "successes" — diminished activity and strength of the repression-targeted protest organizations. Furthermore, hearings during the mid-1970s in Congress such as those by the Church Committee exposed unconstrained past police state tactics and proposed legislation to curb such abuses. The legislation, however, was more symbolic than effective.

With the resumption of Cold War militarism in the late 1970s and particularly after Reagan's triumph, the internal police state apparatus was given an increased budget and broadened mandates to target dissenters.[3] The American Civil Liberties Union's Executive Director (Glasser, [1985]) highlights several ominous official measures and proposals that seriously threaten democratic rights. These include an Executive Order by President Reagan authorizing the CIA to carry on surveillance and other covert activities *inside* the United States; and the creation of several new computer files to track such undesirables as people believed to be "anti-authority," people "'believed' to be 'associated'" with those "'suspected' of being 'terrorists,'" and "associates" of "suspected white-collar criminals." Most frightening was a new law proposed by the Reagan Administration

> that would give the Secretary of State sweeping authority to label U.S. and foreign organizations as "terrorist" and would subject Americans who "support" such groups to up to ten years imprisonment. Neither "terrorist" or "support" is clearly defined in the legislation, and the courts are barred from reviewing the validity of the definition.

By April 1985, anti-interventionist organizations such as the Committee in Solidarity with the People of El Salvador (CISPES) were already being designated by the FBI as engaged in "terrorism." Moreover, this designation (Jones, 1985:3) was being accompanied by systematic harassment intended to intimidate supporters.[4] Infiltration and provocation were also employed under the aegis of surveillance that reported on even those whose contacts with CISPES were peripheral. No criminal acts were ever identified.

Repression has not been limited to secular "radicals." The burgeoning movement by Roman Catholics and Protestants to safeguard Salvadoran refugees' "right to life" was also targeted. According to Schultz (1985):

> The response of the Reagan Administration [to the activities of the Sanctuary Movement] has been to indict 16 Sanctuary workers — including two Roman Catholic priests, a Presbyterian pastor, three nuns, and other religious and lay workers. They were charged with conspiracy, aiding and abetting, transporting, harboring and shielding Central American refugees. In addition, 60 refugees being helped by the Sanctuary Movement were also arrested at the same time. . . .
> Conviction on the conspiracy charge alone carries a maximum penalty of 10 years in prison and a fine of $10,000.

Unsurprisingly, then, we discover a resurgence of official lawlessness manifested by targeting of even liberal peace-oriented foreign policy critics. Mackenzie (1985:7) reports that "in violation of FBI guidelines that limit political investigations, the bureau conducted nationwide probes of moderate peace organizations from 1982 at least through 1984. One target, according to FBI documents, was Physicians for Social Responsibility (PSR), a group of 25,000 doctors that advocates a bilateral, verifiable nuclear weapons freeze."[5]

Despite the Reagan Administration's apparent interest in arms control during the 1986–1988 period, there has been no let-up in spying upon and repression (Glick, 1988) of domestic dissenters. Indeed, the expansion of FBI and other intelligence agency resources during the 1980s in absence of congressional challenge implies that virtually no major peace, civil rights, ecological or other reform group is exempt from infiltration at best and disruption at worst. Even the Supreme Court appears to have been ("License," 1988:9–10) on the FBI's target list for domestic surveillance from 1932 at least until 1985!

Evidently the burden of all this surveillance became too large for the FBI to handle alone. As a response to the civil rights and Vietnam era anti-interventionist movements between the early 1960s and the beginning of the 1970s, the FBI and CIA actively encouraged the police in more than a hundred major cities to create "intelligence divisions" (i.e., "Red Squads"). In the immediate aftermath of the Watergate scandal and Vietnam debacle, many of these activities were curtailed and exposed as a consequence of legislation and judicial suits. Subsequently, however, with the revival of militant Cold Warriorism in the late 1970s and especially in the Reagan era, there was an insidious regrowth and expansion of this repressive infrastructure. Donner (1985) lists a number of recent developments indicating that police at all levels of government — local, county, state as well as federal — are compiling dossiers, monitoring and disrupting those critical of the establishment consensus.[6]

Donner proceeds to identify "six major" current "police abuses" — basing his summary upon press leaks, "court testimony of former undercover agents and informers, statements by police officers before Congressional committees, pretrial disclosures, and documents released under freedom of information laws." They are:

> The targeting of groups and individuals engaged in peaceful dissent.
>
> The use of surveillance, photography, mail covers, informers, wiretapping and other questionable tactics in such investigations.
>
> The resort to aggressive tactics, including provocation, disruption and harassment of political protest groups; burglaries, raids and the dissemination of false information about individuals to landlords, employers and other third parties; the theft, photocopying and destruction of documents and correspondence.
>
> The collection of files and dossiers on dissident groups and the dissemination of the information to other law-enforcement agencies.
>
> The absence of a relationship between these practices and the legitimate police functions of law enforcement, crime prevention and maintenance of public order.
>
> The resort to implausible ideological explanations, such as "national security" or "terrorism," to justify the investigations.

Apparently, the range of peaceful dissent under surveillance is as broad as it was in the early 1970s — civil rights, trade unionism, civil liberties, ecology — and as we saw earlier, includes both anti-nuclear and anti-interventionist groups.[7]

Subsequent disclosures confirm (Burkholder, 1988:20, 18, 22) that not only have such practices proliferated, but the possible resurrection of local police "Red Squads" has been encouraged by the FBI. Furthermore, this "local" upsurge in domestic spying upon progressives has been aided by the growth of heavily funded extremist right-wing "intelligence" organizations, private "security" agencies (Shapiro, 1985) and a number of major corporations.[8] Burkholder (1988:20) reports that

> State and local police seemed to have forged partnerships with right-wing citizens and the Federal Bureau of Investigation in their surveillance efforts. John Rees publishes *Information Digest* in Baltimore, a small-circulation journal for police officers, FBI agents, and right-wing groups. Rees is a veteran FBI and police informant and contributor to the John Birch Society's *Review of the News*. His writings have been cited by the Bureau as being crucial in the FBI's controversial probe of the Committee in Solidarity with the People of El Salvador (CISPES).
> Activists and civil libertarians suspect an FBI role in encouraging or coordinating local and state police-intelligence operations around the country. At the same time that the FBI was monitoring CISPES and the Pledge of Resistance, police officers in Orlando and Philadelphia infiltrated the Pledge group and in Chico, California, joined the local CISPES chapter. Standard FBI field-office involvement includes going to local police with a request for help.

Thus the substructure of a tacit police state apparatus which routinely targets not only radicals but liberals has been institutionalized. Intimidating many who would otherwise join such groups, this domestic component of the nascent garrison state awaits only a major political crisis to launch a massive wave of overt repression. New electronic surveillance equipment, widespread use of polygraphs and the exchange of data by rapidly proliferating "security" computer banks in conjunction with the previously mentioned developments have made opponents of militarism and social injustice particularly vulnerable to loss of employment and other, lesser forms of intimidation. For many who are concerned they have probably exerted a chilling effect upon the open expression of such criticism.

Finally, measures to suppress domestic foreign policy criticism extend to the increased denial of visas to prominent foreigners (Schapiro, 1985). This "practice makes the United States the only Western democracy to exclude foreign citizens on ideological grounds."[9]

DECLINE OF SUBSTANTIVE DEMOCRATIC ACCOUNTABILITY

The erosion of genuine democratic discourse on institutionalized militarization and interventionism in American public life since the late 1960s is by no means wholly due to these highly important repressive tendencies. We have already noted the decline of candidate dependence upon party as opposed to corporate PAC financing and support. Etzioni (1984) discusses the plutocratic implications of these developments since the early 1970s. The decline of accountability to ordinary citizens has been powerfully reinforced over the past several decades by the subordination of elite-mass political communications to increasingly contrived manipulative techniques generated by such fields as advertising and applied psychology. Perry (1984) brilliantly demonstrates that in the 1980 national elections such stratagems were masterfully targeted by the Reagan command upon potential voters, who, it might be surmised, became veritable objects of internal psychological warfare techniques.

The same could be said for 1988 when the Bush team employed systematic survey research, computer analysis and consultant expertise to target Dukakis' weaknesses. Dukakis was put on the defensive by Red-baiting and militaristic allusions — "card carrying member of the ACLU," "the L-word," "soft" on crime and "defense," etc. — until the final weeks. In less perfected form, this process has contributed to the erosion of substantive discourse (Edelman, 1964; Klein, 1988) involving genuine issues and therefore elite accountability for almost three decades. Taking a somewhat longer historical perspective, Green (1989:122) recalls:

> A century ago, 80 percent of eligible Americans voted (about the current average turnout among our Western allies). In 1960, it was 63 percent; in 1988, 50 percent; and in the last nonpresidential election, 33 percent. Americans who once crossed the oceans to fight for democracy now don't cross the street to exercise it. How do we know when a democracy is dying? Surely one measure is the number of its residents who consider it worthwhile to choose the representatives who govern their lives. If too few vote, however, will officials know what is in the broadest national interest? Will some communties fail to be heard — while others are heard too loudly? If a 50 percent turnout is still a democracy, is 33 percent? Ten percent? What about when Americans with annual incomes of less than $5,000 are half as likely to vote as those earning more than $50,000, giving the affluent one and a half ballots each compared with the poor?

It might be added that such patterns are also found with even greater disparity for other forms of political participation.

If those who did participate were reasonably well informed, one could argue they functioned as a surrogate — albeit with a marked upscale bias — for fellow non-voters. Yet this is hardly the case. Rosen (1989) explores the simplest levels of public awareness on life or death related nuclear issues. Referring, for example, to the December 1987 INF treaty, he reports:

> . . .[W]hen a national opinion poll a month later asked questions about the treaty's basic provisions, the results showed that more than 90 percent of registered American voters did not know that INF eliminates all U.S. land-based missiles in Europe capable of reaching the Soviet Union. And 75 percent did not know that the treaty says nothing about missiles aimed at the United States.
>
> That poll echoed the results of a CBS/New York Times poll eight years earlier during the U.S.-Soviet negotiations for a second treaty limiting strategic or long-range weapons. A startling 70 percent of Americans were unable to name the two nations involved in those SALT II talks.

Other illustrations include the fact that "81 percent of the American public believes, incorrectly, that U.S. policy prohibits the first use of nuclear weapons, according to a 1984 Public Agenda Foundation study." Or, to go back two years earlier, a "CBS/*New York Times* poll showed that, while most of the population said that it favored the freeze, only 30 percent knew that Ronald Reagan opposed it. . . ." Thus even as quantitatively the level of electoral and other forms of political participation is very low, qualitatively it lacks sufficient cognitive attributes to hold officials accountable. Citizens in such a formal "democracy" are particularly vulnerable, not only to militaristic manipulation, but also to flagrant violations of their Constitutional rights—provisions and legal norms of which they are equally ignorant. Thus examples abound of garrison state disregard for domestic Constitutional restraints.

The disregard for legal restraint extends to blatant disdain for international law—for example, America's violent attacks upon Nicaragua, and refusal of World Court jurisdiction over Managua's complaint that the United States mined her harbors. When the Congress briefly denied aid to the contras, the Reagan Administration subverted this legislative proscription by arranging for "private" assistance. When such officially generated "private" funds proved inadequate due in part ("Exposing," 1988) to corruption, public funds were obtained and illegally converted by equally corrupt high officials. Coffin (1987:1) portrays this as

> a clear case of the confrontation between the President and Congress. Senator William S. Cohen (R–Maine), a member of the investigating committee, calls the affair "a story of betrayal." Two laws and a treaty are relevant:
> • The Neutrality Act forbids American citizens or carriers from sending arms to warring nations with whom we are at peace, without a declaration of war.
> • The Boland Amendment bans the use of public funds to overthrow the Nicaraguan government.
> • The World Court decided that the U.S. actions in behalf of the contras were a violation of international law and ordered the U.S. to "cease and desist." The World Federalist Association points out that "in certifying the United Nations charter, the U.S. agreed to 'comply'; with the decisions of the World Court."
> The Tower Commission and Congressional hearings offer abundant evidence that President Reagan was indeed "the boss" of a vast, complex conspiracy to break the laws.

Most distressing in terms of the garrison state model was the revelation that (Emerson, 1988) a semi-autonomous, quasi-institutionalized network of ruthless "warriors" operated against movements and governments with impunity—virtually out of control.

A parallel financial substructure of approximately $35 billion was created to evade public accountability. Nelson (1988) recalls:

> Last year, reporters for the *Philadelphia Inquirer* . . . exposed what the Pentagon calls its "black budget." *The black budget is literally a secret cache of funds*—secret weapons and money for intelligence agencies. . . . The black

budget is now nearly as big as the entire federal budget for health care. It is much larger than the federal budget for Education, Agriculture, Transportation, and Environmental Protection.

Where and how the funds are concealed is beyond the purview of this chapter. One example—pertinent given the sudden appearance of certain diseases in Cuba several years ago and more recently in Nicaragua—will suffice. Piller (1988:271) notes that Pentagon bacteriological warfare budgets

> have increased nearly sixfold since 1980. And those budgets reflect only a fraction of the hundreds of millions of dollars in Defense Department biomedical research funds that may be directly applied to BW but are hidden in innocuous-sounding programs.

Here we have a case of what might be called lawful secrecy.

At bottom, however, the problem is that in a state so heavily geared for various types of war, secrecy engenders lawlessness. It is not only Reagan's immediate aides like Poindexter, McFarlane and North who subverted congressional proscriptions (Marshall, Scott and Hunter, 1987) on arms transfers, but the Administration's zealous covert action imperative necessarily resulted in its connivance with drug operators. Coffin (1988:1) emphasizes that

> The CIA seems to believe that anyone who fires a gun and swears allegiance to anti-communism can be signed on. The *New York Times* reports that "the Reagan Administration, like its predecessors, has repeatedly subordinated the drug issue to other American interests, from support for insurgents fighting leftist regimes to the belief that punishing drug-producing countries might destabilize them."
>
> A former State Department official in the intelligence area, Francis J. McNeil, told the *Times*, "You have to balance priorities, but the fact is, we have not balanced priorities; we have always put narcotics at the bottom of the totem pole."

Coffin goes on to detail the charges which have been amply aired in the press. The conclusion is that "national security" has been "routinely" employed to obfuscate the substitution of force—naked and manipulative alike—for law. Morley (1988:165–66) deplores this hypocrisy:

> Senior U.S. policy-makers—including Bush—have proclaimed themselves dedicated to the war on drugs, while allowing immunity or leniency to be extended to major suspected drug dealers in the name of "national security." Noriega is only the latest and most famous beneficiary of this routine practice.

He adds that Congressman Glenn English, who held a series of subcommittee hearings on Bush's role in the alleged "drug war" (an appropriate garrison state metaphor), found "the Administration's interdiction efforts over the past eight years have been little more than lip-service and press relations."

Rather than respect international law or congressional authority under the Constitution, the Administration and its supporters have opted to systematically disinform (manipulate) citizens, opinion leaders and legislators alike. In Latin America, for example, the Reagan team purported to support the Contadora group while simultaneously endeavoring to subvert its efforts (Black, 1987) to end military involvement by both the United States and Cuba in Nicaragua. Black quotes from a report that "a secret background paper prepared for a meeting of the National Security Council last year boasted that the Administration had 'effectively blocked Contadora group efforts.'" Even more to the point, they call our attention to the fact that a "report entitled 'In Contempt of Congress' released earlier this year by Sens. Tom Harkin (D–IA) and John Kerry (D–MA) details a systematic record of deception. The report, prepared by the Institute for Policy Studies, reveals 77 instances in which the Congress was deceived or misled by Reagan officials concerning their activities in Central America. The report also cites 15 possible violations of domestic and international law by the administration."

The eclipse of the national legislature — democracy's core institution — is itself symbolic of a garrison state emphasis upon deference to executive strength and prerogative. Nowhere was this more dramatically illustrated than in the deliberate failure of the Iran-Contra committee to pursue numerous avenues of inquiry involving drug traffickers and the Israeli connection. Even more fundamentally, it intentionally failed to dramatize the president's direct responsibility for a conspiracy which further undermined both the rule of law and the democratic process. In reviewing a critical study (Cohen and Mitchell, 1988), Waldman (1988) prophetically concludes:

> Ultimately, the most depressing thing about the Iran-Contra affair was that it didn't seem to matter all that much. In a few months, Reagan will be saying good-bye to a misty-eyed nation. Poindexter's lawyers will be thinking of ever more creative ways of avoiding trial, and North will be getting higher lecture fees and longer ovations. Fundamentally, people value other qualities more than adherence to democratic principles. Someone really fighting for something he believes in is admirable even if he's running an illegal war. Cover-ups, lies, and obstruction of justice are okay as long as you later admit you lied and explain that it was for a good cause. That Americans still admire these men of zeal in spite of the Iran-Contra hearings shows that the committee's failure was monumental.

This outcome was inevitable since the "investigating" committee itself (1) was stacked with pro–Contras; (2) excluded those with special expertise like Kerry; (3) was too big; (4) had many members who were too lazy — thus leaving the main interrogation to lawyers who were not good at raising the political issues; (5) accorded North and Poindexter unprecedented speechmaking and consultative privileges; and (6) most congressmen lacked sufficient courage to openly impugn the good faith of the Chief Executive or his underlings.

For those addicted to a militaristic hegemonial imperative, Manichean reductionism becomes *the* operative decisional framework. Choices are simplistically (Fitch, 1985:42) portrayed: "Either accept the 'loss' of countries . . . or intervene to establish a domestic consensus through more active use of propaganda and/or restrictions on dissemination of opposing points of view." Civilian militarists in the Reagan era lent their active cooperation by imposing new restraints upon the availability of information through widespread use of intimidating (Jussim, 1985) yet unreliable polygraph tests, prosecutions for releasing data to prosecutors (Naureckas, 1988:4-5) or the press, immense publicity for "spy" trials, efforts to undermine the Freedom of Information Act. Also widespread, we may add, was the brazen use of paper shredders, the Fifth Amendment, dilatory obstructionism as well as "Executive Privilege" to withhold evidence from Iran-Contra investigations and trials. With the President setting the example, top officials also impugned the patriotic credentials of anti-militarist groups (e.g., nuclear freeze, some liberal democrats, journalists) who have not yet been intimidated into silence. Ironically, even the head of the Senate's Intelligence Committee opted for inaction when informed (Corn and Morley, 1989:152) that at least one colleague was under electronic surveillance by the National Security Agency. Such practices seem to have become quasi-legitimate in a symbolic milieu emphasizing the importance of "bargaining from strength" along with the "threat of terrorism" which was targeted upon the mass public as well as congress and the media. Or in the words of veteran analyst Christopher Hitchens (1988: 192) "The age of Reagan has made such fabrication and manipulation seem like an echo of the pastoral." We should of course be wary of exaggerating its effects.

Yet one of the most telling consequences, it seems, is (Donner, 1985a: 437) that "over the past three years a substantial number of Democrats in both houses of Congress have abandoned traditional liberal positions, especially in the areas of foreign affairs and national security." Whether or not the change is wholly attributable "to a shift in popular sentiment" in a chauvinistic direction, it means that the beleaguered minority of anti-militarist liberals are now — short of a major fiasco — incapable of halting and possibly even slowing down the juggernaut. We have already underscored — in the B-1 context — that the price of opposing one major weapon system is support for another. Ironically the slowdown in the growth of military spending since 1986 is more attributable to the state's fiscal crisis, Pentagon saturation with unobligated funds, a "$30 Billion Stockpile of Unneeded Material" (Sciolmo, 1990:3), and Gorbachev's unilateral peace concessions than to a major upsurge of liberal Democratic opposition. Liberal Democrats and moderates will get some modest reductions if Soviet retrenchment and the growing de facto budget deficit continue. Thus external and systemic forces, rather than the vitality of the all but emasculated liberals, will play the determinative role.

Less noticed has been bi-partisan support for the militarization of foreign aid at the very time when developing nations are experiencing a widening socio-economic gap as well as an unprecedented financial crisis. One observer ("The Reagan Legacy," 1988:2) cautions:

> U.S. investments in foreign aid, traditionally weighted toward military aid and assistance to strategically placed allies, have become almost entirely a tool of "national security." In the President's FY89 budget proposal, 61% of U.S. foreign aid dollars would be either direct military aid or indirect assistance to strengthen military allies. Only 22% would assist international organizations or support development in needy third world countries....
>
> ...This expansion will create a bureaucratic will to sustain such spending levels in future budgets. Moving the arms race into outer space and into new technologies will cause further hemorrhaging in military spending. The buildup of U.S. interventionary forces around the world will increase the likelihood of U.S. involvement in future conflicts.

Even the lull provided by opposition to "lethal" Contra aid has more to do with the Contras' lack of success, Sandinista concessions and growing Latin American opposition than to any change in United States destabilization objectives. The invasion of Panama served to confirm the Bush Administration's commitment to historic interventionism. Unsurprisingly, most congressional liberals either were silent or overtly supported the aggression.

PUBLIC RELATIONS AND MASS MEDIA SUBSERVIENCE

The systemic failure manifested in the Iran-Contra Affair (and manifested by the subsequent Bush victory) also reflects a disinclination by what Halliday (1985) calls "news hungry and gullible editors" of the mass media to play an autonomous role — another manifestation of the emergent garrison state. Thus Hertsgaard (1985:48), in the course of reviewing an analysis (Perry, 1984) of Reagan's 1980 campaign, zeroes in on the subservience of the national media.

> The skill of Reagan's public relations apparatus at projecting through the news media its version of who Reagan is and what his policies have meant for the nation has been crucial to the president's popularity and re-election.
>
> David Gergen, who helped run Reagan's media operation until resigning as White House director of communications in January 1984, used to say that a president cannot govern successfully if he does not get the right story out through the "filter" of the press. Gergen and his colleagues did their job so well, however, that the news media under Reagan usually resembled a clear windowpane more than a filter. Not only was the administration's preferred self-image generally passed through to the public intact; news stories for the most part offered few hints at how calculated, contrived, and ultimately dishonest that image was.

This acquiescence occurred despite the growing virulence and militaristic belligerence of presidential speeches. Those speeches, whose tone was but one symptom of garrison state pathology, were pinpointed as a telltale sign by Fitch (1985:33) in his content analysis of presidential State of the Union messages. His somewhat alarming conclusion is that "from 1976 to 1982 the average frequency of symbols associated with increased expectations of violence exceeds the average for the cold war years by more than 25%. Despite the relatively moderate tone of President Reagan's State of the Union messages compared to some of his other speeches, there is ample evidence of a renewed sense of peril and heightened expectations of violence unmatched since the end of the war in Korea." These were refocused upon "drug traffickers" and "international terrorism" after the mid-1980s.

The willingness of mass media in the United States to serve as a foreign policy "transmission belt" for elite militarism and interventionism has been documented in detail by Chomsky and Herman (1979) as well as Parenti (1986) more recently. With a few honorable exceptions, the media have acquiesced to the Reagan Administration's disinformation techniques *vis-à-vis* the Soviets as well as domestic liberal opponents (Perry, 1984), who are often manipulated in a way that forces them to opt for either silence or the appearance of being soft on communism and terrorism. Similarly, uncritical mass media reporting on what were clearly "demonstration elections" (Herman, 1984) in El Salvador and Grenada also highlights institutionalized deference to militaristic interventionism abroad complemented by psychological warfare techniques against one's own citizens.

Indeed, a 1982 content analysis by Dorman (1985:18, 21) of main line media treatment of the Soviets revealed that although there was less name calling than in the early 1950s, "with few exceptions [there] was a portrayal of the Soviet Union as a ruthless and intractable adversary."

> Similarly, U.S. journalists widely agreed that the Soviet Union killed both detente and SALT II by the invasion of Afghanistan. They did not consider that U.S. actions — such as moving to establish a new base on Diego Garcia, or selling military equipment for the first time to China, or beginning a trillion dollar defense build-up — might have been interpreted by Moscow as moves signaling Washington's desire to kill detente, thereby leading the Soviets to conclude that they had nothing to lose by their behavior. Nor did the media seriously assay the possibility that SALT II was in deep trouble in the U.S. Senate from the political right long before the invasion and would not have passed under any circumstances.

More ominous, perhaps, is the same author's warning that "today a concerted effort is underway to label the media as soft on communism and to force them into an even more blatant anti–Soviet stance than they usually adopt. Anything less than unreserved red-baiting by mainstream journalism is enough to trigger criticism from hardcore conservative critics."[10] While such stridency has attenuated in the wake of Gorbachev's "peace initiatives" and unilateral concessions, the overall anti–Soviet, anti-leftist bias continues for the most part in the selection of topics, their interpretations and diction.

There is no doubt that the overall ideological bias (Parenti, 1986) of the mass media gradually shifted toward the hard right after the corporate-funded Committee on the Present Danger launched its threat inflation campaign during 1974. Stephen Cohen (1985a:335) aptly recalls:

> Ten years ago, newspaper editorial pages and network television programs regularly featured proponents and opponents of detente. Now, overwhelmingly, they present only representatives of the cold war right and the center, typically a supporter of the Administration and a self-described "defense Democrat." In addition, the recent practice, as on ABC's *Nightline,* of casting a Soviet official in the role of primary anti–Reagan spokesman implies that there is no legitimate American position anywhere between them.

Pinpointing this shift, Gwirtzman (1985:A27) emphasizes that "not since the days of William Randolph Hearst and Col. Robert McCormick has the right-wing viewpoint been more prominent in American journalism. In much of the media, conservative opinion-makers are either even or pulling ahead of their rivals, both in audience and impact."[11]

One consequence of this media shift was the ease with which Bush tarnished Dukakis by accusing him of being a liberal. Yet once Gorbachev's olive branch and unilateral concessions evoked a shift in Reagan's stance, the media for the most part hewed to the "new line." Even then martial fireworks determined the explicit assumption — repeated ad nauseam — that "weakness" dictated the need for domestic reform, arms reductions or the withdrawal from Afghanistan. A more balanced interpretation is provided by Kriesberg (1989).

One of the clearest patterns is the responsiveness of both mass media and mass opinion to elite cues and corporate-funded priorities. This responsiveness produced the decline ("Opinion Roundup," 1984:37) in the percentage of the public believing that military spending was excessive, from 37 percent in the early 1970s to 26 percent a decade later. Although it affected most groups among the population, this shift was considerably greater among the less educated and more television-dependent mass sector of the citizenry — ironically the same people most victimized by urban decay and other manifestations of decline in their living standards. The sharp social program cutbacks in a context of an administration-induced recession and an unprecedented rise in military spending provoked elite budgetary contention during the 1982–84 period. This in turn was reflected by a fall-off in mass support for the Reagan Administration's trillion-dollar armament program at the expense of social security, health, education and housing.

MASS ALIENATION AND NON-PARTICIPATION

One of the major correlates of the garrison state has been mass marginalization from an increasingly unaccountable and plutocratically dominated political system whose rituals and symbols veil an ever more pronounced manipulative asymmetrical dimension.[12] Bush's style and mendacity (Randolph, 1990:5) continue the pattern. And given the socio-economic stagnation or deterioration examined in Chapter 8, even more ordinary citizens sense that the warfare state's priorities are unresponsive to their aspirations for greater economic security. A decline in historic American optimism for higher living standards and quality of life or even a sense of genuine community (Lasch, 1989) has been a direct consequence of such developments. Likewise the spectacular growth of mass political alienation (Gilmour and Lamb, 1975; Warren Miller *et al.,* 1980) since the early 1960s. "Political alienation" refers to a sense of powerlessness, meaninglessness of partisan choices and above all distrust toward major party political elites that had come to characterize between two-thirds and three-quarters of the citizenry by the early 1970s. For the most part this alienation persisted or worsened (Warren Miller *et al.,* 1980) during the succeeding decade.[13] The pervasiveness of such political distrust has in turn been reflected by a spectacular erosion (Lipset and Schneider, 1984; Broder, 1990) of public confidence in major societal institutions, especially the political.[14]

Predictably this has affected the citizens' most important activity in the democratic process. For elections, despite simplification of registration procedures during recent decades, have been rejected by a growing proportion (Nonini, 1988:26–27) of the electorate.

> Some 47.1 percent of those eligible to vote in 1984 did not, in fact. It was only among the remaining 52.9 percent of the eligible population that Reagan's so-called "landslide" vote took place—one which, in net terms, represented a minority of those people eligible to vote. The 1984 election merely reinforced a long-standing trend since the 1960's—the tendency for an increasing number of people eligible to vote *not* to vote, rising from 32.7 percent in 1960 to 47.4 percent in 1980. Recent studies of nonvoters by political scientists strongly suggest that the majority choose not to vote because of their dissatisfaction with the policies and programs of the state, *not* out of any belief that things are going so well that voting would be superfluous.

By the 1988 presidential election, participation had plummeted to an all-time low of 50 percent. This confirmed the United States as having the highest rate of abstention among all industrialized nations.

Even among upper middle class sectors, which have for the most part benefited in short-run socio-economic terms from the warfare state's militarization process, there has been a sharp rise in alienation—more pronounced indeed than among less privileged sectors whose levels have traditionally been, and continue to be, the highest. For there is a societal or generalized disappointment of expectations involving personal safety, fiscal responsibility and civic probity. Sherrill (1988:170) recalls that

Twenty years ago Richard Harris wrote in *The New Yorker,* "Probably the most destructive characteristic of the successful politician is selective cowardice." Since then, the cowardice of our successful politicians has become so accepted and so indiscriminate, that we seldom feel prompted even to comment on it.

The "cowardice" has if anything been intensified by "the unwritten rule of immunity" for both members of Congress and top executive officials who are virtually exempt from successful prosecution or harsh sanctions (if convicted) for bribery.

EROSION OF THE "RULE OF LAW"

This immunity—exceptions notwithstanding—to effective sanctions for routine lawless behavior is reflected by similar tolerance for warfare state executive infractions. Most visible are such presidential acts as those previously discussed in the context of the Watergate and Iran-Contra scandals. Congressional deference and corruption may explain both the rigged hearings and the absence of impeachment proceedings. Other ignored impeachable offenses included (Bowman, 1988:11) presidential violation of the ABM Treaty and the Defense Authorization Bill.

Less dramatically, routine lawlessness occasionally surfaces when "the profit motives of large defense contractors [that] shape national defense policy" are so dominant that Pentagon officials disobey their Commander-in-Chief's directives with impunity. Thus with respect to the inordinately costly ($28 billion) and the then inoperational B-1 bomber, Zachary (1988:18) continues:

> After President Carter seemingly killed the bomber, the gamesmanship escalated. With the aid of Rockwell International, which was slated to build the B-1, Air Force officials defied the president by continuing to fund development work on the bomber with money from other programs....
>
> Kotz (1987) meticulously documents what has long been obvious: Rather than serve its civilian "master," the Pentagon wields enormous clout in the face of opposition from presidents, Congress and the citizenry.
>
> ...The B-1 bomber survived the opposition of four presidents to become "the most expensive airplane in aviation history."...

Given such pervasive power, one would expect relative immunity—at most token punishment—for criminality by key industrial-military complex actors.

Nowhere is this immunity more dramatically illustrated than in the routine persistence of fraud in military recruitment and particularly weapons procurement. Focusing upon both the 1985 GTE case and 1988 disclosures, Kaufman (1988) targets not only non-aggressive Justice Department handling but also the deferential role of what we earlier depicted as a subservient or non-autonomous press:

> In particular, journalists covering the current round of procurement fraud once again failed to focus on the two key aspects of the scandal: the persistence of

criminality in defense contracting and the inability of the legal system to com-
petently prosecute those charged with breaking the law.

In a nutshell, they failed to relate the (deliberate) ineptness of Reagan-era investigations to analogous "patterns of earlier probes of corruption in defense
contracting." Thus a lack of probity in this as in other areas dealt with in
Chapter 6 may be regarded as institutionalized.

THE CORPORATE PROPAGANDA BLITZ

It is of course not simply the rightward bias of the media which accounts
for the militarization of mass attitudes. Since 1973, thousands of Political Action Committees or PAC's — largely rightist in foreign policy orientation — have
devoted millions of dollars (Etzioni, 1984) to propagandizing for a strong
defense against the Soviets. They have operated often independently of particular candidates though many contributed directly to electoral aspirants and
particularly incumbents who themselves have echoed such themes.

Thus, as Fitch (1985:37–39) makes clear, Reagan rode and intensified the
tide of a massively engineered rightist shift in public mood in the wake of the
failure, among other things, to successfully impose a corrupt satellite regime
(McGehee, 1983) upon Vietnam. Contributing to this was the creation of a
"stab in the back" legend (Stanton, 1985; Kimball, 1988) purporting to explain
the American withdrawal from Indochina. Thus, Fitch recalls that:

> Michael Ward (1983) documents a significant decrease after 1962 in both verbal
> and non-verbal expressions of tension between the U.S. and USSR and a sharp
> resurgence in 1979–1980. At the nonelite level, public opinion surveys also
> show the proportion of respondents who consider communism as the "worst
> possible form of government" increased from 44% in 1973 to 59% in 1980,
> with the percentage agreeing that it might be "all right for some countries"
> dropping from 25% to 13%. Those identifying Russia's primary objective as
> "world domination" increased from 57% in 1978 to 69% in 1981 (Kriesberg
> 1982, p. 51). The proportion of respondents with "unfavorable" attitudes
> toward Russia, which had fallen from 91% in 1954 to 30% in 1973, rose again
> to over 60% in the early 1980's (Smith 1983, p. 280). The proportion with
> favorable attitudes toward the Soviet Union decreased from 45% in 1973 to
> only 9% a decade later (Gallup 1983, p. 17).

Indeed, by the mid-1980s, it was not only impossible for politicians to articulate positive views of Soviet intentions, but even the single-issue nuclear freeze
movement had collapsed in the aftermath of Reagan's 1984 juggernaut (which
had come about despite Mondale's conscious effort to be as "tough" as Reagan).
Symptomatic of garrison state culture, the president routinely used martial
metaphors when referring to nonmilitary protagonists and "targets." Even
though garrison state hyperbole was more subdued in the 1988 presidential
campaign, coercive toughness in dealing with the Soviets was a source of

contention between Dukakis and Bush, who unreservedly identified himself with Reagan Administration policies. Soviet concessions for the INF treaty, in Afghanistan and on human rights were portrayed as consequences of the United States military build-up and coercive "muscle-flexing."

THE MILITARY: BUREAUCRATIC ROLES AND PRAETORIAN MISSIONS

Two additional developments of the early 1980s warrant brief mention before closing our overview of this nascent warfare or national security (Barnet, 1981) state. Although we have already discussed the dominance of the industrial-military complex or iron triangle within the state itself—including the origins of Star Wars in military contractor needs for a third generation of tailored effect weaponry—little has been said about the military itself. The Joint Chiefs of Staff may not have been consulted prior to Reagan's announcement of his project for the unrestrained militarization of space. But while rejecting the president's more farfetched claims of a perfect shield, they have willingly embraced this mechanism for greater status and institutional aggrandizement. Pentagon enthusiasm may also be explained by traditional American reliance upon overkill resulting from material excess and technological advantage (Kennedy, 1985) rather than superior strategy and tactics. Their limited professional development and unlimited corporate loyalty are also manifested by the relative indifference of most brass to waste and corruption ("The Pentagon Scandals," 1985:35–40) in the procurement process.

Even more indicative of the Pentagon's substitution of militarism for professionalism (Vagts, 1967) was their decision to operationalize Reagan's belligerent posture by starting 60 to 70 highly provocative major "war games" involving more than half a million personnel. These war-fighting rehearsals gratuitously promote international tensions aimed at the Soviets as well as nationalistic Third World countries—at times they have deliberately violated their (e.g. Libyan, Nicaraguan) territorial sovereignty. According to the Center for Defense Information ("War Games," 1984:2), "the use of war games for political purposes—particularly to intimidate foreign governments, has become a hallmark of the Reagan Administration's gunboat diplomacy."[15] The aggressive lawlessness of such behavior was also evidenced, according to the CDI, by the construction of bases for contra forces within Honduras despite absence of congressional authorization. One could add the naval bombardment of Lebanon and the downing of a scheduled Iranian civilian airliner over the Persian Gulf—a clear violation of international law for which commanding naval personnel didn't even receive so much as a reprimand. As late as 1988, open efforts were being made to overthrow the Panamanian government while an aircraft carrier task force was dispatched to intimidate the Libyan regime despite its call for negotiations. The 1989 invasion of Panama fully established Bush Administration continuity with its predecessor, as did the show of force off the Colombian coast in January 1990.

As of the mid-1980s, the war proneness of even senior officers was underscored by the results of a *Newsweek*-sponsored Gallup poll in June 1984 of 257 American generals and admirals—roughly 25 percent of the total. The results highlight a woeful failure by America's top professionals to assimilate the implications of the excesses, indiscriminate civilian victimization and genocidal atrocities of previous twentieth century major wars, let alone the implications of vast thermonuclear warhead overkill. Fully 36 percent felt there could be a winner in nuclear war or could justify a first strike, or both. The percentage (Kohut and Horrock, 1984:44–45) reached 45 percent for Air Force generals. It was also substantially in excess of 35 percent for all non-service academy graduates, for those with less "career satisfaction" and for general officers with one or two stars. On the other hand, *only 21 percent* of the total agreed there "could not be a winner," America "could not wage tactical nuclear war," and "could not justify a first strike."

Commenting upon the opinion array, *Nation* columnist Christopher Hitchens (1984:40) adds:

> As the armed forces have become a state within a state, and a law unto themselves, there has been a corresponding and strangely unremarked politicization of the officer corps. At a recent Naval War College seminar in Newport, Rhode Island, the air was thick with political statements from military men. Lieut. Gen. Bernard E. Trainor, deputy chief of staff of the Marine Corps, said that he regarded "limited war" with the Soviet Union as an "almost inevitable probability" (a statement that made up in pith what it lacked in grammar). Vice Adm. James A. Lyons, deputy chief of Naval operations and a close friend of Navy Secretary John Lehman, told the audience that the War Powers Resolution is "insidious." In this, he echoed Adm. James D. Watkins, chief of Naval operations, who earlier this year urged Congress to reconsider the resolution as a means of expiating "the Vietnam syndrome of humiliation and defeat." But he went further than Admiral Watkins in publicly warning against "intellectual corruption" and in suggesting that the United States should have stuck by the Shah and Somoza in the hour of their trial.

As Leitenberg (1981), Aldridge (1983) and Falk (1984) demonstrate, this politicization has determined Pentagon action policy since the late 1950s. And as Lt. Col. Robert Bowman (1988) makes clear, it underscores the determination of the Reagan and Bush administrations to militarize space, even if the latter's pace is somewhat slowed due to the American fiscal crisis.

Others have also pointed to the officer corps' overt politicization as a consequence of the breakdown of a sharp division between civilians and the military during World War II—a tendency accentuated with the onset of the first Cold War. Gates (1985:433), for example, notes that "virtually all parties to the discussion agree that Army officers a century ago were significantly less political in their interests and more isolated from civilian society than officers today." Yet even then they actively promoted the expansion of military roles.

This promotion embraced, but was not limited to, suppressing strikes by tens of thousands of American trade unionists. While noting their intrusion into the foreign policy–making process is immensely greater today, Gates fails to mention that the military's historic bias favoring capital continues in our era with a pronounced anti-labor bias manifested at times by active strike-breaking complicity. Even during the late 1970s under the Carter Administration, Pentagon brass vigorously resisted efforts by the American Federation of Government Employees—one of the most moderate unions—to organize non-commissioned ranks. Perhaps more significant were possible violations of the National Labor Relations Act and other labor legislation by the Reagan Administration through deliberate efforts to weaken union representation. For example, when General Dynamics Electric Boat Division ("10,000 Metal," 1988) was struck, the military extended contract deadlines.[16] Similarly, approximately $54 billion (Blaylock, 1988:11) is now being used for contracting out to largely non-union private suppliers. And despite its moderation, little substantive change in this area can be expected from the Bush Administration.

This hostility to collective bargaining and other measures necessary to defend the status, dignity and living standards of working Americans contradicts professional norms that would maximize the quality and morale of the military's manpower base. But more fundamentally, it reflects an evolving symbiotic relationship with the corporate owning class (i.e., the industrial-military complex) which almost alone constrains Pentagon autonomy. Further, it is reinforced by the officer corps' historic antipathy to liberalism. Given the very political character of officer maneuvering (Moore and Trout, 1978) for promotion to higher ranks, it is unsurprising to discover that liberal animus is most pronounced at senior officer levels. Yet service traditions vary so that we find such rightist anti-democratic bias becomes progressively more pervasive among the brass as one moves from the Air Force to the Navy (excepting the Marines) with the least prestigious Army in between. Hostility to the liberal spirit even in this last service is truly enormous—constituting a potential threat to popular movements that may arise to challenge the warfare state. According to a survey (Chase, 1985) of more than 300 active duty army generals, only 7 percent identified themselves as liberal (vs. 66 percent conservative) and merely 10 percent supported the Democratic Party (vs. 49 percent Republican). Obviously, as in many countries where the officer corps tend to be conservative, America's brass are grossly unrepresentative of their citizenry in political terms.

But beyond that and even more significant of the incipient garrison state is the deeply felt alienation of many in the officer elite from civilian institutions and political leaders. Fitch (1985:42) highlights this intense antagonism:

> In post–Vietnam surveys of American military officers, between 67 and 95 percent said they felt the news media were biased against the military; nearly half said "extremely biased" (Sarkesian 1978, p. 44). The proportion of officers who

felt the military was being treated fairly by civilian leaders declined from 45%
in 1971 to only 25% in 1975. The overwhelming majority viewed Vietnam as
an unqualified defeat. Most blamed the civilian leadership for not allowing the
armed forces full use of their military power. Over half characterized civilians
as "soft" and indecisive (Peters & Clotfelter 1978).

He underlines the gravity and militaristic implications of such estrangement
by noting that American officers are in general "far more willing" to militarily
intervene in the developing areas than are civilians. He further notes that the
inability to resolve this "tension is likely to [result in] an erosion of military
respect for the civilian leadership and increased difficulty in sustaining military
acceptance of civilian control."[17]

Certainly, the Reagan Administration's treatment of Colonel North and
Admiral Poindexter in the Iran-Contra scandal contributed to growing military
alienation. Further, the militaristic bias of both the Reagan and the Bush
administrations — especially the latter's decision to invade Panama — has served
to inhibit any latent tendencies to question civilian authority. The Defense
Department Reorganization Act of 1986 effectively (Previdi, 1988) transformed
the service chiefs into a general staff headed by a much strengthened Chairman
of the JCS. Thus civilian control has not only been seriously weakened, but the
possibility — in terms of centralized command authority — for an effective
challenge to civilian rule has been enhanced.

There is also evidence of military high-level contingency planning for major disturbances. As early as 1981 Deputy Secretary of Defense Frank Carlucci
stated (Lindorff, 1988:60) that senior military commanders possessed the inherent authority to impose martial law on their own in the event of a breakdown of law and order which would be a matter of their determination. This
statement utterly ignored "the Posse Comitatus Act [which] bars the military
from engaging in law enforcement." Indeed, as early as 1971 a Pentagon document signed by then Secretary of Defense David Packard unilaterally asserted
two "Constitutional exceptions" to that act. Earlier we noted one of the revelations associated with the Iran-Contra scandal was a contingency plan prepared
by Oliver North. Prepared for the Federal Emergency Management Administration, it anticipated mass arrests and internment in detention camps in the
event of significant opposition to an American invasion of Nicaragua, notwithstanding the absence of a congressional Declaration of War.

THE ECLIPSE OF PRESTIGE AND LEADERSHIP

Ironically, America's militaristic arrogance has actually undermined
American prestige and influence in the Western Hemisphere. In the words of
one prominent Latin American expert (Burns), "at no time in the 20th century
has U.S. leadership in the Americas been less effective or more seriously
challenged." Not only have the majority of Latin American nations forcefully

declared their opposition to the United States–sponsored Contra war against Nicaragua, but they have defied Washington by restoring ties with Cuba and readmitting her to the OAS. Most recently they have excluded Washington from collective negotiations for a common position on their crushing external debt burdens. They also declined to receive Vice President Quayle during his abortive Latin American tour in early 1990.

Erosion of United States prestige and influence has also occurred in the Mideast, where in 1985 Aronson found:

> Today, Reagan's Mideast team finds itself in the embarrassing predicament of being at the center of a Palestine-Jordanian peace strategy that Washington itself inspired with the Reagan plan unveiled four years ago. Yet the Reagan plan was less a framework for Israeli-Arab *rapprochement* than a tactical maneuver aimed at promoting the image of U.S. control over Mideast diplomacy at a time when its Lebanon policy was falling apart.

This for an administration plagued by "incompetence" which forced it into "almost total dependence upon arms sales as the primary tool in its Mideast diplomatic arsenal...." Connivance with the Israeli attack upon the PLO in an allied capital (Tunis), use of air force fighters against an allied Egyptian military transport following the *Achille Lauro*'s highjacking, and a near firefight with Italian paramilitary personnel in the aftermath all served to diplomatically isolate an administration prone to militaristic solutions. So did its de facto 1982 strategic alliance agreement and intimate linkage to Israel. Thus, neither the Rogers Plan nor Schultz's personal visits brought the Palestinian issue to resolution. On the contrary, Washington's 1987 closing of the PLO information office in that city and the State Department's even more lawless refusal to grant Arafat a visa to address the United Nations further isolated the United States. (When the United Nations voted to move its session to Geneva so that Arafat could address the body, the United States was able to garner only one vote besides Israel's in opposition to the move.)

Thus are charted some of the external dimensions of garrison state chauvinism in a world where most civilized states still accord primacy to diplomacy and international law. There is no doubt that such lawlessness and militaristic belligerency in conjunction with disrespect for Reagan's intellectual primitivism have incrementally isolated the United States from New Zealand, Australia and a number of European allies. Commenting upon this decade-long tendency that was exacerbated under Reagan, two scholars (McKinley and Mughan, 1984:256) emphasize that the

> Twin pillars of US antipathy to the USSR rest on increasingly shaky foundations in Western Europe. The simple fact of the matter is that the United States' allies have never fully shared its revulsion against the ideology of socialism. In addition, as their relations with the USSR have become less tense, so has their

fear of its power and military might become less acute and their impatience with the United States' persistently confrontational approach more pronounced. Generally speaking, therefore, the institutionalised superpower stalemate is becoming ever less pertinent to the immediate, primarily economic, concerns of the United States' traditional allies.

Not only has American leadership diminished *vis-à-vis* the Netherlands, Norway, Denmark, Greece, and Canada, but the elites favoring greater independence have broadened their appeal in both Belgium and (Harnhardt, 1984; Radway, 1985) the Federal Republic of Germany.

It is not merely a matter of firm European resistance by 1988 to United States attempts to dictate Common Market economic policy—even at the risk of a trade war—or Europe's resolve to create a fully independent economic policy. By the late eighties Washington was under intense European pressure to accommodate Gorbachev's "peace initiatives" and to accede to both limited arms reductions and some disengagement of forces in Central Europe. And not only has Spain forced American withdrawal from a major air base, but even Bonn has angered United States officers by unilaterally reducing training exercises 50 percent in its territory.

MILITARIZING YOUTH CULTURE

Less noticeable than domestic public and corporate financed psychological warfare aimed at elite and mass publics has been a parallel effort to mold youth attitudes in a more militaristic direction. Meranto and Lippman (1985) provide considerable documentation on the purge of anti-militaristic radical faculty from American colleges between the late 1960s and mid-1980s. Indeed the university in many instances appears well integrated (Feldman, 1988) into the industrial-military complex.

Secondary schools have been flooded with deceptive college ROTC recruiting materials, films and military speakers. In addition there has been a rapid proliferation of "junior" ROTC programs within such schools. According to one report (Hoffman, 1985:27), "nationwide, the number of high school units has grown from 287 in 1980 to 826 in 1985; the number of cadets has increased from 70,000 in 1980 to 131,493 in 1985. And the Pentagon's junior ROTC budget has jumped from $11.3 million in 1980 to almost $25 million in 1985." Adolescents in these units, which project idealized distortions of military careers and functions, practice with real firearms. Simultaneously, they are unwitting objects of lessons in chauvinistic "patriotism and respect for authority." Such political indoctrination is of course reinforced by intense national bias (Fitzgerald, 1980) in secondary school social studies curricula. History, in turn, is continuously rewritten to conform with contemporary policy biases and priorities.

The insidious effects of militarizing youth culture extend, of course, to younger children who have been influenced by the new prominence of jingoistic and Manichean Cold War themes on television and in the cinema (e.g. *Rambo* I and II, *Rocky IV, Red Dawn,* etc.). Even mercenaries are now portrayed as contemporary heroes! Consequently, according to another report ("Did you Know...?" 1985), "the sales of war toys have climbed by 350 percent since 1982 to a record $842 million per year. According to the most recent toy industry figures, war toys are now the leading category of toy sales, making up five of the six best selling toys in the U.S." Recently the overall trend was summarized by supporters (Donnelly, 1989:9) of the Stop War Toys Campaign, launched in 1985:

> In 1982, war toys were 3% of total toy sales (14% of units sold); in 1985 they rose to 19% of sales (16% of units sold); and in 1987 they declined to 10% of total sales (11% of units sold).
> The bad news is that guns and military action video game sales are up and GI Joe is still the number 5 toy (down from number 1 for most of 1987). Violent cartoons still offer children 43 hours of racism, sexism, and militarism each week. The toy manufacturers are still producing more violent toys to entice young children, mostly boys, to bug their parents to buy them.

Although opponents of such toys claim credit for the lessening appeal, a more significant factor may have been a reduction in belligerent rhetoric by national political elites since the Gorbachev accession to power. Whether this trend is temporary remains to be seen.

THE FAR RIGHT: A GROWING MOVEMENT?

Related to the militarization of America's political culture are other infrastructural or systemic alterations. One new development intimately linked to both the emergent garrison state and the hegemonic dominance of the military-industrial complex has been the rise of the "new" or "far" right to the status of a significant force (Bodenheimer and Gould, 1988) in the American political system. Blumenthal (1987/1988:167, 173) recalls that such paranoid extremists had with the onset of the Cold War attained a position of dominance over American conservatism as early as 1952. By 1964 they managed to capture the Republican Party's presidential nomination for Barry Goldwater. And within another decade and a half, "a concept at the fringe of American thought was enshrined in Washington; during the Reagan Administration the extreme became the center."

Integral to the unprecedented emergence of a well funded pre-fascist sector during the past decade has been the growth of a largely reactionary antisecular and evangelical fundamentalist Christian movement with an estimated mass base in excess of 40 million persons. They have been in the forefront of violent attacks upon family planning clinics throughout the country. Although self-styled patriots dedicated to "defense" of God and country, a number of

the most prominent figures in this movement have not shrunk from accepting
foreign aid—millions from (Weaver, 1986) Korean Sun Myung Moon's semi-
fascist "anti-communist" network of front organizations. These now include
Washington's second major daily, *The Washington Star*. And such organizations among others on the "respectable" far right have provided enormous lec-
ture fees and legal defense funds to their overtly undemocratic new militaristic
hero, Col. Ollie North, since his forced dismissal from the Reagan Administration in 1987.

This new right congeries of religious and secular groups has immeasurably
strengthened the de facto fascist right as a whole including such traditional
organizations as the Liberty Lobby and the John Birch Society. Indeed, a
number of former Nazis, racists and open anti–Semites not only hold positions
(Bellant, 1988) in the World Anti-Communist League and American Security
Council, but were even appointed to national posts in the Republican Party
for the Bush campaign "where they hold leadership positions on the
Republican Heritage Groups Council." Their exposure during 1988 embar-
rassed the Bush campaign organization, which then obtained resignations.

At the same time an organized and yet more extreme "know-nothing"
fringe of paramilitary organizations has proliferated in the South, West and
even in Eastern regions of the United States. These organizations include,
among others, three KKK factions, the National Association to Keep and Bear
Arms, the Minutemen, the Christian Patriots Defense League, the Farmer's
Liberation Army, the Populist Party, Posse Comitatus, the American Nazi
Party, the National Agricultural Press Association, the National Socialist
White People's Party, the U.S. Labor Party, the National States' Rights Party,
a sector of the American Agriculture Movement and various "survival" groups.
Brown (1989:49–50) briefly describes violence attributed to several of these
groups during the 1980s. Total armed membership may be no more than ten
or twenty thousand, although some estimates range considerably higher.
Ledbetter (1988:427) notes: "There was more violent crime by 'hate' groups
from 1983 to 1986 than there had been over the previous two decades." By the
mid-1980s, four major private sector mercenary training (Nandy, 1985:31)
camps were in existence—several with CIA ties. Furthermore, in many cases
armaments and training tend to be at a qualitatively higher level than those
of pre–Vietnam era fringe groups.

While recent setbacks of communism have halted the growth of these
violent fringe groups, an upsurge will follow any major economic downturn
in the United States economy during the early 1990s—especially if, as is likely,
the Japanese can be scapegoated along with Jews for the collapse. Already there
has been a very sharp (Oreskes, 1990) rise in overt articulation of anti–Japanese
feelings by Americans. The increase from 8 percent to 25 percent between 1985
and 1990 parallels the growth of mass debt and economic insecurity which was
discussed in Chapter 8. Predictably, the change was most pronounced among

lower middle and working class sectors. The appeal of neo-fascist far right fringe groups, of course, is particularly strong to frustrated veterans, racist ex-convicts and other whites whose social status is or has become marginal. Such marginated sectors were crucial to Hitler's electoral upsurge in 1932 as the depression deepened.

To what degree such elements have sufficient rapport with more respectable upscale interest groups or the Republican Party to elicit protection remains an open question. Certainly Bush's "war on drugs" and his emphasis on traditional morality (including defense of the flag as well as forced school prayer) provide a common basis. Only token, publicity-stunt FBI crackdowns on hate groups occurred in the late 1980s. At the same time there is increasing evidence of overt organizational linkages that may contribute to greater cooperation. Also suggestive is the apparent coordination of recent attacks upon abortion clinics for low income women and such anti-interventionist organizations as the Arab Antidiscrimination Committee. The last and other attacks upon Arabs critical of Israeli expansionism may have been the work of the paramilitary Jewish Defense League.

Where the estimated 500,000 machine guns (NPR, 1985a), ubiquitous plastic explosives, and other high tech equipment — all in private hands — come from is no mystery. While rifles and automatic pistols may be purchased over the counter, it also appears that the United States military itself is one of the primary sources of such weapons. As mentioned in Chapters 2 and 6, by the mid-1980s many hundreds of millions of dollars worth of weaponry had been pilfered ("Black Market," 1985:30) from various depots for sale domestically and internationally.

> In one case, the Justice Department [was] investigating more than 20 people suspected of helping arms traffickers steal several tons of weapons, including grenades, land mines, plastic explosives and artillery, from Fort Bragg, N.C., over the last few years, according to records from Federal District Court in Miami....
>
> ...Federal agents arrested a security guard this summer at the Army's ammunition plant in Lake City, MO, and charged him with unlawful possession of silencers, machine guns and other stolen arms.
>
> The Government has asserted in court records that the guard, Louis George, Jr., stole many thousands of rounds of ammunition. When he was arrested the Government said he had several rooms full of stolen weapons, including about 30 Claymore mines, as well as antitank bazookas, grenades and grenade launchers, among other weapons.

Lax security measures and poor military management are undoubtedly responsible for the impressive flow of sophisticated weaponry to the black market. Further, "when military thieves are discovered, it is often after they have been stealing for years, and in many cases it is the civilian authorities, not the military, who catch them as they try to sell the weapons on the black market."

Despite capture of one major party's national platform in 1984 by the new right elements, the lack of organizational unification among more extreme protofascist and paramilitary groups, absence thus far of a unifying charismatic national leader, and as yet modest numbers of supporters constitute significant impediments to imposition with military support of an overtly authoritarian security state. However, those impediments may be only temporary. Today, the emergence of Ollie North as a national hero awaits only a socio-economic breakdown in the context of political incompetence or paralysis by existing politicians who in the mass view were responsible for years of decline in general living standards.

Earlier in this chapter we examined the breadth and secular rise in the citizen political alienation. Hightower (1989:162) notes:

> It is precisely this kind of high-dollar, high-tech politics that is generating a debilitating cynicism in our democracy. In last fall's deplorable presidential election, not even half of those eligible chose to vote. Two-thirds of those who did vote said they wished there was another choice, and half the voters for each candidate said they were voting *against* the other guy. When half the people don't vote and half of those who do are voting cynically, our democracy is diluted and gravely weakened. National officeholders regularly are elected by only 15 to 25 percent of the people, and governmental policies subsequently reflect the viewpoints of the narrow elite. As long as politics and government fail to address the real needs and aspirations of more than half the people, voter apathy and disaffection will continue to spread, and America is the worse for it. The "no vote" majority is sending a profound political message. There has to be a better way; it is time to try something different.

The implications of the trends delineated in this chapter are highlighted in Lasswell's 1962 reformulation of his thesis.

Fitch (1985:32) reminds us that "in his later work, [Lasswell] argues that in the U.S. or in Europe, the garrison state need not be characterized by the overt abolition of democratic institutions. The external *forms* of democracy might continue to exist, but effective power would be concentrated in the hands of a loosely knit elite of civilianized military officers and militarized civilians, with increasing integration of corollary skill elites—the police, party and interest group leaders, scientists, and educators—into a growing military-industrial complex." The question, then, is what, if anything, can be done to arrest these and related threats to the security of ordinary Americans? Can the multifaceted erosion of liberties, sense of spiritual community and physical safety be effectively challenged? In the final chapter, we shall explore several options after a brief overview of recent trends.

12. Toward an Alternative National Security Approach

Previous chapters of this study have focused upon the historical and contemporary sources of American militarism. Special emphasis has been placed upon its structural relation to a foreign policy configuration denoted by antipathy toward economic nationalism and social radicalism in the developing areas. The perception that civilian instrumentalities of influence (e.g. economic aid, propaganda, cultural exchange, etc.) had failed in a growing number of countries of the South weakened the position of a declining band of principled liberals who opposed a militaristic national security approach. Although grossly inflated by what I have termed the right wing's paranoid projection syndrome, the intensified Soviet effort to attain parity since their apparent Missile Crisis humiliation, in conjunction with greater Eastern support for non-aligned "revolutionary" (i.e. economically nationalist and socially reformist) Third World regimes, was used to justify unrestrained militarization at home and offensive strategic postures abroad between the late 1970s and mid-1908s. The basing of Pershing II first strike missiles in Europe during the 1983–1987 period complemented new naval task forces, bases, maneuvers and the vastly expanded low intensity conflict Rapid Deployment Force to police the South. The CIA psychological and covert negotiations or initiatives had heightened tensions — continuing what Oakes (1983) calls "a slide toward war."

This slide has been halted at least temporarily by Gorbachev's rise to power and his peace initiatives — unilateral concessions in a context of strong international (particularly European) support. While the Reagan Administration was put in a position where it would have appeared ridiculous had no change of stance or INF agreement eventuated, it is true that Reagan himself reacted to this position and to personal encounters with the Soviet leader in a positive manner that enabled him to transcend some of his earlier Manichean stereotypes. Nevertheless, while the Bush Administration has continued this less hostile — even superficially amicable — pattern at least at the rhetorical level, no fundamental changes have occurred with respect to United States policy. Indeed, amity is directly correlated with the degree to which the Soviets and others allow their systems to become less communist, socially radical or economically nationalistic. It similarly hinges upon unilateral Soviet concessions in the

Third World. Thus when balanced or symmetrical proposals (e.g. United States and Soviet mutual withdrawal from bases in the Philippines, Vietnam and elsewhere) are fielded by Moscow they are routinely dismissed by Washington. And Bush's advocacy of maintaining or reducing only slightly the existing enormous level of military expenditures reveals that despite slight policy moderation toward the Angolans and Palestinians, nothing fundamental or structural has changed with respect to the parameters of the American military-industrial complex or quasi-warfare state. As in the case of Panama and perhaps the Andean countries, new rationales (e.g. "drug terrorism") will be generated to domestically secure acquiescence for interventions to impose or reinforce the position of compliant comprador elites. Another ideological metaphor, "Democracy," will similarly be trumpeted by official and media propagandists except when, as in the case of Mexico (Reding, 1989), or Kuwait, repression is systematically applied to nationalist and socially reformist sectors.

In previous chapters we have elaborated the thesis that America's traditional or conventional national security paradigm has become increasingly counterproductive in terms of its own ends. The militarization process's skewing of society's priorities as well as its consequent cultural bias has contributed to the socio-economic deterioration of both mass living standards and the spiritual vitality or cohesion of an increasingly hardened and narcissistic political culture. Similarly, in a direct sense, the chauvinism and strategic animosity essential to the militarization process preclude the respect and mutuality essential to ending the drive for strategic superiority or even constraining Third World militarization including nuclear proliferation. Thus, notwithstanding a cosmetic improvement, the world has become a more dangerous environment for Americans. Unfortunately, despite a gradual shift in public mood against the Reagan-Bush SDI ("New Findings," 1988), a growing awareness of the economic underpinning of security and heightened opposition to inverventionism in Central America, it seems evident that little major improvement can be expected until the Bush Administration or its successor, and those committed to the now institutionalized militaristic national security approach, are confronted by a major unanticipated disaster of sufficient magnitude to force re-examination of traditional assumptions.

SOVIET AND EUROPEAN CHALLENGES TO AMERICAN LEADERSHIP

Understanding why this short-run assessment is pessimistic requires little more than a glimpse at the lost opportunities of the 1980s. Consistent negativism or the absence of reciprocity toward major Soviet initiatives such as a no-first-use-of-nuclear-weapons pledge, the eighteen month unilateral nuclear test ban by Moscow, offers to withdraw most forces from other European countries, proposals for non-offensive military deployments, a 50 percent cut in strategic weapons, demilitarization of space, and a non-intervention regime for developing areas makes the losses abundantly clear to those actively concerned with the pace of global militarization. While the 1987 INF treaty eliminates several hundred delivery vehicles and marks a very positive advance in the area of on-site verification, it neither eliminates nuclear warheads nor even restrains the continuing arms race or diffusion of ballistic missiles and nuclear weapons to the developing nations. Reductions may occur with respect to United States occupation troops in West Germany where their presence and tactical nuclear weapons have grown increasingly unpopular. Yet Washington steadfastly refuses to negotiate in the areas where its superiority is paramount: space militarization, strategic bombers, and naval forces.

Interestingly, the initial 1985 unilateral Soviet decision to suspend nuclear testing was prompted by an American private sector initiative from a major arms control lobbying organization. According to one account ("Soviets Act," 1985:1), the decision

> responds to a proposal by the Washington-based Center for Defense Information, headed by Rear Admirals Gene R. LaRoque and Eugene J. Carrol, Jr. As reported in *The Defense Monitor*, Vol XIV, No. 5, they wrote to President Reagan in November 1984, suggesting a mutual halt to all nuclear weapons explosions on August 6, 1985. The Administration replied that the U.S. did not plan to pursue talks for a complete test ban "at this time," citing verification concerns as well as the belief that "nuclear testing plays an important role in ensuring a credible U.S. deterrent."
>
> In January 1985 CDI sent a similar letter to then–Soviet president Chernenko. The reply, from the presidium of the USSR Supreme Soviet, said a moratorium "undoubtedly would contribute to constraining the nuclear arms race," and expressed willingness to halt tests as of August 6 or even earlier if other nuclear powers agreed.

Thus even prior to Gorbachev's accession there was Soviet interest in syncretic measures to sharply curtail the nuclear arms race. This was also reflected ("Indefensible," 1988:4) by Moscow's 2 percent average annual rise in military expenditures between 1979 and 1986, as compared to 8 percent for Washington. If, as Ullman (1988:134–35) contends, the Soviet Union is well on its way to becoming an "ordinary state," we must confront the problematic likelihood of Washington's prospects for a similar and reciprocal denouement. And this means constructively facing the "deadly connection" between the East-West arms race or more recently the commitment to strategic dominance in the North and military interventionism in the South.

In the first place, even a reformist American leadership in Washington backed by extensive citizen mobilization and, one hopes, a progressive Congress would be confronted by the question of whether the Carter moderate arms restraint policy deserved another try. After all, one of the homilies of American reform centers upon the time necessary before policy innovations are finally institutionalized via piecemeal, incrementalist tinkering with bureaucratic structures and routines. Looking at the matter in terms of America's massive transfers of weaponry to Third World countries, Pierre (1982:69) seems to be fully in tune with such hoary orthodoxy: "The fact is that only a very few are making a serious argument for eliminating all, or even most foreign arms sales. Most reasonable advocates of restraints would propose rather moderate reductions, and only when foreign policy considerations would support them." Betts (1980:83–103) also shares this "realist" perspective, maintaining that "complete restraint is no more possible than disarmament. Like SALT, arms transfer control will succeed only at the margins." Earlier he warns "there have been numerous attempts at international limitation of conventional arms trade since the Brussels Act of 1890. The best of these were innocuous failures, the worst were fiascos." Similar immobility with respect to bold departures was articulated more recently (Nye, 1988) by one of the Harvard-based national security advisers to Democratic presidential candidate Dukakis.

Sober caution of this genre ignores the contemporary interest of major world powers, indeed all leaders, in preventing escalation (Forsberg, 1988) from a Third World or East European civil low intensity conflict to an unwanted global Armageddon — a veritable holocaust if only due to global fallout and climatological effects. Such a mutual security threat was alien to earlier epochs. The problem, as Jacobsen (1982) takes pains to emphasize, is that we cannot confuse — though many do — the realism of earlier epochs with that of today. To do so is to fall victim to what C. Wright Mills in his book *The Causes of World War III* denounced as "crackpot realism." That was in 1960! Since then, as we saw, numerous wars — most of them with major power involvement — have raged in the Third World. Not only have we also recorded several American threats to use nuclear weapons during the past three decades, but pressures in the United States to expand both the Korean and Vietnam wars were narrowly averted. And here we temporarily ignore the trillions of dollars — vitally needed for socio-economic purposes — that have been siphoned off by the global militarization process as well as the East-West arms race. Today in a land where literally millions are homeless or malnourished, a single stealth B-2 subsonic first-strike bomber costs ("The Brave," 1988) upwards of a half billion dollars. Mills was indeed prophetic.

Although the progress since the Cuban Missile Crisis has been toward a more unstable (i.e., first strike or "counterforce") balance of terror, an ominous prognosis for nuclearism was not alien to some of the genuine realists even during Mills' era of the optimistic 1950s. Einstein himself admonished (IPPNW, 1983) that everything had changed except our way of cognition: "We shall require a substantially new manner of thinking if mankind is to survive." And at the very onset of this mindless Cold War drive for perpetual strategic superiority to enforce a global Pax Americana, one of the foremost political scientists (indeed a founder of the realist school of world politics), Hans J. Morgenthau (1951:88–89), cut to the core of Washington's fixation upon being a global counterrevolutionary gendarme by drawing a sharp distinction between "genuine" revolution and its considerably rarer appearance as the "spearhead of foreign imperialism." Cautioning that "against genuine revolution only the health of our, and our allies', social institutions can insure us," Morgenthau then articulated a prophetic warning:

> If we allow ourselves to be diverted from this objective of safeguarding our national security, and if instead we conceive of the American mission in some abstract, universal, and emotional terms, we may well be induced, against our better knowledge and intent, yet by the very logic of the task in hand, to raise the banner of universal counterrevolution abroad and of conformity in thought and action at home. In that manner we shall jeopardize our external security, promote the world revolution we are trying to suppress, and at home make ourselves distinguishable perhaps in degree, but not in kind, from those with which we are locked in ideological combat.

Not coincidentally, this apprehension was shared by the only army general and war hero to serve as United States president during the twentieth century. Eisenhower had presided over the allied victory against Naziism, and at the very onset of his first term as Commander in Chief, ended hostilities in Korea. His refusal during 1954 to unilaterally send combat troops or employ atomic bombs in Vietnam earned him the epithet of pacifist from Cold Warrior militarists then and since.[1] He not only successfully opposed the coordinated Anglo-French and Israeli invasions of Egypt, but also adamantly rebuffed military-industrial pressures to sharply increase arms spending for most of the 1950s.

Stephen Ambrose (1984: 49–50), author of *Eisenhower the President,* recalls that the general's "great fear" was "that the arms race would lead to bankruptcy of the spirit and the pocket-book." Notwithstanding his perhaps overzealous admiration, Ambrose makes several additional points that enrich our perspective:

> Shutting down the Korean War, he kept the Department of Defense at around $40 billion per year for seven years (compared with $237.5 billion for 1984), much to the benefit of the economic health of the society.
>
> A protracted arms race paid for by deficit financing would inevitably lead to national bankruptcy through inflation, Eisenhower believed. And he believed a consequence would be dictatorship to maintain the burden of the costs. He told his chief science advisor, "In the long run, no country can advance intellectually and in terms of its culture and well-being if it has to devote everything to military buildup. I do not see much hope for a world engaged in this all-out effort of military buildup, military technology, and tremendous attempts at secrecy."...
>
> He told a group of arms manufacturers who had come to urge him to spend more, "We must remember that we are defending a way of life, not merely property, wealth, and even our homes. Should we have to resort to anything

resembling a garrison state, then all that we are striving to defend could disappear."

It would seem that over the course of two subsequent decades, the wisdom of this combat veteran of two world wars has been at least partially vindicated. This has been the essential argument of our earlier chapters.

Insofar as relations with the Russians were concerned, Eisenhower sought a breakthrough for genuine improvement during the last years of his second term. In some measure those efforts were sabotaged — as they have been many times (Morrison, 1985; Wiesner, 1985) since — by militaristic elements within the bureaucratic state structure. Ambrose (1984:49) records that in 1959 as a United States-USSR summit meeting was being prepared:

> Secretary of Defense Neil McElroy made exactly the same argument to Eisenhower that Reagan uses today to justify putting missiles in Europe — that deploying more weapons near the Soviet Union would push the Soviets toward disarmament. Eisenhower's rejoinder to McElroy was "This [missile] deployment does not serve to reduce tensions between ourselves and the Soviets." The Soviets, Eisenhower pointed out, do not scare easily. They would be sure to match any American buildup and stationing of missiles closer to their borders with a buildup of their own. America and Western Europe would be left less, rather than more, secure.

Of particular interest today is the growing prominence of Eisenhower's outlook among an increasing segment of West European mass and particularly elite opinion (Flynn, 1983; Birnbaum, 1985; Radway, 1985; Wulf, 1985a; Wolfe, 1985). Several NATO allies including the Federal Republic of Germany acceded to United States pressures for Euromissile deployments only with the condition that INF negotiations with Moscow be seriously pursued by the United States.

Even before Reagan's inauguration, Washington suspended test ban negotiations. Since then Reagan's belligerent early 1980s anti–Sovietism, Washington's militant interventionism in the Third World and above all Reagan's use of SDI and negotiations as a domestic propaganda ploy after 1983 against liberal freeze critics had vitiated this "dual track" accord (Schmidt, 1985) and increasingly isolated (Johansen, 1986) the United States from its European allies.[2] As late as February 1990 — after three years of halting responses to an unending flow of initiatives by Gorbachev — it was reported ("U.S. Isolated," 1990:3) that "the United States is alone against European members of COCOM in opposing an easing of Cold War restrictions on the sale of sensitive high technology to the Soviet Union. . . ." Among all 16 NATO allies along with Japan and Australia, Washington's delegates to a meeting on this issue were "genuinely isolated." Clearly, the excesses of American militarism were being viewed by a large and growing minority of polite Europeans as a threat to their own security. Similarly, Reagan's efforts to curtail trade and, until late 1985, cultural exchange with the Soviets, had exacerbated tensions (Richman, 1983), cost American workers an estimated 400,000 American jobs ("Economics of Military Spending," 1984:11), and engendered resentment as well as desires for greater autonomy among alliance partners.

Symptomatic of the naked contradiction between Reagan-Bush "realpolitik" and the need for genuinely new thermonuclear realism was the failure of most NATO allies to endorse the Star Wars race to militarize space.[3] The collapse of American prestige subverted the nation's leadership to the extent that a year and a half after the Star Wars announcement, only the United Kingdom—led by the unpopular rightist government of Margaret Thatcher—had endorsed the destabilizing scheme. The United Kingdom's Labour Party, which is growing in strength and likely to form the next government by 1992, is committed to rejection of Star Wars as well as removal of many United States bases in Britain. Like their Social Democratic counterparts in the FRG and other moderates, Britain's new Labour leadership is firmly dedicated to vigorously seeking global arms control before nuclear proliferation and Third World militarization, in the context of continued interventionism and an uncontrolled East-West arms race, intersect during a crisis to create the holocaust no one wants. Given these and similar developments elsewhere, the Reagan Administration had little choice but to respond affirmatively to Gorbachev's unilateral concessions for an INF agreement.

The failure to constructively address the issue of Third World interventionism by the United States under Bush or his predecessors has, as emphasized previously, stymied a breakthrough on strategic counterforce weaponry. Yet both this and SDI may ultimately be ignored by Gorbachev as the Soviets become totally preoccupied with domestic reform.

PROSPECTS FOR LIMITING WEAPONS PROLIFERATION TO THE THIRD WORLD

While Betts and others in the realist or realpolitik school mistakenly attribute Carter's arms restraint fiasco to faulty moralistic premises and exaggerated notions of what could be attained in the real world, most reformist critics argue that his failure was occasioned by internal conflict and a lack of determination to implement policies, or by policies that were themselves too limited. Thus Landgren-Backstrom (1982:209–210) contends that sales to European allies also should have been included. In her view, the main flaw of the Carter policy may have been that it was solely designed to limit the sale of arms to Third World countries—excluding the NATO allies and others in the industrialized world. Although recognizing that a United Nations conference on arms transfer limitations at present would be "a radical proposition," she nevertheless believes that "some kind of recipients' agreement might be possible to abstain from devoting resources to the import of next generations of certain weapons...." Such a conference along with a European shift to more defensive weaponry for both their own militaries and exports would in her opinion enhance global security.

Cannizzo (1980:187–195) also sees some merit in a defensive criterion for distinguishing among various weapons systems:

> Thus it is possible, theoretically, to transfer a limited number of arms that are nonthreatening but that provide adequate protection. This process is only partially objective, since some states (e.g., Israel, South Africa, South Korea, Taiwan) are more paranoid than others, and "adequacy" is to some extent in the eyes of the beholder. But through rational discourse and negotiation, backed by statistics and other relatively objective data on systems' performance, the upper limits could be defined and translated into actual weapons.

Although not too hopeful, she urges a suppliers' agreement to "regulate" exports so as not to upset regional balances by introducing sophisticated, and particularly offensive, weapons. Exports which were destined for high tension areas or which could not be absorbed technically would be proscribed, as would those to "enemy" states. Cannizzo also concedes that "even if these four regulations could be negotiated into a suppliers' agreement, the viper's pit at the arms bazaar would not be turned into a nest of garter snakes. There would, undoubtedly, still be much of an unsavory nature that would continue to attract criticism. Yet a major step in organization and regulation would have been accomplished, and that is, in the view of many, the prerequisite to any more stringent type of control." Her pessimism however is dominant: "vague restraints are not the answer," and arms reductions are "not a very real possibility at this time nor in the foreseeable future."

Others whose historical vision was delimited by the early Reagan era revanchist milieu include Pearson (1981:43), who emphasized the need for renewed restraint with an incremental framework:

> Certainly a strong case can be made for even more stringent restraints since arms transfers frequently do not bring the type of influence abroad major powers have sought. Both Americans and Russians have been rudely expelled in recent years by longstanding arms customers and clients. Alternate arms sources are increasingly available, even for sophisticated weapons. Costs are mounting and might bankrupt some Third World states. However, spokesmen in both the Carter and Reagan Administrations have seen Soviet "successes" in the Third World as due to U.S. passivity and weakness rather than to unique and isolated local or regional conditions.

One might add that those victimized by the zero-sum paranoid projection syndrome seldom balance, as Pearson does, Soviet failure against the inflated range of successes. Furthermore, declining relative Soviet arms exports, Gorbachev's internal reform commitments and tolerance for much greater independence in East Europe, and Moscow's constructive record at the previously discussed CAT negotiations as well as the impressive Soviet "peace initiatives" since then clearly indicate the desirability of Soviet participation in any conference to limit weapons exports.

Gansler (1980:214), with a note of both urgency and optimism, counsels that "the significant parties in arms-control talks should be France, England, and (in some areas) the Soviet Union. If sincerely and properly pursued (including full coverage in the foreign press), such negotiations would be extremely difficult but could be highly effective. Interim agreements would be a positive first step, even if the United States had to give up a small share of its current market." He ends by warning that "time is very important, since more and more new suppliers are entering the field."[4] If that was true when Gansler wrote, it is even more so today — particularly with respect to the Middle East cauldron. Babst (1988:1) points to the fortuitous escalatory risks due in part to technological modernization:

> Decreasing warning time is forcing many nations to computerize their hair triggers making future war decisions ever more dangerous. Warning time is becoming very short due to the dramatic proliferation of ballistic missiles. For instance, ten Mideast nations alone now possess at least 1,200 surface to surface missiles with ranges up to 2,000 miles. The acquisition of long-range missiles by Saudi Arabia and Syria that can strike Israel in minutes illustrates the danger. Israel, which has nuclear weapons and is perpetually on a high state of alert, has begun discussing "push-button" warfare. Would the first nuclear explosions in space cause an EMP communication blackout between other nuclear powers?

In the event of a crisis, a communication blackout might be misperceived as the onset of a pre-emptive strike — "hotlines" and "risk reductions centers" notwithstanding. By 1990 (Karp, 1989) at least two dozen Third World countries will have acquired, or be in the process of acquiring, ballistic missiles. Almost a half dozen (China, Israel, India, South Africa, Pakistan) either have or can quickly manufacture nuclear warheads, while several others (Brazil, Argentina and possibly Turkey) are moving close to nuclear club membership. All of these countries have direct or indirect military links with the Pentagon.

Betts (1980:82–86, 103) cautions that even multilateral restraints upon arms exports to developing nations might ignore recipients' bona fide needs. Further, in light of the continuing military "modernization" in the North, they would be hypocritical by one-sidedly increasing the relative military power of the North *vis-à-vis* the South. Indeed, complaints at the third five-year review of the Nuclear Weapons Non-Proliferation Treaty (NPT) centered upon the failure of both superpowers to live up to Article VI requiring good faith negotiations to end the arms race and initiate arms reduction. Johnstone (1985:3) stresses that in fact the overwhelming majority attributed violation of Article VI to the militaristic posture of existing United States policy-makers.[5]

This continues (Castrioto, 1989) to be a major impediment to NPT univer-salization. The same American obduracy pertains to Washington's escalation of chemical and biological weapons production.[6] (The former was officially resumed in 1987 after a 30-year hiatus.)

Far from "realism," the new self-created isolationism in psychological space adversely affects Washington's leadership pretensions not only in its European and Anglo-Saxon backyards, but increasingly among the non-aligned majority in the United Nations. In the latter organization as well as the OAS — once a virtual American rubber stamp — resounding majorities con-demned the premeditated United States invasion of Panama in December 1989. Ironically, the commercial motives of reactor exporters in the United States and certain NATO allies will shortly neutralize the one-sidedness of the NPT.[7] Thus, in the absence of multilateral agreements of the type mentioned in preceding paragraphs, the 1990s may become the decade of global nuclearism.

Even some in-house arms control experts like Rand specialist Sereseres (U.S., House, CFA, 1981, 44, 45, 46) imply that the real arms proliferation dynamic today is to be found in a virtually autonomous state-within-a-state, the military-industrial complex. Emphasizing that "security" assistance "is not influence; it only represents presence and access," he suggests the scale of these militarization-related activities is virtually devoid of rationality.[8] By the late 1980s, this had become even more the case. Now drugs and terrorism function as the rationales. Yet his "realism" joins that of Cannizzo in voicing a pessimistic prognosis that "arms restraint agreements among suppliers, recip-ients, or both seem unlikely."

Less concerned with immediate probabilities than with necessity is Klare (1982:67), who directly links continued superpower rivalry with regional insta-bility as the most likely source of thermonuclear war. Assuming what is neces-sary for national security is also possible, he counsels that the United States:

> • Envision a new concept of world security in which regional peace and stability is considered more important than the ascendancy of particular allies;
> • Recognize the mutual advantage of the two superpowers in curbing their military exports to their respective clients in conflict-prone areas of the Third World;
> • Place human rights considerations ahead of "internal security" when deciding on sales of counterinsurgency and paramilitary gear to authoritarian regimes;
> • Provide incentives for the arms corporations to convert production from military to non-military products;
> • Facilitate the export of non-military commodities to the oil-producing countries, and to the Third World in general.

The problem with this approach, those previously delineated and Carter's restraint experiment is that the very tangible dangers are nevertheless both contingent and long run while the costs in terms of further erosion of corporate profits as well as American leverage in the Third World are substantial and immediate. The leverage and "force projection" rationales must then be addressed.

So long as economic nationalism and social radicalism — which receive varying though often quite limited and currently diminishing Soviet support — are defined as overriding threats to American national security, none of these proposals will be more consistently or seriously implemented than were Carter's.[9] At bottom, even Carter's arms control faction shared this counterrevolutionary and procorporate open door bias, and consequently they encountered enormous difficulties in opposing the arguments of militarists when the latter systematically resorted to threat inflation in a milieu characterized by an erosion of Western and particularly American control in various Third World countries or regions. Ronfeldt and Sereseres (1977:25) articulate this conventional wisdom by counseling that "the central importance of military leaders and institutions in Latin American polities . . . suggest[s] that it is important for the U.S. government to maintain constructive relations with them as well as with elites and institutions in civilian sectors."

As long as systematic interventionism to influence civilian sectors remains integral to American policy, it is utopian to expect that the military elites can be excluded. This is invariably so when within such a neo-imperial framework, most non-nationalist regimes lack broadly based legitimacy.[10] Koistinen (1980:124) argues:

> Any attempt to control fundamentally the extraordinary power wielded by the MIC must start not with reforms in procurement or even cuts in the military budgets (although such developments can only be welcome and are long overdue). First the idea that the nation can and should play world policeman must be abandoned, and military solutions to what are essentially social, political, ideological, and economic issues must be foregone. This is not to propose a new form of isolationism or "fortress America," as Cold War Hawks are so eager to charge. Instead, it means a foreign policy of sane and reasonable priorities for the world's major power, reasonable priorities that stand somewhere between attempting to ignore the world and attempting to mold the world in the American image.

Failure to address Koistinen's position — one shared by Forsberg (1984) — that a basic alteration in foreign policy is essential explains why attempts by some arms restraint enthusiasts to attenuate linkages with militaries were overwhelmed by the threat exaggerations of the military-industrial complex, their corporate allies, and a largely unsophisticated media infrastructure that for three decades has been socialized into anti-communist demonology, a procorporate open door or free market ideology with universalistic (Thompson, 1983) pretensions, and what both Sanders (1983) and Wiesner (1985) characterize as a "militarist culture." Devoid of humility, most liberal arms restraint civilianists like Nye (1988) share a consensus that it is legitimate to manipulate elites and domestic power balances within developing nations. This idea is arrogantly masked by such rhetorical symbols as "free world leadership" or "global policeman." It is no wonder that such arms control advocates were put on the defensive in an era of imperial decline.

Just as Truman's containment policy and loyalty purges paved the way for both the arms race and McCarthy's witchhunts, so the bipartisan foreign interventionism of subsequent moderate Democratic administrations and congressional elites down to the present (Klare, 1988; Miller, 1988) have themselves contributed to an enormous military-industrial complex and structured ideological environment that facilitated Reagan and Bush's excesses. Only one American president, as mentioned earlier, appears to have reached the verge of intellectually and psychologically transcending the unquestioned assumptions of containment militarism. Eisenhower's projected 1960 summit with Khrushchev was sabotaged by the U-2 incident. Later, his successor was also on the verge of overcoming militarism. Coffin (1983b:4) recounts that:

> General Shoup, one of the great prophets of his time, was asked by Kennedy to look over the ground in SE Asia and counsel him. General Shoup advised that unless we were prepared to use a million men in a major drive, we should pull out before the war expanded beyond control.
> Kennedy was preparing to take that advice before he was murdered. Some ten days before assassination, Kennedy took Senator Wayne Morse (D–Ore.) into the rose garden, where they would not be overheard or "bugged," and told him, "Wayne, I've decided to get out. Definitely!"

That decision in tandem with Kennedy's previous detente openings during the post–Missile Crisis months — indeed his concessions to the Soviets during the height of the crisis itself — may have reflected the President's "inchoate and still largely intuitive grasp that security of East and West is indivisible, that absolute national security is impossible in an insecure world," an understanding which "hold[s] out promise of revolutionizing the concept of defense and leaving behind the obsession with containment." Only such a perspective, in the view of Sanders (1983:45), Forsberg (1984), LaRocque (1988) and Bowman (1988), will enable us to end the increasingly costly, unstable and ever more irrational nuclear arms "modernization" race.

Arms control, then, was doomed so long as it was premised upon perpetuation of the political status quo in developing areas. Thus a foreign policy that assumes radicalism and nationalism are threats to America's national security, and that power projection cum strategic escalatory dominance are essential to promote global interests, is a foreign policy that cannot be reconciled with curbing the insecurity generated by deepening underdevelopment and financial crisis for most Third World countries, or the massive flow of arms to client military establishments in the South. And since, as Landgren-

Backstrom (1982:203) and many others recognize, "arms exports . . . are an integral part of the foreign policy of the respective exporter," effective restraint must begin with the underlying foreign policy goals rather than the instruments. Otherwise, as the weak arms control faction in the Carter Administration discovered, once a plausible case can be made that the goals of maintaining spheres of influence and weakening nationalist or radical movements are not being attained by non-military means it becomes nearly impossible to resist those who would employ all possible instruments including nuclear blackmail or overt military attacks (Grenada, Panama, Libya, Iran) as well as wasteful arms transfers. The fact that weapons exports and military aid are of limited utility or varying effectiveness — even counterproductive and risky at times — does not differentiate arms transfers from any other imperfect instrument for influencing the policies or internal power balance of Third World nations. Thus liberal critiques emphasizing such deficiencies have invariably been facilely countered by militarists.

In view of my earlier discussion of the rising socio-economic and political costs imposed upon American society as well as on developing nations, and the dangers of escalation to ecocide, the following perspective by Sanders (1983:2) posits the needed re-direction of foreign policy:

> Having oscillated from militarism to managerialism and back again, American politics is at an historic crossroads. One way points toward the continuing pursuit of empire, a burden destined to bear an increasingly heavy price even as its returns diminish in the years ahead. The other path turns away from containment altogether, transcending the Machiavellian realism of both lions and foxes in favor of a foreign policy cognizant of the fact that global social justice and national security have become indivisible in an age of transformation and interdependence. While one cannot be sanguine that the latter course will be chosen, the pursuit of militarized security is creating a growing "security gap" of its own at home which has put demilitarized economic and social security at the center of the political agenda. Unlike the heyday of the cold war, the U.S. can no longer have it both ways. Which will prevail depends, in William Appleman Williams' words, on whether the American people can break free from "empire as a way of life."

This real threat to America's socio-economic national security by the current policy is slowly fashioning a political environment favorable to questioning what Sereseres (U.S., House, CFA, 1981:37) identified as its three basic "policy fallacies." First is the view that emanates from Washington concerning the mutuality of interests between the United States and Latin American countries. The mutuality is exaggerated, as reactions to the invasions of Grenada and especially Panama have demonstrated. Nor have most Latin American OAS members been disposed to back U.S. efforts to overthrow the Nicaraguan Government. Second, there is a tendency to project an unrealistic vision of collaboration as a result of an assistance relationship, such as arms transfers.

Third, there has been a tendency to interpret most, if not all, Soviet activities as being part of a play for global domination. Once such conventional wisdom or the prevailing orthodoxy in its global application is accorded the problematic status it deserves at best, we will be freed to at least consider Sanders' (1983:23) alternative perspective that "from its inception, the Pax Americana that emerged from the destruction of World War II embodied the commingled objectives of stabilizing an international economic climate favorable to capitalist expansion, and maintaining political hegemony in areas defined as vital to U.S. geopolitical interests." As such expansionism extends to Eastern Europe, it would be unsurprising if similar "vital interest" definitions were soon applied to that unstable region — one whose prospects for ethnic harmony or even democracy are, to say the least, highly problematic.

Although Sanders' statement may appear too strong or even abrasive to some, it is quite consonant with the conclusions of Magdoff (1969), Eckhardt (1977) and others referred to in Chapters 3, 6, and 9, *viz.*, that in the contemporary period so-called national security policy primarily enhances the profitability of transnational corporations while reducing the socio-economic and physical security of non-owning Americans, many allies and most citizens of developing areas. Ironically, the arms race's dysfunctionality or irrationality for corporate imperialism is itself a new fact. For now it physically imperils even the owning classes of these corporations. If the twentieth century has been an era of war, the prospect of nuclear winter or, short of that, societal devastation implies that corporate elites and bankers will no longer be able to reap profits as they handsomely did during or after two previous world wars. In short, as a few of the more sophisticated corporate "Yankees" now acknowledge, the old game is up. To pursue the present course now will ever more deeply enmesh us in a fatal "social trap."[11]

AN ALTERNATIVE NATIONAL SECURITY PERSPECTIVE?

Johansen's (1983:3) analytical critique of the "national security community's" very conception of "realism" is essential for those who would chart a new course premised upon the indivisibility of security in a thermonuclear age: "'Realism' has become sufficiently out of tune with political realities to cause one foreign policy failure after another. ... The fault lies not in the realists' emphasis on the need to scrutinize the empirical world, but in their failure to observe this basic ground rule." Johansen continues:

> As long as scholars and policy makers operate from a closed, system-maintaining agenda of policy options, humanity will not be able to extricate itself from a major security dilemma. On the one hand, self-restraint in the arms build-up will seem to reduce national power and make one vulnerable to attack. On the other hand, to increase destructive capability will leave oneself and the human species less secure, because weapons innovations usually are imitated by one's adversary. U.S. "breakthroughs" like the atomic and hydrogen

bombs, the intercontinental bomber, the ballistic missile, the multiple warhead delivery vehicle, and the cruise missile inevitably have come back to haunt their creators, who in effect merely purchased a fleeting strategic advantage at the price of greater global instability.

Since, as I have argued, the primary if not exclusive catalyst of the East-West military competition and American militarization is the desire for credible escalatory threats in the South, an alternative national security approach for those seeking to end the nuclear arms race must begin with America's role in developing areas.

In elaborating this alternative, my core assumptions are as follows. First, as implied in previous sections, more radical nationalist and even Marxist regimes in the developing areas do not necessarily threaten (Nye 1988) either the safety or the material welfare of the American people. The diminution of Soviet interest and involvement since the late 1970s—their aid drop being especially pronounced between 1987–1990—along with Moscow's active encouragement of negotiated compromise settlements since 1985 in all Third World regions further underscores this point. Transnational corporate "trickle-down" has diminished due to increasing reinvestment abroad in branch (often runaway) plants or more speculative tax shelters (e.g. Switzerland, Grand Cayman), as well as the trend domestically toward the use of capital earnings for luxury consumption and parasitical rather than productive investment. Moreover, the economic costs of informal empire abroad—postponed by Johnson during the Vietnam War—have ascended (MacEwan, 1989) to the point, through rising debt, interest and tax burdens, declining state services, increasing structural unemployment and hardship, that they have all but ended the historic mass sector rise in living standards and quality of life. The combined government and employer assault upon trade unions has also exacerbated the social deterioration.

Even if "leftist" regimes increase the price of their resources—directly or through taxes upon corporate intermediaries, and this is largely passed on to the public—it is altogether likely that such costs would be more than offset by a massive reduction in America's current half-trillion dollar military-related budget and by conversion of military contractor resources to meet civilian economic and social needs. It would be more difficult too for companies to blackmail American workers by threatening to relocate abroad. Authoritarian nationalist and what Falk (1980) calls "Leninist" regimes such as South Yemen, Cuba, Cambodia and Angola are not ideal by any means, but they do actively promote mass welfare to a far greater extent (Wolpin, 1982; 1983; White *et al.*, 1984; Nagle, 1985) than "moderate" comprador and pro–United States variants.

Moreover they are fiercely nationalistic and if given the opportunity for American trade and friendship, will both become better markets for American goods and themselves resist, as many have successfully, any overbearing Soviet efforts to guide their development — particularly when the alternative of American friendship and intercourse is readily available. Even Vietnam in 1976 sought ties to the United States to avoid undue dependence on the USSR, as did Mao and Ho Chi Minh as early as 1945, Tito in 1948, the Cubans during the Carter era, Ethiopia in 1977, Sandinista leaders in 1980, and Mozambique and Angola since then. Given the domestic economic reform and human rights priorities of the Gorbachev leadership at the close of the 1980s, the "Soviet threat" rationale for intervention seems extinct.

My second assumption is that once "radicalism" is tolerated as an acceptable and perhaps — with ecological (Trainer, 1989:512–15) modifications — the optimal development strategy for many Third World systems, it will be easier to effectively counter proponents of military interventionism in the South. The old realism accepts the inevitability of attempts by large powers to manipulate the policy process of weaker countries. But as Kreisberg (1982) and others have documented, such intervention is viewed as meddling and *not* widely supported by American mass publics — provided they know that billions of their tax dollars are being so used for the ultimate benefit of TNCs. And this is undoubtedly more true today than it was at the height of the Reagan era's threat inflation. There is also broad though less pronounced antipathy with respect to using billions for meddling in other countries with non-military instrumentalities (e.g. so-called "foreign aid") as well. Except for corrupt comprador regimes typified by those of Mexico, Zaire, El Salvador and the Philippines, America will lose few friends and perhaps gain many more by renouncing its interventionism and force projection posture.

Even some members of Congress from relatively unsophisticated heartland districts are cognizant of America's declining prestige and growing moral isolation due to decades of imperialist practice. Coffin (1983c:2) reports:

> Rep. Bill Alexander (D–Ark.), long interested in Central America explains: "virtually every hemispheric American — except, perhaps, those of us who make policy north of the Rio Grande — is aware that the real problem in Latin America is not simply a military one. It is economic, social and political — in that order of importance. Nobody but us gringos who make policy appear[s] to believe in the strategy of suppressing discontent by force of arms. Nobody, that is, but the regimes which have demonstrated an incapacity to maintain order in their own countries without foreign assistance and weapons at the ready.

Worth stressing is his reference group — "gringos who make policy." Seventy percent of Americans do not (Kriesberg, 1982:40) support intervention even to promote civil liberties let alone to further corporate profit-taking. Only when systematic threat inflation is employed by elites (e.g. Noriega as a "druglord") are mass sectors sufficiently frightened to acquiesce in military interventionism. This also assumes short duration and victory. Whereas "Soviet sponsored aggression" or "Soviet dominated regimes" were the traditional Red menace bogies (Joel and Erickson, 1983), more recently "oil-denying" aggression (Saddam Hussein) and "terrorism" have become (Falk, 1988) the vogue.

My third policy assumption is that as Forsberg (1983; 1984) contends, once the United States no longer opposes nationalism and renounces military meddling in the Third World, negotiating a test freeze and *major* arms reduction treaty with the Soviet Union will not appear as utopian as it does now. Neither the United States nor the West Europeans today have territorial conflicts with the USSR directly or concerning post–World War II Eastern European boundaries. Since the need for strategic superiority or escalatory dominance will have been attenuated, it should be possible to limit nuclear arsenals to a few hundred relatively invulnerable slow reaction submarine and perhaps airborne weapons that could be easily withheld for a second (retaliatory) strike. Thus America's nuclear deterrent would be a stable one until such time that it was feasible to eliminate it entirely.

In distinguishing a provocative "war-fighting" nuclear posture from a low-level and stable retaliatory one, Tony Rogers (1988:11) emphasizes that the peace movement would enhance its appeal by taking account of residual fears of the Soviets — a reality that cannot be wished away. Indeed the director of the Center for Defense Information, Adm. (Ret.) Gene LaRocque (1988), recently elaborated a much diminished force-level mix and non-threatening deployment configuration that would be fully adequate for America's defense needs. Analogous alternative security proposals have been elaborated by Col. (Ret.) Robert Bowman (1988), director of the Institute for Space and Security Studies in Washington, and by the New York–based World Policy Institute in the culmination of a three-year study. Similarly, Ullman (1988:137) counsels:

> The West should assume that Gorbachev means what he says when he calls both for equalizing the sizes of conventional forces in Europe at substantially lower levels and for restructuring them so as to emphasize defensive rather than offensive capabilities. Each side, he has said, should eliminate from its arsenals a large proportion of the weapons that most frighten the other.

This would create a climate that was propitious for expanded nuclear free zones, military disengagement and greater emphasis upon non-threatening or defensive weapons deployments (Böge *et al.*, 1984; Wulf, 1985a) in Europe.

The impetus for such changes which already is growing (Wolpin, 1986; Ullman, 1988), would be reinforced in a positive rather than negative manner. An example of negative reinforcement is the drive by Washington (NPR, "Evening," Feb. 13, 1989) to have NATO modernize its nuclear weapons. With the backing only of Thatcher, the arms race intensification proposal by the Bush Administration triggered an unprecedented level of opposition from Scandinavian countries as well as West Germany. The latter's foreign minister called for a 2 to 3 year delay in any decision, responding in part to recent poll results showing 80 percent of West Germans favor removal of all nuclear weapons from the FRG. European sentiment more than ever favors a positive response to Soviet disengagement and arms reduction proposals. Similarly, East-West cooperation to curtail further nuclear proliferation might benefit considerably from an overall lessening of tensions.

The foregoing would be the basis for a national security policy that, as urged by Senator Machias and other civilianists cited at the outset of this study, assigns priority to: 1) increasing the productivity of America's domestic civilian industries; 2) promoting higher levels of socio-economic and cultural welfare for American citizens; 3) enhancing spiritual cohesion across racial, ethnic and class lines by fostering a sense of equity in the distribution of societal burdens as well as rewards; and 4) maintaining military capabilities to defend the continental United States against "clear and present" threats to its physical safety should they ever arise. The $92 + billion in current Pentagon waste and $30 billion excess inventory referred to earlier, in conjunction with a two-thirds reduction in its budget (approximately 70 percent is allocated for non-continental military purposes), would release several hundred billion dollars. The budget deficit could also be eliminated, and the trade imbalance reduced by new investments to raise industrial productivity.

Coffin (1988c:1) emphasizes that "the goal can be reached by giving up our role as world cop. The authoritative Center for Defense Information estimates that only 7 to 8% of our $320 billion annual military cost is for the defense of North America." More bluntly, Coffin urges

> the simplest and most direct strategy is to take a meat ax to military spending, according to a detailed three-year study by World Policy Institute. It insists that one trillion dollars can be safely shifted over the next 10 years from U.S. military budgets. In the first five years, $374.4 billion could be saved, a sum much larger than figures mentioned on Capitol Hill today. The Institute states that our economic crisis cannot be resolved without releasing resources now claimed by our bloated military budget.

Thus without raising taxes, financial resources would be available not only to address the socio-economic needs delineated in Chapter 8, but also to retrain and employ workers as weapons manufacturing facilities were converted to meet long-delayed civilian transportation, housing, ecological and other needs. Barron's (1983:D1, 4) report on Grumman's self-help measures when confronted by a possible temporary halt to F-14 purchases suggests that private initiative might also be counted on in any conversion program.[12] Several studies and feasible approaches to conversion are analyzed by Dumas (1982),

Melman (1983), and Gordon and McFadden (1984). Recently (Coffin, 1990:2) Congressman Ted Weiss submitted a bill — co-sponsored by fifty colleagues — to actually implement such a program.

> Its principal feature is a requirement that any defense plant, base or laboratory of 100 or more employees must develop alternative production plans within a two-year period. The penalty for non-compliance would be ineligibility for future defense contracts. Equal employee and management representation is required.
> The bill would tax defense contractors for the cost of worker adjustment benefits. It would also require military managers and engineers to enroll in professional retraining programs, to "unlearn" the cost-plus mentality. A Defense Economic Adjustment Council would set public works priorities.

Other work (Gleditsch, 1987; Wulf, 1988) on conversion prospects in Norway and West Germany suggests that special programs and perhaps high initial compensation levels would have to be guaranteed to overcome intense opposition in communities that are dependent upon weapons production.

Within the United States, then, it is clear that large initial grants would be necessary for retraining former military personnel as well as some workers and even for investments in new production facilities. Subsidies would also be needed to compensate for a reduction in wages, even though we have seen that only a small fraction of the labor force would be affected.[13] Degrasse (1983) cites numerous studies demonstrating that funds now used to procure weaponry would be less inflationary and generate much greater employment in more labor intensive civilian sectors. In the aircraft and missile industries, only about 20 percent of the cost goes to production workers as wages.

As for firms that couldn't make the transition, the Conrail nationalization (i.e., purchase) approach would seem indicated — and this might be extended to most remaining primary contracting firms per the advice of General Somerville to the War Production Board. Nationalization of this industry would also eliminate a massive publicly subsidized source of arms race propaganda alleging non-existent strategic gaps within a context of threat inflation.

As for arms exports, clearly we cannot reconcile this new defensive, non-imperialistic approach to American national security with Pierre's (1981/1982:286) conventional wisdom alleging "the challenge is to *manage* the process of arms sales so as to enhance international security. Of themselves arms sales are neither 'bad' nor 'good' — it all depends upon how they are used — so that there is no a priori case for either reducing or increasing them." The vast overkill capacity and unprecedented global militarization as well as the crucial diversion of resources suggest there *is* a reasonable a priori case for reduction. Yet Pierre is partly correct in that because there will remain for a period a basically anarchic interstate system, some weapons may be necessary or even "good" in limited circumstances.

A major reduction in arms exports to the South does not, as Betts (1980:86) would have it, reflect "a naive and paternalistic view of the Third World, as if backward countries would not be at each other's throats without the malign impetus of extra available weapons." Certainly there will still be conflicts, even wars. But there is no reason that the United States should exacerbate destructiveness or tensions in other nations by favoring dependent oligarchies or client regimes. Kuwait is the most recent example.

As the preceding chapters make clear, the costs of a massive interventionist superstructure have risen well beyond any economic spillover to the mass of ordinary Americans. This rise in costs is due to pervasive nationalist resistance abroad, the erosion of West European and Japanese quasi-satellite status, the transnationalization of corporate capital and the enhanced domestic leverage of an industrial-military complex now addicted to enormously expensive high-tech weaponry.

In the course of reviewing Paul Kennedy's widely acclaimed *The Rise and Fall of Great Powers* (1987), Dickinson and Schaeffer (1988:26) point to a common dynamic in the fall of a powerful nation: "during its fall, the attempt to maintain political power by force contributed to economic decline and, eventually, economic decline to military failure." In stark terms, they argue — following Kennedy — that:

> the sum total of the United States' global interests and obligations is nowadays far larger than the country's power to defend them simultaneously....
>
> The United States is subject to many of the same forces that led to the fall of previous great powers: when the military becomes overextended it undermines economic competitiveness and contributes to economic decline vis-a-vis other rising states (Western Europe, China and Japan), which results in a more multipolar world, one in which no single state is hegemonic.
>
> ...For the peace movement, Kennedy's findings are salutary. At a time when U.S. military growth has outstripped the economy's capacity to support a global, interventionist military presence, it is in U.S. interests to constrain the military and bring political commitments in line with economic capabilities.

Although Nye (1988) and the Bush Administration reject this thesis, public opinion seems, for a change, to be in closer contact with the new reality. Thus by late 1988, the "Americans Talk Security Survey" reported ("New Findings," 1988:6) that "by a three-to-one margin, the public feels economic power is more important than military power in determining a country's influence in the world." Even more to the point, "many" now believe that a nuclear war is more likely to be triggered by a third-party or "terrorist" attack than by a fanciful pre-meditated Soviet launch. Thus United States links to conventional or nuclear armed repressive powers like Israel (Cobban, 1988) have become the greatest threat to American and global security. Involvement in an East European civil or interstate war would also risk such escalation.

The path to recovering American prestige is non-entanglement or in

Ravenal's (1980) words, that the United States government learn how to "do nothing." If the French, Iranians, or, as now seems quite unlikely, even the Soviets wish to become involved, let them. Respect is the basis for world leadership, and in the long run America will regain the position lost since the final days of World War II. Naziism's drive to destroy the USSR and impose a Thousand Year Reich was exceptional rather than a common occurrence in the world system. Even then Berlin's global ambitions were problematic. Furthermore, in its other dimensions, that great war was catalyzed by Japan's and Italy's aspirations to join France and Britain as colonial powers. Indeed, the major Axis powers had felt—with some reason—cheated or victimized by the Western-dictated World War I "settlement," which was not only vindictive, but violated Wilson's "Fourteen Points" which conditioned Germany's surrender.

While this may not persuade those imprisoned either by the paranoid projection syndrome or virulent anti-communism, fortunately only a minority (15 to 20 percent) of the American public is militarily interventionist and intensely anti–Soviet. Currently ("New Findings," 1988:6) 80 percent of Americans support strategic arms cutback negotiations with Moscow while "many" not only see relations as improving but envisage them as even more cooperative in the future with respect to environmental and other issues. And the proportion has undoubtedly increased since this survey was taken.

Soviet unilateral peace initiatives (INF, Afghanistan, arms concessions) and Gorbachev's style have probably been surpassed by a change in American elite cues in bringing about this mood shift. Even more easily can leadership win mass support for restoring vitality and enhancing the quality of life in America by focusing energies upon this challenge and renouncing interventionism in the affairs of other nations. This does not preclude normal commercial or cultural intercourse with other nations directly and through multilateral organizations. Thus non-interventionism is premised upon international respect, equality and law—principles essential to a global community dedicated to the common security of all.

If outright adoption of a non-interventionist foreign policy eliminating all arms transfers appears too extreme, fortunately there is a slightly less radical alternative that I believe would still be consonant with American safety and welfare, i.e., national security. Two criteria are elaborated here. First, arms transfers could be limited to primarily short-range and light defensive weaponry. At the outset of this chapter, both Cannizzo and Landgren-Backstrom emphasized such a distinction. Betts (1980:89) also observes that "cheap precision guided munitions can be effective against high-volume tanks and aircraft, so a declining amount of funds ... could coincide with absolute and relative increases in the country's military power." Landgren-Backstrom (1982:209) adds that "it is possible to identify certain categories of weapons obviously designed for 'offensive use'—such weapons would be for example

long-range fighter bombers, land-mobile surface-to-surface missiles. The next
step would be to limit production and sale of certain categories of weapons."

An overall strategic rationale distinguishing such weapons as surface-to-
air missiles, short-range fighters, etc., which because of their performance
limitations are non-threatening to other states is elaborated by Johansen
(1983:22–23). Urging immediate elimination "without negotiations" of
weapons which "threaten one's opponent," he counsels that others be "designed and deployed to mount a strong defense." Thus "the idea that offense
provides the best defense 'should be a rule of tactics and not of strategy.'" Such
an alternative national (i.e., mutual) security approach has been analyzed for
a number of possible contingencies with respect to West Germany and Scandinavia by Böge, Wilke and Wulf (1984), Dankbaar (1984), Lutz (1984), and
Wulf (1985).

Several of these peace researchers note that certain weapons like the tank
or armored personnel carrier are neither essentially non-threatening nor
necessarily offensive in nature. This observation brings a second criterion into
play. Both types of weapons as well as troops would have to be *deployed* in
a non-threatening manner. Thus a country would have the option of purchasing non-threatening defensive arms such as SAMs, anti-tank PGMs, short-
range interceptors such as the F-5, etc. Such "high technology" defensive (i.e.,
non-threatening) weapons assigned to small (company- to battalion-sized) yet
coordinated mobile contingents might become, when supplemented by a professional frontier force, the basis of national or "territorial" (Roberts, 1986)
defense systems. If backed by an extensive mobile reserve and possibly a militia
mobilization capability, there would be a credible frontal and in-depth
defense deterrent to any potential aggressor. The aggressor would be confronted by very high costs and unpredictable delays in attaining crucial objectives. Eventually counterattacks would result in attrition once the defender's
reserves supplemented main force units. At the same time, such a force structure combined with non-threatening deployments of both troops and potentially offensive weapons would not provoke fears by neighbors, thus symboliz-
ing a genuine indivisibility of security.

Elaborating upon such an alternative defense doctrine, Wulf (1979) offers
a more graphic description of possible implementation by Third World
nations:

> Besides these infantry units equipped with simple wire guided anti-tank
> missiles, occasionally a small navy for coastal protection is required, whereas the
> protection against possible air attacks lies in the hands of decentralized infantry
> units. The weapons will be produced locally as far as possible. Should imports
> be required, supplier relationships will have to be diversified to forestall possi-
> ble one sided dependencies. . . .
> Since the defenders are not dependent on external assistance the aggressor
> cannot hope to blackmail the defenders into surrender by cutting off . . . the

supply of weapons and parts. On the contrary, the invaders are permanently harassed and attacked by a large number of lightly armed combatants with the intention not necessarily of defending the territory or the border of the country, but of ultimately forcing the aggressors to surrender.

Or, we may add, withdraw.

The small regular armed forces would continue to perform genuine national security functions by training militia and/or reserves as well as coordinating external defense efforts. Tuomi and Vayrynen (1980:257) have extracted key components of Wulf's low-cost and implicitly democratic "people's war" defensive (i.e. non-threatening) strategic posture premised upon maximal self-reliance, minimization of external indebtedness, and enhancing the availability of scarce resources for social welfare. Comparing the "technocratic army" to the "people's army," they find (for example) that the weaponry of the former includes "capital-intensive" equipment such as tanks and aircraft, only partially locally produced, while the people's army relies on smaller, simpler arms (anti-aircraft and anti-tank missiles), mainly locally produced. The technocratic army is a professional and specialized force, permanently mobilized; the people's army uses a militia system "geared to serve also economic functions," with "limited mobilization" in times of peace. The technocratic army has a "hierarchical, centralized" structure, as opposed to the "democratic, decentralized" structure of the people's army. Finally, the strategy of the technocratic force includes offensive "potential for pre-emptive strikes," while that of the people's army is "defensive, reactive."

To the extent that released resources are utilized to improve employment opportunities and living standards, they will broaden regime legitimacy. This in turn may attenuate elite fears of an armed mass-based militia supplementing regular reserves. At the same time, a socio-economically responsive government will over time feel more confident in opening up the system to mass participation beyond rituals. As accountability and citizen integration develop, other defensive possibilities will emerge. One of the most exciting is the training of broad population sectors for non-violent civil resistance or at least non-cooperation with any prospective invader. By 1989 such practices by Palestinians in Gaza and the West Bank were dramatically raising the costs to Israeli occupiers and making such seized territories virtually ungovernable. Indeed, rather than constituting an alternative to armed defense, Salmon (1988) regards planned civilian resistance as a complement which would follow defeat of perimeter forces and be applied mainly in highly populated urban zones while decentralized mobile forces continued fighting in lightly populated areas. Thus the high costs and difficulty of attaining a rapid conquest would function as a powerful yet non-provocative deterrent to any political aggressor. Or, as Salmon (1988) puts it:

> The purpose of both violent and non-violent defense is the same: to make it impossible for the invader to govern and ultimately to cause him to withdraw and allow full national sovereignty to be established.

The beauty of such an approach is that no neighboring state would have reason to feel threatened, and common security could be enhanced as the governing norm for the international community.

Considerable investigation needs to be done on the range of both experiences and possibilities for such alternative defense strategies.[14] China, Nicaragua and Yugoslavia may approximate some of its parameters. Pfaff (1982:6) reports that Yugoslav

> landing fields, potential paratroop drop zones and the coasts are under permanent surveillance. New radar gives or will give them coverage of the whole Eastern Mediterranean and the Black Sea. Their own ships are sheltered in caves cut into coastal mountains, and their aircraft in underground blast shelters. They have taken advice from the Swedes and the Swiss on this.
>
> There is a permanent, regularly exercised, national organization of popular defense, with tanks in factories, small arms stored in advertising agency cupboards and the back rooms of banks. More than a third of the population is actively enrolled. . . .
>
> They have debated whether cities should be given up or defended, whatever the civilian cost, in an invasion. The decision is to fight for the cities, and if necessary to destroy whatever an enemy might use.

Clearly, this is not a strategy of weakness. On the contrary, as Dietrich Fischer points out: "'Strength' has two different meanings which often are not distinguished. Strength can mean the ability to harm others or the ability to resist harm intended by others."

Furthermore, Johansen (1983:23) reminds us that this approach telescopes the problem addressed by Michael Klare in Chapter 2 of striking a neat balance between nations' force levels. For in contradistinction to more traditional deterrent strategies, "a defensive posture can succeed in the presence of an inequality of military power as long as it is an excess of defensive capability over offensive capability. Each country can enjoy its own superiority of defensive power without making other states insecure. No government should be unhappy with defensive inequalities becuase they threaten no one!" In practice, few governments would squander resources upon clearly exorbitant acquisitions of defensive weaponry. Where this did occur, or when range-extending logistical equipment was sought, suppliers could decline sales and emphasize that reliance should be placed upon diplomacy, the United Nations and the World Court as the primary security mechanisms.[15]

Finally, arms exporters such as the United States should set an example for true world leadership by adopting a genuinely defensive weapons mix and force deployment policy—the latter involving abrogation of most existing alliances (except with immediate neighbors) and liquidation of the essentially interventionist (i.e. offensive) global base structure.[16] It is worth reiterating that the value of such a national security approach is its low economic cost, implicit democratic content and above all non-threatening character — essential for the enhancement of global security. These factors have been examined throughout this work from the perspective of their converse — the declining contribution to security flowing from Washington's high cost, nascent garrison state committed to an increasingly unstable counterforce posture essential for interventionist escalatory dominance.

My purpose here has been to provide an alternative national security policy of which arms transfers limited to defensive weaponry and countries whose deployments were non-threatening are but two components. The mechanics of implementation are beyond the scope of this study, yet far from insuperable. Either the United Nations Secretary General or the Stockholm International Peace Research institute could, for example, be commissioned to assess deployments and categorize weapons on the basis of relative offensiveness, i.e., how threatening their potential use was to neighboring states. Thus a fivefold typology might be elaborated to govern such classification:

1) Defensive (e.g. surface-to-air missiles — SAMs)
2) Primarily Defensive (e.g. short-range helicopters)
3) Indeterminate (e.g. heavy tanks)
4) Primarily Offensive (e.g. 50–300 km range ballistic missiles)
5) Offensive (e.g. fighter bombers — F-16E, highly accurate IRBMs or SLBMs)

I do not ignore the difficulty of categorizing many systems whose tactical employment may vary. In all probability, initial consensus would be limited to a small number of weapons in the first and last categories. The difficulties are underscored by Johansen (1983:23), who concedes that

> most weapons fall between these two extreme categories. They can serve both offensive and defensive purposes. Yet the difference in the degree of defensiveness is important. The security policies of Switzerland and Yugoslavia, countries fiercely determined to maintain their national independence without threatening others, illustrate this approach.

Fischer's (1982) description of the Swiss weapons mix suggests that analysis of force deployments and terrain can be helpful at times in making borderline classifications.

Even the ACDA during the Carter era is reported by Pearson (1981:37) as having advocated "defensive as opposed to offensive emphases and force configurations." Such distinctions were endorsed by South American nations well over a decade ago (Ronfeldt and Sereseres, 1977:32) in the Declaration of Ayacucho. By the end of 1988, a similar common security approach had, as we noted in Chapter 5, been adopted by the Soviets. In his December United

Nations address, Gorbachev (Farris, 1988:1, 6) announced a major troop, tank, artillery and aircraft pullout from Central Europe and "the European part of the U.S.S.R." Of equal importance, remaining "divisions" would be reorganized. "Their structure will be different from what it is now; after a major cutback of their tanks, it will become clearly defensive." Scandinavians and West Germans were moving in a similar direction during the early months of 1989.

As far as arms transfers are concerned, in general it would seem prudent to use a restrictive defensive criterion if our purpose is to curtail the militarization process as well as global insecurity flowing from offensive postures and arms races. Further, quantitative ceilings on exports could be dispensed with under this approach. Exports could be further reduced by restricting transfers only to countries which have formally complained to the United Nations Security Council that they fear an imminent attack or, like Nicaragua, were actually defending their territory from external assaults. A recommendation for assistance by that body or the General Assembly might also be required. This would, of course, strengthen the United Nations — a reversal of United States policy for more than a decade. It would also imply Washington's adoption of a "Good Neighbor" (i.e., non-interventionist) Policy toward the Third World — at least in the military area.

Another practical issue hinges upon whether administrative responsibility should be vested in the executive branch of the United States government. Although one may reasonably differ, my own view is that given the inept or blatantly illegal executive performance delineated in Chapters 3 and 5, and the fact that during the 1974–1977 era nearly all initiatives to limit arms transfers originated within the Congress, this body should reserve its authority to approve each transfer above $10 million proposed by the State Department.[17] If necessary, the foreign affairs committees can acquire additional specialized staff from the half-dozen or so peace research institutions within the United States or Western Europe.[18] Again the purpose is to restrict transfers to defensive weaponry and further to reduce them to a minimum rather than to proceed with a business-as-usual approach — one that characterized the Carter experiment.

Beyond a freeze on exports of offensive weapons that are most likely to be viewed as threatening to neighboring countries, another restrictive option exists. Defensive weapons might be exported on a grant or wholly concessional basis only to regimes with good political human rights records or to those which at least demonstrated marked annual improvement in mass welfare, i.e., socioeconomic human rights. The latter might be relatively authoritarian mobilizational systems yet should be devoid of routine use of the more brutal repressive practices such as torture, disappearances and extra-judicial execution by police, army or tolerated death squads. Indeed, where these heinous acts are sufficient to constitute a pattern (as in Mexico or Iran), even electoral competition (likely to be only nominal) would fail to qualify a regime for concessional terms.

Independent human rights assessments are published annually by Amnesty International, while changes in national rankings on various welfare indicators are published by World Priorities. Improvements in the Overseas Development Council's physical quality-of-life index might also be employed as a concessional criterion. This would reward elites who either were actually enhancing the well-being of their citizens or who at least gave counterelites an opportunity to be elected in an atmosphere devoid of intimidation. Enhancing the defensive capabilities of such governments on a partly or wholly concessional basis would in the long run contribute to their development (by not running up more unsupportable external debts), as well as restore American prestige and influence in the developing areas.

To maximize the efficacy of this new approach, Millett's proposition cited in Chapter 4 should be implemented. Since arms denials "are only effective if they are carefully coordinated with all other aspects of our policy, presenting a single, clear message to the individual nations," then economic aid, intelligence, propaganda, and diplomacy should not contradict a restrictive arms export policy. Suitable adjustments should also govern insurance, services and other subsidies for corporate investors.[19] Even then, particularly when no longer using covert action, America's influence or leverage will be, as it should, modest. But in adopting a posture consistently favoring defensiveness, political human rights, or at least mass socio-economic betterment, the United States will in an indirect way promote the safety and well-being of its own society, i.e., its own national security. Not only will the major reduction in America's defense burden allow a genuine reindustrialization as well as significant foreign development aid increases, but the corrosive effect of militarism upon the quality of civic life in America will be removed.

Externally, a non-militaristic source of positive influence and restored world leadership will become the basis for new respect and genuine national pride. Rand experts Ronfeldt and Sereseres (1977:26) proudly declaimed at the zenith of the Carter experiment: "Human rights are a proper and useful emphasis for U.S. foreign policy. Even in South American countries where specific congressional measures have been criticized, there is recognition that the new emphasis has restored a vigorous and progressive image to the United States as a superpower and as a traditional champion of freedom." In short, global respect or admiration should be given precedence over the fear engendered by compulsive neo-colonial power projection, and protection of transnational corporations.

Also germane is the erosion of substantive democratic accountability and civility within our own system — one increasingly characterized by alienation, manipulation and even strident intolerance. Militarism and neo-colonialism are, as I have argued, inherently elitist — and as we saw in the Iran-Contra case, also subversive of democratic values not to mention the Constitution itself. What should be respected by political elites is the continual opposition of the citizenry to arms transfers, military interventionism and non-humanitarian foreign aid. This opposition is evinced by ordinary Americans who for a decade or two have experienced static or deteriorating living standards. Years ago Pierre (1982:71–72) underscored this point:

> Public opinion polls have consistently supported greater restraint. Indeed the largest portion of respondents in polls taken in the late 1970s stated fairly routinely that as a general policy the United States should not sell weapons to other countries at all. . . . Even after the Reagan Administration adopted a new approach, 67 percent opposed giving military assistance to anti-communist allies that violate human rights.

This helps one comprehend why threat inflation and distortion must infuse all manipulative public policy rationales.

As Kriesberg (1982) recognizes, there was a moderate alarmist shift in the public mood between 1974 and 1978, but both he and especially Sanders (1983a) pinpoint domestic elites as the primary catalyst. In the late 1980s dominant elites opted for a more moderate stance, and again the mass mood was receptive. Greenberg (1988:556–57) notes that Gallup surveys indicate the proportion of Americans who wanted Washington to reduce tensions with Moscow rose from 20 percent in the 1978–1982 period to almost 66 percent by late 1987 when the INF accord was signed. A shift in policy that limited arms transfers to defensive weapons would receive broad public support, as would an end to military interventionism in the developing areas. The same could be said for sustained serious efforts involving genuine reciprocity and even modest unilateral initiatives to further improve relations with the Soviets. This in turn would obviate the need for threat inflation, thus enhancing the democratic quality of elite-mass interaction (i.e., accountability) in America. Hence the marked rise in public alienation since the early 1960s (Gilmour and Lamb, 1975; Miller *et al.*, 1980), and the previously discussed fall-off in electoral interest, conceivably might be reversed.[20]

Ultimately, in the wake of such United States foreign initiatives and arms control policy redirection, efforts should be undertaken to convene the United Nations conference envisaged by Landgren-Backstrom. In such a setting, it would no longer be "a radical proposition." If certain suppliers or recipients were uninterested, at least America's hands would be clean! As mentioned before, the United States would still be furnishing the highest quality defensive arms in abundant quantities when a demonstrable need existed. Export magnitudes and weapons mixes might even be based upon desires of the recipient, thus avoiding the chauvinism implicit in determining whether they "really need it."Weapons types would be severely restricted to those of marginal offensive value such as SAMs, anti-tank PGMs, light artillery, mortars, mines, sensors, patrol boats, and short-range or light-load interceptors.

As Ronfeldt and Sereseres (1977:55) wisely acknowledge:

> Important advantages for U.S. interests may accrue from developing U.S.
> policies that stress the potential politico-military benefits, rather than the
> presumed costs, from regional arms diversification. Being one among varied
> suppliers may prove to be a useful position at times. A very close or dominant
> arms transfer relationship may no longer optimize political influence and
> leverage if it ever did. At present, a very close relationship carries the risk that
> a client or superclient may be able to exercise reverse-leverage.[21]

Although the authors' neo-colonial preoccupation with maximizing influence
should be rejected, opening the way to multilateral participation in place of
a compulsive drive for pre-emptive dominance may not only be the first step
toward a successful global arms restraint conference, but also constitute the
beginning of Falk's (1980) noncoercive "global community."

As such it would offer hope for the future of the United States, which today, because of the political elite's addiction to a militaristic "Pax Americana,"
has been tarnished by growing diplomatic isolation abroad and domestic
wariness in a once optimistic nation. Sanders (1983:43) poses the key issue:
"How deeply militarism is rooted in America's political culture has become the
most profound question of our time." Like others (Lumsden, 1972; Chilton,
1986; Klein, 1988), Jerome Wiesner, a former MIT president and special assistant to John Kennedy, underscores (1985:104) the symbolic pervasiveness of
this "garrison state" hegemonial mentality:

> More than 35 years of Cold War language and politics have created a situa-
> tion in which it is difficult to talk rationally about how we arrived at the present
> impasse. A combination of Newspeak words, false information, half-baked
> ideas about successful preemptive attacks and winning nuclear wars, and clair-
> voyant projections of Soviet forces and objectives have obscured rational alter-
> natives to the arms race. In particular, the use of worst-case analysis, supported
> by controlled leaks of secret information, has manipulated Americans into de-
> nying responsibility for the arms race and believing that the Soviets are
> relentless and reckless aggressors. As a result, ordinary citizens conclude that
> they can do nothing to stop the catastrophe they see coming.

No one delegated to the United States the responsibility to police the world.
America's real duty is to promote its own national security in a manner that
does not threaten the safety and mass welfare of other societies. If it does only
that, America will be making a substantial contribution to a more secure global
system—one that someday may attain the quality of an equitable community.

Despite their "failure," the arms controllers in Congress and the Carter
Administration set a valuable precedent. They had the courage to take an initiative. Their real failure was to allow the interventionist foreign policy
framework or assumptions requiring a militarized infrastructure as well as arms
transfers "for influence" to go unquestioned. Hence a mere replication of the

Carter restraint initiative will be equally unsuccessful. The consequences, on
the other hand, of permitting the current approach to go unchecked are
spelled out by Klare (1982f:146) as likely to

> exacerbate all the problems which have become associated with such sales: in-
> tensified local arms races in conflict-prone areas, leading to increased instability
> and a greater risk of regional conflicts; the growing proliferation of high-
> technology arms, leading to ever-increasing levels of violence in whatever con-
> flicts do occur; the further diversion of scarce economic resources to military
> purposes, thereby perpetuating the underdevelopment and indebtedness of
> many Third World countries; and the empowerment of Third World military
> forces, resulting in a continuing dissolution of democratic institutions in favour
> of military rule.

With greater experience, citizen support and, one hopes, wisdom, perhaps
America will succeed in transcending the neo-colonial consensus which enabled those associated with the military-industrial complex and transnational
corporate sectors to isolate and eventually emasculate the arms controllers of
the seventies. It is to this political challenge that the nation must turn. For it
is not sufficient to merely posit an alternative. Needed peace movement innovations must be addressed as well. As matters now stand, fewer than 15 percent of peace organization leaders (Eichner, 1990:201) believed in the
mid-1980s that the movement's tactics had proven very successful. The Bush
team's flagrant disregard of international law and world opinion by invading
Panama, its glacial response to Gorbachev's peace initiative and maintenance
of the SDI program as well as its refusal to substantially reduce the FY1991 proposed military budget have certainly reinforced such convictions.

How to learn from past failures and strengthen the peace constituency is
the most difficult question facing Americans sensitive to the ultimate irrationality and self-destructiveness of their nation's present course. That self-
destructiveness pertains not merely to mass socio-economic austerity, but more
fundamentally to norms of equity, honesty, civility, lawfulness and elite
accountability—indeed the qualitative dimensions of American civilization.
Yet it is obvious that too much is at stake in the short run for the "iron triangle"
to melt before a reasoned critique by outsiders. Nor can this be anticipated as
a consequence of Bush's "kinder and gentler" rhetoric in response to Gorbachev's unilateral concessions and broad range of proposals to promote major
arms cutbacks, military disengagement, an end to the arms race and cooperative undertakings with respect to Third World issues and global ecological
dangers.

Sanders (1983:43) points out that "the real litmus test will come when a
challenge is mounted to the proposition that resistance to empire abroad is *pari
passu* a threat to security at home, the heart of containment orthodoxy." He
goes on to caution, "If the short-lived era of detente and the dynamics of

the post–Vietnam period are any guide, this challenge cannot be expected from managerial [i.e. liberal] elites within the Establishment who share the underlying militarist goal of empire, even as they disagree on the most effective means toward its achievement." Indeed, Petras and Morley (1983:11), like Kaplan and Blechman (1978), document a frightful number of post–World War II instances where both liberal Democratic and Republican adminstrations seriously contemplated resort to nuclear weapons in their bipartisan drive to preserve hegemony (Tarq, 1984; Chomsky, 1987) in the Third World against nationalist and social revolutionary movements. Though liberal elements in the Democratic congressional establishment may function as a weak moderating or restraining force, they will continue to be relatively impotent with respect to fundamentally altering the basic foreign policy parameters. They are literally overwhelmed not only by the chief executive but also by a large majority of "moderate" and conservative colleagues. Among other events, the invasions of Lebanon, Grenada and Panama underscore their impotence as has the de facto defiance of the Central American peace accords by both the Reagan and Bush administrations. Furthermore, they cannot rely upon (Healey, 1988:230) an effective national peace constituency.

DOES THE "PEACE MOVEMENT" HAVE A FUTURE?

Despite improved organization, unprecedented mass alienation and an impressive number of defections by dissident ex-insiders from the garrison state apparatus over the past decade, success has eluded the American peace movement, which is currently in a state of disarray (Healey, 1988; Melman, 1988; McCrea and Markle, 1989) and fragmentation. Indeed a recent (Colwell, 1988) analysis found not only a multiplicity of "peace" organizations, but more seriously conflicting priorities. This was also the case (Perkovich, 1988) with respect to dealing with Soviet domestic vs. foreign policies. Add a national leadership which stresses (Healey, 1988) insider lobbying at the expense of building tightly coordinated constituency linkages in congressional districts and we have a recipe for impotence. The failure of the nuclear freeze movement for the liberal wing, and the ineffectiveness of opposition to Contra aid from the more anti-interventionist leftist sectors, have jointly contributed to general demoralization, as have some of the repressive government policies described in Chapter 11. Indeed, progressives have become nonpersons or are denounced with the epithet "radical," while as the 1988 presidential election campaign demonstrated, the term liberal (Bush's "L" word) has become a euphemism for radical. The absence of significant protest against Bush's effort to use East-West arms control to enhance the Pentagon's "strategic superiority" (e.g. its asymmetry) and killing of thousands with the resurrected "big stick" against Panama, or his failure to prosecute gross lawlessness by the North-Poindexter-Reagan clique all attest to the moribund state of a "peace movement" which twenty years earlier was a force to be reckoned with in

American politics. Indeed the domestic popularity of wars against such mini-states as Grenada and Panama suggests the need for a new direction.

In proposing a number of maximal goals (a ban on all offensively threatening arms exports, nationalization of prime military contractors, etc.) and minimal policy restrictions of exports to defensive (light and short-range) types, (reliance upon SIPRI, AI and UN determinations, etc.) I have sought to avoid prescribing a blueprint. Only a few qualitative changes (e.g. renouncing foreign policy interventionism and its supporting infrastructure of training, bases, personnel and weaponry) have been specified. We are too far from any of them for *a priori* sequential precision. A similar approach is the most one can expect for turning the militaristic juggernaut — albeit a less crude, loosely managed and fast-paced one under Bush — around.

The sharp division among peace activists over Soviet human rights (Perkovich, 1988) has become less important in view of the new glasnost-related tolerance and greater respect for civil liberties by the new Soviet leadership. Yet new fissures may appear concerning Soviet respect for self-determination in the Baltic region and possibly even Eastern Europe. They already exist with respect to drugs, democracy, and military intervention in Central America. Healey (1988) sees the main problem in organizational terms — stressing the need for strong centralized authority and direction. He emphasizes that a social movement's power comes from building a network of base organizations through grassroots campaigns, a process which demands the strongest of national staffs and leaders. The more decentralized the organizing base of the movement, the higher a priority must be put on national strategy and coordination.

The freeze campaign never understood this. Instead it displayed what Solo calls "pathological" organizational behavior. The campaign was deeply ambivalent about power and distrusted leaders. As with other United States social movements, the organizational life of the campaign reflected the fierce individualism and the internalization of an atomized culture, even while rejecting it. To its credit, "the Freeze was able to accomplish what its predecessors had been unable to do — to define nuclear weapons as a major social problem of our time" (McRea and Markle, 1989:150). Yet McCrea and Markle also stress the consequences of its tactical decision to engage in partisan politics:

> Ronald Reagan and his Cold War rhetoric provided a perfect foil for the Freeze. Yet the Reagan foil was a two-edged sword. When the Freeze made his electoral defeat their top priority for 1984, the ensuing landslide marked the Freeze as a marginal not a major, factor in American political life. Thus as Reagan helped to create the Freeze, his political endurance and popularity also delimited its success.
>
> Even before the 1984 elections, the Freeze had lost its impetus. By allying itself with the Democratic party, particularly under the aegis of Edward Kennedy, the Freeze was coopted into the larger issues of party politics. Though

many Freeze advocates saw the House of Representatives resolution as a victory, it was nothing of the sort. The non-binding resolution, full of loopholes, allowed Congress members to go on record for the idea of a freeze, yet still support the military-industrial complex. In sum, the Freeze tried to influence electoral and congressional processes, but instead became controlled by the very forces it was trying to shape.

Subsequently, the Freeze suffered a sharp erosion of membership and financial contributions from foundations. Foundation funding, McCrea and Markle (1989:153) add, "was crucial in two ways for SANE and Freeze: external funds allowed the organizations to grow and flourish, but at the same time exercised a conservative influence over movement strategy and tactics." In decline, the two organizations merged in 1988 and were forced to reduce their national staff by one-third the following year.

Other peace researchers including Klare (1985a) emphasize the importance of coalition building with labor, minorities and environmentalists. A few like Fitch (1985) warn that the advanced nature of the garrison state is such that any effective challenge to its militarism will evoke severe repression. Ironically, as the preceding chapter makes clear, a moderate level of repression has been targeted upon peace and leftist sectors notwithstanding their much diminished influence since the late 1960s. High-intensity repression (Churchill and Van der Wall, 1988) was restricted largely to militant leadership sectors of such radical minorities as blacks, Puerto Ricans and Native Americans.

There is varying merit in all of the contentions of peace researchers. Repression can be resisted (Glick, 1988) and is not invariably successful. Recent changes in Eastern Europe underscore this as well as gross distortion in Western depictions of those systems as "totalitarian." Similarly, despite its "bureaucratic authoritarianism," the pre–Gorbachev human rights situation in the Soviet Union (Lane, 1985; Stephen F. Cohen, 1985; Lewin, 1985; Solomon, 1985) was far better than Stalin's and surpassed that in many of Washington's closest Third World allies. Gorbachev has relaxed admittedly distasteful emigration barriers for Jews (Perkovich, 1988a) and has greatly broadened freedom or tolerance of expression. Soviet official publications like *Pravda* are today enlivened by public debate over reforms as never before. Evtushenko's speech as early as December 1985 to Russian writers had forcefully called for a more libertarian milieu. Between then and 1988, not only has the Soviet system become relatively tolerant of dissent, but as Kessler (1988) makes clear, there are now well over a thousand non-official political groups of various suasions. Even "the Party" encompasses a broad (i.e. pluralistic) rather than narrow range of policy perspectives with de facto factions and publications associated with different tendencies. Without further easing of East-West tensions, little more can be expected. Indeed, Gorbachev's reformers are engaged in a sharp conflict with neo–Stalinist "conservatives" who may soon halt or even reverse the current course. Neo-fascist groups are also growing.

Yet such matters are really none of America's business and in any case peripheral to United States safety and welfare interests that require an end to the arms race. Preoccupation with trying to change domestic Soviet or East European policies also induces one to ignore the fact that in some socio-economic and cultural human rights areas, Soviet practices (Szymanski, 1985; Nagle, 1985) compare favorably with a far wealthier country like the United States. With the same humility America should acknowledge that not many of its ordinary citizens are really concerned about employment or other sanctions upon Soviet dissidents. Furthermore, by giving special salience to political criticisms historically stressed by hypocritical rightists who themselves routinely overlook South African, Salvadoran and Korean or Taiwan's authoritarianism, peace activists would open themselves to charges of naivete and reinforce demonic threat inflation by militaristic sectors.

Finally, while repression-resistant coalition building does point in the right direction, it ignores a fundamental historical lesson and therefore suffers from undue idealism. Nigel Young's (1984) comparative investigation of the failures experienced by Western peace movements yields several interesting findings. Most important is that in large measure anti-war campaigns failed to elicit active support by masses of ordinary citizens, i.e., the modestly educated majority of blue collar workers, lower middle class white collar employees and those residing in rural areas. These movements were essentially elitist in nature. Their appeals found resonance among a minority of the comfortable and relatively sophisticated upper middle class religious or ideological intelligentsia. In Freudian terms, they never penetrated into the mass corpus in sufficient measure to compel militaristic elites to respect the right to life![22]

Three necessary political innovations for a fundamental and lasting militarization turnaround in the West and particularly the United States may be derived from this historical lesson. First, as Gramsci counsels, the hegemony of cultural symbols is crucial to winning a mass constituency. In the past, peace activists have generally opposed or at best ignored patriotic national symbols with which the broad majority strongly identify. At a recent peace symposium (IPIS, 1988:12–13, 16–17) sponsored by the Cambridge-based Institute for Peace and International Security, its co-director, Pam Solo, counseled that:

> The Right has succeeded in using polling data to shape public opinion and promote its policies. It is also successful in contextualizing its political demands and policy proposals within a clear and simple philosophy. For the Right, ideas matter. Language shapes values, attitudes and policies. The Right knows how to use beliefs and myths, and take their ideas into the political culture. By doing this, the Right is defining the political debate. It is determining what is politically possible and acceptable.

Earlier, Robert Manoff, the director of the Center for War, Peace and the News Media at New York University, provided a concrete example drawn from the 1988 presidential campaign:

In this context I note and appreciate the shift in American opinion which we have heard about. Sadly, I do not regard it as transient. We need an enemy as a people. If the Soviets should cease to be that enemy, the Germans and Japanese are already lined up for the privilege. However, I think that the Soviets will continue to serve.

As I consider the elections I realize that this is precisely the meaning of the controversy over the Pledge of Allegiance. 70% of those in the *New York Times* poll disagree with Dukakis on the Pledge, 31% in a Gallup poll think the Pledge is the "most important issue." It has had an enormous impact on Michael Dukakis's prospects for the Presidency.

The debate represents something bizarre, something that polling can't get at. It tells us of some upswelling of deep, basically irrational forces that we ignore at our own peril. I am even moved to ask—apocalyptic implications notwithstanding—whether this exposes to view some really deeply underlying sickness in the American body politic. The Seventh Day Adventists who first objected to the Pledge were correct, it is idolatrous. It is the Golden Calf of American politics right now.

If the non-militaristic approach is indeed the one most consonant with national security, peace movements should appropriate the flag rather than surrender it to the real enemy, *viz.,* apologists for corporations and the iron triangle who are undermining mass safety and welfare while feathering bureaucratic careers and lining their own pockets.

Put differently, anti-militarists need a new "Committee to Activate a Patriotic Majority" or a movement organization with analogous symbols (e.g. Patriotic Progressive Non-Partisan League) that attacks established special interest elites on patriotic grounds.[23] This would vitiate one of the historic vulnerabilities of peace movements—particularly those of an internationalist genre or during eras of repression. Gleditsch (1989:78), himself victimized by state repression for publishing a critical book on Norwegian electronic intelligence, warns: "If freedom of expression becomes severely constrained—as it did under the McCarthy period in the US—this may affect negatively people's willingness to participate in movements which may be labelled as 'unpatriotic.'" By identifying the initial concern as the safety and well-being of Americans while accusing interventionist politicians of being unpatriotic for impoverishing the American "way of life"—both economically and spiritually—through demagoguery masking subservience to profiteering big bankers and corporations, the non-militarization movement can tap two powerful cultural traditions: populism and patriotism. Indeed the shift in public mood toward linking diminished economic well-being with security erosion (IPIS, 1988:10) favors such an approach. Recent findings of the Americans Talk Security Project emphasized public perceptions that Americans "are economically overextended in our commitments to preserve and protect other countries." There is a strong impulse to pull back from that commitment because it is felt to be at the expense of Americans' own economic well-being at home.[24] At the same time, ordinary Americans saw renewed Japanese and German "economic strength [to] offer a greater threat to U.S. national security than does Soviet military strength." And it can be pointed out that their state managers have eschewed squandering anything like the resources that American politicians have upon wasteful military burdens and boondoggles.

Given the pervasiveness of distrust for established elites in conjunction with the marked decline (Lipset and Schneider, 1983) of mass confidence in most major institutions, the setting is propitious for mounting a mass-based challenge to the nascent garrison state.[25] But the point of departure or initial focus should not be against military strength itself nor even interventionism, apart from the latter's domestic effects. These have never been issues that directly evoke intense mass discontent, short of a victoryless war of long duration. Indeed, as Gleditsch (1989:73–76) emphasizes, peace movements in the West have usually collapsed once war began. Further, not only have they been subject to cyclical vicissitudes, but they evoke mass interest only when focused upon a concrete, immediately threatening object that is directly perceived. There is little resonance at the lower middle and working class levels for "arms control" (IPIS, 1988:10) or what is perceived as international idealism. Because of the historic weakness of trade unionism and the absence of labor party politics in the United States, privatism and the possessive individualist ethos of capitalism are especially pronounced (Bellah *et al.*, 1985)—more so even than in Western Europe.[26] The precipitous decline (Moberg, 1989) of trade union membership and influence over the past two decades—and particularly during the Reagan/Bush onslaught—has further reinforced this materialist cultural bias.

Thus any movement seeking structural change must begin with an emphasis upon how interventionist-inspired militarization has misused "the flag" for special interests and directly eroded both American safety (domestically and internationally) and, particularly, average American living standards or economic security. About 80 percent of the United States population have failed to improve their physical well-being over the past decade, while it has worsened for three-fifths of the citizenry.[27] Although this trend has been most marked—as we saw in Chapter 8—for the lower class, it has in lesser measure affected and also increased the sense of economic insecurity of those *below* the upper middle professional-managerial class (i.e. the top 10 percent). Thus Schudson (1988:794) stresses that Gans' *Middle American Individualism* describes attitudes and values widely shared by "middle Americans."

> These are the majority of Americans who, in terms of class, sit between the poor and the upper middle class. They are, generally speaking, high school graduates but not necessarily college graduates, with family incomes between $15,000 and $45,000, working in a wide array of blue-collar and white-collar, industrial, bureaucratic and clerical positions. This broad swath of the American population is deeply concerned about economic security. Their version of individualistic values stems more from this than from anything else.

Distrustful of large institutions and oriented primarily to family and to a microsocial world of informal groups, they seek control over their lives

Primary *stress,* then, should be upon harm to Americans rather than injustice to foreigners. The latter should be added, but only as a secondary reason. Put differently, the initial psychological target should be to improve domestic mass living standards. This may appear a trifle base, but we must realize that both militarism and untempered predatory — now largely deregulated — capitalism have adversely affected the spiritual levels of the American population, with some exceptions. Counter-traditions of cooperativism and community remain, but have been eroded since World War II and particularly in the late twentieth century.

A potentially effective patriotic mass movement should stress specific measures and changes which will directly enhance mass well-being. Navarro (1985:49) pinpoints this crucial strategic imperative for those who would transcend the current anti-liberal political climate:

> It would be erroneous to conclude from this analysis that the solution demands proposals for the establishment of programs aimed primarily at these lower income groups. This approach would only strengthen the perception of "interest-group" politics and would be exploited by the corporate class. The solution is to develop programs that benefit all members of the working population including those groups. In other words, there is an enormous and urgent need to resurrect the class practices of the New Deal.

The author argues, with some merit, that the previously mentioned electoral abstentionism has been a reaction to the failure of both major parties to champion such working and lower middle class interests as higher purchasing power, employment security, and a reformed health delivery system.[28]

One New Deal legacy, the legitimacy of collective bargaining, should also be reaffirmed. For trade unions in general have remained as important supporters of the types of programs which are at the core of a new populist movement. Furthermore, while the number of employees on strike dropped by a third between 1982 and 1989 ("Vital," 1990:63), there has been a major upsurge in public support during the 1985–1989 period for strike actions — even in essential services.

Movement building should be carried out independently and within trade unions, cooperatives, civic associations and even the Democratic Party, which is a nebulous and essentially opportunistic electoral umbrella less totally dominated by the corporate sector than the Republicans. When rightist "conservatives" and "neo-liberals" respond that there is a fiscal shortage (i.e., a budgetary deficit) that prevents new government spending for a second "New Deal," *they* can be forced upon the defensive. In short, the money is there and should come from now highly militarized foreign aid and excessive military expropriation of the people's wealth which impoverishes increasing numbers while endangering everyone's life. It is shown (Bauer, 1985) not only that the big banks rather than recipient countries have been the primary foreign aid beneficiaries, but also that these same financial institutions have frequently flouted the law (another useful patriotic symbol) by habitually laundering drug money. Indeed, much of the deficit can be blamed upon a congressional giveaway to the rich via massive tax reductions in the early 1980s. Again the "special interest" symbol must be redirected toward the fat cats and militarists.

People can then be shown *how* interventionism and the military-industrial complex are contributing to the decline of their safety and welfare. Portraying the multinational corporate owning class as "anti-national" and oppressive will naturally flow from a simple analysis of how the United States came to be in its current situation. A mass constituency can be developed by underscoring job or wage losses in America due to blackmail threats or the actuality of runaway plants, with the brief addition that moving abroad is attractive to companies because they are unpatriotic (i.e., they are loyal only to their own enrichment). Further, they use the Marines and other interventionist units to keep wages and taxes low by strengthening repressive military establishments and anti-reformist parties in developing areas.

By stressing "bread and butter" or economic security issues at home while secondarily linking their attainment to ending interventionism and its global military infrastructure, a mass-based prosperity movement will enter the realm of possibility. Its support can be reinforced by invoking spiritual appeals to such values as generosity, justice for others, genuine respect for America and community at home. The peace or anti-militarization issue must be easily perceived as a route to greater personal economic and socio-cultural opportunities. Only in this way can interventionism and militarization issues be made appealing to many ordinary as opposed to a few affluent citizens.

An "American Citizens Progressive Alliance" or "New Patriotic Non-Partisan Movement" may begin as a "Blue-Green" or citizens' coalition encompassing a broad range of individuals in various parties, cooperatives, civic associations and trade unions. Its style should exude affirmation and optimism. So long as primary emphasis is upon economic enhancement measures of general applicability for all ordinary people rather than (Navarro, 1985) for special sectors, its potential to become a dominant force within the New Democratic party will be strengthened. By dramatizing populist and, less explicitly, socialist traditions that inspired many New Deal measures aimed at benefiting the common man, the pseudopopulism of the Republican new right will be discredited as will the moderate neo-liberalism of the Democratic party's dominant faction.

Advocating the need for a "Second New Deal" with a concomitant "Good Neighbor Policy" to fulfill the egalitarian promise of the first, an anti-imperialist movement can anchor itself solidly in what most Americans regard as a proud tradition. It can stress that this new movement, because of its independence from corporate capital, can transcend constraints that subverted full implementation of many New Deal programs. This time a world war will not be necessary to fully overcome economic stagnation and insecurity. The coalition should not shrink from full employment, progressive tax reform, and national health insurance as immediate goals, nor from extending public ownership not only to the major military contractors, but also to any transnational corporations that subvert the economy by disinvesting. Tax policy can also be employed to deter such job-destroying behavior just as rigorous anti-trust enforcement can impede the takeover of America's more efficient small firms by conglomerates. Unpatriotic blackmailing of the citizenry by exporting needed capital, whether to unnumbered Swiss bank accounts or elsewhere, should, like tax evasion, be grounds for both nationalization and enforced penal sanctions. A cooperative vision of restored community may emerge in the process to catalyze a genuinely democratic spiritual rebirth.

Besides appropriating the cultural symbols of America's patriotic heritage and focusing them in the first instance upon measures to enhance mass welfare, a corollary strategic imperative is to confront the Soviet issue rather than endeavor to ignore it. James Weinstein (1985:14) properly calls attention to this salient reality in the context of the peace movement's ill-fated decision to heighten expectations while "appearing supportive" of Reagan in his November 1985 meeting with Gorbachev—an act which must tacitly accept the president's "premise about the Soviet threat." Not only is this "disingenuous," but it ignores the fact that

> the effects of the Cold War, whether the arms race or neocolonial intervention in Central America, cannot effectively be opposed without confronting the Cold War's central myth—that there is a Soviet threat to the security of the American people. . . .
> Appearing supportive of the president in the coming weeks won't help revive the peace movement. Sooner or later it will have to confront the myth of a Soviet threat. The longer it waits, the weaker it will become.

The right will certainly react by substituting more deeply hidden conspiracies for its discredited demonic portrayals. And while this has become progressively more difficult due to Gorbachev's policy changes, more subtle rationales will surface. Hence Soviet reforms and changes are attributed to American "strength." Similarly, the reforms are painted as a likely source of greater long-term Soviet "strength" and "potential threat."

As Bodenheimer and Gould (1988) make evident, one of the salient structural obstacles to change is the penetration of America's far right into the state apparatus with a broad private and heavily financed supporting infrastructure. In terms of political rights, a non-militarization movement should stress that the Soviets have progressed since the Tsarist era and particularly during the post–Stalin era. It may be admitted that despite the impressive relaxation of constraints under Gorbachev, they have quite a distance to go before full socialist democracy is attained. Yet domestic Soviet policies are no more America's business than the way Americans treat persons of color, the poor or women is a Soviet responsibility. Further, the movement should emphasize that improving relations strengthens (Stephen F. Cohen, 1985; Solomon, 1985; Perkovich, 1988) reformist (i.e., anti–Stalinist) tendencies in the USSR as well as tolerance of autonomy in Eastern Europe. Recently, establishment experts supporting the Bush Administration have elaborated similar views (Barnet, 1990:4) with respect to China. And in any case there are persuasive reasons (Kriesberg, 1989; Hough, 1990) for concluding that Soviet foreign policy changes flow from the primacy accorded to domestic restructuring rather than Pentagon intimidation or strength.

Finally, an emergent movement must stress the historical absence of an inherent threat to American security in Soviet policy toward Europe (Nasser, 1989) or the developing areas. Even if his assessment is overly benign, there is more than a grain of truth in James Weinstein's (1985:14) observation that

> most Soviet gains in the Third World are a result of its being the only nation able and willing to give substantial aid to anticolonial revolutions, all of which have unstintingly been opposed by recent American administrations. And so far, in every case where a Third World country — from Egypt to Mozambique — has wanted out of the Soviet orbit, it has simply walked out. Isn't it time that someone acknowledge this in polite society, and that we start drawing appropriate conclusions?

In Chapter 5 we examined the very limited post-1950s decline in Soviet influence. Since the accession of Gorbachev, the Soviets themselves have accorded an even lower priority to Third World areas while redirecting attention to promoting a reintegration with Western Europe along with domestic reform. More significantly, as the traditional Soviet sphere of influence in Eastern Europe has greatly weakened, Moscow has focused most of its resources upon domestic ethnic cleavages which seriously threaten the Soviet Union's federal system. Hence the task here should be much less formidable.

I do not minimize the obstacles. Some of these have been mentioned earlier in our discussion of repressive garrison state tendencies. Others flow from disunity and traditional sectarianism on the left. Struggles will even have to be directed against bureaucratic dominance of major American trade unions whose officials enjoy careerist perks and patronage as a consequence of their willing subservience to warfare state interventionism. Thus efforts by Victor Reuther (Moberg, 1985), a founder and former high official of the United Auto Workers, to raise some of the "bread and butter" costs of imperialism to members of his own relatively progressive UAW elicited repressive reactions by union officials.

And finally, there is a self-created major impediment in the previously mentioned propensity of many anti-militarists to put the (foreign) cart before the (domestic) horse, which inhibits building the mass support necessary to change policy. The converse approach has been employed with sub-optimal symbolism by Jobs with Peace and hinterland affiliates of the Institute for Defense and Disarmament Studies as the Piedmont Peace Project. Feffer (1988:28) notes that

> In four short years . . . [the] Piedmont Peace Project pushed North Carolina Congressman Bill Hefner's voting record on peace issues from zero to 80 percent, according to the Council for a Livable World. A conservative southern Democrat, Hefner was responding to pressure from constituents who have shown a growing interest in arms control and budget priorities. These constituents, in turn, have become vocal thanks largely to Stout's efforts to make alternatives to the national security state relevant to the grassroots. . . .
>
> Stout's custom-made curriculum focuses not just on military matters, but on economic tie-ins that directly affect rural workers. By emphasizing the growing military budget, the burgeoning trade deficit, and the deplorable working conditions in other countries, Stout can move an audience from protectionism and Japan-bashing to fair trade and nuclear weapons reductions. "In 10 minutes you can get them from cussing the damn foreigners to cussing the American government!" she says.

Suggestive of at least some real interest in such an approach is Alger's (1989:9) report that "other activists have shifted from international to local issues but see their work as fulfilling global objectives. They've moved to the grassroots to build broader coalitions, sensing that people don't listen until they can see the link to themselves."

Of even greater impact may be the patriotic credentials and enhanced legitimacy which former "national security" officials bring to the movement. One of the most prominent is Philip Agee, a former CIA case officer (Muwakkil, 1988:2) who authored *Inside the Company* in 1975 and is a prominent member of the recently organized ex–CIA Association for Responsible Dissent (ARDIS), since renamed the Association of National Security Alumni.

> Although he pioneered the movement to reform the CIA and enthusiastically joins other ARDIS members in urging a halt to all covert operations, Agee says that the problem is deeper than the reform of just one agency of government.
>
> "Since Reagan and Bush were elected in 1980, tens of thousands of Central Americans, Mozambicans and Angolans have been killed in the name of our national security," he said during a recent public appearance. And this is not new, but is a practice which has gone on without pause for the last 40 years. Foreign policy is always a reflection of domestic contradictions.
>
> "Revolutions in Nicaragua and Grenada pose no threats to our security as a nation. But they are threats to the corporate interests who own this country because they are intended to help empower the poor, and that example is extremely dangerous for corporate security," he said. "Therefore, they must be

crushed." Agee said real change can occur in our foreign policy only if corporate interests are reigned in and society is restructured.

Only after white lower middle and working class Americans believe that a non-militarization movement is first and foremost concerned with their well being, and see the relationships, will they actively oppose interventionist measures against the Philippines or Nicaragua.[29] With enhanced dignity and economic security, they will feel less threatened by measures to overcome the effects of racism and sexism.

Over time and with priority upon sustained grass-roots organizing of the mass constituency that has become alienated by the corruption and manipulative techniques of politicians, a progressive new American movement for a Second New Deal can be built. As with other patriotic insurgencies, it can count upon being aided by growing defections from established parties and elite sectors. McGehee, Agee, Stockwell, Clark, Ellsberg and a host of others have already assumed prominent roles in the alternative security movement as have retired senior officers like Admirals LaRocque, Carroll and Marine Col. James Donovan, at the Center for Defense Information. Wiesner (1985:105) underlines this trend, noting that

> most important of all, we are witnessing the emergence, as dissenters, of in-
> creasing numbers of former insiders and experts whose professional loyalty to
> the Establishment has until recently, made them reluctant to speak out against
> policies that worried them. More and more civilian and military officials of the
> past are expressing disagreement with current national defense policies.

Some, of course, limit their "disagreements" to specific means rather than the ends of policy. Even so, they, along with more structural critics, will provide inspiration as the movement outside — the main catalyst — grows.

Yet in addition to the historical opportunity provided by a conjuncture of declining contemporary mass material and spiritual welfare with diminished physical safety (domestically and internationally due to proliferation of both anti-Americanism and nuclear weapons to developing areas) in a political en-vironment characterized by unparalleled levels of mass distrust of established institutional leadership, considerably more will be required for a real move-ment take-off. Success usually requires dynamic leaders in addition to effective organization. Thus, significant challenge at the national level will have to be led by one or more individuals exuding authenticity as well as probity and whose popularity is at least tinged with charisma.[30] And, it may be added, who avoid being assassinated by neo-fascist paramilitary squads.

Furthermore, the psychological inertia of large numbers will have to be traumatized by a financial or military crisis of major proportions. Current trends imply that such an eventuality is likely whether prompted by collective Third World default upon indebtedness; Israeli, South African or other detonation of nuclear weapons; a depression or Watergate-type scandal; or even a currently unlikely military confrontation between the United States and USSR.[31] A reversion to hard-line leadership within the Soviet Union combined with intervention to end a local ethnic or territorial conflict in the Baltic or East European traditional sphere of influence could sharply resurrect a high tension level, particularly following Washington's declaration that the survival of anti-Communist free market regimes in that region was a "vital national security" interest! It is of course during major crises that charismatic leaders emerge. If the alternative security proponents anticipate that future opportunity — perhaps their last — by building a nationwide movement infrastructure today, they may position themselves to seize the moment when it arrives. Then they shall enjoy the inner tranquillity of knowing that their interim efforts have contributed to more humane life opportunities for American citizens and those deserving equal respect elsewhere.

References

Chapter 1. "National Security": Symbolism and Perversion

1. My use of the term "arms transfers" generally follows Pearson (1981:48), who includes "the international transfer of conventional military equipment via grant, credit, or cash sales. Conventional military equipment is considered to be non-nuclear weapons of war, spare parts, ammunition, support equipment, or other primarily military commodities." Occasionally the term will be used more inclusively to refer to infrastructural facilities (e.g. airport construction), military training, coproduction licensing, etc. Rand Corporation specialist Caesar Sereseres (U.S., House, CFA, 1981:37) stresses that "you cannot isolate the arms transfer phenomenon from the broader context of U.S. security assistance objectives and programs in the region. In other words, arms transfers must be linked to U.S. training programs, the status of the Southern Command Headquarters in Panama, and to the military mission systems."

2. Although there were precursors in the late 1950s beginning with Eisenhower's tentative responses to Khrushchev's call for "peaceful coexistence," the era of detente was anticipated by a series of speeches and agreements during eight months preceding Kennedy's assassination. Most observers date it from the late 1960s, which implies a transition period from the first steps to a full-blown declaratory stage. The same may be said of detente's demise. Although the latter is commonly put in the late 1970s, Wallensteen (1985:4) recalls that "In the spring of 1976, Governor Reagan actually forced President Ford to abandon the term 'detente.'" Fitch (1985:34–35) would seem to concur. His content analysis of Presidential State of the Union speeches revealed a very sharp rise of belligerent and "security" rhetoric in 1976 — far above anything since 1952 — in such addresses. He concludes, "The year we have taken to be the beginning of the new cold war era, 1977, also marks the first year since 1964 that proponents of higher military budgets outnumbered advocates of reductions in military spending. . . . It was also the first year since 1968 that defense expenditures actually increased in real dollars."

3. In his view, "militarism is a preference or bias favoring any employment of armed forces beyond what is actually necessary for territorial defense. Similarly, values, practices, rituals and weapons acquisition beyond what is required for the scientific (i.e., most efficient) use of such resources for defense are "militaristic."

4. Among the most prominent are retired admirals Hyman Rickover, Eugene Carroll, and Henry Eccles, General William Fairbourn, Captain James Bush and Colonel James Donovan. All except Rickover are associated with the Center for Defense Information in Washington. Even former Secretary of Defense Robert S. MacNamara echoed (*Kansas City Times,* August 8, 1980) this national security perspective: "To the extent that military expenditures severely reduce the resources available for other essential sectors and social services — and fuel the futile and reactive arms race — excessive military spending can erode rather than enhance it." Significantly, both MacNamara and

(especially) Rickover were targeted by the military-industrial complex with intense defamatory propaganda after they assumed a critical stance.

5. Undue American emphasis upon the importance of overly sophisticated "gold plated" weaponry ignores not only one of the major lessons of Vietnam — that poorly armed yet highly motivated citizen soldiers are a match for superior firepower — but the more general rule that, as Luttwak (1980:19) put it: "technology or no technology, in the reality of warfare, as opposed to paper calculations, the intangibles of leadership, command experience, tactical ingenuity, and skill of troops are much more important than material factors — your firepower, mobility, and so on. From everything we know about warfare, ancient and modern, those intangibles easily dominate. It's not 10 percent around the margin, it's more like 100 or 300 percent."

Chapter 2. Weapons Exports and the Third World Militarization

1. For an incisive analysis reflecting this orientation, see Johansen (1983). It is doubtful that Betts' (1980:82) portrayal of such critics as suffering from "moral absolutism" is any more warranted than the initial clause in his assertion that "crusaders against arms sales often do not take seriously the recipients' military requirements, and see proliferation of weaponry as a counterproductive indulgence that may precipitate the United States into self-destructive involvements in conflict."

2. Klare goes on: "When translated into actual hardware, moreover, we find that the net transfer of war-making capabilities has been truly astounding: according to the CRS, between 1973 and 1980 the industrialized nations provided Third World countries with 19,910 tanks and self-propelled guns; 19,120 armored cars and personnel carriers; 4,830 supersonic combat planes and 4,400 other aircraft of all types; and 30,100 surface-to-air missiles (SAMs)."

3. In this work, I rely as much as possible upon SIPRI rather than ACDA data. Pearson (1981:48) refers to "discrepancies in reported sales data released by ACDA and SIPRI. . . ." The SIPRI data, based on U.S. Commerce Department figures, seem far more indicative of total transfers than ACDA data presumably based mainly on FMS statistics. For a more extensive discussion of data reliability, concealment and ACDA's conservative bias, see Leitenberg (1976:111–116), Brzoska (1981:261–276), and Wolpin (1983:11).

4. LaRocque and Goose continue: "Currently, these same countries are spending over $130 billion per year for weapons and to maintain about sixteen million men under arms. Military expenditures account for roughly 5.5 percent of their gross national product and nearly a fourth of their central government expenditures. At the same time, many continue to have trouble meeting the basic needs of their citizens." The magnitude of resource diversion during the 1981–1984 period is underscored by Third World arms import agreements (USACDA, 1985:42 revised) totaling $139.7 billion in current dollars. Of this, $70.6 was to be imported from NATO countries while the total from all non-communist vendors was $85.2. Warsaw Pact countries accounted for $44.7 and all communist exporters totaled $54.5. The non-communist proportion was 56 percent higher than that of the communists, representing 61 percent of the total. Given their origin, the data, if anything, understate non-communist totals and exaggerate communist ones.

5. "Twenty years ago the Third World accounted for only 10 per cent of world military spending; since then its share has doubled. Its armed forces make up two-thirds of the world total" (Power, 1983:4).

6. "An examination of Indian, Israeli and Brazilian arms production programmes demonstrates that complete self-sufficiency has so far been reached only for some less-

sophisticated weapon systems. Other countries, less advanced than Brazil or India both in general industrialization and in arms production, are even more dependent on foreign collaboration. The South Korean arms industry is almost totally oriented toward US licenses and high-technology imports, even though the general industrial level is fairly advanced. Taiwan's efforts could be described in similar terms and the dependence of Egypt's plans to revive its arms production can best be demonstrated by pointing to the long list of West European and US collaborative projects which were discussed, then partly abandoned and are now once again in the planning stage, mainly in conjunction with US companies" (Wulf, 1979:340).

7. Cf. note 5, Chapter 1.

Chapter 3. American Arms Exports in Historical Perspective

1. In addition, very large sales above a fixed ceiling must be submitted to Congress, which, however, has never exercised a veto on human rights grounds.

2. See, for example, Fleming (1961), Kolko (1969), Wolpin (1973), Kaplan and Blechman (1978), Chomsky and Herman (1979), Eveland (1980), Williams (1980), McGehee (1983).

3. The following also examine various aspects of this anti-nationalist historical legacy: Moon (1926), Williams (1962), La Feber (1963), Gardner (1964), Smith (1960), Magdoff (1969), Fagen (1979), Drinnon (1980), Scheslinger and Kinzer (1982), Herman (1982).

4. Horowitz (1969) and less explicitly Herman (1982) provide theoretical explanations of this policy pattern as do Kolko (1969), Barnet and Muller (1974), Sklar (1980) and Parenti (1988).

5. "As in the case of absolute aid levels, these correlations are uniformly positive . . . when compared with correlations between human rights and absolute aid levels . . . about half of the correlations . . . are of equal strength and the remainder are slightly lower" (Schoultz, 1981).

6. Intensified economic and "covert" warfare during the period 1983–1987 made the "economy scream" (to use Kissinger's infamous goal for Allende's Chile prior to the United States–engineered coup) and forced sharp curtailment of most social welfare and reform programs. The unceasing external pressure and subversive operations (Naureckas, "Secret," 1988) also magnified the effects of Sandinista economic policy errors and administrative inexperience, as did the fateful 1988 hurricane whose unprecedented devastation was not alleviated by a single dollar of U.S. disaster relief.

7. The 105 countries were those with a 1970 population above 500,000 and a per capita GNP below $3000. A few borderline cases (e.g., Gabon) were added. Insofar as the composite classification is concerned, my own independent rankings were compared with Sivard's (1982:17). Because all are based upon judgment and vulnerable to error, convergence or "intersubjective agreement" is always preferable. Furthermore, her criteria for the "highly repressive" emphasize "torture and brutality," as I do for the "violent" category. Where we differed in our classifications, I used Gastil's (1981:25) rankings to reconcile the disagreement. This even though his classifications eschew special emphasis upon regime brutality or violence — what Herman (1982) refers to as "state terror." Further, Gastil's criteria include such liberties as entrepreneurial freedom, a euphemism for capitalist endeavors. Thus I have constructed a "composite index" which statistically correlates strongly with my own rankings (.92), Sivard's (.73), and more moderately with Gastil's (.45). All of these Pearson coefficients are significant at the .001 level. Countries in both the "violent" as

well as the "institutional" categories evidence high repressiveness toward at least one significant political sector opposing the government. In some cases, of course, pre-existing sustained repression has eliminated such opposition groups. The key difference — one that I believe is highly important — between the two categories concerns the disposition toward patterned violence — torture, executions, disappearances, and unusually harsh prison conditions. The third or "minimal" classification pertains to the absence, exceptional or mild resort to suppressive practices. Further, when regimes do not act vigorously against non-official groups — especially those in basic sympathy with the government — the violent activities of such organizations are attributed to the regime. This is particularly common in Latin America and a few other countries such as Thailand.

8. "Structural" violence is (Kohler, 1978:8) "a term used in contemporary peace research and is to be distinguished from armed violence. While armed violence is violence exerted by persons against persons with the use of arms, structural violence is violence exerted by situations, institutions, social, political, and economic structures. Thus, when a person dies because he/she has no access to food, the effect is violent as far as that person is concerned, yet there is no individual actor who could be identified as the source of this violence. It is the system of food production and distribution that is to blame. The violence is thus exerted by an anonymous 'structure.' The measurement of the number of persons killed through structural violence uses statistics of life expectancy. By comparing the life expectancy of affluent regions with that of poor regions, one can estimate how many persons died in a poor region on account of poverty and poverty-related conditions (e.g., lack of doctors, clean water, food, etc.), which can be interpreted as 'structural violence.'"

9. "Open Door" regimes are those whose dominant civilian or military elites enforce policies intended to enhance the profitability of the private corporate sector. Because the latter is dominated by transnational corporations in most underdeveloped areas, so long as indigenous officials acquiesce in such relations their domestic and even foreign policy choices tend to depend upon favorable reactions by such corporations and associated international financial institutions. "Dependency," then, has evolved historically with the growth and extension of corporate capitalism into a world system.

10. One observer (Pearson, 1981:29) recalls that "in the fifteen years from 1963–78 U.S. arms transfers shot from approximately $1.5-billion to over $7-billion; economic interests found a place — albeit probably still secondarily — in U.S. transfer decisions. Sophisticated weapons were far more widely distributed; competition from other arms producers reduced the U.S. share of world arms trade from 50 percent (1968) to 39 percent. U.S. sales to Europe, Japan, Canada, and Australia went from 80 percent of the total (1964) to 14 percent, with the remainder going to the Third World. . . .

"Still, relatively little advanced and sophisticated weaponry had been transferred to the Third World until the Nixon Administration. With the Nixon Doctrine and Henry Kissinger's determination to establish regional police powers, such as Iran, to help the U.S. 'stabilize' regions in the wake of Vietnam, many sophisticated weapons (F-14, F-15, F-4, F-5 aircraft, tanks, air-to-surface missiles, etc.) were sold or transferred on credit to Iran, Saudi Arabia, Kuwait, Korea, Israel, and a number of Third World states. Latin America was included, although the emphasis had previously been on transferring relatively obsolete weapons there in order to dampen arms races and warfare. . . .

". . . The U.S. tried to maintain its influence with increasingly ambitious Latin American military leaders in order to oppose radical revolution."

Chapter 4. Carter's Interregnum: The Eclipse of Liberal Human Rights and Arms Restraint Policies

1. "The premises were that U.S. security assistance programs should not help to sustain such governments; that the denial of arms might provide some external leverage for inhibiting repressive practices in some countries; and, that U.S. political ideals and interests would be better served by minimizing contact and association with security forces blamed for violations of human rights" (U.S., House, CFA, 1981:42).

2. As presented to Congress (Pearson, 1981), the rationale highlighted a Realpolitik national security interest: "Unrestrained arms transfers can generate arms races, increase the likelihood of local conflicts, heighten the danger of great-power confrontation, and divert resources from badly needed economic and social development. In unstable circumstances the political influence sought through arms transfers may be quickly lost and the arms may be used in ways not initially contemplated or in the U.S. interest. Unrestrained arms transfers also pose the continuing risk of the compromise of sensitive military technology. . . . [A] controlled arms transfer policy is necessary to reduce the threat which the uncontrolled proliferation of conventional arms can pose to regional stability and our own security."

3. Thus one arms restraint analyst contends that an agreement between Washington and Moscow to restrict arms exports to the Third World would have been one-sided in its benefits. Betts (1980:87) maintains that the United States rather than the Soviets would be the major beneficiary of such curtailment: "If arms trade outside NATO and the Warsaw Pact was terminated completely, the net benefit would accrue to the United States. The Soviets' ascendancy in marketing would no longer be relevant diplomatically, they would suffer financially from loss of hard currency and greater relative decline in overall trade balance, and the shrinking but still larger disparity in force projection capabilities would give the United States an edge in the third world militarily." Yet even in the absence of such an agreement, Betts (1980:57) is candid enough to acknowledge that the "revival of containment does not justify all sales, because some customers are not proxies of either superpower, and want arms for purposes unrelated to U.S.-Soviet competition. . . . Proponents of arms sales often make dubious arguments about how these sales benefit more than just our pocketbooks. . . ."

4. With respect to Korea, Carter repudiated his early pledge that an American division was to be brought home. Even worse, Hitchens (1985:38) records that "when General Chun seized power in 1980, a South Korean frontline battalion was diverted from the northern border to help secure the dictatorship and put down civilian dissent. That atrocious decision, which weakened the very border defense of which conservatives make such a fetish, was taken with the permission of Gen. John A. Wickham Jr., the U.S. Commander in South Korea."

5. He adds that "only the collapse of the Shah salvaged the attempt to reduce the dollar volume of sales, but within a year, the Afghanistan invasion silenced the conventional arms control lobby for awhile."

6. Pearson (1981:36–37) records that "ACDA was allowed greater input on decisions when it became apparent that their congressional mandated concerns in arms control impact statements—i.e., with regional arms races, escalation of conflict, or arms control agreements—could mesh rather well with DOD concerns about release of sensitive technology and preservation of U.S. control in light of shaky regimes abroad. Hence, compared to the State Department where regional bureaus generally favored sales, DOD had few objections to including ACDA in the inter-agency bargaining and coalition building process. ACDA's concern for regional balances is seen by other agencies as its main contribution to the decision process."

7. "...Such reconsiderations if continued over time could increase the skepticism about sales as foreign policy levers, and begin to erode the sales consensus. Pressure will build for exceptions to formal regulations, but regulations represent both important bureaucratic checkpoints and symbolic statements to administrators and foreign powers."

8. "If the United States or other suppliers were selling too many arms, then customers must have been buying too many. If so, then which customers, and according to what yardstick? The obvious example is Iran, to which many arms controllers did point well before the collapse of the Shah. It is notable, however, that even Carter's ambitious policy of restraint exempted Iran to a great extent, denying a few of the Shah's requests, but maintaining a generous allotment under the aggregate ceiling. Moreover, in one case the Administration maneuvered shabbily to limit a U.S. sale but allowed the Shah to get the hardware he wanted, by agreeing to build the weaponry for a set of frigates but not the hulls (which were to be built in Europe)."

9. "Whether these unnatural efforts by the United States to improve human rights conditions in the hemisphere could have been more effective with the cooperation of European arms suppliers is open to conjecture. The fact is that each regime which was subjected to an arms cut-off by the United States found other sources for its military needs. It is difficult to determine the kind and level of cooperation necessary to make the U.S. position of human rights prevail in the Western Hemisphere. What kinds of weapon acquisitions need to be targeted for denial: The least detectable, least expensive weapons which are operationally used in the violation of human rights? Or, the larger, more expensive, easily detected weapons which fulfill symbolic military functions? A much larger portion of the arms acquisitions is for such weapon systems as aircraft, seacraft, vehicles, and heavy weapons — hardware that has little to do with human rights violation."

10. "The problem was recognized in part when the original policy announcement included so many exemptions and loopholes. But even then the ceiling proved difficult to stay under. Juggling the accounting to do so created the impression of insincerity. Construction costs — which doubled from FY 1977 to 1978 — were excluded although they subsumed runways and naval bases. Ceiling expenditures were also reduced by eliminating packing and shipping charges."

11. "...It soon became clear that the Carter Administration was willing to approve a wide variety of arms sales, that certain countries and commercial sales were excluded from ceilings, and that new accounting methods were being employed in calculating yearly sales totals. While F-16 and F-14 aircraft sales were vetoed, AWACs radar planes and other equipment were quickly approved for the Shah of Iran. As the Administration moved to increase its influence in regional conflicts ranging from the Persian Gulf and Afghanistan to Korea, Southeast Asia, the Horn of Africa, Sahara and Arabian Peninsula, it utilized arms transfers as an integral, not exceptional, foreign policy tool."

12. Brevetti's (1983:91–92) synoptic account, focusing upon Central America, is indicative of this policy trend: "U.S. military aid to El Salvador amounted to $0.1 million between 1953 and 1961, $6.5 million between 1962 and 1969, and $10.2 million between 1970 and 1979. Between 1976 and 1978, under the Carter Administration, legislation was enacted which successfully limited U.S. military support for specific regimes (e.g., Guatemala and El Salvador). Despite these limitations on U.S. supplies, El Salvador successfully stocked its arsenal with purchases from Israel. However, in the context of heightened struggle in El Salvador and the growing consolidation of the Nicaraguan revolution, in 1979 the Carter Administration [abandoned a policy of] constraints in favor of one which directly armed regimes like the one in El Salvador. In

1980, $5.9 million in aid was allocated, and before Carter left office he designated another $5.5 million to be reprogrammed under the 1981 budget."

13. "In Africa particularly, since Carter used arms transfers to counter Soviet intrusions and influence, the inconsistency between the rhetoric of restraint and actual practice became apparent within a few months of his Administration."

14. "These trends have been reinforced by trends in the external world, the international system, that have reduced the U.S. government's ability to control external events: (1) an increased number of nations with security problems that were only marginally related to the East/West confrontation; (2) the emergence of nonindustrialized economic superpowers without the industrial capability to produce sophisticated weapons systems but with large amounts of capital and resources with which to bargain with arms producers; (3) arms supply competitors in Western Europe vulnerable to the nonindustrial economic superpowers and compelled by domestic economic considerations to sell arms; and (4) a perceived reduction in the U.S. government's ability to respond to friends' and allies' assessments of threats to them except through arms transfers."

15. "While European interests in arms sales to Latin America appear to be primarily economic in nature, this is not the case with other important potential suppliers. In particular, the Soviet Union and Israel, and possibly Brazil in the not too distant future, seem to have political interests at stake in their arms export policies. These political interests militate against their potential agreement to arms control restraints." As we shall see, such "establishment" apprehensions—particularly as applied to the Soviet Union—proved to be unfounded.

16. Pierre (1981/1982:283) records, almost with astonishment, that "to the surprise of many, the discussions proceeded quite smoothly. By the end of round three it was agreed that restraints might be both regionally oriented and global, and that restrictions might be 'military-technical' on certain types of weapons or 'political-legal' in nature. These, it was thought, could lead to 'harmonized guidelines' on restraints."

Chapter 5. The Salience of Arms Transfers and Threat Inflation in Reagan's "Containment" Policy

1. As Sanders (1983:1) puts it: "Militarists accused managerialists of suffering from 'Vietnam syndrome,' an affliction responsible for a continuing "failure of nerve" in U.S. leadership. Accordingly, this faction called for the 'rearming of America,' projecting a vast military buildup of both nuclear and conventional forces in hope of regaining the military superiority and credible interventionist threat enjoyed in the halcyon days of the cold war before defeat in Vietnam."

2. It is instructive to note that a Pentagon study (Becker, 1984) concluded that three major efforts by both the Carter and Reagan administrations to economically coerce the USSR and Poland had been total failures. These involved the 1980 grain embargo, a 1982 effort to force Warsaw into default on its external debt, and a clumsy attempt the same year to force an American subsidiary to break its contract to sell gas pipeline compressors. West European governments either refused to join or actively opposed these acts of economic warfare.

3. "During the first two decades of the nuclear arms race, when the United States had an overwhelming first-strike capability by default, frightening the Russians was not a problem. There was nothing they could do about it. Now that they can destroy us in a half-hour, a U.S. first-strike capability might place Soviet weapons in a use-them-or-lose-them situation" (Moreland, 1985:197).

4. Like Bowman (who ran the AF Star Wars research program in the Pentagon under the Ford and Carter administrations) and many other critics, John Pike (1985), associate director for space policy of the Federation of American Scientists, shares Morrison's apprehensions. Pike, after noting that "Star Wars" is "generally regarded as requiring a level of perfection that is not likely to be achieved," proceeds to pinpoint the real danger to American security inherent in the new "defense" posture: "The Star Wars defense will be vulnerable to direct attack, including attack by other space weapons. The defensive umbrella will be more effective in reducing the effects of a retaliatory drizzle than a torrential first strike. This increases incentives to strike first in a time of crisis. The short reaction times of these systems increase the risk of accidental war.

"*Arms race or arms control?* Defenses can be overwhelmed by a massive increase in the number of attacking weapons. These offensive arms will be cheaper than the weapons needed to defend against them. Star Wars will fuel the offensive arms race and make negotiated limitations on these weapons impossible."

5. A revealing analysis of this presidential targeting directive, which more than two and a half decades ago prescribed what could be a first strike "counterforce" strategy, is provided by Leitenberg (1981). Cf. Aldridge (1983).

6. See, for example, U.S. House, CFA, 1981:10, 13–14; U.S., Sen., CFR, *Conventional Arms Sales,* 1981:15–16, 32–33; U.S., Sen., CFR, *Arms Sales Package,* Pt. 1, 1981:17, 57, 61, 83, 186, 190; Pt. 2, 1981:2, 30, 32–37.

7. Why this occurred is pinpointed by Jeremy Stone (1985:48) in his review of Strobe Talbott's *Deadly Gambits* (New York: Knopf, 1984) — an interview-based account of administration decision-making prior to collapse of the "talks": "The dominance of political over military realities is everywhere. Burt says of the Pershing II while it is not ready for deployment: 'We don't care if the goddam things work or not. . . . After all, that doesn't matter unless there's a war. What we care about is getting them in.' Consider, also, Talbott's overall summary: 'In the Reagan Administration, only when arms control was a political exercise, either within the U.S. or within the alliance, did it capture the President's attention.'

"Indeed, the White House and the defense secretary seemed very slow to learn the most elementary things about arms control. At a National Security Council meeting, Talbott says, the defense secretary and the National Security adviser both asserted that SALT is obstructing U.S. weapons programs. But when asked by the chairman of the Joint Chiefs which ones, they could not specify. Chairman General David Jones said to a colleague: 'These guys have got a lot to learn.' And they still do."

8. "Buried in an otherwise unremarkable publication titled *NATO and the Warsaw Pact* is an interesting appraisal of Soviet military spending. According to the report, from 1970 to 1976, the years of detente, spending increased annually by about 5 percent in real terms. Since 1976: 'Overall growth of Soviet military spending is estimated to have declined to less than half the annual average rate of the early 1970's. This slowdown mainly reflects a less rapid rate of growth in procurement expenditure although a decline in rate of growth can also be observed in other categories of expenditure.'"

Equally revealing is the Pentagon's release in March 1985 (Coffin, 1985:4) of a report by the Undersecretary of Defense "comparing the U.S. and the Soviet Union in the 20 most significant military technologies. Was the U.S. behind or ahead or about the same? It is astonishing that almost no one talked about the content of that report. It was a bombshell. In the 20 major military technology categories, the U.S. leads in 15. And in how many categories did the Soviets lead? Exactly none." Thus the disparity has widened slightly over that displayed as of 1983 in Table 9.

9. "Reducing or abolishing U.S. and Soviet 'power projection' forces designed

for use outside Europe would complement and strengthen defense-oriented changes in the forces deployed in Europe. Technically, dismantling certain forces and equipment now deployed in Europe—not just withdrawing and rebasing them elsewhere—can be implemented and verified more easily, and will provide far stronger obstacles to breakout, if post-reduction ceilings are defined globally, not regionally. In addition, the longer-term political goals of nonoffensive defense—developing a stable peace, demilitarizing foreign policy, and ending reliance on nuclear weapons as a means of preserving the peace—cannot be fully realized unless U.S. and Soviet conventional policies are more thoroughly restricted to what each side needs to defend against aggression by the other. This more profound change requires a halt to U.S. and Soviet military intervention in the Third World, radical reductions in interventionary forces, and a change in the relationship between the Soviet Union and Eastern Europe."

10. The war games, according to former Secretary of Defense James Schlesinger, assumed the United States will go nuclear early. They further reflected the "Reagan Administration's belief that it is possible to prevail in a nuclear exchange in which up to 160 million Americans would die immediately."

11. Ohlson (1982:204–205) records that between the periods 1967–71 and 1977–81, the French and Italian shares of major weapon exports rose from 7 percent and 1 percent to 12 percent and 5 percent respectively. Both "Italy and FR Germany are two ... examples of growing arms exporters.... As a group, the Third World arms exporting nations continue to grow, the leading arms exporters being Brazil, which is responsible for 46% of the total Third World arms exports, followed by Israel with 21%." Yet by the mid-1980s, France and the United Kingdom had further increased their shares and emerged as major suppliers while according to ACDA (1988:134) both the Federal Republic of Germany and Italy had a diminished role.

12. France's Mitterand finally suspended military exports to South Africa in 1985 due to intense international criticism. But unlike France, Israel is no mere ally of the United States. Because American grants, loans and trade preferences are the *sine qua non* for avoiding total collapse of a highly militarized economy, Israeli dependency is sufficient to designate that country as a "satellite" of the U.S. Thus the linkages identified by Alexander Cockburn (1985:103) may be regarded as acceptable to American policy-makers. He refers to "Israel's arms exports, which came to about $1 billion worldwide and of which South Africa accounted for about one-third. In a paper prepared for the Jaffe Institute for Strategic Studies at Tel Aviv University, Aharon Klieman estimates that Israel's annual arms sales to South Africa amount to $350 million.... Those figures on Israeli-South African trade exclude a good deal, such as remittances sent home by the Israelis who are technical advisers to South Africa on its nuclear programs and on military, intelligence and security matters...."

13. Dorman's study of Soviet treatment by mainstream U.S. media in 1982 found that despite an absence of name-calling reminiscent of the 1950s, "with few exceptions, [there] was a portrayal of the Soviet Union as a ruthless and intractable adversary.... Similarly, U.S. journalists widely agreed that the Soviet Union killed both detente and SALT II by the invasion of Afghanistan. They did not consider that U.S. actions—such as moving to establish new bases on Diego Garcia, or selling military equipment for the first time to China, or beginning a trillion dollar defense buildup—might have been interpreted by Moscow as moves signaling Washington's desire to kill detente, thereby leading the Soviets to conclude that they had nothing to lose by their behavior. Nor did the media seriously assay the possibility that SALT II was in deep trouble in the U.S. Senate from the political right long before the invasion and would not have passed under any circumstances.... Today a concerted effort is underway to label the media as soft on communism and to force them into even more blatant anti–Soviet stance than

they usually adopt. Anything less than unreserved red-baiting by mainstream journalism is enough to trigger criticism from hardcore conservative critics."

14. Even though the agreement stipulated that Pakistan would end its indirect aggression preventing the movement of weapons and armed combatants into Afghanistan the United States continued to "covertly" maintain the operation under the aegis of Inter-Services Intelligence, an agency of Pakistan's Army. See Lifschultz (1988:492).

15. Forman (1985:11) recalls: "Despite the serious potential of the Soviet action [the unilateral test ban of July], the U.S. dismissed it within 10 minutes, according to Secretary of Defense Caspar Weinberger. Weinberger appeared on national television on July 29 to denounce the Soviet initiative as a propaganda hoax. His charge was echoed by National Security Advisor Robert McFarlane that evening on ABC News *Nightline*. McFarlane cited Intelligence data showing a dramatic increase in Soviet testing prior to the moratorium.

"During the following days all the news media joined in labeling the Soviet move as blatant propaganda, with the *New York Times* sinking to new lows in its editorial denouncing Soviet premier Mikhail Gorbachev's proposal.... For the next month, with the noble exception of columns by Tom Wicker and Mary McGrory, not a voice of dissent was heard in the media. The Soviet initiative was turned into a non-event and assigned to the dustbin of political propaganda.

"Now, after a mysterious pause of two months, we are dutifully informed, in a *New York Times* article on October 3 by Leslie Gelb, that the administration's case was false. The Gelb article makes the following points:

"• Despite Administration statements that Moscow stepped up its nuclear tests before proposing the moratorium, intelligence experts estimated that Russian testing up to August was 'average.'

"• McFarlane's charge that the Soviets suddenly speeded up their testing was not true.

"• Problems with verification are not the reason for U.S. refusal to stop nuclear testing. Richard L. Wagner Jr., the Defense Department's secretary in charge of nuclear weapons programs, is quoted: 'Even if effectively verified, a comprehensive test ban would not be in the interests of the U.S.'

"• The U.S. wants to keep testing so it can develop the Trident II warhead and important components of the Star Wars program."

16. If Carter can be faulted for failing to use arms transfers as an "exceptional" rather than ordinary foreign policy instrument, the balanced civilianist national security approach of this administration nevertheless contrasts markedly with the offensive zeal (Klare, 1982a; Bello and Hayes, 1983) and primacy accorded military means (militaristic bias) of Reagan's. LaRocque and Goose (1982:20) recall that: "In his first year in office, President Reagan: 'convinced Congress to increase U.S. military aid to Third World governments at the very time cuts were being made in U.S. domestic social programs:

'convinced Congress to repeal prohibitions on military aid, based on human rights records, to Pakistan, Argentina, and Chile;

'approved a $1.1 billion deal with Pakistan for forty F-16 fighter aircraft (another $1.6 billion in military loans is planned for the next five years);

'approved a $615 million sale to Venezuela of twenty-four F-16s (the first sale by the U.S. of highly advanced jet aircraft to any Latin American country);

'approved for the first time the sale of lethal military equipment to the People's Republic of China;

'passed the largest arms sale ever through a reluctant Congress, an $8.5 billion deal with Saudi Arabia, including AWACs aircraft and Sidewinder missiles.'"

Other measures that connote a qualitative difference are summarized by Pierre

(1981/1982:277–278), including the rescinding of Carter's "leprosy letter"; requests to Congress for increased "security assistance" and a "Special Defense Acquisition Fund," both to be used to finance certain arms sales; and a request to raise the dollar levels requiring reporting of proposed military sales to Congress.

He proceeds (281–282) to focus upon two salient changes: "downplaying" human rights as well as nuclear non-proliferation concerns. Others who stress a hiatus symbolized by the primacy accorded to military means include Gliksman (1981:36) and Ohlson (1983).

Chapter 6. *Military-Industrial and Transnational Corporate Interests*

1. Thus we find a Rand expert testifying (U.S., House, CFA, 1981:43) that "arms transfers (FMS credit/cash, commercial, or grant) cannot be isolated from the U.S. military mission system, the military training program (IMET), advisory activities, and the status/function of the Southern Command — headquartered in Panama, and responsible for administrative, training, and operational activities in support of security assistance efforts throughout Latin America. Arms transfers are very much a part of a complex of military, security, and political relations between the United States and Latin America."

2. "As a member of Eisenhower's Science Advisory Committee, I saw firsthand how individuals from government and military industries collaborated with members of Congress to defeat the president's efforts [to control the arms buildup]. They killed the nuclear-test-ban negotiations with arguments ranging from the need for the neutron bomb and peaceful nuclear explosions to the possibility of Soviet cheating by testing behind the moon or even the sun. Eisenhower cancelled the B-70 bomber and then reinstated it after being subjected to enormous pressure by the political leaders of the Republican Party. . . .

"President John Kennedy had to contend with similar opposition when he continued Eisenhower's efforts to achieve a halt to nuclear testing. In fact, opposition to his efforts was much more intense. . . . [P]ressure from Congress, the Defense Department, and outside groups caused Kennedy to build a much larger Minuteman missile force than was necessary, even after reconnaissance made it clear that the suspected missile gap did not exist. . . .

"Lyndon Johnson decided in 1967 to buy a modest-sized anti-ballistic-missile system to protect the country from a Chinese military attack and, incidentally, himself from an increasing attack by Republicans during the 1968 presidential election. . . .

"President Gerald Ford and his secretary of defense, James Schlesinger, proposed, because of military pressures, to produce what they called a 'limited, strategic, war-fighting capability' that Schlesinger ultimately admitted to Congress was planned for 'a highly unlikely contingency.' President Jimmy Carter gave up his opposition to the MX missile in the hope of getting the SALT II Treaty through Congress.

"Such pressure groups no longer need to operate on the president. President Ronald Reagan not only accepts the ideas of the groups that Eisenhower warned against, he has become their most articulate spokesman. . . ."

The Bush election demonstrates the American public's complicity in the arms buildup, since he ran on the Reagan Administration's record. The latter's INF Treaty removed but 4 percent of Soviet and American missiles. Yet it excluded warheads and in no way slowed the arms race either on earth or in space.

3. "One immutable law of Pentagon force planning is that the Joint Chiefs of Staff will generate requirements greater than the existing force, irrespective of the

strategy in vogue at the time. It is the inevitable result of a cycle that a former official calls 'incestuous amplification.'

"It begins with the services each going through an elaborate itemization of the number of ships, planes and divisions they want. These listings are stapled together to produce the whole. Real trade offs—say, giving up a wing of Air Force F-15 fighters for an extra Army division—do not intrude on this stylized ritual. The process is additive, and the result is an inflated 'requirements menu' with a five-year cost of about a trillion dollars more than the existing force. Naturally, any peacetime defense budget compared to this target appears woefully inadequate.

"The perception of a cash shortage stems also from the seductive notion that we can fight a 'sanitary' war using complex (and costly) weapons—sophisticated target-acquisition devices, computers, long-range missiles, etc.—that will whittle down a numerically superior foe before he can use his own arms. . . .

"This video-game vision would be fine were it not for a few real-world problems. Not only are these expensive and difficult-to-maintain systems vulnerable to saturation attacks, they can be thwarted in cheap and unpredictable ways, as Iran is doing by using simple radar reflectors to lure Iraqi Exocet missiles away from their intended targets, the oil tankers at Kharg Island. It is also doubtful that our heavy investment in this 'beyond visual range' technology will be used in a shooting war, where the rules of engagement dictate positive identification of the target before shooting. This means that the pilot must make sure the blip on his radar screen is an enemy plane, not a buddy. But combat at such close quarters does not require complex technology: short-range missiles and cannons are brutally effective. More importantly, aircraft stripped of all the electronic 'black boxes' and heavy long-range missiles are much more agile. Greater effectiveness does not necessarily come at greater cost."

4. The B-2 may be another example. Coffin (1990:3) notes that "In Senate debate, Alan Cranston (D–Cal.) pointed out that the real cost of the B-2 Stealth bomber is one billion dollars for each of the 132 planes planned. The *Los Angeles Times* states that the U.S. 'would spend 14 times as much to hit a target with the B-2 as it would have to spend to hit the same target with alternative weapons at hand.' Cranston added: 'The fact is that we do not need this aircraft in order to ensure a stable nuclear triad deterrent against the Soviet Union. New information placed on the public record in Congressional debates makes clear that the B-2 lacks any essential mission. . . .'"

5. "A recent Airforce study confirms argument by the IAM and UAW that military contractors are attacking unions with false claims of labor costs. The study shows that contractors charge the government as much as 20 times their hourly labor costs. For example, at Pratt and Whitney, a division of United Technologies, the cost of a 'standard hour' of labor on its TF-30 aircraft engines was found to be about $10. By the time overhead, administrative expenses, and a 13% profit margin was added, the hourly price charged to the government was $195. Other companies included in the report were G.E., General Dynamics, Rockwell International, Lockheed, and Boeing" ("Economic Clips," 1984:11).

6. "Defense problems in accounting and reporting foreign military sales disbursements and collections were disclosed in 1976 when the services transferred responsibility for maintaining detailed sales accounting records to the Security Assistance Accounting Center. Since then, these differences have increased. . . .

"Sixty-one foreign customers may have been overbilled because their trust fund cash balances were $565 million higher than their sales cash accounting record balances. . . .

"Also, 36 other foreign customers may have been underbilled because their trust fund cash balances were $943 million lower than the detailed sales cash accounting records."

7. Pearson (1981:42) reports, "Surprisingly, the State Department has been able to identify only a few significant cases in which other suppliers of weapons made sales . . . equivalent to those which were denied by the U.S. There were only three major examples: French fighter sales to Ecuador; French fighter sales to Pakistan after the U.S. A-7 refusal; U.K. Jaguar aircraft sales to India after U.S. refusal to sell deep strike aircraft or authorize Swedish Viggen sales. Such British or French sales might have gone through without U.S. denials since customers often consider alternate produces simultaneously."

8. Gauhar states that while the "phenomenal growth of arms and military expenditure in the developing countries is usually justified on political and strategic grounds . . . the obvious correlation between the wealth of a country and its propensity (or compulsion) to spend that wealth on arms is often ignored. To put it bluntly: political and strategic conditions remaining the same, a country coming into wealth tends to (or is made to) apply its sudden riches to military purposes. . . . If a country has the money, arms merchants would find and, if necessary, 'create' the requisite security climate to induce or compel it to undertake higher military expenditures and higher arms imports. . . .

"To illustrate, take the Middle East which saw a sharp increase in its income due to a rise in oil prices in the seventies. The value of major weapons imported in the region was U.S. $196 million in 1961. By 1980 the value had risen to a staggering U.S. $5,414 million, registering an increase of — hold — on — over 2,762 percent! The five year moving average shot up from U.S. $327 million to U.S. $4,342 million. Can one explain this massive increase, to which there was no parallel in any other part of the world during the period, except in terms of the oil wealth which the manufacturers of military weapons decided to appropriate? Admittedly tensions were created, even crises unleashed, but they were part of the West's high-pressure arms marketing strategy.

"Two decades of profligate arms spending did not resolve any dispute in the region, nor did any country acquire a greater sense of security. All that happened was that oil was converted into guns."

9. Pierre (1982:37) underscores this point by noting that "an oil embargo was possible in 1973 when prices [were excessively low and] began leaping up. The prodigious surplus wealth that has since come, to Saudi Arabia, for example, has woven a web of dependence on the West in which it is now ensnared. An oil embargo [now] or a politically motivated price increase would impair its own investment portfolios."

10. Data generated by Vaupel and Curhan (1973), Eckhardt (1977:7–8) gives us some idea of the magnitude involved and then proceeds to posit some implications: "The 261 largest MNC's in the world since 1900 (those with more than $400 million sales per year, and at least 25% equity in branch plants in at least six countries in 1967) had over 16,000 branch plants in 1967, compared with 600 prior to the first world war. About 57% of these branch plants had their home base in the United States, and most of the rest had their home bases in England, West Germany, Japan, Switzerland, Netherlands, France, Belgium, Canada, Luxembourg, Sweden, and Italy (in the order of greater to fewer branch plants). About 36% of these branch plants were located in the Third World, the rest being located in the Western World. . . .

"According to Magdoff (1969), the United States is the world's largest exporter and importer of goods, services, and capital (p. 69). In 1967, there were over 300 overseas branch banks in 55 countries, 90% of which were owned by the First National City Bank, Chase Manhattan, and the Bank of America (p. 73). Almost three times as much money was taken out of the Third World as was invested there (p. 198). . . .

"It might be argued that U.S. banks and other businesses are entitled to make a profit on their investments. But this argument assumes that it is U.S. money that is being invested abroad. Actually, both in Brazil and Canada in 1957, 75% of the U.S. capital invested in these two countries was obtained from within these countries themselves, 47% of the U.S. firms in Canada raising 100% of their capital in Canada (Frank, 1969:50).

"...The U.S. had 3,401 military bases in 30 foreign nations in 1969 (Magdoff, 1971:134) to protect U.S. ownership and control of 40% of the world's resources by 5% of the world's people, suggesting that the U.S. was helping itself to 8 times more of the world's pie than it was justly entitled to eat."

11. Not only has a world capitalist slowdown contributed to a slackening of markets and prices for Third World exports, but growing protectionism also impedes earnings. At the same time interest rates have been high until recently, high cost capital-intensive technology has also driven up debt and the situation has been further exacerbated by both continued import of "luxury" goods and what is euphemistically called capital flight. Although hard data are difficult to come by in this area, estimates range that up to about 50 percent of the $1.3 trillion Third World external debt has been used for investments that have been often illegally recycled by politicians, military officers and business elements to "safe" havens in the advanced capitalist countries of the North. One recent example pertains to the Philippines, where such revelation may have been integral to a CIA operation to force Marcos out in favor of moderate politicians who appeared more likely to be effective in containing the fast developing support for the communist-led nationalist movement. According to one report (Guyot, 1985:19), many millions of dollars were funneled into American real estate and other holdings by Marcos and his close supporters.

12. Even where the Administration has portrayed foreign leaders (as in the cases of Nicaragua and Libya), in demonic terms, opinion polls in the United States have consistently revealed a large majority opposing intervention. Because of this and the recalcitrance of many Latin American and West European governments, by 1985 Reagan's policy-makers opted for provoking or simulating incidents involving purported attacks upon American "honor" (i.e., lives or property). This would resemble the alleged "threat" to the "lives and safety" of American medical students in Grenada prior to the Pentagon's 1983 invasion and incarceration of the island's government, and the staged incident in Panama prior to the invasion.

13. The authors of "Inflating" (1983:57) recall those halcyon days: "The number of U.S. and NATO forward-based systems capable of nuclear strikes against the Soviet homeland had increased by 1955 to more than 500, and the Eisenhower Administration had begun to emphasize American willingness to rely on the U.S. nuclear advantages to deter communist threats around the world."

14. The Draper Commission's Report (U.S. President's Committee, 1959) emphasized such a distinction. Unsurprisingly then, Falk (1984:195) informs us that "Daniel Ellsberg, a former government official with responsibility in the nuclear policy area, confirms the extent to which American presidents were prepared to use nuclear weapons in non-defensive roles and far beyond what the American people were ever allowed to understand. He writes: 'when I did most of my working plans in '59, '60, and '61 ... I assumed that I was reading basically retaliatory plans.... The generals knew better. They knew that these plans were not at all for retaliation because, on the contrary, the Russians had no ability to strike first, so all these plans were really initiative plans, first-strike plans.'" Cf. Aldridge (1983), and Leitenberg (1981).

15. "What role does Cuba play in the development and implementation of U.S. arms transfer/security assistance policies for Latin America? The answers depend on the

manner in which the Cuban threat is defined. Cuba maintains one of the largest standing armed forces in Latin America. It has sent expeditionary forces halfway around the world, and this famous island '60 miles from American shores' is a virtual fortress protected by the latest in Soviet military — mostly defensive — hardware. Several billion dollars worth of Soviet military equipment (including MIG-23s, F-Class Submarines, guided missile patrol boats, cargo troop transports, assault helicopters, T-62 tanks, and an elaborate SAM system) have produced only one incidence of conflict with a hemispheric neighbor — that being the Bahamian patrol boat incident in 1980. Further, no country in Latin America is reported to have sought military hardware as a means to counter Cuban military power. (The Venezuelan desire to purchase F-16s may draw attention to the Cuban factor to seek a favorable outcome.) As a matter of fact, not even the United States has made efforts to enhance defense capabilities against Cuban military capabilities in various strategic sites in the Caribbean Basin, including the Panama Canal.

"Cuba as a threat factor in assessing U.S. arms transfer policies comes in the form of Fidel Castro's politico-military policy style — not in the form of MIGs, SAMs, M18s, and other advanced weaponry. Cuba's security assistance / arms policies are flexible, centralized, and responsive to opportunities that develop. Aside from being opportunistic, the Cuban style is to be discriminate in its support of, and allocation of resources to, revolutionary movements in the region — especially the Caribbean Basin (U.S., House, CFA, 1981:29–30)."

16. Pearson goes on to note that five years later, the "estimate was 5% while by 1984 it may have reached 8% though this also reflects the continued decline in competitiveness of civilian exports — itself an indirect consequence of the militarization process."

17. "The Treasury study found that the impact on broad economic aggregates of any plausible policy curtailing arms exports is likely to be modest; and that the moderate adverse effects could be easily countered by slightly more expansionary monetary and fiscal policies. The estimated percentage decline in total employment by 1983 would be 0.1 irrespective of whether the 40 percent reduction in military sales was achieved immediately or spread over four years (resulting in a 34 percent reduction). The job displacement would be essentially limited to three industries — ordnance, aircraft, and communications equipment — and would be most strongly felt by professional and technical employees, rather than by semiskilled or unskilled workers. . . .

"The Congressional study concluded that large savings do not generally result from U.S. foreign military sales, and that the individual cases in which exports do produce substantial savings in a given weapon's total program costs tend to be exceptional. For a few weapons systems, the savings from foreign sales may come to 8 percent of total research and development costs. These savings are primarily from sales of high technology systems, which employ newly developed and specialized technology, particularly advanced fighter aircraft and missiles. However, for the great majority of sales — ships, ammunition, artillery, military equipment, and services, for which early research and development costs have already been absorbed — there appear to be little or no cost savings. The relationship between any restraints on arm sales and weapon costs to the U.S. Department of Defense will therefore depend less on the total dollar volume of sales than on what portion of sales is of newly developed, high technology items."

Chapter 7. Official "Security" Rationales and Liberal Critiques: The Underlying Imperial Dimension

1. "The old theory was that by withholding training, logistics, and spare parts we could get a nation to do more or less what we wanted in the international arena. Such

a 'blackmailing' technique has certainly worked in the past, but today there are two factors operating against it. First, there are alternative sources. When the Soviet Union apparently told Egypt that it would no longer overhaul the engines of the Soviet-supplied MIG-21 jet fighters, China agreed to supply the parts to Egypt free of charge. All signs point to a broadening of the arms supplier market, and often with similar (licensed) equipment. Second, most countries are now aware of the problems that withholding of logistics support can bring, and are asking for a 'total package.' For example, Iran asked that repair depots be set up for maintaining the Hawk Missile System, that personnel and managers be trained, and that manufacturing facilities be established."

Even so, by October 1980, the Islamic Republic had initiated negotiations with the Reagan-Bush campaign for future weapons deliveries desperately needed to keep more than a small number of jet fighters in action. United States–sanctioned Israeli as well as American shipments during the period 1981–86 were supplemented by those from a half-dozen other suppliers. See Alexander Cockburn (8/13–20/88:120–21).

2. By April 1984, "just days before Nicaragua brought its complaint," the United States (Cook, 1985:15) "made an abortive move to withdraw from World Court jurisdiction on matters concerning Central America for a two year period. After this petition was rejected by a unanimous vote, the U.S. proceeded to serve six months notice of its withdrawal from the World Court's jurisdiction except in cases of voluntary submission. The court ruled anyway by unanimous decision that Washington had violated international laws in mining Nicaragua harbors."

3. I base my decision on these judgments. The AWACs and the F-15 enhancement package could make a difference in the defense of the oil facilities but certainly would not stop a truly determined effort. Not a single witness has been willing to say that the AWACs, the F-15's and the F-15 enhancement equipment would make the oil facilities invulnerable.

"To the extent AWACs would make a difference, that difference would be best realized by an arrangement involving the most capable, the most sophisticated and not downgraded AWACs in Saudi Arabia, but under U.S. control.

"Loss of the AWACs to the Soviet Union would be very valuable to them and compromise of the AIM-9L missiles could have equally serious security implications. Even stringent security precautions would not suffice if Saudi Arabia were to fall victim to an attack by its neighbors or, as some of us feel could happen, of internal dissidence.

"Clearly the Israelis will have to take steps to meet the threat posed by Saudi-owned AWACs, including outlays for jamming and for better air defense. In other words, we would give one set of weapons to one side and we will have to give a responsive set to the other side.

"The AWACs and F-15 enhancement package would encourage another arms spiral in the Middle East and Israeli reaction could lead to effort by Syria and Iraq for more and better equipment. It could cause the new Egyptian Government to press for still more equipment to insure that it is not lagging behind the new round of arms purchases.

"Finally, by showing that we will sell the best and most sophisticated equipment, the proposed sale would undercut any efforts to constrain the sale of sophisticated defense equipment around the world."

4. Looking at the corporate dimensions, Klare (1982e:40) amplifies the "economies of scale" rationale — one that is, however, relevant only to the *early* production runs: "As weapons become more sophisticated and complex, arms sales are increasingly used to pass on to other countries the costs of research and development and production start-up, thus reducing the price America must pay for its own equipment. Foreign military sales also reduce costs by increasing the quality of arms produced at a

given facility, spreading overhead expenses over a larger number of units, and thereby reducing the average cost per weapon.

"These savings have become particularly critical in the past few years, as the rise in R&D and production costs of new high-technology arms have surpassed all expectations and have threatened the survival of several major defense programs, such as the Grumman F-14 carrier-based fighter and the Boeing E-3A AWACs (airborne warning and control system) radar plane."

5. Or in the words of one distinguished West German security analyst (Wulf, 1985a:14–15): "While American critics complain about West European parochialism, most West Europeans — even conservative governments — want to dissociate themselves from the United States global involvements and interventions. Illegal actions that undermine other countries' sovereignty — as against Nicaragua — or arrogant interventions as symbolic acts of power politics — as in Grenada might have created some domestic political gain in the U.S.; in the Atlantic Alliance they are a source of disunity. Chauvinism, in European eyes, is encouraged by President Reagan."

6. See Tables 2 and 10.

7. Betts (1980:92, 98) contends that "some radical analysts have seen the integration of [the] arms trade with general economic trends as evidence of continued 'feudal dominance' of the international system by the great powers. The rise of OPEC casts doubt on the usefulness of this characterization." Although he cannot be faulted for not acknowledging the decline and virtual collapse of OPEC in and since 1985, Betts touches the heart of the issue by subsequently conceding that "if we need to cultivate external markets in order to maintain the viability of industries in the Western democracies, we actually validate Lenin's theory of imperialism." Yet he proceeds to posit: "An alternative interpretation to Lenin's, more appropriate for a post-colonial world, is that a hegemonial policy conflicts with one motivated by industrial profit. The first requires tailoring production to the supplier's own needs, and willingness to manipulate and cut off sales and make grants. The second requires catering to customer needs, maximizing sales, and making no free gifts. The United States still fits the first pattern, while the British have moved from the first to the second. . . ." He not only exaggerates the U.K.-U.S. policy differences (e.g. London's refusal to sell weapons to Nicaragua) but ignores intra-alliance rivalries. Similarly, there is cognizance neither that American hegemonialism serves transnational corporate global interests, nor that both policies may be operative and in occasional conflict.

8. Belgium broke ranks and did sell a shipload of rifles. The ship exploded in Havana's harbor — probably one of the more successful (Agee, 1975) CIA operations. Brussels' role, on the other hand, reflects what Wulf (1985a:15) calls traditional "intercapitalist rivalry and competition" among NATO powers — a recurrent phenomenon associated with U.S. attempts to impose embargoes on East-West trade. West Europeans and the Japanese have ever more persistently opposed such economic warfare as ineffective and an obstacle to lessening tensions.

9. Black and Matthews report: (1985) "The French recognized that, as one official put it, 'The Managua government has no desire to count entirely on Cuba and the Soviet Union to supply its defense needs.' The French sales agreement, signed that December, was modest: two Alouette-3 helicopters, two coastal patrol boats, forty-five troop transport trucks, one hundred STRIM-89 helicopter-mounted rocket launchers and 7,000 rocket rounds. It also offered training for ten Nicaraguan pilots and ten naval officers. The materiel, the French stressed, was purely defensive, and none of it could be transferred to a third party. All told, the package was worth $15.8 million.

"Washington's reaction was fierce and immediate. Secretary of State Alexander Haig told French Foreign Minister Claude Cheysson that he regarded the deal as 'a stab in the back.' . . . One French high-technology export firm complained that its markets in at least three countries had been cut off as a result of the sale. Under intense pressure, Mitterrand caved in and told Reagan in a private meeting in April 1982 that delivery of the helicopters would face 'indefinite delays.' The French ruled out any future sales to Nicaragua."

10. The Dominican Republic represents a prime example of such continuity. Chomsky (1985:15) recalls that "Woodrow Wilson began a major counter insurgency campaign which ended in the early 1920's and which led to the Trujillo dictatorship, one of the most brutal and vicious and corrupt dictatorships that we managed to install in Latin America. In the early 1960's it looked as though there was going to be a move towards democracy. There was, in fact, a democratic election in 1962. Juan Bosch was elected, a liberal democrat. The Kennedy Administration was very cool. The way it reacted is interesting. . . . The American embassy blocked . . . land reform, labor organizing, anything that could have developed public support against a military which was pretty certain to try another coup. . . . As a result, the predicted military coup took place and Washington, which was essentially responsible for the success of the coup, shortly after it, recognized the new government. A typical military dictatorship of the type we like was established. In 1965, there was a coup by liberal, reformist officers, a constitutionalist coup, which threatened to restore democracy in the Dominican Republic, so we . . . sent troops. A bloody and destructive war took place . . . and we again succeeded in establishing a terror-and-torture regime. The country was also, incidentally, brought totally within the grip of American corporations."

Chomsky omits mention of the Pentagon and CIA role in encouraging (Wolpin, 1982) the Air Force–led coup against Bosch. This may explain Washington's failure to impede its success despite appeals for intervention. The latter had been employed to keep Bosch's rightist predecessor in office. Elsewhere, however, Chomsky (1985:14) does recount the role of both the Kennedy and Johnson administrations in subverting the democratically elected Brazilian government. Cf. Agee (1975).

11. Illustrative of such assessments—whose pessimism seldom, however, yields recommendations for sharp curtailment of weapons flow—is the congressional apologia (U.S., House, CFA, 1981:34) of Millett: "The reality is that providing or failing to provide arms has a limited and, in the case of such major regional powers as Brazil and Mexico probably minimal impact on internal politics, civil-military relations and willingness to cooperate in regional defense efforts. . . .

"While the provision of arms rarely, if ever, produces the hoped-for degree of positive influence, refusal to approve transfers can have decidedly negative results. Arms cut-offs directed against the Dominican Republic in 1960–61, against Cuba in the same period, against the Somoza dictatorship in Nicaragua in 1978–79 and currently against the government of Guatemala have all failed to modify the internal practice of those regimes. On the contrary, in each case the internal policies became more repressive and United States influence probably declined. . . .

"Once in possession of arms, Latin America's armed forces, like those of the rest of the world, tend to determine the use of such weapons according to their own interests and not those of the United States."

12. At least two meanings have been ascribed to this phenomenon. The first is suggested by Ronfeldt and Sereseres (1977:53), who caution: "It is rarely true that the more arms the United States transfers to a country, the more leverage the United States obtains. This is especially the case for governments that have become skilled at negotiating with the United States and that have the option of resorting to alternative suppliers. Yet even recipients that are almost totally reliant on U.S. supplies may not lack a capacity to bargain and manage U.S. influence attempts. Indeed, U.S. economic

and military assistance programs in the 1960's seem to have provided an important training ground for foreign elites to learn how to negotiate with U.S. bureaucracies, to exploit U.S. objectives and programs, and at times to exercise 'reverse leverage.'"

Pearson (1981:38), in turn, aptly describes another dimension of such reverse leverage. "Analysts might conclude that three F-5's could do the job of one F-15 in a Third World state, and reduce costs while restricting release of technologies. Yet they might still recommend the F-15 because the greater number of planes would overtax the recipient's piloting or servicing capability. Hence, U.S. defense bureaucrats are put in the position of thinking for recipients in determining whether force proposals are 'appropriate' to the situation. However, reverse pressure is applied through Congress in some cases (notably Israel—which is treated as a quasi-ally under P.D. 13—and Taiwan) if the recipient or other concerned states object either to a sale or denial."

Others who willingly perform a sub-hegemonial regional role can also exercise reverse leverage. Thus Klare (1982c:44) reports that "several State Department officials told me that while they had felt that the Shah's arms purchases were excessive, they were afraid to tell him so for fear of the deleterious effect this might have had on U.S.-Iranian relations."

13. Indeed their influence was so limited that Schoultz (1981:155) concluded, "Congress is relatively unconcerned with the causes of human rights violations; rather it has preferred to avoid the issue and simply to obligate the president to conduct foreign assistance programs in a manner which will 'avoid identification of the United States . . . with governments which deny to their people internationally recognized human rights.'"

14. Bird and Holland (1985a:400) provide illuminating background detail on the (U.S.)-Pakistani weapons flow, including the sequence of events and likely denouement of this tragic conflict, affirming that "a more diplomatic approach might bring the Russians a lot closer to ending the war. They have long indicated a willingness to work out a timetable for the withdrawal of their 115,000 troops. . . . The war is not going well for the Mujahedeen, the Moslem fundamentalist guerrillas, even though the C.I.A. has provided them with a reported $250 million in aid this year and Congress just approved an additional $300 million in emergency funds over the next two years. Much of the aid has been siphoned off by C.I.A. intermediaries and Pakistani officials.

"So far, every attempt at negotiating a settlement of the war has been aborted by the United States . . . presumably to reap the propaganda benefits from a continuing Soviet intervention. . . .

"In the spring of 1983, the Russians indicated they would agree to a staged withdrawal in return for Pakistan's assurances that the Afghan insurgency would be halted. The Russians even said that President Babrak Karmal, whom they had installed, would be willing to step aside in favor of a transitional figure. They planted no illusions that Afghanistan would be allowed to follow an independent course in its foreign relations.

"Pakistan's initial response to the offer was positive. Then in stepped the Reagan Administration. [Selig] Harrison explains, 'Pakistan did not seriously test Soviet terms for a force withdrawal in 1983, losing its heart for diplomatic brinkmanship at the eleventh hour in the face of U.S., Saudi and Chinese disapproval.'

". . . At a press conference in April, U.S. Ambassador to Pakistan Deane Kinton said that he was 'baffled' by those in Pakistan who were pressing for direct talks with the Karmal regime. A month later, Pakistani Prime Minister Mohammed Khan Junejo ruled out any kind of bilateral talks."

Ironically, little had changed by 1990 despite the withdrawal of Soviet troops, new leadership in Kabul and the death of Zia.

Chapter 8. The Domestic Costs of Pentagonism: Whither the American Dream?

1. Thurow says: "While one would think that there would be less political resistance to job programs than there would be to welfare programs (and that is true for the general amorphous public), precisely the reverse is true when it comes to special-interest groups. Most of these special-interest groups are producer groups, and they are much more willing to see general tax revenue go for expanded welfare programs than they are to see government actively working to create jobs or working to alter the distribution of earnings." On the growing corporate dominance of the national legislature, see Sherrill (1988), and Broder (1990).

2. Thurow again: ". . . an implicit compromise was worked out during the Nixon Administration. Programs would be expanded to help the poor, but they would be welfare programs and not programs that required any fundamental restructuring of the economy. After correcting for inflation, income transfer payments to persons rose 156 percent in the eight Nixon-Ford years — more than twice as much as they had risen in the eight years of the Kennedy-Johnson Administration. After correcting for inflation, income transfer payments actually fell 9 percent under Carter. Despite these statistical facts of life, the Democrats were tagged as the party in favor of putting people on welfare. Congressional Democrats had voted for the increases and Reagan, not being willing to extend the implicit compromise made by Nixon and Ford, made attacks upon a welfare mentality a central theme of his campaigns."

3. According to one report ("Taxes," 1985:4), "in 1950, the average worker worked just over two hours out of an eight-hour day to earn the money necessary to pay taxes to the federal, state, and local governments. Today, after four years of Reaganism, the average worker spends approximately three hours a day working to pay taxes. The real tax burden on working Americans has increased by almost 50% over the last 35 years."

4. Thus it was found ("Taxes," 1985:4–5) that "by 1984, workers earning $10,000 lost an average of 28% of their income due to the Reagan 'tax cut,' once social security taxes and inflation were factored in. Those in the $15–20,000 bracket lost 3%; and those in the $20–30,000 bracket held even. Only those with income over $30,000 received any relief from the federal tax burden."

5. As quoted from R. Kuttner, *The Economic Illusion,* Boston: Houghton Mifflin, 1984, p. 189. Coffin (1985a:2) cites a statement by Republican Congressman Dan Coats of Indiana that "in 1959, the median-income family of four with one wage earner paid 3.4% of its income in Federal taxes. Today the same family pays 11.8% . . . a more than threefold increase."

6. Of the corporations, Coffin writes: "Robert McIntyre of Citizens for Tax Justice reports: 'In the 60s, when the economy and capital investment were growing at record rates, taxes paid by American corporations covered the cost of about one-fourth of all government spending other than Social Security.' Last year, the figure was just 8.8%.

"In 1983, 129 companies with profits totalling $45 billion paid an effective tax rate of 4/5ths of 1%. The average effective rate for individuals was 12%."

Illustrative of tax loopholes for individuals is Coffin's (1990a:4) report that "the 100 taxpayers with the most capital gains income in 1985 received an average tax break of $13 million per person. That is the difference between the capital gains taxes they paid and what they would have paid if capital gains were taxed the same as ordinary income. The Joint Tax Committee also reviewed the top 1,000 tax returns for 1985 and found that the average tax benefit under prior law to these taxpayers was about $4 million each. (Senator George J. Mitchell, D–Maine)"

7. Thurow (1985:49) links this lack of equity to the poor productivity performance, contending that "the changes that will be necessary to make the economy more efficient are congruent with what needs to be done to make the economy more equitable. All of our major international competitors have found this to be true. None have slower productivity growth; all (with the possible exception of France) have a much more equal distribution of income. While the ratio of average income between the top and bottom decile of income is 14 to 1 in the United States, it is only 6 to 1 in West Germany. What can be achieved in Germany can be achieved in the United States." By the late 1980s, the situation in America was even more inegalitarian than at the time of Thurow's comparison.

8. Less well known in the United States are the rapid Soviet advances in civilian technology. Buchan (1984:49) records Soviet license sales to Japan, Great Britain, and the United States for such products as cattle feed additive, polymer pins for orthopedic use, and offshore drilling equipment. He warns that "Western companies — in energy, mining, metallurgy, mechanical and hydraulic engineering, and, to some extent, medicine and biochemistry — risk doing themselves a business injury if they ignore what the Soviet Union has to offer and their Western competitors do not. Steelmaking has held up better in Japan than in most industrialized Western countries, possibly because Nippon Steel, Kobe Steel, and other Japanese companies have been the Soviet Union's best non–Communist customers for techniques such as continuous casting and electroslag remelting." Cf. Gorbachev (1987:83–95).

9. Arguing that more equitable treatment for the less privileged is crucial, he maintains that "the poor American productivity performances come not so much from less 'hard' productivity (inferior technology) but from less 'soft' productivity (poorer motivation, less cooperation, adversarial relations rather than teamwork). . . . But what worker or manager will sacrifice to make a company successful ten years from now if he or she knows that there is a high probability that they will not be around in ten years?"

10. "This occurs at a time when long-term unemployment remains at high levels. Labor Department data shows that there are now 1.3 million long-term unemployed (those out of work more than half a year and still looking for a job). More than 5.6 million officially counted unemployed people are without benefits."

11. Ferguson and Rogers continue: "What happens to those who have exhausted unemployment benefits? In over half the states, families of the unemployed in which both parents are present are ineligible for welfare aid, even if the family is impoverished. In most of these states, unemployed two-parent families are also ineligible for any Medicaid coverage for themselves and their children, no matter how low their income."

12. So were tax "reforms." "When the Reagan Administration designed its 1981 tax and expenditure package, it claimed that the supply-side response to the tax cuts would be so rapid that no one's income would decline. As predicted by others, it did not work that way. Families with incomes below $40,000 had their incomes reduced; families with incomes above $40,000 had their incomes enhanced. . . . Since the American savings rate did not go up in the aftermath of the 1981 tax cut, the tax cut package was inefficient as well as inequitable. . . ."

13. Other recent studies reveal that (Muwakkil, 1985), "the gap between the rich and the poor is wider than ever before recorded. 'The poorest 40 percent of U.S. families received just 15.7 percent of the national income in 1984,' notes Bickerman. 'This is the lowest percentage the Census Bureau has ever recorded. The middle 20 percent received 17 percent, which is also the lowest ever. Meanwhile, the top 40 percent received 67.3 percent of the national income, the highest percentage ever recorded.'"

14. Muwakkil (1985) notes that "while the overall poverty rate was 14.4 percent in 1984, for blacks it was 33.8 percent. Poverty among black children reached 51 percent—the highest rate ever recorded. Of the black children living in poverty-stricken families, 70 percent of those families were headed by women."

15. "At public institutions, 18 per cent of the freshmen took remedial reading courses; 22 per cent, remedial writing courses; and 27 percent, remedial math courses. At private colleges and universities, the comparable figures were 9 percent for reading, 12 per cent for writing and 15 per cent for math.

"At colleges with open-admission policies, 30 per cent of the freshmen took remedial math, while at colleges with selective policies, the figure was 13 per cent.

"At two-year colleges, 23 per cent of the freshmen took remedial writing; at four-year institutions, the comparable figure was 17 per cent."

16. According to one (Coleman, 1985:C1) report, "The average [suicide rate] for all groups is about 12 in 100,000. But it has been generally declining since 1950, especially for those over 44 years old.

"Young people represent the chief exception to the trend, and their increased rate has of late received widespread attention. In the 1970's, the suicide rate doubled for white males from 15 to 24 years old. The rate has also risen for young black men, to over 20 in 100,000 among those 25 to 34 years old. This is the highest for any age group among blacks, who overall have lower suicide rates than whites.

"Still, overall rates remain highest among the elderly, said Lee Robins, a psychologist at Washington University Medical School in St. Louis. The rate for those 75 or older is still more than three times the rate of that among the young."

17. Average costs in excess of $100,000 for new homes put them beyond the reach of ordinary Americans. With respect to the affordability of rental housing, Hartman (1985) provides additional data and insights: "The median rent/income ratio rose from 22 to 29 percent between 1973 and 1983, according to the most recent annual housing survey.

"Ten point three million renter households pay 35 percent or more of their income for rent; 6.3 million pay 50 percent or more; 4.7 million pay 60 percent or more." (Try feeding and clothing a family adequately with that burden.)

Despite a softening of the real estate market in the late 1980s, the situation remained acute for lower income (Coffin, 1990:2) sectors: "During the 1980s, public-housing funds dropped from $27.9 billion to $9.7 billion; HUD-subsidized housing starts fell from 144,348 to 17,080. By 1986, an estimated seven million households were paying half or more of their income for rent; more than five million households below the official poverty line were paying at least 70% of their income for rent. (Ethan B. Kapstein, Harvard's Institute for Strategic Studies)"

18. "For example, the decline of infant mortality has slowed down since 1981. This is a result, among other factors, of the 1979–82 recession and also of the reduction of social expenditures that affected primarily but not exclusively the low income groups within the working class. The cuts under Carter and very much under Reagan have affected both Great Society programs (such as Medicaid) and New Deal programs (such as Medicare). . . . This reduction of social expenditures further enlarged the number of people who do not have any form of private or public insurance coverage. In 1984, this figure went up to an appalling 38 million people (nearly 20 percent of the total population), the largest number and largest percentage of uncovered population in any Western developed society. Moreover, 100 million Americans do not have catastrophic insurance coverage. If they have to face a major health care expenditure, they are in deep trouble."

Chapter 9. *Constraining Third World Socio-Economic Development Prospects*

1. "...over three-quarters of arms transfers in the past decade went to Third World countries. Of the ninety-four developing nations that imported arms in 1978, more than one-third were among the poorest nations in the world, with average annual per capita income of under $500.... [A]t the same time the rapid growth in arms imports has evidently canceled out most of the increases in developmental aid; arms purchases have risen twice as fast as gains in development assistance. The developing countries that are not oil exporters have had a sharply rising external debt, yet continue to invest in foreign arms. Moreover, spending on military forces, even when modest as a percentage of the GNP, is often very substantial when compared to governmental spending on other, often urgent, needs such as public health, housing, or education. There is, therefore, a solid basis for the belief that considerable amounts are being spent on the purchase of arms which could be better used for other purposes."

2. The domestic power of such comprador-oriented elites in most "moderate" Third World nations — reinforced by Western arms transfers — suggests the wisdom of Pierre's (1982:37) caveat: "But would the money not spent on arms purchases then be spent on economic and social needs? There is no guarantee that the savings incurred from reducing expenditure on defense would be wisely used for the common good." Without arms aid, however, eventually an economically nationalist and socially radical regime would probably replace that of the existing obligarchy and catalyze many (Wolpin, 1981) of these changes.

3. "This loss of life exceeds the number of deaths per year from even the largest military conflicts, World War I and World War II. The point is not, however, to minimize the human tragedy of war, but to illustrate the enormity of the human death too that is produced through social inequality, both within nations and between nations."

4. "Alcock and Young (1974) distinguished between economic, military, and political imperialism for 26 nations, finding that military imperialism (number of troops stationed on foreign soil) could be equated with political imperialism (more than five colonies). These two forms of imperialism were highly correlated with the number of international conflicts from 1945 to 1968.... Economic imperialism (number of MNCs with subsidiaries in the Third World) was significantly correlated with wealth. Since the gap between the rich and poor nations was steadily growing, it was 'assumed that their richness had developed from and continues to depend upon the poverty of the third world — the exploited' (p. 78), so that economic imperialism contributed to the structural violence of poverty, as did political imperialism, since the colonies all had a much lower standard of living than the imperial country (except for the Soviet Union). Consequently, all three forms of imperialism tested in this study contributed to violence, either behavioral or structural or both."

5. Although this was Smalldone's general conclusion, non-economic variables which at times exhibited moderate or strong coefficients were: 1) domestic political and military conflict in S.W. Asia but not the Horn of Africa (Schrodt); 2) "national military strategy and policy such as diversification of arms suppliers and tradeoffs between weapon inventories and sophistication on one hand, and larger, better trained armed forces on the other" in Zaire and Zambia (Leh); 3) "military-strategic factors (civil strife, regional tensions, regime type, defense expenditure)" (Avery and Picard); "political violence and instability, namely armed attacks, deaths from political violence, assassinations, guerrilla war, and riots" (Avery); "military regimes aligned with the Communist bloc." Interestingly, none of these studies appear to treat promotional activities by supplier country attaches/advisors or "arms merchants" as a variable!

6. One of the several neo-colonial objectives (Wolpin, 1973) of IMET is to tie foreign officers to the purchase of weaponry sold by United States military contractors.

7. "Of the developing countries in this survey, 22 out of the 78 which were independent in 1960 were under military-controlled governments."

8. Ohlson's (1982:219) overview from economic and arms reduction perspectives emphasizes that "local production of weapons is, as a rule, more expensive than importing a comparable weapon. This is particularly true for the production of major weapons incorporating high-technology components.

"The most commonly evoked arguments for an indigenous arms industry do not stand up to reality: self-sufficiency is unattainable. Rather, it normally results in a move from direct dependence on arms imports to technological dependence.

"The investment in a domestic arms production capacity creates — from a disarmament point of view — a vicious circle, the end result being that the producer becomes dependent on the ability to export arms. Third World arms exports, therefore, are primarily determined by pressing economic considerations."

9. Thus Richardson (1988) reports that "since the end of the Vietnam War in 1975," Hanoi had "a large number of troops ... working on development and agricultural plantations and in military industries that also produced goods for the civilian economy." Further, as relations improved with China and ASEAN countries, it was decided to begin a 25 percent reduction in the army involving 300,000 men during 1988 in order to release new resources for economic development.

Chapter 10. Fomenting Arms Races and Warfare in the Underdeveloped Areas

1. "Despite this record of terrorism, not one of the countries where repression was practiced failed to receive a substantial flow of arms from obliging supplier nations. In the most recent reporting period, 1975–1983, over two-thirds of all arms exported to the Third World went to countries with repressive governments. The largest supplier, according to US official estimates, was the Soviet Union (especially to Syria, Iraq, and Libya); the next in rank were the US and France, which supplied arms to a larger number of repressive governments but generally in smaller quantities."

2. "Sometimes the question whether or not an arms race even exists is open to interpretation. The Shah insisted that Iran's massive defense buildup was not aimed at such Persian Gulf states as Saudi Arabia and the United Arab Emirates, but was the consequence of the need to respond to, and deter, his immediate neighbors, the Soviet Union, Iraq, and Afghanistan. Saudi Arabia also disclaimed being in an arms race with Iran. Yet the Saudis were deeply concerned with the Shah's military aggrandizement, and this concern had a major impact on their decision to increase and modernize their armed forces. Moreover, as their request for the F-15 demonstrated, even if they did not intend or wish to match Iran fully, for reasons of both pride and politics they sought clear assurance of equal access to American arms."

3. With respect to the first factor — probably the primary motivation for this initiative — Pearson predicts "the availability of scaled down models or slightly retarded systems will tend to keep costs down and hence sales are likely to rise steadily."

4. Although in the Reagan and Bush era this is the primary type of warfare that the Pentagon engages in, official definitions seem to preclude only an unlimited conventional or nuclear conflict with a major power. Klare (1988:95) informs us that "Lieut. Col. Peter Bond of the Army wrote in 1986 ... [that] 'L.I.C. is a very broad concept that spans the spectrum of conflict from relative peace to conventional war.' Included

in this spectrum, according to Pentagon officials, are terrorism and counterterrorism; guerrilla war and counterinsurgency; pro-insurgency (or U.S. support for anticommunist rebels in the Third World, such as the anti–Sandinista *contras*); antidrug operations; border conflicts and minor skirmishes of all sorts; naval show-of-force operations in contested waterways (such as the Persian Gulf); and other contingency operations. As now conceived, L.I.C. as a doctrine has stretched to the point that it embraces almost any sort of short-term military activity that a President might seek to undertake—War Powers Act or no."

5. Although initial CIA paramilitary intervention was begun during 1979, months prior to the entry of Soviet troops in December, Harrison (1981/1982) underscores the reverse leverage exercised by Zia's dictatorship: "Reagan Administration spokesmen have argued that Islamabad can be persuaded to serve as a conduit for U.S. aid to Afghan resistance only if the United States accedes to Pakistani arms requests. But mounting evidence indicates that Islamabad has been quietly funneling Chinese, U.S., Saudi, and Egyptian aid to the resistance since early 1980. Pakistan's posture on the Afghan aid issue has been and will continue to be determined primarily by pressures from other Islamic countries and by growing Pakistani economic dependence on Washington and Riyadh.... In reality, however, by aggravating Indo-Pakistani tensions, the United States is increasing the danger that a conventional war in South Asia will escalate to the nuclear level. Already, the passions aroused by the F-16 issue have greatly strengthened those in India who argue for the development of a nuclear arsenal."

6. Leventhal emphasized that "the greatest danger" is proliferation through the diversion of nuclear material intended for peaceful use. He notes that in the 1990s, "if current reprocessing plans proceed, more explosive plutonium will have been separated from the spent fuel of commercial nuclear power plants than now exists in the U.S. and Soviet weapons stocks." This plutonium can be used for bombs, as can uranium (also used to power reactors, though less available than plutonium). It is "widely acknowledged" that the IAEA, which has no police authority in the NPT, is incapable of detecting and preventing diversion of nuclear materials to weapons programs. Even experts (Goldblat, 1989:373–74) who exhibit greater confidence in the present efficacy of the IAEA warn that it may not be structured and financed to confront new challenges: "Application of safeguards is becoming ever more demanding, because new countries are acquiring uranium enrichment technology, the stockpile of separated plutonium is growing, and the quantity of plutonium in easily reprocessable spent reactor fuel is also increasing. Laser uranium enrichment (easy to disguise), remotely controlled reprocessing plants and large-scale heavy water production may make safeguarding technically harder and certainly more expensive. New safeguards techniques will have to be developed to deal with installations being decommissioned. The present 'zero real growth' policy, applied to the IAEA budget, does not permit all those activities which are necessary to ensure continued credibility of the safeguards system."

7. San Juan (1985:23), for example, reported that "U.S. officers in the [Clark and Subic] bases not only train, equip and supervise the Marcos military but also assist ongoing counterinsurgency operations. All these obviously lay the groundwork for immediate and massive introduction of U.S. troops—joint exercises are conducted regularly into the conflict between the Filipino people and the isolated, beleaguered Marcos clique or any of its successors."

8. "The big powers acquire a special interest in the survival of regimes to which they sell large quantities of advanced weapons. Should any of these countries face defeat in a local war, the credibility of their supplier is inevitably threatened, producing pressures to intervene. And the pressures are bound to increase if there is any risk that the supplier's military secrets will fall into the hands of an enemy."

9. This crisis, a little more than a decade after the Cuban Missile Crisis, also involved a red alert. After the Soviet threat to defend Cairo, Kissinger induced Israeli forces led by Sharon to halt their advance. Rather than accept the implications of parity, the American right joined by centrist Zionist sectors initiated a campaign within months to restore strategic superiority. Sanders (1983) in great detail describes the establishment of the Committee on the Present Danger in 1974 and the major role it and the supporting military industrial complex played in subverting detente. Needless to say, the collapse of the corrupt Thieu regime in Vietnam and Portuguese colonialism's withdrawal from Africa reinforced their propaganda barrage.

10. It would presumably occur if United States and local troops were being forced back. To avoid this, so-called conventional forces are being massively expanded to ensure prolonged conventional superiority in any theater. Commenting upon this aspect of Reagan's militarization drive, Seligman (1983:118) notes that "the single most important [doctrinal change] appears to be abandonment of the belief, long implicit in U.S. military planning, that any war with the Soviet Union would be short. . . ." Two facets of the military planning are enlarged weapons inventories and increased R&D for technological improvements. By the end of the decade, DOD profligacy, incompetence and corruption had resulted in (Sciolino, 1990:3) "a $30 billion stockpile of unneeded material." Some was allegedly held for possible sale "to friendly countries."

11. External encouragement (as in the case of invasion by South Africa, Somalia, Iraq, the Contras, and Israel between the mid-1970s and mid-1980s) may partially account for the high incidence of attacks despite a marked decline in success rates for initiators. Sivard (1987:28) records that "in the 20th Century, starters on average have won 39 percent of the wars. In the current decade, however, only 11 percent of the starters of wars appear to be winners."

Chapter 11. The Nascent American Garrison State

1. "The demand for conformity and for collective sacrifice will be legitimated by the expectation of violence. The vulnerability of modern centralized technology to terrorism and sabotage will be used to confirm the importance of vigilance against internal as well as external enemies."

2. Reviewing Hougan's *Secret Agenda,* Easterbrook (1985:58–60) emphasizes that "Hougan recites the ever-intriguing fact that the D.C. police officer who actually made the Watergate arrests appears to have been tipped—possibly by someone who was intending to make the CIA, not Nixon, look foolish. The officer, a former employee of the National Security Agency, had volunteered out of the blue to work the graveyard shift that fateful night even though he had already worked a shift, and then parked his patrol car by the Watergate.

"Another event, which occurred in early June 1972, was the headline news that a D.C. grand jury was investigating a political call-girl ring. . . . The ring was said to be based in the Columbia Plaza apartments, a block from the Watergate, and many fun-filled calls were placed through a phone in DNC headquarters that had been set up as a private line. That phone, Hougan maintains—not O'Brien or McGovern—was the burglars' real target. They wanted dirt on any Democrats who might be involved, and also advance warning if anyone in the White House was going to be implicated. (When caught, the burglars were on their fourth, not first, entry into the complex.) In turn, Hougan suggests information from the tapes was destined primarily for the CIA, not the White House. Earlier he places this in a context of the spying mania and infighting which characterized the "national security state" at the time. . . .

"...In brief, he [Hougan] presents a substantial (though not conclusive) case that Howard Hunt was not working for Nixon at all, but was still answering to his old firm, the CIA, planted, in fact, to spy on the White House. Hunt with his ill-fitting red wig has always been played in the press as a bumbler. Suppose that was part of Hunt's act?"

3. Even during the mild Carter era purge, the CIA and FBI retained their partial de facto autonomy. As Bird and Holland (1985:640) stress, this autonomy, along with impressively enhanced appropriations, has been extended to the military (army) intelligence apparatus: "Intelligence is reputed to be the fastest-growing item in the Federal budget. The final version of the fiscal 1986 intelligence bill authorizes a total of at least $10 billion for the spy agencies. Aside from the high price tag, the bill contains a dubious provision that, on a twelve-month experimental basis, lets the Pentagon spend any profits earned by counterintelligence front operation. Previously, all the money taken in by dummy businesses set up to provide cover for U.S. agents, entrap foreign spies and the like had to be turned over to the Treasury Department. The measure will allow Army counterintelligence to do what the C.I.A. and the F.B.I. have been doing for decades, namely, run covert operations with funds that have not been subjected to Congressional scrutiny. Why the Senate is permitting this practice at a time when the Army is investigating the possible embezzlement of $150 million from counterintelligence operations is a mystery. Members of the Senate Intelligence Committee refuse to say who initiated the measure."

4. "The Network recently released its third 'Harassment Update.' The report documents numerous visits and phone calls to activists by the FBI and cases of tampered mail. Several offices have been broken into, including a few in Arizona around the time that the sanctuary trial opened there. The IRS has also begun audits of several solidarity activists and has investigated the bank account of activist and author Grace Paley. At least one person has lost their apartment, another their job, due to FBI pressure.

"FBI head William Webster acknowledged as much in testimony before Congress last spring. He said the FBI had conducted about 100 interviews with people returning from Central America, mostly Nicaragua."

5. "Current FBI guidelines instituted in 1983 permit bureau probes of groups with potential for violence, but confine investigations of peaceful groups to 'protect lawful and peaceful political dissent.' The FBI files on the doctors' organization, heavily censored before release under the Freedom of Informaiton Act, contain no allegations of violence by PSR. The 1982 FBI investigation of the physicians' group was 'administrative,' rather than criminal in nature, according to the documents....

"The FBI probe of the physicians began in 1967. The bureau attempted to link the PSR to the Communist Party. The investigation became dormant in the mid-1970s, and started again in 1982."

6. These developments included an undercover investigation by the Orange County, Fla., Sheriff's Department into the Central Florida Nuclear Freeze Campaign (1983); infiltration of the Clamshell Alliance (an anti-nuclear power group) by the New Hampshire State Police (1980); spying by the Georgia Bureau of Investigation on persons demonstrating against the death penalty (1983 and 1984 — justified by "Georgia's newly enacted Anti-Terrorism Task Force Act"); infiltration of striking copper miners in Arizona by that state's Criminal Intelligence Systems Agency (1983 — under a state statute intended "to facilitate investigation into drug trafficking"); and state police infiltration of a peaceful demonstration held by the religious group Covenant for Peace in Michigan, a state whose Police Intelligence Unit "was officially disbanded in 1976."

7. Referring to a 1976 court suit involving prior activities by the Memphis Police Department, Donner informs us that "according to one surviving memorandum, the D.I.U. had concentrated on 'local subversion, disorders, civil rights activist activities,

and union and Negro coalition activities.' Among its targets were colleges, the Communist party, Operation PUSH (People United to Save Humanity), the A.C.L.U., a number of motorcycle gangs, the Southern Christian Leadership Conference, the Black Panther Party and the Memphis Public Employees Union.... The D.I.U. had also gathered personal information: license plate numbers, salaries, debts, bank balances, marital status and the names of close associates, using bank records, credit checks, telephone company checks and other sources."

8. "The revival of political surveillance is being spurred by those on the ultraright, where rooting out subversives has long been a top priority. In the 1960s police departments in most major American cities — including New York, Philadelphia, Chicago, Detroit, Cleveland, Buffalo and Birmingham — cooperated with right-wing groups. They exchanged information, and in some cases police helped paramilitary groups like the Minutemen evade arrest by Federal authorities. The Chicago transmittal files show that the Chicago police requested data on subversives from the Minutemen after the group's leader, Robert B. DePugh, offered them access to its records....

"... [P]rivate surveillance is not confined to right-wing extremists spying on their political enemies. Beginning in the late 1970s, public utilities, through in-house and hired operatives, have monitored organizations and individuals protesting the use of nuclear power as an energy source. These operations have frequently been launched with the cooperation of police, sheriffs' deputies and state troopers. Nor, in assessing a political surveillance threat, can we ignore the rapidly growing number of security personnel serving private industry, now reportedly exceeding that of the nation's urban police forces. History teaches us that they too can become a countersubversion militia, acting either independently or in collaboration with the police."

9. "The McCarran-Walter Act sets out 33 reasons for excluding individuals from the United States, combining prostitutes, paupers, and the insane with ideological undesirables and homosexuals. Of the two political sections in the Act, one permits the exclusion of individuals associated with the Communist party or affiliated organizations. The other section can be used to exclude individuals considered a danger to the 'welfare, safety, or security of the United States,' or whose entry is deemed 'prejudicial to the public interest.'...

"The State Department maintains what is probably the world's largest blacklist, a global computer network known as the Automated Visa Lookout System (AVLOS).

"There are about a million names in AVLOS, according to the Legislative and Intergovernmental Affairs Office of the State Department."

Applications for waiver have been occasionally granted over the years to those willing to undergo a humiliating procedure. Only after the 1986–1988 second "thaw" in Soviet-American relations was there a relaxation of criteria for such approvals. Even so, Yasir Arafat — recognized throughout the world as a legitimate leader of the Palestinian nationalist movement — was illegally denied a visa to address the United Nations.

Because of its clear violation of international human rights covenants (e.g. the Helsinki accords), the McCarran-Walter Act was finally amended in 1989.

10. Specificity on this point is not hard to find. Cohen (1985a:335), for example, points out that the consequence of intimidating detente-oriented journalists is that "debate is again being stifled by censorious crusaders.... Such intolerance has even crept into some once civil-tongued newspapers and magazines. Not long ago, a *New York Post* editorial accused ABC of 'doing Yuri Andropov's job.' And *The New Republic* said of a leading American expert on the Soviet Union, 'With such Sovietologists, who needs the Soviets?'"

11. "The conservative viewpoint now has a firm anchor in the two most important opinion centers of the nation, New York City and Washington. The metamorphosis

of the *New York Post* from a left-wing to a right-wing tabloid since its acquisition by Rupert Murdoch has given new strength to conservative political candidates and heightened tension on issues of street crime and civil liberties. While The *Washington Post* is still dominant in the capital, Congressmen and Administration officials are now exposed to the Rev. Sun Myung Moon's *Washington Times,* which supports the Administration's domestic and foreign policies, with the Government of El Salvador and the rebels in Nicaragua as its special causes.

"The *Wall Street Journal,* whose circulation is nationwide, champions supply-side economics and a return to the gold standard. The fast-growing and lively *USA Today,* while not strongly ideological, gears its articles to the themes of President Reagan's 1984 campaign, including national pride and financial self-advancement.

"On opinion pages, once dominant liberal voices such as Walter Lippman, James Wechsler and Murray Kempton have given way to a new group of articulate conservatives, led by William F. Buckley Jr., James J. Kilpatrick and George Will."

12. Much of the upper class—particularly the "new rich" sector—is devoid of a sense (Lapham, 1988) of noblesse oblige. Given that and heavy political dependence upon corporate dominated campaign funding from Political Action Committees (PACs), the upper class has in many instances become the major transjurisdictional de facto constituency of congressional representatives. Indeed, a true symbiotic relationship exists with congressional incumbents, who can only rarely be defeated. In his review of Stern's (1988) *The Best Congress Money Can Buy,* Sherrill (1988:172) adds that "eighty percent of all PAC money goes to incumbents." The latter in many cases can now extort contributions from particular PACs—reversing the flow of accountability. The same reviewer homes in on a less obvious yet more insidious affront to citizen accountability: "Another position for screwing the democratic process is taken by those politicians who, needing little or no money to win re-election themselves, use their hefty PAC contributions to win power within Congress. The money they take is handed out to other members." In the aftermath of Watergate, the Reagan Administration's financial corruption and influence peddling episodes along with its arrogant disregard of the Constitutional authority vested in Congress—as symbolized by the Iran-Contra affair—have elicited what might be termed cynicism from the educated and informed portion of America's electorate.

13. Etzioni (1984:270–71) reminds us that "people's feelings . . . are reflected in public opinion polls which show that in 1981, 55 percent of the people agreed with the statement that the Democratic Party and its leaders 'care more about special interest groups than about the majority of the people,' and 57 percent said the same about the Republican Party. A significant percentage of the population felt even more strongly: 35 percent felt that the Democratic Party and its leaders 'tend to be corrupt,' and nearly half—49 percent—felt that way about the Republican Party."

14. Etzioni (1984:272) attributes this disenchantment to the growing dominance of "plutocratic" (i.e., corporate) interests. He notes "the general retreat from institutions that took place in the United States beginning in the mid-sixties, and that encompassed all institutions, from the family to labor unions, from the parties to churches. In 1966, 43 percent of adult Americans expressed a great deal of confidence in the leaders of the major American institutions, including medicine, unions, Congress, and the Executive branch. (The percentage is based on an average score for nine institutions.) By 1979, only 23 percent still expressed confidence in these institutions. While the decline slowed down, and recently there have been some upswings, the measure stood at 23 percent as of November 1983. A revival of political parties is much more likely to take place within the context of a general resurgence of faith in institutions."

15. "The evolution of U.S. war games under the Reagan Administration reveals

a particularly dramatic growth in preparation for intervention in Third World countries." The CDI adds that "a military strategy which requires that the U.S. be capable of fighting any number of future wars and a foreign policy which relies on the threat of military coercion is dangerous and needlessly expensive."

16. According to one report ("Corporations," 1984:13), "spurred by the Pentagon, Department of Defense contractors carry on anti-labor and union-busting practices. The Pentagon seeks to blame its escalating costs on 'excessive wages.' In 1983, Pentagon officials began to assist major aerospace firms in trimming wage increases and cutting back fringe benefits. They tried to tie aerospace wages to the lower average manufacturing wage rates paid in the area. . . .

"Another Pentagon anti-union practice is to support employers against workers in strike situations. When the Amalgamated Clothing and Textile Workers Union struck J.P. Stevens, the Pentagon expanded its purchases of Stevens' products. When the union was pitted against Farah, the military bought more jeans from the company. When the United Farm Workers Union was conducting a grape boycott, the Pentagon bought more grapes. When the Amalgamated Transport Union fought Greyhound for seven weeks, the Pentagon purchased more of its bus services."

17. Instructive on this point is Janowitz's (1960) finding that West Point cadets were socialized into the view that congressional oversight or control was a nuisance they had to put up with. Similarly, one must bear in mind that the Pentagon has itself spent billions since then to propagandize executive officials, congresspersons, opinion leaders, and the citizenry.

Chapter 12. Toward an Alternative National Security Approach

1. They conveniently ignore his threats at the time of the Suez invasion and his authorization of CIA paramilitary subversive operations (McGehee, 1983) against nationalistic — yet initially friendly — governments in Iran, Guatemala, Vietnam, Indonesia, Laos, China, Cuba and the Dominican Republic, among others. His administration also provided massive military aid to France for her doomed efforts to destroy national liberation movements in Algeria and Indochina.

2. After describing Norwegian and Swedish government humanitarian contributions to beleaguered Nicaragua, Wald (1985:A34) adds: "Americans should understand that the Reagan Administration's policies toward Nicaragua have not won the approval of our friends and allies in Western Europe. Our disregard of international law and our recent refusal to recognize the decisions of the World Court in the Hague on Nicaragua are added sources of their dismay and our nation's increasing isolation."

Looking at reactions to the overall Administration posture, Birnbaum (1985:20–21) surveys some basic trends: "The numerous European leaders who appear to accept U.S. primacy in the Atlantic Alliance often justify this at home as being a means to influence American opinion. Because fundamentally most Europeans do not find credible the United States' claim to world leadership. The chauvinism encouraged by President Reagan is, in European eyes, not merely an expression of American immaturity and tastelessness. Their most profound concern is that the United States does not accept the need to coexist with the Soviet Union. The Europeans see a confrontation as leading to catastrophe. . . .

"While the peace movement did not block Euromissile deployment, that will be the last military decision imposed by NATO's technocrats: matters of arms, strategy and tactics are now subject to public scrutiny. The parties of the European center and right have exhausted nearly all their political credit in enforcing the Euromissile decision, and

European governments are increasingly at pains to avoid giving the impression of blind subservience to the United States. Even during the Euromissile debate, they strenuously resisted the Reagan Administration's attempt to interfere in their trade with the Soviet bloc."

3. Pike (1985:3) notes that "Star Wars will not protect Europe, Japan or other U.S. allies. These countries, because of their proximity to the Soviet Union, are much more difficult to defend than North America. Continuation of the SDI program will reduce the strength and undermine the solidarity of NATO."

4. This trend is examined in Chapter 2 and to a lesser measure in Chapter 9. It is not yet insurmountable for, as we saw, most Third World producers remain technologically dependent upon major Western powers or the USSR. And in any case, they comprise no more than a half dozen countries.

5. "Inga Thorsson, the Swedish chair of the first treaty review 10 years ago, told an international freeze movement conference in Geneva that there can be 'no progress' on a freeze, much less disarmament, 'so long as the present U.S. administration exists.'. . ."

6. "A chemical weapon ban has also been blocked by 'absurd and extravagant verification demands' on the part of the U.S. . . . (U.S. negotiators insist on inspection of state-owned, but not privately-owned, chemical plants, meaning in practice Soviet but not American)."

7. "Nuclear technology and material have been exported to countries that have not formally renounced nuclear weapons by signing the NPT for 'essentially commercial rather than political' motives, claimed Nigerian Ambassador Bariyu Adeyemi, 'particularly at a time when the nuclear industry is facing serious economic problems.' The Nigerian noted that 'international efforts to stop the spread of nuclear weapons are now being systematically endangered by commercial pressures.'"

8. "Nor can the United States gain 'influence' in any way commensurate with the arms and training provided. What is certain is that the United States runs the risk of becoming involved in local political conflicts and unwanted identification with the internal security tactics of security assistance 'allies.'

". . . Seeking 'influence,' posturing that the Soviets seek world domination, or defining instability, violence, and anti–Americanism in terms of Communist ideology and subversion tactics is not a security assistance/arms transfer doctrine. What often fuels the pace and direction of security assistance is the self-perpetuation of the bureaucracy itself."

9. Soviet and associated East European economic support has become rather substantial—perhaps the real threat—since the early 1960s. For example, a recent report ("CMEA," 1985:4) notes that "CMEA has helped 14 Arab countries build over 2,000 major economic projects, and another thousand are on the drawing boards. Among them: Algeria: the Al-Hajar metallurgical complex, a mining and concentrating complex, a mercury mining and producing enterprise; Egypt: a metallurgical plant and an aluminum plant; Iraq: assistance in drilling, equipment for oil fields, pipelines and refineries." Ownership is vested in the recipient governments, which generally pay off credits extended through an annual share of output. As we have seen, American and other transnational corporations retain an indefinite equity, raise most capital through local or international borrowing, and recover many times their original investment directly and via other mechanisms such as transfer pricing. Cf. Nagle (1985:221–93).

10. Hence Ronfeldt and Sereseres (1977:39) predicted that "the lessening of U.S. influence in Latin America and the expansion of intra-regional relations probably mean that, military diplomacy, based in part on the acquisition of prestigious weapons, will

be increasingly significant in the conduct of intra-hemispheric relations and in the resolution of potential conflicts."

11. Social Trap theory posits a conflict between short-run advantage vs. long-run rationality. According to Costanza (1984:79–80), decision makers "behave contrary to their own self-interest while making what appear to them to be rational decisions." People generally enter traps "because of misperceived costs and benefits." Drawing upon the work of several researchers, Costanza identifies six conditions that generate such misperception: "(1) 'time delay' traps occur when benefits and costs are misperceived because they are separated in time; (2) 'ignorance' traps occur through simple ignorance of real costs and benefits; (3) 'sliding reinforcer traps' occur when costs and benefits change gradually with time, but this change is not adequately perceived; (4) 'externality' traps occur when the actions of others change the cost and benefit framework.... (5) 'collective' traps occur when costs and benefits perceived by individuals are not equivalent to costs and benefits to the collective ... and finally (6) 'hybrid' traps occur from combinations of the previous causes." While all appear germane to our plight, the third may be most pertinent.

12. "Since the LTV battle, Grumman has turned its attention to rebuilding older aircraft, at least in part because it felt its future with its Navy contracts was [not] assured.

"It has also moved to strengthen its nonaerospace operations, which analysts criticized as its least successful, by building a small truck that gets 40 miles to a gallon of gasoline; broadening its line of fire engines, and winning a higher share of the yacht market...."

13. Concerning arms exports, Pierre (1982:71) offers the following perspective: "It is noteworthy ... that of the top ten contractors with the Department of Defense in 1977, only one, the Northrup Corporation, was heavily dependent upon foreign sales.... A careful, albeit necessarily limited, analysis of available data and studies on American arms sales abroad as a percentage of total exports, as a source of employment, as a way of reducing unit costs for U.S. forces, as a means of recouping research and development expenses, and in terms of broad economic aggregates involving trade and balance of payments, leads to an inescapable conclusion: economic considerations are not of sufficient importance to be an overriding, or in some cases even a major factor, in overall foreign policy considerations in dealing with arms transfers."

14. A project, "Non-Provocative Defense for Third World Development," involving such research, was initiated during 1989 at the International Peace Research Institute, Oslo, by Miles D. Wolpin.

15. Pierre (1982:55) recalls that under the Carter Administration's arms restraint policy, "Pakistan was denied permission to purchase 110 A-7 fighter-bombers, on the grounds that the sale would have introduced a more advanced weapons system into South Asia and run the risk of starting a new round in a regional arms race, but it was indicated that in their place the United States would consider sympathetically the A-4 or F-5 aircraft, both of which have less range and offensive capacity."

16. Johansen (1983:22) maintains that "...a defensive system, unlike nuclear deterrence encourages stability. As discussed earlier, deterrence bears the fatal destabilizing flaw of threatening an opponent, even to the point of committing national suicide. Nuclear deterrence relies on vindictiveness. It has no credibility without willingness to retaliate after being destroyed oneself, even though retaliation can no longer save one's society or do more than further crush civilization and the environment. A continuously credible deterrent functions with confrontation, brinksmanship, and arms buildups."

17. Pierre (1982:51) doubts that Congress can effectively exercise such oversight — though his vision is constrained by the type of politicians who have traditionally

dominated that institution: "Congress has given itself the right to make individual arms transfers subject to its disapproval, rather than the right to approve sales to foreign countries before they are completed. This power of rejection, which requires concurrent resolutions will be used only sparingly as it inevitably involves judgements on foreign policy that can best be made by the president and his advisors. . . . Congress has sought to make certain that arms transfers are subject to close scrutiny of Capitol Hill, and has put the executive branch on notice that prospective sales must be justifiable. In this way the Congress has served as an inhibiting factor on some prospective sales that were likely to be seen as excessive."

18. A list is available from the UNESCO affiliated International Peace Research Association. Some of the more well-established ones with long-standing interests in these matters include SIPRI, PRIO, TAPRI, IPS and the WPI.

19. Optimally a "job compensation tax" could be imposed upon new direct or indirect foreign investments whenever the unemployment rate domestically exceeded 2 percent. These funds would be used for labor-intensive government investments or programs to enhance the quality of life.

20. A July 1983 Gallup poll (*Syracuse Post-Standard,* August 4, p. A-10) revealed that fewer than 20 percent of American citizens believe members of Congress have "high moral standards." In fact, University of Michigan Survey Research Center polls in each national election year since the late 1950s reveal a progressive decline in public trust of the government. For example, those who felt they could "trust the government to do what is right" (Miller *et al.,* 1980) "most of the time" or "always" declined as follows: 1964, 74 percent; 1972, 53 percent; 1980, 25 percent. Similarly, those who thought that "the government is pretty much run by a few big interests looking out for themselves" rather than for "the benefit of all the people," increased as follows: 1964, 29 percent; 1972, 53 percent; 1980, 70 percent. This is also consistent with the erosion of confidence in both major parties. Those *disagreeing* with the proposition that both were "only interested in people's votes but not their opinions" dropped sharply over the years: 1968, 51 percent; 1972, 40 percent; 1980, 35 percent. Etzioni (1984) contends that the rise of largely corporate special interest PACs has, in tandem with the traditional weakness of both parties, eroded the little autonomy that still existed so that today private ("plutocratic") and public power intermesh almost perfectly. Mass perceptions of this, then, seem relatively realistic.

21. An example of this "reverse-leverage" in the portentous form of nuclear blackmail was Israel's apparent threat (Cobban, 1988:424–25) to use atomic bombs if the United States refused a massive weapon resupply during the October War (1973). Equally incisive is Johnstone's (1988:11) analysis of Israel's manipulation of the "international terrorism" issue to leverage Washington into backing Tel Aviv's territorial expansionism.

22. As Stein (1978) takes pains to stress, this was equally true for Vietnam. All long-duration wars are increasingly unpopular as gross inequities of sacrifice become apparent. An absence of clear-cut victory exacerbates this trend, as do high visible costs and of course obvious battlefield failures.

23. See the Committee's "Call to All Americans" (1985).

24. A February 1988 Gallup survey (Greenberg, 1988:556) reported only 6 percent "of the voters thought defense was the most important problem facing the nation. The economy and budget deficits were viewed as considerably more important." The proportion of Americans who wanted the U.S. Government to reduce tensions with Moscow increased from 20 percent between 1978 and 1982 to almost two-thirds by late 1987. They remained, however, quite wary or cautious with respect to major weapons reductions.

25. In the course of reviewing Gans' *Middle American Individualism*, Schudson (1988:794) notes, "The most prominent feature of middle Americans' political activity is what Gans calls 'organizational avoidance.' Unlike the upper middle class, they participate very little in formal voluntary organizations. They distrust both big business and big government. This is a tradition of long standing although Gans does observe that the combination of social decentralization — people moving to areas of lower density where a home-and-outdoors-centered life is more possible — and organizational centralization where formal organizations grow increasingly hierarchical and so become more distant, may reinforce and accelerate organizational avoidance."

26. This contemporary cultural ethos is brilliantly dissected from a socialist perspective by Lasch (1979).

27. Wicker (1988:A27) summarizes Census Bureau findings that between 1967 and 1987, the poorest one-fifth of American families' share of total income decreased from 5.5 percent to 4.6 percent while the next 60 percent dropped from 54.1 percent to 51.7 percent. Fichtenbaum (1988:8) recalls that "in 1973 real average weekly wages were $198.35 measured in 1977 dollars, but by 1988 real median weekly wages declined to $168.75 — a 15% drop." And despite the so-called recovery, Serrin's (1989:84) reassessment of Department of Labor figures results in "an unemployment rate of nearly 14 percent, not 5.4 percent, as the B.L.S. would have us believe — and still other jobless people could be added in." These trends are examined at length in Chapter 8. Serrin also notes that "about two-thirds of the jobless are not currently receiving unemployment benefits."

28. According ("Determine," 1988:2) to "a May 1987 Gallup poll, the top three priorities for which people wanted to spend their tax dollars were: public elementary and secondary schools, medical research, and pollution and environmental control. Fewer Americans are measuring strength in terms of military might alone. A fall 1987 poll for the World Policy Institute found a 3-to-1 majority agreeing that economic power is more important than military power in determining a country's influence. And a recent report on Southern swing voters reflected their hope that the next President would turn his attention to making American industries and workers more productive and competitive."

Similarly, Nye (1988:122–23) reports that "a *Newsweek* poll published on February 22, 1988, showed economic nationalism rising in the United States, with one-half of the respondents favoring trade barriers to reduce the flow of foreign products into the country. In fact, protectionism in America is on the rise; the percentage of U.S. imports that are protected rose from 8 per cent in 1975 to 21 per cent in 1985."

29. The same may apply to increased electoral participation by the largely non-voting lower socio-economic mass sectors. Navarro (1985:43–44) calls attention to the deplorable fact that "the United States has the highest abstention rate in the Western world; 50 million eligible citizens did not register in 1984 and 35 million of those who registered did not vote. Of these 85 million nonvoters, 46 percent consider themselves independent, 80 percent are white, 83 percent have a high school education or less, 72 percent are between the ages of 18 and 44, 50 percent are between the ages of 18 and 29, and 32 percent live in the South. Another characteristic of U.S. politics is that the working class votes less than the other classes. In 1980, 77 percent of white-collar professionals voted, compared with only 44 percent of blue-collar workers. This class abstentionism hurts the Democrats more than the Republicans. Its importance appears clearly when one considers that in 1984, if Blacks and Hispanics with only a high school education or less and the unemployed had voted in the same percentages as those who earn more than $25,000, Mondale would have won." The same could have been said for 1988 when these patterns intensified in a context of even higher overall abstention rates.

30. Ideally with a southern style and background, the only long term prospect, who ironically has a successful record as the Texas Agriculture Commissioner and is forging a progressive populist coalition within the Democratic Party, is Jim Hightower. See Denison (1989).

31. The two most likely types of crisis are an Israeli-Arab conflagration or an unexpected financial collapse in the United States. MacEwan (1989:6) notes that Reagan reversed neither the continued decline in GNP growth (4.7 percent in the 1960s, 2.8 percent in the 1970s, 2.5 percent in the 1980s), nor the drop in expenditure on new plants and equipment (11.4 percent of GNP in 1979–1981 compared to 10.2 percent for 1985–1987). Even worse in this context, not only has non-financial sector debt risen "from 142% of GNP in 1980 to 185% in 1987," but there has been "a huge and persistent foreign trade deficit and a large increase in foreign debt. The trade deficit reached an all time high of $160 million in 1987, and was only slightly lower in 1988. At the end of 1987, net U.S. foreign debt (the difference between the value of U.S.-owned assets abroad and foreign-owned assets in the United States) stood at over $400 billion."

Bibliography

Abelda, Randy, and Cynthia Manse, 1988. "Can We Talk Tax?" *Dollars & Sense*, October, pp. 9–11.

Afheldt, Horst, 1988. "New Policies, Old Fears." *Bulletin of Atomic Scientists*, September, pp. 24–27.

Agee, Philip, 1975. *Inside the Company: CIA Diary*. New York: Bantam Books.

Agrell, Wilhelm, 1984. "Small but Not Beautiful." *Journal of Peace Research* 21, no. 2, pp. 157–67.

"Aid to El Salvador," 1982. *America*, 146 (February 13), p. 105.

Albee, George W., 1985. "The Answer Is Prevention." *Psychology Today*, February, pp. 60–64.

Albrecht, Ulrich, 1983. "Soviet Arms Exports." *World Armaments and Disarmament: SIPRI Yearbook, 1983*. New York: Taylor & Francis. Pp. 361–69.

_____, Peter Lock and Herbert Wulf, 1974. "Armaments and Underdevelopment." *Bulletin of Peace Proposals*, (V): 173–85.

Aldridge, Robert, 1983. *First Strike*. Boston: South End Press.

_____, 1986. "Is U.S. In a Launch on Warning Position Now?" *Peace Research Reviews*.

Alger, Chadwick F., 1989. "A Grassroots Approach to Life in Peace." *Peace Review*, Summer, pp. 5–10.

Ambrose, Stephen E., 1984. "Even Ike Knew Better." *Mother Jones*, November, pp. 49–50.

"America Becomes Less Equal," 1985. *The New Republic*, February 28, p. 7.

Amnesty International, 1981. *Amnesty International Report: 1981*. London: Amnesty International Publications.

_____, 1982. *Amnesty International Report: 1982*. London: Amnesty International Publications.

Amott, Teresa, 1988. "Economy in Review: The 6% Solution." *Dollars & Sense*, November, pp. 6–8, 24.

_____, 1989. "War of Attrition: Long Applications Keep Welfare Lines Short." *Dollars & Sense*, January-February, pp. 20–21.

Anthony, Jan, 1989. "The Trade in Major Conventional Weapons." *SIPRI Yearbook 1989: World Armaments and Disarmament*. London: Oxford University Press. Pp. 195–225.

"Anti-Bases Campaigns Move Ahead," 1988. *Disarmament Campaigns*, September/October, pp. 2–3.

"The Anti-Sleaze Crusade," 1990. *U.S. News & World Report*, February 19, p. 22.

Arkin, William M., and Richard W. Fieldhouse, 1985. "Focus on the Nuclear Infrastructure." *Bulletin of the Atomic Scientists*, June/July, pp. 11–15.

Arlinghaus, Bruce E., 1983. "Arms Transfers to Africa in the 1980s." In *Arms for Africa: Military Assistance and Foreign Policy in the Developing World*. Ed. by Bruce E. Arlinghaus. Lexington MA: D.C. Heath. Pp. 223–27.

Aronson, Geoffrey, 1985. "Reagan's Arms Bazaar Style Leaves Mid-East Policy in Chaos." *In These Times,* October 2–8, p. 9.

Auerbach, Stuart, 1990. "U.S. Prods Jakorta on AT&T." *International Herald Tribune,* February 15, p. 15.

Babst, Dean, 1988. "Push Button Warfare." *Nuclear Alert,* Fall, p. 1. [Nuclear Age Peace Foundation, Santa Barbara CA.]

Bagley, Bruce Michael, 1989–90. "Dateline Drug Wars: Colombia—The Wrong Strategy." *Foreign Policy,* no. 77 (Winter), pp. 154–71.

Ball, Nicole, 1988. *Security and Economy in the Third World.* Princeton NJ: Princeton University Press.

————, and Milton Leitenbert, 1979. "The Foreign Arms Sales of the Carter Administration." *Bulletin of Atomic Scientists,* February 1979, pp. 31–36.

Barden, J.C., 1990. "In U.S., a Half Million More Youths on the Run Each Year." *International Herald Tribune,* February 6, p. 3.

Barnet, Richard J., 1983. *The Alliance: America, Europe, Japan.* New York: Simon & Schuster.

————, 1981. *Real Security.* New York: Simon & Schuster.

————, and Ronald Muller, 1974. *Global Reach: The Power of Multinational Corporations.* New York: Simon & Schuster.

Barnett, A. Doak, 1990. "Bush Is Right to Keep Lines Open to China." *International Herald Tribune,* January 23, p. 4.

Barron, James, 1983. "Grumman's Navy Quandary." *New York Times,* June 1, pp. D1, 4.

Barsky, Arthur J., 1989. "Health Myths, and Realities." *Privileged Information,* January 1, pp. 3–4.

Batra, Ravi, 1988. *The Great Depression of 1990.* New York: Dell [1987].

Bauer, P.T., 1984. *Reality and Rhetoric: Studies in the Economics of Development.* London: Weidenfeld and Nicolson.

Beck, Joan, 1988. "Americans Can Fly to Moon, but Earth Still Mystery." *Watertown Daily Times Sunday Weekly,* August 7.

Becker, Abraham S., 1984. *Economic Leverage on the Soviet Union in the 1980s.* Santa Monica CA: Rand Corp. R-3127-USDP.

Bellah, Robert, Richard Madsen, William Sullivan, Ann Swidler, and Steven Tipton, 1985. *Habits of the Heart.* Berkeley: University of California Press.

Bellant, Russ, 1988. *Old Nazis, the New Right and the Reagan Administration: The Role of Domestic Fascist Networks in the Republican Party and Their Effect on U.S. Cold War Politics.* Cambridge MA: Political Research Associates.

Bello, Walden, 1988. "U.S.-Philippine Relations in the Aquino Era." *World Policy* 5, no. 4 (Fall), pp. 677–702.

————, and Peter Hayes, 1983. "Tensions in the North Pacific." *The Nation* 237, no. 9 (October 1), pp. 274–76.

Bennett, Jonathan, 1985. "Chemical Carnage Gets Green Light from OSHA." *Guardian,* January 16, pp. 3, 9.

Bensky, Larry, 1988. "The Morning After." *The Nation,* August 13/20, pp. 135–37.

Berman, Daniel, 1988. "Occupational Health and Safety and the Permanent War Economy." *IPRA Newsletter,* April/July, pp. 19–21.

"Better Health Per Dollar," 1988. *International Herald Tribune,* November 24, p. 4.

Betts, Richard K., 1980. "The Tragicomedy of Arms Trade Control." *International Security* 5, no. 1 (Summer), pp. 80–110.

Bird, Kai, and Max Holland, 1985. "Capitol Letter: The Profits of Spying." *The Nation,* December 14, p. 640.

_____, and _____, 1985a. "Dispatches." *The Nation,* October 26, pp. 400–01.

Birnbaum, Norman, 1985. "Europeanization of Europe." *Bulletin of the Atomic Scientists,* January, pp. 20–21.

_____, 1985a. "Herr Kohl Meets His Watergate." *The Nation,* January 12, pp. 9–12.

Black, George, and Robert Matthews, 1985. "Arms from the U.S.S.R.—Or From Nobody." *The Nation,* August 31, pp. 129, 148–49.

Black, Jan Knippers, 1987. "Central America: The Larger Scandal." *Cross Currents,* Summer/Fall, pp. 287–302.

"Black Market Sales Rise in Arms Stolen from U.S. Military Bases." *New York Times,* September 29, pp. 1, 30.

Blaylock, Kenneth, 1988. "Trade Union Rights at Home and Abroad." *LRA's Economic Notes,* January-February, pp. 10–12.

Blumenthal, Sidney, 1987/1988. "Dateline Washington: The Conservative Crackup." *Foreign Policy,* no. 69 (Winter), pp. 166–87.

Bodenheimer, Thomas, and Robert Gould, 1988. *Rollback: Rightwing Power in American Foreign Policy.* Boston: South End Press.

Böge, Volker, Peter Wilke, and Herbert Wulf, 1984. "How to Stop the Arms Race: A Proposal for Independent Steps Toward a New European Peace Order." Falkenstein, Hamburg, FRG: Institute for Peace Research and Security Policy of the University of Hamburg.

Borosage, Robert L., 1976. "The Central Intelligence Agency: The King's Men and the Constitutional Order." In *The C.I.A. File.* Ed. by Robert L. Borosage and John Marks. New York: Viking/Grossman. Pp. 125–41.

Bowman, Robert M., 1985. *Star Wars: Defense Or Death Star?* Chesapeake Beach MD: Institute for Space and Security Studies.

_____, 1987. "The Smoking Gun Is on Videotape." *Space and Security News,* December, p. 1.

_____, 1987a. "What's Really Behind SDI?" *Space and Security News,* December, p. 15.

Bowman, Robert M., Lt. Col., 1988. "Everything You Always Wanted to Know About 'Star Wars': THE TRUTH." *Space and Security News,* June, pp. 8–16, 25–33.

_____, 1988a. "The Myth of Soviet Conventional Superiority." *Space and Security News,* June, p. 6.

_____, 1989. "Bush Era Begins." *Space and Security News,* January, p. 1.

"The Brave New World of Stealth Warfare," 1988. *U.S. News and World Report,* November 28, pp. 20–28.

Brennan, Hope, and Meg Dooley, 1988. "Where Have All the Nurses Gone?" *Columbia,* December, pp. 14–19.

Brevetti, Vincent, 1983. "The Political Economy of U.S. Intervention in El Salvador." *New Political Science* 11 (Spring), pp. 85–98.

"Briefing: Global Storm Clouds Menace Recovery," 1983. *In These Times,* August 24–September 6, p. 5.

Brinkley, Joel, 1988. "Shamir Denounces U.S. Acceptance of PLO As 'Blunder.'" *International Herald Tribune,* December 16, pp. 1, 6.

Broder, David S., 1990. "Democracy: While Others Learn It, America Needs to Repair It." *International Herald Tribune,* January 3, p. 4.

Brogan, Patrick, and Albert Zarca, 1983. *Deadly Business: Sam Cummings, Interarms, and the Arms Trade.* New York: Norton.

Brown, Dee, 1972. *Bury My Heart at Wounded Knee.* New York: Bantam.

Brown, Richard Maxwell, 1989. "Historical Patterns of Violence." In *Violence in*

America: Protest, Rebellion, Reform. Vol. 2. Ed. by Ted Robert Gurr. Newbury Park: Sage. Pp. 23–61.

Brown, Robert McAfee (Rev. Dr.), 1988. Balfour Brickner (Rabbi) and Rosemary Radford Ruether (Dr.). "Letter." New York: Witness for Peace.

Bruck, Connie, 1988. *The Predators' Ball: The Junk Bond Raiders and the Man Who Staked Them.* New York: Simon & Schuster.

Brzoska, Michael, 1981. "The Reporting of Military Expenditures." *Journal of Peace Research* **18**, no. 3, pp. 261–76.

————, 1989. "The Impact of Arms Production in the Third World." *Armed Forced & Society* **15**, no. 4 (Summer), pp. 507–30.

Buchan, David, 1984. "Technology: The Soviets' Civilian Advances." *World Press Review*, December, p. 49. Reprinted from the *Financial Times* of London.

Buckley, James L., 1981. "Arms Transfer and the National Interest." *Department of State Bulletin* **81** (July), pp. 51–53.

————, 1982. "Proposed Sale of Aircraft to Venezuela." *Department of State Bulletin* **82**, no. 206 (April), pp. 84–85.

Buckley, Kevin P., 1990. "Noriega: The Makings of an Interesting Interview." *International Herald Tribune*, January 2, p. 4.

Burkholder, Steve, 1988. "Red Squash on the Prowl." *The Progressive,* October, pp. 18–22.

"Bush Cautions on Arms Cuts," 1990. *International Herald Tribune,* February 7, p. 1.

"Business: The Man in the Middle," 1988. *U.S. News and World Report,* December 12, pp. 67–69.

"Call to All Americans Who Love Their Country," 1985. *In These Times,* November 6–12, p. 12.

Campos Harriet, Fernando, 1963. *Historia Constitucional de Chile.* 3d ed. Santiago: Edi. Juridica de Chile.

Cannizzo, Cindy, 1980. *The Gun Merchants: Politics and Policies of the Major Arms Suppliers.* New York: Pergamon.

Cassen, R.H., ed., 1985. *Soviet Interests in the Third World.* Beverly Hills CA: Sage.

"Catching Up with the Polls," 1988. *The Bottom Line* [NYSUT], November 25, p. 2.

Cavanagh, John, 1983. "Whisky Barons Smuggle Arms to South Africa." *Counterspy* **7**, no. 4 (June–August), pp. 50–54, 59.

Cepeda, Susanna, and Ed Glennon, 1983. "The New Budget: Reaganomics Continued." *Sane World,* March, pp. 1–4.

Chamorro, Edgar, 1987. *Packaging the Contras.* New York: Institute for Media Analysis.

Chase, James, 1988. "Philippines: The Tangle Is Growing." *International Herald Tribune,* December 16, p. 4.

Chase, Randell D., 1985. "A Study of the Social Origins of a United States Military Elite: The U.S. Army." M.A. Thesis Findings presented to Northeast Regional Meeting of the Inter-University Seminar on Armed Forces and Society, April 13, SUNY-Albany.

Chicago Tribune, 1983. "Soviets Use Arms for Influence." *The Watertown Times,* NY, August 6, p. 4.

"Child Poverty: Nation Is Lost Among Equals," 1988/89. *On Campus,* December/ January, p. 4.

Chilton, Paul, 1986. "Nukespeak: Nuclear Language, Culture, and Propaganda." In *The Nuclear Predicament.* Ed. by Donna Uthus Gregory. New York: St. Martin's. Pp. 127–42.

Chomsky, Noam, 1985. "Intervention in Vietnam and Central America: Parallels and

Differences." Transcribed speech, March 19, for the Harvard/Radcliffe Committee on Central America and the Central America Solidarity Association.

_____, 1985a. "Cyprus: A Potential Cuba of the Mediterranean?" *In These Times,* January 9–16, p. 19.

_____, 1987. *The Culture of Terrorism.* Boston: South End Press.

_____, 1988. "The Palestinian Uprising: A Turning Point?" *Scandinavian Journal of Development Alternatives* 7, no. 4 (December), pp. 5–28.

_____, and Edward Herman, 1979. *The Washington Connection and Third World Fascism.* Boston: South End Press.

Churchill, Ward, and James Van der Wall, 1988. *Agents of Repression: The FBI's Secret War Against the American Indian Movement and the Black Panther Party.* Boston: South End Press.

"CIA Says Growth Rate of Soviet Military Spending Down," 1985. *New World Review,* January-February, p. 7.

Clark, James, 1984. "International Education: A Time for Concerted Action." *International Programs Quarterly* 1, no. 1 (Fall), pp. 12–16.

Cloward, Richard A., and Frances Fox Piven, 1985. "The Registration Strategy—I: Trying to Break Down the Barriers." *The Nation,* November 2, pp. 433–37.

"CMEA and the Arab Countries," 1985. *Update USSR,* August, p. 2.

Cobban, Helena, 1988. "Israel's Nuclear Game." *World Policy Journal* 5, no. 3 (Summer), pp. 415–34.

Cockburn, Alexander, 1985. "Beat the Devil." *The Nation,* August 17/24, pp. 102–03.

_____, 1985a. "Beat the Devil." *The Nation,* September 21, pp. 230–31.

_____, 1988. "Beat the Devil." *The Nation,* March 26, pp. 402–03.

_____, 1988a. "Beat the Devil." *The Nation,* June 18, pp. 852–53.

_____, 1988b. "Beat the Devil." *The Nation,* August 13/20, pp. 120–21.

_____, 1988c. "Beat the Devil." *The Nation,* September 26, pp. 226–27.

Cockburn, Andrew, 1983. *The Threat: Inside the Soviet Military Machine.* New York: Random House.

Cockburn, Leslie, 1988. *Out of Control.* New York: Atlantic Monthly Press.

Coffin, Tristram, 1983a. "The Not-So-Secret War in Central America." *The Washington Spectator,* March 15, pp. 1–3.

_____, 1983b. "Notes from an Editor's Desk Drawer." *The Washington Spectator,* June 15, p. 4.

_____, 1983c. "The Noise Outside the Window." *The Washington Spectator,* August 1, p. 1.

_____, 1985. "Sparks from Capitol Hill." *The Washington Spectator,* August 15, p. 4.

_____, 1985a. "What About Tax Reform." *The Washington Spectator,* August 15, pp. 1–3.

_____, 1985b. "Pentagon Fraud, a Safe Game." *The Washington Spectator,* December 1, p. 2.

_____, 1987. "Reagan's Constitutional Crisis." *The Washington Spectator,* August, pp. 1–4.

_____, 1988. "A Spreading Drug Epidemic." *The Washington Spectator,* August 1, pp. 1–3.

_____, 1988a. "The High Cost of Health." *The Washington Spectator,* April 15, pp. 1–4.

_____, 1988b. "The Issues That Count." *The Washington Spectator,* July 1, pp. 1–3.

_____, 1988c. "Time to Pay the Piper." *The Washington Spectator,* January 1, p. 3.

————, 1988d. "The Job Ahead." *The Washington Spectator,* March 1, pp. 1–4.

————, 1990. "Converting the Bomb Factories." *The Washington Spectator,* February 1, pp. 1–3.

————, 1990a. "FYI, Items of Interest from Spectator Files." *The Washington Spectator,* February 1, p. 4.

Cohen, Stephen F., 1983. "Sovieticus." *The Nation* **237,** no. 7 (September 17), pp. 200.

————, 1985. *Rethinking the Soviet Experience: Politics & History Since 1917,* New York: Oxford University Press.

————, 1985a. "Sovieticus." *The Nation,* October 12, p. 335.

————, 1986. *Sovieticus: American Perceptions and Soviet Realities.* New York: Norton.

————, 1988. "Will We End the Cold War? The Next President's Historic Opportunity." *The Nation,* October 10, pp. 293, 306–14.

Cohen, William S., and George J. Mitchell, 1988. *Men of Zeal.* New York: Viking.

Coleman, Daniel, 1985. "Clues to Suicide: A Brain Chemical Is Implicated." *New York Times,* October 8, pp. C1, 7.

Colwell, Mary Anna, 1988. "Characteristics of Peace Movement Organizations Citing Promotion of Social Justice in the United States and Worldwide as a Major and Important Good." Paper presented to the 17th annual COPRED Conference, October 16–19, at Manhattan College, Bronx NY.

Committee Against Government Waste, 1985. "Official Military Parts Price List." (Washington DC, 499 S. Capitol St., S.W., Suite 102.)

"Commodities and Manufacturers: What the Long Run Shows About Their Trade." *Research News* [World Bank], June, p. 1.

"Conservatives Urge Bush to Take Lead on Homeless," 1988. *International Herald Tribune,* December 16, p. 3.

"Conventional Arms Transfers in the Third World, 1972–81," 1982. *Department of State Bulletin* **82** (October), pp. 51–64.

Conyers, John, and Frank Collins, 1983. "Launch First, Ask Questions Later." *In These Times,* August 10–23, p. 16.

Cook, Mark, 1985. "Reagan's War on Trial in World Court." *The Guardian,* October 2, p. 15.

Cooling, Benjamin Franklin, 1977. *War Business and American Society: Historical Perspectives on the Military Industrial Complex.* Port Washington NY: Kennikat.

Cooper, Gloria, 1988. "Briefings: The Great American Flood." [Review of *Leaking: Who Does It? Who Benefits? At What Costs?* By Elie Abel. New York: Twentieth Century Fund, 1987.] *Columbia Journalism Review,* March/April, pp. 59–60.

Corn, David, 1988. "The Same Old Dirty Tricks." *The Nation,* August 27/September 3, pp. 157–60.

————, and Jefferson Morley, 1988. "Beltway Bandits." *The Nation,* January, p. 851.

————, and ————. "Beltway Bandits: The Case of the Bugged Senator." *The Nation,* February 6, p. 152.

"Corporations and Unions," 1984. *Economic Notes,* September, pp. 12–13.

Cortright, David, 1975. *Soldiers in Revolt.* Garden City NY: Anchor/Doubleday.

Costanza, Robert, 1984. "Nuclear War and the Theory of Social Traps." *Journal of Peace Research* **21,** no. 1, pp. 79–86.

D'Amato, Alfonse M., 1984. "Letter to Constituents: Dear Fellow New Yorker." Washington: U.S. Senate.

Dammerell, Reginald G., 1985. *Education's Smoking Gun.* New York: Freundlich.

Dankbaar, Ben, 1984. "Alternative Defense Policies and the Peace Movement." *Journal of Peace Research* **21,** no. 2, pp. 141–55.

Day, Adrian, 1988. "A Blueprint for Building Your Portfolio." *Adrian Day's Investment Analyst*, March, pp. 1–7.

DeBenedetti, Charles, 1983. "A CIA Analysis of the Anti-Vietnam War Movement: October 1967." *Peace and Change* 9, no. 1 (Spring), pp. 31–42.

DeCormis, Anna, 1983. "World Debt Crisis." *Guardian*, August 10, p. 21.

DeGrasse, Robert W., 1983. *Military Expansion, Economic Decline*. New York: Council on Economic Priorities.

————, with Paul Murphy and William Ragen, 1982. *The Costs and Consequences of Reagan's Military Build-Up*. New York: Council on Economic Priorities.

Dellums, Ronald V., 1983. "Unconscionable Costs." *Democratic Left* 11, no. 1 (January), pp. 3–4.

Denison, Dave, 1989. "Jim Hightower Interviewed." *In These Times*, February 15–21, pp. 12–13.

"Determine Your Priorities," 1988. *Peace Links Connection*, Spring, pp. 1–2.

Dickinson, Torry, and Robert Schaeffer, 1988. "Stretched Out: An Overreaching Military Contributes to America's Decline as a Great Power." *Nuclear Times*, July/August, pp. 25–26.

"Did You Know...?" 1985. *COPRED Peace Chronicle*, August/September, p. 20. Source: *International Fellowship of Reconciliation Report*, July/August 1985.

"Did You Know That," 1988. *Bottom Line Personal*, November 30, p. 9.

————, 1989. *Privileged Information*, January 1, p. 7.

Dinges, John, 1982. "Why We Are in Guatemala." *Inquiry*, November 1982.

Dixon, Marlene, 1983. "The Trojan Horse: Transnational Banks and the International Debt Crisis." *Our Socialism*, 1:3 (May): 6–12.

"Does America Need an Army," 1989. *U.S. News and World Report*, December 11, pp. 22–28.

Domhoff, G. William, 1967. *Who Rules America?* Englewood Cliffs NJ: Prentice Hall.

Donnelly, Kate, 1989. "War Toys Update." *The Nonviolent Activist*, January/February, p. 9.

Donner, Frank J., 1980. *The Age of Surveillance: The Aims and Methods of America's Political Intelligence System*. New York: Alfred A. Knopf.

————, 1985. "The Return of the Red Squads." *The Nation*, October 12, pp. 329, 339–42.

————, 1985a. "Rambo Plays the Capitol." *The Nation*, November 2, pp. 437–40.

Dörfer, Ingemar, 1983. *Arms Deal: The Selling of the F-16*. New York: Praeger.

Dorman, William A., 1985. "Soviets Seen Through Red-Tinted Glasses." *Bulletin of the Atomic Scientists*, February, pp. 18–25.

Dorsen, Norman, ed., 1984. *Our Endangered Rights: The ACLU Report on Civil Liberties Today*. New York: Pantheon.

Draper, Theodore, 1983. *The Present As History*. New York: Random House.

Drinnon, Richard, 1980. *Facing West: The Metaphysics of Indian-Hating and Empire Building*. Minneapolis: University of Minneapolis Press.

Duffy, Thomas M., 1985. "Literacy Instruction in the Military." *Armed Forces and Society* 11, no. 3 (Spring), pp. 437–67.

Dumas, Lloyd, ed., 1982. *The Political Economy of Arms Reduction: Reversing Economic Decay*. Boulder CO: Westview.

Dunn, John M., 1961. "Military Aid and Military Elites: The Political Potential of American Training and Technical Assistance Programs." Unpublished Ph.D. dissertation, Princeton University.

Dye, Thomas, 1983. *Who's Running America? The Reagan Years*. Englewood Cliffs NJ: Prentice Hall.

"Early Warning: Arms," 1988. *World Peace Review,* Nov., p. 4.

Easterbrook, Gregg, 1985. "Political Booknotes: Secret Agenda." *The Washington Monthly,* February, pp. 58–60.

Eberwine, Donna, 1988. "Alternative Security: A Common Space." *Nuclear Times,* May/June, pp. 26–27.

Eckhardt, William, 1975. "Primitive Militarism." *Journal of Peace Research* 12, pp. 55–62. Referred to in "Peace Research Network," *COPRED Chronicle,* July 1984, p. 10.

————, 1977. "Global Imperialism and Global Inequality." Oakville, Ontario: Canadian Peace Research Institute. St. Louis MO: Peace Research Laboratory. Paper presented at University of Denver Conference on "Global Inequality," June 1977.

————, and E. Azar, 1977. "Major World Conflicts and Interventions." Paper presented at the annual meeting of the Peace Science Society (International), Southern Section, Chapel Hill NC, April 1977, and at the annual meeting of the Canadian Peace Research and Education Association, Fredericton NB, June 1977.

————, and C. Young, 1974a. "Psychology of Imperialism." *Journal of Contemporary Revolutions* 6, no. 3, pp. 90–102.

————, and ————, 1974b. "Civil Conflict, Imperialism, and Inequality." *Journal of Contemporary Revolutions* 6, no. 2, pp. 76–95.

————, and ————, 1975a. "Civil Conflict and Imperialism." Paper presented at the annual meeting of the Peace Science Society (International), Northeastern Section, Ottawa.

————, and ————, 1975b. "Primitive Militarism." *Journal of Peace Research* 12, pp. 55–62.

————, and ————, 1977. *Governments Under Fire: Civil Conflict and Imperialism.* New Haven: Human Relations Area Files.

————, 1989. "22 Wars Last, Research Lab Says." *St. Louis Post Dispatch,* January 8.

"Economic Clips," 1984. *Economic Notes,* November, p. 11.

————, 1985. *Economic Notes,* April, pp. 14–15.

————, 1985a. *Economic Notes,* May-June, pp. 14–15.

————, 1988. *LRA's Economic Notes,* January-February, pp. 14–16.

————, 1988a. *LRA's Economic Notes,* March-April, pp. 14–15.

————, 1988b. *LRA's Economic Notes,* July-August, pp. 14–16.

"Economics of Military Spending," 1984. *Economic Notes* 52, no. 9 (September), pp. 8–11.

"The Economy in Numbers," 1984. *Dollars & Sense* 102 (December), p. 10.

"The Economy in Numbers: Adding Up the Tax Breaks," 1988. *Dollars and Sense,* October, p. 23.

"Economy in Review: The 6% Solution," 1988. *Dollars & Sense,* November, pp. 6–8.

Edelman, Murray, 1984. *The Symbolic Uses of Politics.* Urbana: University of Illinois Press.

Edsall, Thomas Byrne, 1989. "Irish Power." *Dissent,* Summer, pp. 403–405.

Ege, Konrad, 1983. "Reagan's 'Misstatements': Fueling the Push for Military Superiority." *Counterspy* 7, no. 4 (June-August), pp. 15–20.

————, 1983a. "Eyewitness Afghanistan." *Counterspy* 8, no. 1 (September-November), pp. 46–58.

Eichner, Klaus, 1990. "The U.S. and the West German Peace Movements of the Eighties: A Comparison." In *Towards a Comparative Analysis of Peace Movements.* Ed. by Katsuya Kodama and Unto Vesa. Brookfield VT: Gower. Pp. 193.

Eisenhower, Dwight D. (Gen.), 1953. Address Before the American Society of Newspaper Editors, April 16, 1953.

Emerson, Stephen, 1988. *Secret Warriors: Inside the Covert Military Operations of the Reagan Era.* New York: Putnam.

Emery, Richard, 1985. "Curbing New York's Police." *New York Times,* May 7, p. A31.

Etzioni, Amitai, 1984. *Capital Corruption: The New Attack Upon American Democracy.* New York: Harcourt, Brace, Jovanovich.

———, 1988. "More Injustice for the Poor." *The Nation,* October 10, pp. 304–06.

Evangelauf, Jean, 1985. "Enrollment in Remedial Courses Jumps at 63 Percent of Colleges That Offer Them." *The Chronicle of Higher Education,* February 13, p. 3.

Evans, David, 1984. "A Runaway Pentagon." *New York Times,* October 3.

Evans, Rowland, and Robert Novak, 1983. "Schultz Clears Way for Israel to Develop New Jet Fighter." *New York Post,* May 16, p. 31.

Eveland, William Crane, 1980. *Ropes of Sand: America's Failure in the Middle East.* New York: Norton.

Everest, Larry, 1988. "The Gulf Between Pretense and Reality." *In These Times,* July 20-August, pp. 8–9.

Exposing the Shadow Government: A Declaration of Evidence by the Christic Institute. Washington DC: The Christic Institute.

Fagen, Richard R., 1979. *Capitalism and the State in U.S.-Latin American Relations.* Stanford: Stanford University Press.

Falk, Richard, 1980. *A World Order Perspective on Authoritarian Tendencies.* New York: World Policy Institute.

———, 1984. "Nuclear Weapons and the End of Democracy." In *Toward Nuclear Disarmament and Global Security.* Ed. by Burns H. Weston. Boulder CO: Westview. Pp. 194–204.

———, 1988. *Revolutionaries and Functionaries: The Dual Face of Terrorism.* New York: Dutton.

Fallows, James, 1981. *National Defense.* New York: Random House.

Farris, Fred, 1988. "Gorbachev Pledges to Trim Forces by 500,000 Men and 10,000 Tanks." *International Herald Tribune,* December 8, pp. 1, 6.

Feffer, John, 1988. "Policy for People." *Nuclear Times,* May/June, p. 28.

Feldman, Jonathan, 1988. *Universities in the Business of Repression: The Academic-Industrial-Military Complex and Central America.* Boston: South End Press.

Ferguson, Thomas, and Joel Rogers, 1985. "Labor Day, 1985." *The Nation,* September 1985, pp. 164–65.

Fichtenbaum, Rudy, 1988. "Family Income and Expenses." *Economic Notes,* November-December, pp. 8–10.

Fischer, Dietrich, 1982. "Invulnerability Without Threat: The Swiss Concept of General Defense." *Journal of Peace Research* **19,** no. 3, pp. 205–25. Also reprinted in *Toward Nuclear Disarmament and Global Security: A Search for Alternatives,* Ed. by Burns H. Weston. Boulder CO: Westview, 1984. Pp. 504–32.

———, 1984. *Preventing War in the Nuclear Age.* Totowa NJ: Rowman & Allanheld.

Fitch, J. Samuel, 1985. "The Garrison State in America: A Content Analysis of Trends in the Expectation of Violence." *Journal of Peace Research* **22,** no. 1, pp. 31–45.

Fitchett, Joseph, 1988. "National Security Gives Protectionists a Weapon." *International Herald Tribune,* December 16, pp. 1, 14.

———, 1990. "Experts Say Closure of Bases Will Not Harm U.S. Efficiency." *International Herald Tribune,* January 30, p. 8.

Fitzgerald, Frances, 1980. *America Revised.* New York: Random/Vintage.

Fleming, D.F., 1961. *The Cold War and Its Origins.* Vols. 1, 2. Garden City NY: Doubleday.

Flynn, Gregory, 1983. "Public Opinion and Atlantic Defense." *NATO Review* **31**, no. 5, pp. 4–11.

"Following in Boxo's Footsteps," 1988. *In These Times,* September 21–27, p. 5.

Forman, Alex, 1985. "Disinformation as an Accepted Way of Life." *In These Times,* November 6–12, p. 11.

Forsberg, Randall, 1983. "A Nuclear Freeze and a Noninterventionist Conventional Policy." In *Education for Peace and Disarmament.* Ed. by Douglas Sloan. New York: Teachers College Press.

———, 1984. "Confining the Military to Defense as a Route to Disarmament." *World Policy Journal* **1**, no. 2 (Winter), pp. 285–318.

———, 1988. "Toward a Nonaggressive World." *Bulletin of the Atomic Scientists,* September, pp. 49–54.

Frank, Andre Gunder, 1969. *Latin America: Underdevelopment or Revolution?* New York: Monthly Review.

Friends Committee on National Legislation, 1988. "Figures." Spring, p. 3.

Furniss, Edgar S., Jr., 1957. *Some Perspectives on American Military Assistance.* Princeton NJ: Princeton University Press.

Galbraith, J.K., 1988. "Morning Report: Interview." Washington: NPR.

Gans, Curtis, 1988. Review of *Why Americans Don't Vote* [By Frances Fox Piven, Richard A. Cloward. Pantheon]. *The Washington Spectator,* October, pp. 54, 56.

Gansler, Jacques, 1980. *The Defense Industry.* Cambridge MA: MIT Press.

Gardner, Lloyd C., 1964. *Economic Aspects of New Deal Diplomacy.* Madison WI: University of Wisconsin Press.

Garten, Jeffrey, 1990. "Japan: The Friction with America Has Only Begun." *International Herald Tribune,* January 31, p. 6.

Gastil, Raymond F., 1981. *Freedom in the World: Political Rights and Civil Liberties: 1981.* Westport CT: Greenwood.

Gates, John M., 1985. "The 'New' Military Professionalism. *Armed Forces & Society* **11**, no. 3 (Spring), pp. 427–36.

Gauhar, Altaf, 1982. "The Cost of a Soldier." *South* **21**, (July), pp. 8–14.

"Geography Lessons, Where Are You?" 1985. *On Campus* (American Federation of Teachers), March.

George, Nina, 1985. "Suffer Little Children, To Come Unto Impoverishment." *The Guardian,* August 21, p. 8.

George, Susan, 1984. *Ill Fares the Land: Essays on Food, Hunger and Power.* Washington: Institute for Policy Studies.

Geras, N., 1983. *Marx and Human Nature: Refutation of a Legend.* London. As quoted in Miliband (1985:29).

Gerth, Jeff, 1985. "U.S. Weapons Makers Ring Up Healthy Profits." *New York Times,* April 9, pp. D1, 13.

Gibson, James William, 1988. *The Perfect War: The War We Couldn't Lose and How We Did.* New York: Vintage.

Gilmour, Robert S., and Robert B. Lamb, 1975. *Political Alienation in Contemporary America.* New York: St. Martin's.

Glasser, Ira, [1985]. "Letter." New York: ACLU.

Gleditsch, Nils Petter, 1987. "The Local Impact of Reduced Military Spending: A Case Study of Norway." In *Forum International* **11** (World Congress of Sociology: The Military). Ed. by Jurgen Kuhlmann. Vol. 7. Munich.

———, 1989. "The Rise and Decline of the New Peace Movement." In *Towards a Comparative Analysis of Peace Movements.* Ed. by Katsuya Kodama and Unto Veso. UK: Dartmouth and Tampere; Finland: TAPRI. Pp. 73–88.

Glick, Brian, 1988. *The War at Home: A Counter-Insurgency Manual for U.S. Activists.* Boston: South End Press.

Gliksman, Alex, 1981. "Trends in American Arms Transfers." *National Defense* **352**, no. 4 (October), pp. 34–39, 81.

Goldblatt, Jozef, 1989. "Nuclear Non-Proliferation: A Balance Sheet of Conflicting Trends." *Bulletin of Peace Proposals* **20**, no. 4 (Fall), pp. 369–88.

Gorbachev, Michael, 1987. *Perestroika.* New York: Harper & Row.

Gordon, David M., 1985. "Four More Years — A Look Ahead." *The Nation,* January 26, pp. 79–84.

Gordon, Suzanne, and Dave McFadden, 1984. *Economic Conversion: Revitalizing America's Economy.* Boston: Ballinger.

Green, Mark, 1989. "Progressive Values for America." *The Nation,* January 30, pp. 109, 117–18, 122, 124–26.

————, and John F. Berry, 1985. "White-Collar Crime Is Big Business." *The Nation,* June 8, 1985, pp. 689, 704–07.

Greenberg, Stanley B., 1988. "The '88 Election: The Struggle for a Democratic Vision." *World Policy Journal* **5**, no. 3 (Summer), pp. 543–65.

Greider, William, 1988. *Secrets of the Temple: How the Federal Reserve Runs the Country.* New York: Simon & Schuster.

————, 1988a. "The Money Question." *World Policy Journal* **5**, no. 4 (Fall), pp. 567–614.

Greve, Frank, and Ellen Warren, 1984. "Secret Army Unit Allegedly Flies in Latin America." *The Philadelphia Inquirer,* December 16, p. 1.

Guyot, Erik, 1985. "Marcos Blusters While Cronies Hedge Their Bets." *Guardian,* August 21, pp. 19, 21.

Gwirtzman, Milton, 1985. "Conservatives Are Not Heard?" *New York Times,* March 15, p. A27.

Haile-Mariam, Jacob and Bernhanu Mingistu, 1988. "Public Enterprise and the Privatisation Thesis in the Third World." *Third World Quarterly* **10**, no. 4 (October), pp. 1565–87.

Halliday, Fred, 1983. *The Making of the Second Cold War.* Washington DC: Institute for Policy Studies.

————, 1985. "Managing the News in the East and West." *In These Times,* October, p. 17.

Halloran, Richard, 1983. "Aide Acknowledges Waste in Pentagon Spending." *New York Times,* July 13, p. A13.

Hammond, Paul Y., David J. Louscher, Michael D. Salomone, Norman A. Graham, 1983. *The Reluctant Supplier: U.S. Decision-Making for Arms Sales.* Cambridge MA: Oelgeschlager, Gunn & Hain.

Hanhardt, Arthur M., 1984. "The Prospects for a German-German Detente." *Current History* **83** (November), pp. 380–83 + .

Hansen, Fay, 1984. "International Labor: Trends in Foreign Investment." *Economic Notes,* November, pp. 9–10.

Harrington, Michael, and Mark Levinson, 1985. "Are We Two Nations? The Perils of a Dual Economy." *Dissent,* Fall, pp. 417–26.

Harris, Fred R., and Roger W. Wilkins, eds., 1988. *Quiet Riots: Race and Poverty in the United States.* New York: Pantheon.

Harrison, Selig S., 1981/82. "Fanning Flames in South Asia." *Foreign Policy,* no. 45 (Winter), pp. 84–102.

Hartcher, Peter, 1988. "Guess Who's Carrying a Bigger Stick? An Invisible Military Giant Is Growing." *World Press Review,* July, pp. 20–22.

Hartley, Keith, 1983. *NATO Arms Cooperation: A Study in Economics and Politics.* Winchester MA: Allen & Unwin.

Hartman, Chester W., 1985. "The Frightening Reality." *The New York Times,* November 19, p. A34.

Hartung, William, and Rose Nimroody, 1985. "Cutting Up the Star Wars Pie." *The Nation,* September, pp. 200–02.

Hawkins, Beth, 1988. "Former U.S. Envoy Charges Inaction on Crimes." *The Tico Times* [San Jose], April 8, p. 5.

Healey, Richard, 1988. "Research & Analysis: Melted Freeze." *Nuclear Times,* November-December, p. 23.

Health Care—Why the Crisis?" 1989. *The Plain Truth,* March, pp. 3–6.

Hechinger, Fred M., 1985. "Schools and the War on Poverty." *New York Times,* April 23, p. C10.

Heilbroner, Robert, 1985. "The State and Capitalism." *Dissent,* Fall, pp. 438–42.

Hempel, Bill, and Susan Tiffany, 1989. "The Secret of Living Well Within Your Means." *Privileged Information,* January 15, pp. 1–2.

Henwood, Doug, 1989. "The Austerity Agenda: Have We Really Been Binging?" *The Nation,* January 9/16, pp. 43–44.

Henze, Paul B., 1985. *Communist Ethiopia—Is It Succeeding?* Santa Monica CA: Rand Corporation, p. 7054.

Herman, Edward, 1982. *The Real Terror Network.* Boston: South End Press.

———, and Frank Brodhead, 1984. *Demonstration Elections: U.S. Staged Elections in the Dominican Republic, Vietnam and El Salvador.* Boston: South End Press.

Hersh, Seymour M., 1983. *The Price of Power: Kissinger in the Nixon White House.* New York: Simon & Schuster.

Hershey, Robert H., Jr., 1988. "F.S.L.I.C.'s Need Put at $50 Billion." *New York Times,* August 4, p. D1.

Hertsgaard, Mark, 1985. "Political Machines." *Columbia Journalism Review,* January-February, pp. 47–51.

Hightower, Jim, 1989. "Raising Issues, Hope and Hell." *The Nation,* February 6, pp. 160–64.

Hill, Norman, 1988. "The Loss of Jobs and the Rise of the Underclass." *American Educator,* Summer, pp. 16–19.

Hilts, Philip J., 1988. "U.S. Life Expectancies Vary." *International Herald Tribune,* December 16, p. 3.

———, 1990. "Backward on Bath Control." *International Herald Tribune,* February 16, p. 3.

Hitchens, Christopher, 1983. "Minority Report." *The Nation,* September 24, p. 230.

———, 1984. "Minority Report." *The Nation,* January 19, p. 38.

———, 1988. "Minority Report." *The Nation,* September 19, p. 192.

Hoffman, Carl, 1985. "Playing Soldier: ROTC Goes to High School." *The Progressive,* September, pp. 27–28.

Hoffman, Erik P., and Robin F. Laird, 1982. *The Scientific-Technological Revolution and Soviet Foreign Policy.* New York: Pergamon.

Hofstadter, Richard, 1965. *The Paranoid Style in American Politics.* New York: Alfred A. Knopf.

Hoivik, Tord, 1979. "The Demography of Structural Violence." Oslo: PRIO.

Hoopes, Townsend, 1988. "A Golden Chance to Reduce Arms in Europe." *New York Times,* September 2, p. A27.

Horn, Patricia, 1989. "Measure for Measure: Deciphering the Statistics on Income and Wages." *Dollars & Sense,* January-February, pp. 10–11.

Horowitz, David, 1969. *Empire and Revolution*. New York: Random House.
————, ed., 1969a. *Corporations and the Cold War*. New York: Monthly Review.
Horton, John, 1988. "The Perfect War." [Review of *The Perfect War: The War We Couldn't Lose and How We Did*, by James William Gibson.] New York: Vintage. *Monthly Review*, November, pp. 49–53.
Hougan, Jim, 1985. *Secret Agenda*. New York: Random House.
Hough, Jerry, 1985. "Russia and the Third World: The Revolutionary Road Runs Out." *The Nation*, June, pp. 666–68.
————, 1990. "Gorbachev Is Fine, Thank You." *International Herald Tribune*, January 23, p. 4.
Houweling, Henk W., and Jan G. Sicama, 1988. "The Risk of Compulsory Escalation." *Journal of Peace Research* 25, no. 1, pp. 43–56.
Hovey, Harold A., 1965. *United States Military Assistance: A Study of Policies and Practices*. New York: Praeger.
Howley, John, 1984. "Facts and Figures: Calculating Unemployment." *Economic Notes* 52, no. 11 (November), pp. 4–5.
Huggins, Martha K., 1987. "U.S.-Supported State Terror: A History of Police Training in Latin America." *Crime and Social Justice*, nos. 27–28.
Hveem, Helge, and Raino Malnes, 1980. *Military Use of Natural Resources: The Case for Conversion and Control*. Oslo: International Peace Research Institute.
In Contempt of Congress: The Reagan Record of Deceit & Illegality on Central America, 1985. Washington DC: Institute for Policy Studies.
"Indefensible Figures," 1988. *Money Matters*, Spring [CA: Working Assets Money Fund. Source: CD 1].
"Inflating the Assessing of Soviet Strength," 1983. [Review of *Soviet Strategic Forces: Requirements and Responses*. Washington DC: Brookings Institution, 1982.] In *Counterspy* 7, no. 4 (June-August), pp. 57–58.
"International Recruitment," 1988. *International Herald Tribune*, November 29, p. 6.
International Security Yearbook, 1983/4, 1984. Ed. by Barry M. Blechman, Edward N. Luttwak and Joel S. Wit. New York: St. Martin's.
"Investment Update: Europe," 1984. *New York Times*, December 10, Sec. D.
IPIS, 1988. *Plenary Summaries—Restructuring US–USSR Relations: Moving Beyond the Cold War*. Regis College, Denver, Colorado, September 23–25, 1988. Cambridge MA: The Institute for Peace and International Security.
IPS, 1988. *The Real Security Education Program: A Workshop on U.S. Security Policies: Discussion Guide*. Washington DC: Institute for Policy Studies.
IPPNW, [1983]. International Physicians for the Prevention of Nuclear War. Boston MA.
Jacobsen, Carl Gustav, 1982. "The Nuclear Era: Perception and Reality—A Century Apart?" *Journal of Peace Research* 19, no. 1, pp. 21–36.
Janowitz, Morris, 1960. *The Professional Soldier*. New York: Free Press.
Jenkins, R., 1970. *Exploitation: The World Power Structure and the Inequality of Nations*. London: MacGibbon Kee.
Joel, Judith, and Gerald Erickson, eds., 1983. *Anti-Communism: The Politics of Manipulation*. Minneapolis MN: Marxist Educational Press (Ford Hall—University of Minnesota).
Johansen, Robert C., 1979. "The Arms Bazaar: SALT Was Never Intended to Disarm." *Harper's Magazine*, May, pp. 21–29.
————, 1983. *Toward an Alternative Security System: Moving Beyond the Balance of Power in the Search for World Security*. New York: World Policy Institute.
————, 1986. "The Reagan Administration and the U.N.: The Costs of Unilateralism." *World Policy Journal* (Fall), pp. 601–41.

Johnson, Haynes, 1989. "The Contradictions of Panama." *International Herald Tribune,* December 26, p. 6.

Johnstone, Diana, 1983. "In Print: The Wizards of Armageddon, by Fred Kaplan." *In These Times,* August 24-September 6, pp. 17, 22.

_____, 1985. "Reagan's Proliferation Politics." *In These Times,* September 18-24, pp. 3, 22.

_____, 1985a. "A Dangerous New Chemical Dependency." *In These Times,* December 25-January 15, pp. 3, 8.

_____, 1988. "The U.S. Ties That Blind: Israel and Terrorism." *In These Times,* December 14-20, p. 11.

Jones, Jeff, 1985. "Harassment Update: FBI Going After Solidarity Activists." *The Guardian,* November 27, p. 3.

Jonquieres, Guy De, 1985. "Can Europe Catch Up?" *World Press Review,* August, pp. 27-29.

Jordan, Amos A. and William A., 1984. *American National Security: Policy and Process.* Baltimore MD: Johns Hopkins University Press. Pp. 1-80.

Judis, John B., 1983. "Thaw in East-West Relations Stopped Cold." *In These Times,* September 21-27, p. 3.

_____, 1988. "Charting Reagan's Trek on Stormy Seas of Trade." *In These Times,* May 18-24, p. 9.

Juffer, Jane, 1988. "Dump at the Border: U.S. Firms Make a Mexican Wasteland." *The Progressive,* October, pp. 24-29.

Julie, Loebe, [1985]. "Letter: Dear Fellow Taxpayer." Washington: Committee Against Government Waste—Taxpayers Against Wasteful Military Spending.

Jussim, Daniel, 1985. "The Privacy Invaders: Lies, Damn Lies—and Polygraphs." *The Nation,* December 21, pp. 665, 682-84.

Kahn, Joe, 1985. "Economic Trends: The National Debt." *Economic Notes,* May-June, pp. 11, 15.

Kaldor, Mary, 1981. *The Baroque Arsenal.* New York: Hill and Wang.

Kaplan, Fred M., 1982. *Dubious Specter: A Skeptical Look at the Soviet Nuclear Threat.* Washington DC: Institute for Policy Studies.

_____, and Barry M. Blechman, 1978. *Force Without War.* Washington DC: Brookings Institution.

Karas, Thomas H., 1983. *The New High Ground: Systems and Weapons of Space Age War.* New York: Simon & Schuster.

Karliner, Joshua, 1989. "Central America's Other War." *World Policy Journal* 6, no. 4 (Fall), pp. 787-810.

Karp, Aaron, 1989. "Ballistic Missile Proliferation in the Third World." In *SIPRI Yearbook 1989: World Armaments and Disarmament,* New York: Oxford University Press. Pp. 287-318.

Kaufman, Richard F., 1988. "Deadline: Letting the Justice Department Off the Hook ... Again." *Nuclear Times,* November-December, pp. 1-2, 9-10.

Kegley, Charles W., Jr., and Eugene R. Wittkopf, 1982. "The Reagan Administration's World View." *Orbis* 26, no. 1 (Spring), pp. 223-44.

Kelley, Kevin, 1988-1989. "Leveraged Buyout Craze: Is It Selling Out Economy?" *In These Times,* December 21-January 10, p. 3.

Kelly, John, 1983. "Casey's Terrorism Math." *Counterspy* 7, no. 4 (June-August), pp, 8-11.

Kemp, A., 1976. *Multinationals, Arms and Violence: Limits to Violence.* Paper, No. 13. Oakville, Ontario: Canadian Peace Research Institute.

Kende, Istvan, 1973. *Guerres locales en Asie, en Afrique et en Amérique.* Budapest:

Centre pour le Recherche de l'Afro-Asie de l'Académie des Sciences De Hongrie.

————, 1983. "New Features of the Armed Conflicts and Armaments in Developing Countries." *Development and Peace.*

Kennan, George, 1948. "Policy Planning Staff (PPS) 23." U.S. Department of State, February 24.

————, 1982. *The Nuclear Delusion: Soviet-American Relations in the Atomic Age.* New York: Pantheon.

————, 1988. "PSR: Kennan on Deterrence and Mass Neurosis." *Nuclear Times,* May/June, pp. 33–34.

Kennedy, Paul, 1985. Review of *For the Common Defense: A Military History of the United States of America* [New York: Free Press]. *New Republic,* February 11, pp. 32–33.

————, 1987. *The Rise and Fall of the Great Powers.* New York: Random House.

Kerr, Peter, 1988. "The American Drug Problem Takes on Faces." *New York Times,* July 10, p. 5.

Kessler, Meryl, 1988. "Gorbachev's Dilemma: The Paradox of Perestroika." *World Policy Journal* 5, no. 4 (Fall), pp. 651–76.

Kidd, Jack (Maj. Gen., USAF, Ret.), 1988. *The Strategic Cooperation Initiative.* Charlottesville VA: Three President's Publishing (801 East High Street, Suite B).

Kilborn, Peter T., 1985. "Competitiveness Panel Finds 20-Year U.S. Lag." *New York Times,* February 13, pp. D1, 9.

————, 1990. "More and More for American Women, One Job's Not Enough." *International Herald Tribune,* February 16, p. 3.

Kimball, Jeffrey P., 1988. "The Stab-in-the-Back Legend and the Vietnam War." *Armed Forces and Society* 14 (Spring), pp. 433–58.

Klare, Michael T., 1972. *War Without End: American Planning for the Next Vietnams.* New York: Random/Vintage.

————, 1982. "The Global Arms Trade." *New Catholic World,* March/April, pp. 64–67. Reprinted by the Institute for Policy Studies, Washington DC, 1982.

————, 1982a. "The Weinberger Revolution." *Inquiry,* September, pp. 25–28.

————, 1982b. "Why Not Impose a Freeze on Costly, Deadly Conventional Weapons, Too?" *The Des Moines Register,* April 16. Reprinted by the Institute for Policy Studies, Washington DC, 1982.

————, 1982c. "The Political Economy of Arms Sales." *Economic Forum* 13, no. 1 (Summer), pp. 33–47.

————, 1982d. "The Worst Is Yet to Come." *Bulletin of the Atomic Scientists* 82, no. 6 (June), pp. 45–46.

————, 1982e. "Expensive Arms Are Not So Smart." *The Chicago Tribune,* May 17. Reprinted by the Institute for Policy Studies, Washington DC, 1982.

————, 1982f. "Opening the Floodgates: The New U.S. Arms Sales Policy." In *Militarization and Arms Production.* Ed. by Helena Tuomi and Raimo Vayrynen. London: Croom, Helm. Pp. 139–47.

————, 1982g. "Non-Nuclear Arms, Nuclear Threat." *Newsday* (Long Island), November 28, p. 44.

————, 1983. "Stoking the Nuclear Fire." *MERIP Reports,* no. 112 (February), pp. 3–4.

————, 1984. *American Arms Supermarket.* Austin: University of Texas Press.

————, 1985. "New Merchants in the Arms Bazaar." *Bulletin of the Atomic Scientists,* 41:1 (January): 15–17.

_____, 1985a. "Road Map for the Peace Movement." *The Nation,* June 29, pp. 783, 800–02.

_____, 1988. "A Blueprint for Endless Intervention." *The Nation,* July 30/August 6, pp. 77, 95–98.

_____, and Cynthia Arnson, 1981. *Supplying Repression: U.S. Support for Authoritarian Regimes Abroad.* Washington DC: Institute for Policy Studies.

_____, 1989. "America's New 'Grand Strategy' — Back to World Policeman." In *Surviving Together: The Olaf Palme Lectures on Common Security 1988.* Ed. by Radmila Nakarada. Lund: Lund University Peace Research Institute, pp. 157–65.

Klein, Bradley S., 1988. "After Strategy: The Search for a Post-Modern Politics of Peace." *Alternatives* 13 (Summer), pp. 293–318.

Kohler, Gernot, 1978. *Global Apartheid.* New York: World Policy Institute.

Kohut, Andrew, 1984. "Generally Speaking: Surveying the Military's Top Brass." *Public Opinion,* October/November, pp. 42–45.

Koistinen, Paul A.C., 1980. *The Military-Industrial Complex: A Historical Perspective.* New York: Praeger.

Kolko, Gabriel, 1969. *The Politics of War.* New York: Random House.

Kornbluh, Peter, 1987. *The Price of Intervention: Reagan's Wars Against the Sandinistas.* Washington DC: Institute for Policy Studies.

Kotz, David, 1988. "Corporatist Vision Fills Economic Void." *In These Times,* October 12–18, p. 16.

Kotz, Nick, 1987. *Wild Blue Yonder: Money, Politics and the B-1 Bomber.* New York: Pantheon.

Kozol, Jonathan, 1985. *Illiterate America.* Garden City NY: Anchor/Doubleday.

Kriesberg, Louis, 1982. "Recent U.S. Public Views of Foreign Policy: Data for Peace Action." *Peace and Change* 8, no. 45 (Fall), pp. 39–56.

_____, 1984. "Efforts at Deescalating the American-Soviet Conflict." Paper presented at the International Studies Association Annual Meeting in Atlanta (March).

_____, 1989. "Domestic Conditions Major Source of Soviet Change." *The Charleston Gazette,* April 28, p. 7A.

Kutzik, Alfred, 1984. "Facts and Figures: Calculating Poverty." *Economic Notes* 52, no. 111 (November), p. 2.

Labaton, Stephen, 1990. "Banks in Panama Resist U.S. Over Drug Profits." *International Herald Tribune,* February 7, p. 1.

LaFarge, Phyllis, 1988. *The Strangelove Legacy: Children, Parents and Teachers in the Nuclear Age.* New York: Harper & Row.

LaFeber, Walter, 1963. *The New Empire.* Ithaca NY: Cornell University Press.

Landau, Saul, 1988. *The Dangerous Doctrine: National Security and U.S. Foreign Policy.* Washington DC: Institute for Policy Studies.

_____, 1988. *The Dangerous Doctrine: National Security and U.S. Foreign Policy.* Washington DC: Institute for Policy Studies.

Landgren-Backstrom, Signe, 1982. "Global Arms Trade: Scope, Impact, Restraining Action." *Bulletin of Peace Proposals* 13, no. 3, pp. 201–10.

Lane, David, 1985. *State and Politics in the USSR.* New York: New York University Press.

Lapham, Lewis H., 1988. *Money and Class in America: Notes and Observations on Our Civil Religion.* London: Weidenfeld & Nicholson.

LaRocque, Gene R., 1988. "What Should We Defend? A New Military Strategy for the United States." *The Defense Monitor* 17, no. 4, pp. 1–8. Also appears as "What Is Ours to Defend?" *Harpers,* July, pp. 39–50.

————, and Stephen D. Goose, 1982. "Arming the Third World." *Worldview* **25** (October), pp. 19–21.

LaRue, L.H., 1987. *Political Discourse: A Case Study of the Watergate Affair*. Athens: University of Georgia Press.

Lasch, Christopher, 1979. *The Culture of Narcissism*. New York: Random House.

————, 1989. "Give Youth Cause to Believe in Tomorrow." *International Herald Tribune*, December 29, p. 7.

Lasswell, H., 1962. "The Garrison State Hypothesis Today." In *Changing Patterns of Military Politics*. Ed. by S.P. Huntington. New York: Free Press, pp. 51–70.

Lawrence, Ken, 1984. "From the Hessians to the Contras: Mercenaries in the Service of Imperialism." *Covert Action Information Bulletin* **22** (Fall), pp. 10–11.

————, 1985. "The New State Repression." *Covert Action Information Bulletin* **24** (Summer), pp. 3–11.

Ledbetter, James, 1988. "The Policy Jocks." *The Nation*, October 31, pp. 426–30.

Lee, Rensselaer W., III, 1988. "Why the U.S. Cannot Stop South American Cocaine." *Orbis* **32**, no. 4 (Fall), pp. 499–520.

Leitenberg, Milton, 1976. "Notes on the Diversion of Resources for Military Purposes in Developing Nations." *Journal of Peace Research* **8**, no. 2, pp. 111–16.

————, 1981. "Presidential Directive (P.D.) 59: United States Nuclear Weapon Targeting Policy." *Journal of Peace Research*, 28, no. 4, pp. 6–8.

LeRachman, Robert, 1989. "A Letter to George Bush: F.D.R. Changed, and So Can You." *The Nation*, January 30, pp. 117–18.

————, 1981. "Presidential Directive (P.D.) 59: United States Nuclear Weapon Targeting Policy." *Journal of Peace Research* **18**, no. 4, pp. 6–8.

————, 1982. "Efforts at Reducing Military Expenditure in the United States, 1960 to 1978." In *Militarization and Arms Production*. Ed. by Helena Tuomi and Raimo Vayrynen. London: Croom, Helm, pp. 108–38.

Lens, Sidney, 1970. *The Military Industrial Complex*. New York: Pilgrim.

————, 1983. *The Maginot Line Syndrome: America's Hopeless Foreign Policy*. Cambridge MA: Ballinger.

Lernoux, Penny, 1988. "Guatemala's New Military Order." *The Nation*, November 28, pp. 556–60.

"Lessons from the Trenches," 1990. *U.S. News & World Report*, February 26, pp. 50–55.

Leventhal, Paul, 1985. "Flaws in the Non-Proliferation Treaty." *Bulletin of the Atomic Scientists* **41**, no. 8 (September), pp. 12–15.

Levinson, Mark, 1985. "A Toad for Breakfast." *Dissent*, Fall, p. 395.

Lewin, Moshe, 1985. *The Making of the Soviet System: Essays in the Social History of Interwar Russia*. New York: Pantheon.

"License to Spy," 1988. *The Progressive*, October, pp. 9–10.

Lifschultz, Lawrence, 1988. "Bush, Drugs and Pakistan: Inside the Kingdom of Heroin." *The Nation*, November 14, pp. 477, 492–96.

Lifton, Robert F., and Richard A. Falk, 1982. *The Political and Psychological Case Against Nuclearism*. New York: Basic.

Lindorff, David, 1988. "Could It Happen Here?" *Mother Jones*, April, p. 60.

Lippard, Lucy R., 1983. "The Other Nicaragua." *In These Times*, September 21–27, pp. 12–13, 22.

Lipset, Seymour M., and William Schneider, 1983. *The Confidence Gap: Business, Labor, and Government in the Public Mind*. New York: Free Press.

"List of 'Diploma Mills,'" 1985. *On Campus*, American Federation of Teachers, October, p. 6.

Looney, Robert, 1989. "Have Third-World Arms Industries Reduced Arms Imports?" *Current Research on Peace and Violence* 10, no. 1, pp. 15–26.

―――――, and P.C. Frederiksen, 1983. "Defense Expenditures and Economic Growth in Developing Countries." *Armed Forces and Society* 9, no. 4 (Summer), pp. 633–45.

Los Angeles Times, 1983. "Pentagon: Drain on the Economy." *The Syracuse Post-Standard,* August 4, pp. A1, A11.

"Losing Ground in Latin America," 1990. *U.S. News and World Report,* January 22, pp. 20–23.

"Lost on the Planet Earth," 1988. *Newsweek,* August 8, p. 31.

Lumsden, Malvern, 1980. "Militarism: Cultural Dimensions of Militarisation." In *Problems of Contemporary Militarism.* Ed. by Asjborn Eide and Marek Thee. London: Croom, Helm. Pp. 356–69.

Luttwak, Edward, 1980. "Quoted in *Forbes.*" From *National Defense.* By James Fallows. New York: Random/Vintage, 1981. Pp. 16.

Lutz, Dieter S., 1984. "A New European Peace Order as a System of Collective Security." *Journal of Peace Research* 21, no. 2, pp. 169–80.

Lynde, Catherine, 1988. "Public Capital, Private Profits." *Dollars & Sense,* November, pp. 20–21.

McAfee Brown, Robert, Balfour Brickner and Rosemary Redford Ruether, 1988. *Letter.* NY: Witness for Peace.

McClintook, Michael, 1985. *The American Connection.* Vol. 1, *State Terror and Popular Resistance in El Salvador.* Vol. 2, *State Terror and Popular Resistance in Guatemala.* London: Zed. Distrib. by Biblio Distribution Centre, Totowa NJ.

McCrea, Frances B., and Gerald E. Markle, 1989. *Minutes to Midnight: Nuclear Weapons Protest in America.* Newbury Park: Sage.

MacEwan, Arthur, 1989. "Out on a Limb: Can Bush Manage a Recession?" *Dollars & Sense,* January-February, pp. 6–9.

―――――, 1989. *Debt and Disorder: International Economic Instability and U.S. Imperial Decline.* New York: Monthly Review Press.

McGehee, Ralph W., 1983. *Deadly Deceits, My 25 Years in the CIA.* New York: Sheridan Square.

McGowan, William, 1985. "Free Speech and the Border Patrol." *New Age Journal,* January, pp. 56, 59.

Mack, A., 1974. "Comparing Theories of Economic Imperialism." In *Testing Theories of Economic Imperialism.* Ed. by S.J. Rosen and J.R. Kurth. Toronto: Heath. Pp. 35–55.

Mackenzie, Angus, 1985. "Is the Freeze Subversive?" *Guardian,* August 21, p. 7.

McKinley, R.D., and A. Mughan, 1984. *Aid and Arms to the Third World: An Analysis of the Distribution and Impact of U.S. Official Transfers.* New York: St. Martin's.

McMahan, Jeff, 1985. *Reagan and the World: Imperial Policy in the New Cold War.* New York: Monthly Review Press.

Magdoff, Harry, 1969. *The Age of Imperialism: The Economics of U.S. Foreign Policy.* New York: Monthly Review Press.

―――――, 1971. "Militarism and Imperialism." In *Readings in U.S. Imperialism.* Ed. by K.T. Fann and D.C. Hodeges. Boston: Sargent. Pp. 127–38.

―――――, and Paul M. Sweezy, 1988. *The Irreversible Crisis.* New York: Monthly Review Press.

Makhijani, Arjun, 1985. "U.S. Nuclear Strategy: Pied Piper to Armegeddon." *The National Reporter* [formerly *Counterspy*] 9, no. 1 (Winter), pp. 10–11.

Mandel, Michael, 1988. "Is Productivity a Problem?" *Dollars & Sense,* November, pp. 16–19.

Marbach, William D., 1985. "The New Arms Race? Congress Hands Reagan a Win on Chemical Weapons." *Newsweek,* July 1, p. 42.

Marshall, Jonathan, 1983. "Missiles That Fizzle." *Inquiry,* March, pp. 25–27.

————, Peter Dale Scott, and Jane Hunter, 1987. *The Iran-Contra Connection.* Boston: South End Press.

Marshall, Tyler, 1983. "Arrival of First F-16s. Helps Give U.S. Stock Sharp Rise in Pakistan." *International Herald Tribune,* May 17, 1983, p. 5.

Mashinot, Beth, 1985. "In Short." *In These Times,* May 8–14, p. 4.

Medvedev, Roy, 1980. *On Soviet Dissent.* New York: Columbia University Press.

Mellethin, F.W. von, and R.H.S. Stolfi, with E. Sobik, 1984. *Nato Under Attack.* Durham NC: Duke University Press.

Melman, Seymour, 1974. *The Permanent War Economy.* New York: Simon & Schuster.

————, 1983. *Profits Without Production.* New York: Alfred A. Knopf.

————, 1985. "The Butter That's Traded Off for Guns." *New York Times,* April 22, p. A19.

————, 1988. *The Demilitarized Society: Disarmament and Conversion.* Montreal: Harvest Home.

Meranto, Philip J., Oneida J. Meranto, and Matthew R. Lippman, 1985. *Guarding the Ivory Tower: Repression and Rebellion in Higher Education.* Denver CO: Lucha.

Metz, Tim, 1988. *Black Monday: The Catastrophe of October 19, 1987 . . . and Beyond.* New York: Morrow.

Meyerson, Harold, 1989. "Why the Democrats Keep Losing." *Dissent,* Summer, pp. 305–11.

Miles, Sara, 1987. "Towards Post-Reagan Low-Intensity Conflict." In *Surviving Together: The Olaf Palme Lectures on Common Security 1988.* Ed. by Radmila Nakorada and Jan Oberg. Lund: Lund University Peace Research Institute, pp. 145–55.

Miliband, Ralph, and Marcel Liebman, 1985. "Reflections on Anti-Communism." *Monthly Review,* July-August, pp. 1–29.

"Military Construction Aids Air Force Update Effort," 1983. *Aviation Week & Space Technology,* February, pp. 63–64.

Miller, John and Ramon Castellblanch, 1988. "Does Manufacturing Matter? Can We Afford to Lose Our Industrial Base?" *Dollars & Sense,* October, pp. 6–9, 11.

Miller, Marc S., 1988. "New Toys for Robocop Soldiers." *The Progressive,* July, pp. 18–21.

————, 1988a. "U.S. Third World Policies Threaten Permanent War." *In These Times,* September 21–27, p. 17.

Miller, Warren E., Arthur H. Miller, and Edward J. Schneider, 1980. *American National Election Studies Data Sourcebook: 1951-1978.* Cambridge MA: Harvard University Press.

Moberg, David, 1985. "UAW Boycotts One of Its Founders." *In These Times,* November 27-December 10, p. 6.

————, 1989. "Hard Times for Labor." *Dissent,* Summer, pp. 323–32.

Moffitt, Michael, 1983. *The World's Money.* New York: Simon & Schuster.

Mokhiber, Russell, 1988. *Corporate Crime and Violence: Big Business Power and the Abuse of the Public Trust.* Sierra Club.

Moon, Parker T., 1926. *Imperialism and World Politics.* New York: Columbia University Press.

Moore, David W., and Thomas B. Trout, 1978. "Military Advancement: The Visibility Theory of Promotions." *American Political Science Review* 72 (June), pp. 452–68.

Moran, T.H., 1974. "The Theory of International Exploitation in Large Natural Resource Investments." In *Testing Theories Imperialism*. Ed. by S.J. Rosen and J.R. Kurth. Toronto: Heath. Pp. 163–81.

"More Budget Gimmicks," 1990. *International Herald Tribune*, January 31, p. 6.

Moreland, Howard, 1985. "Are We Readying a First Strike." *The Nation*, March 16, pp. 297–300.

Morgenthau, Hans J., 1951. *In Defense of the National Interest*. New York: Alfred A. Knopf.

Morley, Jefferson, 1988. "Bush's Drug Problem — And Ours." *The Nation*, April 27/September 3, pp. 149, 165–69.

_____, and Malcolm Byrne, 1989. "The Drug War and 'National Security.'" *Dissent*, Winter, pp. 39–46.

Morrison, David C., 1985. "Energy Department's Weapons Conglomerate." *Bulletin of the Atomic Scientists* 41 no. 4 (April), pp. 32–36.

Muwakkil, Salim, 1985. "Drop in Poverty Rate Hides Rising Injustices." *In These Times*, September 25–October 1, p. 5.

_____, 1988. "Hail to the Chief of Intelligence." *In These Times*, November 16–22, p. 2.

Nagle, John D., 1985. *Introduction to Comparative Politics: Political System Performance in Three Worlds*. Chicago: Nelson Hall.

Nairn, Allan, 1983. "The Guns of Guatemala." *New Republic*, April 11, pp. 17–21.

Nandy, Pritish, 1985. "America's 'Guru of Mercenaries': Inside a Private School for Saboteurs and Assassins." *World Press Review*, December, pp. 30–32.

Nasser, Alan G., 1989. "The Atomic Bomb, the Cold War, and the Soviet Threat." *Monthly Review*, December, pp. 1–8.

National Conference of Catholic Bishops, 1983. "Excerpts from U.S. Bishops' Pastoral Letter on War and Peace." *New York Times*, May 5, p. B16.

"NATO: As the 'Ratchet Turns,'" 1985. *The Nation*, March 2, p. 230.

"NATO and Warsaw Pact Forces: Conventional War in Europe," 1988. *The Defense Monitor* 17, no. 3, pp. 1–8.

Naureckas, Jim, 1988. "In Brief." *In These Times*, August 3–16, pp. 4–5.

_____, 1988. "Secret Diplomacy." *In These Times*, August 3–16, pp. 4–5.

Navarro, Vicente, 1985. "The Road Ahead." *Monthly Review*, July-August, pp. 30–58.

Nelson, Jill, 1988. "Letter: Dear Caring American." Jobs with Peace Campaign National Office. Boston MA: 76 Summer Street, 02110.

"New Findings — Americans on National Security," 1988. *Peace Links Connection*, Winter, p. 6.

"New Union Strategies in Meatpacking," 1988. *Economic Notes*, January-February, pp. 6–9.

"News the Media Missed," 1988. *Confidential: Report from Zurich*, December, pp. 11–15.

Nincic, Miroslav, 1985. "The American Public and the Soviet Union: The Domestic Context of Discontent." *Journal of Peace Research* 22, no. 4, pp. 345–57.

"No Kidding," 1988. *In These Times*, September 21–27, p. 5.

Nonini, Don, 1988. "Everyday Forms of Popular Resistance." *Monthly Review* 40, No. 6 (November), pp. 25–36.

NPR (National Public Radio), 1984. News Report based upon U.S. Department of Justice Release.

_____, 1985. "Morning Edition: Interviews." February 8.

_____, 1985a. "Morning Edition." October 29.

_____, 1988. "Morning Edition: Drug Use." January 14.

_____, 1988. "Morning Edition: Poison and the Pentagon." April 5.

_____, 1988. "Morning Edition: Arms Sales to the Middle East." August 18.

_____, 1988. "All Things Considered: Amnesty International." October 4.

_____, 1988. "All Things Considered: Illiteracy." October 10.

_____, 1988. "Morning Edition: American Voting Participation." October 26.

_____, 1988. "Morning Edition: Illiteracy." November 2.

_____, 1988. "All Things Considered: UNICEF." December 20.

_____, 1988. "Morning Edition: Savings and Loan Bailouts." December 29.

_____, 1989. "All Things Considered: Chemical Weapons." January 2.

_____, 1989. "Morning Edition: Chemical Weapons." January 6.

_____, 1989. "All Things Considered: U.S. Chemical Weapons." January 7.

_____, 1989, "All Things Considered: Bailing Out Savings and Loan Institutions." January 10.

_____, 1989. "All Things Considered: Justice Department Report Accuses Meese of Ethical Improprieties." January 17.

_____, 1989. "All Things Considered: West Europe's Push for Accommodation with the East." February 13.

Nye, Joseph S., Jr., 1988. "Understanding U.S. Strength." *Foreign Policy*, 72 (Fall), pp. 105–29.

Oakes, John B., 1983. "Reagan's Slide to War." *New York Times*, September 29, p. A31.

Odell, S.J. "Correlates of U.S. Military Assistance and Military Intervention." In *Testing Theories of Economic Imperialism.* Ed. by S.J. Rosen and J.R. Kurth. Toronto: Heath. Pp. 143–61.

Odom, William E., Lt. Gen., 1988. "It's Time to Create a Border Control Department." *U.S. News and World Report*, December 12, p. 22.

Ohlson, Thomas, 1982. "Third World Arms Exporters—A New Facet of the Global Arms Race." *Bulletin of Peace Proposals* 13, no. 3, pp. 201–20.

_____, and Eva Loose-Weintraub, 1983. "The Trade in Major Conventional Weapons." In *World Armaments and Disarmament: SIPRI Yearbook, 1983.* New York: Taylor & Francis. Pp. 267–350.

_____, and Rita Tullberg, 1983. "World Military Expenditure and Production." In *World Armaments and Disarmament: SIPRI Yearbook, 1983.* New York: Taylor and Francis. Pp. 129–60.

Okitu, Saburn, 1989. "Japan's Quiet Strength." *Foreign Policy* 75 (Summer), pp. 128–45.

Oreskes, Michael, 1990. "A U.S. Poll Finds 'Real Erosion.'" *International Herald Tribune*, February 7, p. 1.

Organski, A.F.K., and Jacek Kugler, 1980. *The War Ledger.* Chicago: University of Chicago Press.

"Opinion Roundup," 1984. *Public Opinion*, December/January.

_____, 1984a. *Public Opinion*, August/September.

PBS, 1988. "Frontline: Poison and the Pentagon." April 5.

Pacific Forum, 1984. *U.S.-China Relations and the Future of the Asian Pacific Region.* Honolulu: Pacific Forum.

Page, Benjamin, 1984. *Who Gets What from Government.* Berkeley: University of California Press.

Paine, Christopher E., 1984. "Arms Control Poker." *Inquiry*, June, pp. 16–18.

Parenti, Michael, 1984. "U.S. Intervention: The World as 'Our Oyster.'" *New World Review*, May-June, pp. 11–15.

_____, 1985. "Anti-Sovietism in the U.S. News Media." *New World Review*, November-December, pp. 26–29.

_____, 1986. *Inventing Reality: The Politics of the Mass Media.* New York: St. Martin's.

_____, 1988. *The Sword and the Dollar.* New York: St. Martin's.

Parry, Robert, with Rod Nordland, 1988. "Guns for Drugs? Senate Probers Trace an Old Contra Connection to George Bush's Office." *Newsweek,* May 23, pp. 22–24.

Paul, Jim, 1983. "The Egyptian Arms Industry." *MERIP Reports,* No. 112 (February): 26–27.

Pear, Robert, 1989. "U.S. Sales of Weapons to Third World Jump as Moscow's Decline." *International Herald Tribune,* September 2, p. 3.

Pearson, David, 1984. "K.A.L. 007: What the U.S. Knew and When We Knew It." *The Nation,* August 18/25, pp. 105–24.

Pearson, Frederic S., 1981. "U.S. Arms Transfer Policy: The Feasibility of Restraint." *Arms Control* 2, no. 1 (May), pp. 25–65.

Peiris, Denzil, 1982. "Special Report: The Tender Touch." *South,* August, pp. 35–38.

"The Pentagon Scandals," 1985. *World Press Review,* August, pp. 35–40.

Perera, Victor, 1985. "Uzi Diplomacy." *Mother Jones,* July 1985, pp. 40–48.

Perkovich, George, 1988. "Peace and Freedom." *Nuclear Times,* November/ December, pp. 14–18, 24.

_____, 1988a. "Soviet Jewry and American Foreign Policy." *World Policy Journal* 5, no. 3 (Summer), pp. 435–67.

Perry, Roland, 1984. *Hidden Power: The Programming of the President.* Beaufort Books.

Peters, Charles, 1988. "Tilting at Windmills." *Washington Monthly,* March, pp. 6–9.

Peters, Thomas J., 1987. "Robert Reich Takes on Rambo [Review of *Tales of a New America* by Robert Reich. New York: Random House 1987]." *Washington Monthly,* March, pp. 51–56.

Peterzell, Jay, 1984. *Reagan's Secret Wars.* Washington: Center for National Security Studies.

Petras, James, 1987. "The Anatomy of State Terror." *Science & Society* 51, no. 3 (Fall), pp. 314–38.

_____, and Morris Morley, 1983. "Third World Crisis Is Nuclear Trigger." *In These Times,* October 26–November 1, p. 11.

Pfaff, William, 1982. "Yugoslavia, for One, Would Like to Be Left Alone." *International Herald Tribune,* December 10, p. 6.

_____, 1989. "Washington's Trivial Pursuits Magnify the Pursued Nuisance." *International Herald Tribune,* October 17, p. 4.

Pierre, Andrew J., 1981/82. "Arms Sales: The New Diplomacy." *Foreign Affairs* 60, no. 2 (Winter), pp. 266–86.

_____, 1982. *The Global Politics of Arms Sales.* Princeton NJ: Princeton University Press.

Pike, John, 1985. "The Case Against 'Star Wars.'" *In These Times,* March 20–25, p. 3.

Piller, Charles, 1988. "Lethal Lies About Fatal Diseases." *The Nation,* October 3, pp. 271–72, 274–75.

Piven, Frances Fox, and Richard Cloward, 1982. *The New Class War: Reagan's Attack on the Welfare State and Its Consequences.* New York: Pantheon.

"Political Booknotes," 1988. *The Washington Monthly,* March, pp. 59–60.

"Poor Students Defer College Dreams," 1988. *The Connection* (UUP/NYSUT), November 3, p. 2.

Power, Jonathan, 1983. "Can the Third World Have Guns and Plowshares?" *International Herald Tribune,* May 6, p. 4.

Previdi, Robert, 1988. *Civilian Control vs. Military Rule.* New York: Hippocrene.

Radway, Lawrence, 1985. "U.S. Forces in Europe: The Case for Cautious Contraction." *SAIS Review* **5**, no. 1 (Winter/Spring), pp. 227–42.

Rand Corporation, 1985. *Rand Checklist*, no. 333 (May), p. 11.

Randolph, Eleanor, 1990. "It Isn't Necessary for Bush to Lie." *International Herald Tribune*, February 15, p. 5.

Raskin, Marcus G., 1979. *The Politics of National Security*. New Brunswick NJ: Transaction.

Ravenal, Earl C., 1980. "Doing Nothing." *Foreign Policy* **39** (Summer), pp. 28–39.

————, 1983. "Taking the Sting Out of the Nuclear Threat." *Inquiry*, October, pp. 20–24.

"Readers Report: Letters to the Editor," 1987. *Space and Security News*, December, pp. 3–5.

"The Reagan Budget," 1982. *America*, February 20, pp. 124–25.

"The Reagan Legacy," 1988. *Friends Committee on National Legislation Washington Newsletter*, April, pp. 1–2.

Reding, Andrew, 1989. "Mexico Under Salinas." *World Policy Journal* **6**, no. 4 (Fall), pp. 685–729.

"Regional Report: The Middle East Arms Bazaar," 1988. *World Press Review*, June, p. 40.

"Repairs: Don't Delay," 1988/89. *On Campus*, December/January, p. 3.

Reston, James, 1988. "25 Wars Are Still Going On." *New York Times*, June 3.

Richardson, Michael, 1988. "Vietnam Plans Huge Reduction in Army." *International Herald Tribune*, December 6, pp. 1, 6.

Richman, Sheldon, 1983. "What's Wrong with Red Trade?" *Inquiry*, October, pp. 25–29.

————, 1984. "The Culture of Intervention." *Inquiry*, March/April, pp. 12–13.

Ridley, Scott, 1988. "Idaho Battles Weapons Plants." *The Nation*, November 14, pp. 484–86.

Rimland, Bernard, and Gerald E. Larson, 1981. "The Manpower Quality Decline: An Ecological Perspective." *Armed Forces and Society* **8**, no. 1 (May), pp. 21–78.

"The Rising Burden," 1988. *Dollars and Sense*, November, p. 23.

Roberts, Adam, 1986. *Nations in Arms: The Theory and Practice of Territorial Defense*. London: Macmillan.

Rogers, Paul, 1988. "Does START Live Up to Its Name? Opening the Door for New Generations of Arms." *World Press Review*, July, pp. 23–25.

————, 1988. "The Nuclear Connection." *Bulletin of the Atomic Scientists*, September, pp. 20–22.

Rogers, Tony, 1988. "Dilemmas for the Peace Movement." *Peace & Security*, Spring, pp. 10–11.

Rolfe, David, and Judith Vidal-Hall, 1988. "Will the Seven Become Four." *World Press Review*, October, p. 52.

Ronfeldt, David, and Caesar Sereseres, 1977. *U.S. Arms Transfers, Diplomacy, and Security in Latin America and Beyond*. P-6005. Santa Monica CA: Rand Corporation.

Rosen, Jay, 1988. "Deadline: Dilemma for National Security Reporters, Is Anybody Listening?" *Nuclear Times*, November/December, pp. 3–5.

————, 1989. "Phantom Public Haunts Nuclear Age." *Bulletin of the Atomic Scientists*, June, pp. 16–19.

Rosen, S.J., 1974. "The Open Door Imperative and U.S. Foreign Policy." In *Testing Theories of Economic Imperialism*. Ed. by S.J. Rosen and J.R. Kurth. Toronto: Heath. Pp. 117–42.

Rosenfeld, Megan, 1988. "Expert on Children Addresses America's Wars." *Watertown Daily Times,* April 14, p. 4.

Rothschild, Matthew, 1985. "No Place for Scruples." *The Progressive,* November, pp. 26–28.

Rothstein, Richard, 1988. "Give Them a Break: Third World Debtors and a Cure for Reaganomics." *New Republic,* February 3, pp. 20–24.

Russett, Bruce, 1984. "Why Do Arms Races Occur?" In *Toward Nuclear Disarmament and Global Security.* Ed. by Burns H. Weston. Boulder CO: Westview. Pp. 69–90.

Ryan, Sheila, 1982. "The Reagan Budget: Money Is Policy." *MERIP Reports,* no. 105 (May), pp. 14–21.

Sabin, A.G., 1987. *Shadow Or Substance?* Adelphi Paper No. 222. London: International Institute for Strategic Studies.

Said, Edward W., 1981. *Covering Islam.* New York: Pantheon.

————, and Christopher Hitchens, eds. *Blaming the Victims: Spurious Scholarship and the Palestinian Question.* New York: Verso.

Salmon, Jack, 1988. "Can Non-Violence Be Combined with Military Means for National Defense?" *Journal of Peace Research* 25, no. 1, pp. 69–80.

Sampson, Anthony, 1977. *The Arms Bazaar: From Lebanon to Lockheed.* New York: Viking.

Sanders, Jerry W., 1983. *Empire at Bay: Containment Strategies and American Politics at the Crossroads.* New York: World Policy Institute.

————, 1983a. *Peddlers of Crisis: The Committee on the Present Danger.* Boston: South End Press.

San Juan, E., Jr., 1985. "Leftists: Wake Up to Philippine Revolt!" *Guardian,* December 4, p. 23.

Sarios, Beatrice, 1988. "Putting Study of Geography Back on the Map." *Watertown Daily Times: Sunday Weekly,* September 18.

Schaffer, Ronald, 1980. "American Military Ethics in World War II: The Bombing of German Civilians." *Journal of American History* 67, no. 2 (September), pp. 318–30.

Schapiro, Mark, 1986. "The Excludables." *Mother Jones,* January, pp. 29–32, 51.

Scheer, Robert, 1982. *With Enough Shovels: Reagan, Bush and Nuclear War.* New York: Random House.

Schell, Jonathan, 1982. *The Fate of the Earth.* New York: Knopf.

Schlesinger, S., and S. Kinzer, 1982. *Bitter Fruit: The Untold Story of the American Coup in Guatemala.* Garden City NY: Doubleday.

Schmid, Alex P., 1985. *Soviet Military Interventions Since 1945.* New Brunswick NJ: Transaction.

Schmidt, Helmut, 1985. "Blueprint for 1985: A Formula for Bridging the East-West Gap." *World Press Review,* April, p. 40.

Schmidt, William, 1988. "Penalty Accords in Job Safety Cases Assailed." *New York Times,* April 3, p. 24.

Schneider, Kenneth, 1988. "U.S. Says Pollution from A-Arm Plants Poses Grave Threat." *International Herald Tribune,* December 8, p. 3.

Schoultz, Lars, 1988. *National Security and United States Toward Latin America.* Princeton NJ: Princeton University Press.

Schudson, Michael, 1988. "Pumping Polyester." *The Nation,* June, pp. 794–95.

Schultz, Gastav H., [1985]. "Sanctuary." San Francisco CA: National Sanctuary Defense Fund.

"Science Faculty: A Dwindling Supply," 1988/89. *On Campus,* December/January, p. 3.

Sciolino, Elaine, 1990. "Pentagon II: A $30 Billion Stockpile of Unneeded Material." *International Herald Tribune,* February 6, p. 3.

Selders, George, 1987. *Witness to a Century.* New York: Ballantine.

Seligman, Daniel, 1983. "The War on the U.S. Defense Budget." *Fortune,* April 4, pp. 116–28.

Selvin, Paul, 1988. "Campus Hacks and the Pentagon." *The Nation,* November 28, pp. 563–66.

Serrin, William, 1989. "The B.L.S. Numbers Game: Playing Down Unemployment." *The Nation,* January 23, pp. 84–88.

Severo, Richard, and Lewis Milford, 1989. *Wages of War: When America's Soldiers Came Home — From Valley Forge to Vietnam.* New York: Simon & Schuster.

Shanker, Albert, 1988. "Where We Stand: Advertisement." *New York Times,* August 28, p. E7.

————, 1988/89. "Where We Stand: Illiteracy — It's Not All Discouraging Words." *On Campus* [AFI], December/January, p. 7.

Shapiro, Bruce, 1985. "Teaching Cops About Terrorism." *The Nation,* October 12, pp. 344–46.

Shaw, Linda S., Jeffrey W. Knopf, and Kenneth A. Bertsch, 1985. *Stocking and Arsenal: A Guide to the Nation's Top Military Contractors.* Investor Responsibility Research Center, Inc., 1319 F St., N.W., Suite 900, Washington DC 20004.

Shenfield, Stephen, 1985. "Soviets May Not Imitate Star Wars." *Bulletin of the Atomic Scientists,* June/July, pp. 38–39.

Sherrill, Robert, 1988. "Deep Pockets [Review of *The Best Congress Money Can Buy* by Philip M. Stene. New York: Pantheon, 1988]." *The Nation,* August 27/September 3, pp. 170–72.

————, 1988a. "White Collar Thuggery." [Review of *Corporate Crime and Violence: Big Business Power and the Abuse of the Public Trust* by Russell Mokhiber. Sierra Club Books.] *The Nation,* November 28, pp. 568–74.

Shields, Lynn, 1988. "Endangered Species: The Uncertain Future of Low-Income Housing." *Dollars & Sense,* November, pp. 9–12.

Shipler, David K., 1983. "Israel Is Quietly Expanding Links with Nations Throughout Africa." *New York Times,* August 21, pp. 1, 11.

Singer, J. David, 1981. "Accounting for International War: The State of the Discipline." *Journal of Peace Research* 17, no. 1 (1981), pp. 1–18.

SIPRI, 1982. *The Arms Race and Arms Control.* Stockholm International Peace Research Institute. Cambridge MA: Oelgeschlager, Gunn & Hain.

————, 1982a. *World Armaments and Disarmament: SIPRI Yearbook 1982.* Stockholm International Peace Research Institute. London: Taylor & Francis.

————, 1984. *Armaments Or Disarmament?* Bergshamra: Stockholm International Peace Research Institute.

————, 1988. *SIPRI Yearbook 1988: World Armaments and Disarmament.* Stockholm International Peace Research Institute. Oxford UK: Oxford University Press.

————, 1989. "[Weapons] — Basic Checklist." August 29, 09:24:06. From Herbert Wulf.

Sisón, José María, 1988. "Revolutionary Prospects in the Philippines." *Monthly Review,* December, pp. 1–24.

Sivard, Ruth Leger, 1981. *World Military and Social Expenditures, 1981.* Leesburg VA: World Priorities.

————, 1982. *World Military and Social Expenditures: 1982.* Leesburg VA: World Priorities.

_____, 1985. *World Military and Social Expenditures: 1985*. Washington DC: World Priorities.

_____, 1987. *World Military and Social Expenditures, 1987–88*. Washington DC: World Priorities.

Sklar, Holly, 1980. *Trilateralism: The Trilateral Commission and Elite Planning for World Management*. Boston: South End Press.

_____, 1984. *Reagan, Trilateralism and the Neoliberals: U.S. Policy in the 1980s*. Boston: South End Press.

Small, Melvin, 1980. *Was War Necessary? National Security and U.S. Entry Into War*. Beverly Hills CA: Sage.

Smalldone, Joseph P., 1983. "U.S. Arms Transfers and Security-Assistance Programs in Africa: A Review and Policy Perspective." In *Arms for Africa: Military Assistance and Foreign Policy in the Developing World*. Ed. by Bruce E. Arlinghaus. Lexington MA: Heath. Pp. 179–220.

Smith, Robert F., 1960. *The United States and Cuba: Business and Diplomacy*. New Haven CT: College and University Press.

Smith, Ron, Anthony Humm, and Jacques Fontanel, 1985. "The Economics of Exporting Arms." *Journal of Peace Research* **22**, no. 33, pp. 239–47.

Snyder, Julian M., 1988. "IML Bulletin." *International Moneyline*, September, p. 6.

_____, 1988a. "1989 Forecast." *International Moneyline*, December, pp. 1–10.

"So Who's Counting?" 1988. *Bulletin of the Atomic Scientists*, September, p. 17.

Sollen, Robert, 1989. "A World at War." *The Nation*, January 9/16, pp. 46–47.

Solomon, Norman, 1985. "Americans Shouldn't Be Too Quick to Mock Soviet Peace Groups." *In These Times*, September 25–October 1, p. 12.

Sorley, Lewis, 1983. *Arms Transfers Under Nixon: A Policy Analysis*. University Press of Kentucky.

"Sorry Marks for Nursing Homes," 1988. *U.S. News and World Report*, December 12, pp. 92–3.

"Soviet Economy," 1983. *Counterspy* 7, no. 3 (March-May), p. 6.

"Soviets Act on U.S. Group's Proposal," 1985. *Update USSR*, August, p. 1.

Spechler, Diana R., 1978. *Domestic Influences on Soviet Foreign Policy*. Lanham MD: University Press of America.

"Special Report—Safe Banking," 1988. Potomac MD: Phillips Publishing Inc., 7811 Montrose Rd., 20854.

Spencer, Miranda, 1988. "Harboring Doubts: The U.S. Navy Is Planning New Home Ports for Its Nuclear Fleet." *Nuclear Times*, November/December, pp. 8–11.

"Spy Dust Memories," 1985. *The Nation*, September 7, pp. 163–64.

Squires, Gregory D., 1988. "Trickle-Down Won't Stop Poverty from Growing." *In These Times*, September 21–27, p. 16.

Stanton, Shelby L., 1985. *The Rise and Fall of an American Army in Vietnam: 1965–1973*. Presidio Novato CA: Presidio.

Stares, Paul B., 1985. *The Militarization of Space: U.S. Policy, 1945–1984*. Ithaca NY: Cornell University Press.

Steffens, Dorothy R., 1984. "So Who's Better Off?" *New World Review*, August, pp. 18–19.

Stein, Arthur A., 1978. *The Nation at War*. Baltimore: Johns Hopkins University Press.

Stevenson, Gail, 1989. "Structural Adjustment Lending and Outward-Oriented Growth: Some Remarks." *Bulletin of Peace Proposal* **20**, no. 4, pp. 421–34.

Stone, I.F., 1985. "I.F. Stone." *The Nation*, January 12, p. 17.

Stone, Jeremy J., 1985. Review of *Deadly Gambits* by Strobe Talbott. *Bulletin of Atomic Scientists* **41**, no. 1 (January), pp. 47–48.

Stork, Joe and Jim Paul, 1983. "Arms Sales and Militarization." *MERIP Reports,* no. 112 (February), pp. 5–15.

"Students' Interest in Humanities Continues to Wane," 1988. *The Connection* (UUP/ NYSUT), November 3, p. 2.

Sweezy, Paul M., and Harry Magdoff, 1983. "International Finance and National Power." *Monthly Review,* October, pp. 1–13.

Szymanski, Albert, 1984. *Human Rights in the Soviet Union.* London: Zed.

Targ, Harry R., 1984. *Strategy of an Empire in Decline: Cold War II.* Minneapolis MN: Marxist Educational Press (Ford Hall, University of Minnesota).

Tarnoff, Peter, 1989. "Why All This Sudden Nostalgia for the Cold War." *International Herald Tribune,* September 20, p. 4.

Taubman, Philip, 1983. "Honduras Wants Large Increase in U.S. Arms." *New York Times,* June 10, p. A10.

"Taxes," 1985. *Economic Notes,* February, pp. 4–5.

"Teen Suicide: The Alarming Statistics," 1985. *On Campus* (American Federation of Teachers), February, p. 7.

"10,000 Metal Trades Workers Tell General Dynamics: 'Dump the Lump,'" 1988. *LRA's Economic Notes,* July-August, pp. 14–16.

"Thatcher Arms Pinochet," 1983. *Counterspy* **8,** no. 1 (September-November), pp. 6–8.

"Third World Must Cut Arms Bills," 1989. *Jane's Defense Weekly,* October 7, p. 741.

Thom, William G., 1984. "Sub-Saharan Africa's Changing Military Environment." *Armed Forces and Society* **11,** no. 1 (Fall), pp. 32–58.

Thompson, E.P., 1983. "Letter to America: On Peace, Power and Parochialism." *The Nation,* September 24, pp. 225, 238–44.

_____, 1985. "Peace and Human Rights." *The Nation,* September 14, pp. 206–08.

Thurow, Lester C., 1985. "The 'Big Trade-Off' Debunked: The Efficiency of a Fair Economy." *The Washington Monthly,* November, pp. 47–54.

_____, 1990. "Time to Halt America's Economic Drift." *International Herald Tribune,* February 13, p. 4.

Tirman, John, 1985. "A Way to Break the Arms Deadlock." *The Nation,* February 16, pp. 167–71.

Tobias, Sheila, ed., 1982. *What Kinds of Guns Are They Buying for Your Butter?* New York: Morrow.

"Tomorrow: George Bush Shows He Is His Own Man," 1988. *U.S. News & World Report,* November 28, p. 33.

Trainer, F.E., 1989. "Reconstructing Radical Development Theory." *Alternatives* **14,** no. 4 (October), pp. 481–515.

TRB, 1983. "Views from Backstage." *New Republic,* April 18, p. 6.

"Trends in the Minimum Wage," 1988. *LRA's Economic Notes,* March-April, pp. 12–13.

Tuomi, Helena, 1983. "Transnational Military Corporations: The Main Problems." In *Militarization and Arms Production.* Ed. by H. Tuomi and Raimo Vayrynen. London: Croom, Helm. Pp. 138–60.

_____, and Raimo Vayrynen, 1980. *Transnational Corporations, Armaments and Development.* Research Report No. 22. Tampere, Finland: Tampere Peace Research Institute.

Ullman, Richard H., 1988. "Ending the Cold War." *Foreign Policy,* pp. 130–37.

Ungar, Sanford J., 1985. "The Military Money Drain." *Bulletin of the Atomic Scientists,* September, pp. 31–34.

"Unilateralism as a Road to Disarmament," 1985. *Gandhi Marg* **73** (April), pp. 3–6.

"Unionization in Industry," 1985. *Economic Notes,* October, pp. 1–3.

UNSG, 1982. *The Relationship Between Disarmament and Development.* Department of Political and Security Council Affairs, United Nations Centre for Disarmament. Report of the Secretary-General. New York: United Nations.

USACDA, 1979. *World Military Expenditures and Arms Transfers: 1968–1977.* Washington DC: U.S. Arms Control and Disarmament Agency, Department of Defense.

_____, 1985. *World Military Expenditures and Arms Transfers, 1985.* Washington DC: U.S. Arms Control and Disarmament Agency, Department of Defense, Oct. 29, errata revision.

_____, 1988. *World Military Expenditures and Arms Transfers, 1987.* Washington DC: U.S. Arms Control and Disarmament Agency, Department of Defense.

_____, 1989. *World Military Expenditures and Arms Transfers: 1988.* Washington: Dept. of Defense, Arms Control and Disarmament Agency.

U.S. Congress, House of Representatives, 1981. *U.S. Arms Transfer Policy in Latin America.* Hearing before the Subcommittee on International Security and Scientific Affairs of the Committee on Foreign Affairs. Oct. 22, 1981. 97th Cong., 1st Sess.

U.S. Congress. Senate. Committee on Armed Services, 1981. *Military and Technical Implications of the Proposed Sale of Air Defense Enhancements to Saudi Arabia.* Report of the Hearings Together with Additional Views of the Committee on Armed Services. Oct. 22, 1981. 97th Cong., 1st Sess., Report No. 970242. Washington DC: GPO.

U.S. Congress. Senate. Committee on Foreign Relations, 1981. *Arms Sales Package to Saudi Arabia.* Hearings on the AWACS and F-15 Enhancements Arms Sales Package to Saudi Arabia. Parts 1, October 1, 5, 6, 14, and 15, 1981. 97th Cong., 1st Sess. Washington DC: GPO.

_____, 1981. *Arms Sales Package to Saudi Arabia.* Hearings before the Committee on Foreign Relations, on the AWACS and F-15 Enhancements Arms Sales Package to Saudi Arabia. Part 2, October 1–15, 1981. 97th Cong., 1st Sess. Washington DC: GPO.

_____, 1981. *Conventional Arms Sales.* Hearing before the Committee on Foreign Relations, July 28, 1981. 97th Cong., 1st Sess. Washington: GPO.

"U.S.-China Joint Comminique," 1982. *Department of State Bulletin* 82, no. 2067 (October), pp. 19–22.

U.S. Department of Defense, 1982. *Foreign Military Sales, Foreign Military Construction Sales and Military Assistance Facts as of September 1982.* Washington DC: Security Assistance Agency, Dept. of Defense. Published by Data Management Division, Comptroller, DSSA.

_____, 1983. *Annual Report to the Congress.* Report of the Secretary of Defense Caspar W. Weinberger to the Congress on FY 1984 Budget, FY 1985 Authorization Request and FY 1984–88 Defense Programs. February 1, 1983. Washington DC: GPO.

U.S. Department of State, 1981. *Country Reports on Human Rights Practices.* Report submitted to the Committee on Foreign Relations, U.S. House of Representatives by the Department of State, February 2, 1981. Washington DC: GPO.

U.S. G.A.O., 1980. *Correct Balance of Defense's Foreign Military Sales Trust Fund Unknown.* Report by the Comptroller General to the Chairman, Committee on Appropriations, House of Representatives. GGMSD-80-47.

_____, 1982. *U.S. Security and Military Assistance: Programs and Related Activities.* Report by the U.S. General Accounting Office. GAO/ID-82-40. June 1, 1982. Gaithersburg MD: GAO.

"U.S. General Speaks Out on Removal," 1989. *International Herald Tribune,* November 28, p. 3.

"U.S. Isolated in COCOM on Soviet Trade," 1990. *International Herald Tribune,* February 16, p. 3.

U.S. President's Committee to Study the United States Military Assistance Program, 1959. *Composite Report.* Washington DC: GPO.

"U.S.-Soviet Military Facts," 1988. *The Defense Monitor* 17, no. 5, pp. 1–8.

USSR, 1985. State Committee for Foreign Economic Relations. *USSR and Developing Countries: Economic Cooperation.* Chicago: Imported.

"U.S. Troops in Europe," 1988. *International Disarmament Campaigns,* July, p. 3.

"Updates: Another Bad Year for the Poor," 1988. *Dollars and Sense,* November, p. 5.

"Veterans Work for Peace in Nicaragua and Vietnam." 1988. *International Disarmament Campaigns,* July, p. 4.

Vagts, Alfred, 1967. *A History of Militarism.* New York: Free Press.

Van Alstyne, Richard W., 1965. *The Rising American Empire.* Chicago: Quadrangle.

Vaupel, J.W., and J.P. Curhan, 1973. *The World's Multinational Enterprises: A Sourcebook of Tables Based on a Study of the Largest U.S. and Non U.S. Manufacturing Corporations.* Cambridge MA: Harvard University Press.

"Vital Statistics," 1990. *U.S. News & World Report,* February 25, p. 63.

"Waging War on Campus Crime," 1988/89. *On Campus* (American Federation of Teachers), December/January, p. 8.

Wald, George, 1985. "Letter to the Editor." *New York Times,* p. A34.

Wald, Matthew L., 1989. "Complainers at U.S. Nuclear Plants Say They Were Sent to Psychiatrists." *International Herald Tribune,* August 8, p. 3.

Waldman, Steven, 1988. "The Committee That Couldn't Shoot Straight." *Washington Monthly,* September, pp. 43–50.

Wallensteen, Peter, 1982. "Armed Forced Are Not Only for War." *Journal of Peace Research* 19, no. 1, pp. 83–88.

———, ed., 1988. *States in Armed Conflict, 1988.* Uppsala: Department of Peace and Conflict Research, Uppsala University.

———, 1985. "Focus On: American-Soviet Detente: What Went Wrong?" *Journal of Peace Research* 22, no. 1, pp. 1–8.

"War Games," 1984. *The Defense Monitor* 13, no. 7, pp. 1–7.

Weaver, Carolyn, 1986. "Unholy Alliance." *Mother Jones,* January, pp. 14–17.

Webster, William, 1988. "Interview: Morning Edition." National Public Radio, August 10.

Weede, Erich, 1988. "Redistribution and Income Inequality in Industrial Democracies." *Journal of Conflict Resolution,* 25:4, December, pp. 639–54.

Weinberg, Steve, 1985. "Trashing the FOIA." *Columbia Journalism Review,* January-February, pp. 21–27.

Weinstein, James, 1985. "Editorial." *In These Times,* October 2–8, p. 14.

Weinstein, Martin E., ed., 1982. *Northeast Asian Security After Vietnam.* Urbana: University of Illinois Press.

Weisskopf, T.E., 1974. "Capitalism, Socialism, and the Sources of Imperialism." In *Testing Theories of Economic Imperialism.* Ed. by S.J. Rosen and J.R. Kurth. Toronto: Heath. Pp. 57–82.

Wenger, Martha, 1983. "U.S. Backs Morocco's Saharan War." *Counterspy* 7, no. 4 (June-August), pp. 53–55, 59.

Weschler, Lawrence, 1985. "Perspectives: Is Defense Spending Strangling U.S.?" *In These Times,* January 9–15, p. 17.

"Western Nations' Arms Exports," 1988. *International Herald Tribune,* December 16, p. 14.

Westing, Arthur H., 1982. "War as a Human Endeavor: The High Fatality Wars of the Twentieth Century." *Journal of Peace Research* **19**, no. 3, pp. 261–70.

"What's Next: Social Problems and the Deficit," 1988/89. *On Campus* (American Federation of Teachers), December/January, p. 4.

Where Your Income Tax Money Really Goes, 1988. New York: War Resisters League.

"Whispering About Sex," 1988. *International Herald Tribune,* August 2, p. 4.

White, Gordon, Robin Murray, and Christine White, 1984. *Taking the Socialist Path: Revolutionary Socialist Development in the Third World.* Lexington KY: University of Kentucky Press. Dist. by Harper and Row.

Whynes, David K., 1979. *The Economics of Third World Military Expenditures.* London: Macmillan.

Wicker, Tom, 1983. "A Policy Revealed." *New York Times,* September 19.

————, 1988. "Let 'Em Eat Swiss Cheese." *New York Times,* September 2, p. A27.

————, 1989. "Prisoners: In Poland, in America." *International Herald Tribune,* October 14–15, p. 4.

Wiesner, Jerome B., 1985. "A Militarized Society." *Bulletin of the Atomic Scientists,* August, pp. 102–05.

Williams, William A., 1962. *The Tragedy of American Diplomacy.* New York: Dell.

————, 1980. *Empire as a Way of Life.* New York: Oxford University Press.

Wilson, William Julius, 1987. *The Truly Disadvantaged: The Inner City, The Underclass and Public Policy.* Chicago: University of Chicago Press.

Winslow, George, 1988. "Junk-Bond Junkies Get a Bottom-Line Fix." [Review of *The Predators Ball: The Junk Bond Raiders and the Man Who Staked Them* by Connie Bruck. New York: Simon & Schuster, 1988.] *In These Times,* December 7–13, p. 20.

Wise, Tim, 1988. "Land Reform for the Landed." *Dollars & Sense,* November, pp. 12–15.

Witt, Matt, 1989. "A Stake in Foreign Workers' Rights." *International Herald Tribune,* September 7, p. 9.

Wofsy, Leon, 1985. "Can the Cold War Be Ended Peacefully?" *In These Times,* March 15, Op-Ed page.

————, 1988. "Gorbachev's New Thinking and World Politics." *Monthly Review,* October, pp. 18–31.

Wolfe, Alan, 1985. "Letter from Copenhagen: Why Danes Think We're Crazy." *The Nation,* May 11, pp. 560–62.

Wolpin, Miles D., 1973. *Military Aid and Counterrevolution in the Third World.* Lexington MA: Heath.

————, 1982. *Militarization and Social Revolution in the Third World.* Totowa NJ: Allanheld, Osmun & Co. (Littlefield, Adams & Co.).

————, 1983. *Militarism, Internal Repression and Social Welfare in the Third World.* Oslo: International Peace Research Institute. Revised Version: *Militarization, Repression and Social Welfare in the Third World.* Beckenham, Kent, UK: Croom, Helm, 1986. U.S. Distributor: St. Martin's.

————, 1983a. *State Terrorism and Repression of the Third World.* Oslo: International Peace Research Institute. Revised Version: "State Terrorism and Repression in the Third World: Parameters and Prospects." In *Government Violence and Repression.* Ed. by George A. Lopez and Michael Stohl. Westport CT: Greenwood, 1986.

————, 1983b. "Socio-Political Radicalism and Military Professionalism in the Third World." *Comparative Politics* **15**, no. 3 (April) pp. 203–10.

————, 1986. "Security Implications of a New European Peace Order." *Current Research on Peace and Violence.*

————, 1986a. "State Terrorism and Repression in the Third World: Parameters and Prospects." In *Government Violence and Repression.* Ed. by Michael Stohl and George Lopez. Westport CT: Greenwood.

"Working-Class Families," 1985. *Economic Notes,* April, pp. 1–5.

World Bank, 1988. *World Debt Tables: External Debt of Developing Countries.* Vol. 1. *Analysis and Summary Tables.* Washington DC: World Bank.

"Worth Noting," 1989. *The Bottom Line* (NYSUI), January 6, p. 4.

"Wrong on Afghanistan," 1990. *International Herald Tribune,* February 6, p. 4.

Wulf, Herbert, 1979. "Dependent Militarism in the Periphery and Possible Alternative Concepts." In *Arms Transfers in the Modern World.* Ed. by Stephanie G. Neuman and Robert E. Harkavy. New York: Praeger.

————, 1985. "Arms Transfer Control: The Feasibility and the Obstacles." Hamburg, FRG: Institute for Peace Research and Security Policy (Falkenstein).

————, 1985a. "A Europeanist Approach to Security and Disarmament." Hamburg, FRG: Institute for Peace Research and Security Policy (Falkenstein).

————, 1988. "The West German Arms Industry and Arms Exports." *Alternatives* **13**, pp. 319–35.

Zachary, G. Pascal, 1988. Review of *Wild Blue Yonder: Money, Politics and the B-1 Bomber* by Nick Kotz (New York: Pantheon). *In These Times,* May 25–June 7, p. 18.

Zunes, Stephen, 1988. "Looking at Israel in a Broad Historical Context." *In These Times,* September 14–20, p. 16.

Zwick, Jim, 1982. *Militarism and Repression in the Philippines.* Montreal: Centre for Developing Area Studies, McGill University.

Index